Atlantic Cataclysm

In this comprehensive work, David Eltis offers a 2,000-year perspective on the trafficking of people, and boldly intervenes in the expansive discussions about slavery in the last half-century. Using new and underexplored data made available by slavevoyages.org, Eltis offers compelling explanations of why the slave trades began and why they ended, and in the process debunks long-held assumptions, including how bilateral rather than triangular voyages were the norm, and how the Portuguese rather than the British were the leading slave traders. Eltis argues that two-thirds of all enslaved people ended up in the Iberian Americas, where exports were most valuable throughout the slave trade era, and not in the Caribbean or the United States. Tracing the mass involvement of people in the slave trade business from all parts of the Atlantic world, Eltis also examines the agency of Africans and their experiences in the aftermath of liberation.

David Eltis is Professor Emeritus at Emory University and the University of British Columbia. He is a founding member of www.slavevoyages.org, a publicly accessible transatlantic slave trade database. His three previous books have won twelve prizes, including the Frederick Douglass award.

Atlantic Cataclysm

Rethinking the Atlantic Slave Trades

DAVID ELTIS

Emory University and University of British Columbia

Shaftesbury Road, Cambridge CB2 8EA, United Kingdom

One Liberty Plaza, 20th Floor, New York, NY 10006, USA

477 Williamstown Road, Port Melbourne, VIC 3207, Australia

314–321, 3rd Floor, Plot 3, Splendor Forum, Jasola District Centre, New Delhi – 110025, India

103 Penang Road, #05–06/07, Visioncrest Commercial, Singapore 238467

Cambridge University Press is part of Cambridge University Press & Assessment, a department of the University of Cambridge.

We share the University's mission to contribute to society through the pursuit of education, learning and research at the highest international levels of excellence.

www.cambridge.org
Information on this title: www.cambridge.org/9781009518970
DOI: 10.1017/9781009518963

© David Eltis 2025

This publication is in copyright. Subject to statutory exception and to the provisions of relevant collective licensing agreements, no reproduction of any part may take place without the written permission of Cambridge University Press & Assessment.

When citing this work, please include a reference to the DOI 10.1017/9781009518963

First published 2025

A catalogue record for this publication is available from the British Library.

A Cataloging-in-Publication data record for this book is available from the Library of Congress

ISBN 978-1-009-51897-0 Hardback

Cambridge University Press & Assessment has no responsibility for the persistence or accuracy of URLs for external or third-party internet websites referred to in this publication and does not guarantee that any content on such websites is, or will remain, accurate or appropriate.

"In God we trust. All others must bring data."
attributed to W. Edward Deming

To Suzan
In remembrance and expectations of all our voyages

Contents

List of Figures	*page* viii
List of Tables	x
List of Maps	xii
Preface	xiii
Acknowledgements	xx
List of Abbreviations	xxiv
1 Atlantic Slave Trading and World History	1
2 The Americas and Atlantic Slave Trading: The Iberians and the Rest	46
3 Europe and Atlantic Slave Trading	101
4 The Portuguese System	153
5 Africa, Africans, and the Slave Trade	196
6 Abolition: A Leninist Interpretation	247
7 Freedom?	292
Conclusion	355
Index	365

Figures

1.1	Deformation as a mark of enslavement?	page 35
2.1	Share of transatlantic captives taken from Africa by location of home ports of vessels carrying them	50
2.2	Panning for gold in Mato Grosso	77
3.1	Profile of the steam-powered slave ship *Cicerón*	109
3.2	Time profile of French transatlantic slave voyages	120
4.1	Image of the Liverpool slave ship *Brooks* according to the "Society for Effecting the Abolition of the Slave Trade: Description of a Slave Ship" (London, 1789)	154
4.2	The *Marie-Séraphique* (ID 30941) showing the barricado midships	155
4.3	The slave deck of the *Marie-Séraphique* (ID 30941) during the transatlantic voyage as drawn by one of the ship's officers	156
4.4	Contemporary image of the *Isla de Cuba* (ID 4961)	190
4.5	*Albanez* (ID 3483). Detained in 1845 with 600 captives, fewer than half of whom are shown in the image	191
4.6	Image of the *Diligente* (ID 2588), showing approximately half the number of captives on board at the time of detention	191
5.1	Slave-trading compound at Loango, north of the Congo estuary, 1771	211
6.1	References to "slaves" in seventeenth- and eighteenth-century newspapers by decade distributed according to whether the slaves were European ("White") or African ("Black")	280
7.1	Liberated Africans on board HMS *Daphne*, 1868	293
7.2	Liberated African children on board HMS *Daphne*, 1868	294
7.3	Liberated Africans on board HMS *Undine*, 1883	294

List of Figures

7.4 Catherine Zimmerman Mulgrave, seated third from the left. Photograph, 1873 — 325
7.5 Samuel Ajayi Crowther (center) visiting the "Wilberforce Oak" (Keston, Kent) in 1873, along with leading members of the Church Missionary Society in Sierra Leone and Nigeria — 326
7.6 Headstones of a prominent Liberated African in Freetown, Sierra Leone — 327
7.7 Liberated Africans in St. Helena fifty years on from their arrival on the *Aventureiro* (ID 4031) in 1850 — 328
7.8 Survivors of the *Wanderer* (ID 4974) photographed in 1908 — 329
7.9 A further survivor of the *Wanderer* (ID 4974) in 1908 — 329
7.10 Survivor of the *Clotilde* (ID 36990): Oluale (Charlie Lewis) disembarked at Twelvemile Island, Alabama, in 1860; photographed in 1900 — 330
7.11 Survivors of the *Clotilde* (ID 36990): Abache (Clara Turner) and Kossola (Cudjo Lewis) disembarked at Twelvemile Island, Alabama, in 1860 — 331
7.12 Survivor of the *Clotilde* (ID 36990): Pollee Allen disembarked at Twelvemile Island, Alabama, in 1860; shown in c. 1912 — 332
7.13 Survivor of the *Clotilde* (ID 36990): Kossola (Cudjo Lewis) disembarked at Twelvemile Island, Alabama, in 1860; shown at home c. 1927 — 333

Tables

2.1 Captives carried from Africa and the location of home port of vessels carrying them, 1520–1866 ('000'). *page* 49
2.2 Enslaved persons per crew member by flag of slave ship, 1613–1830   67
2.3 Total cost of purchases of the enslaved in 1770 relative to total output of plantations in the Caribbean in current pounds sterling for the major Northwest European slave trading powers   75
2.4 Estimated arrival of enslaved people in the Americas by jurisdiction   89
2.5 Slaves arriving in the Americas by broad region and slaves arriving under the Spanish flag direct from Africa, 1520–1867   93
3.1 Estimated size of the transatlantic traffic carried on in the first 130 years of its existence in three major European regions from which slave voyages were launched   108
3.2 Transatlantic slave voyages owned by major state-sponsored chartered companies   129
4.1 Mortality rates by age/sex groupings   175
4.2 Impact of naval suppression on average number of slaves captured per vessel, 1808–1850, compared to mean number of captives on vessels not captured   182
4.3 Slaves embarked per crew member on board when vessel left home port, by national flag, 1751–1810   185
5.1 Time spent in days by vessels trading for slaves on African coast   207

5.2	Transatlantic movement of people across the Atlantic from regions that became Western African nation-states, and from Portugal and Britain, 1519–1850	217
5.3	Value of imports per person in select regions in the Atlantic world c. 1800 in pounds sterling	228
7.1	Regions of disembarkation of Liberated Africans: Initial place of arrival and subsequent movements, 1800–1867	299
C.1	Enslaved populations of the African diaspora and Indian Ocean c. 1800	360

Maps

7.1 Locations of languages of Liberated Africans leaving
northern Bight of Biafra ports, 1808–1847 *page* 302
7.2 Locations of languages of Liberated Africans leaving
the Bight of Benin and the Gold Coast, 1810–1848 304
7.3 Locations of languages of Liberated Africans leaving Upper
Guinea, 1808–1847 305

Preface

At one level this book is a sequel to my *The Rise of African Slavery in the Americas*, published almost a quarter-century ago. A large part of it takes up the story of the emerging anti-Black prejudice that made four hundred years of transatlantic slavers drawing on Africa possible. It carries the narrative of this prejudice through the slave trade era and into the period of virulent racism that has shaped Black lives in the Americas down to the twentieth century. But in a more important sense it is an attempt to persuade fellow-scholars and the general public to recognize the enormous advances in knowledge represented by www.slavevoyages.org, only a sliver of which existed in the form of a CD-ROM when *The Rise of African Slavery* first appeared. Since then, slavevoyages has not only dramatically expanded its coverage of the transatlantic slave trade, but, more significantly, added four completely new databases to the 36,200 transatlantic ventures, and is about to extend coverage into the Indian Ocean.

Nevertheless, many traditional interpretations have yet to be questioned. To address all of these would require a much longer book than this one. But as slavery and the slave trade have moved closer to the center stage of public interest in the last half-century, the gap between public awareness of the horrific traffic and what the sources now reveal has tended to widen rather than shrink. At the scholarly level the new information has enriched the work of those writing micro-histories rather than reconfiguring the larger canvas. In geographic terms, it is true that the weight of scholarship has shifted slightly to the South Atlantic. Nevertheless, historians continue to focus too heavily on West Africa as the major source of slaves, as well as Europe as the starting point of most slave-trading voyages, and North America or the Caribbean as the major recipients of their human cargoes.

The databases on the peoples associated with slaving voyages have generated new information about participation in the business. We already knew that several Liverpool families were each responsible for carrying off 50,000 enslaved people from Africa and that each of the major organizational centers on both sides of the Atlantic also had major families, albeit dispatching somewhat smaller numbers. What we now know is that almost all ports in Europe and the Americas had many smaller investors with a wide range of occupations. These included clerks, apprentices, and businesses often in related maritime activities such as rope- and sail-making. In the huge Brazilian trade, ownership stakes might be held by crew. If we add to these the firms and their workers who made the trade goods, awareness of and participation in the slave trade was very broadly based. This same pattern holds true for Africa. The Enslavers database also includes Africans who appear in slave ships' trade books as sellers of the enslaved in a wide spectrum of African ports. Typical sales involved one to five captives and many different sellers. Yet the current literature still stresses the role of major merchants and African rulers colluding in the expulsion of millions across the Atlantic. This view needs qualifying. Acceptance of the trade in all three continents was broadly based.

The second new database is for the enslaved. A treasure trove of the names of Liberated Africans for the nineteenth century written down by officials of courts established to suppress the slave trade allow us to identify the language to which the name belonged. This in turn enables us to indicate the approximate geographic origin of the enslaved individual. This new data allows us to argue that captives could well have begun their horrific journey somewhat closer to the coast than is often claimed in the literature.

In this work, I first provide a wider context for the slave trade era with an overview of slave trading around the globe in the millennium preceding the first slave ship to cross the Atlantic from Africa. The point here is to locate the slave trade among the many cataclysmic events that humans have inflicted on each other. Steven T. Katz has exhaustively made the comparative case for modern times with his work on the twentieth-century Holocaust, but no one has taken on the period preceding

---

[1] Steven T. Katz, *The Holocaust and New World Slavery: A Comparative History*, 2 vols (Cambridge, 2019–21). Also, David E. Stannard, "True Believer: The Uniqueness of Steven T. Katz," *Journal of Genocide Research*, 22 (2020): 391–409, doi: 10.1080/14623528.2020.1719734.

European expansion to the Americas.[1] For slavers, much like warmongers, the basic drive to extend one's power over others was always present, but technological advances – in this case the ability to cross oceans – made the consequences of this impulse so much more devastating than the huge transcontinental land-based slave trafficking that existed in Eurasia in the preceding centuries. Similarly, the extensive maritime slave trading that existed across smaller bodies of water such as the Mediterranean, Black Sea, Baltic, North and Irish Seas may have lasted longer than their later transatlantic counterpart but was certainly smaller in volume. The traffic in the so-called "Mediterranean Atlantic" beginning in the early fifteenth century comprised a stepping stone toward transatlantic slave trading in terms of geography, organizational structures, and of course scale. Nevertheless, it is certainly possible for scholars to draw useful comparisons between the Mongols in medieval Eurasia and the Europeans in the later Atlantic world.[2]

The chapters that follow take on a structure that differs from the typical scholarly monograph on the traffic in enslaved people. Chapter 2 argues that the Americas constituted the keystone of the transatlantic slave trade. After Australasia, the Americas easily comprised the most lightly populated landmass on Earth. They then experienced major population declines in the aftermath of European conquests, brought about by the introduction of Old World pathogens and the conquerors' exploitation of native populations. For the occupiers this meant there was a labor problem that steadily worsened in the two centuries after 1492, given that the Americas also had abundant natural resources together with high land-to-labor ratios in global terms. Therefore, while Europeans initiated the Atlantic slave trade, what was for Europeans the New World comprised the source of demand for labor that sustained the movement of people around the Atlantic for nearly four centuries. The Americas were not only the source of a massive increase in demand for labor in the sixteenth-century Atlantic world, but they also had a major role in increasing supply. I refer here not to the enslavement of Indigenous Americans – though that, too, occurred on a grand scale – but rather to the organization of transatlantic slave-trading voyages. No less than seventy ports in the Americas, from Portland, Maine, in the north to Montevideo in the south dispatched at least one slave voyage to Africa. Three of the four busiest organizational slave-trading ports in global history, Rio de Janeiro, Baía de Todos os Santos (now Salvador) and Pernambuco (now

---

[2] See the twenty-three essays in *CWHS*, vol. 2.

Recife) were all located in the Americas, not Europe. Moreover, measured by total exports the most valuable colonies for most of the slave trade era were not English, French, or Dutch, but rather Spanish. Even prerevolutionary St. Domingue's sugar, coffee, and indigo could never surpass the value of gold and silver extracted by Spain from its American possessions.

While Europe's role in the slave trade may have been secondary it can scarcely be described as minor. The traffic was broadly based, with ninety-six European ports dispatching at least one voyage to Africa. Almost every port large enough to initiate transoceanic trade participated in the business. Owners, their employees and, most important, the public had unquestioning support for the business until the last quarter of the eighteenth century. The Portuguese and Spanish created the Atlantic slave-trading system, and they were the last to abandon it. They dispatched more voyages and carried off far more enslaved women and men than did the British throughout the era. As firstcomers, the Portuguese expanded south and west from the so-called Mediterranean Atlantic and occupied the choicest locations for obtaining and selling captives, from which these Iberians were never dislodged. Such locations allowed the Portuguese to accumulate more of their captives on land rather than on ships, reduced rebellions and mortality, and enabled them to dominate the shortest route from Africa to the Americas, namely to Brazil. Their major loss, the fort at Elmina on Africa's Gold Coast, was never a major source of captives. Spain had a much smaller African presence – a few coastal slaving stations – but its domination of the intra-American slave trade meant that it received more slaves than all the British Caribbean possessions together. And in Africa, late-starting north European slave traders had to find new regions and longer routes over which to conduct their business rather than supplanting the Portuguese. A central result of the new data is to question the old idea of the more capitalist-driven northwest Europeans taking over from precapitalist Iberians.

Overturning one trope leads to the questioning of another. Iberian dominance in the colonial Americas as indicated by colonial trade figures (including the number of slaves traded) inevitably undermines the argument that the economic development of Western Europe depended on the slave systems of the Americas. It was Britain, not Spain or Portugal, that led the Industrial Revolution, even though the American possessions of both Iberian countries separately extracted and exploited far more African captives than did the British or the French. Rather than Atlantic slave systems stimulating European economic development, it was the growth of Britain, the Netherlands, and France that allowed these nations to establish their own slave systems in the face of Iberian competition. As argued below, paradoxically, the Portuguese always remained the most efficient and overall the largest of the national groups of slave traders.

The successful Iberian systems were rooted in the organization of the voyage as much as having first choice over places to buy and sell captives. Contemporary illustrations and new documentary sources allow us to examine conditions on board during the passage to the Americas. It extends the analysis of the differences between the Portuguese and their competitors to the conditions experienced on the voyage. Those familiar only with the northwestern European business will find it surprising that most Portuguese slaving voyages had enslaved or formerly enslaved Africans among their crew. Many of these held a small financial stake in the captives, often as part-payment of wages. Because of the specificity of the African regions on which the Portuguese drew, there were usually some crew members on board who were able to interact with those confined to the slave deck. Thus, not only did the enslaved spend less time on board but they were also less likely to believe they were to be eaten by their captors or deposited in a completely strange environment. A close analysis of resistance and onboard defensive measures suggests that the northwestern Europeans never came close to matching the efficiencies, in effect the lower costs, of the Portuguese system of buying Africans and putting them to work in the Americas.

The discussion of Africa does not offer a big-picture alternative to what readers can find in the existing historiography. Rather, it more modestly examines some of the better-known interpretations of Africa's role in the external traffic in the light of the new data. Modesty, however, does not preclude expressing disappointment with some of the current findings. With one or two major exceptions, currently accepted interpretations largely reflect the ideas of the great Africanist scholar, Walter Rodney, formulated well before the dramatic increases in available information on the slave trade. Much of the current literature does not provide sufficiently for African agency. Generally, the new data reveals a sense of equality between buyer and seller on the African littoral, at least until late in the slave trade era. It now seems unlikely that European slave traders were able to "dump" cheap goods on gullible African consumers in exchange for human merchandise. More important, Africanists have yet to take on board new population estimates for African regions in 1850 and match these with new estimates of the exodus of people that are now available. It now seems unlikely that outside influences transformed the nature of slavery in Africa.

A major subtheme of the book is the widely based support for the slave trade apparent on all the continents involved in it. Surviving trade books show that capturing and selling captives in Africa were activities that involved large numbers of Africans beyond just the ruling elite. Modern commentators have too often mistaken the natural desire of an individual to avoid enslavement with reservations about slavery itself. Anti-slavery, much less abolitionism, was scarcely widespread. Before this era the myriad of workers in both the slave trade and in industries supplying it, as well as investors, government officials, and the great majority of intellectuals, all saw little difference between buying people and buying commodities such as wheat, whale meat, or other products made accessible by long-distance commerce. Differences of opinion on slavery throughout all continents involved in the business were confined to eligibility for enslavement rather than whether slavery itself should exist, at least prior to the late eighteenth century.

This brings us to the question of the ending of the traffic taken up in Chapter 6, which does offer an alternative approach to abolition. Drawing on thousands of references in English newspapers in the century after 1688, it establishes the gradual shift from a preoccupation with the enslavement of Europeans, largely in North Africa, to one that focused on enslavement of Africans on both sides of the Atlantic. This trend was reinforced by the fact that much of the newspaper coverage of Black slavery comprised graphic reports of very violent revolts on board slave ships. Chapter 6 also tracks patterns in the naming of slave ships over a century and a half – now readily available in the slavevoyages database – to establish the increasing engagement of slave traders with a range of African rulers. These patterns were well established by the mid eighteenth century and show the erosion of the concept of Africans as outsiders, a critical prerequisite to recognizing that Africans should not be enslaved. As for the political execution of abolition, the chapter downplays the importance of the St. Domingue slave rebellion and the emergence of Haiti, but carefully tracks the interplay between revolts in the Caribbean and the initiatives of British abolitionists at the metropolitan center. Counterfactually, abolition of both the slave trade and slavery itself could not have happened without these two key elements.

For more than 200,000 Africans, attempts to suppress the slave trade by armed intervention had serious implications. Found on board intercepted slave ships, and adjudicated by British and international courts, the "re-captive" Africans were not freed, but rather distributed across the Atlantic world under encumbrances ranging from "apprenticeships" to, in some cases, a status analogous to full chattel slavery. For the latter group, release from a slave ship was truly meaningless. The final chapter tracks the wide range of outcomes for re-captive people and compares these to the experiences of the nearly 6 million people of African descent in the Americas who were emancipated in the century after the 1791 outbreak of the St. Domingue Rebellion. A second comparison group is the millions of poor whites who began to migrate to the Americas en masse after 1830. Such comparisons contextualize what freedom meant to survivors of the slave trade. The chapter delineates the expectations of the governments that declared the captives emancipated and compares these with the aspirations of the newly released Africans and African Americans themselves. It finds that neither the officials administering emancipation, nor most of its supposed beneficiaries came close to getting what they wanted. The reason for this, as the comparison with European migrants makes clear, was the persistence of the same anti-Black attitudes that initiated the transatlantic slave trade in the sixteenth century.

So, the argument returns to its starting point. Of course, those who were emancipated avoided a remaining lifetime of forced labor (except for a few thousand "rescued" by Brazilian and Cuban cruisers prior to their quick and permanent absorption into slave plantations). Twenty-six years after abolition in the District of Columbia, Frederick Douglass declared, "I denounce the so-called emancipation as a stupendous fraud."[3] And indeed, no person of African descent had the rights of a poor European migrant arriving in New York or Quebec City. In one sense this volume is about the decline of anti-Black racism over four centuries, but in another sense, as a modern audience should know well given today's Black–White disparities in income, incarceration rates, life expectancies, and police shootings, there are yet many miles to travel.

---

[3] For the full speech, see www.historyisaweapon.com/defcon1/douglassfraud.html. The argument here is similar to that in James Walvin, *A World Transformed: Slavery in the Americas and the Origins of Global Power* (Berkeley, CA, 2022), though I have a different view of the slavery in the millennium preceding 1500.

Acknowledgements

In 1979 during my thesis defense at the University of Rochester, Gene Genovese commented with some justification that my work read not so much as a thesis, but rather as an appendix to a thesis. Mercifully, he signed off anyway. Several books and many articles later, if Gene's remark continues to resonate it is because of YouTube, and especially my appreciation of the dazzling videos of the late Swedish epidemiologist, Hans Rosling and his family in support of his worldview that "The world cannot be understood without numbers. But the world cannot be understood with numbers alone."[1] In no field does this aphorism resonate more than in studies of slavery and slave trading in global history.

A long-time association with www.slavevoyages.org with its now five databases currently containing details of 212,661 people, over half of whom are African or African American, and 66,800 voyages that carried enslaved people, inevitably means incurring huge debts. The late Philip Curtin started my journey by donating 2,313 IBM punch cards (one per voyage) shortly after he published his 1969 *Atlantic Slave Trade: A Census*, while at the same time Herbert S. Klein was beginning to establish databases from the archives of the Arquivo Histórico Ultramarino in Lisbon, and the Archivo Histórico Nacional in Madrid. Stephen D. Behrendt, the late David Richardson, and the late Manolo Florentino became principals in the process of vastly broadening the range of British and Brazilian voyages by donating the fruits of their own archival labors and helping to shape the user interface that allowed the

---

[1] *Factfulness: Ten Reasons We're Wrong about the World – and Why Things Are Better than You Think* (New York, 2018), p. 192.

public to access their data. Steve has sent a steady stream of corrections and new references over the decades. In the crucial years spent moving the project to the web, Martin Halbert and Katherine Skinner of the Emory Library were central to winning a National Endowment for the Humanities (NEH) award. Between 2008 when the transatlantic slave trade database went live on the web and 2011 when www.african-origins.org was launched, the project began its turn from an exclusive focus on the voyages of slave ships to the people on or managing those voyages. This shift of emphasis could not have happened without Richard Anderson, Nafees Khan, Ugo Nwokeji, Kwesi J. DeGraft-Hanson, Daniel Barros Domingues da Silva, Olatunji Ojo, Henry B. Lovejoy, Liz Milewicz, Marcy Alexander, but above all Phil Misevich, who led the way on the African names project and has done most of the editing of users' contributions to the language identifications of African names over the last twelve years. Data for maps in Chapter 7 is largely his work.

In a real sense, www.slavevoyages.org and www.african-origins.org, with which it is now merged, were not the creation of any single scholar or institution. The consortium that now maintains the site with their financial contributions comprises ten institutions in addition to Emory, but this is essentially a stewardship. The real "owners" are rather the community of scholars who work on the Atlantic slave trades and the interested public that use, contribute to, and exploit their work. Contributors of data to voyages and African names number in the thousands and cannot all be named here. Funding agencies that underpinned this activity are in chronological order the Social Sciences and Humanities Research Council of Canada, the National Endowment for the Humanities, the Andrew W. Mellon Foundation, the Arts and Humanities Research Council of the UK, the American Council of Learned Societies, the Casa de Rui Barbosa Foundation of Rio de Janeiro, and the Hutchins Center for African & African American Research. Henry Louis Gates, Randall Burkett, and the late Barbara Solow provided a home for the development of the transatlantic slave trade database at Harvard in 1992, and ever since, Professor Gates has provided critically important periodic interim funding, as well as advice on content. I cannot imagine what the site would look like without his thirty years of support. And while most of this paragraph is about www.slavevoyages.org, I find it impossible to separate out work on the voyages site from the writings on the pages that follow here.

The addition of the intra-American slave trade database has had a major impact on our understanding of the Black Atlantic and, more specifically, many of the arguments made in the following pages. This, too, could not have happened without the careful work of Alex Borucki and Greg O'Malley. Dave Wheat has kept up a stream of new information about voyages in the early transatlantic slave trade over the last decade, as well as commenting on the complete manuscript. Jorge Felipe and Marial Iglesias Utset have guided me through the still widely underappreciated and massive slave trade to Cuba. Leonardo Marques has navigated me through the scholarly shoals of the South Atlantic historiography. Jane Hooper was always on hand to answer queries about the Indian Ocean world. Jelmer Vos contributed masses of slave-trading data from the AHU in Lisbon and the BNA in London, and for two decades has given insightful advice. Craig Perry took a course with me on Atlantic slavery at Emory, yet over the years since I have learned more from him about medieval slavery than he did from me in that course.

I have benefited from the expertise of many readers. Jim Walvin not only read the complete manuscript but gave me sage advice on publishers. Richard Anderson gave Chapter 7 a particularly careful reading. The late David Brion Davis commented on a preliminary version of Chapter 6. John Thornton reviewed the whole manuscript. Both he and Ewout Frankema gave invaluable comments on Chapter 5. I have been especially lucky to collaborate with Nick Radburn, another who read the complete manuscript and whose influence in this work is clearest in Chapter 4. Pieter Emmer also corrected many errors as he, too, engaged with the complete 520 typescript pages.

Both the site and my own work have benefited enormously from a close association with programmer Domingos Delmonica that started in Emory when he was completing his PhD and continued after his return to Brazil a decade ago to establish his own business. Designers and software engineers Yang Li, videographer, Steve Bransford at Emory, Jane Webster of Newcastle University, author of the best book on this topic and John Mulligan at Rice have not only made the site attractive and usable but also brought to my attention unsuspected elements of the data. The Emory Center for Digital Scholarship has supported all my endeavors even though I moved to emeritus status twelve years ago. Beyond the call of duty, these included the hospitality of the co-director, Allen Tullos and his wife, Cynthia Blakeley after I moved from Atlanta. Their advice on polishing my completed manuscript was critical. When I moved to Vancouver I was warmly welcomed by the late Danny Vickers, then chair of the History Department of the University of British Columbia. The collegial UBC scholarly community and especially the excellent Library made the final preparation of the manuscript relatively painless.

Acknowledgements xxiii

Two scholars especially have been constant and supportive companions in my own journey of discovery. Paul Lachance worked with me on the CD-ROM and had two fellowships at Emory while we moved the data to the web. He was involved in every major decision about the design of the site in its Emory phase, and prepared the imputed values and the estimates page prior to the movement of the project to Rice. His SPSS skills are simply better than mine. We have, in addition, coauthored a series of papers and he has read and improved much of my sole-authored work prior to publication. We lived for two decades separated by a short bike ride along the Ottawa Rideau canal path. Such proximity turned into one of the foundation stones of this study.

The second of the two goes back even further. This book is the first of my written works since 1975 that the late Stan Engerman was, for health reasons, not able to read in draft format several times over. For this reason, I feel as much trepidation over this publication as I did my first – which happened before I met him. His knowledge of and contribution to the scholarship of slavery was peerless, but just as important was his talent for phrasing criticisms in a nonconfrontational manner. Apart from his own huge contribution to economic history, no scholar has been as active, astute, or generous a critic as he has over the past half century. I cannot better the words of Peter Coclanis when he wrote, "the work of almost every student and scholar of economic history has been improved because Stan Engerman has read or commented on it. If any scholar in any field merits disciplinary canonization, it is he."[2]

Errors, needless to say, are my own.

---

[2] Peter Coclanis, review of "*Slavery in the Development of the Americas*, by David Eltis, Frank D. Lewis, and Kenneth L. Solokoff," *Journal of Southern History*, 71 (2005): 660. He was, of course, aware of Stan's Jewish origins!

Abbreviations

African-Origins	Database of African names, now part of www.slavevoyages.org/past/database/african-origins
AHNA	Arquivo Histórico Nacional de Angola, Luanda, Angola
AHU	Arquivo Histórico Ultramarino, Lisbon
ANOM	Archives Nationales d'outre-mer, Aix-la-Chapelle
BNA	British National Archives
BL	Bodleian Library, Oxford
BrL	British Library
CWHS	*Cambridge World History of Slavery* (2011–2021) Vol. 1 edited by Keith Bradley and Paul Cartledge Vol. 2 edited by Craig Perry, David Eltis, Stanley L. Engerman, and David Richardson Vol. 3 edited by David Eltis, and Stanley L. Engerman Vol. 4 edited by Seymour Drescher, David Eltis, Stanley L. Engerman, and David Richardson.
GAA	Amsterdam City Archives
HCA	High Court of Admiralty
Huntington	Huntington Library, San Marino, California
I-Am	Intra-American slave trade database – part of www.slavevoyages.org
ID	Unique identification number assigned to a voyage or an individual in www.slavevoyages.org
MCC	Middelburgsche Commercie Compagnie – *Zeeuws Archief* (Middelburg, Netherlands)

NARA	US National Archives Records Administration
NBER	National Bureau of Economic Research, Boston, MA.
PP	Great Britain, Parliamentary Papers
PAST	People of the Atlantic Slave Trade at www.slavevoyages.org/past/
RAC	Royal African Company
Rawlinson	Rawlinson manuscripts, Bodleian Library, Oxford.
SCIR	Maxine Berg and Pat Hudson, *Slavery, Capitalism and the Industrial Revolution*
Slavevoyages	www.slavevoyages.org.
TSTD	Transatlantic slave trade database – part of www.slavevoyages.org.

I

Atlantic Slave Trading and World History

We begin with the largest of canvases to ask where the transatlantic slave trade lies in the rich and extensive annals of inhumane behavior around the globe. Europeans and their descendants in the Americas and the Indian Ocean carried off and enslaved close to 13 million Africans from sub-Saharan Africa in the 450 years between about 1450 and 1867.[1] Even after the dramatic decline of the Indigenous populations of the Americas in the two centuries following European contact in 1492, Europeans themselves proved reluctant to participate in transatlantic migration. Indentured servants, convicts, and all those owing obligations to work off labor debts to others always comprised a small share of total transatlantic migrants in the early modern era. Prior to 1820 the share of completely free migrants in this broad picture was much smaller again. Thus, for the greater part of this period merchants seeking to exploit the riches of what for Europeans was a newly discovered continent, resorted to slave labor, a form of coercion that had largely disappeared in their home countries by 1500.

Extraordinarily, faced by a labor shortage, peoples of European descent resuscitated this most violent and inhumane manifestation of all terms of labor, but applied them almost exclusively to the Indigenous populations of the Americas and sub-Saharan Africa. But why did sub-Saharan Africans seemingly accommodate this European prejudice? As Nathan Huggins, the first director of the W.E.B. Du Bois Institute pointed out and as I developed

---

[1] Note that new work by Marc Eagle and David Wheat on the early Iberian trade will likely mean that the 12.5 million total that Paul Lachance and I estimated in 2010 (see www.slavevoyages.org/voyage/downloads#estimates-spreadsheet/2/en/) should be increased by a quarter million to 12.75 million.

further in an earlier book, it happened because the rich and diverse cultures of the Indigenous Americas and of sub-Saharan Africa could not accommodate a pan-American or pan-African identity before the twentieth century. Just as Indigenous peoples in the Americas did not know they were American, in Huggins' striking words, Africans sold other Africans because they did not know they were African.[2] In 1859, the Africans on the *Clotilda*, among the last brought to the Americas on a slave ship, still "did not call their homeland Africa."[3] Even terms such as "Igbo" or "Yoruba" emerged in the diaspora, not Africa. Sigismund W. Koelle, the missionary who compiled *Polyglotta Africana* based on interviews with Liberated Africans in Sierra Leone found "that they had never heard it [the term Igbo] till they came to Sierra Leone ... and know only the names of their respective districts of countries."[4]

Such cultural dissonance, and, of course, profit maximization on both sides of the transaction that consigned people to a slave deck, were responsible for more than forty thousand voyages, 1519–1867, dispatched first to Africa and then to a plantation colony. The inhumanity, violence, and disastrous long-term consequences of this traffic are difficult to grasp by those living today in free societies with historically low violent crime rates. First there was the terror and killing inflicted in the capture of enslaved peoples and their transport to the coast. Then, almost 2 million Africans died at sea – a staggering mortality unmatched on transoceanic voyages carrying only Europeans. Most perished from the dehydrating effects of dysentery. Others succumbed to infectious Guinea worm or dracunculiasis, "their entrails filled and gnawed with worms; some small and flat, others ... monstrous in length and size; some vomited in a bunch and others in a quantity of twelve to fifteen at a time."[5] Human actions

---

[2] Nathan Huggins, *Black Odyssey: The Afro-American Ordeal in Slavery* (New York, 1977), p. 20.

[3] Sylviane Diouf, *Dreams of Africa in Alabama: The Slave Ship Clotilda and the Story of the Last Africans Brought to America* (New York, 2007), p. 50.

[4] Diouf, *Dreams of Africa*, p. 38. As the title of the book suggests, interviews with the survivors in later life indicate that Africa "became" the homeland about which they dreamt. Sigismund W. Koelle, *Polyglotta Africana; or, A Comparative Vocabulary of Nearly Three Hundred Words and Phrases, in More than One Hundred Distinct African Languages* (Graz, 1963), pp. 7–8. For the emergence of the term "Yoruba," see Richard P. Anderson, *Abolition in Sierra Leone: Rebuilding Lives and Identities in Nineteenth-Century West Africa* (Cambridge, 2020), pp. 161–65.

[5] Jean-François Carës, "Aux sources de l'histoire de la traite négrière: l'exemple de l'expédition catastrophique du Roi Guinguin (1764–1766)," *Mémoires de la société d'histoire et d'archéologie de Bretagne*, 92 (2014): 101–30, quote p. 110. See ID 30789. The vessel was named after the king of Badagry, who supplied the captives.

were often more deadly than Guinea worms. The tenth slaving voyage of the Dutch West India Company ship, *Leusden*, in 1738 foundered in the estuary of the Maroni River in Suriname with 664 Africans captive below deck. Fearing the chaos that might result as the ship went down within sight of land, the captain ordered the hatches nailed shut before abandoning ship. But first he made sure that the enslaved people that he himself owned, together with the company's gold (taken on board at Elmina, now in Ghana), were secure on the boat that carried them to safety.[6] Such horrors continued to the very end of transatlantic slave trafficking. In 1861, the St. Helena colonial engineer John Charles Melliss was the first British official to board the *Ardennes*, a newly captured slave vessel. He wrote:

> [T]he whole deck, as I picked my way from end to end, in order to avoid treading on them, was thickly strewn with the dead, dying and starved bodies of what seemed to me a species of ape that I had never seen before ... (yet) the miserable, helpless objects being picked up from the deck and handed over the ship's side, one by one, living, dying and dead alike, were really human beings. Their arms were worn down to about the size of a walking stick. Many died as they were passed from the ship to the boat, but there was no time to separate the living from the dead.[7]

In this nearly four-century-long gallery of inhumanity, the murder of the *Leusden* captives stands out as the worst recorded atrocity of all the 40,000-plus transatlantic slave voyages that occurred before 1867. Unsurprisingly, violence bred violence. In the sixty or so recorded slave revolts in which the captives gained at least temporary control of the vessel, all but one or two of the crew were slaughtered as an incentive to the surviving crew to navigate a return to Africa. In a couple of such instances, a now-captive European kept a journal before expiring, at which point the vessel drifted in the Atlantic as the Africans gradually succumbed to hunger and thirst. In one case, fifteen African survivors plus the sailor's journal were eventually picked up mid-Atlantic and taken to

---

[6] Leo Balai, *Slave Ship Leusden: A Story of Shipwreck, Mutiny, and Murder* (eBook, 2015), chapter 12. For a similar if marginally less murderous case, see the London-based *Phoenix*, ID 75976, which foundered mid-Atlantic. The captain and 36 crew were saved by a passing merchant ship, leaving the 332 people on the slave deck to drown (*Gazette de France*, Jan. 10, 1763, p. 13, https://digipress.digitale-sammlungen.de/view/bsb10485553_00015_u001/3?cq=n%C3%A8gre).

[7] Probably the *Ardennes* (ID 4842). Quote is from John Charles Melliss, *St. Helena: A Physical, Historical, and Topographical Description of the Island, including Its Geology, Fauna, Flora, and Meteorology* (London, 1875), pp. 30–31.

Bristol in the United Kingdom. From Bristol, the Africans likely continued their journey to a lifetime of plantation labor. The most successful slave-ship rebellion in history occurred on a French ship, the *Regina Coeli*, in 1858. The vessel's 391 captives took control of the ship, killed all the crew, and escaped. Many found their way to Monrovia, the capital of Liberia. The almost six hundred shipboard rebellions that we *do* know about were unsuccessful. Failure was inevitably followed by even more horrific violence, as captain and crew exacted a retribution constrained only by the need to preserve the human merchandise for sale in the colonies.[8]

Survivors of these transoceanic horrors might well have thought that they were not particularly fortunate. They could expect long hours of gang labor on plantations enforced by whipping and other cruelties. If family life was possible, it was insecure. North of Brazil it meant there was virtually no possibility of parents or children escaping servitude, except by running away. It is nearly one hundred years since Ulrich Bonnell Phillips – then the leading White authority on slavery in the US – argued that the slave trade improved the lives of Africans by bringing them to the Americas.[9] Since then both research into and recognition of the enormity of the horrors of the business have expanded dramatically. There is probably no field of history that can match the gains in knowledge and the shifts in scholarly attitudes that have taken place in the study of slavery in the Atlantic world. We now know the structure, dimensions, and impact of the abominable business. Most importantly, we can grasp something of the experiences of those forcibly removed from sub-Saharan Africa as well as their descendants to a degree previously unimaginable. As I will demonstrate, the study of slavery and the slave trades in the four centuries after 1450 has moved to center stage for both scholars and the general reader.

But these advances have not occurred without some costs. One is the steady erosion of the comparative component in more recent research. Slavery outside this four-century interval and beyond the confines of the

---

[8] Francois Renault, *Liberation d'esclaves et Nouvelle Servitude: Les rachats de captifs africaines pour le compte des colonies francaises apres l'abolition de l'esclavage* (Abidjan, 1976), p. 158 points out that French merchants continued to purchase Africans on behalf of planters in the French islands in the Indian Ocean until well into the 1890s. See Chapter 7 for a fuller discussion of this issue. The *Regina Coeli* case is discussed in Chapter 5. For the enabling role of identity shifts in the slave trade see my *The Rise of African Slavery in the Americas* (Cambridge, 2000), pp. 1–28.

[9] Ulrich Bonnell Phillips *Life and Labor in the Old South* (Boston, 1929), pp. 188–217.

Atlantic has not received the same attention. For example, scholars of the Indian Ocean world, where slavery and the slave trade had a much longer history, have referred to the "tyranny of the Atlantic" in the discipline, by which they mean the disproportionate research funding it receives.[10] A second issue is raising the profile of the slave trade in the catalogue of catastrophic cruelties that our species has inflicted on itself. The scale of the Atlantic slave trades ensured that four out of every five people arriving in the Americas from across the ocean before 1830 were African, not European. Cumulatively, migration from Europe exceeded arrivals from Africa only in the following decade. For more than three centuries, the repopulation of the Americas after the demographic collapse induced by Old World disease was by Africans, not Europeans.[11] However, only in the temperate Americas – southern Brazil and what became the southern US – did the two flows of people overlap significantly. Overwhelmingly, Africans both departed from and arrived in tropical regions, but the disease environment of Africa was not the same as in the tropical Americas. Moreover, the grueling labor Africans were required to perform in the low-lying wetlands where sugar grew best ensured higher Black mortality. Disease, malnutrition, and sheer exhaustion killed untold numbers. Sugar ensured a much larger inflow of Africans to the Americas than Europeans, but by 1800 only the Black populations of the US, Barbados, and probably Antigua had achieved an intrinsic positive natural rate of growth.[12] In the Americas as a whole, descendants of the smaller European migration came to heavily outnumber their African counterparts. This chapter attempts to set the horrors of the slave trade against the backdrop of the preceding millennium.

A broad comparative approach to what might be called the repeopling of the Americas helps explain why the trafficking of people first from

---

[10] Richard Allen, "The Constant Demand of the French: The Mascarene Slave Trade and the Worlds of the Indian Ocean and Atlantic During the Eighteenth and Nineteenth Centuries," *Journal of African History*, 49 (2008): 47. See also the Introduction to *CWHS*, vol. 2: 1–24.

[11] For the debate on the impact of Old World diseases on New World populations, see most recently Alexander Koch, Chris Brierley, Mark M. Maslin, and Simon L. Lewis, "Earth System Impacts of the European Arrival and Great Dying in the Americas after 1492," *Quaternary Science Reviews*, 207 (2019): 13–36. Bibcode: 2019QSRv.207...13K. doi: 10.1016/j.quascirev.2018.12.004.

[12] For this concept, see Jack Eblen, "Cuban Population," in Eugene D. Genovese and Stanley L. Engerman (eds.), *Race and Slavery in the Western Hemisphere: Quantitative Studies* (Princeton, NJ, 1975), pp. 211–14. For slave populations, Barry W. Higman, *Slave Populations of the British Caribbean, 1807–1834* (Baltimore, MD, 1984) is still the foundational work.

Africa to the Americas (and soon thereafter between ports within the Americas) has had such a great and enduring influence on the modern world. This despite all the famines, conquests, wars, attacks on minorities, and viciously suppressed rebellions that in the previous millennium created such historical shatter zones of human misery. Yet the grim and ongoing legacy of the violent slave trade should not prevent us from locating what was effectively the forced repopulation of the Americas against the backdrop of inhuman behavior in recorded history. The very term "inhuman" seems inappropriate given the prevalence of the practice of slavery in our past. Scholars can cite the occasional thinker who had reservations, but up to 250 years ago, and in most parts of the world long after that, slavery was regarded as an unfortunate condition, one to be avoided, but certainly not one to be abolished. If not quite a universal practice, it was seen as a quintessentially human practice. A first step toward understanding what happened in the Atlantic world – especially to Africa and Africans – is to recognize what this massive, forced migration had in common with what had gone before, as well as how it differed. Even a brief examination of global slavery and slave trades over the last two millennia – instead of the more usual focus on the Atlantic world alone since 1450 – reveals perspectives and contexts usually missing from specialist works.

Walter Scheidel has estimated the traffic in enslaved people into the Roman Empire at three or four hundred thousand per year at its peak. That was three times the level of traffic from Africa to the Americas in 1829 – the year of the highest annual total recorded for the transatlantic slave trade.[13] And when pagan peoples invaded and destroyed the now Christianized Roman Empire, beginning in the late fourth century, it is quite possible that in some years the reverse flow of captive Roman citizens into "barbarian" territories was of similar magnitude.

Historians of the Atlantic and the Americas have tracked the movement and evolution of what Philip Curtin called the plantation complex – the nexus of tropical produce, forced labor, and large estates.[14] Several centuries after Europeans learned of sugar production during the Crusades, that complex moved westward through the Mediterranean Sea, then out into the Mediterranean Atlantic bounded by the Atlantic Islands, before landing in São Tomé in the Gulf of Guinea, then making the leap to New Spain, Brazil, and the Caribbean. After 1450, when sugar production

---

[13] Walter Scheidel, "The Roman Slave Supply," in *CWHS*, vol. 1: 287–310, 293.
[14] Philip D. Curtin, *The Rise and Fall of the Plantation Complex* (Cambridge, 1990).

reached Madeira and the Canaries, it began its four-century-long dependence on enslaved labor. Despite these links between the medieval and the early modern world, most historians still see the large-scale forced movements of people – the "many middle passages" – as a post-1600 phenomenon unique to the last few centuries.[15]

Northern Europe provides an even bigger discontinuity between medieval and post-1600 worlds for most historians of the Atlantic. Slavery supposedly died out in this region before the English, the Dutch, the Scandinavians, and the French revived and reconstituted it in a particularly violent and exploitative form in their overseas colonies. The larger literature on slavery still sees the medieval period as something of a hiatus between the Roman Empire and the plantations of the European Americas – a hiatus that is firmly rooted in the Western-languages scholarship of the last two centuries. Few recent scholars have explicitly made this argument, but a cursory survey of *Slavery and Abolition*'s annual bibliography of slavery that began in 1981, and in the 1990s attempted to incorporate all titles published since 1900, confirms that during the twentieth century no less than 95 percent of the listed items in this bibliography dealt with slavery before or after the medieval millennium.[16] Coverage of Asia, the Indian Ocean world, Amerindian societies and Oceania has increased significantly in recent years, but so, too, have publications on coerced labor in all periods and geographic regions. Thus, in a comparative sense, the temporal focus of scholarship on slavery over the past two millennia has changed little.

Humanity's oldest surviving work of literature, the *Epic of Gilgamesh*, fragments of which appear on 4,200-year-old clay tablets from northern Iraq, contains references to enslaved status.[17] Slavery is thus in its fifth millennium of recorded history. It certainly did not disappear between 450 and 1450 CE; it merely took on different forms and appeared in different types of socioeconomic structures. Large landholdings and mines worked by forced labor were indeed largely absent in medieval Eurasia. The notable exception was the sketchily documented Zanj people, who were forced to

---

[15] See Emma Christopher, Cassandra Pybus, and Marcus Rediker (eds.), *Many Middle Passages: Forced Migration and the Making of the Modern World* (Berkeley, CA, 2007).
[16] Joseph C. Miller, *Slavery and Slaving in World History: A Bibliography*, 2 vols (Armonk, NY, 1993 and 1998). Data for other years taken from Thomas Thurston, "Slavery: Annual Bibliographical Supplement," published in the last issue of each year in *Slavery and Abolition*.
[17] Albert Tobias Clay (ed.), and Morris Jastrow (trans.), *An Old Babylonian Version of the Gilgamesh Epic* (New Haven, CT, 1920), line 154.

clear salt from marshes in ninth-century Mesopotamia. However, the incidence of enslaved labor in households for both domestic and sexual labor appears to have increased across the Old World. The phenomenon of enslaved peoples in temples appeared in Buddhist societies with few antecedents in the ancient world, and none whatever in the later Americas, unless we shoehorn the vast Jesuit slaveholdings in the Iberian Americas into this category. In addition, the medieval millennium saw the high point of enslaved people used in military contexts. Slave soldiers in the Delhi Sultanate, Mamluk Egypt, and the Janissaries of the Ottomans are well known. But given that every elite soldier in the Middle East and Asia required a support corps of tens and in some cases hundreds of enslaved people to minister to his needs, it is probable that the global share of persons in bondage over the whole course of history peaked at some point in the medieval millennium, rather than in the early modern Atlantic world. Certainly, in the millennium before 1420 it is possible that nowhere in the world was there a settled society (i.e. one based on agriculture) that lacked enslaved women and men.[18]

Both the medieval and the early modern eras experienced prolonged periods of economic growth, the first curtailed by global plague, and the second, encouraged by industrialization, continuing into the modern era. Increased urbanization, expanding trade networks, and the growth of centers of learning were common to both. Scholars have argued for a twelfth-century renaissance in Europe and the Arab world, leading to some historians positing the evolution of a first "world system" in the thirteenth and early fourteenth centuries. Still, no scholar foregrounds slavery and the slave trade either as a cause or a consequence of this phenomenon.[19] By contrast, one cannot imagine the later and more widely known era of European overseas expansion without attempts to link slavery with economic expansion – either as cause or effect.

But to what extent was slavery in the two eras sufficiently alike to warrant comparison? Property-in-persons and coerced labor have

---

[18] Ali Anooshashr, *The Ghazi Sultans and the Frontiers of Islam: A Comparative Study of the Late Medieval and Early Modern Periods* (Abingdon-on-Thames, UK, 2008). See the essays in Reuven Amitai and Stephan Conerman (eds.), *The Mamluk Sultanate from the Perspective of Regional and World History: Economic, Social and Cultural Development in an Era of Increasing International Interaction and Competition* (Göttingen, 2019). Note that while "slave soldiers" were bought they were normally freed upon successful completion of their military training.

[19] Janet L. Abu-Lughod, *Before European Hegemony: The World System A.D. 1250–1350* (Oxford, 1989) argues that eastern societies could easily have become the progenitors of a modern world system.

appeared in such a range of forms in history that no consensus definition of slavery is possible. Joseph Miller's specification of slavery as a "practice" or a "strategy" rather than an "institution" has proved influential. But if practices are "socially constructed and accepted ways of doing things," the distinction is not helpful for the purpose of comparing the two periods.[20] How is such a practice so defined different from an institution? More useful is anthropologist Edmund Leach's view of another fundamental human practice – marriage – which also took a wide variety of forms. Marriage, he argued, was "a bundle of rights" with such variations that a universal definition is quite impossible. To take just one aspect, think of the almost infinite variations of polygamy in societies in the Americas alone. Analysis can take place only in a specific cultural context, an assessment that assuredly applies to slavery as well, but one that does not inhibit comparisons.[21] The type that is most readily recognized today – the chattel bondage characteristic of the European-dominated Americas and classical Greece and Rome – was certainly not the predominant form of slavery in global history. As already noted, in the Indigenous Americas, much of Africa, and the Islamic world, an incorporative form of the institution prevailed. While plantation slavery aimed primarily at extracting labor, the incorporative variety evolved in part as a device to extend the size and prestige of a lineage, a fictive kin-group, or a religion, in a social environment where a fulfilling life without such associations was inconceivable. And if, in the first, it was difficult for a captive or her descendants to exit enslaved status, in the second, full integration of an enslaved person or her descendants into the host society was normally a definite possibility. In this work we avoid a definition of slavery, but we know it exists when a person is traded or captured and subsequently owes lifelong obligations to another.

Much of Asia fits neither model. In China, Korea, the long-lasting Khmer Empire, and seventeenth-century Japan, enslaved peoples had few prospects of changing status. They were created by foreign conquest, the judicial system (convicts), or were simply drawn from the lowest social stratum of "base" people. Nevertheless, the concept of property in

---

[20] Joseph C. Miller, *The Problem of Slavery as History: A Global Approach* (New Haven, CT, 2012), pp. 2–4; Nathan Hofer, *The Popularisation of Sufism in Ayyubid and Mamluk Egypt, 1173–1325* (Edinburgh, 2015), pp. 14–19.

[21] Edmund R. Leach, "Polyandry, Inheritance, and the Definition of Marriage," in Leach (ed.), *Rethinking Anthropology* (London, 1961), pp. 105–13; see David S. Reynolds' review of Sarah M. S. Pearsall, *Polygamy: An Early American History* (New Haven, CT, 2019) in the *New York Review of Books*, April 19, 2019, pp. 27–28.

persons that characterized slavery in the European Americas and the Islamic worlds never evolved in China. Slavery in the Indian subcontinent was different again, as we might expect given the heavy Islamic influence beginning in the mid thirteenth century. The institution there occupied a large conceptual middle ground between the incorporative slavery of Africa and Islam on the one hand, and East Asian systems of coerced labor on the other. Collective ownership of enslaved peoples by Hindu and Buddhist monastic lineages survived alongside ownership by individuals. Medieval Islamic incursions extended both military and court slavery. But Islamic, Hindu, and Buddhist communities legally sanctioned enslaved holdings and transfers of property-in-persons. They also imposed responsibilities on owners. The law might circumscribe both ownership and treatment. Slaves in some jurisdictions might have the right to inherit, to own, and to dispose of their own property.[22]

Here I argue that most enslaved peoples were not obtained either by purchase or conquest. Perhaps the common denominator across cultures and time was the existence of a marketplace in which individuals were traded. In the medieval millennium, the term "slave" or its equivalent was not reserved solely for instances in which an owner assumed title to *all* the individual rights of the enslaved. The term could also describe other forms of social dependency in which only some degrees of unfreedom were subject to transfer. Many markets must have witnessed buyers and sellers where each had a slightly different idea of what was being traded. Nevertheless, such markets could not have existed without both parties to a transaction sharing a common understanding that their exchange involved a commodified person – as, for example, on the African coast in the early modern period where both the buyers of the enslaved (Europeans) and sellers (Africans) viewed the people they traded as outsiders to their own societies.

Debates over the definition of slavery have not proved very productive and for our comparative purposes here, we do not need a definition of slavery applicable across cultures. It is sufficient to note the wide distribution and vibrancy of markets for the enslaved across the major continents, from ancient history to the early twentieth century. These were clearance centers for future units of labor, sexual exploitation, social prestige, expansion of the kin group, and other purposes, but also, from the enslaved's perspective, humiliation, deracination, and physical abuse.

---

[22] Pamela Crossley, "Slavery in Early Modern China," in *CWHS*, vol. 3: 187; Indrani Chatterjee, "British Abolitionism from the Vantage of Pre-colonial South Asian Regimes," in *CWHS*, vol. 4: 441–65.

Even without a definition of slavery we can discern some contrasting geographic patterns in the movement of enslaved people over the globe in the last millennium and a half. In the early modern Atlantic world, an ocean separated the major markets and the enslaved flowed overwhelmingly from east to west. In medieval Eurasia we do see cases of Chinese captives sold in Black Sea markets, presumably having arrived there in a series of stages. Slaves travelled mainly by land throughout this era, albeit frequently following riverine routes, but seas such as the Irish and North Seas, the Mediterranean, the Caspian and Black Seas and the Indian Ocean all had very active slave trades in different periods. Predominantly, however, the enslaved moved on a north–south axis rather than east–west. A series of empires and powerful states stretched from Spain through the Mediterranean, the Tigris–Euphrates region, the Turkic states, and through the Khmer Empire of southeast Asia to China.[23] This belt comprised several dynasties and was occasionally subject to conquest from the north. It drew captives from the less densely populated and poorer regions such as northern Europe, the Caucasus, and central Asia, as well as from the south (Africa, India during the Muslim incursions, and Korea). Victims of Viking raids ln Iceland might sell in Baghdad.

Further east, the Turkic polities of the Samanids and Ghaznavids conducted extensive raids – the Saminids in central Asia, while the Ghaznavids drew heavily on northern India. Key markets, often bordering on bodies of water, constituted transit or staging points for the enslaved. Examples in the period included Dublin, Tana on the Sea of Azov, Caffa in the Crimea peninsula, Baku in Azerbaijan, and Alexandria and Venice in the Mediterranean. In the Indian Ocean, Aden and Zabid in Yemen, and Zayla in Somaliland hosted large slave markets. The city of Guangzhou in China had a centuries-long presence of Africans, perhaps brought by Arabs, beginning no later than the tenth century – long before Admiral Zheng He's voyages to the sub-continent. However, the extreme south of China, Korea, Inner Mongolia and Central Asia supplied most of the externally generated enslaved peoples to mid-millennium China, in yet another north–south axis. Within North Africa, the pre-Atlantic traffic moved on both axes, east toward Egypt, the Red Sea and Mesopotamia,

---

[23] For the Khmer see Radhakrishna Choudhary, "Slaves and Serfs in Medieval Cambodia (Circa 400–1300 A.D.)," *Proceedings of the Indian History Congress*, 28 (1966): 520–31, and James C. Scott, *The Art of Not Being Governed: An Anarchist History of Upland Southeast Asia* (New Haven, CT, 2009), pp. 6, 50–51, 250, 280.

and on the better known six major south-to-north routes that Paul Lane describes.[24]

Both the early modern Atlantic and medieval Eurasia experienced cataclysmic periods of enslavement. European incursions into the Atlantic and eventually the Americas peaked in the 1701 to 1850 period, when 80 percent of the transatlantic traffic occurred. This expansion of maritime bondage resulted in the startling fact that far more enslaved people than free left the Old World for the Americas in this century and a half. The medieval equivalent of this upheaval involved the conquests of the nomads of Central Asia – first the Mongols, then the Khanates, and later the Turks. These events had huge consequences for enslavement as well as, of course, unleashing violent death and social disruption. In neither case were the enslaved an important component at the beginning of imperial expansion. But both generated an apotheosis of violence, the first transcontinental, the second, transoceanic. The military adventures of the Mongols under Chinggis Khan (d. 1227) and Tamerlane (d. 1405) all involved high mortality. Chinggis Khan killed countless citizens of captured cities in the event of their resistance. He enslaved many more besides. Tamerlane's subsequent conquests in the late fourteenth century led to possibly the largest contiguous territorial empire in history. The later European disruption of Atlantic peoples destroyed three-quarters of the population of the Americas and triggered violence and enslavement in Africa. Just as European empires brought an Atlantic market for enslaved peoples into existence, so the Mongol Empire strengthened and supplied an integrated market for both commodities and enslaved Eurasian people.[25]

Without claiming cause and effect, it is striking that arguably two of the most catastrophic sociopolitical events in global history are, in some senses, antecedents of the two superpowers of the mid twenty-first century – China in the East and the United States in the West. Finally, both power centers came to abandon outside sources of forced labor. The China that the

---

[24] Don J. Wyatt, *The Blacks of Premodern China (Encounters with Asia)* (Philadelphia, PA, 2010), pp. 20–22. For Africa, see Map 22.1 in Paul J. Lane, "Slavery in Africa c. 500–1500 CE: Archaeological and Historical Perspectives," in *CWHS*, vol. 2: 531–52.

[25] The death, destruction and enslavement of imperial expansion was exacerbated by yet another East–West parallel – the epidemiological impact of Mongol and European expansion. The Pax Mongolica, which saw East–West trade expand dramatically, also provided ideal conditions for the spread of the *yersinia pestis* bacterium that killed 100 million people during the Black Death. European expansion to the Americas had a comparable effect on the Indigenous population of the Americas.

Mongols helped shape, and of which they had become an integral part by the fifteenth century, had only a tiny fraction of their population enslaved. China no longer drew on external sources for their "base" people. In the West, likewise, Americans, even before independence, quickly came to rely on internal sources for new captives – in the form of natural population growth. Yet the parallels extend only so far. Amid all the claims that slavery was an essential prerequisite of economic growth in America (and an earlier literature that makes similar links for the preceding British case), no one considers chattel slavery when discussing the economic rise of China.

As these comments suggest, comparisons between eras inevitably raise questions of scale.[26] We do know the approximate numbers of captives moving around the Atlantic world after 1500, as well as the broad demographic patterns in the major European colonies of the Americas. In Africa, however, there is no such data for the slave trade era, apart from tallies of the enslaved who were forced to leave for the Americas. Instead, demographers depend on backward projections of twentieth-century data, applying various assumptions in their models. The most reliable of these, by Frankema and Jerven, comprise a modification of Patrick Manning's foundational work.[27] For the end of the slave trade era in 1850, they estimate a continental population of 114 million broken down by modern country, which, after allowing for the large swathes of the north, northeastern, central, and southern parts of the continent that could not have supplied captives to the Americas, means approximately 59 million people living in potential catchment zones. In the peak years of 1701 to 1850, an annual average of 60,600 captives left Africa for the Americas. Deaths prior to boarding the slave vessel through violence, or passage through regions with unfamiliar disease environments, amounted, perhaps, to an additional third of this total, but there is no

---

[26] John C. Caldwell and Thomas Schindlmayr, "Historical Population Estimates: Unravelling the Consensus," *Population and Development*, 28 (2002): 183–204; United States Census Bureau, "Historical Population Estimates, revised July 5, 2018," www.census.gov/data/tables/time-series/demo/international-programs/historical-est-worldpop.html; Jean-Noel Biraben, Essai sur l'évolution du nombres des hommes," *Population*, 34 (1979): 13–25. The sixth edition of the widely cited Massimo Livi Bacci, *A Concise History of World Population* (Hoboken, NJ, 2017) still draws on Biraben's essay.

[27] Ewout Frankema and Morten Jerven, "Writing History Backwards or Sideways: Towards a Consensus on African Population, 1850–2010," *Economic History Review*, 67 (2014): 907–31; Patrick Manning, "African Population: Projections, 1850–1960," in Karl Ittmann, Denis D. Cordell, and Gregory H. Maddox (eds.), *The Demographics of Empire: the Colonial order and the Creation of Knowledge* (Athens, OH, 2010), pp. 245–75.

hard data on this phase of the traffic.²⁸ If Africa lost 81,000 people a year to the transatlantic slave trade, then annual population loss was between .01 and .02 of a percentage point, or 1.5 per thousand per year, assuming that the population remained at about 59 million during these 150 years of maximum impact. Including the trans-Saharan and Indian Ocean world (IOW) slave trades in this computation increases these rates slightly, though the IOW traffic probably became significant only in the late eighteenth century.²⁹

In the seventeenth century these catchment regions within Africa would certainly have contained fewer than 59 million people, an assessment based on what we know about the arrival of new crops from other parts of the globe in the preceding centuries. Images of an unchanging African agriculture before the twentieth century are clearly erroneous. As John Caldwell and Thomas Schindlmayr have argued, "the majority of food eaten in sub-Saharan Africa is non-indigenous and was eaten by no one there 500 years ago." By the early eighteenth century, European slave-ship captains seeking provisions familiar to their captives prior to the voyage were able to buy Asian rice, manioc, and maize on the Western African coast, none of them native to Africa.³⁰ The superior nutritional content of these foodstuffs gradually gaining acceptance across much of the continent would have enabled population growth even during the years when the transatlantic slave trade was at its height. In addition, we now know that the female component of the forced migration was only one third, and this is a key metric in determining the impact of emigration on a population. While some slave trade scholars argue that the slave trade reduced the African population, few modern historical demographers subscribe to this position – in contrast to their mid twentieth-century predecessors.³¹

---

²⁸ See below, p. 217.
²⁹ Ralph A. Austen, "The Mediterranean Islamic Slave Trade out of Africa: A Tentative Census," *Slavery & Abolition*, 13 (1992): 214–248; for higher estimates, see Paul E. Lovejoy, *Transformations in Slavery: A History of Slavery in Africa*, 3rd edition (Cambridge, 2011), pp. 46–48; Gwyn Campbell "Slavery and the Trans-Indian Ocean World Slave Trade," in Himanshu Prabha Ray and Edward A. Alpers (eds.), *Cross Currents and Community Networks: The History of the Indian Ocean World* (Oxford, 2007), pp. 286–305.
³⁰ Jevan Cherniwchan and Juan Moreno-Cruz, "Maize and Pre-colonial Africa," *Journal of Development Economics*, 136 (2019): 137–50.
³¹ Quote is from Caldwell and Schindlmayr, "Historical Population Estimates," 185. See also John C. Caldwell, "Major Questions in African Demographic History," in Christopher Fyfe and David McMaster (eds.) *African Historical Demography: Proceedings of a Seminar Held in the Centre of African Studies, University of Edinburgh* (Edinburgh, 1985), pp. 7–22. Augustine S. O. Okwu. *Igbo Culture and the*

The dearth of demographic material anywhere in the world before 1600 is such that the early modern Atlantic world seems data-rich by comparison. It is generally accepted that the medieval global population was much lower than its eighteenth-century successor – perhaps 260 million in the year 1000 CE, of whom at least 200 million lived in Eurasia. About one third of this total lived in China under the early Song dynasty (CE 960–1279).[32] China, the largest polity in Eurasia, enslaved both Chinese and non-Chinese people at different times in the medieval era, with both state and private individuals as owners. But as noted above, chattel slavery as practiced in the later Atlantic world fits poorly with categories of dependency as they evolved in China. "Base people" comprised 5 percent or less of the imperial Song population. Setting aside eunuchs and concubines – groups that were not considered base – and given that not all base people were enslaved, the incidence of slavery in China must have fallen below the enslaved ratios of contemporary Islamic and Christian regions, as well as eastern societies such as Korea.[33] The incursions of Jurchens, Jins, and Mongols into China that destroyed the Song dynasty would have seen temporary increases in the incidence of slavery.

Meanwhile, Orlando Patterson has estimated that mid tenth-century Western Europe alone was home to 3.4 million enslaved peoples (15 percent of a total population of 22.5 million). The majority were native Western Europeans.[34] Islamic populations filled much of the vast space between the receding Byzantine territory and the western boundaries of the Song, and although Islam viewed freedom as the original condition of humanity, enslaved peoples were ubiquitous across the Muslim Middle East, northern India, and much of central Asia. They labored in a wide variety of roles. Scholars have identified servile labor existing in religiously diverse southern India, where slavery was often associated with temples. Reliable estimates are impossible, but if even 10 percent of the Old World

---

Christian Missions (Lanham, MD, 2010) is a recent work that revives Adu Boahen's argument for a major depopulating impact (*Britain, the Sahara and the Western Sudan 1788–1861* [Oxford, 1964]).

[32] Colin McEvedy and Richard Jones, *Atlas of World Population History* (London, 1978) provides continental breakdowns. Don Wyatt, "Slavery in Medieval China," in *CWHS*, vol. 2: 277, for Chinese population figures.

[33] Frederick W. Mote, *Imperial China, 900–1800* (Cambridge, MA, 1999), pp. 366–67; Seung B. Kye, "Slavery in Medieval Korea," in *CWHS*, vol. 2: 295–312. The temple slavery of Buddhists was more widely established outside China than within.

[34] Orlando Patterson, *Slavery and Social Death: A Comparative Study* (Cambridge, MA, 1982), p. 157.

population was enslaved in the year 1000 CE, then at 20 million (one tenth of 200 million) there would have been far more enslaved peoples in Eurasia than at any time in the Americas in the four centuries after 1450. But the rate/ratio of enslavement was higher in the Americas. Given that the Americas accounted for just 2.5 percent of the global population in 1804 (a benchmark year chosen by Barry Higman) a different assessment, one built on ratios rather than aggregate totals yields a different picture. In 1804 the relatively lightly populated Americas had approximately 13 percent of its people enslaved – a larger proportion, no doubt, than any continent in the history of the world. To a greater extent than elsewhere, slavery built the Americas, but would the development path have been different if all migrants had been free?[35]

Turning from populations (stocks) to forced migrations (flows) does not improve the quality of the medieval data that is available. For the movement of enslaved peoples within Eurasia in the medieval millennium, we rely mainly on the records of chroniclers who were often dependents of the great men about whom they wrote. In such records "the numbers of slaves reported as captured ... should be divided by ten, or even a hundred."[36] A few Chinese people on sale in Black Sea ports, the aforementioned African captives in Guangzhou, and the Greek woman in the Sultan of Java's harem noted by Ibn Battuta, testify to a vast trading network matching, if not exceeding, the range of slaving routes in the later Atlantic.[37] But they also point to the interconnectedness of markets for the enslaved. Unlike in the transatlantic traffic, no single slave trader carried his human chattel from one end of Eurasia to sell at the other. Enslaved people acquired and sold via war and conquest dominate the sources. Meillassoux's model of slavery as being associated with predatory states could be generalized across the ages. If one polity had the ability to overcome another, then war, violent death, or some form of social debasement and dependency for the survivors would surely follow – a situation that probably holds for slavery everywhere.[38] James C. Scott has argued

---

[35] B. W. Higman, "Demography and Family Structures," in *CWHS*, vol. 3: 479–507; and Higman, "Demography," in *CWHS*, vol. 4: 20–48, especially, pp. 23–24.

[36] See Introduction, in *CWHS*, vol. 2: 2, 9.

[37] Hamilton A. R. Gibb, *The Travels of Ibn Battuta, A. D. 1325–1354*, 2 vols, vol. 2, passim (Farnham, UK, 2017); Marina A. Tolmacheva, "Concubines on the Road: Ibn Battuta's Slave Women," in Matthew Gordon and Kathryn A. Hain (eds.), *Concubines and Courtesans: Women and Slavery in Islamic History* (Oxford, 2017), pp. 167, 173.

[38] Claude Meillassoux, 'Rôle de l'esclavage dans l'histoire de l'Afrique occidentale,' *Anthropologie et Sociétés*, 2 (1978): 117–48.

that "all Southeast Asian states in history have been slaving states" and "wars (were) about the seizure of as many captives as possible,"[39] especially women. In the later Atlantic world such conflicts occurred as a prelude to the enslaved embarking on the African coast. While many similar wars occurred in the Americas, especially the Caribbean, the victory of one party over another – say the British over the French in the eighteenth century – may have resulted in existing enslaved peoples changing hands. Nevertheless, the losers in the conflict did not themselves become enslaved. In Eurasia, by contrast, at least until the emergence of increasingly impermeable "no-slaving zones" late in the medieval period, slave owners as well as enslaved peoples on the losing side could normally expect to face servitude (or extended servitude in the case of the already enslaved).

For the Aztecs, the Viking raiders, the Umayyad Caliphate, the Latin kingdoms in the aftermath of Christendom's resurgence, the Ghaznavids in India, and the string of Mongol victories to the east, enslavement followed from raids and conquest. The same would be true later with Europeans in the Americas. But prisoners of war and civilians treated as booty – the spoils of war – fed into the Eurasian network of markets for the enslaved. Nevertheless, war captives cannot have been the most important source of slave labor. What other sources were there? Conquered groups frequently supplied enslaved people to the victors as tribute. Self-enslavement brought on by extreme deprivation appears to have been universal though not numerically significant, as were judicial enslavement and kidnapping. In fact, all five of the enslavement mechanisms that appear in Sigismund Koelle's report of his interviews with Liberated Africans in nineteenth-century Sierra Leone are to be found in medieval sources, even though the documentary record suggests that armed struggle and its consequences was the principal route to enslavement.[40]

Yet this catalogue of pathways to oppression omits the probable major source of slaves in global history: birth. Almost all discussions of slavery in specific contexts explore the ways in which individuals became enslaved. The current conventional meaning of the verb "to enslave" implies that people had at some point lost their free status. In a reality that modern

---

[39] Scott, *The Art of Not Being Governed*, p. 24.
[40] P. E. H. Hair, "The Enslavement of Koelle's Informants," *Journal of African History*, 6 (1965): 193–203. Abandoned children or the practice of parents selling their offspring into servitude is one enslavement mechanism that does not show up in Africa (even though famine-stricken communities must have resorted to such sales). It was certainly more common in east Asia.

scholars today almost never recognize, the implications of the hereditary nature of slavery throughout history, at least until the twentieth century, guaranteed that birth was the main source of slaves in almost all societies. Even the word "captive" is problematic. In eras when slave raids and war-generated captives were the dominant sources, many of those caught up in such tumult already had the status of slaves. Medieval and classical sources provide countless instances of strong states raiding their weaker neighbors, but we hear of the status of the resulting enslaved persons only if they were high-born or later became well-known. People already enslaved in the target society were those most likely to be captured, or more precisely, recaptured.[41] In the transatlantic context given the high incidence of slavery within Africa, many captives dispatched to the Americas would have been already enslaved.

A quick survey establishes that most captives were born into servitude. In the European-controlled Americas three different demographic scenarios played out for people of African descent. First, in the relatively well-documented US case, fewer than half a million captive Africans arrived via the maritime slave trade over 250 years. But by 1865 at least 10 million people had experienced slavery on the North American mainland. More than 90 percent of them were born into bondage, rather than captured and then sold.[42] Second and by contrast, the slave labor force of the Caribbean sugar colonies experienced a much harsher demographic regime. Except for Barbados after 1760, constant inflows of Africans were necessary to prevent the labor force from declining in the face of the exigencies of sugar cultivation. Yet, just prior to emancipation in 1833, and twenty-five years after the slave trade ended, only one in five of the half-million enslaved persons in the British Caribbean could have been African-born.[43] Third, in Brazil, too, few of the enslaved freed in 1888 could have been born in Africa.[44] Most

---

[41] Judith Evans Grubbs, "Child Slaves in Late Antiquity and the Middle Ages," *CWHS*, vol. 2: 158–59. Patrick, enslaved as a boy by the Irish as they raided northwest England, was accompanied to Ireland by "recaptured" male and female slaves belonging to Patrick's father.

[42] David Hacker, "From '20. and odd' to 10 million": The Growth of the Slave Population in the United States," *Slavery & Abolition*, 41 (2020): 840–55. For Brazil, see Robert W. Slenes, "The Demography and Economics of Brazilian Slavery, 1850–1888," unpublished PhD thesis, Stanford University (1975), pp. 297–410, 484–573, esp. p. 317.

[43] Calculated from Higman, *Slave Populations*, pp. 116, 418. Weighted average of ratios are provided for Jamaica, Barbados, Demerara/Berbice, Bahamas, Anguilla, Grenada, and Dominica.

[44] A third demographic structure emerged in Brazil and the Spanish Americas about which much less is known – the first reliable census for Brazil dating only from 1872, sixteen years before slavery was abolished there.

scholars have still not engaged with the fact that almost two thirds of all those taken from Africa to the Americas spent the balance of their lives in Latin America.[45] Here, unlike the US and most of the Caribbean, it was more possible for some slaves to change status over their lifespan via the practice of self-purchase, although manumission rates were always low outside the major cities.[46] The fertility of the Brazilian slave population was lower than that of the Black population of the US South, but high compared to most other regions in the Atlantic world for which data is available. Robert Slenes has used a range of reliable data from the 1870s to calculate an annual fertility rate of 36/1,000. With an enslaved population in 1850 of around 2 million, about 72,000 people per year were born into slavery in Brazil.[47] Annual arrivals from Africa to Brazil between 1801 and 1850 – the peak half-century of the Brazilian slave trade – averaged only 41,000. In the Americas, of course, the slave trade was vital to the expansion of the various plantation economies, but creoles, not Africans, must have dominated the slave labor forces at most points in time.[48]

Slavery in the Americas, and the traffic in people that made it possible, receive far more scholarly attention than does slavery in the rest of the world. Such scholarly focus is perhaps warranted given the high ratio of enslaved people in these places compared to elsewhere, and the high land-to-labor ratios on the continent. Estimates of the pre-contact populations of the Americas have varied widely but even before the "great dying" that European settlement and its accompanying diseases triggered among Indigenous peoples, population densities were likely much lower than on other continents.[49] Imperial systems in the Americas before 1492 certainly maintained enslaved populations that drew in part on tribute slaves supplied by fringe client states.[50] In the aftermath of European conquest, population densities, already low by global standards, fell

---

[45] See Table 2.5.
[46] Self-purchase is discussed more fully in Chapter 2.
[47] Slenes, "Demography and Economics," p. 317. Cuba was the destination of almost two-thirds of the Africans carried into Latin America, but even as the Cuban sugar revolution began in the late eighteenth century significant numbers of urban slaves were able to exercise their rights to *coartación* (self-purchase). See David Eltis and Jorge Felipe, "The Rise and Fall of the Cuban Slave Trade," in Alex Borucki, David Eltis, and David Wheat (eds.), *From the Galleons to the Highlands: Slave Trade Routes in the Spanish Americas* (Albuquerque, NM, 2020), p. 215.
[48] As this suggests, the current practice of referring to slaves as "enslaved persons" is inaccurate. How can a person born into slavery have passed from free to slave status?
[49] Koch et al., "Earth System Impacts of the European Arrival," pp. 13–36: https://doi.org/10.1016/j.quascirev.2018.12.004
[50] Camilla Townsend, "Slavery in Pre-Contact America," in *CWHS*, vol. 2: 553–70.

dramatically, with repopulation occurring via immigration and positive rates of natural growth. Even the Indigenous populations of the Americas experienced natural growth from the late seventeenth century. The inflow of people to the Americas occurred under the auspices of five major transoceanic imperial systems (English, French, Spanish, Portuguese, and Dutch), all of which depended on enslaved labor. As already noted, before 1820 four out of five of the arrivals from the Old World were bonded Africans rather than European free migrants prior to 1820. Except for parts of Oceania, no other part of the known world experienced demographic disaster on the scale of the early Americas. Plagues and famine decimated populations, but nowhere did slavery play such a large role in the subsequent demographic recovery as in the Americas.

In the medieval millennium, plantation slavery was rare, but the same pattern of births constituting the main source of slaves held. Most empires in history have relied on outside populations for their servile labor in their early expansionary phases. But over the course of their imperial existence, they drew on natural increases of their slave populations. Unfortunately, the sources for the medieval millennium are dominated by descriptions of the enslavement process, particularly when this was a by-product of war and imperial expansion. Hard data on natural population growth in medieval empires does not exist. We do, however, have sources that point to the predominance of females in most slave populations. In medieval India, Leslie Orr has found that "[m]ore than half of all [temple] inscriptional references to slaves, where gender is noted, concern the gift or sale of women or of female-headed families." The late medieval Deccan state, Orr continues, "possessed tens of thousands of slaves, mostly women, who had been captured and brought to court from the neighboring non-Muslim kingdoms." Among the Mongols, Michal Biran argues that "female slaves were more valuable, as they could be used not only for herding sheep and cattle but also for ... domestic chores that transformed the produce of the nomadic economy into useful goods ... and as wives or concubines."[51] Genetic analysis of modern near-eastern Arab populations shows the African component arrived via females beginning in the early sixth century. In Mamluk Egypt "female slaves outnumbered male, probably by a significant margin," a profile that emerges even more strongly among Jewish owners in pre-Mamluk Egypt's Geniza documents. Across

---

[51] "Slavery and Dependency in Medieval South India," in *CWHS*, vol. 2: 313–33, quote is from p. 318; Michal Biran, "Forced Migrations and Slavery in the Mongol Empire (1206–1368)," in *CWHS*, vol. 2: 78.

the late medieval Mediterranean world, in response to plague pandemics, the slaves in demand were "especially female ... who could be employed as domestic servants." In northern Europe, David Wyatt argues that while scholars continue to focus on the male agricultural laborer, the medieval traffic in slave women barely declined. The enslaved were principally attached to households where they cohabited with their masters.[52]

Shaun Marmon makes clear the implications for natural population growth of a majority-female slave presence in a predominantly domestic context. "Since the sexual exploitation of female slaves is inherent to the institution of slavery, in all historical contexts, all female slaves were potential sexual slaves" and "slaves only gave birth to slaves."[53] As graphic illustrations of this point, consider just three examples of very different cultures spread across 850 years. The arrival of the Rus (of Swedish origin) in Bulgar, a major slave market in Eastern Europe in 922, was famously described by Ibn Fadlan as being "accompanied by beautiful slave girls for trading. One man will have intercourse with his slave-girl while his companion looks on ... Sometimes indeed the merchant will come in to buy a slave-girl from one of them and he will chance upon him having intercourse with her but will not leave her alone until he has satisfied his urge." Also, Geniza documents from the relatively sedate urban environments of twelfth- and thirteenth-century Egypt show Jewish households stressed by the failure of Jewish law to recognize concubinage to the point that marriage and engagement contracts came to include a "slave woman clause," specifying that "the groom will not retain

---

[52] Susan Mosher Stuard, "Ancillary Evidence for the Decline of Medieval Slavery," *Past & Present*, 149 (1995): 3–28; Gwyn Campbell, Suzanne Miers, and Joseph C. Miller, "Women in Western Systems of Slavery: Introduction," *Slavery and Abolition*, 26 (2005): 161; Leslie C. Orr, *Devotees and Daughters of God: Temple Women in Medieval Tamilnadu* (New York, 2000), pp. 53–54; Orr quote is from Orr, "Slavery and Dependency in Medieval South India," *CWHS*, vol. 2: 323; Ali Anooshahr, "Military Slavery In Medieval North India," *CWHS*, vol. 2: 379–80, quote is from p. 380; Michal Biran, "Encounters among Enemies: Preliminary Remarks on Captives in Mongol Eurasia," *Archivum Eurasiae Medii Aevi*, 21 (2014–15): 27–42; quote is from Biran, "Forced Migrations and Slavery," in CWHS, 2: 78; Stephan Conermann, "Slavery in the Mamluk Sultanate," in *CWHS* vol. 2: 401–402, quote is on p. 401; Debra Blumenthal, "Slavery in Medieval Iberia," *CWHS*, vol. 2: 522; David Wyatt, "Slavery in Northern Europe (Scandinavia and Iceland) and the British Isles, 500–1420," in *CWHS*, vol. 2: 487–88. See also Craig Perry, "The Daily Life of Slaves and the Global Reach of Slavery in Medieval Egypt, 969–1250 CE," unpublished PhD thesis, Emory University (2014).

[53] Shaun Marmon, "Intersections of Gender, Sex and Slavery: Female Sexual Slavery," in *CWHS*, vol. 2: 189.

a slave woman whom she (the bride) dislikes." Across the ages, it does seem that household rather than agricultural slavery is what most enslaved people experienced. Finally, Thomas Thistlewood's plantation record in Jamaica contains a depressing record of sexual assault and rape that was all too common in a plantation society. From his arrival on the island in 1750, through to his death thirty-seven years later, he "engaged in 3,852 acts of sexual intercourse with 108 different slave women," all meticulously recorded in his diary.[54] The absence of consent is the common thread in these three examples. Finally, to return to the Miers and Kopytoff assimilative model useful for understanding post-conquest Islamic – and indeed Amerindian – slavery, it might be assumed that host societies found it easier to integrate and assimilate women and children rather than men.

If most of us were asked to identify the central difference between the predominantly Eurasian slavery of the medieval millennium and the large slaveholdings that characterized the succeeding era in the Atlantic world, we would likely answer, first, that slavery became more extensive in the later period, and second, that the African component of the global slave population increased to the point that the enslaved became overwhelmingly, perhaps exclusively, Black after 1500. But both points are questionable. The enslaved in the Americas always accounted for a small share of the global enslaved population. Barry Higman estimates that in 1800, the global population of chattel slaves had reached 45 million, or 5 percent of the Earth's total. However, only 6 million lived in the Americas.[55] Given that slavery was common in the Indigenous Americas both before and after the destructive European incursion, and that the large Islamic band of polities stretching into southeast Asia continued to thrive after 1500, the transatlantic slave trade by itself, massive though it was, may not have drastically changed the global ratio of enslaved to free.

As for the African-descended share of the enslaved, just more than a quarter of the global total of enslaved persons were of African descent

---

[54] "The Risala of Ibn Fadlan," trans. James Montgomery: http://viking.archeurope.com/settlement/russia/ibn-fadlan/risala-of-ibn-fadlan/; Craig Perry, "Slavery and Agency in the Middle Ages," in *CWHS* 2: 251–53; Trevor Burnard, *Mastery, Tyranny, and Desire: Thomas Thistlewood and His Slaves in the Anglo-Jamaican World* (Chapel Hill, NC, 2004), p. 156. On slavery in pre-contact Indigenous American communities see Townsend, "Slavery in Pre-Contact America," 553–70.

[55] Higman, "Demography." Higman describes his estimate as "best estimates with uncertain margins of error, to be refined by future research" (p. 23). No estimate of slaves in Africa in 1804 exists, but their numbers cannot have been more than a few million. Three million is added here to Higman's total to accommodate the sub-continent.

in 1800. At any point earlier than 1800, the African American component of the global total was inevitably smaller. But what was the pattern in the Old World? Some scholars argue that the exodus of Africans via the trans-Saharan and Indian Ocean came close to matching Atlantic departures, but such claims are dubious, given that evidence of the eastern and northern branches of the African slave trades cannot compare to what is available for the Atlantic traffic.[56] Islamic regions constituted by far the largest market for captives in medieval Eurasia.[57]

What did Africa contribute to the enslaved labor pool of this vast Eurasian region? With the single exception of the area occupied by the Zanj, a variously described Bantu-speaking people in what is now southern Iraq in the ninth and tenth centuries, it seems that people of African descent never constituted a majority population of any part of medieval Islam. We might point to the huge diversity of enslaved people that the region contained, a diversity that only gets wider when we recognize that the term "African" itself encapsulates a vast range of ethnolinguistic groups.[58] Islamic states drew on Circassians, Tartars, Rus, Slavs, Mongols, Turkic peoples, Latin Europeans, and many others. The major group traded in Cairo, the largest slave market in the Mediterranean through most of the medieval millennium, were brought in from Black Sea regions, though about half the slave women in medieval Egypt's Geniza documents were Black or Nubian.[59] For the early period, Michael McCormick's magnum opus, *Origins of the European Economy: Communications and Commerce, AD 300–900*, focuses on European slaves entering the Islamic world, but Jeff Fynn-Paul points to several non-European groups that McCormick overlooks who passed along well-established trade routes

---

[56] Patrick Manning in *Slavery and African Life: Occidental, Oriental and African Slave Trades* (Cambridge, 1990) makes the assumption of equivalency of Atlantic, Indian Ocean world, and trans-Saharan. Gwyn Williams is skeptical, see "The African-Asian Diaspora: Myth or Reality?," *African and Asian Studies*, 5 (2006): 305–24.
[57] Blumenthal, "Slavery in Medieval Iberia," pp. 508–30.
[58] To counterpose "African" with Tartar, Circassian, Mongol etc., as many scholars of medieval Islam do, ignores this diversity. Presumably if gold production in fourteenth-century Mali had resulted in a north-to-south traffic in slaves sourced in the Mediterranean and beyond, "Whites" would have become the umbrella term for Scandinavians, Slavs, Circassians, etc. within the Mali empire itself, as it expanded northward along the Niger Valley. The best attempt at separating myth from reality on this topic is John E. G. Sutton, "The African Lords of the Intercontinental Gold Trade Before the Black Death: Al Hasan bin Sulaiman Kilwa and Mansa Musa of Mali," *Antiquaries Journal*, 77 (1997): 221–42.
[59] Hannah Barker, *That Most Precious Merchandise: The Mediterranean Trade in Black Sea Slaves, 1260–1500* (Philadelphia, PA, 2019), p. 2; Perry, "Daily Life of Slaves," pp. 40–41.

only one of which connected with sub-Saharan Africa.[60] Early Islam's (the Abbasid Caliphate) use of African soldiers has attracted considerable scholarly attention, but not all of these were slaves. By the later Mamluk era in Egypt and in the Delhi Sultanate in North India the African component was much smaller, replaced by purchases from the Black Sea region, Turkic areas, and Central Asia.[61] Less is known about the origin of the numerous non-combatant slaves that supported the military elite. Africa may have quickly become the sole external source of slaves when the Europeans took over the Americas, but Africans appear to have had no significant presence in the United Mongol Empire (1206–1260) or the subsequent Khanates of the Mongol Commonwealth.

Manuals on buying slaves offer further insights into the origins of Islamic slaves. A treatise by an eleventh-century Baghdad physician identifies "women of India, Sind, the Maghrib, several regions of sub-Saharan and coastal Africa, three towns of Arabia (Mecca, Medina and Taif), Yemen, Qandahar (Afghanistan), Allan (Caucasus) and the Daylam region (northern Iran) … as well as Turkish, Greek (presumably Byzantine) and Armenians." Other guides to buying for the Mamluk era offer stereotypical descriptions of a similarly wide range of peoples.[62] The etymological evidence also points away from Africans, but this time not toward a multiethnic mélange of peoples, but to a specific alternative group. In the later Middle Ages, both Latin languages and Arabic began to roll together the terms for a slave on the one hand and, on the other, the name of the ethnic group on which both Latins and Arabs had come to largely depend. That term was not "African," "Black," "negro," "nigra" or any derivatives of these words, but rather Slavic peoples, whose name forms the stem of the word slave in all western languages – the Latin term for "Slav" being *esclavus*. Arab terminology, too, quickly came to integrate the status of slave with the ethnicity of most people who occupied that status. Thus, "saquiliba" (Arabic صقالبة) denoted both Slavic and enslaved.

---

[60] Michael McCormick, *Origins of the European Economy: Communications and Commerce, AD 300–900* (Cambridge, 2001), pp. 759, 768; Jeff Fynn-Paul, "The Greater Mediterranean Slave Trade," CWHS, vol. 2: 27–52.

[61] Bayarsaikhan Dashdondog, "The Black Sea Slave Trade in the 13th–14th Century that Changed the Political Balance in The Near East," *Golden Horde Review*, 7 (2019): 283–94.

[62] Matthew S. Gordon, "Slavery in the Islamic Middle East (c. 600–1000 CE)," CWHS, vol. 2: 337–61; Stephan Conermann, "Slavery in the Mamluk Sultanate," CWHS, vol. 2: 383–405.

None of these sources allow us to pin down either a number or a specific ratio, much less a trend over time, but they do make it unlikely that Africa was a dominant source of slaves for the medieval Islamic world. Nor does this contradict evidence of the stigma of black skin that periodically surfaces in the medieval sources, and arguably intensified in the later Middle Ages. Adherents of all three Abrahamic religions do show increasing evidence of prejudice against Black people over the millennium. The bizarre story of the Curse of Ham gained currency, wherein Abraham condemns the offspring of Canaan, the son of Ham, to be slaves in perpetuity for a trivial offence on the part of Ham. A discourse on color symbolism begins in Christendom and Islam in which Black is equated with evil and White with good. But the Black descendants of Cush, brother of Canaan, are deemed innocent in early rabbinic writings, and writers continue to see black skin as a function of climatic factors as did their classical-era predecessors.[63]

Turkic and Sudanic peoples formed the bulk of the elite Mamluks, but other states that used elite enslaved military units in India and the Middle East drew on those of African descent. More important, none of the societies adhering to the Religions of the Book had legal systems based on somatic norms. Antarah ibn Shaddad, born a Black slave, became a famous knight as well the best-known poet in the pre-Islamic near east. The freedman, Bilal ibn Rabah, likely an Ethiopian, was the Prophet's close companion and is regarded as the first caller to prayer. In Christendom, one of the three kings attending the birth of Christ had become portrayed as Black by the end of the medieval period. And the well-known cult of St. Maurice, the black knight, could scarcely have flourished in the face of such discrimination. Thirteenth-century literary romances *Parzival* by Wolfram von Eschenbach and the anonymous Dutch *Moriaen* illustrate the increasing European engagement with and ambivalence toward "Ethiopians," and perhaps a growing epidermal racism. But nothing in the medieval Eurasian written record in any way suggests that only Blacks should be enslaved, and thus nothing foreshadowed the situation that emerged in the Atlantic world in the century after 1420.[64]

---

[63] The best discussion and partial dismissal of the Curse of Ham scholarship is Steven T. Katz, *The Holocaust and New World Slavery*, 2 vols., vol. 1: 22–23, n. 60.

[64] See the discussion in David Brion Davis, *Slavery and Human Progress* (Oxford, 1984), pp. 23–51; Steven A. Epstein, "Attitudes toward Blackness," in *CWHS*, vol. 2: 214–39. The best guide to the rise to dominance of Black slavery in the Atlantic world continues to be the *magna opera* of David Brion Davis, which draws on the full range of Western thought on the

After 1500, with the acceptance of Christianity or Islam by the peoples of eastern Europe, the steppes and much of northern Africa now complete, the Latin West and the Arab world did draw more heavily on Africa for enslaved people. Even though slaves usually accounted for only a small share of most Asian populations (Korea was an exception), the typical slave prior to the nineteenth century was Eurasian and female – not African (or Slavic) and male – given the enduring importance of Asia in global demography. The modern world may visualize peoples of African descent when they think of slaves in a historical context, but in fact this group has never come close to forming most of the world's population of enslaved peoples. The extraordinary slave ratios in the eighteenth-century Caribbean populations were highly exceptional in the context of global history. What also follows is that despite the transoceanic slave trade, the enslaved population of the Old World always vastly exceeded that of the New.

The exclusive association of black skin with slavery, discussed more fully below, was not established until the early seventeenth century, and never took firm root in the Islamic world and points east. The first sale of a sub-Saharan African as a chattel slave certainly occurred BCE. Among the last were those accompanying their Nigerian owners to Saudi Arabia on a *hajj* in the 1930s (and perhaps later), where they were sold – having been forced into the role of an animated traveler's check for their owners.[65] For most of this span of more than two millennia, Africans were no more likely than people on other continents to be enslaved and sold into a long-distance slave trade. When Jacopo Tintoretto (the elder Tintoretto) painted his stunning and widely acclaimed "San Marco libera uno schiavo," known in English as "The Miracle of San Marco," in mid sixteenth-century Venice, the slave in the foreground was White, and two

---

topic and fully recognizes that the African share of slaves used in the Middle East and Indian Ocean Worlds rapidly increased at the same time. For the emergence of color as a racial marker in the late Middle Ages see Geraldine Heng, *The Invention of Race in the European Middle Ages* (Cambridge, 2018), pp. 181–256. Heng also has one of the better definitions of race making: "the strategic, epistemological, and political commitment ... to demarcate human beings through differences among humans that are selectively essentialized as absolute and fundamental, in order to distribute positions and powers differentially to human groups." (Heng, "The Invention of Race in the European Middle Ages I: Race Studies, Modernity, and the Middle Ages," *Literature Compass*, 8 (2011): 268.)

[65] Alaine S. Hutson "'His Original Name Is ... ': Remapping the Slave Experience in Saudi Arabia," in Sabine Damir-Geilsdorf, Ulrike Lindner, Gesine Müller, Oliver Tappe, and Michael Zeuske (eds.), *Bonded Labour: Global and Comparative Perspectives (18th–21st Century)* (New York, 2017), pp. 133–62. For specific cases see Hutson's database at www.remapdatabase.org/.

of the onlookers in the background were not only Black, but well-dressed merchants to boot.[66] The transatlantic slave trade was already four decades old when the painting was finished in 1548. In European eyes a slave could be white and a Madonna, black.[67]

From the early seventeenth to the late nineteenth century in a large part of the Western world, a slave had to be someone of African descent. Even the Portuguese, whom much of the literature has viewed as having the most malleable of attitudes toward skin color, came to associate slavery with African descent. In 1670 captured Portuguese soldiers in the hands of the Soyo army in West Central Africa were offered the option of becoming slaves or being killed, and "they replied proudly that 'Whites will never serve Blacks'; they were then put to death."[68] While the corollary never held, being Black usually ensured a status somewhere below full citizenship, especially throughout the Americas. In modern-day slavery this association of skin color with enslavement, at least in the popular perception, seems to have at last disappeared. While de facto slavery still exists in parts of Africa, the victims of human trafficking – and most are still predominantly female – can be of any origin. In terms of the multiethnicity of modern-day slaves – except perhaps for concentrated numbers of temporary debt slaves in South Asia – we seem to have returned to the enlightenment of the early Middle Ages.[69]

Why, four centuries ago, would the diversity of people enslaved by the Latin West shrink to comprise Africans alone? Slavery itself was entrenched in both the medieval millennium and in the four centuries of the Atlantic world that seamlessly emerged from it. In one sense, as we have seen, it did not become less diversified, given Africa's more than 1,500 distinct spoken languages, hundreds of distinct systems of beliefs, and huge genetic and phenotypic variation shaped by a wide range of

---

[66] The dramatic perspectives in the picture brought Tintoretto instant celebrity status. San Marco was the patron saint of Venice. Venetian Renaissance paintings include an abundance of subjects of African descent. Marcio Manziale, "La Cena in Emmaus," painted between 1495 and 1507, has one of its five major subjects as Black. Similarly, one fifth of the figures are Black in Pablo Caliari detta Paulo Veronese, "Banquet in the House of Levi," which is really a depiction of the Last Supper (all in the Galleria dell'Academia, Venice).

[67] See Michael Duricy, "Black Madonnas: Origin, History, Controversy," University of Dayton: https://udayton.edu/imri/mary/b/black-madonnas-origin-history-controversy.php.

[68] John K. Thornton, *A History of West Central Africa to 1850* (Cambridge, 2020), p. 185.

[69] Kevin Bales, "Contemporary Coercive Labor Practices – Slavery Today," in *CWHS*, vol. 4: 655–78, and the extensive literature cited there; the Borgen Project, "10 Facts about Human Trafficking in Africa": https://borgenproject.org/human-trafficking-in-africa/.

climates, diets, and exposures to infectious disease. But in geographic terms the point cannot be doubted.

Three factors help account for the narrowing of Western eligibility requirements to sub-Saharan Africa. Historians have discussed the first two at some length, while the third requires more attention. First, more than three-quarters of the people carried off across the Atlantic and Indian Oceans disembarked in colonies producing sugar and its derivatives. As already noted, the cultivation of sugar cane began BCE in the Pacific and gradually spread after the Crusades via India and the Arab world into the Mediterranean. Over the course of a further two centuries, Europeans spread the complex across the Atlantic and the real price of refined sugar declined substantially as the use of slave labor rapidly expanded. Where long-distance trade had mostly centered on luxury products, after 1500 the produce of tropical plantations, chiefly sugar, gradually came within the range of ordinary consumers. Consumer choice drove the expansion of the plantation complex. Stimulants such as coffee, tea, sugar, tobacco, and a range of alcoholic beverages had become mass consumption items by the end of the era. Working classes came to see such items as necessities, even though their overall impact on health was likely negative. Prior to the advent of sugar beets in the nineteenth century, refined cane sugar was a commodity that Europeans could access only through long-distance trade. The human craving for a cheap sweetener thus lies at the foundation of the sugar plantation complex, as well as the slave trade that sustained it.[70] Accounting for the demand for slaves, however, explains nothing about where those enslaved peoples were to be captured.

The second factor is geographic. The sugar complex made its way into the Atlantic, as the Portuguese learned how to navigate the oceans of the world. In the age of sail the great gyres and the associated wind patterns determined all transoceanic transportation. The Earth's rotation ensures that a single vast spiral dominates each of the northern and southern sectors of the great oceans. North of the equator in the Atlantic the gyre turns clockwise, and to the south, and separated from it by the doldrums, the gyre moves counterclockwise. As the Portuguese discovered, to sail west (or in returning, east) across the Atlantic one must first sail south

---

[70] Philip D. Curtin, *The Rise and Fall of the Plantation Complex: Essays in Atlantic History*, 2nd ed. (Cambridge, 1998), pp. 34–185. While the widely cited *Sweetness and Power: The Place of Sugar in Modern History* (New York, 1985) by Sidney Mintz, hints at such items boosting worker energy during the Industrial Revolution, any calculation of the calorie count of well-documented British sugar imports shows that such an impact could only have been trivial.

(or north). To reach the Americas from Africa south of the equator, one must first sail north (or, in returning from the New World, south).[71] Despite the circuitous route, Western sub-Saharan Africa was closer to the Americas than any other well-populated landmass, and during the sixteenth century, ocean-going technology had made the transatlantic crossing routine. It became suddenly quicker and less costly to transport three or four hundred people from the well-populated forest zones of West Africa to northeast Brazil, than to form a caravan to cross the desert to the Mediterranean coast.

If consumer demand for sugar and the Atlantic's oceanic patterns – two factors scholars *do* emphasize – were pre-requirements of a transatlantic slave trade, they were not sufficient in themselves to make it happen. The third and most important factor in narrowing European conceptions of who could be enslaved was a sense of the otherness of Black Africans that appears to have held among all Europeans who aspired to trade with Africans on their Atlantic shores. As I argued in a previous book, Europeans had become reluctant to impose slavery on other Europeans, even if those others were convicted murderers, rebels, heretics, or prisoners of war. In Jeff Fynn-Paul's terms, by the end of the Middle Ages both Christendom and the Islamic powers of North Africa and the Middle East had become "perfect no-slaving zones," by which he means co-religionists could not be enslaved.[72] We know that galley slaves based in Spanish America could be Moriscos, North Africans, or orthodox Christians, but were their offspring also slaves? A documented instance of a white-skinned chattel slave, complete with subsequent progeny who were also enslaved, has yet to emerge from the archives of the Atlantic world. By contrast, light skinned mulattos could be slaves, as could their children.

A fuller understanding of the shift toward exclusively African enslavement requires us to step outside both the medieval millennia, and the

---

[71] Daniel Domingues Da Silva, "The Atlantic Slave Trade to Maranhão, 1680–1846: Volume, Routes and Organization," *Slavery and Abolition*, 29 (2008): 477–501; and Alfred Crosby, *Ecological Imperialism: The Ecological Expansion of Europe, 900–1900*, 2nd ed. (Cambridge, 2004), pp. 195–216.

[72] Eltis, *Rise of African Slavery*, chapter 2; Fynn-Paul, "Greater Mediterranean Slave Trade"; in an echo of *Rise of African Slavery*, Seymour Drescher has further reviewed the moral, political, and institutional barriers that inhibited enslavement of Europeans (Seymour Drescher, "White Atlantic?: The Choice for African Slave Labor in the Plantation Americas," in David Eltis, Frank D. Lewis, and Kenneth L. Sokoloff (eds.), *Slavery in the Development of the Americas* (New York, 2004), pp. 31–69. However, the author sees his essay as a critique rather than what it really is – an elaboration of the original argument.

1500–1800 era, and look briefly at the evolution of *Homo sapiens*. As is well known, a range of hominids, including *Homo erectus*, Neanderthals, and eventually *Homo sapiens*, evolved first in Africa before populating the Euro-Asian landmass. *Homo sapiens* emerged over a period from about 500,000 to 300,000 years ago, but at separate locations. Advances in DNA analysis have, rather counterintuitively, destroyed the consensus on the timing of the exit from Africa that used to exist.[73] Considering the above discussion, however, the first point to note is that if all hominids, including *Homo sapiens*, originated in Africa then they must have been black-skinned. The obsession over the causes of black skin that has preoccupied Western intellectuals over the last millennia shows a Eurocentric preoccupation with the wrong question. The issue should rather have been what caused white, red, or yellow skin.[74]

Black migration out of Africa meant a series of journeys that were overwhelmingly one-way and comprised a series of constant goodbyes. The final stages by sea through to the settlement of Hawaii and New Zealand occurred about one thousand years ago. We now know that *Homo sapiens* interacted with earlier versions of humans who had migrated well before the main exodus of *Homo sapiens*, Neanderthals and Denisovans, especially. "Interaction" in this context no doubt meant a great deal of violence over millennia in addition to extensive interbreeding.[75] As the last ice age ended about 11,500 years ago, rising water levels impenetrably sealed off huge sections of global populations from each other. The cultural implications of these tectonic events were

---

[73] The paleoanthropologist consensus on the "out of Africa" explanation of *Homo sapiens* may also be coming under pressure. See Madelaine Böhme, Rudiger Braune, and Florian Breier, *Ancient Bones: Unearthing the Astonishing Story of How We Became Human* (Vancouver, BC, 2020).

[74] See, most recently, the preface in Henry Louis Gates and Andrew Curran (eds.), *Who's Black and Why: A Hidden Chapter in the Eighteenth-Century Invention of Race* (Cambridge, MA, 2022), pp. ix–xiii.

[75] Eleanor Scerri et al., "Did Our Species Evolve in Subdivided Populations across Africa, and Why Does It Matter?" *Trends in Ecology and Evolution*, 33 (2018): 582–94; Rolf Quam, "Fossil Jawbone from Israel is the Oldest Modern Human Found Outside Africa," *The Conversation*, January 25, 2018; Ann Gibbons, "Trove of Teeth from Cave Represents Oldest Modern Humans in China," *Science*, October 15, 2015; Genelle Weule, "How Do We Know How Old the Indigenous Madjedbebe Rock Shelter Is?" *Science*, July 19, 2017. The ability to access nuclear DNA (from the nucleus of a cell) as opposed to mitochondrial DNA (the DNA lying outside the nucleus of a cell) has permitted a much clearer picture of human migration to emerge in the last two decades or so. On violence between *Homo sapiens* and Neanderthals, see Nicholas R. Longrich, "War in the Time of Neanderthals: How Our Species Battled for Supremacy for Over 100,000 Years," *The Conversation*, November 2, 2020.

enormous and continue to shape social tensions in our modern world. Migration meant that the number of languages and cultures in the world peaked – probably just prior to 1500. Ocean navigation enabling return voyages, as evidenced by the exploits of Admiral Zheng He and Columbus, initiated the reintegration of global populations, a process still in its very early stages in the twenty-first century. Cultural diversity, as evidenced by language loss, has been in decline ever since return voyages became not only possible, but routine, and will no doubt continue.[76]

The isolation of the Americas and the late arrival there of *Homo sapiens* also ensured that for four centuries after 1492 America continued to have by far the largest land-to-labor ratio in the temperate world. Historically these are not the conditions under which individuals usually work voluntarily for others for any extended period.[77] Slaves certainly existed in probably every Indigenous society in the Americas, but even in the Indigenous empires of Central and South America, they were very much in the minority. To believe that America's resources would have entered the global economy without empire, slavery, racism, extreme violence, and unequal income distribution is to ignore global history. As explored further in Chapter 2, a transoceanic slave trade could have happened without Western Europe and without Africa, but not without America.

The key difference between the initial dispersion and the later reintegration of peoples was the time span involved. Whereas migration by land had occurred over millennia, and new languages and cultures emerged gradually, transoceanic migration brought peoples who were very different from each other, culturally and physically, into sudden contact. Oceans had ensured that many societies had developed without awareness of continents other than their own. The reactions in northwestern Europe to peoples and cultures previously beyond reach differed from the reactions of their Iberian neighbors to the south, who were still accustomed to living with multiethnic enslaved people. Consider the contrast with England, which became the first country in Europe to permanently expel its Jewish population (in 1290), then became the first to expel Black people (in 1599 and 1601). Despite repeated incursions by various

---

[76] See the February 21, 2017, edition of www.smithsonianmag.com/smart-news/four-things-happen-when-language-dies-and-one-thing-you-can-do-help-180962188/.

[77] Evsey Domar, "The Causes of Slavery and Serfdom: A Hypothesis," *Journal of Economic History*, 30 (1970): 18–32.

mainland European peoples stretching from the Bronze Age to the Norman Conquest, Geraldine Heng identifies England as the "first racial state in the West." It appears almost inevitable that a few decades later its colonies in the Americas presided over one of the most oppressive and, in racial terms, rigidly defined slave regimes in recorded history. In this they were joined by the Dutch and the French.[78]

By contrast, the Reconquista in Iberia, and the slave-trading prowess of both Genoa and Venice throughout the Mediterranean and Black Seas, ensured that the multiethnic conception of slave eligibility, characteristic of the medieval millennium and earlier, was abandoned much more slowly in southern Europe than in the north. People of African descent comprised 10 percent of the Lisbon population in 1480, not all of whom were enslaved. Official arrivals of enslaved Africans to the port averaged 2,000 a year between 1490 and 1516.[79] But at the same time the *degredados*, sent to a lifetime of labor in overseas Portuguese possessions, and the galley slaves at work in the sixteenth-century Spanish Caribbean, were certainly Europeans, many of whom were orthodox Christians or Jews.[80]

Among the maritime powers of Europe, the Portuguese, Spanish, and Italians had the strongest connections with sub-Saharan Africa in the late medieval period. Not surprisingly, they also developed slave systems and laws in the Americas based on the Castilian code, Siete Partidas, of 1265. This contained an escape hatch or two to freedom missing from similar codes in the slave colonies of their northern neighbors. David Wheat has argued that the pre-plantation Spanish Caribbean (lasting in Cuba's case until well into the eighteenth century) was settled by Blacks and Whites together. Blacks were certainly early victims of the slave trade. But by the early seventeenth century, large free populations of African descent in major cities, and the rural areas that provisioned them, have led Wheat to

---

[78] Geraldine Heng, *England and the Jews: How Religion and Violence Created the First Racial State in the West* (Cambridge, 2019), chapters 1 and 3. Anti-Jewish riots that saw extensive damage to properties in Manchester, Bolton, and other cities occurred as recently as 1947, despite fresh knowledge of the Holocaust (*Financial Times*, January 16, 2020). The most recent interpretation of Queen Elizabeth I's expulsion edicts sees them as an attempt to establish a slave trade in Africans. See Emily Weissbourd, "Those in Their Possession": Race, Slavery, and Queen Elizabeth's "Edicts of Expulsion," *Huntington Library Quarterly*, 78 (2015): 1–19.

[79] Alastair C. de C. M. Saunders, *A Social History of Black Slaves and Freedmen in Portugal, 1441–1555* (Cambridge, 1982), pp. 4–34; Ivana Elbl, "The Volume of the Early Atlantic Slave Trade, 1450–1521," *Journal of African History*, 38 (1997): 44–46.

[80] David Wheat, *Atlantic Africa and the Spanish Caribbean, 1570–1640* (Chapel Hill, NC, 2016), pp. 181–215.

describe Blacks as "surrogate settlers." New Spain did have a modest sugar complex in the first century after the Spanish reached the mainland. But most Blacks, enslaved and free, mostly "Latinized," and living in both the familiar towns (*pueblos*) and surrounding rural areas (*partidos*), had quickly come to form most of the non-Indigenous population of the early Spanish Americas. The practice of *coartación* (or self-purchase) remained in place through to the abolition of slavery in the late nineteenth century, even as the Spanish sugar and Brazilian coffee plantation complexes reached their respective apogees.[81] Self-purchase notwithstanding, slaves held in the Americas by Western European powers quickly came to be exclusively African and exclusively employed in the export economy and the activities that the export economy enabled. Africans in the Spanish Americas came to be clustered around export activities, urban centers enriched by such activities, or in areas that were strategically important in protecting routes to Europe – as in early Cuba and the Rio de la Plata. Differences between Iberian and non-Iberian systems in the Americas were slight compared to differences between slavery in the Americas and slavery in the rest of the world.

The horrors of the slave trade were thus in part the result of people separated by vast and unnavigable bodies of water developing different perceptions of how they saw themselves in relation to others. Slavery and the traffic in slaves evolved without much discussion or self-reflection within the societies that adopted these practices. If an opportunity to acquire captives occurred, it would be taken. Questions of morality arose only over eligibility for enslavement, not the practice itself. For major groups such as those living in Christendom and under Islam, and in various east Asian imperial polities, the identity point is obvious, particularly when counterposed with the inhabitants of meso-Americas and sub-Saharan Africa, where no such overarching identity existed. As already noted, no Indigenous American identified themselves as American. No one living in sub-Saharan Africa identified as African. Until the late eighteenth century throughout the world eligibility for enslavement was always the central question, not the practice of slavery itself.

---

[81] Eltis and Felipe, "Rise and Fall," p. 215. In the brutal aftermath of the La Escalera conspiracy in Cuba in 1843–44, Joseph Crawford, the British consul in Havana, wrote, "one of the sixteen shot lately in Matanzas left 1,200 dollars in his box and several others left money enough to purchase their freedom had they pleased to do so," Joseph Crawford to Lord Aberdeen, Jan. 17, 1844, BNA, FO84/520. This could not have happened in the British Americas. Note that *coartación* was always far more likely in an urban environment than on a sugar estate.

To summarize, three factors shaped the cataclysm that was the transatlantic slave trade: first, consumer desire for the products of plantations; second, rapid diffusion of new maritime technologies facilitating reintegration of global populations; and third, the fact that Africans and Indigenous Americans had a much narrower conception of who was ineligible for enslavement than had Europeans. But almost as important in explaining what happened in the Atlantic world after 1500 were the differences in perceptions of self *within* Christendom. Britons and Iberians may have seen themselves as Europeans, and thus ineligible for enslavement, but they had different codes, both formal and informal, governing their relations with Africans. It was inconceivable that the English would have occupied Jamaica or the Dutch, Surinam, with the same settlement pattern that prevailed in Spanish Cuba, much less that they would have institutionalized self-purchase for their slaves and overseen the emergence of colonial populations comprising an intermixture of indigenes, people of African descent, and Europeans. Miscegenation has negative connotations in English and Dutch completely missing from its Spanish-language counterpart, *mestizaje*. Strikingly, several Latin American countries have embraced the concept of the mestizo as central to the formation of new national identities in the era of independence. English-speaking countries in the Americas would have found this impossible.

The centuries-long evolution of identity and its implications for the exclusive enslavement of Africans in the Atlantic world, as well, eventually, as in much of Islam, helps explain the continuing impact of Atlantic slavery on the modern world. Of all the many past horrors, the trafficking of people first from Africa to the Americas, and soon thereafter between ports within the Americas, has had one of the most enduring influences on the modern world. Contemporaneously, famines, conquests, wars, attacks on minorities, and suppressions of rebellions also created vast zones of human misery.[82] But the cursory overview of global history presented here does underscore that those historical perspectives on slavery and the slave trade changed over time. According to the Old Testament, all but one of the twelve tribes of Israel were enslaved in Egypt. Enslavement and exodus are core elements of Jewish ritual, but enslavement of ancestors is not one of the many issues that separate Jews from non-Jews today. In China, Korean women were prized as concubines for centuries, as well as the eastern Khanates both before and after the Mongol conquests. These women

---

[82] A question posed most recently by Katz, *The Holocaust and New World Slavery*, 1: chapter 2 for the slave trade.

Atlantic Slave Trading and World History 35

FIGURE 1.1 Deformation as a mark of enslavement? Reproduced with the permission of the US National Anthropological Archives, Smithsonian Institution, BAE GN 03084.
"A flattened head was a mark of beauty among some indigenous groups living along the Lower Columbia River in the nineteenth century. Such groups saw round-headed individuals as potential enslaved persons. Indigenous groups in British Columbia by contrast saw flattened heads as marking the potentially enslaveable. The flattening was the result pressure applied to an infant's forehead and occiput. Epidermalization of slave status – the norm in the Atlantic World between 1600 and 1888 – has been highly unusual over the several millennia in which slavery across the globe has flourished."

were forced into sexual slavery across east Asia and beyond. But while the Japanese exploitation of Korean "comfort women" in World War II remains a bitter issue between the two countries, the earlier and vastly larger scale of exploitation perpetrated by China does not. And Western intervention in the Balkans in the 1990s was not complicated by memories of long centuries of Latin slave trading in Slavic regions.[83] More recently, the mark of slavery in parts of what is now coastal British Columbia was a flat head brought about by applying pressure to the head of infants.

---

[83] Recent tensions between Japan and South Korea focus on Japanese extraction of forced labor in the first half of the twentieth century. The vastly greater and longer-lasting exploitation of Korean women is not a modern issue.

Yet among the Wakashan and Chinookan-speaking Indigenous societies in the Lower Columbia River area to the south, a flat head signified membership of a group that *owned* slaves. Warfare and enslavement had created this situation, yet resentments, indeed, memories, of these physical distinctions of enslaved and enslaver do not appear to inform modern interactions of these two groups.[84] By contrast, the enslavement of Africans in the Atlantic continues to feed into deep modern social inequities, most recently with the higher viral infection rates during pandemics among African Americans.

Is it still useful, though painful, to ask when the Holocaust and the transatlantic slave trade will come to be treated with the detachment that historians assume in evaluating, say, the slave trade generated by the Roman, Mongol, Islamic, and Latin empires? The short answer to this question is no time soon. A slightly longer answer, on Atlantic slavery at least, is that perhaps it might happen when Black/White income differentials disappear, or when Black/White ratios in prison populations – as well Black/White victims of police shootings of unarmed people or awaiting execution on death row – come to reflect Black/White ratios in the general population. This view does not come from a belief in progress (though in material terms this cannot be questioned), and it certainly does not mean that racism will eventually disappear. Sadly, anyone looking back over 3,000 years of racist stereotyping in the written record must conclude that, while overall violence has declined, the target populations of discrimination, often based on physical appearance, will not disappear. Instead, they may well continue to shift, just as they have throughout global history.

It will not have much impact on current racial inequalities, but it is worth recognizing that every one of the nearly 8 billion people on the Earth today are descended from Black people. It is equally certain that all of us have both a slave and a slave owner in our ancestral heritage. The Legacy of British Slavery group at University College, London, began life with a mission to identify all British slave owners. In addition, www.slavevoyages.org has now developed user interfaces that do the same for owners of slave ships of every nation. These show the very wide distribution of participation in ventures

---

[84] Robert H. Ruby and John A. Brown, *Indian Slavery in the Pacific Northwest* (Spokane, WA, 1993), pp. 23–25 and passim. Note that Russian serf owners claimed that their serfs had black bones as opposed to their own white variety (Peter Kolchin, "In Defense of Servitude: American Proslavery and Russian Pro-serfdom Arguments, 1760–1860, *American Historical Review*, 85 (1980): 811.

designed to sustain and enforce coerced labor. Bondspeople were frequently owned collectively, thus spreading slaveholding further across the community. Monasteries and temples in South and Southeastern Asia owned thousands of slaves, many given to monks as a testament of lay piety. Kinship groups were even more important collective owners in Indigenous African and American societies. In Brazil, many enslaved people were themselves owners of enslaved people.[85]

For evidence of the *slave* status of non-Africans, researchers must dig deeper, but no modern ethnic or national group can possibly be free of such ancestry. The enslaved normally accounted for a small share of a society. But as already discussed, slavery was ubiquitous, ancient, and female. The temporary nature of bondage in many historical societies has also ensured wide descent lines. While, say, 10 percent of a population may have been enslaved in each society, they would not have been the same 10 percent over a lifetime, and not all manifestations of slavery in Asia were hereditary. Orlando Patterson describes the phenomenon of "social leakage," by which he means the high manumission rates in some slaveholding societies. In the Islamic World, much of non-Islamic Africa, and the Indigenous Americas, gradual erosion of slave status over time can be observed as slaves (or their descendants) slowly integrated into the community to be replaced by others. But the central reason for the widespread descent from slave status of all modern populations was the majority-female component of most servile groups. Records dating to the second millennium BCE indicate that some two-thirds of bond-persons in Babylonia were female.[86]

It is therefore not surprising that presidents George W. Bush and George Herbert Walker Bush had a direct ancestor, one Thomas Walker, who owned and captained slave ships sailing from Bristol between 1784 and 1791 before he emigrated to the new republic.[87]

---

[85] Patterson, *Slavery and Social Death*, pp. 9, 120–21, 210–21, 124–26, 132–33. Debt slavery – accounting for the largest numbers of what are termed "modern slaves" – today lasts on average five years. Historically, however, it has formed a major path to permanent slavery across Asia, but intergenerational transfers of debt servitude were rare, and such slaves did not reproduce themselves. See also Muhammad A. Dandamaev, *Slavery in Babylonia* (DeKalb, IL, 2009), p. 560.

[86] Daniel C. Snell, "Slavery in the Ancient Near East," *CWHS*, vol. 1: 6–7, 10.

[87] See Simon Akam, "George W. Bush's Great-Great-Great-Great-Grandfather Was a Slave Trader," Slate.com, June 20, 2013: www.slate.com/articles/life/history_lesson/2013/06/george_w_bush_and_slavery_the_president_and_his_father_are_descendants_of.html. This source correctly identifies the ancestor as Thomas Walker (the origin, perhaps, of the second given name of George Walker Bush). However, there were two Thomas Walkers captaining slave ships in the 1780s and 1790s – one based in Liverpool and one

What has received less attention is that, some centuries earlier, the West Country of England, the ancestral home of the Bush family, very likely participated in other kinds of slave trafficking, as either slave traders or as victims of slave traders, or both. Meanwhile, Icelandic children were sold in the Bristol region as late as the early fifteenth century, and, before 1100, English slaves captured by Irish raiders were sold in other parts of Europe and in the Mediterranean. Irish-Scandinavian Dublin had a major slave market in this era. Bristol, for a few decades the major slaving port in Europe for transatlantic slaving ventures, thus had a centuries-long experience of both importing and exporting captives, well before it began to send slave ships to Africa in the late seventeenth century. According to the Domesday Book survey of 1086, one in five people in England's West Country were enslaved (as opposed to an overall average for England of about one in ten). And as late as the early twelfth century, monks visiting Bristol were warned that Irish merchants on ships in the harbor were likely to kidnap and carry off the unwary to slavery. The families that organized the later African trade, including the eighteenth-century Walkers before they emigrated, could easily have had ancestors enslaved in England and counted in the Domesday Book. Some perhaps were dispatched to Ireland. Others, according to a widely cited letter of Pope Gregory I, were sent to the slave markets in late sixth-century Rome.[88]

It was not just the Irish Sea and its surrounding territories that saw slavery and slave trading continuing without abatement for centuries after the fall of Rome. As we have seen, slave routes crisscrossed the Old World (and probably parts of the New) during the 450–1450 era. For the global slave trading that preceded European contact with the Americas, large blind spots remain, and will forever lie beyond the light of scholarship. We

---

in Bristol. The Bush ancestor is the latter, and thus the author attributes eleven voyages to Walker instead of the true number of four (see www.slavevoyages.org, IDs 17917, 17999, 18029, and 18070). Some economists now argue that most rich and powerful people in Western society have tended to have the same surname as their rich and powerful predecessors of many generations ago (Gregory Clarke, *The Son Also Rises: Surnames and the History of Social Mobility* [Princeton, NJ, 2015]), but the consensus still seems to be that extreme wealth accumulation by one individual dissipates within four subsequent generations.

[88] David Pelteret, *Slave Raiding and Slave Trading in Early England* (Cambridge, 1981), pp. 112, 114; Wyatt, "Slavery in Northern Europe," 30; Nicholas J. Higham, *The Convert Kings: Power and Religious Affiliation in Early Saxon England* (Manchester, UK, 1997), pp. 65–66; Georges Duby, *Rural Economy and Country Life in the Medieval West* (Columbia, SC, 1968), pp. 37–39.

will never know, for example, the demographic impact of the disruptions stemming from Mongol conquests, or the extent and direction of slave trading in the early Indian Ocean. In some important respects, however, the advantage lies with the earlier period. For the traffic that kept the slave markets of Eurasia supplied for a millennium before 1450, the sources typically tell us much more about the origins of enslaved people than is available for early modern Africa, as well as the conflicts that led to their capture. While we know the region of embarkation for more than half of the vessels that brought captives to the Americas, for fewer than 1 percent of these arrivals do we have homelands in the interior of Africa. Except for seventeenth-century Angola, we have only sketchiest information on the wars and raids that generated the Africans dispatched to the Americas. Prior to 1807, at least, African records that might reveal this information simply do not exist. While scholars now recognize the "many middle passages" in the making of the modern world – the convict trade from Europe, contract laborers from Asia, as well as the enslaved from Africa – only a few medievalists focus on the largely terrestrial movement of forced labor across Eurasia that preceded these migrations. These, too, were "middle passages," albeit not transoceanic. Medievalists are much more likely to reference events in the post-1500 Atlantic world than are scholars of the later Atlantic to draw parallels with, say, the Mongol Empire. Yet a comparative review of earlier slave-trading activities and their trans-oceanic African successors does provide both context and continuities between medieval slave trades and the cataclysm that subsequently engulfed the tropical Atlantic world.[89]

The broad pattern running through all written records on slavery is that power imbalances between polities or world religions usually resulted in violence, and at least the partial enslavement of the weaker of the two. The first reference from Mesopotamia describes women and child captives being distributed among members of the court and the army generals of Babylon or sold to those who could afford them after a successful war. Most adult males were presumably killed after capture. If we set to one side the necessarily short-term Nazi enslavements in the Holocaust, then the last such case of a power imbalance triggering enslavement occurred in the more remote reaches of Polynesia. Beginning in 450, Polynesian farmer

---

[89] Christopher et al. (eds.), *Many Middle Passages*; for the medieval period, see the essays by Jeff Fynn-Paul, Michal Biran, and Hannah Barker, cited earlier in *CWHS*, vol. 2: 27–52, 76–99, 100–22.

migrants with identical technologies began sailing east. After centuries-long island-hopping, their descendants reached New Zealand and the tiny Chatham Islands, 500 miles west of New Zealand at about the same time – 1000 CE. The two groups of migrants then evolved in isolation of each other over the next eight centuries. The Maori used intensive farming to establish a technically advanced, warlike, and highly stratified society in New Zealand. Meanwhile, the Chatham Islanders – the Moriori – reverted to hunter-gatherer status in the face of poor soil conditions, but abundant shellfish, nesting seabirds, and seals. In the 1830s the Maori learned of the existence of the Moriori from European sealers. They thereupon invaded the Chatham archipelago and slaughtered or enslaved all the estimated 2,000 inhabitants. This enslavement lasted until 1863. "It was" said a Maori leader, "in accordance with our custom."[90]

Between Ancient Mesopotamia and the Chatham Islands of 1863, and no doubt well before the written record began, not much human migration occurred without violence. It is unlikely that Neanderthals negotiated their peaceful takeover by *Homo sapiens*. It is equally improbable that the hunter-gatherers of the Philippines voluntarily yielded their territory to Austronesian-speaking farmers several centuries prior to the written record.[91] The mix of Neanderthal and Denisovan genetic material that we carry today was probably the result of the familiar pattern of raids and warfare that dictated only the women and children of the Neanderthal and Denisovan target population would survive. The maritime manifestation of both human occupation and reoccupation of the globe remained the same from Homer's Greece through to Irish, Viking, and Islamic raiders and farmer migrants in parts of Indonesia. With one dramatic exception all used the same violent measures.

---

[90] See Jared Diamond, *Guns, Germs, and Steel: The Fates of Human Society* (New York, 1997), chapter 2, and Moriori and the Trustees of the Moriori IMT Settlement Trust and the Crown, "Deed of Settlement of Historical Claims": www.govt.nz/assets/Documents/OTS/Moriori/moriori-deed-of-settlement-initialled.pdf, pp. 29–33.

[91] The overwhelming evidence of violent death in the archeological record suggests that intergroup violence was always endemic – a subject still of intense debate among anthropologists and archeologists that Steve Pinker's *Better Angels of Our Nature: Why Violence Has Declined* (New York, 2011) has intensified. The Kenya Turkana Lake evidence from ten thousand years ago adds weight to Pinker's view (Marta Mirazon Lahr, Frances Rivera, R. K. Power, and Aurélien Mounier, "Inter-Group Violence Among Early Holocene Hunter-Gatherers of West Turkana, Kenya," *Nature*, 529 (2016): 394–98; Douglas P. Fry, and Patrik Söderberg, "Lethal aggression in mobile forager bands and implications for the origins of war," *Science*, 341 (2013): 270–73.

Jonathan Gottschall's generic description of the earliest of these five examples applies to them all:

> Fast ships with shallow drafts are rowed onto beaches and seaside communities are sacked before neighbors can lend defensive support. The men are usually killed, livestock and other portable wealth are plundered, and women are carried off to live among the victors and perform sexual and menial labors.[92]

For several millennia Gottschall's description held, but the big exception was the African slave trade. For the most part, the embarkation points for European and Arab slave merchants on the African coast were places where captives could be purchased, rather than bases for launching raids to capture them. Raiding and other sources of captives, of course, occurred, but off-site and certainly off-camera, as it were. The role of the major African embarkation points was akin to that of Venice or Caffa described earlier.

The Europeans who took over or invaded the early modern Atlantic and maritime southeast Asian worlds had a more complex self-justification for their actions than did the Maori. This involved religious proselytization and an Ulrich Bonnell Phillips-like conception of Africa as a place so savage that slavery elsewhere would save not only souls, but bodies. However, in the end, such justifications are little more than "according to our custom," particularly with respect to eligibility for bondage. In both the East and the West, Europeans frequently came across pre-existing institutionalized slavery and slave trading. Writing of the traffic that the Dutch found (and quickly joined and expanded) when they arrived in the Indonesian archipelago in the seventeenth century, François Valentijn described the slave trade as the "world's oldest trade."[93] In the West, early expansion into the Atlantic tapped into an ancient trans-Saharan traffic in people. In terms of enslavement, Europeans became the Mongols of the oceans. Like the Maori, wherever power imbalances permitted, Europeans organized a slave trade as in the early traffic in indigenes from southern to northeastern Brazil. Where the imbalance was *not* pronounced – as on the Western African coast described in Chapter 5, and in addition to most of the Asian landmass – they bought rather than raided for people.

---

[92] Jonathan Gottschall, *The Rape of Troy: Evolution, Violence, and the World of Homer* (Cambridge, 2008), p. 1. For one of the best and most accessible later versions of the experience at the personal level, see Ólafur Egilsson, trans. Karl Smári Hreinson and Adam Nichols, *The Travels of Reverend Olafur Egilsson: The Story of the Barbary Corsair Raid on Iceland in 1627* (Reykjavik, 2008).

[93] François Valentijn, *Oud en Nieuw Oost-Indiën*, 5 vols (Amsterdam, 1724–26), vol. 2: 42. For the original reference to the "oudsten handel, in de wereld," see Markus Vink, "'The World's Oldest Trade': Dutch Slavery and Slave Trade in the Indian Ocean in the Seventeenth Century," *Journal of World History*, 14 (2003): 132.

Ordinary Europeans, rather than rapacious capitalists and rulers, were ultimately responsible in first, responding strongly to the lower prices for products that plantation slavery ensured, and second, refusing to migrate in large numbers to the tropical Americas. Relative freedom for Europeans meant extreme oppression for many Africans. And the cataclysmic decline in the Indigenous population of the Americas linked European consumers directly with the African slave trade. Europeans had the option of not signing up for plantation labor, except, it may be assumed, for wages that would have greatly reduced both plantation profits and output. It is striking that the early modern commercially minded states and their elites refrained from enslaving even marginalized Europeans. Instead, European expansion meant the destruction of two-thirds of the Americas' Indigenous population by the second half of the seventeenth century. It meant the forcible removal of 12.75 million Africans to another continent. And it meant many more dying in the disruption caused by the traffic.

Nevertheless, the slave trade as it evolved in the Atlantic world was simply a maritime – and much better documented – version of what had been happening on land for millennia. Europeans moved far greater numbers of people over far greater distances than had ever before happened in global history. These numbers and distances were not exceeded until the mass migration of Europeans to the Americas began in the mid nineteenth century. Yet in neither the medieval nor early modern eras was slave trading among the worst examples of man's inhumanity to man. Historians can easily point to cataclysmic events in the last two millennia of global history that had a much greater demographic impact than the transatlantic slave trade: the 40 million Amerindians who died in the sixteenth century alone, or the 20 million people who died in the 15 years of the Taiping Rebellion, to cite just two relatively short-term catastrophes that bookend the era of Atlantic trafficking.

Four novel features help explain the enduring impact of the Atlantic slave trade on modern life – as opposed to other atrocities in history. It was not the number of enslaved people that separates slavery in the Americas from slavery in the Old World, but rather the exceptionally high proportions of such populations that were enslaved in most American regions. Such societies have been rare in history. So it makes sense that the only successful slave revolt in global history – in St. Domingue, now Haiti – should occur in such an environment. A second novelty was the 340-year exclusive focus on a single geographic source for captives: sub-Saharan Africa. This was a place of dizzying cultural complexity. In 1850, Africa was inhabited by just 5 percent of the global population but was home to

25 percent of all global languages.[94] As already argued, such cultural diversity ensured that no one living in Africa without contact with Arabs, Europeans, or Asians could possibly have conceived of themselves as African, sub-Saharan African, or having an identification with any region larger say than early Mali or the Sokoto Caliphate. Even among non-Africans, the term "African" only gradually came to replace other generalized nomenclatures such as "Blacks," "Blackamoors," or variants of the word "Negro." The system in which they were held came to be known as "racial" slavery, even though it is absurd to refer to Africans or their descendants as comprising a race. This helps explain why, against all the historical evidence, for most people slavery is still associated primarily with people of African descent.

A third novel feature is that the transatlantic traffic is the only large-scale slave trade in history that, at least until its last three decades, was predominantly comprised of adult males. New World plantation owners preferred to buy males. African sellers preferred to retain females.[95] Europeans solved the security issue thrown up by attempts to move large numbers of men across long distances by adding defensive features to slave vessels. Finally, the fourth novelty is the persistent question of the connection between historical practices of slavery and slave trading and the emergence of part of the modern economically developed world. Some scholars, and increasingly most of the modern media, see a strong causal connection between slavery and the economic rise of the West, even though three thousand years of recorded history suggests that a reverse of this cause-and-effect relationship would be much more plausible. By this, I mean that a global historical perspective points to prosperity invariably enabling slavery, rather than slavery having had an essential role in enabling prosperity.[96] All these distinctive features are issues that are taken up more fully in the chapters that follow.

---

[94] According to www.ethnologue.com, Nigeria contains 335 distinct languages today even as language diversity shrinks around the globe. In the words of the distinguished linguist, Kay Williamson, who spent most of her life there, the Niger Delta is a linguist's paradise.

[95] David Eltis and Stanley L. Engerman, "Fluctuations in Sex and Age Ratios in the Transatlantic Slave Trade, 1663–1864," *Economic History Review*, 46 (1993): 308–23.

[96] The grim legacy of slavery in the US, accurately described in best-selling books such as Clint Smith's *How the Word Is Passed* (New York, 2021), does not undermine this fundamental point. Note that even in colonial North America, the high per capita incomes relative to Britain allowed colonists to embrace slave labor, see John J. McCusker and Russell R. Menard, *The Economy of British America, 1607–1789* (Chapel Hill NC, 1985), pp. 51–70; Alice Hanson Jones, *The Wealth of a Nation to Be* (New York, 1980), pp. 71–9.

Finally, a note on terminology and methodology. The foregoing survey makes clear the continuity of enslavement practices across the ages and suggests that the peak number of enslaved people on the globe probably occurred before the plantation complex moved into the Mediterranean Atlantic, much less the Americas. In the last two decades, historians have begun to use the terms "first slavery" to refer to slavery in the Americas before circa 1800 and "second slavery" to what happened after (or because of) industrialization.[97] These phrases reflect the ingrained Eurocentrism of the World-systems school of scholars, first established by Immanuel Wallerstein.[98] Slavery in the Americas before 1800 shared far more with its post-1800 successor than with its pre-1500 antecedent (and with its very extensive, non-European contemporary systems of bondage). How would the experience of working in the cane fields of eighteenth-century Jamaica have differed from the same environment in nineteenth-century Cuba? The history summarized in this introduction establishes that the global peak of slavery occurred before 1492. How could slavery in the Americas between 1500 and 1800 possibly have been the "first slavery"? Forcing the history of slavery into such a framework and viewing prosperity as the result of slavery when it was more often its cause, distorts historical reality.

Many recent historians have expressed concern over what they see as the dominant role of statistics in the study of the slave trade. As the outlines of both the transatlantic and intra-American slave trades have come into focus in the last few decades, revealing new issues and paradoxes, historians from James Walvin to Stephanie Smallwood have worried that the figures fail to convey the "human" element in the terrible sequence of events that transferred millions from one side of the Atlantic to the other. Marcus Rediker, calls such an approach "a violence of abstraction" – by which is meant writing about slavery without showing its devastating human toll – that has "dehumanized … reality."[99] For Toby Green, quantification inhibits scholars from "thinking through … the cultural, political and social consequences of this phenomenon [meaning the slave trade]." Vincent Brown

---

[97] Dale Tomich, 'The "Second Slavery": Bonded Labor and the Transformation of the Nineteenth-Century World Economy," in Francisco O. Ramirez (ed.), *Rethinking the Nineteenth Century: Contradictions and Movements* (New York, 1988), pp. 103–37; and most recently the essays in Dale W. Tomich (ed.), *Atlantic Transformations: Empire, Politics and Slavery in the Nineteenth Century* (Albany, NY, 2020). This approach is particularly influential among Brazilian scholars.

[98] For an introduction see Gregory P. Williams, *Contesting the Global Order: The Radical Political Economy of Perry Anderson and Immanuel Wallerstein* (Albany, NY, 2020).

[99] Marcus Rediker, *The Slave Ship: A Human History* (New York, 2007), p. 12; Barry Unsworth, *Sacred Hunger* (London, 1992), p. 353.

sees quantification as rendering "the deadly migration of Africans somewhat like the chalk outline of a murder victim." Most critics are less melodramatic and simply resort to tired variations of "these people were not mere commodities," as they most certainly were not.

Yet trying to imagine scholarship on the slave trade and, indeed, the Atlantic world, in the last half century without knowing the size, direction and mortality/morbidity of this largest forced migration in history is rather like battling disease without the discipline of epidemiology, or climate change without long-run data on temperature. No discipline other than history would tolerate such a position. Would our appreciation of the horrors and sufferings of the slave trade be greater today if we did not know its dimensions? My argument rests firmly on the belief that one must know what a phenomenon is before one can think through "the cultural, political and social consequences" of that phenomenon. This in turn cannot happen without data as Jennifer Morgan's critique of such data sources makes plain.[100] Scholars have agonized over drawing on archives created by exploiters and racists. But given the ubiquitous acceptance of slavery until relatively recently, everyone was at least a potential exploiter including, in Brazil, some enslaved people and former slaves. For every abolitionist-inspired Solomon Northup, there were many millions of White, Black, Indigenous American, and Asians whose experience of enslavement before 1800 did *not* erode their subsequent willingness to become slave owners. They, too, helped create the pre-1800 archives.[101]

---

[100] Almost every major scholar in the field has at some point criticized efforts to establish reliable data for the trade as "dehumanizing." To respond to this criticism, the current editors of www.slavevoyages.org created a committee to humanize the language of the site. At the same time, almost everyone who writes on the trade draws on the site's data. See Rediker, *Slave Ship*, p. 12; Unsworth, *Sacred Hunger*, p. 353; Stephanie E. Smallwood, *Saltwater Slavery: A Middle Passage from Africa to American Diaspora* (Cambridge, MA, 2007), p. 5; Paul E. Lovejoy, "Extending the Frontiers of Transatlantic Slavery, Partially," *Journal of Interdisciplinary History*, 40 (2009): 65; James Walvin, *Questioning Slavery* (London, 1996), p. 103; Toby Green, *The Rise of the Trans-Atlantic Slave Trade in Western Africa, 1300–1589* (Cambridge, 2012), pp. 4–5. See also Gesa Mackenthun, "Body Counts: Violence and Its Occlusion in Writing the Atlantic Slave Trade," *Papers from the Francis Barker Memorial Conference. Essex University Internet publication* (2001): Vincent Brown, *The Reaper's Garden: Death and Power in the World of Atlantic Slavery* (Cambridge, 2008), p. 29. But how can establishing the dimensions of inhumanity be dehumanizing?

[101] See Jennifer L. Morgan, *Reckoning with Slavery: Gender, Kinship, and Capitalism in the early Black Atlantic* (Durham, NC, 2021), pp. 29–50. Oddly, Morgan is also unhappy with what she sees as the small sample size of the age-sex data of captives in slavevoyages. At approximately 10 percent of all voyages, it is a far bigger sample than what epidemiologists have used to underpin the mountain of research behind, say, improved life expectancy and living standards since 1900.

2

The Americas and Atlantic Slave Trading: The Iberians and the Rest

The first recorded landing of enslaved Africans in what is today the US did not occur in Jamestown in 1619, but rather Puerto Rico a century earlier.[1] While the slave vessels involved began their voyages from the Iberian peninsula and followed a triangular route, the phrase "triangular trade" does not come close to capturing the complex reality of the routes that distributed enslaved Africans across the Atlantic world. A decade after these first voyages, the United States mainland received its first enslaved Africans, but not from Africa. A Spanish expedition from Hispaniola landed near Sapelo Sound, Georgia, and established the settlement of San Miguel del Gualdape, if "established" is the correct word given that it survived less than two months. This mix of transatlantic and intra-American origins of the US' Black population was therefore in place within three decades of Columbian contact. This bifurcated pattern of arrivals held true for every part of the Atlantic littoral of North and South America but was not reflected on the slavevoyages site until 2018 when the intra-American slave trade database joined its transatlantic counterpart.[2]

Across the US and indeed across the Americas, it is likely that every port large enough to organize and dispatch even a coastal commercial voyage was involved in buying and selling slaves before slave trading became illegal. Trading slaves in the Americas was as ubiquitous on water as it was

---

[1] The *Santa Catalina* (ID 42996) in 1519, see www.slavevoyages.org/voyages/89YpU2Jt.
[2] Jane Landers, *Black Society in Spanish Florida* (Urbana, IL, 1999), pp. 12–13. Between 1516 and 1618, more than 7,000 captives disembarked in Puerto Rico direct from Africa (https://slavevoyages.org/voyages/umzVoceI) as well as others from metropolitan Spain. Territories that became the US may have accounted for a small share of the total slave trade but that small segment endured for 341 years – longer than in any other country.

on land. Some smaller communities such as Bristol, Rhode Island, even entered the business after it became illegal, because the abolition laws were easier to avoid in the minor maritime centers. Between 1519 and 1866 transatlantic slave voyages set sail from places as far north as Ventspils in modern Latvia (ID 26441) and as far south as Rio de la Plata, a latitude range of 95 degrees. The east-west span of departures was almost as large, ranging from Odessa in the Crimea to Cartagena. Every continent bordering the Atlantic, including Africa, dispatched slaving expeditions.[3] These vessels serviced slave markets that were no less scattered – from Boston, Massachusetts, to Carmen de Patagones in southern Buenos Aires province, and east to the Iberian peninsula. And most of these destinations served as both entrepôts and final transatlantic markets. Thus, as suggested above, some 15–20 percent of the enslaved underwent further movement by land and/or sea that might see them crossing the Caribbean on another vessel or entering the Pacific via Cape Horn, trekking over the Andes, or the Panama Isthmus, with final disembarkations in Chile, Callao in Peru, and, for a very few, across the Pacific to the Philippines. Vivid accounts of two such journeys into the Pacific – separated by two centuries and at either end of South America – are now in print.[4]

Written and media presentations on this slave trade, both fictional and scholarly, remain fixated on the supposed triangular pattern of the typical slave voyage with the apex anchored in Europe.[5] The first half-century of the transatlantic traffic was indeed very much based in Europe, mostly Lisbon and Seville and their satellite ports. Well over 90 percent of the slaves in this early period came from Senegambia, in the northern part of sub-Saharan Africa and the region closest to the optimal sailing route from Europe to America. The early triangular trade initially comprised

---

[3] African ports are listed as the ports of departure of 186 voyages. See https://slavevoyages.org/voyages/ootkhPHb.

[4] Linda A. Newson and Susie Minchin, *From Capture to Sale: The Portuguese Slave Trade to Spanish South America in the Early Seventeenth Century* (Leiden, 2007), pp. 101–234; Greg Grandin, *Empire of Necessity: Slavery, Freedom, and Deception in the New World* (New York, 2014), pp. 171–202, 211–22. Grandin assumes the leaders in a slave revolt central to his book were Islamic, but the African names evidence discussed in chapter 7 below make this extremely unlikely.

[5] Sean M. Kelley, "New World Slave Traders and the Problem of Trade Goods: Brazil, Barbados, Cuba and North America in Comparative Perspective," *English Historical Review*, 134 (2019): 303–33, offers the correct counter to this tendency. And for a rare book-length study that focuses on the South Atlantic, see Luiz Felipe de Alencastro, *The Trade in the Living: The Formation of Brazil in the South Atlantic, Sixteenth to Seventeenth Centuries* (Albany, NY, 2018).

a very flat triangle entirely confined to the North Atlantic. Ships sailed from Iberia to the Canary Islands followed by the circum-Caribbean and then a return to Iberia. Although the labor force in the silver export sector was mainly Indigenous and heavily concentrated on the American mainland, vessels sailing to the Caribbean from Spain did not have to go far out of their way to obtain African slaves. The sixteenth-century Caribbean and circum-Caribbean became populated by people of Senegambian descent based on trade patterns that were a relatively simple extension of what had been established in the Mediterranean Atlantic since the mid fifteenth century – all based firmly in Europe.[6]

Nevertheless, a quick overview of the traffic shows that while Europe colonized the Americas, it was not in fact the center of the transatlantic traffic in people. We can now say that probably more slaves were carried off from Africa in vessels with home ports on the western side of the Atlantic Ocean than in Europe. Table 2.1 distributes the overall TSTD estimates of captives carried off from Africa by the ports from which the slaving expedition was launched. As the final row in the table indicates, while the organization of the transatlantic traffic was split between the continents of Europe and America, most of these ventures were based in the Americas.

Figure 2.1 shows the trend over time in terms of the percentage shares that European and American-based slave voyages held (the shares sum to 100). The surge in the Brazilian traffic in the early seventeenth century temporarily put the control of the trade in the Americas, but the explosive growth of the Caribbean plantations quickly reversed this pattern mid-century. Abolition of the slave trade initially affected Europe more than the Americas and this largely explains the re-emergence of the Americas' dominance after 1800. Except for the early trade and the late eighteenth century, the organizational bases of the trade were distributed more or less equally across the Atlantic traffic, but overall, the Voyages database shows that a traffic that had begun in the Iberian peninsula in first half of the sixteenth century eventually shifted to the Americas and for the last forty years of its existence was located there almost entirely.

Column 4 of Table 2.1 shows that more than half of all Africans who crossed the Atlantic disembarked in Cuba and Brazil, but column 2 also shows that Europe was not heavily involved in how they got there. Slave ships sent out from other American slave-holding regions supplied a smaller but still significant share of their incoming slaves. Brazilian and Rio Platense

---

[6] Wheat, *Atlantic Africa*, pp. 20–67.

TABLE 2.1 *Captives carried from Africa and the location of home port of vessels carrying them, 1520–1866 ('000')*

Regions where captives disembarked	Location of home port of slave vessels and numbers carried			All continents ('000')
	Europe	America	Africa	
Europe	10.8	0.0	0.0	10.8
Mainland North America	375.4	97.0	0.0	472.4
British Caribbean	2,601.6	157.4	4.1	2,763.4
French Caribbean	1,310.3	16.3	1.9	1,328.4
Dutch Americas	502.2	12.0	0.0	514.2
Cuba	127.6	762.4	0.0	890.0
Puerto Rico	28.5	3.1	0.0	31.3
Spanish circum-Caribbean	372.1	0.0	0.0	372.1
Rio de la Plata	63.8	19.2	0.0	83.0
Other Spanish Americas	214.9	0.0	0.0	214.9
Danish Americas	115.9	14.0	0.0	129.9
Amazonia	162.7	0.0	0.0	162.7
Brazil other than Amazonia	0.0	5,369.4	0.0	5,369.4
Africa	0.0	178.9	0.0	178.9
Total	5,885.6	6,629.8	6.0	12,521.4

Source: Number of captives embarked for each broad destination region is from http://slavevoyages.org/tast/assessment/estimates.faces?yearFrom=1501&yearTo=1866 These are distributed across the regions in which the home ports were located according to ratios derived from http://slavevoyages.org/tast/database/search.faces?yearFrom=1514&yearTo=1866&ptdepimp=10000.20000.30000.40000.50000.60000.80000. Worksheet available from the author.

merchants owned the vessels that introduced 30 percent of the Rio de la Plata inflow. On the North American mainland, almost one-fifth of arrivals direct from Africa disembarked from colonial (and later US) ships. Even in the British Caribbean traffic, dominated as it was by Liverpool, London, and Bristol owners, nearly 6 percent of all Africans arrived on colonial vessels. But this figure understates West Indian involvement given that the *Elizabeth and Sarah* (id 75411), leaving from London in 1724, had five owners, four of whom were residents of St. Kitts.[7] Moreover, thirty of the

---

[7] www.slavevoyages.org/voyages/JsOe4V9o. The owners were Roger Baker, Gideon Devrede, Robert Pemberton, Joseph Symonds, and Pecock Walker. See British State

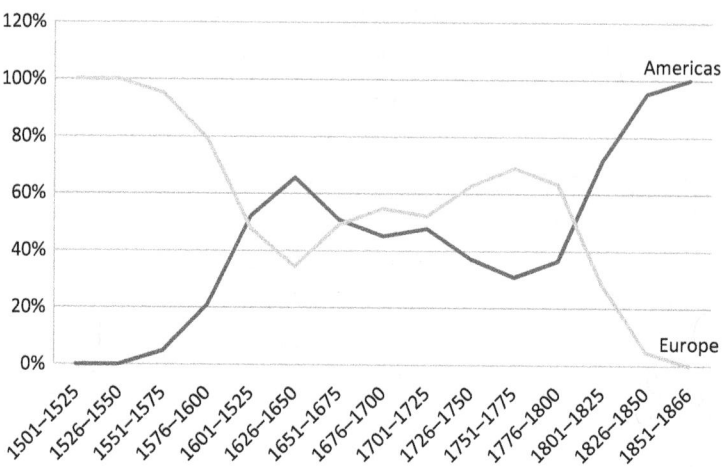

FIGURE 2.1 Share of transatlantic captives taken from Africa by location of home ports of vessels carrying them
Source: Alex Borucki, David Eltis, and David Wheat, "Atlantic History and the Slave Trade to Spanish America," *American Historical Review*, 120 (2015): 433–61.

wills of merchants dispatching slave ships from London are described as "of Barbados," "of Jamaica," or "of Antigua." Two thirds of British colonial slave vessels left from West Indian ports – mainly Bridgetown, Barbados, and Kingston, Jamaica – rather than from New England. The transatlantic slave traffic based in the colonial Caribbean has largely escaped scholarly attention. While Rhode Island's role in the business prior to US independence is well known, the so-called New England rum ships brought far fewer slaves to the Americas than did their Caribbean counterparts.

As well as occupying the organizational center of the slave trade, the Americas were central to the business in a much more profound sense. Three continents shared access to the Atlantic Ocean: Africa, Eurasia, and America[8] though people in only two of the three were aware of each other before 1492. For more than 350 years after that year the largest maritime coerced migration in history bridged the Atlantic and bound the three

---

Papers at www.british-history.ac.uk/cal-state-papers/colonial/america-west-indies/vol23/, pp. 68–89. The ship that brought Richard Ligon to Barbados in 1647 subsequently went direct to Cacheu in modern Guinea-Bissau to buy slaves on its return journey [Richard Ligon, *The True and Exact History of the Island of Barbadoes* (London, 1673), p. 22].

[8] This work adopts the Latin American convention of treating the Americas as a single continent.

together. The keystone in that bridge was America rather than Europe. It may seem a commonplace to say that without that continent there would have been no slave trade, but there are deeper meanings. The fact that there was a continent called America that had remained isolated from significant interaction with the rest of the world for tens of thousands of years virtually guaranteed the epidemiological apocalypse that enveloped the Indigenous population after 1492. It also made highly likely that in the absence of Western Europeans the resources of America would have become available to one or more of the many other post-Iron Age cultures of the Old World (both east and west) as soon as the invaders had figured out a way of making return transoceanic voyages. A long list of peoples has claimed to have reached the Americas in the medieval millennia, some with stronger evidence than others.[9] The counterargument is not the absence of documentation, but rather that there is no archeological evidence of a demographic disaster before the Spanish invasion. Any sustained contact with Old World biota – Asian, African, or European – would surely have triggered such an impact, just as it did between 1492 and 1680. And when this demographic catastrophe did occur, the scale would surely have been lessened after 1492 if contact with the Old World had happened in preceding centuries. In addition, because the New World had much lower population densities than any other continent in the world (holding climate zones constant), any labor used to exploit America's abundance of resources would very likely have been coerced in the aftermath of renewed contact between the continents. For four centuries after 1492 America continued to have by far the largest land-to-labor ratios in the temperate world, and historically these are not conditions under which individuals usually work voluntarily for others for any extended period.[10]

The implication of the argument is that a Eurasian culture other than Western Europe could have navigated its way to the resources of America, perhaps an Asian, Russian, or African society. Likewise, there were possible alternatives to sub-Saharan Africa as a source of labor. More systematic use of convicts and indentured servants from within Western Europe, or perhaps Slavic or South Asian labor was possible. Moving such labor to where its value to the elite was maximized would of course

---

[9] In order of probability – Vikings, Basques, West Country English, Africans, Polynesians, and, according to President Erdogan of Turkey, Islamists (who could indeed have been Africans). See www.globalresearch.ca/before-columbus-how-africans-brought-civilization-to-america/5407584, and www.theguardian.com/world/2014/nov/17/muslims-beat-columbus-america-better-get-in-line.

[10] Domar, "Causes of Slavery and Serfdom," pp. 18–32.

have required a long sea journey that few would have undertaken voluntarily. Without Western Europe, and without Africa, the development of the Americas would have taken a different path. But several millennia of isolation and the "portmanteau biota," of micro-organisms and animals that accompanied migrants from the Old World would have ensured depopulation of the continent in any event.[11] Old World technology and the ubiquity of slavery globally, already discussed, made some form of coerced labor in the aftermath of demographic collapse in America highly probable. Without Europe, exploitation of American resources would have occurred later and proceeded more slowly than it did, but exploitation and development there would certainly have been. To believe that America's resources would have entered the global economy without empire, slavery, racism, and unequal income distribution is to ignore global history. Only if Columbus really had sailed to the East Indies in 1492 – if indeed America had not existed – could there have been less forced migration in the world after that date. A transoceanic slave trade would have happened without Western Europe and without Africa, but not without America. This, together with the fact that the Americas dispatched most of the transatlantic slave voyages and was the recipient of almost all the resulting captives, is the reason why the New World takes precedent over the Old in this reinterpretation of Atlantic slave trades.

No existing interpretations of the slave trade allow for this counterfactual emphasis on the Americas. The last century of scholarship on Atlantic history has been structured around European expansion and – in the last several decades – the pushback against that expansion on the part of the peoples it subjugated, as well as the new nations that eventually emerged there. Europe is still seen as the main instigator of the plantation complex it sustained. Goods traded for slaves may have come from around the world, but in the traditional view they passed through European ports first. There, they were sorted into appropriate cargoes, incorporated into slaving ventures, and the slaves for which they were exchanged were distributed across America under European flags. A small North American-based trade has a bit role in this interpretation and claims far more scholarly attention in the English-language literature than does its many times larger Brazilian-based counterpart. Scholars therefore see the resources (capital, expertise, financial services, and most of the merchandise) as coming predominantly from the North Atlantic, and the benefits (plantation produce, bullion, and, above all, profits) accruing mainly to Europe.

---

[11] Crosby, *Ecological Imperialism*, pp. 89–90.

DISPATCHING TRANSATLANTIC SLAVE VOYAGES

As already noted, there is some truth to the traditional narrative in the first half-century of the traffic. The distribution of natural resources across the Americas was just as important as the oceanic gyres described in the previous chapter. The Spanish conquistadors looked for connections with the Indies for the simple reason that transoceanic journeys were expensive and only exotic products could bear the costs of transportation to Europe. While extending imperial control over first, the Caribbean, then New Spain and Peru and Bolivia, it was logical that Spain's primary interest would be in precious metals. Agricultural produce, whether animal or vegetable, could not by itself bear the cost of shipping from the Caribbean to Europe until the seventeenth century. Moreover, after the plunder phase of the conquest the earliest export complexes of America were isolated. After the Spanish found silver at Zacatecas, Mexico, and Potosí, Bolivia, in the mid-1540s, the most lucrative of these resources were remote – located hundreds of miles from the Atlantic Ocean and in awkward topography.

Generally, how a commodity is produced determines both settlement patterns and the social institutions that subsequently evolve.[12] Of all sixteenth-century economic activities that required capital – ranging from hard-rock mining at one extreme to hunting and fishing at the other – the Spanish project was by far the most capital-intensive. Locating, then mining, precious metals, organizing the necessary Native American labor, and shipping the refined output safely back to Europe constituted activities well beyond the capacities of early sixteenth-century entrepreneurs, whether single or in companies – even those in northern Italian city-states. No city-state could have created the infrastructure necessary to exploit Potosi. With the single exception of the Iberian Americas, European overseas ventures in the 1500s comprised trade, plunder, and some fishing, rather than the establishment of new centers of production. Only the most powerful of European states could contemplate such an undertaking. By comparison, the Portuguese Empire, memorably described as "occupying a multitude of territories without possessing them,"[13] remained huddled in three pockets on the shores of the Atlantic in 1600, with sallies beyond these enclaves establishing

---
[12] Stanley L. Engerman and Kenneth Sokoloff, *Economic Development in the Americas since 1500: Endowments and Institutions* (Cambridge, 2012), pp. 1–30.
[13] Daviken Studnicki-Gizbert, *A Nation Upon the Ocean Sea: Portugal's Atlantic Diaspora and the Crisis of the Spanish Empire* (Baltimore, MD, 2007), p. 5.

varying and impermanent spheres of influence.[14] Not surprisingly, most American gold and silver output before 1600 was the product of a state monopoly, just as it had been under the Inca state.[15]

As the conquest proceeded, Spanish America evolved into two distinct but mutually dependent economies. The Lowlands included the Caribbean and the low-lying mainland; the Highlands generated most of the transatlantic exports. The former produced some precious metal – gold in early Española and El Chocó, Columbia – but they mostly catered to the needs of the Highlands by supplying provisions, including sugar and tobacco, from large *rancheros* and other *latifundia*. The Caribbean, especially Havana, also provided a first line of defense against European competitors for the Spanish. A quarter of a million Spanish immigrants arrived in the New World before 1640, but twice this number of African captives disembarked. Not many of either group worked directly in the export sector. The state monopoly over production extended to licensing of the slave trade, with some licenses specifying monopoly rights, and some not. La Casa y Audiencia de Indias in Seville acted as the organizational center. But this did not prevent the merchant or landowner in the Spanish Americas dispatching the occasional slave voyage to Africa in this period. The first known slave voyage organized in the Americas left Puerto Rico in 1551 financed by *vecinos* in San Juan. The *Nuestra Señhora de los Remedios* (id 42987) brought between seventy and ninety captives from the Cape Verde Islands in December of the following year.[16] Thereafter almost every plantation colony established after that Spanish century began sending its own slave vessels to Africa even as European-based merchants entered the business, including Barbados, South Carolina, New York, Virginia, and Brazil.

After the earliest years, there were few barriers to entry to the slave-trading business. Compared to most transoceanic branches of maritime trade the ships themselves were small and the areas open to the traffic on the African coast were vast enough that no single power (European or African), much less an individual slave trader, could restrict access. Between 1562 and 1866 ninety-five separate American ports ranging from Maine in the North Atlantic to Montevideo in the South fitted out

---

[14] Thornton, *History of West Central Africa*, pp. 1–88; Alencastro, *Trade in the Living*, pp. 39–116.

[15] This statement holds down to 1800 and for pre- as well as post-conquest America,

[16] Marc Eagle and David Wheat, "The Early Iberian Slave Trade to the Spanish Caribbean, 1500–1580," in Borucki, et al., *From the Galleons to the Highlands*, pp. 61–62.

and dispatched slave ventures to Africa. These ports were concentrated overwhelmingly in the regions of the continent that imported the most slaves. Despite the widespread misapprehension that New England slave traders played a major role in the business, fewer than 7 percent of all departures from ports in the Americas set out from New York and points north.

Slave traders based in Europe began to lose ground to their American counterparts well before 1600. The key factor was the movement of the sugar plantation complex from São Tomé in the Gulf of Guinea to Pernambuco (Recife), Brazil, around 1560, and a little later further south to Bahia de Todos os Santos (Salvador).[17] At first this new export center also relied heavily on Indian labor. Planters in northeastern Brazil enslaved thousands of Native Americans, some from far to the south. Bandeirantes were the first slave traders to meet the relatively modest labor needs of the late sixteenth-century Brazilian sugar sector. For a few decades a south-to-north slave trade was operating on both sides of the Atlantic before the east-to-west transatlantic movement to Brazil got underway. On the eastern side of the ocean, it brought sub-Saharan Africans and Canary Islanders to Europe and, further south, from Angola to São Tomé in the Gulf of Guinea; while on the western side it brought Native Americans from temperate to tropical Brazil, and from the northern states to the English Caribbean. On the eastern shores of the Atlantic this south-to-north trade was based in Lisbon and Seville, and on the western side merchants in Brazilian and Eastern Caribbean ports organized the traffic.

The exact genesis of the Americas-based slave trade to Africa will likely never be known. Probably some enslaved people with sugar-making skills accompanied milling equipment carried from São Tomé

---

[17] São Tomé was a major source of sugar in the sixteenth century, but it is easy to exaggerate its importance given later developments. Toby Green in *A Fistful of Shells: West Africa from the Rise of the Slave Trade to the Age of Revolution* (Chicago, IL, 2019), pp. 169–77, argues for a significant slave trade to the island from what became the Slave Coast. In fact, there was very little slave trading from the Bight of Benin at this time. While the region did supply slaves to São Tomé, and while the slave population of the island may have briefly attained twelve thousand at its peak prior to the major 1595 slave rebellion, this number could have been reached with arrivals of only a few hundred a year over the nearly century-long rise of the sugar sector, most of whom came from the Bight of Biafra and Angola rather than the Bight of Benin. See Gerhard Siebert, "São Tomé & Príncipe: The First Plantation Economy in the Tropics," in Robin Law, Suzanne Schwarz, and Silke Strickrodt (eds.), *Commercial Agriculture, the Slave Trade & Slavery in Atlantic Africa* (Woodbridge, UK, 2013), pp. 72–74.

to Pernambuco and Vera Cruz around the mid sixteenth century, but the evidence is circumstantial.[18] Northeast Brazil was the point in the New World closest to Africa, but the very first *engenhos* (sugar-mills) in Brazil and in Vera Cruz have left evidence only of Amerindian, not African slaves. However, the first arrival of enslaved people from Africa was probably in Bahia in 1550, even though it was the captaincy of Pernambuco that saw the most rapid development of Brazilian sugar. The Portuguese queen regent issued a royal decree in 1559 permitting the governor of São Tomé to sell up to 120 slaves to each *senhor de engenho* in Pernambuco.[19] By 1580, one third of *engenhos* labor was of African origin, and 5,800 lived in the captaincy. But not until 1620 was Africanization of the workforce complete.[20] After the São Tomé slave rebellion in the late 1590s almost all sugar in European markets was produced in Brazil.[21] Information on specific slave ventures for this early period is scattered, with the first recorded transatlantic slave voyage dating to 1574, but clearly African slaves had been arriving for some years prior to this. TSTD has records of ten voyages bringing or intending to bring slaves into Brazil between 1574 and 1620, and a further ten for the following decade, ending early in 1630 with Dutch occupation of Pernambuco. These twenty voyages carried off an estimated 5,200 slaves, though the projected total for arrivals in Brazil in these years, at 232,000, is many times greater than this small sample. The derivation of this estimate is explained elsewhere,[22] but the important point here is that every one of the

---

[18] Daniel B. Domingues da Silva and David Eltis, "The Slave Trade to Pernambuco, 1560–1851," in David Eltis and David Richardson (eds.), *Extending the Frontiers: Essays on the New Transatlantic Slave Trade Database* (New Haven, CT, 2008), pp. 95–129: Christopher Ebert, *Between Empires: Brazilian Sugar in the Early Atlantic Economy, 1550–1630* (Leiden, 2008), p. 12, comments "Brazilian sugar appears to have gained increasing notice in international markets after about 1570, and its ascendancy from that time on is indisputable."

[19] Mauricio Goulart, *Escravidão Africana no Brasil: Das origins à extinção do trafico* (São Paulo, 1975), p. 99; Gerald Cardoso, *Negro Slavery in the Sugar Plantations of Veracruz and Pernambuco, 1550–1680* (Washington, DC, 1983), pp. 76–78.

[20] Stuart B. Schwartz, "A Commonwealth within Itself: The Early Brazilian Sugar Industry, 1550–1670," in Stuart B. Schwartz (ed.), *Tropical Babylons: Sugar and the Making of the Atlantic Worlds, 1450–1680* (Chapel Hill, NC, 2004), pp. 156–200; Francisco Augusto Pereira da Costa, *Arredores do Recife* (Recife, 2001), p. 126.

[21] Seibert, 'São Tomé and Príncipe," 54–78.

[22] For the derivation of the total volume of the Brazilian slave trade see David Eltis and David Richardson, "A New Assessment of the Transatlantic Slave Trade," and Domingues da Silva and David Eltis, "Slave Trade to Pernambuco," both in Eltis and Richardson, *Extending the Frontiers*, 1–62; 95–129.

twenty ventures in the sample was launched from Brazil – Pernambuco, Bahia, or Rio de Janeiro.[23] The chronology of the first recorded slaving ventures from each follows what we know to have been the development sequence of the sugar complex in the Americas: Pernambuco, Bahia, and then Rio de Janeiro by the end of the century.

Cultivating and processing sugar for export to overseas markets was certainly capital-intensive, but it was not hard-rock mining as in New Spain or Peru. Mining gold and silver in the highlands of New Spain and Peru and getting it to Europe remained beyond the reach of individual merchants, in contrast to a plantation located on the coast of the South Atlantic or a Caribbean island, both of which were clearly well within grasp. If merchants could finance a plantation they could certainly invest in a slave-trading venture direct to the African coast. In Brazil the wealth that sugar and later tobacco generated, initially from Native American labor, also provided the capital that enabled a direct trade with Africa. As well as the complexities of growing and processing, sugar in effect sustained the cost of two transatlantic journeys – one to bring labor from Africa, and the other to carry plantation produce to Europe. Of all sixteenth-century Europeans, the Portuguese possessed the most extensive pool of expertise in both making sugar and trading slaves. Portuguese São Tomé was Europe's main source of sugar in 1550, to be replaced by Brazil before the end of the sixteenth century.[24] In addition, Portuguese officers, ships, and trading posts on the African coast had undergirded the Spanish slave trade from its inception. While the Portuguese state granted land and the Dutch much of the shipping, private merchants established both the plantations and the slave trade. By 1575, the Portuguese had founded what was to become the largest transshipment point for African captives ever at Luanda. Except for the brief Dutch occupation of Pernambuco and Angola, the Portuguese, more precisely the Brazilian grip on the South Atlantic gyre remained secure for the better part of the next three centuries.

The Dutch attacked and attempted to conquer what in 1630 was the largest of the three Brazilian sugar complexes – Pernambuco. Portuguese resistance and several years of Dutch consolidation meant a temporary suspension of the transatlantic traffic, at least to Pernambuco. When

---

[23] http://slavevoyages.org/tast/database/search.faces?yearFrom=1560&yearTo=1630&mjslptimp=50000.
[24] Eddy Stols, "The Expansion of the Sugar Market in Western Europe," in Schwartz (ed.), *Tropical Babylons*, p. 260.

a Dutch slave trade to Brazil eventually got underway in 1637, it, too, was based entirely in Brazilian ports. Between 1631 and 1654, not one of the 142 slaving ventures to Brazil in www.slavevoyages.org set sail from Europe. The Dutch were the most powerful maritime nation in the world at the time, but they had quickly adopted the Portuguese pattern and located their Atlantic slave trade in the Americas. The Portuguese retook Pernambuco while the Dutch conquered Surinam from the English, a cession recognized in the Treaty of Breda in 1667. Whereas Pernambuco was located just south of the equator, the conquered territory was located just north of the line. Here, too, the Dutch organized a plantation complex complete with a transatlantic slave traffic that this time endured to the late eighteenth century. Strikingly, almost all slave voyages to the ceded territory left from Europe. Thus, two branches of the slave trade conducted largely under the same flag – that of the Netherlands – using the same marine technology and hauling thousands of people from and to the same continents nevertheless used organizational bases separated by almost 5,000 miles of ocean. Moreover, the two systems were largely mutually exclusive throughout most of the slave trade era – slave ships based in Europe rarely supplied Pernambuco, and, until the 1790s, slave ships based in the Americas never supplied the Dutch Guianas. And what held for Pernambuco also held for the whole of Brazil south of Amazonia. Max Menz and Diego Martins have found details of 75 previously unknown vessels leaving Lisbon for Luanda and Benguela between 1719 and 1807. Assuming all these were slave ships we need to note that over the same period 2,442 voyages left Angola for Brazil.[25] Virtually all nineteenth-century voyages were based in Brazil. Likely fewer than 10 percent of the Africans taken to Brazil over three centuries were on vessels based in Europe.[26]

The organizational heart of the transatlantic slave trade in the Americas was already located in Brazil by the mid seventeenth century, a dominance that continued unchallenged through to the ending of the Brazilian traffic in 1851. And in the wider Atlantic world over the whole slave-trading era, vessels from the top three South Atlantic ports of Rio de Janeiro, Bahia de Todos os Santos (now Salvador), and Pernambuco (now Recife) carried off far more enslaved Africans

---

[25] www.slavevoyages.org/voyages/2yvutlMg.
[26] The traffic from Lisbon to Luanda is being tracked by Jesus Bohorquez and Maximiliano Menz. See their "State Contractors and Global Brokers: The Itinerary of Two Lisbon Merchants and the Transatlantic Slave Trade during the Eighteenth Century," *Itinerario*, 42 (2018): 403–29, and more recently in Menz, *Senhor Da Morte: Capitalismo, Guerra E Tráfico De Escravos. Portugal, Angola E Brasil (1640–1770)* (São Paulo, forthcoming), chapter 5.

than the combined total of ships leaving the three leading British ports of Liverpool, London, and Bristol together with the major French port of Nantes. More than one in four of the enslaved Africans brought to the Americas over 360 years disembarked from slaving ventures that had set out from these three Brazilian ports, almost all of them on bilateral voyages.[27] Lisbon traders did have a big presence in the trade, but it was limited to the African embarkation ports of Luanda, Benguela and Bissau. These merchants even provided credit to bring captives from the African interior. But the transatlantic phase of the traffic remained at the risk of merchants in Brazil.[28] Nothing better illustrates the misplaced emphasis of the literature, both scholarly and popular, on the triangular trade and Europe as the dominant centers of the slave-trading business.

For ports in the Atlantic world most dependent on slavery and the slave trade for their existence we must turn to Brazil, rather than northwest Europe or Iberia. Even after ignoring the virtual absence of hard data for the first century of slave-trading data in Bahia and Rio de Janeiro, each port dispatched more voyages to Africa than did Liverpool, or London, or Amsterdam. And whereas these and other European ports were developing a multitude of trading connections around the globe during the slave trade era, Brazilian coastal cities had only the coastal trade and a tenuous connection to the Far East as alternatives to ferrying enslaved people and the produce they created. Like their European counterparts, both Brazilian ports filled their departing slave ships with trading merchandise generated in their hinterlands. Recent work by Kristin Mann, Lisa Castillo, and Luis Nicolau Parés establishes that given the range and diversity of investors, few people in Salvador were far removed from the commerce. Salvador de Bahia was a slave-trading society. This was a city entirely dedicated to bringing in enslaved people from Africa, and to facilitating the export of plantation produce as well as the importation of whatever merchandise could be obtained in return. Kristin Mann concludes, "that few free people in Salvador were far removed from the slave trade, including after it became illegal, and many freed men and slaves had connections to the commerce, as

---

[27] David Eltis and David Richardson, *Atlas of the Transatlantic Slave Trade* (New Haven, CT, 2010), p. 39; Alencastro, Trade in the Living, pp. 185–252.
[28] Joseph C. Miller, *Way of Death: Merchant Capitalism and the Angolan Slave Trade, 1730–1830* (Madison, WI, 1988), pp. 257, 285–6, 295–6, 299–300, 311–12, 315–17; idem, "Capitalism and Slaving: The Financial and Commercial Organization of the Angola Slave Trade, according to the Accounts of Antonio Coelho Guerreiro," *International Journal of African Historical Studies*, 17 (1984): 1–56.

well."²⁹ To anticipate a later discussion, with such an exclusive and centuries-long focus on slavery and the slave trade and the economic growth that both delivered, it is indeed odd – from the perspective of the new historians of capitalism – that industrialization did not begin in Brazil rather than 5,000 miles to the northeast.³⁰

Sugar production spread from Brazil to the most easterly of the Caribbean islands, Barbados, in the early 1640s. A plantation economy based on tobacco and cotton, drawing on European indentured labor, was already in existence there, but by 1643 the island was exporting some sugar.³¹ If the Brazilians moved from Indigenous to African labor over a sixty-year period, the British and French made a transition from White indentured to Black slave labor in half this time. The first ship on record carrying slaves direct from Africa arrived in Barbados in 1641. Outfitted in London, it predated the first recorded sugar exports from the island. However, a continuous slave traffic based on the island began only in 1644, with according to George Downing of Downing Street fame, 1,000 slaves arriving the following year.³² In August of 1644, and therefore in the vanguard of the British slave trade, the first known slave venture dispatched from British America left Bridgetown for the Rio del Rey in what is now southeastern Nigeria. In the following year a small vessel left from St. Kitts for the same African region. In the first decade of the Barbados traffic a quarter of all captives brought to the island arrived on Barbadian vessels and a further 12 percent on ships based in New England.³³ Just 25 years after the Plymouth Colony settlers disembarked,

---

²⁹ Luis Nicolau Parés, "Entre Bahia e a Costa da Mina, libertos africanos no tráfico illegal," in Giuseppina Raggi, João Figueirôa-Rego, and Roberta Stumpf (eds.), *Salvador da Bahia: Interações entre América e África (séculos XVI–XIX)* (Salvador, 2017), pp. 13–50; Lisa Earl Castillo, "Mapping the Nineteenth-Century Brazilian Returnee Movement: Demographics, Life Stories and the Question of Slavery," *Atlantic Studies*, 13 (2016): 25–52: www.tandfonline.com/doi/abs/10.1080/14788810.2015.1110677?tab=permissions&scroll=top; Kristin Mann, *Transatlantic Lives: Slavery and Freedom in West Africa and Brazil*, chapter 3 (forthcoming); Mann, "Salvador, 1800–1850: uma sociedade dependente do tráfico de Africanos: Duas perspectivas familiares," in João J. Reis and Carlos da Silva Jr. (eds.), *Poder e dinheiro na era do tráfico* (Salvador, Brazil, forthcoming). Quote is from this last reference.
³⁰ See the next chapter for further development of this point.
³¹ Russell R. Menard, *Sweet Negotiations: Sugar, Slavery, and Planation Agriculture in Early Barbados* (Charlottesville, VA, 2006), pp. 1–28; Larry Gragg, "To Procure Negroes: The English Slave Trade to Barbados, 1627–1660," *Slavery & Abolition*, 16 (1999): 65–84.
³² Cited in Bernard Bailyn, *New England Merchants in Seventeenth Century* (Cambridge, MA, 1955), p. 85. For the transition in Brazil, see Alencastro, *Trade in the Living*, pp. 117–42.
³³ Pat Stafford and David Eltis, "Barbados and the Slave Trade," *Journal of the Barbados Museum and Historical Society*, 68 (2022): 1–17.

Boston was dispatching slave vessels to Africa, including one named *Gift of God* that no doubt had Puritan owners. By the end of the century Barbados had dispatched more than a hundred vessels to Africa,[34] and merchants in Antigua and Nevis had dispatched others direct to the African coast. Overall, a quarter of the 356 slave voyages recorded as disembarking slaves in Barbados down to 1700 began their voyages in the Americas, mainly Barbados.[35] Such a ratio is certainly a lower-bound estimate given that most pre-1698 voyages violated the Royal African Company (RAC)'s English monopoly over the slave trade. Illicit Caribbean-based ventures are more likely to have left no trace in the historical record.

We have much less detail of slave ships leaving the French Lesser Antilles. But we do know that the Black population of St. Kitt's, Martinique, and Guadeloupe came to match that of the White in the early 1660s, shortly after that same pattern had emerged in Barbados. But here the slave traders were more likely to have been Dutch than French. All but one of the twenty-one recorded disembarkations of captives in the French Antilles before 1666 were from vessels setting out from Dutch ports.[36]

As the frontier of the sugar complex moved west through the Caribbean so, too, did the home ports of Caribbean slave traders. Kingston, Jamaica, exported sugar to London for the first time in 1669, but except for a single voyage in 1687 the slave trade based on the island did not get underway until the Company's monopoly was relaxed in 1698. Beginning in 1699 there followed eighty documented slave voyages from Kingston, mostly in the first half of the eighteenth century. The smaller ports of Montego Bay and Martha Brae quickly joined in. The RAC was nevertheless a latecomer to the traffic based in the Americas, dispatching its first voyage – from Bridgetown – in 1679, but managing an average of only one voyage a year from that location for the rest of the seventeenth century.

---

[34] Slavevoyages shows eighty-nine voyages as setting out from Barbados, but there are another forty that arrived at the island with slaves without an identified home port, but have all the characteristics of a Barbadian vessel.

[35] Stafford and Eltis, "Barbados and the Slave Trade." For the data, see http://slavevoyages .org/tast/database/search.faces?yearFrom=1514&yearTo=1700&mjslptimp=34200, and then set the tables tab to "Broad region where voyage began."

[36] Laurence Verrand, "Premiers esclaves aux Petites Antilles d'après les chroniques et récits de voyages francais (XVIIe siècle)," in Philippe Hrodĕj (ed.), *L'esclave et les plantations de l'établissement de la servitude à son abolition. Hommage à Pierre Pluchon* (Rennes, 2009), pp. 85–102; www.slavevoyages.org/voyages/x8NLrCyA.

The major Caribbean organizational center of the slave trade developed late in the era. Havana merchants had established a major presence in the intra-American slave traffic in the later eighteenth century. Aided by British and US withdrawal from the transatlantic business and a rapidly expanding sugar economy after the collapse of St. Domingue, they were able to evolve into major transatlantic slave traders in the decade after 1807. Cuban-based merchants dispatched more than 1,500 voyages to Africa in the nineteenth century and carried off almost half a million enslaved people. Ninety percent of these voyages either left from Havana or were Cuban-owned. In just sixty years Havana became more important in the slave trade than any European port except for the three major English centers and Nantes, all of which had traded on the African coast for a century prior to Cuban involvement. Merchants in Santiago de Cuba, Matanzas, Trinidad de Cuba, and other Cuba out-ports organized their own ventures. A wide investors base evolved in the nineteenth century. The British Commissioner to the Mixed Court reported 108 slave-ship departures in 1828 and 1829, the failure of some of which "made many shopkeepers in Havana bankrupt because of their slave trade speculations." A quarter-century later the successful disembarkation of 479 captives in Havana from the *Pierre Soulé* meant that $85,000 in profits were shared among forty-eight investors, some of them in Africa.[37]

Although the northern continental colonies got into the business quite early, they remained minor players for the first century relative to their competitors to the south.[38] The early vessels brought slaves to the New England and New York markets – the very first perhaps carrying Africans, not from Africa but from the Caribbean in 1638. One was the *Desire*, which first brought the few male survivors of the Pequot War in 1637 to Barbados and then returned to Boston with a miscellaneous cargo that included Africans.[39] Down to 1700 only one transatlantic slave voyage left the mainland British colonies for every three from the Caribbean. All mainland ports together sent out at least thirty-six slaving ventures to

---

[37] W.S. Mcleay to Palmerston, Jan. 1, 1830, BNA, FO84/107; Commander Crabbe to the US Secretary for the Navy, Feb. 14, 1857, House Executive Document, 7, 36–2, p. 520.

[38] The best, indeed, the only account of the involvement of North Americans over the full duration of the transatlantic slave trade is Sean M. Kelley, *American Slavers: Merchants Mariners and the Transatlantic Commerce in Captives, 1644–1865* (New Haven, CT, 2023). Much of the following two paragraphs is based on this source.

[39] James Savage, Richard Dunn, and Laetitia Yaendle (eds.), *Journal of John Winthrop 1630 to 1694* (Cambridge, MA, 1996), entry for February 26, 1638, "Mr. Peirce in the Salem ship, the *Desire*, returned from the West Indies after seven months. He had been at Providence [island] and brought some cotton, and tobacco and negroes, etc., from thence, and salt from Tertugos." See www.slavevoyages.org/voyages/6J6xWe9X.

Africa in the seventeenth century, two-thirds from Boston and New York, the latter beginning its two-century-long span as a transatlantic slave-trading base in 1663 while it was still Dutch. Initially New Englanders sold their slaves in the Caribbean; New Yorkers, by contrast, brought slaves back to their own city. Yet as with their sugar-planting Caribbean compatriots, tobacco farmers and rice planters, they were able to sponsor transatlantic ventures to fetch the labor they needed. Chesapeake planters dispatched a small slave vessel to Africa in 1652 from the Wye River and followed up with a further four recorded ventures down to 1698, all of them in violation of the RAC's English monopoly. Other Chesapeake merchants partnered their London counterparts on ventures that left from the English capital.[40]

Between 1680 and 1721, New York merchants established a slave trade with Madagascar, and here, too, the last such venture, was owned jointly by New York and London merchants, in this case Jewish.[41] Further south within a couple of years of the first rice exports from Charleston, Charleston vessels were reported buying slaves in the Gambia without paying the 10 percent duty to the RAC required by the 1698 legislation.[42] None of this activity came close to supplying the labor needs of the rapidly expanding British North American plantation sector, but even in its earliest phase of growth, some plantation owners had the capital and expertise to blur the line dividing planters and slave merchants, and effectively met some of their own labor requirements.

The North American mainland slave-trading business began to expand in the 1720s and overtook the West Indian competition in the 1740s. The first Newport voyage dates from 1701, but it took several decades for New England rum to compete with the Barbadian product. Not until the 1720s did Newport become a significant base for slaving ventures. Rhode Islanders nevertheless held two-thirds of the mainland business by mid-century. As Sean Kelley points out, while eleven merchants owned one-fifth of the voyages dispatched, ownership in Rhode

---

[40] See voyage IDs 21124, 21125, 21393.
[41] The 1721 voyage by the *Crown Gally*, ID 75307, sailed from London, brought in 120 captives and was a financial disaster. See Eli Faber, *Jews, Slaves, and the Slave Trade: Setting the Record Straight* (New York, 1998), pp. 132–34; BNA, C104/13, pt 2 and C104/14, pt 2.
[42] "The whole trade of the River lyeth in the hands of the tennpercent [sic] ships who are here at this present seven in number some from Carolina & the rest from England who daily increase the price of slaves in this River." Extract of a letter from Messrs Nathan Pile, Thomas Rayner & Richard Oakely, James Island, Gambia, March 4, 1700, BNA, T70/175, f. 23.

Island was broadly based and few of the merchants specialized in the business. Moreover, New England became a major shipbuilding center during the eighteenth century. While historians have focused on the role of US-built ships in the illegal slave trade of the nineteenth century, it is not generally recognized that over one-third of the British slaving fleet in the third quarter of the eighteenth century was built by North American mainland shipbuilders.[43]

By the end of the eighteenth century, Charleston-based slave ships had become more numerous than those sailing from New England, aided by a developing northern abolitionist movement that had begun to restrict the northern traffic. For a decade before 1808, Charleston became the entry point for the largest inflow of slaves into the mainland of any decade in American history as the new South, created by the 1803 Louisiana Purchase, became available to US slaveholders. For a few years Charleston and Havana were competing for slaves directly: some slave-ship captains checked out both ports before deciding where to sell. Between 1808 and 1820, the year that the US made slave trading a capital offence, US citizens and ports remained active in the slave trade though at a seriously reduced level and without introducing many slaves into the US itself. They were particularly involved in the Cuban slave trade where some ship owners like the d'Wolfs had plantations and, as with the well-documented voyage of the *Abaellino* in 1818,[44] sent out their vessels with Spanish registration papers. Cuban and Spanish owners became dominant in the Cuban trade between 1810 and 1820, even before slave trading became a capital offence. US participation declined sharply, before reviving again in the late 1830s. Renewed participation took the form of supplying fast sailing ships and, in a reversal of the pattern in the 1810s, facilitating the supply of US registration papers to Brazilian and Cuban slave ships. US papers would allow vessels to escape the attentions of the British navy on at least the outbound voyage. Direct US ownership of transatlantic slave ventures was rare by this time.[45]

The advantages of using the Americas as an organizational base are obvious. In the eighteenth century, round-trip voyages from Caribbean

---

[43] Kelley, *American Slavers*, pp. 77–108. For shipbuilding compare voyage numbers in https://slavevoyages.org/voyages/lqUDO3GB with those in https://slavevoyages.org/voyages/gd0Fz9d1.

[44] ID 37297. Buch to James D'Wolf, Dec. 6, 1818, Edward Spalding Papers, University of Miami.

[45] Leonardo Marques, *The United States and the Transatlantic Slave Trade to the Americas, 1776–1867* (New Haven, CT, 2016), pp. 139–84.

home ports lasted nine months, compared to 15 months for voyages setting out from Europe. Brazilian and North American slave ships returned to home port within a year, and by the mid nineteenth century in just five months.[46] The most important part of the voyage from the standpoint of its profitability – the return trip – lasted on average forty-two days compared to the seventy-seven days for the middle passages of European-based vessels following the triangular route. Mortality and morbidity data – the key elements governing profitability in the business – are not up to the task of allowing us direct comparisons but given the much faster Atlantic crossing they likely favored the Americas-based trafficker. America also had the advantage of abundant supplies of timber. While the British carried almost eight times more slaves across the Atlantic than vessels setting out from their colonial possessions, as already noted, the latter built over one-third of the British slaving fleet during the slave trade era. It is probable that a similar ratio of colonial to metropolitan built vessels held for slavers sailing under the Portuguese/Brazilian flags.

As for trade goods, some European manufactures reached Angola direct from Lisbon and in the late eighteenth century these averaged about 40 percent of Luanda's imports. The South Atlantic gyre ensured that East Indian textiles were cheaper in Rio de Janeiro than in Lisbon.[47] There were ready products at hand in the Americas in high demand on the African coast. *Cachaça* (alcohol), tobacco, bullion, and provisions were plentiful, with *cachaça* predating Barbadian rum exports by at least half a century.[48] The first recorded New England slave vessel disembarked slaves in Barbados in 1645, but it was provisions, rather than rum, that underpinned the early North American mainland trade. A New England ship carrying rum was captured off Succondee on the Gold Coast in 1687 by the RAC, but it may have got its rum in Barbados.[49] The typical trading

---

[46] For 1701–1800, 8,372 European-based voyages averaged 446.7 days (SD = 134.5); 526 Brazilian voyages took 367.7 days (SD = 139.8); 216 North American mainland trips lasted 353.9 days (SD = 129.6); while 37 Caribbean vessels completed round trips in 368.9 (SD = 118.0)

[47] Rudy Bauss, "Textiles, Bullion and Other Trades of Goa: Commerce with Surat, Other Areas of India, Luso-Brazilian Ports, Macau and Mozambique, 1816–1819," *Indian Economic & Social History Review*, 34 (1997): 275–87: https://doi.org/10.1177/001946469703400301.

[48] Gustavo Acioli Lopes, "Brazil's Colonial Economy and the Atlantic Slave Trade: Supply and Demand," in David Richardson and Filipa Ribeiro da Silva (eds.), *Networks and Trans-Cultural Exchange: Slave Trading in the South Atlantic, 1590–1867* (Leiden, 2015), p. 68; Alencastro, *Trade in the Living*, pp. 114–16.

[49] BL, Thomas Draper, Succondee, February 25, 1687, Rawlinson mss, c 745, ff. 437–38.

cargo of these vessels, including those sailing from New York to Madagascar in the late seventeenth century was "bread, flour, butter, pork, Barbados rum, and Madeira wine."[50] Barbadians had drunk "mobby," fermented from sweet potatoes, before the sugar regime, but by the late 1640s rum had taken over and indeed became the island's currency.[51] Where ships from Europe had always included brandy or English spirits among their trade goods, Africans preferred Barbadian, and eventually, Jamaican rum when it became available – the equivalent in Africa of *cachaça* from Brazil.[52] Finally, for several decades from the beginning of the eighteenth century the commodity that trumped all others was Brazilian gold. Some London-owned ventures would sell their slaves to Bahian vessels on the Gold Coast and in the Bight of Benin and then return directly to London with gold.[53]

The Eurocentric thrust of slave trade historiography has ensured the sidelining of the Americas, especially on the issue of the funding and crewing of voyages. The wider literature recognizes high land-labor ratios in the Americas relative to Europe and the consequences of this for higher wages and capital costs in the New World. As Jacob Price noted, the Americas "retained the frontier characteristics of cheap land, scarce capital, and dear labor."[54] But the literature does not consider how slave traders adjusted to such resource patterns. One crude proxy for wage costs is the tons per crew ratio that TSTD makes it possible to

---

[50] Edward Searle, Commenda, February 12, 1696, ibid, c 747, f. 63. As late as 1720 a New York venture (*Crown Gally*, ID 75307), owned jointly by London and New York merchants bought 240 slaves in Madagascar with a cargo of provisions – see the very detailed accounts, some in Yiddish, in BNA, C104/13, pt 2.

[51] "Small vessel from Barbados here ... trades only rum and sugar" (BL, William Cross, Commenda, Jan. 26, 1687, Rawlinson Papers, c745, f. 430); Carl Bridenbaugh and Roberta Bridenbaugh, *No Peace Beyond the Line: The English in the Caribbean, 1624–1690* (Oxford, 1972), pp. 50–51.

[52] American rum was cheaper on the coast than English spirits (BL, Steede and Gascoigne, Barbados, July 1, 1686, Rawlinson Papers, c. 745, f. 373; Dalby Thomas, Cape Coast Castle, April 28, 1704, BNA, T70/28, f. 35).

[53] As London slave trader Humphry Morice instructed one of his captains, "you cannot but be sensible how much it will be for my advantage to turne of & sell your Cargoe of Goods, and the Negroes you purchase for Gold, whereby the great Loss that often happens by the Mortality of Negroes will be avoided, as well as the Loss in returns from the West Indies, which you well know runs away with all the profit of a voyage made by the Sale of Negroes," cited in Matthew D. Mitchell, *The Prince of Slavers: Humphrey Morice and the Transformation of Britain's Transatlantic Slave Trade, 1698–1732* (London, 2020), p. 158. For an annual series of Brazilian gold production 1721–1807, see Leonor Freire Costa, Maria Manuela Rocha e Rita Martins de Sousa, *O Ouro do Brasil* (Lisboa, 2013), pp. 192–94.

[54] Jacob Price, "Credit in the Slave Trade and Plantation Economies," in Barbara Solow (ed.), *Slavery and the Rise of the Atlantic System* (Cambridge, 1991), p. 295.

TABLE 2.2 *Enslaved persons per crew member by flag of slave ship, 1613–1830*

Flag of ship	Mean	SD	n (differences significant at the 1 percent level)
Portugal/Brazil	14.2	7.0	360
Great Britain	10.1	4.3	1,024
Netherlands	8.1	2.3	132
France	8.5	3.1	1,367

Source: TSTD

calculate. At the height of the slave trade – 1751–1800 – slave vessels leaving the North American mainland had similar ratios to those leaving Brazil. These were 23 percent higher than for crews leaving British and French ports. But the big difference between the Americas and Europe in labor productivity was in the number of enslaved people per crew member. On Portuguese vessels there was one crew for every 14, a ratio which was between 40 and 70 percent greater than their northwest European competitors.

On the capital front, mercantile credit ultimately based in London, Amsterdam, and Paris underpinned the British, Dutch, and French slave trades at relatively low interest rates. In addition, creditors in most of the British Caribbean could seize plantations in the event of non-payment of debt. This was not an option in Latin America, where creditors' claims were limited to the produce of the plantation, and debt financing of voyages was therefore more restricted.[55]

Distinct regional solutions to these financing issues evolved. Before 1775, New England merchants operated the smallest slave ships in the business, averaging below 70 tons[56] and often sailing between Upper Guinea and North America. They were among the smallest of all transoceanic sailing vessels. New England ships also had the highest tons per crew ratios in the slave trade. Although the average British slaver was more than twice the size of its colonial counterpart, the two

---

[55] Price, "Credit in the Slave Trade," pp. 296–97; Russell R. Menard, "Law, Credit, the Supply of Labor, and the Organization of Sugar Production in the Colonial Greater Caribbean: A Comparison of Brazil and Barbados in the Seventeenth Century," in John J. McCusker and Kenneth Morgan (eds.), *The Early Modern Atlantic Economy* (Cambridge, 2000), pp. 159–61.
[56] See www.slavevoyages.org/voyages/siFuwYIZ.

groups (New England and British) had a comparable slaves per crew ratio. In addition, colonial ships could buy slaves at major British forts on the Gold Coast, where fewer men on board were required (see Chapter 4) and sell at major British Caribbean markets. Given the more than one hundred British American shipbuilding sites specified in the slavevoyages database, it seems clear that cheaper and smaller ships, and a degree of British naval protection off Africa enabled the New Englanders to compete with the more heavily capitalized British slave trade centers.[57]

A second response to relative labor and capital scarcity in the Americas emerged in the Caribbean. The TSTD shows that in the seventeenth century 128 slaving ventures set sail from British Caribbean ports compared to just thirty from the North American mainland. Here, too, vessels dispatched from British islands to Africa averaged just half the size of their London-based counterparts and were thus cheaper to fit out. But in this instance European capital *was* available. In the early British and French Caribbean there were strong links between establishing plantations and sending out slave voyages, with both activities funded in part by metropolitan merchants. London and Bristol merchants bought up land and introduced slaves at the same time.[58] Of thirty-seven documented slave-ship owners (other than the London-based RAC) setting out from seventeenth-century Barbados, half were proprietors of sugar plantations and only five can be identified as local merchants without English connections. Later in the eighteenth century, Caribbean involvement was limited to the funding or part-funding of ventures that left from Europe. For example, the Freemasons of Guadeloupe dispatched the *Franc-maçon* (ID 32744) from Le Havre, which was destroyed off Gabon by a slave uprising.[59] This was the branch of the slave trade of the Americas with the strongest connections to a major European slave-trading center, but that branch was also a relatively small component of the larger picture. The problem with

---

[57] François Crouzet estimates that by the time of abolition of the slave trade in 1807 the total tonnage of the overall US merchant fleet amounted to 60 percent of its British counterpart ("America and the Crisis of the British Imperial Economy, 1803–1807," in McCusker and Morgan, *Early Modern Atlantic*, p. 305).

[58] Richard Dunn, *Sugar and Slaves: The Rise of the Planter Class in the British West Indies, 1624–1723* (New York, 1972), p. 272; Larry Gragg, *Englishmen Transplanted: The English Colonization of Barbados, 1627–1660* (New York, 2003), pp. 132–41.

[59] Chloe Duflo-Ciccotelli, *La franc-maçonnerie en Guadeloupe, miroir d'une société coloniale en tensions 1770–1848* (Bordeaux, 2021), p. 174. My thanks to Sandra Willendorf for this reference.

small was the risk, as the Freemasons discovered. On mainland North America the owner of the snow *Tulip* (ID 25371) wrote in 1762 after a third unsuccessful venture from Annapolis, "there are more disasters in those Voyages than any others whatever."[60]

The major Caribbean organizational center for the slave trade turned out to be not British but rather Spanish, and here ties to European capital were much weaker. Havana was the port in the Americas with longest-lasting connection to Africa, Cuba being one of the first markets for enslaved Africans to open in the Americas and certainly being the last to close. Before the 1790s the island depended on foreign slave traders for almost all its supply of enslaved people. Yet 87 percent of Cuba's total influx from Africa arrived between 1790 and 1866, putting Havana second only to Rio de Janeiro as the world's premier slave trading port of the nineteenth century. The development of Havana in the thirty years after the gradual implementation of the Bourbon reforms in 1789 and the parallel opening up of trade in Brazil after the Portuguese court moved to Rio de Janeiro in 1807 was just extraordinary. The income generated by Cuba's sugar and Southeast Brazil's coffee economies reached unprecedented levels by the second quarter of the nineteenth century.[61]

In the mid 1820s only three ports in the Americas had populations larger than 100,000 – Havana, Rio de Janeiro, and New York – figures that put them in the top five most populous cities in the Americas. All three were larger than Liverpool at the time of British abolition.[62] Such port cities backed by the plantation output of their hinterlands – sugar, coffee, and cotton respectively – could raise the capital and provide the myriad services necessary to launch slave-trading expeditions to Africa.[63] As we have seen in the case of Bahia, that the hinterlands comprised intensive agriculture rather than industrial manufacturing mattered little. Both could support the capital requirements of

---

[60] Elizabeth Donnan, *Documents Illustrative of the Slave Trade to America*, 4 vols (Washington, 1930–33), vol. 4: 42, n.

[61] David Eltis, *Economic Growth and the Ending of the Transatlantic Slave Trade* (New York, 1987), pp. 283–89; Jorge Felipe Gonzalez, *Foundation and Growth of the Cuban-based Transatlantic Slave Trade* (forthcoming).

[62] Mary Karasch, *Slave Life in Rio de Janeiro* (Princeton, 1987), pp. 60–3; *Darby's edition of Brookes' Universal Gazetteer* (Philadelphia, 1823), p. 518; *Cuadro estadístico de la siempre fiel Isla de Cuba correspondiente al año de 1827* (Habana, 1829), p. 47.

[63] For the growth of these ports into major bases of the slave trade see Felipe Gonzalez, *Foundation and Growth*; John Harris, *The Last Slave Ships: New York and the End of the Middle Passage* (New Haven, CT, 2020), pp. 23–92; Marques, *United States*, pp. 106–38.

a vibrant slave trade. Moreover, by the nineteenth century the laws restraining creditors from taking possession of plantations no longer existed. Eventually, therefore, New York and Havana joined the Brazilian port cities as major centers serving prosperous hinterlands that could finance their own ventures. Between them New York, Havana, and Rio de Janeiro sent out 2,460 slaving ventures in the last half-century of the traffic, even though the New York component was severely restricted by increasing US sanctions against the traffic.[64] John Harris and Leonardo Marques have laid out the innovative risk-averting strategies that New York and Havana traders adopted.[65] In the final quarter-century, these voyages – two dozen of them on steam ships carrying more than 1,000 captives at a time – were double the size of their eighteenth-century counterparts, averaging 552 enslaved persons at embarkation as opposed to 283.[66]

The three environments for launching slaving ventures described above nevertheless applied to fewer than half of all voyages leaving the Americas for Africa. Seven thousand ventures set out from Brazil (excluding nineteenth-century Rio de Janeiro) and these drew on a yet different pattern used only in the Portuguese South Atlantic.[67] As argued at greater length in Chapter 4, the South Atlantic slave-trading system had lower costs that were unrelated to wage rates for crew and expensive credit. Distances were shorter, voyages faster, slave rebellions fewer, losses from wars and piracy rarer, and slaves carried, both per crew member and per ton, greater than for ventures originating in the North Atlantic. In addition, as first European comers in the South Atlantic, the Portuguese claimed a tenuous, but enduring and exclusive sovereignty over two of the three

---

[64] https://slavevoyages.org/voyages/TLto9yX1. In late colonial Rio de la Plata, we see nascent signs of Buenos Aires and Montevideo joining this group. With a joint population of c. 70,000 at independence in 1810, their merchants dispatched twenty-seven voyages to Africa between 1777 and 1837 – mostly before 1811 when abolition kicked in (Lyman L. Johnson, *Workshop of the Revolution: Plebeian Buenos Aires and the Atlantic World, 1776–1810* (Chapel Hill, NC, 2011), p. 8; Alex Borucki, "The Slave Trade to the Rio de la Plata, 1777–1812: Trans-Imperial Networks and Atlantic Warfare," *Colonial Latin American Historical Review*, 20 (2011): 81–107; https://slavevoyages.org/voyages/axA2H9Zz.

[65] Harris, *Last Slave Ships*, pp. 23–55; Marques, United States, pp. 139–218.

[66] https://slavevoyages.org/voyages/GJGgjWY8 for 1841–1866; https://slavevoyages.org/voyages/GtciOoau for 1701–1800.

[67] Calculated by taking all departures from Brazil (see https://slavevoyages.org/voyages/tGR7UVBw) and subtracting slave vessels leaving Rio de Janeiro after 1810, compared to voyages leaving Rio after 1810 (https://slavevoyages.org/voyages/Zp6TBIla) plus vessels leaving North America, including Caribbean for the whole period – https://slavevoyages.org/voyages/pnaPhFxP.

biggest African embarkation points in the trade, in the form of Luanda and Benguela. Between them, these ports with a combined population of 4,000 in the late eighteenth century, accounted for almost 30 percent of all transatlantic departures from Africa. Just as the Spanish were able to occupy the richest parts of the Americas for themselves, so the Portuguese on the other side of the Atlantic were able to lay first claim to the ports that supplied the most enslaved people. In doing so they developed relations with Africans in the hinterland that no other European nation could match.[68] *Lançado* traders of mixed Portuguese and African heritage helped link African sellers in the interior with Brazilian buyers on the coast who maintained barracoons where Brazilian vessels embarked captives. Dutch, English, and French slave-ship captains typically dealt directly with Africans resident on the coast, although both Dutch and English contacts did involve limited numbers of traders of mixed descent.

But if the funding requirements of a voyage in the South Atlantic were more modest, a second advantage was that Brazilians were able to tap into a wider range of small investors than any of their competitors. The contrast between the major French and English ports on the one hand and the Brazilians on the other was indeed dramatic. The www.slavevoyages.org site contains records of 15,000 owners of slaving ventures located in ports around the Atlantic. Slavers from Bahia carried off approximately the same number of Africans as vessels from Liverpool – between 1.3 and 1.4 million – though of course Bahia was active in the traffic for a longer period. However, the ownership structure and funding in the two ports was completely different. For Bahia, TSTD identifies 1,091 investors in 2,799 ventures. The Liverpool records are somewhat more complete, with 1,876 individuals investing in 4,669 voyages. The largest Bahian owner was João Ferreira Souza, active between 1709 and 1736, followed by Jose de Cerqueira Lima trading between 1801 and 1839. They had ownership stakes in vessels that embarked 17,053 and 12,618 slaves respectively. However, such numbers as these would not have placed the pair in the top sixty ranking of Liverpool slave traders. William Boat's ships transported 55,352 slaves in the years 1744–1795, and Thomas Hodgson's vessels carried off 52,339 captives between 1752 and 1805.[69]

---

[68] Eltis and Richardson, *Atlas*, p. 90.
[69] The PAST UI on www.slavevoyages.org contains 1,092 owners for Bahia, and 1,875 for Liverpool.

The more interesting question is the structure of investment in the two ports. This can be explored with the Gini coefficient, commonly used to measure income or wealth inequality, with zero indicating complete equality and one, complete inequality. Instead of income, here we assess investment in the slave trade. Using the raw data, the Gini index for Liverpool is 0.35, and for Bahia, 0.31, suggesting that investment in the second-largest Brazilian slave-trading center was only slightly more equally distributed than in Liverpool. But the raw data in TSTD includes only the principal investors and ignores the large number of minor participants – including slave-ship crew, shopkeepers, and indeed even the enslaved crew on board the typical Brazilian slaving vessel.

The earliest examples of the participation of small investors comes from the customs records of the Cape Verde Islands in the early sixteenth century. The *Madanela Cansyna* left Santiago in December 1513 with 125 slaves bound for Castile. Twenty-five owners sailed with their chattel, all but two were Portuguese and among them were both merchants and crew.[70] This pattern has recently been brought to center stage for the later period by Mary Hicks. It emerges from trials of captured vessels rather than shipping records where only the principals are identified. Hicks' impressive data supports her claim that "[s]laving merchants drew extensively on a variety of familial and patronage ties to kin, friends, and dependents in order to complete cargoes," and gives instances of trading cargoes owned by dozens of investors some of whom were themselves enslaved persons.[71] Very few of these individuals are included in the PAST databases in TSTD, which is biased toward the large investor. It will require a major research effort to ever identify more than a handful of them. But the practice was extensive enough that

---

[70] Trevor P. Hall, *Before Middle Passage: Translated Portuguese Manuscripts of Atlantic Slave Trading from West Africa to Iberian Territories, 1513–1526* (Leiden, 2016), pp. 192–94.

[71] Mary E. Hicks, *Captive Cosmopolitans: Black Mariners and the World of South Atlantic Slavery* (Chapel Hill, NC, 2024); Hicks, "Financing the Luso-Atlantic Slave Trade, 1500–1840: Collective Investment Practices from Portugal to Brazil," *Journal of Global Slavery*, 2 (2017): 273–309. Quote is from p. 279. For the broader issue of slaves owning slaves, see João José Reis, "Slaves Who Owned Slaves in Nineteenth-Century Bahia, Brazil," Mecila Working Paper Series, No. 36, São Paulo, 2021: The Maria Sibylla Merian International Centre, http://dx.doi.org/10.46877/reis.2021.36. The Portuguese government encouraged a pattern of dispersed investment (Pierre Verger, *Trade Relations Between the Bight of Benin and Bahia from the 17th to the 19th Century* [Ibadan, 1968], p. 81).

the typical Brazilian-based slaving venture had a great many more investors than French, Dutch, and English voyages. In the major northwestern European ports partnerships of ten or more are rare. The TSTD Enslavers database shows that only 93 out of 21,700 voyages sailing from northwest European ports have ownership information that falls into this category.

Hicks also describes the common practice of allowing crew to make private investment in slaves, or sometimes allotting them cargo space, as an alternative to receiving wages. English and French principals typically allowed captains and, less often, surgeons small numbers of "privilege" slaves to be transported free, but rarely extended the option to ordinary seamen and never to seamen who were also slaves. Remuneration for non-officered crew in English, French, and Dutch slave ships took the form of wages.[72] One exception in the very early English slave trade is the *Brazil Frigate* (ID 21750), which set off from Luanda for Pernambuco in 1658 with 1,200 Africans – easily the largest number of people ever carried by any English slave ship. Ordinary seamen on this venture did indeed buy slaves on their own account. However, this English ship was hired by the Governor of Angola, João Vieira, so that the voyage can be classed as Portuguese rather than English, and it is thus probable that Portuguese practices prevailed. Such strategies meant that principal investors in Brazil could adapt to both the high-wage and the capital-scarce environments of the Americas relative to their European and North American competitors. If the crew were investors, albeit small, and half their number at least on Bahian slave ships, were of African descent – including many crew members – then the complications for a class-based (or even race-based) interpretation of the slave trade, or even the Atlantic world, seem clear enough.

As for the racial composition of crews, the emergence of Black sailors in the English-speaking plantation Americas has received considerable attention and was far more common than on voyages leaving Old World ports. Enslaved sailors on privateers based in North America could receive part of any prize money that captures generated.[73] But in North America, Black sea-captains were rare, and instances have yet to emerge of Black crew members on slave ships having roles as investors or in reassuring the enslaved in their own language that they were not to be

---

[72] BNA, HCA13/73, ff. 306–53.
[73] W. Jeffrey Bolster, *Black Jacks: African American Seamen in the Age of Sail* (Cambridge, MA, 1997), pp. 102, 114.

eaten at the end of the voyage. There is certainly no parallel in the English, Dutch, and French slave trades to the *NS da Penha de França*, which left Pernambuco in 1812 with a *pardo* (mixed-origins) captain and fifteen crew. The only White on board was a sailor from Porto in Portugal.[74] The extensive appendices to Mary Hicks' book suggest that just under half the crew on slave voyages leaving Brazil were Black and half of these were enslaved. We know that the average crew on these voyages was 21.6,[75] and that TSTD shows at least 9,628 ventures left Brazilian ports for Africa. If just ten of the crew on average were *pardo* or *preto* (Black) then close to 100,000 Africans and Black Brazilians crewed slaving voyages to Brazil.[76]

We do not know how many of these were investors, in the sense of receiving all or part of their wages in the form of enslaved people or fractions thereof, but Hicks' work makes it clear that the practice was not only extensive but also supplemented by a traffic in African products, especially textiles that crew members were allowed to trade for and to transport to Brazil in their sea chests.[77] But small investors were not confined to Brazil. In Havana, *accionistas* (shareholders) with "shares as low as $100 ... eagerly sought for by clerks in public and mercantile houses."[78] There were more small investors in the North Atlantic slave trades than the literature recognizes, but nothing on the scale of the Brazilian and Cuban business. These financing and hiring strategies were critical to the ability of the slave traders of the Iberian Americas to defend their dominant role in Atlantic slave trading in the face of

---

[74] It is significant that the most widely read books on the slave trade – Rediker, *Slave Ship*, Basil Davidson, *The African Slave Trade* (Boston, 1980); Daniel P. Mannix, *Black Cargoes: a History of the Atlantic Slave Trade, 1518–1865* (London: 1963) and Hugh Thomas, *The Slave Trade: the Story of the Atlantic Slave Trade, 1440–1870* (New York, 1997) – give short shrift to the South American traffic. Some fascinating issues cannot be explored if scholars of the slave trade insist on treating the English and US slave trades as typical. I thank Marial Iglesias Utset for the reference to the NS *da Penha de França* at BNA, HCA42/406/391. ID is 52119.

[75] Calculated from https://www.slavevoyages.org/voyages/k1vIgw6n.

[76] Interest in the multiracial crews of slave ships has increased in recent decades. See Emma Christopher, *Slave Ship Sailors and their Captive Cargoes, 1730–1807* (Cambridge, 2007), pp. 51–90 for access to the now extensive literature, and see pp. 231–38 for her three appendices that list 153 Black sailors in the Bristol, Liverpool, and Rhode Island slave trades between 1748 and 1807. Yet such numbers are utterly trivial compared to the Blacks on Portuguese slave ships, a topic that until the publication of Hicks' essays and now her monograph, this literature has yet to address.

[77] Hicks, *Captive Cosmopolitans*, chapter 7.

[78] R. Jameson to Castlereagh, Sept 1, 1821 (enc.), BNA, FO84/13.

competition of the ports of northwestern Europe. There can be little doubt that their competitors had far greater access to credit and capital markets.

Indebted planters feature prominently in the histories of the French, British, and Dutch tropical colonies. Distressed estate sales and spectacular bankruptcies are almost a trope.[79] Given that most slave traders advanced credit to plantation owners and, especially in the French case, waited for years for repayment, how could planters afford to finance slave voyages? Successful businesses have always drawn heavily on credit and renewing the slave labor force always constituted the largest single expense for owners in the first century or so of a sugar colony's existence. Borrowing was an essential part of normal business. The value of labor force purchases may be viewed against a backdrop of total output. Table 2.3 shows the value of captives arriving in the Caribbean in 1770

TABLE 2.3 *Total cost of purchases of the enslaved in 1770 relative to total output of plantations in the Caribbean in current pounds sterling for the major Northwest European slave trading powers*

	British	French	Dutch
Value of total output of plantations	£2,669,000	£3,819,000	£573,000
No. of slaves arrived, 1769–1771	99,062	46,281	18,368
Annual mean	33,021	15,427	6,123
Price of prime slaves in Americas	£44.3	£44.3	£44.3
Price of average slave in Americas	£31.0	£31.0	£31.0
No. of price obs. (complete cargo)	22	3	14
Total cost of slaves	£966,915	£441,662	£189,813
Cost of enslaved/total output (row 7/row 1)	0.36	0.12	0.33

Sources: Enslaved: https://www.slavevoyages.org/voyages/QLL4mvbl. Total output: David Eltis, "The Slave Economies of the Caribbean: Structure, Performance, Evolution and Significance," in Franklin Knight (ed.), *General History of the Caribbean – UNESCO*, 4 vols. (New York, 2007), vol. 3: 178–202. For slave prices in 1770, North America see https://www.slavevoyages.org/voyages/BdQbcvoQ.

---

[79] Pieter C. Emmer, "Surinam and the Decline of the Dutch Slave Trade," *Revue Française d'Histoire d'Outre-Mer*, 226–27 (1975): 245–51; Lowell J. Ragatz's book, *Fall of the Planter Class in the British Caribbean, 1763–1833* (New York, 1928) underpinned the decline thesis which dominated the British Caribbean historiography during the twentieth century; Nicholas Radburn, "Guinea Factors, Slave Sales, and the Profits of the Transatlantic Slave Trade in Late Eighteenth-Century Jamaica: The Case of John Tailyour," *William and Mary Quarterly*, 72 (2015): 243–286. muse.jhu.edu/article/580882.

relative to the total product of the British, French, and Dutch Caribbean in that year. Overall, even assuming most of these purchases were bought on credit, the debt load does not appear crippling, and Lorena S. Walsh's assessment of the Chesapeake plantocracy that serious planter indebtedness was limited to early careers and was rare in later life was probably generally true across the Americas.[80] Nothing in the French, British, and Dutch slave trades matched the financing system in the Portuguese traffic. Hicks' findings revise our understanding of that traffic.

THE INTRA-AMERICAN SLAVE TRAFFIC

Sugar plantations and their ancillary activities accounted for most of the transatlantic slave trade and almost all of them were located within thirty miles of salt water. The survivors of the transoceanic passage would therefore have reached the property of their new owners on foot in much less time than it took for them to reach the African coast from their point of enslavement. Some plantation records link the enslaved persons with name of the vessel that brought them from Africa.[81] In 1787 Robert Hibbard, agent to the Duke of Chandos purchased "twenty prime young men" in Kingston from the *Brooks* (ID 80666, and later to become the iconic subject of a misleading abolitionist pamphlet) for the Hope estate located just three miles to the north and now the Mona campus of the University of the West Indies. In St. Domingue, Jean-Joseph de Laborde, perhaps the wealthiest slave owner in the eighteenth-century Caribbean with his 1,400 slaves, had two plantations in the southern peninsula of St. Domingue, one just six miles from les Cayes where Laborde bought Africans from the *Naïade* in 1769 (ID 31564). Only four of them were still alive a quarter-century later.[82]

However, not all prospective slave buyers had access to markets large enough to accommodate transatlantic slaving ventures. And some that did, like Cuba, were subject to imperial regulations that for

---

[80] Lorena S. Walsh, *Motives of Honor, Pleasure, and Profit: Plantation Management in the Colonial Chesapeake, 1607–1763* (Chapel Hill, NC, 2010), p. 236. For a more complete view of the slave trade's position in the thirteen colonies and early republic, see Lawrence Officer and Samuel H. Williamson, "The Antebellum Slave Trade: Numbers and Impact on the Balance of Payments": www.measuringworth.com/sam/Slavetrade.pdf.

[81] Huntington, Stowe mss, vol. 26, Robert Hibbard, Nov. 10, 1787.

[82] Trevor G. Burnard and John D. Garrigus, *The Plantation Machine: Atlantic Capitalism in French Saint-Domingue and British Jamaica* (Philadelphia, 2016), pp. 22, 165; "Etat des Négres, Négresses, Négrillons, et Négrittes Existans sur la Premier Habitation de Monsieur Laborde ce Mai 10, 1793," BNA, HCA30/381.

centuries inhibited direct trade with Africa. Some minor plantation products such as tobacco, rice, indigo, and coffee were also accessible by water. But the rest of the market for slave labor, amounting, perhaps, to 20 percent of the total demand in the Americas, lay far away from the ocean in the Spanish American highlands and the gold-bearing regions of Minas Gerais, Goiás, and Mato Grosso of Brazil. As Figure 2.1 shows, panning for riverine gold was not as capital intensive as hard rock mining for silver.[83]

A workforce of about fifty is displayed, not much different from the requirements of a moderate sized *engenho* or a seventeenth-century Barbados plantation. The remote location of the "mining factory" depicted was a challenge, given that western Mato Grosso is not just the center of Brazil, but of South America, too. But gold was the least bulky of the precious metals and compared to a sugar-mill, the required infrastructure for its extraction was not beyond the resources of a single investor. Leo Marques has written of the owner, José Paes Falcão das

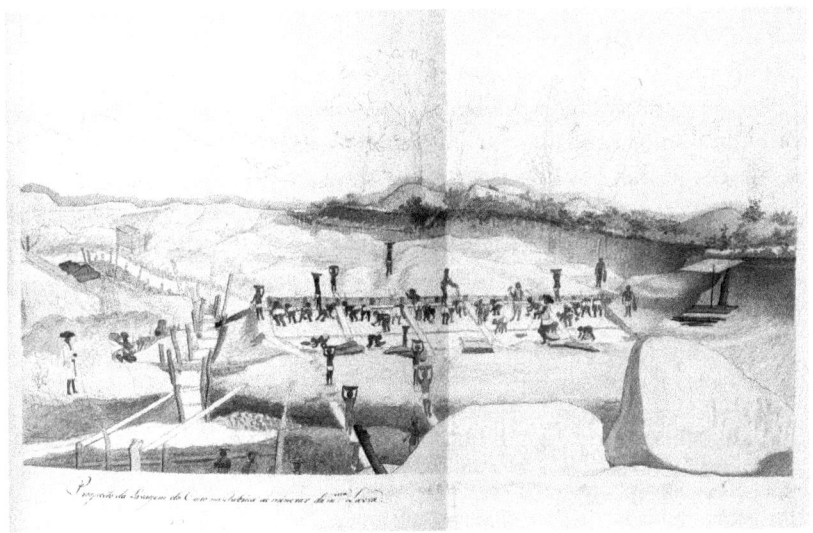

FIGURE 2.2 Panning for gold in Mato Grosso.
"Prospecto da lavagem do ouro na fábrica de minerar da mesma lavra," Source: Universidade de Lisboa/Museu Nacional de História Natural e da Ciência, PT-MUL-RMJBA-TC-02-0007.

[83] I am indebted to Leonardo Marques for drawing this image to my attention.

Neves, who a few years later owned two "mining factories and a total of 116 slaves some of whom were employed in a *cachaça* distillery." However, for the enslaved Africans forced to travel to these remote regions, the passage across the ocean constituted less than half their total journey in terms of time.[84]

A further underlying pattern saw slave emporia in the tropics such as those in the Caribbean and in Rio de Janeiro supplying slaves to smaller markets in both the tropical and temperate Americas. The first transatlantic voyages did not reach the Spanish American mainland until the 1540s. Small groups of Africans arriving in New Spain before that point transshipped from Cuba and Hispaniola. The Rio de la Plata began receiving captives from Rio de Janeiro before the end of the sixteenth century. Between 1640 and 1790, Spanish America was heavily dependent on the intra-American trade. Many vessels carried just a single slave, others such as the *San Fortunato el Nuevo* carried hundreds – in one instance, 973 people from Curacao to Portobelo in 1669.[85] Even before the mid seventeenth century a major intra-American trade in slaves developed. We now know that Spanish supplies of enslaved people were sustained by a trans-imperial intra-American slave trading operation first established by the Domenico Grillo and Ambrosio Lomellino partnership of Genoa, the basic structure of which endured into the late eighteenth century. First the Dutch and then the British and Portuguese were the dominant vendors.[86] But Spanish-flagged ships were far more prominent in this business than in the transatlantic trade. In sharp contrast to the transatlantic business almost as many Africans moved to their ultimate destination under the Spanish flag as under the British.[87]

Yet the Dutch accounted for more than 60 percent of all the recorded intra-American traffic before 1700, most of it originating at Curacao

---

[84] Leonardo Marques, "A fronteira do ouro e a degradação do Outro nos confins do Brasil colonial (Mato Grosso, século XVIII)," in Alexsander Gebara and Leonardo Marques (eds.), *História das mercadorias: trabalho, meio ambiente e capitalismo mundial (séculos XVI-XIX)* (São Leopoldo/RS, 2023), pp. 555–68. The best overview of the intra-American traffic is Gregory O'Malley and Alex Borucki, "Patterns in the Overall Intercolonial Slave Trade across the Americas Before the Nineteenth Century," *Revista Tempo*, 23 (2017): 313–48.

[85] ID 110684, www.slavevoyages.org/voyages/kFYxVazf.

[86] Alejandro García-Montón, *Genoese Entrepreneurship and the Asiento Slave Trade, 1650–1700* (New York, 2022), pp. 98–136. Note that the Genoa links did not extend to Africa.

[87] www.slavevoyages.org/voyages/IGBKuXkI. The major role of the Spanish is one of the few points that escapes the attention of García-Montón.

with a smaller stream from St. Eustatius. Curacao, a near desert of an island in the southern Caribbean, along with the similarly infertile St. Eustatius, received 82,000 captives direct from Africa in the second half of the seventeenth century, almost as many as the whole of the French Caribbean plus Jamaica combined. Ninety-five percent of these Africans were destined for reshipment to the Spanish American mainland, which, for some, meant a further ocean voyage from Panama to Callao in Peru.[88] Barbados was the British counterpart to Curacao until the second decade of the eighteenth century. Strikingly this small island, along with Jamaica, was in the top five jurisdictions in the Americas in terms of arrivals of Africans, following Brazil, Cuba, and St. Domingue.[89] Unlike the Dutch islands, Barbados combined a thriving plantation sector with a major slave-trading entrepôt role. In 1715, John Ashley, the RAC agent for Barbados, wrote that typically 5,500 slaves per annum arrived at Bridgetown (remarkably close to the mean slavevoyages annual estimate for the island, 1711–1715), of whom 1,400 were sold on to other sugar islands, mainly French, and 900 to the North American mainland.[90] However, Jamaica quickly took over as the major slave entrepôt in the Caribbean during the eighteenth century. Of the 1 million Africans brought to the island between 1701 and 1800, 200,000 were subsequently re-embarked on smaller vessels, three-quarters to the Spanish-speaking regions. With the Dutch largely abandoning the internal Caribbean traffic after 1730 to focus on Surinam, the British became the dominant slave trader within the Caribbean. In addition to Jamaica's expanded role, they opened free ports in Grenada and Dominica acquired from France in 1763 where ships of any nation could buy slaves free of duty.[91] The Danes followed suit and the island of St. Thomas became yet a further, if minor, slave entrepôt, especially during wartime.

---

[88] Wim Klooster, "Curaçao and the Caribbean Transit Trade," and Han Jordaan, "The Curaçao Slave Market: From Asiento Trade to Free Trade," both in Johannes Postma and Victor Enthoven (eds.), *Riches from Atlantic Commerce: Dutch Transatlantic Trade and Shipping, 1585–1817* (Leiden, 2003), pp. 203–58. For a sample early seventeenth-century journey to the Pacific see Newson and Minchin, *From Capture to Sale*, pp. 187–234.

[89] Stafford and Eltis, "Barbados and the Slave Trade," 1–17.

[90] Huntington, Stowe mss, ST9, p. 43, John Ashley, no date but c. 1715. The Barbados data are under-represented in the intra-American slave trade database on slavevoyages.org.

[91] The best discussion of the English Navigation Laws is still Lawrence A. Harper, *The English Navigation Laws: A Seventeenth Century Experiment in Social Engineering* (New York, 1939). For their impact on the colonies, see especially pp. 394–404.

After the low-lying sugar regions, the gold- and silver-producing highlands of the Americas comprised the second largest source of demand for enslaved labor in the Americas before 1800. Between 1540 and 1640 more than four out every five Africans brought into the Spanish Americas disembarked at Veracruz, Cartagena, Portobelo or Rio de la Plata, venues that were starting points for a strenuous further journey often by sea or through rugged landscape.[92] The enslaved were employed in the alluvial extraction of gold in Chocó, Columbia, and from the late seventeenth century in Minas Gerais, Brazil. However, the labor force in the much larger silver-mining sector of Spanish America was not African, but rather overwhelmingly Indigenous and came from levies on local communities called *mita labor* – a system that, in South America at least, the Spanish took over from the Inca Empire.[93] The processing of silver in Zacetecas employed some Africans, as indeed did sugar plantations in the lowland Vera Cruz region. However, Africans, mostly enslaved, flooded into these areas not to labor in mines or plantations, but rather to urban areas to work at a wide range of tasks – including manufacturing. When the Panama City council complained of the shortage of labor in the 1640s after Portuguese withdrawal from the Spanish Empire, mining was only one of the sectors primarily affected. Sawmilling, pearl fishing, ranching, agriculture, and transisthmian transportation were listed as more important.[94] But all this activity was ultimately sustained by the prosperity stemming from the high levels of silver production throughout the colonial era.[95] Like almost everywhere else in the Americas, free people who could afford to buy slaves generally did so.

Portuguese merchants probably managed the greatest share of the intra-American slave trade over the whole era of Atlantic slave trading. The Portuguese colony of Côlonia do Sacramento facilitated the transfer of at least 47,000 slaves to the Rio de la Plata region between 1680 and Spanish annexation of Côlonia in 1777, and thereafter Portuguese sold a further 26,000 to Platense merchants down to 1810. Many of these Rio

---

[92] https://slavevoyages.org/voyages/tPmHs7Lb.
[93] Camilla Townsend, "Slavery in the Pre-Contact Americas," *CWHS* 2: 553–70.
[94] Petition by Panama's city council, Panama City, 8-VIII-1646, AGI, Pan-amá, Leg. 31, n° 46, cited by García-Montón, *Genoese Entrepreneurship*, p. 102.
[95] For the traffic in African slaves within New Spain and the gradual shift from African to creole slaves see Pablo Miguel Sierra Silva, "The Slave Trade to Colonial Mexico: Revising from Puebla de los Ángeles, 1590–1640," and Sabrina Smith, "Slave Trading in Antequera and the Interregional Slave Traffic in New Spain," both in Borucki et al (eds.), *From the Galleons to the Highlands*, pp. 73–102, and 127–47.

de la Plata arrivals were then taken to the Potosí region and others by sea to Spain's Pacific colonies.[96] But the major Portuguese role in this traffic played out on land rather than the ocean. After the discovery of gold in Minas Gerais in the late 1690s, hundreds of thousands of African slaves arriving in Bahia and Rio de Janeiro were sold on to the newly opened gold producing regions. The traffic in captives to these two ports during the thirty-five years before 1696 saw a combined total of 6,100 people per year disembarking. But in the sixty-five years 1696 to 1760, when gold production is thought to have peaked, the annual average more than doubled to 14,415, suggesting that Brazilians perhaps moved half a million Africans inland, a distance of at least 215 miles.[97] Over the whole colonial era this phase of coerced migration could easily have reached a million. Initially the route from Rio went through Paratí and took six weeks through rugged terrain, but in 1701 a new road cut the journey by half. But even then such a journey would have excluded the very young as well as older people. The Jesuit André João Antonil described these two routes, plus a third from Bahia, in his foundational work on Brazilian slavery. Bahia was further away from the gold production sites in the interior, but the route was easier to travel.[98] The enslaved moved in batches not dissimilar to those grouped together on a voyage and, given that police approval of such movements was necessary, records for the nineteenth century at least have survived.

The intra-American traffic attained its greatest importance in the nineteenth century, and again the Portuguese had a major role. After 1800 the major plantation crops of the Americas became cotton, grown overwhelmingly in the US South, sugar centered on Cuba, and coffee in southeast Brazil, all heavily dependent on slave labor. However, in the

---

[96] Alex Borucki, "From Asiento to Spanish Networks: Slave Trading in the Rio de la Plata, 1700–1810," in ibid, 177–200. See also Grandin, *Empire of Necessity*, chapters 18, 21, 22. See chapter 7 below.

[97] This assumes sugar production in Bahia and Rio de Janeiro remained constant. Thus, 523,000 is certainly an upper bound estimate. The fundamental work on silver in Spanish America is the three-volume set, *The Royal Treasuries of the Spanish Empire in America* co-authored by John Jay Tepaske and Herbert S. Klein (Durham, NC, 1982). Tepaske's summary and conclusions about overall silver production and exports are in *A New World of Gold and Silver*, edited by Kendall W. Brown (Leiden, 2010), pp. 12–15, 305–15. For the opening of Minas Gerais' and then Goías' gold production, Charles R. Boxer's classic account is still useful – *Brazil's Golden Age, 1695–1750* (Berkeley, CA, 1969), pp. 30–60, 267–70.

[98] See Kempton Evans Webb, *The Geography of Food Supply in Central Minas Gerais* (Washington, DC, 1959), pp. 30–34; Andre João Antonil, *Brazil at the Dawn of the Eighteenth Century* (Amherst, MA, 2012), part 3, chapters 11, 12, and 13.

wider Atlantic world an abolitionist movement developed almost in lockstep with these new slave markets, the impact of which was to gradually restrict the international slave trade and more specifically access to Africa. Two of the three new major plantation centers, the US and Brazil, not coincidentally the largest countries in the Americas, turned to domestic sources of slaves. A major movement of slave labor occurred from the US Old South to the New after the invention of the cotton gin and Jefferson's Louisiana purchase. More than 600,000 slaves were moved to the New South in the forty years after 1820, of whom 150,000 were traded, perhaps one half by sea.[99] This was a maritime slave trade that lay beyond the reach of the British navy as it attempted to suppress the slave trade after 1807.

A parallel situation developed in Brazil with the northeast of the country assuming the role of the Old South and the rapidly expanding coffee plantations of the southeast providing the new market for enslaved labor. Whereas US slave traders could no longer access Africa after 1807, Brazilian planters maintained their access to African captives until 1851. Thereafter, a major interstate traffic quickly developed that according to Robert W. Slenes saw the transfer of 200,000 slaves from the northeast to the southeast, though as Slenes is careful to point out, most of these came from employment outside the sugar-producing sector.[100]

Cuba, by contrast, had no reserves of slaves to match those in Brazil and the US. Cuban planters nevertheless tried to access slaves that were already in the Americas. Cuban plantation owners certainly drew on the labor force of the declining Cuban coffee sector as it faded in response to Brazilian competition, but this was scarcely a replacement for Africa. They also provided a welcome new home for some Jamaican and Bahamian planters and their slaves in the 1820s as British slave owners tried to escape their government's tightening restrictions on slavery in the British Empire.[101] The British were by now attempting to shut down not just the slave trade but slavery itself. David Turnbull, English consul in

---

[99] Jonathan Pritchett, "Quantitative Estimates of the United States Interregional Slave Trade, 1820–1860," *Journal of Economic History*, 61 (2001): 467–75. For the personal details of 78,481 enslaved caught up in this and the Brazilian coastwise traffic, see www.slavevoyages.org/past/database/oceans-of-kinfolk. For the voyages on which they travelled, see www.slavevoyages.org/voyages/7KLnU3s5.

[100] Slenes, "Demography and Economics," pp. 120–78, but especially p. 169, n. 39. For details of 12,730 voyages involved in this traffic see www.slavevoyages.org/voyages/EB5BkVob.

[101] Joseph Crawford to Lord Palmerston, Dec. 31, 1848, BNA, FO84/722, in which Crawford provided an inventory of all British slave owners resident in Cuba.

Havana in the early 1840s, claimed that enough slaves had moved illegally from the British islands that plantations in the Holguin area of Cuba used English as the working language.[102] Numbers from this source cannot have exceeded a few thousand, however, and the Cuban authorities turned to other sources outside Cuba. A traffic with the Yucatán peninsula brought in a few thousand Indigenous slaves. Between 1809 and 1818 at least sixteen Portuguese ships brought three thousand African slaves from Bahia, but this trade, too, failed to take off.[103] In the 1840s, Cuba opened a traffic in indentured labor from China, but onboard abuses were such that the Chinese government suspended the trade. And when these efforts failed the slavers attempted to defeat the abolitionists by using a range of subterfuges to revive slaving links with Africa,[104] and did so with some success. Cuba was the last region in the Americas to give up the transatlantic slave trade.

The British government largely stymied a fourth major nineteenth-century branch of the intra-American trade. An abolitionist-inspired Order-in-Council in 1805 followed by legislation in 1806, 1807, and 1824, severely restricted the movement of slaves to fertile underdeveloped territories acquired in the Napoleonic Wars. The British had obtained possession of Trinidad, Demerara, Essequibo, and Berbice, all of which had small populations and unexploited soils. Planters in the older sugar colonies of the British Eastern Caribbean and Jamaica immediately began to migrate to these newly acquired colonies, a movement that was at first restricted and then banned outright except for enslaved personal servants. In the event about 25,000 British slaves were forced to make the move between 1803 and the abolition of slavery in 1833. Migrations such as this were always associated with higher mortality and lower fertility for the enslaved. But as an indication of what might have happened one has only to look at later developments. From the late 1830s the British allowed the sugar colonies to bring in indentured labor from India. Ninety percent of this inflow went to these territorial prizes of war. Trinidad and Demerara between them produced nearly half of British sugar by 1860, a figure that

---

[102] "Report from the Select Committee of the House of Lords appointed to consider the best means which Great Britain can adopt for the final extinction of the African slave trade," *Parliamentary Papers*, 1850, vol. IX: 75–79; David Turnbull, *Travels in the West: Cuba, with Notices of Porto Rico and the Slave Trade* (London, 1840), pp. 162–63; BNA, Attorney General's Office, Bahamas, Dec. 2, 1841, FO313/33; Richard R. Madden to James Stephen, Jan. 1, 1841.
[103] https://slavevoyages.org/voyages/a1IR09Fo.
[104] Harris, *Last Slave Ships*, pp. 137–81.

was one-third of Cuba's output.[105] Without restrictions this intercolonial slave traffic might easily have seen one-third or more of Britain's 700,000 Caribbean slaves forcibly relocated in the nineteenth century.

Almost all those caught up the intra-American traffic before the nineteenth century had recently arrived from Africa. The main exceptions were the post-1807 branches from the Old to the New South, and from northeast to southeast Brazil where the African share of the population was low. We can therefore get some idea of the probability of an African being involved in a significant post-oceanic journey by comparing the rough estimates discussed above (omitting the late US and Brazilian data) with the 10.7 million enslaved Africans that survived the transatlantic slave trade. Approximately 1.5 million were subjected to a further long-distance journey in the aftermath of disembarking from a transatlantic vessel, about 14 percent of all arrivals. The only full-length study of any branch of the intra-American is Greg O'Malley's foundational coverage of the British traffic between the Caribbean and mainland colonies. O'Malley estimates that about 15 percent of all Africans entering what became the US arrived via the Caribbean, a ratio that this discussion suggests might be appropriate for the whole of the Americas.[106]

In summary, the Americas was the center of a huge intra-American trade in slaves, conducted by both land and sea. All this business was organized in the Americas by merchants with little direct involvement in the transatlantic slave trade. It required substantial capitalization and credit, very little of which came from Europe, and it falls naturally into four branches. First, the temperate regions to both the north and south of the tropical Americas always received a substantial portion of their African captives from slave emporia located in the tropical Americas. A second branch was in Spanish America. Because it lacked footholds in Africa and because of its own misguided attempts to regulate the slave trade, Spanish America came to depend heavily on such entrepôts, almost always Dutch or British, prior to 1789. A third stream developed in response to the discovery of silver in what is now Bolivia in the mid

---

[105] David Eltis, "The Traffic in Slaves Between the British West Indian Colonies, 1807–1833," *Economic History Review*, 25 (1972): 55–65; William A. Green, *British Slave Emancipation: The Sugar Colonies and the Great Experiment, 1830–1865* (New York, 1976), p. 249.

[106] Gregory E. O'Malley, *Final Passages: The Intercolonial Slave Trade of British America, 1619–1807* (Chapel Hill, NC, 2014); O'Malley, "Beyond the Middle Passage: Slave Migration from the Caribbean to North America, 1619–1807," *William and Mary Quarterly*, 66 (2009): 125–72.

sixteenth century, and gold in Minas Gerais 150 years later. A huge overland traffic in slaves flourished in South America, long before the much better-known coerced migration from the Old South to the New in the nineteenth-century US. The Buenos Aires/Montevideo axis acted as the hub for the first of these, and Rio de Janeiro and to a lesser extent Bahia anchored the second. A final intra-American stream was triggered by attempts to end the transatlantic slave trade, beginning in 1807. Abolition of the transatlantic business triggered a large internal trade in slaves both in the US and Brazil. and would have induced yet a third from the older to the newly acquired British Caribbean colonies, but for the actions of imperial officials and abolitionists in 1805–1807.[107] Much of the nineteenth-century intra-American traffic is best understood as a surrogate for a transatlantic traffic that was no longer permitted.

Finally, we should note that the intra-American trade was critical for merchandise as well as slaves. Adrian Pearce has shown that the value of this traffic was three or four times larger than previously thought and that Spanish traders from the colonies sailing to the British Caribbean free ports after 1760 ran most of it. It was not just slaves sent to the British Caribbean that ended up in the Spanish Americas, but much of the merchandise showing up in British records as being sent to the British Caribbean as well. As we show in the following section, historians of the trade in both merchandise and people have made insufficient allowance for the scale of these intra-American movements.[108]

RECEIVING SLAVES

Before 1540 transatlantic voyages disembarked overwhelmingly in Puerto Rico and Hispaniola, but the first gateway to the Pacific, Nombre de Dios, saw initial arrivals as early as 1531, while Cartagena's dominance as entrepôt for the Pacific was a post-1570 phenomenon. The first recorded disembarkation in Veracruz occurred in 1546, but New Spain must have received captives before this date given that by mid-century the slave trade to Spanish America had largely switched from the Caribbean islands to

---

[107] David Richardson, *Principles and Agents: The British Slave Trade and Its Abolition* (New Haven, CT, 2022), pp. 233–44.
[108] Adrian Pearce, *British Trade with Spanish America 1763–1808* (Liverpool, 2014). For US shippers, benefiting as middlemen in the trade between Britain and the Spanish colonies during the Napoleonic Wars, see Javier Cuenca-Esteban, "British 'Ghost' Exports, American Middlemen, and the Trade to Spanish America, 1790–1819." *William and Mary Quarterly*, 71 (2014): 63–98.

the mainland. The 1550s also saw the first impact of a European war on the Atlantic slave trades when hostilities between France and Spain, 1552–1559, temporarily interrupted the steady half-century-long expansion of the business. Indeed, from this point down to 1815 dramatic swings in the volume of the traffic every three or four decades – readily observable in the timeline at http://slavevoyages.org/estimates/M85jaRPs – were invariably the result of conflict in Europe. The number of voyages carrying slaves doubled in the 1580s compared to the previous decade and almost doubled again in the 1590s. Vessels by now might still carry a range of cargo and passengers, but while the size of the vessels remained unchanged, the number of slaves on board as the ship left Africa now averaged 360.[109] By this time mainland markets in the Spanish circum-Caribbean, the Pacific (accessed by the Isthmus of Panama), and, since the mid 1580s, Rio de la Plata, absorbed almost all the Africans that survived the crossing, all of whom now left from sub-Saharan Africa rather than the Iberian peninsula. With the slave trade to Brazil also well underway, the major features of the transatlantic traffic would remain unchanged for the next 250 years.[110]

Origins and destinations would of course change over time. The intra-American traffic data allows us to examine the final distribution of Africans in the Americas. We begin by reiterating the now widely accepted point that far more Africans than Europeans arrived in the Americas prior to 1820. We do not have estimates of annual breakdowns for European migrants, but the disparity in the aggregate totals is so great that we are probably secure in saying that arrivals from Africa exceeded those from Europe in every one of the years between 1520 and 1820. On a cumulative basis, the European migrant total did not overtake the African until the mid nineteenth century. The two Atlantic slave trades distributed 10.7 million Africans across the Americas. Combined with the devastating decline in the Indigenous population that reached a nadir in the late seventeenth century, these slave trades ensured that demographically, at least, the Americas was an extension of Africa not of Europe for much of the early modern period.[111]

---

[109] https://slavevoyages.org/voyages/x1O2OM5Q (n = 1,245).
[110] Marc Eagle, "The Early Slave Trade to Spanish America: Caribbean Pathways, 1530–1580," in Ida Altman and David Wheat (eds.), *The Spanish Caribbean and the Atlantic World in the Long Sixteenth Century* (Lincoln, NE, 2019), pp. 139–62.
[111] David Eltis, "Free and Coerced Transatlantic Migrations: Some Comparisons," *American Historical Review*, 88 (1983): 251–80; see also the essays in David Eltis (ed.), *Coerced and Free Migration: Global Perspectives* (Stanford, CA, 2002).

Overwhelmingly, slaves were sold on to the most prosperous parts of the Americas. Such regions were prosperous because they produced a range of products that consumers in the rest of the world wanted. Most of the plantation produce came to Europe, while southeast Asia received much of the gold and silver of the Americas, in exchange for high-end textiles, spices, and other luxury goods that Europeans desired. The evils of the slave trade therefore stemmed not from profit-seeking merchants, but rather from ordinary consumers coupled with their obliviousness toward how plantation labor was acquired and enforced. As argued in a later chapter, Europeans were well aware of slavery, but for most of the slave trade era were prepared to act against it only insofar as Europeans were among the enslaved, as in North Africa.

The relatively small net benefits that consumers derived from these slave-produced items compounded the evils of the traffic. Sugar, rum, coffee, and small quantities of rice and indigo added little to the feeding, clothing, and housing of Europeans. Cotton from the US was an exception but in no sense did it depend on the transatlantic slave trade for its labor. Production by the enslaved determined income in the Americas far more than in Europe. In a land-abundant environment slavery ensured that employers would have access to labor that free persons could choose to avoid. In the Spanish American highlands in the first 120 years of the slave trade landowners drew mainly on Amerindian Indigenous communities for labor, mostly *corvée*, for the silver mines. Silver production was nevertheless strongly correlated with arrivals from Africa in the Spanish American mainland (Rio de la Plata and Spanish circum-Caribbean combined). Some enslaved Africans did produce exports of cacao, pearls in Venezuela, gold in New Grenada, and hides in Cuba by mid sixteenth century and later the Rio de la Plata, but the greater share of African labor in Spanish America worked outside the export sector, producing many of the goods that were traded between the highland and lowland Spanish colonies. Compared to mainland North America, Spanish America was highly urbanized even before the conquest. Mexico City, Guanajuato, Querétaro, Lima, Buenos Aires, and Havana were larger than New York, Boston, and Philadelphia as late as 1820. *Obrajes* (workshops) in these cities and foodstuff production beyond city limits employed both free and enslaved Africans, but these activities could not have existed without the massive silver production in New Spain and Mexico. In the following century, an equally strong correlation emerged between slave arrivals in Bahia and Rio de Janeiro combined and Brazilian gold production between 1691 and 1800, but in this case African slaves did produce the gold.[112]

The sugar-producing islands of the Caribbean absorbed 4.8 million people forcibly displaced from the African continent.[113] When the slave trade was no longer possible, planters introduced contract laborers from India and China instead, beginning in Trinidad in 1808 and ending only when first the Chinese government and then the government of India banned the traffic over a century later. Nevertheless, a further million migrants, mostly indentured, left for sugar-producing regions around the world – from Mauritius in the Indian Ocean to Hawaii in the Pacific, but largely to the Caribbean, Surinam, and British Guiana. There are no parallels in global history of a single crop triggering migration on such a scale, most of it coerced and all of it long-distance.[114]

As noted earlier, Barbados was the Caribbean bridgehead for sugar cultivated by slaves. There is little evidence of either Dutch or Brazilian involvement on the island in the 1640s, but there is an indirect link. One side effect of the Dutch attempt to seize Brazil and Angola was a prolonged transatlantic war between Portugal and the Netherlands, beginning in 1630. Of the twelve quarter-centuries between 1500 and 1800, 1626–1650 is the only one in which the volume of the transatlantic traffic declined from the previous quarter-century – an undoubted side effect of hostilities between the two leading slave-trading countries of the time. We have no data but sugar output in Brazil certainly declined as well. With England at peace with both combatants until 1652, the war allowed London merchants to establish sugar plantations, with the first recorded slave ship disembarking in 1641 in

---

[112] Ten-year totals of gold and silver, 1521–1640 taken from TePaske, *New World of Gold and Silver*, p. 21 correlated with ten-year totals of slaves arriving in the Spanish circum-Caribbean generated a Pearson Product-Moment correlation co-efficient of 0.834 significant at 1 percent. For Brazil, the same variables 1691–1770, generated a Pearson product moment coefficient of 0.854 significant at the 5 percent level. For African employment in Peru dominated by agriculture, building trades and transportation, see Frederick P. Bowser, *The African Slave in Colonial Peru, 1524–1650* (Stanford, CA, 1974), pp. 88–109. Bowser's findings of the wide range of African occupations are consistent with those of David Wheat's more recent book, Atlantic Africa *and the Spanish Caribbean*, see especially pp. 255–65. Once more we see that large-scale purchases of the enslaved were enabled by the mining sector even though relatively few enslaved Africans worked in the mines.

[113] http://slavevoyages.org/estimates/twb9ORNP.

[114] Stanley L. Engerman, "Economic Change and Contract Labor in the British Caribbean: The End of Slavery and the Adjustment to Emancipation," *Explorations in Economic History* 21 (1984): 146; Walton Look Lai, "Asian Contract and Free Migration to the Americas," in Eltis (ed.), *Coerced and Free Migration*, pp. 229–58.

TABLE 2.4 *Estimated arrival of enslaved people in the Americas by jurisdiction*

Brazil	4,864,372
Jamaica	1,019,595
Cuba	983,000
St. Domingue (now Haiti)	773,543
Barbados	493,162
US	388,747
Rest of the Americas combined	2,180,234
Total arrivals in the Americas	10,702,653

Source: http://www.slavevoyages.org/estimates/d44aJCIZ.

Barbados. The "Compagnie des Îles d' Amérique" commissioned a vessel that landed sixty-three Africans in Guadeloupe in 1643, presumably for tobacco cultivation.[115] There is no evidence of a significant sugar culture on the French islands until the following decade when the Dutch and Brazilian connection with Martinique and Guadeloupe was established. Dutch slave ships began to arrive in the former in 1651 and in Guadeloupe in 1659. In 1654, 250 Dutch Jews expelled from Pernambuco arrived in Martinique with sugar cane. The few enslaved that arrived before this date worked on tobacco and cotton and were outnumbered by *engagés*, the French equivalent of indentured servants. The Caribbean received more African slaves than Brazil in the second half of seventeenth century – an estimated 463,000 – with the tiny island of Barbados, arguably the first to introduce gang labor to sugar cultivation, receiving the largest share (156,000).

Astonishingly, as Table 2.4 shows, over the three- and one-half centuries of the trade's duration, only four other jurisdictions in the Americas received more African captives than Barbados. And if we divide the number of captives disembarking by the area of the hinterland of the receiving port then we can say that Bridgetown was easily the leading slave-trading center not only in the early modern Americas but probably in the three-thousand-year written record of sales of the enslaved around the globe. Even more surprising, the island achieved this dubious distinction despite entering the

---

[115] Voyageid 21707; ANOM, F2A13, "Actes des délibérations de la Compagnie des Iles d'Amérique, pp. 444 and 463, 4 février 1643 et 7 octobre 1643."

traffic late (1640 as opposed to Puerto Rico in 1519) and leaving it early (1807, as opposed to 1867 in the case of Cuba).[116]

But Barbadian development was dwarfed when the plantation complex extended its range into the western Caribbean. The western half of Hispaniola became formally French in 1697 and proved to be extraordinarily fertile. Two western Caribbean colonies, Jamaica and St. Domingue, received a combined total of 1.6 million enslaved Africans in the eighteenth century alone. If we include Barbados and Martinique in this group then these fragments of Caribbean territories with a combined landmass less than half the size of Portugal, received over 2 million people, or one in five of all who were forcibly disembarked in the Americas. Not all the arrivals worked in the sugar sector. As already noted, many of those going to the English islands were soon dispatched to the Spanish possessions, and some of those who remained labored on other crops or worked in service industries ancillary to sugar. After 1750 St. Domingue became not only the premier sugar producer in the world but also the Caribbean leader in the production of all other plantation products – coffee, indigo, and cotton, a dominance that it took a violent revolution to end.

The rebellion that overthrew the St. Domingue plantocracy was a defining moment for the Atlantic world. However, historians have failed to recognize one unfortunate consequence. The conflagration – literally – that began in the northern province of St. Domingue in August 1791 had no perceptible impact on volume of the transatlantic slave trade. The major decrease in the traffic that occurred by 1794 was the result of war in the wider North Atlantic, not rebellion in what was to become Haiti. St. Domingue's competitors – specifically, Jamaica, Cuba, and Brazil – immediately began to increase their slave purchases in Africa. The revolution kick-started the massive expansion of sugar production in Cuba and of coffee in southeastern Brazil. Jamaican planters also expanded their output of both crops. They all did so by drawing on the transatlantic slave trade. Jamaican annual arrivals from Africa, which had averaged 10,800 between 1782 and 1791, jumped to 15,900 in the next decade despite the transition from the peacetime 1780s to the war-torn 1790s. In the twelve months beginning in January 1793, just sixteen months after the revolution, the planters bought the largest annual number of Africans ever to arrive on the island – 28,300 or a staggering 8 percent of Jamaica's total

[116] Eltis, *Rise of African Slavery*, pp. 29–84; Stafford and Eltis, "Barbados and the Slave Trade," 1–17.

slave population.[117] Fourteen years later, British abolition of the slave trade in 1807 meant that they and their fellow planters in Trinidad and Demerara could no longer keep pace with their Cuban and Brazilian competitors. But even with the inability to bring in more African labor after 1807, Jamaican output did not fall far behind that of Cuba until the British abolished slavery itself in 1833.

The British occupation of Havana in 1762 is often mistakenly singled out as the trigger for the explosive growth of the Cuban sugar sector.[118] But the Haitian Revolution and the effective suppression of their own slave colonies by the British themselves first in 1807 and then in 1833 were the true catalysts, just as British orchestration of international opposition to the international slave trade helped cut off Cuba's access to Africa in 1867. Together St. Domingue's slaves and British abolitionists framed the rise and fall of the Cuban slave trade.[119] By 1860, Cuba was the leading global source of sugar, Brazil the global leader of coffee, and the US South similarly of cotton. Cuba had introduced nearly a million slaves, 90 percent of them after 1790, and Brazil another 2 million in just the first half of the nineteenth century. The Brazilian sugar economy held its own until late in the slavery era, and the cotton and rice sectors in Amazonia also used slave labor. As we have seen, the United States also depended on a slave trade, in this case the intra-American trade, but natural growth of the US slave population came close to matching that of White Americans after 1800 and ultimately the natural population growth of the US Black population proved to be the major source of new labor in most cotton-producing states.

Ever since slave trafficking in the Atlantic was shut down, research into the topic has overwhelmingly focused on the transatlantic business in the North Atlantic. The South Atlantic and the intra-American trades have received relatively little scholarly attention. Books by Mauricio Goulart and Frederic Mauro established the importance of the former in the middle of the last century, but even including all the late Joseph Miller's formidable publications and the growing contributions of younger

---

[117] For an annual series of arrivals in Jamaican ports, 1782 to 1795, see www.slavevoyages.org/estimates/NTAoPe2S.

[118] Franklin Knight, *Slave Society in Cuba during the Nineteenth Century* (Madison, WI, 1970), but see the Eltis and Felipe essay "Rise and Fall," in Borucki et al., *From the Galleons to the Highlands*, pp. 201–22.

[119] For the rise to dominance of the Cuban sugar economy and slave trade, see Manuel Moreno Fraginals, *The Sugarmill: the Socioeconomic Complex of Sugar in Cuba* (New York, 1976); Felipe Gonzalez, *Foundation and Growth*.

scholars Mariana Candido, Roquinaldo Ferreira, and Carlos da Silva, the imbalance between the north and south Atlantic historiographies has continued to grow.[120] Post-1640 Spanish America is similarly neglected, with, for example, very little appearing on Africans in Mexico between Colin Palmer's 1976 book and Pablo Miguel Sierra Silva's monograph of 2018. The most recent update of www.slavevoyages.org does offer some corrective to this imbalance. Table 2.5 incorporates the latest data for the transatlantic slave trade into the European Americas as it existed in the eighteenth century. Row 6 shows estimates for that part of the intra-American traffic that disembarked slaves in Spanish territories and row 7 shows the distribution of total disembarkations after allowing for these intra-American flows.[121]

Spanish America was the destination of the first as well as the last enslaved Africans to cross the Atlantic, but even so it is rather extraordinary that Africa added more to the Spanish American population than to the British colonies. Even more striking is the dominance of the Iberian Americas in this broad picture. Almost two-thirds of the survivors of the Atlantic slave trades spent the rest of their lives in Brazil and Spanish America.[122] The northwestern Europeans – the British, Dutch, and French – came into the business late, left it early but, while involved, sold on over half a million Africans to the Iberians from their American entrepôts. Measured by US conceptions of race, they helped Brazil to become the largest Black country in the world after Nigeria. By contrast, in Spanish America outside Cuba, Africans arrived early and lived among a large Indigenous population. For the most part an intermixing of Indigenous peoples, Africans, and Europeans (*mestizaje*) has made identification of their modern descendants difficult except for some locations in Mexico, Columbia, and Venezuela.

Finally, we should note the impact of differences in attitudes toward race between Iberian and other Europeans. These did help shape the Atlantic slave trades. The peoples of Europe closest to West Africa – the

---

[120] Frédéric Mauro, *Le Portugal et l'Atlantique au cviie siècle (1570–1670): Etude économique* (Paris, 1960); Mauricio Goulart, *Escravidão africana no Brasil* (São Paulo, 1950).

[121] Palmer, *Slaves of the White God: Blacks in Mexico, 1700–1839* (Cambridge, MA, 1976); Sierra Silva, *Urban Slavery in Colonial Mexico: Puebla de los Ángeles, 1531–1706* (Cambridge, 2018). By far the best survey of slavery and the slave trade in Latin America contains little on the central importance of the intra-American slave trade. See Herbert S. Klein and Ben Vinson III, *African Slavery in Latin America and the Caribbean*, 2nd edition (Oxford, 2007).

[122] More precisely, 63.3 percent.

TABLE 2.5 *Slaves arriving in the Americas by broad region and slaves arriving under the Spanish flag direct from Africa, 1520–1867*

	United States	British Caribbean	French Caribbean	Dutch Americas	Danish Americas	Spanish Americas	Brazil	Totals	Slaves arriving under Spanish flag
pre-1581	0	0	0	0	0	84,900	4,100	89,000	84,900
1581–1640	100	100	0	0	0	444,900	261,400	706,500	222,500
1641–1700	15,000	308,000	38,700	124,200	18,100	61,700	523,000	1,088,700	21,700
1701–1760	188,900	807,000	393,700	162,700	20,500	56,800	1,084,600	2,714,200	300
1761–1820	184,200	1,173,200	640,500	154,300	62,300	298,900	1,696,600	4,210,000	133,600
1821–1867	500	11,000	47,300	3,500	8,100	558,800	1,269,400	1,898,600	563,100
Total	388,700	2,299,300	1,120,200	444,700	109,000	1,506,000	4,839,100	10,707,000	1,026,100
Adjustment for intra-American trade	64,066	−247,500	−19,000	−115,900	−47,800	+566,300	−136,100		
Total after adjustment	452,766	2,051,800	1,101,200	328,800	61,200	2,072,300	4,703,000		

Source: Gregory E. O'Malley, "Beyond the Middle Passage: Slave Migration from the Caribbean to North America, 1619-1807," *William and Mary Quarterly,* 66 (2009): 125–72, but especially, 166; http://slavevoyages.org/tast/assessment/estimates.faces?yearFrom=1501&yearTo=1866, with modifications. For column 6 see text, and for row 8 see Alex Borucki, David Eltis and David Wheat, "Notes on the Estimates of the Intra-American Slave Trade to the Spanish Americas," and "IntraAmertoSpanAmer.xlsx," at https://www.slavevoyages.org/voyage/downloads#estimates-spreadsheet/2/en/.

Note: The Spanish and British totals have been adjusted to reflect the changing status of Trinidad. On the 2010 estimates page of Voyages, Trinidad is classed as part of the British Americas even though British occupation began only in 1797. Here, the 16,500 captives taken there before 1797 are reassigned to the Spanish Americas.

Portuguese and Spanish – established slave empires where it was possible for the enslaved, especially in urban environments, to buy their own freedom, even when their sugar and coffee plantation economies were at their expansionist peaks. Strikingly, this pattern continued even when abolitionist pressures restricted supplies of new labor.[123] As noted in Chapter 1, slave codes in both empires incorporated the Castilian code, which provided for self-purchase. *Coartación* was always more likely in urban centers on which the scholarship necessarily focuses, and in Cuba some estimates put the incidence at just 1 percent of the slave population a year. Moreover, as in the Islamic world, obligations to the former owner continued after freedom. But there was nothing equivalent in the English, Dutch, and French Americas. In Brazil, the practice was certainly widespread. The growing literature on Africans returning to Africa after gaining their freedom is almost exclusively concerned with return voyages beginning in Brazil and Cuba. Except for rare cases like Catherine Zimmermann-Mulgrave (see Chapter 7), there were very few such returnees from the British, French, and Dutch Americas.[124] In Brazil, especially, *coartación* boosted the slave trade to the Iberian Americas as owners sought replacement labor. By the 1870s, Brazil had 1.5 million free Blacks, by far the largest number of any jurisdiction in the Americas prior to abolition. Reliable estimates of the numbers that were freed in earlier periods are not yet possible but were certainly much higher than in Cuba.

ECONOMIC SIGNIFICANCE

The literature on the slave trade focuses on the great benefits that Europe received from the transatlantic slave trade. But with all the mines and plantations and most of the slave trade based in the Americas, it is hardly surprising that the main beneficiaries of this massive forced system lived on the western side of the Atlantic rather than in Europe. Absentee ownership was relatively rare outside the British and French Caribbean

---

[123] For the Cuban case see Eltis and Felipe, "Rise and Fall," p. 215; for Brazil, see Slenes' computation on self-purchase in the second half of the nineteenth century, "Demography and Economics," pp. 484–573. For manumission in colonial Brazil see Stuart B. Schwartz, "The Manumission of Slaves in Colonial Brazil: Bahia, 1684–1745," *Hispanic American Historical Review*, 54 (1974): 603–35.

[124] Note that even Catherine Zimmerman-Mulgrave came to Jamaica as a Liberated African rather than an enslaved person. See www.slavevoyages.org/voyage/essays#vignettes/catherine-zimmermann-mulgrave-a-slave-odyssey/1/en/.

and even within these two broad regions was less common than is usually imagined. Transatlantic trade and income were highly correlated with slavery in the Americas. As argued in a later chapter, Europe already had a diversified and well-developed economy by the early modern period. The addition of a few sectors that added so little to existing European diets and lifestyles – an alternative sweetener (sugar), additional stimulants (coffee, rum, tobacco), a new dye (indigo) – is unlikely to have generated a revolution in either consumer behavior or investment patterns. In the labor- and capital-scarce environment of the Americas, however, the impact on the Americas of producing these items was of much greater significance.

It is possible to assess this impact for benchmark years. Beginning with the North American mainland, Alice Hanson Jones' detailed work on probate records showed that the southern colonies were better off than the north in the late colonial era. In the South, slave-grown tobacco, rice, and indigo production enabled significantly higher living standards for the free population. Wider intercolonial comparisons across the Americas reveal more dramatic differences. Barbados generated per capita product (including the enslaved) at least 50 percent greater than in England at the end of the seventeenth century. Seventy years later the net worth per free person in Jamaica was almost ten times greater than in the southern US (for slave and free together).[125] All the export economies of the Caribbean probably had a higher per capita income than Britain in both 1700 and 1770, and Britain had the highest income of any of the eighteenth-century imperial powers.[126] Juan Pérez de la Riva has suggested that the western region of Cuba, wherein was to be found most of the sugar complex, had

---

[125] McCusker and Menard, *Economy of British America*, pp. 56–61; Alice Hanson Jones, *Wealth of a Nation*, pp. 71–79; David Eltis, "The Total Product of Barbados, 1664–1701," *Journal of Economic History*, 55 (1995): 321–38. See also Eltis, "The Slave Economies of the Caribbean: Structure, Performance, Evolution and Significance," pp. 178–202.

[126] Modifications of "social tables" for England and Wales for 1688 and 1759 can be found in Peter H. Lindert and Jeffrey G. Williamson, "Revising England's Social Tables, 1688–1913," *Explorations in Economic History*, 19 (1982): 385–408. Dividing the national income for 1688 and 1759 by population estimates in E.A. Wrigley and R. S. Schofield, *A Population History of England, 1541–1871: A Reconstruction* (Cambridge, 1981), p. 533. Table A 3.3 yields a per capita figure of about 11 pounds sterling (current prices) compared to 14 or 14.5 pounds in the Caribbean for 1700 and 1770, respectively. These are all in current prices but adjusting for inflation would not change much. For a similar exercise using real values and focusing on the British Americas that comes to conclusions broadly consistent with this discussion, see Stanley L. Engerman, "Notes on the Pattern of Economic Growth in the British North American Colonies in the Seventeenth,

a per capita income of $350 in 1862, about the same as Sweden, France, Switzerland, and England in 1955.[127] This was maybe an overstatement, but in 1850 the per capita output of Cuba must have ranked among the top half-dozen of the world's nations.[128] As might be expected, the ending of slavery in both St. Domingue/Haiti (1802) and Jamaica (1834) resulted in dramatic declines in per capita output. Haiti is discussed later, and there is no national income data for the new nation in the nineteenth century. With per capita exports of no more than £0.7 pounds sterling and a large domestic subsistence sector, per capita product in Haiti was likely to have been the lowest in the Caribbean.[129] Most of the present income gap between Caribbean and North Atlantic countries appeared in the late nineteenth and twentieth centuries. Eisner's estimates for Jamaica in 1850 and Moohr's for British Guiana for 1852 are much closer to the mid nineteenth-century British figure than is Eisner's 1930 estimate for Jamaica to the British figure for that year. But both the Jamaican and the British trends were upwards.[130] Why the elite established slavery and the slave trade is clear enough from these patterns.

Perhaps the most important finding is that Spanish American preeminence long predated the nineteenth-century Cuban sugar revolution. The English Committee for Foreign Plantations for the mid 1660s marvelled at

---

Eighteenth and Nineteenth Centuries," in Paul Bairoch and Maurice Levy-Leboyer (eds.), *Disparities in Economic Development since the Industrial Revolution* (New York, 1981), pp. 46–57.

[127] Juan Pérez de la Riva, "Aspectos demográficos y su importancia en el proceso revolucionario del siglo XIX," in *Unión de Periodistas de Cuba* (Havana: Ciencias Sociales, 1968), pp. 30–49 cited in Francisco López Segrera, "Cuba: Dependence, Plantation Economy and Social Classes, 1762–1902," in Manuel Moreno Fraginals, Frank Moya Pons, and Stanley L. Engerman (eds.), *Between Slavery and Free Labor: The Spanish-Speaking Caribbean in the Nineteenth Century* (Baltimore, MD, 1985), pp. 85–86.

[128] Laird Bergad, *Comparative Histories of Slavery in Brazil, Cuba, and the United States* (Cambridge, 2007), 18; "Introduction," in Eltis, Lewis, and Sokoloff (eds.), *Slavery in the Development of the Americas*, pp. 1–6; Eltis, *Economic Growth*, pp. 235–36; Stanley L. Engerman, Stephen Haber and Kenneth L. Sokoloff, "Inequality, Institutions and Differential Paths of Growth among New World Economies," in Claude Menard (ed.), *Institutions, Contracts and Organizations: Perspectives from New Institutional Economics* (Cheltenham, UK, 2000), pp. 108–34.

[129] Eltis, "Slave Economies of the Caribbean: Structure, Performance, Evolution and Significance," p. 117.

[130] Gisela Eisner, *Jamaica, 1830–1930: A Study in Economic Growth* (Manchester, UK, 1930), p. 289; Michael Moohr, "The Economic Impact of Slave Emancipation in British Guiana, 1832–1852," *Economic History Review*, 25 (1972): 588–607. https://doi.org/10.2307/2593950; Brian R. Mitchell, *British Historical Statistics* (Cambridge, 1988), pp. 845–46. Note the subtitle of Eisner's book.

Barbados ... being then (1625) an intire wood with greate trees wch by the incomparable Industry of the Planters is brought to that perfection so that years since they shipped out of that Island ... as many ... goods in tunnage yearly as the Spaniards doe out the two famous empires of Mexico and Perew ... and out of there famous islands of Porto Rico, Española, Jamaica when it was theres, and Cuba.[131]

The comment, of course, ignored the contribution of the enslaved, but the idea of an island a little more than twenty miles long and fourteen miles across at its widest point producing more exports than the whole of the Spanish Americas is as striking today as it was then. The assessment receives some corroboration from the dramatic drop in the price of sugar in the second half of the seventeenth century as Barbados sugar reached Europe.[132] Nevertheless, the opinion, or rather boast, was simply wrong. Historians have failed to recognize that exports to Europe from the Spanish Americas had a far greater value than those from their British, French, Dutch, and Portuguese counterparts. In 1700, the total output of the non-Hispanic Caribbean amounted to £1.7 million or 7.6 million pesos.[133] In the Spanish possessions, by contrast, bullion production alone averaged 8 million pesos annually from 1696 to 1700, an amount that made them also more valuable to Spain than Brazil was to Portugal, and more valuable than both mainland and Caribbean colonies together were to the British. It is no surprise that "nominal wages and prices were on average much higher than in Western Europe or in Asia," and comparable to colonial North America.[134]

---

[131] "A discription of ye Careeby Islands," n.d. but ca. mid-1660s. BNA, CO 324/1, p. 184.
[132] Richard Pares, "Merchants and Planters," *Economic History Review*, Supplement 4 (1960): 70, n. 2.
[133] Calculated from Eltis, "Slave Economies of the Caribbean," pp. 110, 118. The Caribbean total does include the Spanish Antilles, though removing them would not change our relative assessment.
[134] Ibid. For bullion production and shipments, see Tepaske, *A New World of Gold and Silver*, data from p. 315. For exchange rates, see John J. McCusker, *Money and Exchange in Europe & America, 1600–1775: A Handbook* (Chapel Hill, NC, 1978), 104, 106. For a similar argument on the importance of Spanish colonies, see Javier Cuenca-Esteban, "Statistics of Spain's Colonial Trade, 1747–1820: New Estimates and Comparisons with Great Britain," *Revista de Historia Económica*, 26 (2008): 323–54. For relative living standards, see Leticia Arroyo Abad, Elwyn Davies, Jan Luiten van Zanden, "Between Conquest and Independence: Real Wages and Demographic Change in Spanish America, 1530–1820," *Explorations in Economic History*, 49 (2012): 149–66. For US comparisons, see Engerman and Sokoloff, *Economic Development in the Americas since 1500*, pp. 9–56. Note that smuggling disproportionately affected Spanish trade and thus Spanish data may understate Spanish preeminence. On this, see Willem Klooster, "Inter-Imperial Smuggling in the Americas, 1600–1800," in Bernard Bailyn and Patricia L. Denault (eds.), *Soundings in Atlantic History: Latent Structures and Intellectual Currents, 1500 to 1830* (Cambridge, MA, 2009), pp. 141–80. Klooster argues for universal smuggling in the Atlantic world, but his examples still suggest the preeminence of the Spanish in this activity.

Seventy years later, the supremacy of the Spanish was only slightly eroded. The total annual value in pesos of French Caribbean output in 1770 was 23.1 million, and of British output, 16.2 million, whereas the Spanish Empire generated exports worth close to 31 million pesos – 29.2 million of which was bullion. Even if we include the thirteen mainland colonies in the British total, the Spanish Americas still come out well ahead – though they no longer outproduced all their competitors combined. The cession of Jamaica to Britain in 1655 and St. Domingue to France in 1697 did not apparently enable the British and French to catch up prior to the era of independence; Spanish America grew vigorously until at least 1800.[135] Thereafter, as we have seen, the Cuban sugar replaced mainland bullion. Enslaved Africans were certainly used in the gold mines of New Granada, but "free" Indigenous labor predominated in silver mines of New Spain and Potosí.[136] Even though African labor had never produced much silver, the income that bullion generated underpinned a demand for enslaved people throughout the Spanish Americas. It helped make Spanish America the second biggest destination for the slave trades of the Atlantic World.

We cannot easily locate Brazil in this league table of infamy except to reiterate that it easily comprised the major market for slaves in the Americas. The pre nineteenth-century data, when gold production was at its height, unfortunately does not permit us to say much more than this, particularly the lack of reliable population and pricing information. Obviously, it was home of the first and longest-lasting slave sugar plantation complex on the continent, and possibly the source of most of the world's gold for a time in the eighteenth century, as well as coffee in nineteenth century. The transatlantic slave trade continued until 1852, and trafficking from the northeast to southeast of the country until the 1880s. Once gold exports began, then both as colony and independent nation Brazil must have rivalled Spanish America in the value of its exports and thus probably exceeded those of its better-documented rivals in the Caribbean. The Brazilian agricultural renaissance of the later eighteenth century and beyond is reflected in the time profile of arrivals from Africa, given that the decline in gold exports at this time occurred without any decline in the slave trade. Brazil has yet to be fully integrated into the history of slavery in the Americas. Comparative

---

[135] Engerman and Sokoloff, *Economic Development in the Americas*, p. 10 on comparative GDP and p. 45 on comparative populations.

[136] See most recently, Paola Vargas Arana, "The Resistance of West African Women in the Antioquia Mines of New Granada," in Paul E. Lovejoy, Henry B. Lovejoy, Érika Melek Delgado, and Kartikay Chadha (eds.), *Regenerated Identities: Documenting African Lives* (New Jersey, 2022), pp. 223–51.

scholarship in Brazil on the African diaspora in the Americas has focused on race rather than slavery.[137]

Sugar plantation owners in the Americas generated considerably more income than did slave traders and we should return to the question of links between the two groups. The state-owned mines in Spanish America used Indigenous labor so we would not expect such links there. Likewise, gold producers in Brazil do not show up as owners of slave ships. As we have seen, Barbadian and Chesapeake planters did initiate slaving ventures, but once a plantation colony was established, there was usually little overlap between growing and processing produce and buying slaves in Africa. Few of the major English slave-trading families acquired significant holdings in plantations. Their names cannot be found among those compensated by the British government in the aftermath of the 1833 abolition act.[138] When Portuguese slave traders sold up their assets and abandoned Rio de Janeiro to return to Portugal as a direct result of the ending of the Brazilian slave trade in 1852, they did so without any apparent impact on the plantation sector. The *grand blancs* of St. Domingue, many of whom lived in France, do not appear to have invested in the slave trade.[139] Both the New England slave trade and its rejuvenated successor based in Charleston in 1804–1807 were no different. Even when South Carolina reopened its ports to the transatlantic traffic in 1803, the value added to the US national product (output values minus input values of a given activity) of the traffic could only have been small.[140]

---

[137] For estimates of values and volumes of Brazilian plantation output in the nineteenth century, see Eltis, *Economic Growth*, pp. 284–89.

[138] See 'Centre for the Study of the Legacies of British Slavery' at www.ucl.ac.uk/lbs/search/ though the title of this project is potentially misleading given the fact that the British were themselves enslaved in the early middle ages and again in North Africa from the sixteenth to the eighteenth centuries.

[139] Robert Louis Stein, *The French Sugar Business in the Eighteenth Century* (Baton Rouge, LA, 1988), p. 57; Gabriel Debien, *Les Colons de St. Domingue et la Revolution* (Paris, 1953). For a case study, see Paul Burton Cheney, *Cul de Sac: Patrimony, Capitalism, and Slavery in French Saint-Domingue* (Chicago, IL, 2017). The names of the leading slave traders in each French port are available at www.slavevoyages.org/past/.

[140] Adjusting for value added, slave traders could not have accounted for more than 0.2 of 1 percent of colonial income, with a more probable ratio falling well below one-tenth of 1 percent. TSTD shows a total of 31,257 enslaved people disembarked in British North American mainland ports between 1770 and 1774 or 6,250 per annum, and price information exists for eighty-five shipments of captives sold in the Americas in these years (https://slavevoyages.org/voyages/WAbblEyr). This yields a total value of £226,100 received by slave traders in current values or £2.3 million in 1980 prices ($10.2 million in 1980 dollars assuming an exchange rate of $4.44 = £1). The contribution of any activity to national income is the value added by that activity – or the cost of

Except in the very early days of a plantation colony, successful slave traders around the Atlantic world tended to diversify their activities into other forms of commerce, but even in the Americas the latter would rarely involve plantation ownership. Some exceptions appear in Cuba in the nineteenth century, but slave trading, both transatlantic and intra-American, was a service to a much larger sector producing much more highly valued exports. Julián Zuluetta invested in at least eighteen large slave-trading ventures in the last quarter-century of the Cuban slave trade, but his main business was the four large sugar estates with a combined labor force of over 2,000 captives, acquired after he emigrated from Spain in 1832. Likewise, the twenty voyages sent out by major plantation owner Pedro Martinez during the thirteen years 1828–1840 comprised a sideline. Most investors, including the now well-documented Portuguese Company in New York in the late 1850s, were not plantation owners. In contrast, the Zangronis, Hermano & Cía firm of slave traders, operating from Havana for a half a century from the 1810s, had some plantation investments but do not appear to have been plantation owners.[141] The firm dispatched twenty-seven slaving voyages to Africa, but these were unlikely to have been the core of their commercial activities. Trade, agriculture, and mining apparently required different skill sets and there is no evidence of vertical integration in the sugar business.[142]

---

output less the cost of inputs. Carrying slaves across the Atlantic was expensive, but let us assume a value added of one quarter of total sales – certainly too high. For the mainland colonies Alice Hanson Jones estimated a per capita figure of $804 in 1980 prices and an aggregated GNP of $1,892 million [Hanson Jones, *Wealth of a Nation*, pp. 54, 63, 71; McCusker and Menard, *Economy of British America*, pp. 56–57. Ratios are for 1803–1807 when South Carolina reopened its ports to transatlantic trafficking. From 1791 through to 1807 the US shipping industry (shipbuilding as well as freight services) experienced one of its most rapid growth periods in history. US shippers squeezed out British competition in many ocean-going sectors (slave trading and whaling included). Between 1803 and 1807 the American merchant fleet averaged 1.1 million tons in size while TSTD tells us that the 280 US slave ships that were operating in these years averaged 144.9 tons. Thus, slave vessels accounted for less than one-third of 1 percent of all US shipping. [François Crouzet, "America and the Crisis of the British Imperial Economy, 1803–1807," in McCusker and Morgan (eds.), *Early Modern Atlantic*, pp. 278–315.]

[141] Manuel Barcia, "'Fully capable of any iniquity': The Atlantic Human Trafficking Network of the Zangroniz Family," *The Americas*, 73 (2016): 303–324; Harris, *Last Slave Ships*, pp. 56–92.

[142] Luiz Felipe de Alencastro, "Prolétaires et Esclaves: Immigrés Portugais et Captifs Africains a Rio de Janeiro, 1850–1872," *Cahiers du Centre de Recherhes Ibériques et Ibero-Americaines de l'Université de Rouen*, 4 (1984): 148; Alencastro, "La Traite Négrièr et L'Unité Nationale de Brasilienne," *Revue francaise d'Outre-Mer*, 46 (1979): 415. For other leading slave traders see Thomas, *Slave Trade*, pp. 641–49; Felipe Gonzalez, *Foundation and Growth*.

3

Europe and Atlantic Slave Trading

THE STRUCTURE OF EUROPEAN SLAVE TRADING

Public history sites – both virtual and physical – as well as much of the scholarly literature continue to misrepresent the evolution and structure of the Atlantic slave trades. Just as few have recognized the importance of the Americas as the organizational base of the traffic, even fewer are prepared to recognize the significance of the overall dominance of the Iberians in Atlantic slavery. Mainstream views of the centrality of the Dutch, the British, and the French to Atlantic slavery are misplaced. Such views continue to project Iberia as pioneering the mass forced migration of Africans to the Americas, but also see the northwest Europeans as overtaking the Iberians and perfecting the business. Accordingly, with their invasion of Brazil in 1630, the Dutch quickly assumed the role of chief supplier of Africans to the vast Spanish Empire, followed by the English. Further, from 1640 the English presided over their own rapidly expanding Caribbean sugar complex that within two decades was purportedly sending more sugar to Europe than the whole of Brazil. When the French joined in, they grew sugar in the western half of Hispaniola even before the Spanish ceded them what became the colony of St. Domingue in 1697. Within a little more than half a century St. Domingue was generating more plantation produce than the whole British Caribbean. These northwestern European nations had the richest slave plantation colonies sustaining a coerced population exodus of 5.3 million people from Africa, which they organized between 1640 and 1807. At the top of this system of exploitation, was "a small, high and mighty Atlantic ruling class of merchants, planters, and political leaders."[1] Such a dramatic pattern enabled the rapid growth of the West.

Most of this mainstream interpretation of Atlantic slavery and more specifically the Atlantic slave trades that supported it, is incorrect. In short, an interpretation that has emerged from half a century of data collection embodied in www.slavevoyages.org suggests rather that slavery and the slave trade in the Atlantic world were dominated by the Iberian nations, and it was the prior economic growth of northern Europe (and its offshoots in the Americas) that allowed the nations of that region to temporarily break into an already well-established Atlantic system. That system was over a century old when the Dutch intruded. It is true that for eighty years, down to the dissolution of the union between the Spanish and Portuguese crowns, the share of the slave trade based in Europe as opposed to the Americas declined steadily, but as late as 1640 the Iberian peninsula was the source of 80 percent of transatlantic slaving voyages. Of all the European maritime powers expanding into the transoceanic world, the Iberians had the advantage of being firstcomers – the Spanish in the Americas, and the Portuguese in Africa – advantages that the Iberians enjoyed almost to the ending of Atlantic slave trading.[2]

Iberian domination of the Americas lasted well beyond the breakup of the Iberian union in 1640. When the most powerful state in Europe first came to the Americas, it did not choose to settle lightly populated Patagonia, Roanoke Island, or the St. Lawrence River. Instead, it went straight to the most heavily populated (and therefore resource-rich) central Americas and quickly took over the two most powerful Indigenous polities in the Americas (the Aztec and Inca empires). From this point until at least 1800 Spanish America was the largest, richest, most heavily populated, as well as the most urbanized European imperial domain in the New World, stretching eventually from California to Cape Horn. As we have seen in Chapter 2, the Spanish maintained their economic preeminence among Europeans

---

[1] Rediker, *Slave Ship*, 14.
[2] Malyn Newitt (ed.), *The Portuguese in West Africa, 1415–1670: A Documentary History* (Cambridge, 2010), pp. 1–24; Sanjay Subrahmanyan, "Holding the World in Balance: The Connected Histories of the Iberian Overseas Empires, 1500–1640," *American Historical Review*, 112 (2007): 1359–85. Kenneth Maxwell made the call for a new focus on the South Atlantic system, thirty years ago the response to which can only be called muted: see Maxwell, "The Atlantic in the Eighteenth Century: A Southern Perspective on the Need to Return to the 'Big Picture,'" *Transactions of the Royal Historical Society*, 3 (1993): 209–36. This argument is consistent with Alencastro's findings, in *Trade in the Living*.

occupying the Americas down to the end of the colonial era. It is not surprising that until 1760 (and probably beyond) they also attracted far more immigrants from Europe to their American possessions, on a cumulative basis, than did the British, French, and the Dutch combined. More important in the present context, during the slave trade era the Spanish introduced more African slaves into their territories than the English did to the whole of the British Caribbean, though they did so under foreign flags. Moreover, after allowing for the intra-American traffic, and including the traffic to Brazil, no less than 63.3 percent of the people carried off from Africa were held in slavery in the Spanish and Portuguese Americas. Histories of the Atlantic world have never recognized these basic facts.[3]

As the first European nation with the transoceanic skills that carried them from Ceuta in North Africa in 1415 and to Japan in 1543, the Portuguese found themselves in a parallel position to the Spanish on the African coast.[4] No European power at the time could hope to conquer an Old-World sub-continent, especially a well-populated West Africa, but they *were* able to select the African regions with the combination of offshore islands and hinterlands amenable to modest military interventions and interactions with a range of African cultures. By the early seventeenth century, the Portuguese had occupied islands off the West African coast stretching from Arguim in the north to Luanda in the south and including the ten Cape Verde islands, Ile Principe, São Tomé plus the fort of Elmina. These they easily retained after 1650 in the face of northern European incursion with the single exception of Elmina.[5] The success of

---

[3] For transatlantic migration see David Eltis, "Free and Coerced Migrations from the Old World to the New," in Eltis (ed.), *Coerced and Free Migration*, pp. 62–63. The terms "first" (referring to Iberian-dominated) and "second" (northern European-dominated) Atlantic appear in P. C. Emmer, "Dutch and the Making of the Second Atlantic System," in Barbara L. Solow (ed.), *Slavery and the Rise*, pp. 75–96; the late Elinor G. K. Melville argued that " [t]he Spaniards remained primarily agro-pastoralists of the temperate highlands and latitudes; they avoided the humid tropical lowlands where possible," unlike the Portuguese in Brazil (Melville, "Land Use and the Transformation of the Environment," in Victor Bulmer-Thomas, John H. Coatsworth, and Roberto Cortés Conde (eds.), *The Cambridge Economic History of Latin America* (Cambridge, 2006), p. 125). More crudely (but just as erroneously), Robin Blackburn, in his widely read *Overthrow of Colonial Slavery, 1776–1848* (London, 1988), contrasted the "vigour" of the English and French colonies with that of the Spanish where the creole elite were "sunk in provincial torpor" (pp. 16–17). The 63.3 percent is calculated from Table 2.5.
[4] Charles R. Boxer, "Second Thoughts on the Anglo-Portuguese Alliance, 1661–1808," *History Today*, 36 (1986): 22.
[5] Pierre Verger, "Rôle joué par le tabac de Bahia dans la traite des esclaves au Golfe du Bénin, *Cahiers d'études africaines*, 4 (1964) 4: 352.

this system was perhaps due less to the occupation of island bases than to the interactions between Portuguese and Africans. These were of a kind that other Europeans were unable to replicate to quite the same extent. For many years the Gulf of Guinea islands (Príncipe and São Tomé) were controlled from Luanda rather than Lisbon. The links between these island bases and the mainland sources of captives, as well as the Upper Guinea coast, were established and maintained by *lançados* or *tangomãos*, (usually Portuguese men who married African women) *grumetes* (Portuguese-speaking Africans), and *pombeiros* (in Angola, traders of mixed Portuguese and African heritage). Many were integrated into African communities, and some were women.[6] The Portuguese thus developed a method for obtaining slaves in sub-Saharan Africa that ensured steady supplies at lower shipping costs and with little interference from European competitors, issues that are discussed more fully below. The northern powers were left with virtually no bases in Africa that extended beyond the range of a cannon-shot fired from one of their coastal forts, and with fewer intermediaries between themselves and the African traders who supplied the captives. Even these forts were largely confined to the Gold Coast.

Iberian domination of Atlantic slavery evolved naturally from slavery in the Iberian peninsula. Although enslavement as a practice had seriously diminished in northwestern Europe, the Baltic Crusades generated new supplies of enslaved people from the late twelfth century. Yet thereafter what looks like a major shift in values occurred. In the mid fourteenth century bubonic plague killed up to half the population of Europe and greatly increased the land-labor ratio. As we have seen in the Americas, these were conditions conducive to *more* slavery, not *less*. As might be expected, real wages began to rise, at least in England and the Netherlands from the late 1370s, surpassing previous peaks.[7] But in striking contrast to

---

[6] Newitt (ed.), *The Portuguese in West Africa*, pp. 12, 21, 79–80, 206, 208, 227. For *lançados*, see Linda Newson, "Africans and Luso-Africans in the Portuguese Slave Trade on the Upper Guinea Coast in the Early Seventeenth Century," *Journal of African History*, 53 (2012): 2–10; Newson, "Bartering for Slaves on the Upper Guinea Coast in the Early Seventeenth Century," in Toby Green and José L. Nafafé (eds.), *Brokers of Change: Atlantic Commerce and Cultures in Pre-Colonial Western Africa* (Oxford, 2012), pp. 259–84; Michał Tymowski, *Europeans and Africans: Mutual Discoveries and First Encounters* (Leiden, 2020), pp. 224–59; George E. Brooks, *Eurafricans in Western Africa: Commerce, Social Status, Gender, and Religious Observance from the Sixteenth to the Eighteenth Century* (Athens, OH, 2003), pp. 68–101; Peter Mark, *"Portuguese" Style and Luso-African Identity: Pre-Colonial Senegambia, Sixteenth-Nineteenth Centuries* (Bloomington, IN, 2002).

[7] Robert C. Allan, "The Great Divergence in European Wages and Prices from the Middle Ages to the First World War," *Explorations in Economic History*, 38 (2001): 411–47.

the second serfdom of early modern Eastern Europe, slavery and serfdom *declined* rather than expanded. As serfdom and slavery declined, wage labor increased and even in Sweden, where slavery endured longest, the practice went into decline. Nevertheless, juxtaposing the violence within Europe in the centuries between 1500 and 1815 and the explosive growth in Europe's ability to move people across oceans, it is astonishing that not a single European forcibly dispatched overseas carried the heritable status of an enslaved person. Slavery frequently waxed and waned in global history, and physical resistance and abolitionist sentiments never accounted for its decline. In post-Black Death Europe slavery did not re-emerge even though its preconditions – labor shortages and high land-to-labor ratios – were clearly in evidence.[8]

We cannot solve this puzzle in part because historians have paid far more attention to the decline of serfdom than to the disappearance of slavery. Clearly, the institution of slavery remained thoroughly familiar to Europeans even as it declined. Europeans were held captive in North Africa, and utopian thinkers from Thomas More to the radical Levelers had asserted that the idle in society – those who refused to work – should be made "common servauntes [ie slaves] of the commonwealth" a principle that the English Parliament briefly incorporated into statute law in 1547. In France, Louis X's oft-cited 1315 ordinance did not in fact free all slaves in his domain; the French free-soil tradition emerged much later. The Spanish may have made the enslavement of native Americans illegal but both sides in the well-known Vallodolid debates between de las Casas and Juan Ginés de Sepúlveda in 1550–51 agreed on the essential morality of forcibly moving Africans to the Americas. As did the Portuguese when more than a century later they followed the Spanish lead. Moreover, debates on liberties in England drew heavily on conceptions of their opposites – villeinage and slavery. Awareness of chattel bondage remained ever present in late medieval Europe and continued seamlessly into the early modern era. But the issue in all discussions was who should be eligible for enslavement, not whether enslavement should exist.[9]

---

[8] Wyatt, "Slavery in Northern Europe," 482–507; Edgar Melton, "Manorialism and Subjection in Eastern Europe," in *CWHS* 3: 297–323; Richard Hellie, "Russian Slavery and Serfdom, 1450–1804," *CWHS* 3: 275–96; Domar, "Causes of Slavery and Serfdom," pp. 18–32.
[9] Michael Guasco, *Slaves and Englishmen: Human Bondage in the Early Modern Atlantic World* (Philadelphia, 2014), chapter 1, quote is on p. 33; Richard W. Davis, "Introduction," in Davis (ed.), *The Origins of Modern Freedom in the West* (Stanford, CA, 1995), pp. 1–7; Sue Peabody, "An Alternative Genealogy of French Free Soil," *Slavery and Abolition*, 32

Europe was defined as much by the Mediterranean as the northern seas. Western Europeans may have given up enslaving each other, and were themselves liable to enslavement in North Africa, but neither pattern of behavior had any anti-slavery implications. The border between Islam and Christendom ensured that while slavery and the slave trade had diminished somewhat in Europe, there was no break in continuity. European expansion to the Americas began in the "Mediterranean Atlantic" or "Atlantic Triangle," an area defined by the Atlantic Islands and the Southwestern European and North African coastlines.[10] Just as the first several thousand slaves introduced to Cuba were Indigenous Americans from the mainland,[11] so the very first captives brought into Portugal via the Atlantic Ocean were the now extinct Guanches, the Indigenous people of the Canaries. This happened in the early 1420s and was followed by the Moors, more precisely "blackamoors," or Berber peoples from as early as 1441. After 1450 the traffic drew on sub-Saharan peoples with the first mainland embarkations occurring at Arguim. Iberia saw the Black component of its slave population gradually rise over the fifteenth century, but slaves and slaveholders alike still came from a strikingly diverse range of backgrounds, including Orthodox Christians, Slavs, and Muslims. Spanish authorities strove to keep the Americas Catholic, but the enslaved component of settlement in the early Spanish Americas reflected some of this diversity so that not all the enslaved were African.[12] As eastern sources of slaves dried up with the Ottoman conquests, Portuguese access to markets in Africa became critical to the needs of Iberia's slave owners. By the time ships began carrying the enslaved direct from Africa to the Americas in 1519 the traffic in the Mediterranean Atlantic was drawing overwhelmingly on sub-Saharan Africa. Numbers carried off to Europe approached 5,000 a year by the second half of the 1510s.[13]

(2011): 341–62; Luis Perdices de Blas and José Luis Ramos Gorostiza, "The Debate over the Enslavement of Indians and Africans in the Sixteenth and Seventeenth Centuries Spanish Empires" in Jorg Alejandro Tellkamp (ed.), *A Companion to Early Modern Spanish Imperial Political and Social Thought* (Leiden, 2020), pp. 295–317.

[10] Felipe Fernández-Armesto, *Before Columbus: Exploration and Colonization from the Mediterranean to the Atlantic, 1229–1492* (Basingstoke, UK, 1987), pp. 96–202; William D. Phillips, Jr., *Slavery in Medieval and Early Modern Iberia* (Philadelphia, PA, 2014).

[11] Felipe Gonzalez, *Foundation and Growth*.

[12] Debra Blumenthal, *Enemies and Familiars: Slavery and Mastery in Fifteenth-Century Valencia* (Ithaca, NY, 2009), pp. 267–77; David Wheat, "Mediterranean Slavery, New World Transformations: Galley Slaves in the Spanish Caribbean, 1578–1635," *Slavery & Abolition*, 31 (2010): 327–44; James H. Sweet, "The Iberian Roots of American Racist Thought," *William and Mary Quarterly*, 54 (1997): 41–66.

[13] Sergi Tognetti, "The Trade in Black African Slaves in Fifteenth-century Florence," in T. F. Earle and K. J. P. Lowe (eds.), *Black Africans in Renaissance Europe* (Cambridge,

Portuguese expansion southward and Spanish invasion of the Americas meant that Lisbon, Seville, and to a lesser extent Cadiz became the organizational centers of the slave trade for a century and a half. The first arrivals had disembarked in Lagos in the Algarve close to sugar-growing regions, but Lisbon became the dominant market for incoming Africans well before 1500. Here, from 1486, the Casa dos Esclavos (Slave House) processed all arrivals and collected a one-twentieth duty. It was the institution in Portugal that came closest to the better-known Spanish Casa de la Contractión (House of Trade) in Seville that licensed all slave voyages to the Spanish Americas. Spain and Portugal attempted tight regulation of the slave trade but before the eighteenth century neither created state-owned joint-stock slave trade companies. Between 1511 and 1640 the slave trade based in Europe was synonymous with the slave trade based in southwestern Iberia. Approximately 2,000 "European" slave ships sailed to Africa from a 250-mile stretch of the coastline between Lisbon and Cadiz. They obtained their captives almost exclusively in the islands-based Portuguese system on the West African coast. In 1519 the *Santa Catalina* (ID 42996) mentioned in Chapter 2 sailed into San Juan, Puerto Rico, from Guinea with just eight captives. All previous transatlantic slave voyages had carried Africans from Europe, not Africa. A further half-dozen voyages direct from Africa were completed by 1526.

A breakdown of departures within Iberia shows that for every slave voyage leaving Lisbon, two left from Seville (including Sanlúcar de Barrameda) or Cadiz, but a vessel leaving Lisbon could have subsequently called at Seville and might be identified in the record as starting its voyage there.

Table 3.1 draws on new voyage data collected by Marc Eagle and David Wheat that revises estimates of the early trade published in 2015. The table allows us for the first time to assess the importance of the early Iberian traffic relative to other better-known branches of the slave trade, including those based in London and the Netherlands. For all three regions in the table, we have a count of the first 130 years of slave-trading activity beginning in 1511 for the Iberians, 1641 for London and

2005), pp. 213–24; John L. Vogt, "The Lisbon Slave House and African Trade, 1486–1521," *Proceedings of the American Philosophical Society*, 117 (1973): 1–16; Hannah Barker, *That Most Precious Merchandise: The Mediterranean Trade in Black Sea Slaves, 1260–1500* (Philadelphia, PA, 2019), p. 150; Ivana Elbl, "The Portuguese Trade with West Africa, 1440–1521," unpublished PhD thesis, University of Toronto (1986), pp. 467–80.

TABLE 3.1 *Estimated size of the transatlantic traffic carried on in the first 130 years of its existence in three major European regions from which slave voyages were launched*

Region of departure	Number of voyages	Average number of Africans carried per voyage	Total number of Africans (col. 1 × col. 2)
Southwestern Iberia, 1511–1640	1,874	352.1	634,551
London, 1641–1770	2,303	276.3	636,210
Netherlands, 1651–1780	1,433	371.5	532,536

Source:
Row 1: www.slavevoyages.org/voyages/tPmHs7Lb – www.slavevoyages.org/voyages/xwBi5b5x
Row 2: www.slavevoyages.org/voyages/iqsxuYCA
Row 3: www.slavevoyages.org/voyages/NN37CFTZ

1650 for the Netherlands. The numbers for southwest Iberia and London are similar in this initial period. But while the traffic from Spain and Portugal continued for more than two centuries beyond 1640, London's traffic lasted for just an additional four decades beyond the initial period, and there was little Dutch slaving after 1780. Column 3 of the table indicates that down to the end of the Union of the Portuguese and Spanish crowns in 1640, the Iberian trade was almost double the size of the total trade based in the Netherlands and larger than the London traffic when that trade was at its height. More intense exploitation of the silver mines in the Americas, and Brazilian sugar plantations gradually replacing Indigenous labor with African meant that the pre-1640 Iberian traffic accelerated quickly to levels that would not have been out of place in the eighteenth century. After allowing for the intra-American traffic, Portuguese and Spanish possessions in the Americas formed the major market for enslaved Africans until the late seventeenth century.

Between the mid seventeenth and the mid nineteenth century, Iberian-based voyages declined dramatically, for reasons explained in Chapter 2. Overall, records exist for 556 slave voyages leaving Lisbon in the two centuries between 1641 and 1842, but over half of these traded in the North Atlantic gyre that crossed the Atlantic from ports on the southern rivers of Senegambia (mainly Bissau and Cacheu) to Amazonia. Others – fewer than two hundred – made the triangular trip from Lisbon to Angola,

Brazil, and back to Portugal.[14] The nineteenth century saw a minor revival of the Iberian traffic despite (or, given Spain's tolerant attitude to slavers, maybe because of) the traffic becoming illegal. We have records of 110 of these nineteenth-century voyages that were illegal in the sense that they sailed in contravention of treaties that Spain and Portugal had signed with the British. Cadiz, Barcelona, Lisbon, and Santander were home ports for 90 percent of these ventures. Two steam ships based in Cadiz carried off 3,600 Africans to slavery in Cuba in just three voyages in the 1860s. The sleek lines of one of these, the *Cicerón*, is shown in Figure 3.1, a far cry from a fifteenth-century carrack, and a testament to the impact of modernity on a business that many scholars and general readers alike view as quintessentially premodern.

The northwest Europeans were slow to loosen the Iberian grip on slaving in the Atlantic world. Initially, French merchants traded mainly on the River Senegal and the English on the Gambia River and Sierra Leone regions. For the English, French, and after 1600, the Dutch, there were two kinds of contact with Atlantic sub-Saharan Africa. One was trade in African produce – hides, ivory, and some gold; the other, activated only in wartime, was in the enslaved that privateers had captured from Iberian slave ships after they had left Africa for the Americas. There is no hard evidence of an English, French, or Dutch slave ship between

FIGURE 3.1 Profile of the steam-powered slave ship *Cicerón*. Source: BNA, FO84/1218, f. 320 (IDs 5052 and 4988). Reproduced with permission of the British National Archives, Kew.

---

[14] The scale of this traffic is being revised upwards. See Maximiliano Menz, "Uma comunidade em movimento: os traficantes de escravos de Lisboa e seus agentes no Atlântico, c. 1740–1771," *CLIO: Revista de Pesquisa Histórica*, 37 (2019): 39–57; Bohorquez and Menz, "State Contractors and Global Brokers," 403–20.

1589 and 1630 sailing to Africa, exchanging that cargo for captives, and selling the enslaved either in the Americas or Europe. Dutch privateers in charge of a captured Spanish and Portuguese slave vessel and in one instance even freed the onboard enslaved on the Brazilian coast because they could not find a market for their human cargo. At present we have records of just twenty-nine transatlantic slaving voyages setting out from Dutch, French, and English ports prior to 1640, compared to 1,819 such ventures that set out from Iberian ports (or bases in the Spanish-occupied Canary Islands) in the same period. Beyond the Atlantic, and well before their invasion of Brazil, the Dutch had established outposts in maritime Asia that had significant slave populations. Early V.O.C. (*Vereenigde Oostindische Compagnie*, 1602–1795) settlements were bases for the shipping of thousands of slaves from the Coromandel Coast and Bengal to Batavia – even in the absence of a full plantation economy.[15] This despite contemporary Dutch writers linking slavery in the Americas and indeed their own situation in Europe with the oppressive weight of the Spanish yoke.

The northwest Europeans started with no bases in Africa, no expertise in slave trading, and after the Dutch withdrawal from Brazil, very little in the way of tropical and sub-tropical territory in the Americas – no more than a precarious grip on a few tiny islands in the eastern Caribbean and some settlements on the South American coastal mainland. Yet within a quarter-century the center of gravity of the European-based traffic shifted dramatically north to first the Netherlands and England, and there, with the additional and slightly later development of the large French and the much smaller Scandinavian slave trades, it remained until 1807. Despite the nearly 500 slave voyages leaving French ports between 1813 and 1830, the traffic was thereafter firmly anchored in the Americas. The transmission of expertise in these matters from southern to northern European slave traders was made possible not by northern Italian city-states, as we might have expected given the latter's dominance

---

[15] Matthias van Rossum, "The Dutch East India Company and Slave Trade in the Indian Ocean and Indonesian Archipelago Worlds, 1602–1795," in David Ludden (ed.), *Oxford Research Encyclopedia of Asian History* (Oxford, 2020): https://oxfordre.com/asianhistory/display/10.1093/acrefore/9780190277727.001.0001/acrefore-9780190277727-e-403?p=emailAo25OyGmoom72&d=/10.1093/acrefore/9780190277727.001.0001/acrefore-9780190277727-e-403 ; Rik van Welie, "Patterns of Slave Trading and Slavery in the Dutch Colonial World, 1596–1863," in Gert Oostindie (ed.), *Dutch Colonialism, Migration and Cultural Heritage* (Leiden, 2008), pp. 155–259. especially 192–95; Joseph J. Mickley, "Some Account of William Usselinx and Peter Minuit," *Papers of the Historical Society of Delaware*, 3 (1881): 5–26.

in the Mediterranean Atlantic. Rather, the Dutch and English learned from each other, especially from the chastening Dutch defeats in Angola and Brazil.

After absorbing the higher costs incurred by trading from a ship rather than a land-based trading factory, the northwest European intrusion supplemented rather than replaced the preexisting Portuguese system. The Dutch did contrive a small overlap with the Portuguese system via a 1661 treaty that provided limited access to the Angolan coast in exchange for Portuguese access to the "Dutch" sections of the Gold and Slave coasts. But 576 transatlantic slave voyages between 1641 and 1665 show the Portuguese dominating Angola, the Bight of Benin, and Upper Guinea. Moreover, despite French and English encroachments in Upper Guinea, 93 percent of Africans leaving Cacheu and Bissau over the course of the slave trade era were on Portuguese vessels, and some of the remainder were on English ships with a license to carry enslaved children to Lisbon.[16] In striking contrast to the East Indies, where many Portuguese outposts were taken by the Dutch and English, the Portuguese held on to their Atlantic system. The northwest Europeans, including the occasional Scandinavian voyage, were forced into initially secondary markets located in the Bight of Biafra and from there south to the Congo River and eventually Côte d'Ivoire and the Gold Coast to the west. Except for the Dutch capture of Elmina – not a major source of slaves initially – the northwest Europeans left the Portuguese enclaves on the coast of Africa untouched, including shared access to Ouidah in the Bight of Benin. As already noted, the combined traffic of English, Dutch, French, and Scandinavian slave traders accounted for a minority of all arrivals of Africans in America.

Two key factors enabled the northwestern intrusion into what for a century and a half had been an almost exclusively Iberian domain. The first was the economic growth of Britain and the Netherlands relative to Portugal and Spain. Growth meant the emergence of more efficient financial intermediaries, with new credit instruments evolving such as bottomry bonds, and risk-reducing insurance contracts. These innovations constituted new ways of linking ultimate lenders to ultimate borrowers and emerged from the broader financial environment as the economy grew. The slaving business drew heavily on these, as did all long-distance trade. Of course, these innovations were refined by the slave traders and other transoceanic merchants. But they did not develop first in the slave trade before being applied to the rest of the economy, as Joseph

---

[16] www.slavevoyages.org/voyages/DIT7cPpB.

Inikori argues.[17] The second factor is the simple correlation between free and coerced transatlantic migration. Willingness of the population of the imperial power to migrate to the tropical Americas was a key determinant of the size of the African slave trade to any given region on the western side of the Atlantic. Plantations could not thrive without slaves, but without enough Europeans to supervise and initially to labor on the estates, they would never have started. In the early modern era, greater proclivity to migrate from Europe meant a greater slave trade from Africa.[18] Dutch migration was greatest in the first half of the seventeenth century, given Dutch incursions into Brazil and Dutch Guiana even though many of the European immigrants were not Dutch.

Many historians think that heritability of status and the term of servitude count for little; that the differences between slave and servant status were trivial. From this standpoint there were "many middle passages" across the oceans of the early modern world, and the experiences and specifically the transportation and use of indentured servants, slaves, and convicts on plantations was identical.[19] For such scholars a capitalist drive for profits in the mid seventeenth century created many kinds of "slaveries," the difference between them obscured by an obsession with the racialized plantation system that did not fully evolve until the eighteenth-century Americas. French *engagés* (indentured servants) were "mainly" kidnapped or defrauded into service in this rendition of history and they were in reality enslaved. The term "indentured servant" was essentially just "a rhetorical cloak" for slavery. Further, those protesting White servants in mid seventeenth-century England were early abolitionists, an argument to which we will return later.[20]

But, tellingly, the exploited were themselves acutely aware of the different terms of labor, as well as the relative status of each. One of the

---

[17] Joseph Inikori, *Africans and the Industrial Revolution in England: A Study in International Trade and Economic Development* (Cambridge, 2002), pp. 314–61.

[18] Robert Louis Stein, "The Free Men of Colour and the Revolution in Saint Domingue, 1789-1792," *Histoire Sociale*, 14 (1981): 7–28; David Eltis, "Introduction: Migration and Agency in Global History," and "Free and Coerced Migrations from the Old World to the New," in Eltis (ed.), *Coerced and Free Migration*, pp. 1–74.

[19] See the essays in Christopher et al. (eds.), *Many Middle Passages*.

[20] John Donoghue, "'Out of the Land of Bondage:' The English Revolution and the Atlantic Origins of Abolition," *American Historical Review*, 115 (2010): 942–74. Donoghue also argues that historians who use the term "indentured servant" are following the lead of slaveholders in disguising the institution's real nature. Donoghue references Galenson's work only for his statistics without engaging with his conclusions. Galenson's data is actually fatal to Donoghue's argument.

core complaints of White servants in Barbados in the mid seventeenth century was that they were Christians and should not be slaving in the fields alongside Africans. Their complaints were not against slavery per se, but against their own "enslavement." Their use of the label "Christian" implied who *should* be slaves – non-Christians – rather than who should not. On the island of Montserrat to which many Irish were sent as servants in the seventeenth century, a detailed 1729 census indicates that the Irish servants and their descendants had become *the* major owners of slaves at a time when Montserrat was approaching its all-time peak sugar production. We should also keep in mind that the most systematic records that historians use for early modern servant migrants are court registrations of indentures dating from 1654 to 1775, mostly created in Europe prior to migration. These suggest that however large the incidence of kidnapping and abuse in the colonies – e.g. the involuntary extension of the term of indentures – most indentured migrants exercised volition over the signing of indentures and did become full citizens at the expiry of their term.[21] Even Portuguese *degredados* and English convicted felons forcibly transported to the Americas, and eventually, Australia, served time-limited terms of labor that were typically seven or fourteen years rather than for life. Most important, no servant or convict complained about the law "which keeps and makes them and there (sic) seed Slaves forever" as African slaves in Virginia did in a 1723 petition to an Anglican bishop.[22] The difference between a slave and an indentured servant was clear to the petitioners, as well as to all other categories of exploited labor. It remains unclear to some historians only because the rhetorical use of the term "slavery" to describe severe work conditions was as common in sixteenth- and seventeenth-century Europe as it is today. Clearly, the expansion of slavery depended not just on the migration of the free, but also on the migrants having a strong sense of their own status.

---

[21] Marianne Wokeck, "Irish and German Migration to North America in the Eighteenth Century," in Eltis, *Coerced and Free Migration*, pp. 152–75; David W. Galenson, *White Servitude in Colonial America: An Economic Analysis* (Cambridge, 1982), pp. 1–19, 183–93. Irish immigrants were already part of the elite by the early eighteenth century. Africans were not. Donald Harmon Akenson, *If the Irish Ran the World: Montserrat, 1630–1730* (London, 1997), pp. 117–53.

[22] The hardness of their masters, they said, kept them from following the Sabbath: "wee doo hardly know when [Sabbath] comes." See Thomas N. Ingersoll, "'Releese us out of this Cruell Bondegg': An Appeal from Virginia in 1723," *William and Mary Quarterly*, 51 (1994): 777–82. For *degredados*, see Timothy J. Coates, *Convicts and Orphans: Forced and State-Sponsored Colonizers in the Portuguese Empire, 1550–1755* (Stanford, CA, 2001), pp. 21–41.

Dutch slaving in the Atlantic was at a continuous disadvantage from the scarcity of free migrants, and so, too, was the French before 1763.[23] The former had four phases. The first as described in the previous chapter supplied Brazil and ended with their effective loss of control over Pernambuco in 1647 and Luanda the following year. The second briefly saw them selling in a wide range of markets before other European powers enforced mercantilist restrictions that closed their ports to non-nationals. Between 1650 and 1674, the Dutch carried off nearly 100,000 people from Africa despite having no significant plantation colonies of their own. Third, from 1662 to 1715 Dutch slave ships sold mainly to Spanish America via their base in Curaçao in the southern Caribbean, though they were also responsible for a large share of the enslaved being taken to the nascent French colonies.[24] Dutch plantations in northern South America offered a new market in the second half of the seventeenth century, and thus the fourth and final phase of Dutch slave trading saw an almost exclusive focus on these possessions after 1715 and through to the 1790s. For slave markets the French, Dutch, Danish, and English were left for the most part with the Bights and the coast north of the Congo River – where there was no Portuguese land-based presence. For a very brief five years the Dutch did take over a major part of the Portuguese Atlantic slave-trading system. They held bases just off the African coast – São Tomé and Luanda – as well as Elmina Castle but taking over all the *lançado* networks that supplied these Atlantic ports with slaves was beyond them. Moreover, by the 1770s the Dutch were sending more produce ventures than slave ships to Africa in another trend that has escaped historians.[25]

Whereas the Dutch tried and failed to take over the existing Portuguese system, the English – much the weaker maritime power in the mid seventeenth century – tried to replicate it from the real estate and the maritime space that the Portuguese had not occupied. A key element in the strategy was the maintenance of trading alliances with Portugal in one of the

---

[23] For the dramatic increase of White immigration to St. Domingue after 1763, see Stein, "Free Men of Colour," 14.

[24] Half of all arrivals in Cayenne between 1660 and 1690 were on Dutch vessels and, in 1664, 637 residents of the island had Dutch creditors. See William Jennings and Martijn van den Bel, "La traite négrière à Cayenne, 1660–1690," *Bulletin de la Société d'Histoire de la Guadeloupe*, 186 (2020): 27–53. https://doi.org/10.7202/1072360ar and Klooster, "Inter-Imperial Smuggling," p. 158.

[25] Geoffrey Harteveld, "'Op Africa Gevaaren': Een verkenning van de Nederlandse scheepvart op Guinea voor de tweede helft van de achttiende eeuw, 1756–1791," Unpublished MA thesis, Leiden University, 2013), appendix.

longest-running bilateral diplomatic links in European history. It was not surprising that the relationship emerged when the Dutch were at their strongest (and the Portuguese at their weakest) with the marriage of Charles I and Catherine of Braganza in 1662. The Treaty of Methuen in 1703 further strengthened commercial ties between the two countries and helped preserve the long-standing Portuguese slave-trading system in the Atlantic. In the late eighteenth century, a major English merchant in Lisbon financed Portuguese voyages to Asia. The diplomatic links culminated in the Strangford Treaty of 1810 that gave British manufactured goods preferential access to Brazilian markets more than a century after the Methuen Treaty.

In the late seventeenth- and eighteenth-century Atlantic, it was the English who came closest to emulating the Portuguese system. Both countries had lower income levels than the Dutch and fewer remnants of the feudal ties to the land that restricted emigration from other European countries. The potential for transoceanic migration from England and Ireland was considerable and with English imperial ventures in Asia trailing those of the Dutch, the chief destination for English migrants became the Caribbean, and eventually mainland North America.[26] These regions were peripheral to the Spanish imperial thrust and thus poorly defended. The English counterpart to Brazil became Barbados, Jamaica, the Leeward Islands, and eventually the US South. Migration from Europe to the tropical Americas led inevitably to a slave trade from Africa. English indentured servants enabled more extensive plantations in the Americas that the Dutch were never able to match in their own territory. Then, as the flow of servants slowed in the English Caribbean after 1660, British slave traders stepped up their deliveries of African slaves to the point where nine out of ten Africans on all British slave ships disembarked in the British Americas, a similar ratio to the Portuguese within their own system.

But unlike the Portuguese, almost from the outset of the expansion of their slave trade the English were also supplying the Spanish Empire with enslaved labor via the intra-American slave trade. Perhaps most of the Africans disembarked in Barbados in the 1660s by the Company of Royal Adventurers were subsequently carried to Spanish America according to the terms of a contract between the Company and the Genoese *asientistas*, Grillo and Lomellin, signed in London. The Dutch, however, were the

[26] For a fuller discussion of the domestic determinants of emigration from the Netherlands and Britain in the early modern era see Eltis, *Rise of African Slavery*, pp. 29–56.

major national group supplying the Spanish before 1720. They sold more than half the captives they carried off from Africa in foreign colonies along with all those taken to Dutch Caribbean Islands, especially Curaçao, that were sold on to the Spanish Americas.[27]

English attempts to encroach on the Portuguese in Africa began after Thomas Thurloes, the RAC agent in the Gambia in 1678, noted that he was buying more captives from *lançados* than from Africans.[28] A few years later John Booker, a new agent at James Island in the Gambia wrote that he "hath cleared severall persons to live as Portuguese in the Country."[29] And indeed, Upper Guinea with its fractured political structures had a culture in which individual European traders were most likely to marry into African families and establish small-scale slaving businesses, but none of these traders fronted networks that matched those of the *lançados* on which the Portuguese could draw. The Dutch, French, and English slave traders made no impression on the Portuguese hold over supplies of the enslaved coming through either Cacheu and Bissau in the north or Angola and Mozambique in the south. Apart from the short-lived Dutch occupation of Luanda, almost all enslaved people leaving these ports before 1830 did so under the Portuguese flag.[30]

The English and the French also had limited success in breaching the system at its western end. Between 1661 and 1760, at least nine British slave ships sold, or tried to sell, slaves in Brazil.[31] Some of these sporadic attempts to introduce captives into the Portuguese Empire ended in confiscation. An alternative strategy quickly emerged. Francis Cock, a former employee of the RAC, wrote from Bahia in 1706, "[t]hat it is not safe to send English ships thither with slaves That if ye Compy will order any slaves to be put on board Portuguese ships and order them thither he will take care of them they are a very good Commodity and returns may be

---

[27] For English data see https://slavevoyages.org/voyages/yxenNo7U; for Dutch see https://slavevoyages.org/voyages/4EN5tXdB; for Portuguese, see https://slavevoyages.org/voyages/2ZPmkNW8; García-Montón, *Genoese Entrepreneurship*, pp. 121–25.

[28] BNA, March 15, 1678, T70/10, f. 1.

[29] BNA. John Booker, Gambia, June 17, 1691, T70/11, p. 69. See also BNA, John Freeman and Henry Greenway, York Island, Sherbro, March 18, 1703, T70/14, f. 60 who wrote "Sayes he is ready to begin an Enterprize in yor Service in the Susa Country from which all ye Chiefe of yo Trade Comes." The letter continued "The Portuguez are alarmed … at this & have made new offers of trade."

[30] www.slavevoyages.org/voyages/yCF8l2zP.

[31] https://slavevoyages.org/voyages/8mD5daVO. One of the nine occurred after a successful mutiny when the crew sold the captives in Pernambuco. See loose papers in BNA, HCA15/19, and HCA23/23.

made to Lisbon." The offer was repeated by James Blaney later that year. There was an immediate response. Roberto de Costa, Francis Cock and John Dowker sent gold and 280 tobacco rolls from Bahia in return for slaves. And several similar transactions occurred subsequently. Blaney reported "a very large number of Negroes Shipt by Mr. Duffield to Brazill" in 1714.[32] Most of the estimated 105 captives disembarked from the NS do Monserrat e Piedade in Bahia in 1721 were on the company's account, and smaller batches totaling 230 on four separate Portuguese ships followed in the same year.[33] But overall, the numbers involved were not large and might be described as confirming rather than threatening the Portuguese system. The only partial success the English achieved was in the minor traffic in enslaved children between Upper Guinea and Lisbon, which continued down to the Marquis of Pombal's abolition of the slave trade to Portugal in 1761.[34] French efforts to penetrate the Portuguese system were similarly unsuccessful.[35] Both the British and the French extended their slave-trading activities to include all embarkation points on the African coast outside Portuguese control, but they did not come close to breaching the Portuguese system's informal boundaries.[36]

The English accordingly avoided Portuguese factories in Africa. In the two decades after 1641 they obtained a few hundred captives at points where they already had long-standing connections for the African produce trade such as the River Gambia, Sierra Leone, and the Gold Coast.

---

[32] BNA, Cock to RAC, April 25, 1706, T70/5, f. 26; BNA, James Blaney to RAC, Cape Coast Castle, Nov. 14, 1714, T70/5, f. 25; BNA, idem, Whydah, Jan. 12, 1714, T70/3, f. 10; BNA, Dalby Thomas to RAC, Dec. 31, 1706, T70/5, f. 27.

[33] BNA, T70/885, f. 86, "Ledger for William's Fort, Whydah," April 3, 1721, "By adventures to Brazil Sent per four vessels per journal, 230 Slaves"; f. 85 mentions 99 slaves sent via Capt. Jose de Torres (id 51632).

[34] Francis Moore, *Travels into the Inland Parts of Africa* (London, 1738), p. 67; BNA, William Hickes, Dec. 12, 1709, T70/5, ff. 65–6. TSTD has records of 23 voyages from Upper Guinea to Lisbon between 1714 and 1758; Eleven of these were by London-based ships. See www.slavevoyages.org/voyages/PENBMIbB.

[35] See Joseph Blaney, Martin Hardrett and William Rogers, Whydah, to RAC, May 22, 1714, BNA, T70/5, f.102v; The Dryade (id 32891), a Compagnie des Indes vessel, called at Pernambuco in 1726 on its way to St Domingue from Whydah (Archives Nationales, MAR/4JJ/27, piece 10, MAR/JJ/69, piece 17).

[36] For British slave ships attempting to sell in Brazil, see https://slavevoyages.org/voyages/8mD5daVO. For similarly intended French slavers, see https://slavevoyages.org/voyages/qUFLCR10. Note, too, the RAC's discussion of making "Tryall of English Tobacco twisted into Rolls of 8olbs each as the Portugueze do theirs," BNA, Dalby Thomas, Feb. 12, 1704, T70/14, f. 23; and BNA, John Chaigneau, Cape Coast Castle, to RAC, July 31, 1708, T70/5, f. 53.

However, they opened a wholly new source of slaves in the Bight of Biafra that accounted for almost 70 percent of their captives in these twenty years. Initially, Old Calabar and to a lesser extent, New Calabar and the Rio del Rey were easily the most important individual markets. Thus, the charter generation of the Barbados population comprised indentured servants from London, and enslaved Igbo and Ibibio. The latter initiated a transatlantic slaving corridor between a 150 kilometer stretch of Africa lying east of the Niger Delta on the one hand, and, on the other, the English Americas. This link endured for almost 170 years; 85 percent of the ships trading in the Bight of Biafra in this era flew the British flag.

Even excluding what must have been several thousand British-purchased slaves arriving in Brazil on Portuguese vessels, we can say that for seven of the eighteenth-century decades the British carried off more Africans than did the Portuguese, and when the slave trade was at its pre-nineteenth century height between 1761 and 1807, well over half the ventures leaving Europe did so from Britain. As described in the previous chapter, some were sold on to foreign territories, mainly Spanish. Moreover, British occupation of foreign colonies during warfare was usually followed by an immediate jump in slave arrivals in the occupied colony, as in Guadeloupe, 1759–63, Havana, 1762–63, and Trinidad, 1797.[37] If the British had not left the trade abruptly in 1808, there seems little doubt that they, and probably US merchants as well, would have finally begun to make inroads into the Portuguese system. In one of the great ironies of the slave trade era, given Portuguese dependence on Britain in the Napoleonic Wars, it is not difficult to imagine a pro-slave trade Britain insisting on a clause in the 1810 Strangford Treaty with Brazil that would have at last allowed British voyages into the bilateral Brazil–Africa voyage system of the South Atlantic. What was possible and desirable in 1710, however, was clearly impossible in 1810. For British slave traders this was a huge missed profit-generating opportunity.

Three English ports dominated in sequence not just the English trade, but traffic from the whole of Europe: London before 1720, Bristol from the later 1720s, and Liverpool from the mid 1740s to 1807.[38] Less well

---

[37] For Guadeloupe, see www.slavevoyages.org/voyages/HkwCjT9F; for Cuba, www.slavevoyages.org/voyages/5pnH5VT4; for Trinidad, www.slavevoyages.org/voyages/ToOHXkxR.

[38] For Bristol, see David Richardson, "Slavery and Bristol's 'Golden Age'," *Slavery & Abolition*, 26 (2005): 35–54; for Liverpool's dominance, see Stephen D Behrendt, "Human Capital in the British Slave Trade," in David Richardson, Suzanne Schwarz, and Anthony Tibbles (eds.), *Liverpool and Transatlantic Slavery* (Liverpool, 2007), pp. 66–97,

known is the wide geographic range of ports involved in the business. The West Country provided the best locations for departures for Atlantic destinations. Prevailing westerlies in the English Channel could add weeks to outbound voyages from both Dutch and English Channel ports. It is not surprising that all seventeen English slave voyages recorded in the sixteenth century left from Plymouth and that a sugar refinery was operational in Bristol in 1606 long before British occupation of Barbados.[39] The early dominance of Amsterdam and London as Atlantic ports emerged from their links with mainland Europe and their specialist services for merchants, not their geographic location. In England, West Country vessels sailed from Lyme, Exeter, Topsham, Poole, Falmouth, Dartmouth, Cowes, and the Channel Islands, as well as Plymouth. They carried off more than 10,000 African captives before 1763. However, the most heavily involved outside the big three were Lancaster (eighty-three recorded voyages) and Whitehaven (a further sixty-four). Another thirteen ports in England dispatched at least one voyage to Africa, including Hull, Stockton, and Newcastle upon Tyne on the east coast. Vessels from four Scottish ports accounted for almost another 5,000 African departures between 1716 and 1766. The major pattern is that apart from the early West Country activity, all the minor ports moved into the trade as it expanded in the first half of the eighteenth century. Like New England slavers, their vessels were small – averaging less than 200 Africans embarked – and traded overwhelmingly in Upper Guinea and Gold Coast ports rather than the Bights and Angola regions that attracted the much larger Liverpool slavers. Despite dispatching a total of 243 voyages, they, like Bristol and London, ultimately could not compete with Liverpool. But once more we see merchants and seamen in almost every port large enough to engage in transoceanic trade viewing the slave trade as providing investment and employment possibilities.

The French intrusion into the Portuguese Atlantic was the latest to develop. Figure 3.2 displays the trend over time in their slaving ventures. The intermittent but dramatic gaps are entirely explained by wars, during which French slave ships remained in port or took out letters of marque to harry English shipping. The underlying upward trend from the mid 1720s tracks the remarkable rise to global dominance of St. Domingue in the

and Nicholas Radburn, *Traders in Men: Merchants and the Transformation of Britain's Slave Trade, 1701–1807* (New Haven, CT, 2023), pp. 19–58.

[39] I. V. Hall, "Bristol's Second Sugar House," *Transactions of the Bristol and Gloucestershire Archaeological Society*, 68 (1949): 110–64.

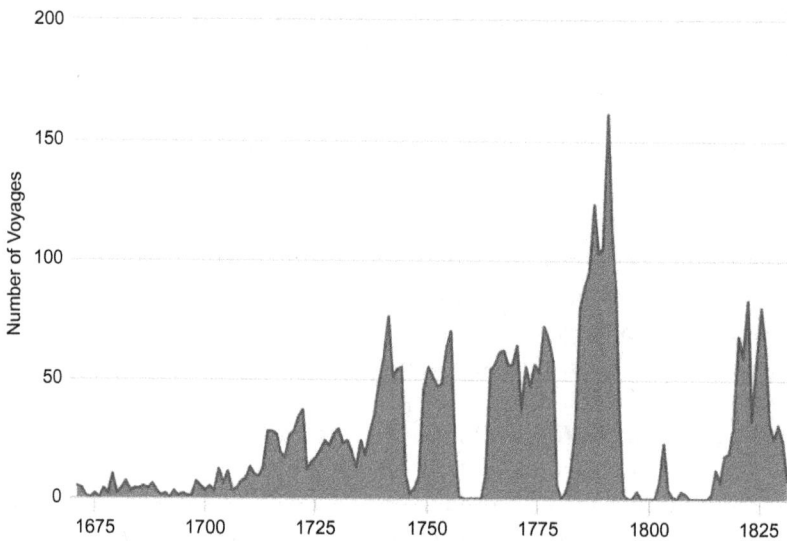

FIGURE 3.2 Time profile of French transatlantic slave voyages
Source: www.slavevoyages.org/estimates/MmfdnJTA

production of all tropical produce except rice. While the sudden ending in 1830 reflects the July monarchy's decision to enforce abolition of the traffic.

French and English settlement of the Lesser Antilles began at about the same time and depended initially on tobacco and cotton. In sharp contrast to the English Caribbean, however, before 1700 approximately similar numbers of European settlers (mainly *engagés*) and African slaves arrived in St. Kitts, Martinique, and Guadeloupe.[40] As this suggests, sugar cultivation was slower to take hold on the French islands than in the English Caribbean. Moreover, before 1670 the twenty-five slave voyages recorded as disembarking in the French Americas were all Dutch. Indeed, sugar production was boosted by the final expulsion of the Netherlands from Pernambuco in 1654, which saw several hundred Dutch Sephardic Jews relocate to Martinique and Guadeloupe together with their slaves.[41]

---

[40] For French arrivals see Eltis, "Free and Coerced Migrations," pp. 62–63 and the sources cited there. Gabriel Debien's analysis of 6,200 *engagé* contracts in in Les engagés pour les Antille (1634–1715) (Paris, 1952), pp. 248–49 suggests that arrivals from France peaked before 1665, just prior to a surge in slave arrivals from Africa, for which see www.slavevoyages.org/voyages/DoZqeHZo.

[41] J. Rennard, "Juifs et Protestants aux Antilles françaises au XVIIe siècle," *Revue d'Histoire des Missions*, 20 (1933): 436–62, esp. 437–9; I. S. Emmanuel, "Les Juifs de la Martinique

Arrivals in the eastern Caribbean under the French flag began in 1671, though there may well have been some unrecorded French interloper landings before this date. Despite French settlement in what became St. Domingue, Martinique remained the main destination for Africans until 1715. From then until the 1791 uprising, St. Domingue absorbed four out of every five of the 840,000 slaves disembarked in the French Americas, all of them on French ships, except for 21,500 taken into the colony on captured British vessels during the periodic eighteenth-century Anglo-French conflicts. To these should be added the nearly 20,000 brought into Guadeloupe by the British during their occupation of the island, 1759–1763.[42]

After disappearing from the oceans during the Revolutionary Wars, French slave traders re-entered the business briefly in 1802 to 1804 and more substantially, as Figure 3.2 shows, in 1813–30.[43] But in this final phase Cuba now assumed the dominant market role formerly occupied by St. Domingue. This was the only occasion in the history of the French slave trade when French slavers made a substantial contribution to the slave populations of non-French territories.[44] A further distinctive feature of this period is that one-fifth of the post-1812 total, left from French *Caribbean* ports, where probably it was easier to evade official anti-slave trade sanctions than in France. The French flag continued to be used in the slave trade after 1830, but always as a flag of convenience. Portuguese, Spanish, and Brazilian investors sometimes attempted to pass as French, given that the French refused British requests for the right to stop French vessels off Africa to check the authenticity of their papers.

Within metropolitan France the pattern of wide geographic dispersion of slave-trading ports was like that in Britain. Although the French government issued *lettres patentes* in 1716, permitting merchants in only five ports to participate in the business – Rouen, La Rochelle, Nantes, Bordeaux, and St, Malo – slaving ventures left from twenty-two different French locations in the eighteenth century. In the seventeenth century, the

---

et leurs co-religionnaires d'Amsterdam au XVIIe siècle," *Revue des Etudes Juives*, 123 (1964): 511–16; Filipa Ribeiro da Silva, "Crossing Empires: Portuguese, Sephardic, and Dutch Business Networks in the Atlantic Slave Trade, 1580–1674," *The Americas*, 68 (2011): 7–32. Two Portuguese slavers even sailed to St. Domingue in the 1780s.

[42] www.slavevoyages.org/voyages/Cg4Zohno.

[43] Eric Saugera, "Guerres et traites françaises aux côtes d'Afrique de la Revolution à Napoléon," *Revue française d'histoire d'outre-mer*, 408-413 (2020-2021): 1–624.

[44] The 10,000 Africans taken to Spanish America by the Compagnie de l'Asiente, 1702–1713 notwithstanding.

leading port for all Atlantic trade had been La Rochelle. Nantes was scarcely involved in the early traffic, but aided by additional duty relief from Brittany, it dispatched 1,714 slaving ventures between 1697 and 1831. Together with three other French ports – La Rochelle, Bordeaux, and Le Havre, each sending out between 440 and 480 voyages – these four major centers accounted for 78 percent of the nearly four thousand recorded French slaving voyages.[45]

Behind such growth and dispersion lay subsidies. Unlike Britain and the Netherlands, French slave traders received major relief from duties on both outbound cargoes to Africa and on colonial produce returned from the Caribbean. Between 1716 and 1784, these *acquits de Guinée*, as they were called, could be sold on to merchants trading directly with the American colonies. In 1784, the system was replaced by a direct subsidy on the tonnage of the slaving vessel causing, unsurprisingly, a dramatic and fraudulent increase in the reported size of French slave ships, as well as the nominal registration of some British slave ships in French ports. The French revolutionary government abolished this subsidy with the decree of July 27, 1793. But for most of the ancien régime and through four years of revolution, France subsidized its slave trade and earned the distinction of being the only government in the Atlantic world to do so. The fact that duty relief was not extended to merchants in the colonies perhaps accounts for the absence of a colonial-based slave trade in the French Atlantic before 1800.[46]

The Portuguese and Spanish accommodated the intrusion of seventeen thousand Dutch, English, and French slaving voyages into their Atlantic slave systems rather well. The territorial integrity of their possessions on both sides of the Atlantic remained largely intact through to the nineteenth century and their access to the forced labor of Africans was never at risk. Moreover, Portuguese slave trading expanded steadily in both north and south Atlantic gyres in the eighteenth century. The traffic into the Spanish empire did decline significantly even after allowing for the vibrant intra-American traffic in the Caribbean and South America, but this was

---

[45] https://slavevoyages.org/voyages/bW111hKX.
[46] Jean Tarrade, *Le commerce colonial de la France a la fin de l'ancien régime* (Paris, 1972), pp. 92–94. The sudden rise in reported tonnage is apparent in Jean Mettas, *Rèpertoire des Expéditions Nègriers Françaises au XVIIIe Siècle*, ed. Serge Daget, 2 vols (Paris, 1978–84). TSTD excludes the spurious tonnage data for 1784–1793 reported in this source. The clearest explanation of the tonnage subsidy and its impact is in Thomas Clarkson to the Comte de Mirabeau, Nov. 17, 1789, Huntington, Clarkson Papers, mss., CN 36. For the 1793 decree and its impact see Éric Saugera, "Guerres et Traites, Introduction," *Revue d'Histoire Française d'Outre-Mer*, 408 (2020): 30–33.

not because of Spanish inability to compete. Rather, the Spanish benefited from the rebound in the Indigenous populations that began in the second half of the seventeenth century. The recovery ensured *corvée* and eventually free labor enabled the silver mines to increase their output through to the end of the eighteenth century. When their European and North American rivals withdrew from the slave trade in the early nineteenth century the Spanish and Portuguese were able to seamlessly re-establish their former dominance and take the slave trade briefly to new heights. The overall peak year in 350 years of transatlantic trading occurred in 1829, not in the late eighteenth century, when the British and French traffic were at their respective heights.

Iberian resilience and resurgence in the face of prolonged competition from innovative and well-financed Dutch, British, and French was rooted in three key advantages: the enduring success of the Iberian imperial project in the Americas, their command of goods vital for obtaining slaves, and the impact of abolition. The previous chapter has already tracked the strong growth in output in Latin America relative to the overseas possessions of the other European colonial powers. As for trade goods, both Spanish and Portuguese America produced commodities that comprised universal global currencies – silver and gold. These gave them easy access to global markets, especially to Asian textiles.[47] In the eighteenth century the silver bought slaves in the intra-American trade. After 1807 when the Spanish re-entered the transatlantic trade, American bullion formed part of their trading cargoes from Cuba to Africa.[48] In addition, the oily, spicy sweet tobacco of northeastern Brazil when cured, wrapped in thick strands around a rod, coated in molasses, bound usually in goat skin, and weighing 80–90 lbs a unit, became an indispensable trade good on the Gold Coast and the Bight of Benin. The Portuguese may not have conquered Africa, but in the sixteenth century and for the last 170 years of the transatlantic traffic they were able to assemble trading cargoes based on gold from first Mina in West Africa and later Brazil, as well as rolls of tobacco that apparently

---

[47] Bohorquez and Menz, "State Contractors and Global Brokers," 406–20, and Bohorquez, "Linking the Atlantic and Indian Oceans: Asian Textiles, Spanish Silver, Global Capital, and the Financing of the Portuguese–Brazilian Slave Trade (c. 1760–1808)," *Journal of Global History*, 15 (2020): 31–33 establish the vital importance of American bullion for slave merchants whose interests ranged from Brazil and the Rio de la Plata to Calcutta as well as Angola.

[48] David Eltis, "Trade Between Western Africa and the Atlantic World before 1870: Estimates of Trends in Value, Composition and Direction," *Research in Economic History*, 12 (1989): 220. Bullion is estimated at 38 percent of trading cargoes leaving Cuba in 1828.

could not be produced elsewhere.[49] The third element preserving the Iberian system was, paradoxically, abolition. Starting with Danes in 1792 and continuing with the British and the Americans in 1807, the Dutch in 1815, and the French in 1830, the northwestern intrusion came to a voluntary end. Consequently, in the nineteenth century, the business returned to its fifteenth-century Iberian and multinational roots.

EUROPEAN ATTITUDES TOWARD THE SLAVE TRADE

Within the framework of national participation, there lies the question of who was involved in the slave trade, and, beyond that, the extent to which their attitudes to the business differed from those of the general population. The coverage of slavery in the media, the destruction of statues associated with slavery, and the thrust of respected academic projects such as "Legacies of British Slave-Ownership" and, more recently "Legacies of the British Slave Trade: The Structure and Significance of British Slave Trade Investment, 1550–1807," implicitly suggest that enslavers held values that were different from the general population and are thus uniquely culpable for past horrors. Underlying this attitude is the unstated conviction that we can best understand the past by the applying the values of the present to any historical analysis. In fact, an examination of those involved in forcibly moving 12.75 million Africans from their sub-continent homes shows that they were neither small in number, nor high and mighty in social status. Until the mid nineteenth century there is no evidence that any significant segment of the population shared modern attitudes to the African diaspora. Worse, among abolitionists, there was no shortage of a racism matching that of the slave traders.[50]

---

[49] See Vitorino Magalhaes-Godinho, *Économie de l'empire portugais aux XVe et XVIe siècles* (Paris, 1969), pp. 228–243. See also the T70 references on pp. 162–63 and Mitchell, *Prince of Slavers* chapter 4 and Appendix; John L. Vogt, "The Early São Tomé-Principe Slave Trade with Mina, 1500–1540," *International Journal of African Historical Studies*, 6 (1973): 453–67. For tobacco, see Carl A. Hanson, "Monopoly and Contraband in the Portuguese Tobacco Trade, 1624–1702," *Luso-Brazilian Review*, 19 (1982): 149–68; Pierre Verger, *Flux et reflux de la traite des nègres entre le golfe de Bénin et Bahia de Todos Os Santos du XVII au XIX' siècle* (Paris, 1968), p. 11. Hanson writes "Together with bullion, tobacco became the principal item of exchange for products from the Far East and for slaves taken from the west coast of Africa." Quote is on p. 149.

[50] See the description of Haiti in 1802 by Henry Brougham, later Lord Chancellor at the time of the 1833 abolition act, in his *An Inquiry into the Colonial Policy of the European Powers*, 2 vols (Edinburgh, 2003), especially vol. 1. Brougham was perhaps the most racist abolitionist of all, but one that Maeve Ryan, in her excellent *Humanitarian*

The diversity of the merchandise, the geographic range of production sites, and the composition of the slave-trading firms speak to the awareness of all Europeans and their acceptance of the extension of slavery around the Atlantic world. The European-based maritime slave trade with Africa continued uninterrupted through to its three-hundred-year peak in the late eighteenth century without significant opposition in either sub-continent – European or sub-Saharan Africa. Black people, including slaves, could be seen in all the larger European slaving ports, with 10 percent of the Lisbon population comprising Blacks in the early sixteenth century.[51] From modern perspectives awareness of such a presence was a case of an abolitionist dog that did not bark. In the Netherlands, England, and France, the transatlantic slave trade continued across three centuries with not even a Vallodolid-type discussion on who should be enslaved. Nor was there anything equivalent to the 1555 protest in the Portuguese case of Dominican friar Fernão Oliveira in his *Arte da Guerro do Mar*. In northwest Europe it was truly an "unthinking decision" in Winthrop Jordan's well-known comment on the adoption of racial slavery in the English colonies.[52]

Thousands of workers across Europe depended on merchandise traded for slaves for their livelihoods. Long before the mass petitions against the trade in the abolitionist era a major petitioning campaign *in favor* of the slave trade in 1707–1713 gets much less attention.[53] In the early eighteenth century the

---

Governance and the British Anti-Slavery World System (New Haven, CT, 2022) omits from her review of abolitionist attitudes toward Africans.

[51] Rik van Welie, "'What Happened in the Colonies Stayed in the Colonies": The Dutch and the Slave-Free Paradox," in Philip Misevich and Kristin Mann (eds.), *The Rise and Decline of Slavery and the Slave Trade in the Atlantic World* (Rochester, NY, 2016), pp. 100–107; Dienke Hondius, "Black Africans in Seventeenth Century Amsterdam," *Renaissance and Reformation*, 31 (2008): 87–105; Pieter Emmer and Ernst van den Boogart, "The Dutch Participation in the Atlantic Slave Trade, 1596–1650," in Henry A. Gemery and Jan S. Hogendorn (eds.), *Uncommon Market: Essays in the Economic History of the Atlantic Slave Trade* (New York, 1979), pp. 353–57.

[52] Winthrop D. Jordan, *White Over Black: American Attitudes toward the Negro, 1550–1812* (Chapel Hill, NC, 1968), p. 44. This was arguably a second case of the abolitionist dog not barking; the first being the aftermath of the plague in the fourteenth century when neither serfdom nor slavery expanded in Europe when we would have expected it to do so (again a decision made without discussion). The first resulted in a freer environment for Europeans, the second in the quick development of a massive enslavement for Africans. For Oliveira, see Alencastro, *Trade in the Living*, p. 157, and for other Portuguese reservations, see pp. 165–84. The Valladolid debate (1550–1551) was the first published discussion of the rights and treatment of indigenes in the Americas.

[53] See Seymour Drescher, *Abolition: A History of Slavery and Antislavery* (Cambridge, 2009), p. 250; Richard Huzzey, "A Microhistory of British Antislavery Petitioning." *Social Science History*, 43 (2019): 599–623.

issue was not abolition, but the ending of the monopoly of the Royal African Company, a measure that would greatly stimulate the expansion of the slave trade. Petitioners on both sides of this issue naturally assumed there was nothing immoral about the business. The House of Commons received two hundred petitions from forty communities outside London, most of them centers of woolen manufacturing. Organizers favored numbers over social status so that many literate spinners and weavers must have signed.[54] In a startling inversion of their nineteenth-century efforts to suppress the slave trade, between 1731 and 1787 thirteen fully commissioned naval vessels and one transport vessel commissioned by the British government carried more than one thousand enslaved Africans from mainly the Gold Coast to Barbados. These no doubt comprised speculative ventures by the ships' officers.[55] A few years later hundreds of sailors from slave ships rioted against their employers in what was then (1775) the largest slave-trading center in the world – Liverpool. Yet the issue was not the slave trade itself but wages – in other words the distribution of revenue that the slave trade generated.[56]

On the continent of Europe, there was no significant worker opposition to the slave trade until the nineteenth century and even then, no mass petitioning of national legislatures. As explained in Chapter 6, French abolition of slavery in 1794 was a bourgeois measure and is best understood as a reaction to the St. Domingue Rebellion rather than a reflection of domestic hostility to slavery.[57] As noted in Chapter 6, during the French Revolution slave-ship owners renamed their vessels *Assemblée Nationale*, *Soldat Patriote*, *Bon Citoyen*, *Révolution*, *Nouvelle Constitution*, and *Mirabeau*, without any apparent sense of the tension between the revolutionary ideals embodied in the name and the wretched business that these vessels carried on.

As the Liverpool riot suggests, workers in the industry themselves could be counted in the thousands. But slave ships constituted a tiny part of the merchant navy of any country. In Middelburg, an average of one slave vessel left port every month. In Liverpool at the slave trade's peak, an

---

[54] William A. Pettigrew, *Freedom's Debt: The Royal African Company and the Politics of the Atlantic Slave Trade, 1672–1752* (Chapel Hill, NC, 2013), pp. 118–26. Pettigrew argues that the dispute "produced more petitions and more pamphlets than any other issue relating to trade policy during the ... quarter century after 1688" (p. 118).
[55] www.slavevoyages.org/voyages/jWnQJD7J and www.slavevoyages.org/voyages/yoWGBg8K.
[56] Gomer Williams, *History of the Liverpool Privateers and Letters of Marque with an Account of the Liverpool Slave Trade* (Montreal, 2004, first published London, 1897), pp. 555–60.
[57] See the essays in Gert Oostindie (ed.), *Fifty Years Later: Antislavery, Capitalism and Modernity in the Dutch Orbit* (Leiden, 1995) for the absence of anti-slavery on the part of the Dutch worker.

average of 2.5 slaving ventures left each week, at a time when hundreds of vessels cleared from both ports weekly. But slave vessels were heavily manned, especially in wartime. In 1786 and 1787, years of peace, a total of 419 slave ships set sail from European ports on voyages that would take between one and two years to complete. They were manned by a mean of 35 crew, suggesting a workforce of 14,670 at sea – with no doubt three or four times this number remaining in port having made the voyage possible by building, fitting out, and provisioning the ship.[58]

But it was not just the size and wide distribution of the workforce across Europe enabling the slave trade that is striking. A review of the evolution of investment in the business shows a similar pattern. In the mid sixteenth century the English merchant community in Seville numbered at least one hundred. The first English sugar plantation owner shows up in early sixteenth-century La Palma in the Canaries, not in seventeenth-century Barbados. Along with other English merchants, the owner, Thomas Maillard, traded in slaves, sixteen of whom are listed in his will.[59] Robert Thorne owned many slaves in Andalusia and the Canaries more than fifty years before the famous Hawkins' transatlantic voyages of the 1560s. More important were the Pinellis of Genoa, the Florentine Berardi brothers and Bartolomeo Marchionni (who first represented the Cambini bank, and then operated independently in Lisbon after the bank's 1482 bankruptcy). These merchants financed businesses that employed slave labor in Andalusia as well as the Canary Islands, along with Spanish partners.[60] A Genoese company in Seville funded ventures intended to carry 4,000 individuals from Africa to the Americas, including the very first recorded voyage direct from Africa, owned by Genoa's Polo de Espindola. The licenses, issued by Charles V in 1518, were first granted to the Flemish Laurent de Gouvenot. Ten years later, the Spanish Crown awarded an *Asiento* (contract) for four years to Heinrich Ehinger and Hieronymus Sayler, agents of the German Welser family. Eventually, despite an eighty-year war for independence from the Spanish, Dutch capital also became involved.[61] And two thousand

---

[58] https://www.slavevoyages.org/voyages/zKPSqoLS.
[59] Gustav Ungerer, *The Mediterranean Apprenticeship of British Slavery* (Madrid, 2008), pp. 15–69 surveys English slave owners in the Mediterranean Atlantic. He identifies 50 settling in Sanlucar de Barrameda alone between 1512 and 1540 under the patronage of the Duke of Medina Sidonia.
[60] Ruth Pike, *Enterprise and Adventure: Seville and the Opening of the New World* (Ithaca, 1966), pp. 2, 99–127.
[61] Marc Eagle and David Wheat, "The Early Slave Trade to Spanish Caribbean," in Borucki et al (eds.), *From the Galleons to the Highlands*, pp. 53–57; Hall, *Before Middle Passage* provides a logbook of one of the slavers involved in the slave trade to Europe (see his

Portuguese merchants were based in Seville by 1600, including many *conversos* (former Jews). Overseas ventures were European rather than Iberian enterprises, with continuing Genoese involvement. Within Iberia it is often impossible to separate Spanish from Portuguese ownership except via the issuer of the license, a permit that was typically resold more than once before the voyages it authorized left port.[62]

Equity in individual voyages was similarly widely distributed. After 1640, patterns of ownership remained international through to the end of the slave trade era. But whereas before 1640 the non-Iberian component was mainly northern Italian, German and Flemish, after 1640 the pan-European character was expressed via new national groups entering the business under their own flags, including small states such as the Duchy of Courland (now Latvia) and, prior to Napoleon's reorganization of Germany, Brandenburg. Unlike the early Iberians, each of the northwestern nations used state-sponsored chartered companies with nationally defined monopoly rights to break into the slave trade.[63] All of them eventually incurred losses that put them out of business. Table 3.2 lays out the contributions to the slave trade of the more important of them.

The ultimately disastrous Dutch venture into Brazil and Angola undermined the original Dutch West India Company founded in 1621, and in 1648 the Dutch revoked its monopoly access to the African coast. Despite this, in 1674 a second reorganization of the West-Indische Compagnie created the only Dutch institution allowed to trade in slaves across the Atlantic. Some Dutch "free" traders had already moved their operations to the Baltic and conducted business under the label of Swedish, Danish, Brandenburg, and Courland chartered companies. Others became "interlopers" sailing illegally from Dutch ports. The monopoly of the reorganized (or Nieuw) WIC was finally eliminated in 1734. Although Dutch plantations had emerged in Surinam, Demerara, Essequibo, and Berbice, the Dutch company continued to supply enslaved labor to the Spanish via

---

chapter 7) and a Cape Verde custom receipts book for the years 1513–1516. For later Genoese involvement see García-Montón, *Genoese Entrepreneurship*.

[62] Until the 1560s when a regular slave traffic to Brazil got underway almost all voyages left from Iberia or the Canary Islands. See Linda A. Newsom, "The slave-trading accounts of Manoel Batista Peres, 1613–1619: Double-entry bookkeeping in cloth money," *Accounting History*, 18 (2013): 345.

[63] On the paucity of private English slaving ventures to Guinea before 1640, see Paul E. H. Hair, "The Experience of the Sixteenth-Century English Voyages to Guinea," *Mariner's Mirror*, 83 (1997): 3–13, DOI: 10.1080/00253359.1997.10656625; Richard Jobson, *The Golden Trade: or a discovery of the River Gambra and the Golden Trade of the Aethiopians* (London, 1623), p. 112.

TABLE 3.2 *Transatlantic slave voyages owned by major state-sponsored chartered companies*

Name	Years operating	Voyages disembarked	Slaves carried
First West-Indische Compagnie	1630–1652	157	46,961
Company of Royal Adventurers	1662–1672	104	26,925
Royal African Company	1673–1731	652	187,123
Second West-Indische Compagnie	1674–1750	379	184,097
Compagnie du Sénégal	1677–1721	85	22,932
Vestindisk-guineiske Kompagni	1696–1755	36	9,771
Compagnie de l'Asiente	1703–1713	28	9,745
South Sea Company	1714–1740	118	41,123
Compagnie des Indes	1720–1750	123	44,833
Companhia Geral do Grão Pará e Maranhão	1756–1791	151	29,464
Companhia Geral de Pernambuco e Paraiba	1760–1787	160	60,432
Total		1,995	666,076

Source: Row 3: www.slavevoyages.org/voyages/fETO5qLc Row 4: www.slavevoyages.org/voyages/8nfHZoPv slavevoyages.org/voyages/RibGyfaC;

the entrepôt of Curacao Island until 1715, before leaving the business totally in 1734 very heavily indebted. Its 386 slave voyages had carried off 187,000 captives to the Americas in addition to forty-eight ventures shipping nothing but African produce.[64]

The French dalliance with state-sponsored chartered companies enforcing monopoly rights was more complicated. Colbert's Compagnie des Indes Occidentales lasted only eight years. From 1672 the Compagnie du Sénégal was awarded exclusive rights to trade north of the Sierra Leone River only, and in 1685 the Compagnie de Guinée (becoming in 1701 the Compagnie de l'Asiente) held monopoly rights to the rest of West Africa. Altogether eight separate French chartered companies sent out 283 voyages that carried off an estimated 83,000 captives from Africa.[65] None of these companies survived

---

[64] Table 3.2; Pieter C. Emmer, "The West India Company, 1621–1791," in Leonard Blussé and Femme Gaastra (eds.), *Companies and Trade, Essays on Overseas Trading Companies during the Ancien Régime* (Leiden, 1981), pp. 71–95.
[65] www.slavevoyages.org/voyages/OqCouJWX.

for long, however, and by the end of the second decade of the eighteenth century the French traffic was largely in the hands of private merchants based in Nantes, La Rochelle, St. Malo, Bordeaux, and Le Havre, a reality recognized by the Crown's *lettres patentes* of 1716 and 1717. A few state-chartered companies in Portugal emerged with monopoly rights. The Marquis de Pombal tried to create monopolies centered on each of the major Brazilian ports in the 1750s. Only the company serving the smaller markets of Maranhão and Para (the Companhia Geral do Grão-Pará e Maranhão) and Pernambuco (the Companhia Geral de Pernambuco e Paraíba) had brief success – but their monopolies did not survive Pombal's fall from power in 1777. These chartered companies were easily the largest slave traders in the Portuguese business, accounting for almost 2,000 voyages overall, as Table 3.2 shows.

The English monopoly slave-trading companies are usually classed as failures, but the Company of Royal Adventurers (1662–1672), the Royal African Company (1672–1731), and the South Sea Company (1713–1740) dispatched a total of 876 slaving ventures, to which should be added at least 418 intra-American voyages carrying captives mainly from Jamaica to the Spanish American mainland for the South Sea Company. This third joint-stock company had been formed in anticipation of Spain granting the *Asiento* contract to Britain in the 1713 Treaty of Utrecht – albeit with the King of Spain coming to hold 28 percent of its stock. When the terms of the treaty were announced, crowds in London celebrated wildly. None of this reckons with the 222 produce voyages that the RAC sent out that returned directly to London with ivory, gold, and dyewoods. Alone of all the companies mentioned here, it actually paid a dividend of 10 percent on its stock between 1676 and 1688 and was regarded as just as secure as its much larger East Indies counterpart. Yet, paradoxically, the English were the first to begin a shift to de facto free trading in slaves when, in 1689, the common law Court of King's Bench refused to recognize the RAC's right to confiscate the property of merchants trading in violation of the Crown's prerogative-sponsored monopoly.[66] Ultimately the RAC could not survive without the monopoly. The South Sea Company fell victim to the vicissitudes of the Anglo-Spanish relationship so this, too, was ultimately a financial failure.[67]

---

[66] Pettigrew, *Freedom's Debt*, p. 30; Aboulaye Ly, *La Compagnie du Sénégal* (Paris, 1958); Guy Chaussinand-Nogaret, *Les financiers de Languedoc au XVIIIe siècle* (Paris, 1970).

[67] Hugh Thomas, "The Treaty of Utrecht and the Slave Trade," in Trevor J. Dadson (ed.), *Britain, Spain and the Treaty of Utrecht 1713–2013* (Leeds, UK, 2014), pp. 52–56.

These digressions on chartered companies are important here because the stock of the three largest of these companies was widely held. The West-Indische Compagnie (both new and old), the Royal African Company, and the South Sea Company had many thousands of shareholders with perhaps most of those investing in the last of this trio losing heavily in the South Sea Bubble.[68] Each had a long tail of small investors – in the RAC's case 5,000 shareholders along with 358 directors from the commercial elite – during its seventy-year existence. One of the directors, John Blunt, was one of two co-founders of the South Sea Company; and several others were directors of both companies. Most RAC ventures used vessels that the company had hired for the purpose, the owners of which received a portion of the slaves that survived the voyage as payment – thus widening further the pool of those with a direct interest in the slave trade. Yet despite these impressive numbers, it is easy to establish that private investment enabled and sustained the traffic. Overall, a total of at least 40,000 transatlantic slave voyages occurred over the 350-year-long transatlantic slave trade era. State sponsored company ventures could have accounted for only 5 percent of these.[69]

As in the Americas, any port large enough to organize a transoceanic voyage invested in a slaving venture when it became legally possible to do so. Ninety-two separate ports stretching from Tønsborg in southern Norway to Trieste in Italy, dispatched at least one expedition during the slave trade era.[70] By the time the European slave trade reached its late-eighteenth-century peak a dramatic consolidation had taken place, with only 26 of these ports remaining engaged, ships from two of which, Liverpool and Nantes, accounted for almost half of the people carried off from Africa between 1781 and 1790. And in the next decade Liverpool alone accounted for well over half of all slave-ship departures not just from Britain, but from the whole of Europe.

An even more striking consolidation is apparent if we focus on owners rather than places. Slavevoyages.org contains the names of 30,000 captains and owners of slave ships, two-thirds of them based in Europe. The "People of the Atlantic Slave Trade" project (PAST) has edited this data, as well as adding biographical information when available. Preliminary

---

[68] For the wide ownership base of the Dutch companies in the overlapping fields of slavery and privateering see Franz Binder, "Die Zeelandische Kaperfahrt, 1654–1662," *Proceedings of the Zeeland Society of Sciences*, 42 (1976): 40–92, especially p. 43.
[69] https://slavevoyages.org/voyage/about#methodology/coverage-of-the-slave-trade/1/en/.
[70] https://slavevoyages.org/voyages/zKPSqoLS.

analysis suggests that slave-trading companies owned and operated by individuals existed after the chartered company era, but that private equity was vested in families rather than corporations. The great bulk of the slave trade comprised partnerships formed for a single voyage, with different prominent multigenerational families playing key roles in each port. Equity holdings were fluid and constantly shifting yet allowed for the small investor.

The largest incorporated entity (apart from the state-sponsored chartered companies) was Zeeland's MCC, which dispatched 112 voyages between 1730 and 1797 carrying 31,000 captives. At any given time, the company had roughly 400 shareholders, about half of whom held fractions of a share.[71] In Amsterdam after the withdrawal of the WIC from slave trading, the partnership of father and son, Jochem Matthijs Smitt and Coenraad Smitt, carried off 12,000 enslaved Africans to Suriname over a thirty-year period.[72] The Rotterdam firm of Coopstad and Rochussen took 21,246, almost all to the Dutch Guianas between 1749 and 1789.[73] The ships of Jacques- François Begouën of Le Havre carried off 19,255 enslaved people. The Nairac family of Bordeaux took 17,623 others and in Nantes, the Montaudoins carried 23,956 in the first half of the eighteenth century, with the Bouteillers assuming the dominant role thereafter with 22,335 enslaved. But a dozen families in Liverpool invested in voyages that carried much larger numbers. The largest individual investor was William Boats, whose vessels carried off 55,361 people, with the largest family being the Gregsons, all of Liverpool. The Gregsons were responsible for transporting 136,000 captives on 401 ventures. Generally, the major Liverpool families – the Aspinalls, the Hodgsons, the Tarletons, the Earls, and William Davenport – carried off twice as many or more captives than their largest continental counterparts. The latter would not have made the top ten of Liverpool owners, nor would any of the slave traders of the Americas.[74] This did not stop direct British investment in the slave trade ending abruptly in 1807.

---

[71] Koen van der Blij, "Shareholders in the Dutch Eighteenth-Century Atlantic Trade," in *The Low Countries Journal of Social and Economic History*, 19 (2022): 79–81.

[72] Ramona Negrón and Jessica den Oudsten, *De grootste slavenhandelaren van Amsterdam* (Zutphen, 2022).

[73] www.slavevoyages.org/voyages/cJX7thoK.

[74] All ownership data in this and the next paragraph are readily available at www.slavevoyages.org/enslaver/shnqg9TF. Note, too, that most of these families have streets named after them in their respective cities.

Most leading families entered the traffic early and their investments grew with the trade. Typically, the distribution of ownership was wider in the first half of the eighteenth century than in its closing decades as the larger families increased their dominance. Liverpool slave merchants tended to have parents who were of more modest origins than those in the major continental centers and came from towns in their port's hinterland. In France and the Netherlands, the early investors appear to have been merchants or local dignitaries and/or persons with positions in local government. In Liverpool, by contrast, the fathers of the founders of the top ten major families tended to come from more modest origins; in David Pope's words "few came from either a wealthy or a poor background." Only two of them were merchants or local officials and the occupations of "porter," "mariner," "yeoman," "brewer," and "barber" appear in the record, together with "gentleman/lawyer." Further, Pope's analysis of wills indicates that "participation in the slave trade did not guarantee vast wealth. Few of the leading Liverpool slave merchants ... achieved enormous wealth." Pope's list of ninety-four leading eighteenth-century Liverpool slave trade merchants, a list confirmed by the recently launched PAST user interface, shows that only twenty-two left estates valued at more than £10,000.[75]

Yet this focus on the large investor misses a key feature of investment in the slave trade. Across Europe, including Liverpool, the most striking feature of the distribution of equity is the exceptionally long tail of small investors, defined as those with interests in no more than two ventures. Of course, the slavevoyages.org data on ownership does not give us the amount invested. An interest might be as little as a one thirty-second share, whereas a major investor might be the sole owner of a venture. Treating all investors as equally important therefore understates inequality. But the purpose of this exercise is to show the number of people interested in the business rather than to calculate relative levels of investment. Across the Atlantic world, owners of slave voyages invested in an average of only eight ventures during their careers.[76]

In the Netherlands over 90 percent of those with equity in the slave trade had stakes in no more than two voyages. In his only recorded

---

[75] On Liverpool's dominance see David Pope, "The Wealth and Social Aspirations of Liverpool's Slave Merchants of the Second Half of the Eighteenth Century," and Behrendt, "Human Capital" both in Richardson et al., *Liverpool and Transatlantic Slavery*, pp. 66–97 and 164–226, quotes from p. 168. For more on major Liverpool and Nantes owners see Radburn, *Traders in Men*, pp. 28–35.

[76] Calculated from www.slavevoyages.org/past/enslavers.

investment, Theunis Reijersz, a compass maker, was one of nine owners of the *Vergulde Zon*, which in 1668 delivered 215 captives to Curacao on their way, no doubt, to Spanish America.[77] Individuals primarily in other professions such as sailmaker Albert van der Veer and wine merchant Andries van der Poest also made small investments. In Bordeaux the ratio of small investors was just under 80 percent of total owners. Then there is the example of the *Saint George* (ID 24929) of Chester, which had ten owners of the venture from Bonny to Barbados in 1753, three of whom were "apprentices."[78] Scattered information on fathers' occupations, also from PAST, again reveals middling sorts of origins – a sea captain, an apothecary, a stockbroker, and a couple with interests in Cape Breton – not surprising given Bordeaux's links with French Canada. In the largest French port, Nantes, the small investor ratio was close to three-quarters. For the two hundred investors identified in Lisbon between 1781 and 1830, small investors comprised 79 percent of the total. In the early English trade, even when the Royal African Company was at its most successful (between 1672 and 1712), we still have the names of 450 individuals who invested in transatlantic slaving ventures sailing independently of the RAC, mostly from London.[79] The outlier in this brief survey was, as we might expect, Liverpool, which at 50 percent had the lowest small-investor ratio of all major European slaving ports. Despite Liverpool's importance, however, it seems that overall, at least two-thirds of those Europeans with a direct financial interest in the business comprised minor investors, even though their investments could not have provided the bulk of slave trade financing. Their role has attracted little scholarly attention.[80]

The larger investors – defined as those holding equity in at least three voyages – included families already well-established in shipping and trade that had nothing to do with the slave trade. Pieter van Wickevoort was a director of the WIC, but his primary interest, together with his son, was

---

[77] See the IDs P_10829_0362, P_10829_0466, P_10840_0091 in PAST. Van Wickevoort & Van de Blocquery was the company with the Baltic and whaling interests.

[78] Maurice M. Schofield, "Chester Slave Trading Partnerships, 1750–1756," *Transactions of the Historic Society of Lancashire and Cheshire*, 130 (1980): 187.

[79] Pettigrew, *Freedom's Debt*, pp. 227–39.

[80] However, Pope, probably overstates the case in "Wealth and Social Aspirations," p. 184, when he argues "the vast majority [of Liverpool slave traders] were small investors who quickly disappeared from the trade." Joseph Inikori reflects the erroneous majority view in the historiography in arguing that fewer than a dozen rich merchants controlled the Liverpool traffic (Inikori, "Market Structure and the Profits of the British African Trade in the Late Eighteenth Century," *Journal of Economic History*, 41 (1981): 744).

the Baltic and whaling trades. Both the original and the Nieuw WIC shared investors with the Dutch East India Company (the VOC) and captains, too. The most complete set of financial records for a major trader – the Davenport papers – indicate a wide range of business investments that generated more than one-third of William Davenport's net income. It is highly probable that very few traders relied exclusively on slaves for their income.[81] In the nineteenth century national flags became less important as ownership reverted to multinational groups, with vessels sometimes sailing with faux papers or often without any papers at all. There is no evidence of the major Nantes families re-entering the post-1814 business as the French traffic revived. As already discussed, the organizational base of the traffic shifted back to the Americas, but investors on the scale of the large eighteenth-century Liverpool families never emerged elsewhere. Moreover, in Rhode Island, Sean Kelley has calculated that 71 percent of seagoing ventures owned by individuals identified as slave traders between 1768 and 1775 had nothing to do with the slave trade.[82] The new data on ownership suggest that the Atlantic world had very few merchants who specialized in slave trading.

As argued in Chapter 2, Portugal's pattern of equity in the slave trade was quite unique in Europe and had more in common with ownership in Asian and Brazilian commerce than with the rest of the European trade. It is particularly striking that the Portuguese and Spanish dominated the Atlantic slave trade from beginning to end without ever developing the large family firms present in British and French slave trafficking. By far the largest single slave-trading firm in Portugal was the Companhia Geral do Grao Para e Maranhão. Between 1755 and 1788, it forcibly removed almost 30,000 people from the Bissau and Cacheu region in Upper Guinea using the northern Atlantic gyre. Ownership data is, however, inadequate for analysis for the pre-1700 era. For the long eighteenth century to 1812, data exist for just over half of the 676 slaving ventures recorded as leaving Portugal. The Para and Maranhäo company owned 151 of this sample. The top 10 percent of owners accounted for only 35 percent of captives. A further 227 slave vessels set sail from Iberian ports between 1813 and

---

[81] Radburn, *Traders in Men*, 36–38, 210–13; Pope, "Wealth and Social Aspirations," pp. 185–86; Jane Longmore, "'Cemented by the Blood of a Negro'? The Impact of the Slave Trade on Eighteenth-Century Liverpool," in Richardson et al., *Liverpool and Transatlantic Slavery*, pp. 227–51.

[82] Sean M. Kelley, "A 'Slaving Port'?: The Captive and Conventional Trades in Newport, Rhode Island, 1768–1775," in Kenneth Morgan (ed.), *The Routledge History of the Modern Maritime World since 1500* (forthcoming in 2025).

1865 – four-fifths from Lisbon and Cadiz – and yet no individual investor can be linked to more than ten of these ventures. Nevertheless, such data exaggerates the degree of ownership concentration, given that the record frequently contains only the name of the principal owner.

In addition, Portuguese slave traders made extensive use of sea loans, a medieval credit instrument where the lender assumed the risks of the loan and the borrower repaid the principal and interest only if the venture was successful with amounts tied to a specific vessel and voyage.[83] Interest rates were extremely high compared to borrowing rates in northern Europe, but the option was available to large and small investors alike. There is abundant evidence of seamen, skilled workers, and small traders, some organized into societies, using sea loans to engage in transoceanic trade.[84] Moreover, as described in the previous chapter, crew members made small ventures in lieu of wages. As a consequence, vessels left Africa with numerous small batches of slaves on board with a different owner for each batch, a practice that runs through the Lusophone slave trade from the *Madanela Cansyna* in 1513 to the 25 voyages mentioned in letters written between 1848 and 1850 from Bahia and found in King Kosoko's house in Lagos at the end of the Brazilian slave trade.[85] Equity in the Portuguese-dominated South Atlantic traffic must have been much more widely distributed than was its North Atlantic counterpart, widespread though ownership and participation was in Britain and the Netherlands. Certainly, private equity was responsible for the great majority of slave-trading ventures based in Portuguese and Brazilian ports. But the line

---

[83] Or much older again. "This type of loan was not much different from the antique bottomry loans whose essential elements are already described in the Hammurabi code issued around 2250 BC ... " Quentin van Doosselaere, *Commercial Agreements and Social Dynamics in Medieval Genoa* (Cambridge, 2009), p. 129.

[84] Hicks, *Captive Cosmopolitans*, chapter 4; Bohorquez. "Linking the Atlantic and Indian Oceans," 24–29. Bohorquez argues that sea loans effectively integrated the Indian and Atlantic Ocean pools of credit, but most of his examples are from Asia rather than the transatlantic slave trade.

[85] Olatunji Ojo, "Document 2: Letters Found in the House of Kosoko, King of Lagos (1851)," *African Economic History*, 40 (2012): 37–126. The year name and IDs of the vessels are: 1848 *Andorinha*, ID 3778; *Calumnia*, ID 3772; *Mequelina*, ID 4585; *Segunda Andorinha*, ID 3788. 1849 *Rosita*, ID 3963; *Pardal, Italia, União* (no IDs); *Segredo*, ID 3961; *Vencedora*, ID 4776; *Bom Destino*, ID 3962; *Igualdade*, ID 3966. 1850 *Bom Destino*, ID 4597; *Vencedora, Andorinha, Felicidade* (no IDs); *Esperanca*, ID 4971; *Industrie* (no ID); *Polka*, ID 4599; *Mosquito*, ID 4598; 3a *Andorinha, Diligente, Andorinha Feliz* (no IDs); *Mariquinha*, ID 4607; *Uniao* (no ID); *Liberal*, ID 4612; *Dos Amigos (Irmaos)*, ID 4617.

between capitalists and workers in such ventures is awkward if not impossible to divine.[86]

The closest parallel to this Portuguese pattern may be observed in the small Brandenburg traffic where the Brandenburg African Company tolerated crew members including junior officers holding private ventures in the business.[87] Clearly only a small minority of Europeans invested in the slave trade and the above analysis is not intended to suggest that small investors contributed the bulk of financing for the business. Rather the intention is to demonstrate that a wide range of people invested in an activity that appeared to them to be no different from trading in farm animals or in inanimate commodities. Risk, profit, and loss were the sole considerations. If the returns from the slave trade were somewhat higher than in other lines of business, it was not because of investors avoiding the business for moral reasons. In the rapidly developing pamphlet and newspaper cultures of the seventeenth- and early eighteenth-century, Dutch, French, and British voices such as Willem Usselinx, Jean Bodin, Thomas Tryon, and John Atkins casting doubt on slavery and the slave trade between 1560 and 1760 win a lot of attention. They are seen as precursors of the abolitionist critique that began to receive mass support in the last quarter of the eighteenth century, but this in no way deterred investors even in the twenty years prior to abolition. Boycotts of sugar beginning in 1792 there may have been, but there is no trace of boycotts of shares in slaving ventures even as late as 1807.

Finally, we should note that for more than a millennium Christians were held in slavery in North Africa, and Muslims likewise in Europe, as well as after 1600 in the Americas also. Some were redeemed, most were not. The Barbary corsairs ensured that the number of Europeans held in such captivity increased along with the growth of the transatlantic slave trade. Sailing ships navigating the English Channel to and from the Atlantic often spent weeks waiting for favorable winds, particularly westbound vessels. Channel ports became safe havens, with "the Downs,"

---

[86] Menz, "Uma comunidade em movimento"; Bohorquez and Menz, "State Contractors and Global Brokers"; Ribeiro da Silva, "Crossing Empires: Portuguese, Sephardic, and Dutch Business Networks"; Bohorquez, "Linking the Atlantic and Indian Oceans," 19–38; Bohorquez, "Para além do Atlântico Sul: fundamentos institucionais e financeiros do tráfico de escravos do Rio de Janeiro em finais do século XVIII," *Revista de Historia*, 178 (2019): 1–4.

[87] Craig Koslofsky and Roberto Zaugg, "Ship's Surgeon, Johann Peter Oettinger A Hinterlander in the Atlantic Slave Trade, 1682–1696," in Felix Brahm and Eve Rosenhaft (eds.), *Slavery Hinterland: Transatlantic Slavery and Continental Europe, 1680–1850* (London, 2016), pp. 25–44.

a shallow anchorage off Deal, being the most prominent. In the first week of November 1721, among the ships taking shelter were four who had or were intending to have a human cargo. Two of them were naval vessels full of redeemed – meaning purchased – English slaves from Salé in modern Morocco, one of the principal centers of the Barbary corsairs. A third was a Maryland-bound vessel carrying sixty-two convicts – coincidentally, shortly to experience a spectacular rebellion by prisoners. The fourth was a Royal African Company vessel on its way to buy 200 slaves for Jamaica. This small group of British ships, conceivably anchored next to each other, encapsulated the European solution to the labor shortages following on from overseas expansion. These vessels were buying both White and Black captives, the naval ships bound for England and freedom, and the slave ship to Africa/Caribbean and slavery. The convict group had intermediate status in that its members were banished for seven- or fourteen-year terms. Given that convicts would have been sold on arrival (but were nevertheless not slaves), what we have here are three varieties of the extreme commodification of humanity. More important in this context, no European would have seen anything remarkable, much less ironic, in this juxtaposition of voyages. If pressed, a European observer – like the Maori chief 114 years later in the Chatham Islands, mentioned in Chapter 1 – may well have said "it was in accordance with our custom."[88]

Thousands of captains, seamen and even some owners of slaves were themselves enslaved during the slave trade era without this having any apparent impact on their views of slavery. Claas Jacobs was enslaved in Morocco but continued in the slave trade when eventually redeemed – rising to captain the slaver *Lea* in 1787.[89] A century earlier the Earl of Inchiquin was captured and enslaved by Barbary pirates for a year, but when redeemed became Governor of Jamaica and suppressed a slave uprising there in 1691.[90] James Irving captained the slave ship *Anna* in 1789, was captured en route to Africa, enslaved and sold to Mawlay 'Abd al- Rahman, son of the Emperor of Morocco. Ransomed almost

---

[88] Daily Courant, November 5, 1721; Deal, November 8, 1721. For the Hamilton see https://slavevoyages.org/voyages/GkLNpf9h.

[89] Amsterdam City Archives, 5075, inv.nr. 12437, October 14, 1777; https://slavevoyages.org/voyages/o2Kt7R4F. See also the case of Pieter Allards Grootschaar in Amsterdam City Archives, 5075, inv.nr. 6749, August 13, 1712.

[90] *Dictionary of Irish Biography*: https://dib.cambridge.org/viewReadPage.do;jsessionid=6462AF96298C5E77B42F9B41AD039D9D?articleId=a6502; Diary of Samuel Pepys, entry for Nov. 28, 1661.

two years later, he returned to the trade immediately as captain of the *Ellen*. Irving noted the large number of enslaved crews of French ships working in the fields where he was held.[91] Later abolitionist John Newton was also enslaved and forced to work on an African plantation but captained three slave voyages after his release, all of them after experiencing a profound religious experience.[92] Pieter Grootschaar captained two West-Indische Compagnie voyages before spending seven years enslaved in North Africa. There is no evidence that any of these men changed their minds about the slave trade. True, slave-ship captain John Newton did become an abolitionist, but his conversion to the cause occurred many years later.[93] Near-death experiences made no difference, either. Stephen Deane captained eight voyages to the Gambia and thence to South Carolina or Georgia between 1765 and 1773. The seventh was ended by a slave revolt that destroyed the vessel and left only two survivors in a ship's boat on the open sea, one of whom was Captain Deane, the other an African captive. Undeterred, Deane returned to England and obtained the command of another slaving expedition, this one completed to the satisfaction of the owners, and presumably himself.[94] Not covered here are the thousands of captives of European descent, not connected directly to slavery and the slave trade who were held by the Barbary pirates. One can scour their narratives, too, without finding, at least until the age of abolition, any traces of abhorrence of slavery as opposed to an abhorrence of being enslaved.[95]

Captivity stories are of course scattered throughout the history of slavery, including in the Bible. But personal experience as either an enslaver or an enslaved person did not lead any to question the institution's legitimacy, an issue taken up again in Chapter 5 in the African context. In not one case did the experience of enslavement provoke a reaction in the captive other than that slavery was one of life's risks to be avoided at all costs yet taken advantage of when possible. In this respect most of the eighteenth

---

[91] Voyage IDs 80295, 81242. For Irving's diary, see Suzanne Schwarz (ed.), *Slave Captain: The Career of James Irving in the Liverpool Slave Trade* (Liverpool, 1995), and on his continued pro-slavery views, see especially pp. 42, 66–67.
[92] Bernard Martin and Mark Spurrell (eds.), *The Journal of a Slave Trader (John Newton)* (London, 1962), p. 63.
[93] See Eltis, *Rise of African Slavery*, pp. 233, 299–300; Schwarz, *Slave Captain*, 68. For Grootschaar, see www.slavevoyages.org/enslaver/vpLlNMv4.
[94] *Gentleman's Magazine*, October 1773, p. 523; Lloyd's List, June 18, 1773; *South Carolina Gazette*, May 31, 1773.
[95] See especially the many cases discussed in Paul Baepler (ed.), *White Slaves, African Masters: An Anthology of American Barbary Captive Narrative* (Chicago, IL, 1999), passim.

century – when abolitionism as a movement originated – was no different from the preceding four millennia, back to when the first written evidence of slavery in Mesopotamia has survived. Over this period, it is likely that very few captives indeed became convinced by their experience as a slave that slavery itself should not exist.[96] Modern attitudes to the slave-free dichotomy where anyone enslaved is automatically assumed to be opposed to slavery, make it impossible to understand the shared mindset of most Europeans and Africans of the pre-1800 era on this issue.

The group of people with a direct interest in the trade constituted a wide cross section of European society – from rich to poor, from Quakers to Catholic priests, from political radicals to monarchists, from ordinary seamen to Humphry Morice, Governor of the Bank of England, and sponsor of eighty-three slave voyages. From Queen Anne, the second largest shareholder of the South Sea Company, to the cabin boys on the 653 Royal African Company slave voyages – and certainly not the several hundred shareholders of the RAC over its sixty-year existence – no one had any moral or humanitarian cause to avoid the business. The stream of Europeans migrating to the West Indies to take up supervisory positions on plantations continued well into the abolitionist era. The poet Robert Burns, famed for challenging the social order with often bitter satire, nevertheless resolved to emigrate to a Jamaican plantation. He booked a berth on a ship leaving Greenock in September 1786 and withdrew just prior to departure only because of the sudden and unexpected success of his celebrated first book, *Poems, Chiefly in the Scottish Dialect*. Given his energetic love life in Ayrshire, he might well have sexually outperformed Thomas Thistlewood, his near contemporary, had he embarked.[97]

We do not know the share of the population that owned slaves in the eighteenth-century colonies, but we do know that when Britain compensated its slave owners in the aftermath of the abolition of slavery itself the vast majority of those claiming compensation "owned only a handful of slaves," most of whom will remain unidentified but certainly included many doctors, clergymen, and soldiers' widows across British society.[98] Across the Americas, runaway slaves formed independent societies in remote regions of land-abundant plantation colonies. Called *quilombos*

---

[96] See also the many captivity memoirs of White people captured by the Indigenous peoples of North America.

[97] Burnard, *Mastery, Tyranny, and Desire*; John Campbell Shairp, *Robert Burns* (Cambridge, 2011, first published 1879), p. 27.

[98] Nicholas Draper, *The Price of Emancipation: Slave-Ownership, Compensation, and British Society at the End of Slavery* (Cambridge, 2010), pp. 147, 204.

in Brazil, *palenques* in Spanish America, and maroon communities in Jamaica and Surinam, they survived in many cases through to abolition and down to the present. But they, too, held enslaved people. The Accompong Town maroons in Jamaica petitioned the colonial government in 1840 for compensation for their slaves freed by the British abolition act, unsuccessfully as it turned out. And in Brazil, some slaves were also themselves slave owners for a further five decades after this.[99] Until the late eighteenth century there is no reason to think that conceptions of morality, and more specifically, attitudes to slavery and the slave trade of the above slices of society were any different from those of the rest of the population. Today's value systems are ill-equipped to explore slavery and slave trading of the past. Applying modern values to all historical figures would surely reveal the racist attitudes of every one of such figures. There would be no statues or plaques left standing to anyone living before the late eighteenth century.

Finally, awareness and acceptance of slavery at all levels of society was implicit in consumer behavior. The root cause of the slave plantations in the Americas was not the avarice of powerful slave merchants scattered across Europe's ports and financial centers, but rather the tastes of consumers across the income spectrum. From one perspective – as discussed in Chapter 1 – consumer demand for plantation produce such as tobacco, sugar, coffee, and alcohol, comprised trivial additions to consumer diets. They added nothing to the shelter, core foodstuffs, and clothing of ordinary people. Other tropical goods such as dyes for textiles, rice, and raw cotton *were* core products, but always comprised a tiny share of global output before the nineteenth century. In another sense, as discussed below, they constituted the birth of the non-material needs that encompass status. Cocoa in Spain, coffee in France and the Netherlands, eventually tea in Britain, and tobacco, alcohol, and sugar everywhere in Western Europe had themselves become necessities by the end of the slave trade. As Carole Shammas observes, "almost every overseas settlement controlled by Western Europeans had a direct or indirect relationship to [the] demand for tropical consumer goods."[100] Everyone knew how these were obtained. Against a few isolated individuals expressing reservations

---

[99] Manolo Florentino and Márcia Amantino, "Runaways and Quilombolas in the Americas," in CWHS3, p. 737; Alycia Hall, "Strategic Ties: Family, Land, and Plantation Connections in Maroon Jamaica," unpublished PhD thesis, Yale University (Department of History, 2024).

[100] Carole Shammas, "The Revolutionary Impact of European Demand for Tropical Goods," in McCusker and Morgan, *Early Modern Atlantic Economy*, p. 183.

about holding people as property we have hundreds of thousands of people directly involved in trading people and electing to go to the slave colonies to pursue careers on plantations. In addition, consumption of slave-grown products across all sectors of the population increased rapidly, and huge investment in the tropical plantations occurred. An organized boycott of sugar, largely ineffective, did occur late in the abolition era. Yet as slave plantations spread across the Caribbean after 1640, consumers were happy to take advantage of falling sugar prices, sailors to accept any higher wages associated with a Guinea voyage, merchants to reap new investment opportunities, and governments (national and municipal) to receive higher tax revenues.

IMPACT OF THE SLAVE TRADE ON EUROPE

Everyone in Europe was aware of the horrors of slavery and the slave trade, but what did the traffic contribute to European welfare? We begin with the merchandise that European nations shipped to Africa. Europe consistently produced about half the goods traded on Africa's Atlantic coast – a little more in West Africa, a little less in West Central Africa. Asia and the Americas supplied the other half in roughly equal proportions. These ratios held from the 1680s onward when the Bahian and Pernambuco tobacco traffic became important, and when all Western European countries had established strong trading connections with Asia and the Indian Ocean. No single European nation could supply the extraordinary range of goods and produce that Africans required in exchange for the enslaved. The great diversity of cultures and resources in sub-Saharan Africa ensured a matching diversity in regional consumer tastes that could be met only by drawing on global supply chains. A typical post-1680 slave trading cargo would include items from every continent between the Arctic and Antarctic.

The early voyages leaving Portugal and Spain, even before the transatlantic traffic got underway, exchanged merchandise from all over Europe for enslaved people. The customs accounts for fifteen vessels arriving in Santiago in the Cape Verdes between 1513 and 1515 show textiles from a wide range of European countries as well as containers, both earthenware and metal, dominating the trade goods, with English cloth making up the largest category. Iron and beads, so important in later trade in this region, are absent in these early years, iron because the Portuguese crown banned the sale to Africans of weapons or the materials to make them, notwithstanding the fact that African iron was available from Mende traders and sometimes made its way back to Portugal.[101] By 1526 according to the trade book of a vessel buying slaves in Sierra Leone and the southern rivers of Senegambia, semiprecious beads and brass bracelets, probably German or Italian, had become the third most important merchandise group. By the early seventeenth century East Indian textiles and iron expanded the range of offerings.[102] Later in the century the Royal African Company records show iron, much of it made in Sweden, becoming central to trading in Upper Guinea to the point where "bars" became the unit of account in the region through to the end of the slave trade era.[103] For 1684 to 1692, we have the accounts of a major Luanda slave trader that show textiles – mostly East Indian – accounting for two-thirds of trade goods, with beads and alcohol comprising a further 10 percent. Metals and weapons were of trivial importance.[104]

From 1785 to the end of the traffic we have the best evidence of trade goods in the history of the slave trade, with details of merchandise exchanged for nearly 700,000 captives as recorded in the Luanda custom house.[105] Here, too, textiles predominated – accounting for 54.7 percent of total values – with, as we might expect in a period spanning industrialization, European cloth gradually replacing its Asian competitor. The entry of English, Dutch, French, and American colonists into the business had little effect on the type of merchandise imported into Africa from the Americas. Alcohol and tobacco arrived from the New World, but overall, 50–60 percent of imports comprised English woolens, Silesian linens, Swedish iron bars, Dutch pans and pottery, and sundry other manufactured goods. Metal goods, including weaponry, rarely

[101] Elbl, "The Portuguese Trade with West Africa," p. 454.
[102] See the logbook of the *Santiago*, which carried 108 captives to Lisbon in 1526 from the Cape Verde islands and the customs receipt books for the islands recording slave arrivals from Africa as well a slave-ship departure for overseas markets in the 1510s in Hall, *Before Middle Passage*, pp. 227–40; East Indian textiles formed only 1 percent of Portuguese imports from Asia in the early sixteenth century, rising to only 10 percent by 1700. However, in 1617 the Portuguese sold 15,000 Indian "Guinea cloths" at São Jorge da Mina (Giorgio Riello, *Cotton: The Fabric that Made the Modern World* [Cambridge, 2013], pp. 90–91).
[103] Newson and Minchin, *From Capture to Sale*, pp. 38–49. For an inventory of the Royal African Company fort at James Island in the Gambia see T70/20, ff. 55–56, dated Sept. 27, 1680.
[104] Joseph C. Miller, "Capitalism and Slaving: The Financial and Commercial Organization of the Angolan Slave Trade according to the Accounts of Antonio Coelho Guerreiro (1684–1692), *International Journal of African Historical Studies*, 17 (1984): 1–52.
[105] Daniel B. Domingues da Silva, *The Atlantic Slave Trade from West Central Africa, 1780–1867* (Cambridge, 2017), pp. 176–99.

reached 10 percent, and alcohol and tobacco accounting for much of the remainder was a pattern that held throughout for Western African imports from Arguim in the north to Benguela in the south.[106] This, despite pronounced regional variations in African consumer preferences. Beads and shells could be vital in initiating trade but were of small importance overall.[107]

Each of the major Western slave-trading countries had their own textile manufacturers so that production was widely distributed geographically. Merchants in major ports like Nantes, Middelburg, and Liverpool placed orders locally for cloth based on the latest reports from West Africa about shifting African tastes. To show the significance of the African market to Europe we can select the five-year period when slave sales on the coast were at their greatest and multiply the number of slaves by the average price per slave. Between 1786 and 1790 – just prior to the St. Domingue slave rebellion – slave traders carried off an extraordinary 505,000 enslaved people, about 4 percent of the total 350-year traffic in just five years. Multiplying the annual totals for these years by the average price gives us the annual value of the trade FOB (free on board) in Europe, when that trade was at its greatest.[108] The five-year total of 65.8 million is in constant pounds sterling (year 1700=100), or L13.1 million a year, but only 55 percent of that annual figure comprised European merchandise. Measured against the total population of Western Europe of 100 million, or that sub-continent's total merchandise exports, this amount is certainly trivial. After converting from official values to real values, exports to Africa account for 1–2 percent of British, Dutch, or French total trade after excluding merchandise exchanged by slave traders for produce rather than people.[109] For most years of the

---

[106] For the 1780s replacing row 3 in table 8 of Eltis, "Trade Between Western Africa," 218, with Daniel Domingues' data for Angola, 1785–1794, makes little difference to the weighted average.

[107] For the continued importance of beads and their provenance in Europe, see Anne Ruderman, "Intra-European Trade in Atlantic Africa and the African Atlantic," *William and Mary Quarterly*, 77 (2020): 211–44.

[108] Data for such a calculation are readily available. Prices from David Richardson, "Prices of Slaves in West and West-Central Africa: Towards an Annual Series, 1698–1807," *Bulletin of Economic Research*, 43 (1991): 55. Slave departures taken from www.slavevoyages.org/estimates/VT7Ysmzw.

[109] Ralph Davis, *The Industrial Revolution and British Overseas Trade* (Leicester, 1979), p. 89; Jan de Vries and Ad van der Woude, *The First Modern Economy: Success, Failure and Perseverance of the Dutch Economy, 1500–1815* (Cambridge, 1997), p. 499; Tarrade, *Le commerce colonial*. For the rising importance of African commodity exports at the end of the eighteenth century, see Angus Dalrymple and Pieter Woltjer,

Europe and Atlantic Slave Trading   145

slave trade era the ratio would have been a small fraction of one percent. In Peter Coclanis' words:

> ... the big story of early modern Europe was local and regional integration, economic integration, of course, but political and cultural integration as well. The most important trades were not the long-distance trades ... but both short-haul trades and less glamorous Continental trades (whether "bulk" or "rich") linking southern Europe to Northern Europe and Eastern Europe to the west.[110]

For particular ports the impact might be different and indeed, our best records for the slave trade derive from the ports that organized and dispatched slave ships, whether official documents, newspapers, or the private papers of slave merchants.[111] Yet, as Coclanis suggests, a broader perspective indicates that the traffic sustaining overseas slavery was relatively small.

The latest attempt to defend the primacy of slavery in the economic development of the Western World is Maxine Berg and Pat Hudson, *Slavery, Capitalism and the Industrial Revolution* or SCIR. However, this publication does not use TSTD correctly and offers arguments that the slavevoyages data do not support.[112] The central claim is that British slavery dominated the economy when the slave trade was at its height, between 1730 and 1807. It is certainly correct that the British transatlantic slave trade was the largest in this period, but in second place the Portuguese were never far behind – in the 1740s, 1776–1785, and again in 1803–1807, the Portuguese recovered their dubious first-place distinction. But, in any event, the slave trade was a relatively small part of the plantation complex. One needs to see where the enslaved ultimately disembarked. Berg and Hudson ignore what slavevoyages tells us about this and, just as important, they ignore the intra-American traffic that now has its own database on slavevoyages. More than one-fifth of disembarkations from British transatlantic slave ships occurred in ports outside the British Empire. Moreover, large numbers of Africans who did land in British territory were quickly sold on to other jurisdictions after their transatlantic passage. Adjusting for these patterns drastically changes our view of the dominant slaving power as the Industrial Revolution unfolded. As Table 2.4 makes clear, the largest

---

"Commodities, Prices and Risk: The Changing Market for non-slave Products in pre-Abolition in West Africa": www.aehnetwork.org/wp-content/uploads/2016/10/AEHN-WP-31.pdf.
[110] Peter A. Coclanis, "Drang Nach Osten: Bernard Bailyn, the World-Island, and the Idea of Atlantic History," *Journal of World History*, 13 (2002): 176.
[111] For Liverpool, see Longmore, "'Cemented by the Blood of a Negro'?" pp. 227–51.
[112] The first reference in SCIR to www.slavevoyages.com confuses the database itself with the estimates page. See p. 34, n. 1.

markets for slaves in the Americas were never British, or indeed French, but were always Brazilian and Spanish American. As argued in Chapter 2, it is likely that the total colonial output of both these regions always greatly exceeded that of Jamaica or St. Domingue, and for most years was greater than the combined total of these two colonies.[113]

There is, however, a more fundamental flaw in SCIR. The body of the text is a 216-page catalogue of what reads like all possible connections between individual slave traders and their businesses on the one hand, and the economy that lay beyond the slave trade on the other. The list must be by far the most complete ever assembled. Example is piled on example. but it is essentially descriptive and is in line with the numerous essay-length studies on Dutch involvement in the business that have appeared recently.[114] Despite the title of SCIR and the strong economic history background of its two authors, their book has a startling lack of analysis. All studies that track slave-trader interactions with the rest of the economy make the implicit assumption that without the slave trade the resources in the contact industry, for example, textiles, would have sat idle. Prices, however, would have adjusted, and many textiles would have found alternative buyers.[115]

Sixty years ago, Robert W. Fogel set out to answer an equally large question.[116] Faced with generations of historians who had stressed the crucial contribution of the railroads to US economic growth, he determined to find just how big this contribution might be. Almost all historians ignore market adjustments in the allocation of resources that would have occurred if an industry or an innovation had not existed. Few of them engage with the concept of value added, which forms the core of modern National Income accounting. Using extensive data collection and large

---

[113] For the French and British cases, see Charles K. Harley, "Slavery, the British Atlantic Economy, and the Industrial Revolution," in A.B. Leonard and David Pretel (eds.), *The Caribbean and the Atlantic World Economy: Circuits of Trade, Money and Knowledge, 1650–1914* (New York, 2015), pp. 161–83.

[114] Karwan Fatah-Black and Matthias van Rossum, "Beyond Profitability: The Dutch Transatlantic Slave Trade and Its Economic Impact," *Slavery & Abolition*, 36 (2015): 1–21; Pepijn Brandon and Ulbe Bosma, "Slavery and the Dutch Economy, 1750–1800," *Slavery & Abolition*, 42: (2021): 43–76, doi: 10.1080/0144039X.2021.1860464. For a paper with a narrower focus centered on Jamaica to which this same critique applies, see Jenny Bulstrode, "Black Metallurgists and the Making of the Industrial Revolution," History and Technology, 2023, doi: 10.1080/07341512.2023.2220991.

[115] The precise amount of the adjustment would depend on the price elasticities of demand and supply. None of the studies in the preceding paragraph make allowance for this effect.

[116] Robert W. Fogel, *Railroads and American Economic Growth: Essays in Econometric History* (Baltimore, MD, 1964).

numbers of simultaneous equations, Fogel's answer was that in 1900 without railroads, US GNP would have been just 5 percent below the actual figure. Resources would have moved into the canal sector, among others, thus ensuring that railroads had only a modest impact on the economy. But Fogel's key finding was that in a modern economy, no single innovation or industry is going to have a large impact. There is no room for such a conclusion in SCIR. Even though Britain never had the largest slave empire and even though the Iberian powers clearly did, but never showed traces of industrialization, the authors are certain that their long list of descriptive links between the slave sector and the rest of the economy is evidence of slavery triggering accelerating economic growth first in Britain.

But the most dramatic indication of the triviality of the slave trade to the economy of any given port comes from Liverpool. In 1799 and 1800, more slave-trading ventures left this port than any other in history. In 1799, the busiest slave-trading year experienced by any single Atlantic port, a slaving voyage left Liverpool every three days. Because we also have a good idea of the Atlantic total traffic in these years, we can say that Liverpool's 267 slaving ventures accounted for almost half the transatlantic slave traffic from all Atlantic ports combined. This is an extraordinary ratio, and we can add tonnage data. TSTD tells us that Liverpool slave vessels averaged 155 tons in 1799–1800. Over two years the gross tonnage of Liverpool's slave-trading fleet at its all-time peak was thus 41,385. How does this compare with other shipping leaving Liverpool in these years? A well-known commercial dictionary of the time provides the answer. A total of 9,264 voyages paid dock duties in 1799–1800 on vessels which had a total tonnage of 878,382. Therefore, slave-trading ventures leaving Liverpool at a time when the port accounted for nearly half the total Atlantic slave trade accounted for 2.9 percent of total shipping and 4.7 percent of total shipping tonnage. At most other times, for example in peacetime, these ratios would have been very much smaller again.[117]

We also have close to complete data on the ownership of slave-trading voyages departing from Liverpool. We know that 950 persons took an equity interest in at least one voyage leaving the port between 1779 and

---

[117] For Liverpool data, see www.slavevoyages.org/voyages/Xoe1tU5e; J. R. McCulloch, *A Dictionary, Practical, Theoretical and Historical of Commerce and Commercial Navigation*, 2 vols (Philadelphia, 1840), vol. 1: 599–600. I thank Steve Behrendt for drawing this source to my attention.

1807, years when industrialization was well underway. As already noted, very few of this group invested in the slave trade alone – perhaps no more than thirty. Involvement in the slave trade must have accounted for a tiny fraction of total wealth in the county of Lancashire where both Liverpool and much of the early English Industrial Revolution were located. By 1750 Liverpool had grown from a seventeenth-century fishing village to the fourth largest city in England but given the above data, the slave trade by itself cannot have been the primary cause. More likely candidates are the port's trading links with Ireland and the Americas broadly defined. Moreover, the port's most dramatic expansion occurred after the slave trade ended. When the slave trade was close to its peak Thomas Clarkson researched the port's economy (1788–1789). He found that the diversity of Liverpool's economy was such that it would comfortably survive abolition, and of course he was correct in that by 1851 Liverpool had become the second largest English city despite the ending of the slave trade. Later in the century, no less than 40 percent of all global trade passed through the port.[118] A few years after Clarkson's assessment, future Lord Chancellor Henry Brougham correctly forecast that "the various other branches of our foreign commerce which are understocked with capital would afford a ready and profitable employment for the small pittance thrown out of the slave trade."[119] Thirty years after British abolition of the slave trade, dock duties in Liverpool were paid by 15,038 vessels with a combined tonnage of almost 2 million (1837). Clarkson and Brougham were proved correct. If the slave trade had never existed, then income, employment, or any indicator of human welfare in Liverpool or England could not have been much different to the historical reality.[120]

But what about the countries apart from Britain? Excluding the Brazilian-based traffic, Portugal was not one of the region's major slave-trading countries after 1640, but it is worth noting that despite a near monopoly of the trade between Europe and Africa in the very early period, as early as 1520 the revenues of the Lisbon slave house and the Lisbon

---

[118] Stephen D. Behrendt and Nicholas Radburn, *History of the Liverpool Slave Trade* (forthcoming), chapter 10; Zoe Dare Hall, "Ferry Across the Mersey," *Financial Times*, May 12, 2023.

[119] Henry Brougham, *A Concise Statement of the Question Regarding the Abolition of the Slave Trade* (London, 1804), p. 35.

[120] For an alternative view, see Barbara L. Solow, *The Economic Consequences of the Atlantic Slave Trade* (Lanham, MD, 2014). The issue was first raised by Eric Williams, *Capitalism and Slavery* (London, 1944).

Guinea house were already falling behind the value of the traffic in gold from Mina in Africa, as well as the East Indian trade.[121] The country's participation in the massive Spanish American project modifies this picture. Down to 1640 we have records of 308 voyages leaving Portugal carrying off 108,000 slaves, but again the annual average of departures during the sixty years of the union of the two crowns was small. It may also, of course, be incomplete.[122] The Spanish and Portuguese Americas cumulatively produced far more exports by value than did their English-speaking counterparts. The importance of Iberian colonial exports to their respective metropolitan economies was far greater than were the British plantation economies to Britain.[123] In the final analysis, all scholars who see slavery as the foundation of quickening growth in the metropole must deal with the Portuguese case. A recent study of that nation's economy during the whole era of the slave trade, 1527 to 1850, generates striking results fatal to the argument that slavery enabled industrial capitalism. Portugal had the smallest population of all west European colonial nations, and thus in per capita terms was the nation with the largest potential per capita gains from slavery and its overseas riches. For more than three centuries Portugal was the leading Atlantic slave trader and, at least until 1825 when Brazil became independent, the possessor of the largest single source of plantation produce in the early modern Atlantic world. By 1750 Portuguese per capita GDP was high by European standards, though still significantly below British and Dutch levels. In the following century the volume of its slave trade and the value of Brazilian coffee exports increased to their greatest ever levels. What happened to per capita GDP in the face of these colonial activities? According to Palma and Reis in a statement surely fatal to those seeing links between slavery and economic growth:

Economic performance slowed down, but population grew strongly, and within half a century all of the GDP per capita and real wage gains were wiped out. Thereafter income per person continued to decline, with the consequence that by the middle of the nineteenth century Portugal became one of the most backward economies of

---

[121] Magalhaes Godhino, *L'economie de l'empire Portugaise aux XVe et XVIe siècles* (Paris, 1969), pp. 228–43; Vogt, "Lisbon Slave House," pp. 1–16.
[122] https://slavevoyages.org/voyages/YcQ8cU5m.
[123] William J. Ashworth, "*The Impact of Transatlantic Trade on the Commercialization of England, 1660–1700,*" in Guillaume Garner and Sandra Richter (eds.), *Wolfenbutteter Arbeiten zur Bacockforschung*, 54 (2016): 33–48; Nuala Zahedieh, *The Capital and the Colonies: London and the Atlantic Economy, 1660–1700* (Cambridge, 2012), pp. 4–33, 184–185, 236–277.

Europe ... Over the long run, there was no per capita growth: by 1850 per capita incomes were not different from what they had been in the early 1530s.[124]

Today, Portugal is the poorest country in the Western EU, despite Portuguese pre-eminence in the Atlantic slave trades. And income levels in its larger Iberian neighbor have always lagged those of Britain, France, and Germany despite its colonies for over three centuries absorbing far more slaves who produced far higher value exports than did its competitors. Major European countries such as Germany and Italy attained developed status without any large-scale dependence on coerced labor; outside Europe, Japan and South Korea likewise. Of the two major modern economic powers slavery was significant in the history of one – the US – and insignificant to the history of the other – China. But in the US case what does "significant" mean? For every enslaved person arriving in North America, seventeen arrived in the Iberian Americas. Moreover, slavery started earlier and lasted longer in the latter. Thanks to natural population growth the US slave population became the largest in the Americas, but colonial North America experienced strong economic growth before the slave labor force became significant (slaves comprised just 6 percent of the total population in 1776) and the US economy grew most rapidly after slavery was abolished eighty-seven years later.

Of the three northwestern European intruders in the Iberian Atlantic, historians have paid least attention to the economic impact of slavery on France. St. Domingue produced more sugar, rum, coffee, cotton, and indigo than the combined British Caribbean in the second half of the eighteenth century. But the French economy was much larger and, in any event, data for the late eighteenth century is not yet available.[125] But we do know that the British invaded St. Domingue in 1793 not to free slaves or end the slave trade but to incorporate the richest colony in the world into their own imperial system. This motivation also lay behind Napoleon's invasion in 1802. It is striking that reviews of the condition of the French economy in the late eighteenth century take no account of the loss of most of the French American colonial empire, the demise of which apparently had no effect on Napoleon's capacity to wage almost two decades of war on the rest of

---

[124] N. Palma and João Reis, "From Convergence to Divergence: Portuguese Economic Growth, 1527–1850," *Journal of Economic History*, 79 (2019): 477–506.

[125] What statistics we have can be found in Paul Bairoch, "L'économie Française dans le contexte Européen à la Fin Du XVIIIe Siècle," *Revue économique*, 40 (1989): 939–64, especially 955–59; Bairoch, "International Industrialization Levels from 1750 to 1980," *Journal of European Economic History*, 11 (1982): 269–333.

Europe. The most rapid industrialization of France before the twentieth century occurred in the 1850s and 1860s after slavery was abolished. For all its preeminence in the annals of slavery in the Americas, the rise and sudden fall of the St. Domingue slave economy, the largest in the plantation Americas, was apparently of small import to metropolitan France, including those Atlantic ports with the closest ties to the colony.

Similarly, the economy of the Netherlands grew very slowly in the second half of the eighteenth century. Historians have been misled by the fact that in this same period the Atlantic share of this trade increased as consumers bought more sugar, coffee, tobacco, and other plantation products.[126] In the 1770s the value of Dutch Atlantic imports surpassed the value of Asian imports even though Surinam plantations were not doing well at this time.[127] This development could not stave off an eighteenth-century decline of the Dutch economy relative to its neighbors, nor permit the Netherlands to experience industrialization ahead of the British. Eventually, the country "joined modern western industrial progress after 1860" about the same time as France, and, we might add, about the same time as the abolition of slavery in both countries.[128]

Too many regions have enforced the most exploitative forms of slavery for long periods of time without developing industrial capitalism, and too many others developed industrial capitalism without chattel slavery. Whatever the explanation for Britain's rise to prosperity and global power in the nineteenth century, slavery cannot have featured as one of the essential explanatory factors. Most economic historians would agree with Eric Hilt that:

[a]nyone wishing to argue for the centrality of slavery in capitalist development needs to consider what could have been possible without slavery and a world without American slavery but with the Industrial Revolution was indeed possible.

---

[126] Jan. de Vries, "The Dutch Atlantic Economies," in Peter A. Coclanis (ed.), *The Atlantic Economy during the Seventeenth and Eighteenth Centuries: Organization, Operation, Practice and Personnel,*" (Columbia, SC, 2005), pp. 1–29, 18–21; and the essays in Gert Oostindie, and Jessica V. Roitman (eds.), *Dutch Atlantic Connections, 1680–1800: Linking Empires, Bridging Borders* (Leiden, 2014).

[127] A. van Sipriaan, "The Suriname Rat Race: Labour and Technology on Sugar Plantations, 1750–1900," *The New West Indian Guide/Nieuwe West-Indische Gids*, 63 (1989): 94–117.

[128] See the special issue of *De Economist*, vol. 148 (2000), but especially Joel Mokyr, "The Industrial Revolution and the Netherlands: Why Did it Not Happen?" pp. 503–20, quote is from p. 503. For trade patterns and decline, see Gert Oostindie and Jessica V. Roitman, "Repositioning the Dutch in the Atlantic, 1680–1800," *Itinerario*, 36 (2012): 132; Wim Klooster and Gert Oostindie, *Realm between Empires: The Second Dutch Atlantic, 1680–1815* (Ithaca, NY, 2018), pp. 224–49.

Historians of capitalism wish to highlight the tragedy of American slavery by claiming it was essential for industrialization. I would argue that it is more tragic that slavery may not actually have been necessary.[129]

Slavery and the slave trade could have triggered accelerated economic growth at the imperial center only if there had been social and economic structures within the imperial power that were able to use colonial growth to make the transition to industrialization. It is these domestic patterns to which the historians of slavery need to direct their attention. To return to the larger argument, the human capital, especially maritime skills, plus the financial intermediaries and services that evolved in London, Amsterdam, and later, Nantes, allowed the northwestern nations to break into the slave trade, but these were not sufficient to displace the Portuguese and Spanish in the Atlantic world. A dispassionate look at the development paths of these five Western European nations suggests that successful participation in the slave trade and, beyond that, slavery in the Americas, was in no way a prerequisite of the sustained and permanent economic growth of Western Europe. What *was* a prerequisite were the institutions generated by the early modern economic growth of northwestern Europe that allowed the region to draw on expanding overseas trade. First causes were thus the domestic changes that enabled the economy to benefit from expanding trade.

---

[129] Eric Hilt, "Economic History, Historical Analysis, and the "New History of Capitalism," *Journal of Economic History*, 77 (2017): 530. Not a single scholar among those linking slavery in the Americas with accelerated growth in Europe – from Eric Williams through to, most recently, Koen van der Blij's otherwise useful essay ["Shareholders in the Dutch Atlantic Trade," *Tijdschrift Voor Sociale En Economische Geschiedenis* 19 (2022): 69–94] has engaged with this central counterfactual critique that lurks at the heart of all discussions of links between slavery and capitalism. The special issue of the journal, *Slavery & Abolition* in 2021, 42 (2021): 1–178, edited by Tamira Combrink and Matthias van Rossum) contains nine essays on "how global slaved-based economic activities and their spinoffs have contributed to economic development throughout Europe." One contributor, Filipa Ribeiro da Silva, in "The Profits of the Portuguese-Brazilian Slave Trade; Profits and Possibilities," does conclude that "[t]he Portuguese-Brazilian case challenges the idea that colonial economies produced only for the benefit of the metropole" (p. 103)." Yet Robin Blackburn has argued that planters could have used free labor with only modestly higher costs. See Blackburn, *The Making of New World Slavery: From the Baroque to the Modern, 1492–1800* (London, 2010), pp. 352–56.

4

The Portuguese System

For five decades after 1807, Freetown in Sierra Leone – the African center of British efforts to suppress the slave trade – contained a floating population of former slaver crews looking to return to their Brazilian and Cuban home ports after the British had detained their vessel.[1] In 1842, five sailors from a recently condemned slave ship stole a new 29-foot open boat just delivered from London for the use of the British officials of the Mixed Commission Courts. As the British Commissary judge related, the men "pulled up to the Rio Pongo where they either kidnapped or purchased five or six slaves, with whom ... they started for Brazil and arrived there in safety." No doubt a 29-foot boat was equipped with some sails, but the letter also specifies rowing. For this case and possibly other open launches in the database, perhaps slaves were forced to propel themselves to the Americas.[2] At the other end of the spectrum of the transoceanic slave experience were twenty-three steam-powered slave ships in the voyages database, averaging 361 tons and disembarking a mean of 1,004 captives – slave trading in the industrial era. One of them is displayed as Figure 3.1. And then there are the clipper ships of 600 tons or more. The *Orion* (ID 4807) had, according to the arresting officer in 1857, "the finest slave deck I have ever seen being about 8 feet in height and clear fore and aft."[3] In addition, blockades by the British squadron had forced it to leave the coast

---

[1] Parts of this chapter first appeared in Nicholas Radburn and David Eltis, "Visualizing the Middle Passage: The *Brooks* and the Reality of Ship Crowding in the Transatlantic Slave Trade," *Journal of Interdisciplinary History*, 49 (2019): 533–65.

[2] See BNA, James Hook, Sierra Leone, to Lord Palmerston, November 11, 1849, FO84/752; http://slavevoyages.org/voyages/sse2CNIZ.

[3] For the 29-ton vessel, see, Admiralty to Lord Aberdeen, Sept. 15, 1842 (enc.) BNA, FO84/441. The average height of the slave deck for 21 intercepted vessels between 1829 and 1860 was just 3.6 feet.

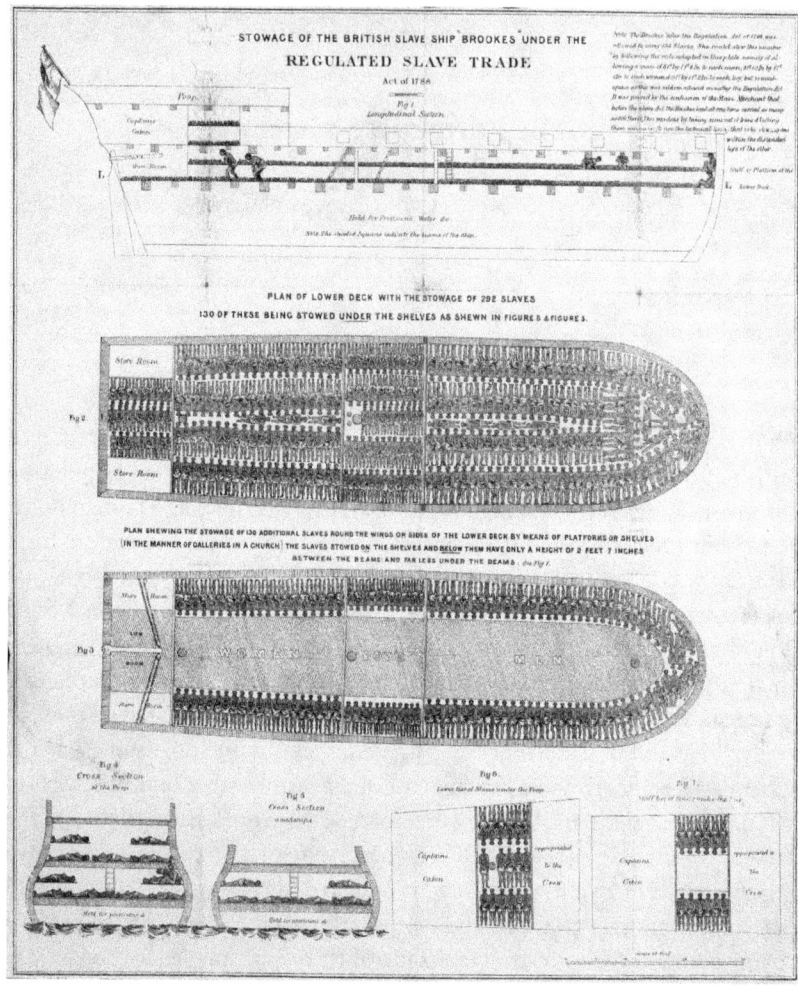

FIGURE 4.1 Image of the Liverpool slave ship *Brooks* according to the "Society for Effecting the Abolition of the Slave Trade: Description of a Slave Ship" (London, 1789). This was an abolitionist pamphlet showing the improbable distribution of captive Africans. Library of Congress, LC-USZ62-44000.

with only two-thirds of its intended captives on board.[4] Compare these with the iconic and highly misleading image of the *Brooks* (ID 80666; Figure 4.1) from 1788 and the very accurate paintings, by contrast, of the

---

[4] Steam ships are at https://slavevoyages.org/voyages/9zTLTFNr. For the *Orion*, see, Admiralty to Lord John Russell, March 13, 1860, enc. Lt. Simpson to Capt. Courtenay, Dec. 1, 1859, BNA, FO84/1123.

The Portuguese System

FIGURE 4.2 The *Marie-Séraphique* (ID 30941) showing the barricado midships. The image is part of the video accessible on the home page of www.slavevoyages.org. Reproduced with permission of Private collections, Nantes History Museum.

Marie-Séraphique (ID 30910; Figure 4.2, Figure 4.3) from two decades earlier, and it is hard to believe that all these vessels (*Marie-Séraphique* through to the *Orion*) were in the same transatlantic business in a short, eighty-five-year period. It is easy to recognize, or to learn to recognize, an East India man, a whaler, a Dutch fluit trading for grain in the Baltic, but not a slave ship, unless the midship barricado attached to the mainmast, as displayed in Figure 4.2, was in position.[5]

In short, because the Atlantic slave trade ranged over 95 degrees of latitude and was shaped by so many environmental factors, regulatory regimes, and changes in technology over time, no less than seventy-four

---

[5] For a fuller critique of the *Brooks'* iconic role in both slave trade scholarship and popular representations of the transatlantic traffic see Radburn and Eltis, "Visualizing the Middle Passage."

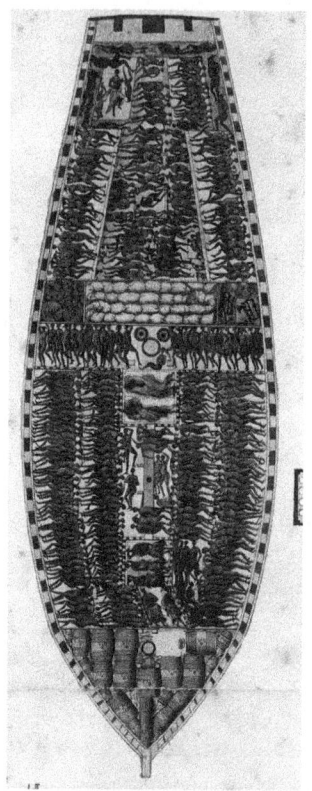

FIGURE 4.3 The slave deck of the *Marie-Séraphique* (ID 30941) during the transatlantic voyage as drawn by one of the ship's officers. The image is part of the video accessible on the home page of www.slavevoyages.org. Reproduced with permission of Private collections, Nantes History Museum.

types of ship (mainly different rigs) can be identified in TSTD.[6] Generally, "sailing ships were fungible: they could operate in various trades and carry mixed cargoes," and moreover were subject to many different ways of measuring tonnage; before the nineteenth century it is difficult to standardize tonnage measurement.[7] Certainly within a given type

---

[6] The five most common in TSTD – bergantim, curveta, schooner, brig, and ship – do account for close to two-fifths of our sample of 23,500 records with identified rigs, but within these categories there was a wide variation in size. See also the discussion in Jaime Rodrigues, *De Costa a Costa: Escravos, Marinheiros e Intermediários do Tráfico negreiro de Angola ao Rio de Janeiro. (1780–1860)* (São Paulo, 2005), pp. 121-33.

[7] Stephen D. Behrendt, Peter M. Solar, Luc Hens, Aidan Kane, Silvia Marzagalli, and Maria Cristina Moreira, "Tons, Tonneaux, Toneladas, Lasts: British and European Ship

(or rig) ships also varied in size. Slavers leaving the North American mainland and the Caribbean before 1800 averaged just half the capacity of their counterparts leaving Europe and Brazil, and on the African coast, vessels trading in Upper Guinea were smaller than those buying slaves east and south of Cape Palmas.

As already stressed, almost every port worthy of the name in the Atlantic-facing world organized and dispatched a ship to Africa for slaves, but in the age of sail, shipbuilding centers and the skills that supported them were even more broadly distributed geographically than were ports and merchants participating in transoceanic trades. Sailing ships were cheap to construct relative to the costs of fitting out and the value of the cargoes they carried. In tropical waters before the adoption of copper-sheathing technology, a hull might survive nine or ten round trips. TSTD records the place of construction for the vessels used in 9,155 voyages. These locations ranged from Calcutta, India to Portobelo, Panama, to Quebec City and Mahone Bay in Canada to Point Askaig in the Western Isles of Scotland and Kronstadt in Russia. Seven hundred in this sample had been taken as prizes in wars, and most had never previously been employed in the slave trade. When looking for a vessel to send to Africa before 1800, investors could quickly adapt almost any ship under 400 tons for the purpose. Owners often built vessels specifically for a slaving venture, but these, too, were of a wide variety of rigs and sizes.[8] In a sense then, there was no such thing as a slave ship, except insofar as it was a ship that carried slaves, but analysis of the records of 36,000 slave voyages and the approximately 12,000 ships that made these voyages, nevertheless make possible new generalizations. These in turn allow us to understand more fully both the patterns of the transatlantic slave trading, and the enslaved experiences that historians have missed.

Tonnages in the Eighteenth and Early Nineteenth Centuries," *Histoire & Mesure*, 35 (2020): 198.

[8] To put the main point here in a different context, any kind of transatlantic mercantile business (manufactured goods from Europe, produce from the Americas), drew on the same range of shipping types and size of vessel. In the illegal slave trade era, Cuban merchants referred to an enslaved person in their correspondence as a *bulto* or in English a "package," in a crude attempt to disguise their activities in the event of capture. The eighteenth-century counterpart to the modern container unit was the barrel. From the standpoint of the slave-trading community a slave was a package or a barrel, albeit a dangerous package that might explode into revolt and destroy the ship, and one that had to be fed and guarded. But if a vessel could carry barrels then it could also carry slaves if modified by the carpenter on its way to Africa. If the specifics of ship size and type varied, this was on account of the differing coastal environments of the major African embarkation regions.

As argued earlier, the transatlantic traffic developed as an extension of the slave trade from Africa to Europe – often called the Old-World slave trade, but it also involved African commodities as well as human beings. Gold, ivory, and other African produce exports to Europe were carried along with captives first to the Americas as well as direct from Africa to Europe. Anthony Hopkins noted that "the Europeans who came to Africa in the fifteenth and sixteenth centuries were interested in goods other than slaves ... and this commerce continued even after the overseas slave trade was well underway."[9] Commodities arriving from Atlantic ports prior to Columbian contact comprised sugar from Madeira (and later São Tomé) as well as mainland produce. For the early years the samples of voyages in the slave trade direct to Europe scattered through Ivana Elb's work indicate a mean human cargo of less than 100.[10] Thus captives were carried on merchant vessels and, if sufficiently numerous and comprising a threatening mix of gender and age, they were no doubt manacled and chained, but in these early years many vessels probably carried more crew than slaves.

A similar pattern is apparent in the early transatlantic traffic. For the first quarter of the sixteenth century, the galleons that left Spanish ports for the Americas carried European merchandise, approved emigrants, and slaves, most, but not all, of the latter being of African descent. In a pattern adopted nearly three centuries later in the British intra-Caribbean trade, passengers were permitted – with royal approval – to bring two personal servants with them.[11] Probably most vessels docking in the Spanish Americas disembarked some captives. When African slaves began to arrive in the Americas direct from Africa rather than Europe in 1520, the mix of slaves and commodities continued. The mean number of captives on board 131 vessels arriving in San Juan, Puerto Rico, between 1520 and 1546 was just sixteen, with only four carrying more than ninety captives. Ships collecting slaves from the offshore bulking centers of Arguim Island and Santiago in the Cape Verde Islands, not only freighted merchandise for the Americas but also picked up gold and perhaps sugar from Madeira, African spices, and ivory. Sixteen slaves carried on just one of the three legs of a voyage from Seville to Africa and the Americas and

---

[9] Anthony G, Hopkins, *An Economic History of West Africa* (London, 1973), p. 89; Eagle and Wheat, "Early Iberian Slave Trade."
[10] Ivana Elbl, "The Portuguese Trade with West Africa," pp. 448–598 for the relative importance of African exports and the evolution of Portuguese trading practices on the African coast.
[11] See Chapter 2 above.

back, could not have been the main interest of investors. In the 1550s detailed records of two large transatlantic vessels suggest that each disembarked more than one hundred slaves in Hispaniola and Vera Cruz respectively. But on arrival they were also found to be carrying huge volumes of wine, olive oil, and a wide range of manufactured goods.[12]

Even when the Iberians began to seek slaves south of Senegambia, first, at São Tomé in the Gulf of Guinea, and then West Central Africa, commodities remained of central importance. Quite apart from African gold that at one stage made up 10 percent of global supplies, São Tomé was Europe's major source of sugar in the mid sixteenth century. The ten slave voyages in TSTD that carried captives from that island to the Americas between 1526 and 1592 were likely carrying sugar from Africa as well as slaves. It is not possible to identify the point at which the value of slaves exceeded that of commodities on a "typical" transatlantic venture, but the main point is that slaves required space not only for themselves but also for provisions and water. European merchants obviously found transporting merchandise to the Americas, and African produce brought to Europe via the Americas, just as profitable as slaves. The value of captives may not have exceeded that of commodities until after 1550. What we can say is that in terms of space provided per captive, the very earliest transatlantic captives must have travelled under conditions better than their successors could have possibly imagined.

The TSTD shows the average number of captives per vessel increasing after 1550 but given the extent of smuggling into the Spanish Americas, this data – drawn from the official record – is not very reliable. Fortunately, between 1575 and 1637 seventy very well documented cases of vessels exist that the colonial authorities suspected of bringing in more slaves than their captains declared were on board. The extensive investigations that followed revealed that on average the seventy vessels disembarked 278 captives (SD = 124.3) as opposed to the 167 that the captains claimed they had imported. After allowing for voyage mortality these ships would likely have embarked between 350 and 400 captives on the African coast. There is no statistically significant difference between the true average of 278 slaves disembarked by this sample and the mean of 263 that TSTD generates for the 10,163 British, French, Dutch, and Danish vessels carried to the Caribbean over the whole period of the slave trade.[13] The conclusion from these comparisons is that a transatlantic slave trade of a type that most scholars would recognize,

---
[12] Eagle and Wheat, "Early Iberian Slave Trade," pp. 47–72.
[13] To view these voyages, see https://slavevoyages.org/voyages/H5DLneVO.

and most of the enslaved had to endure, was fully established sometime between 1560 and 1590. By "type" is meant ships carrying several hundred slaves under intensely crowded conditions, the value of whom far exceeded that of all other commodities on board. Such a system had not existed previously. Thus, the question of a ship built for the primary purpose of slave trading did not arise for more than a century after Europeans began carrying slaves from Africa.

There is, however, a need to reexamine and regroup the 35,800 voyages that occurred after 1560. It has become standard practice to analyze the traffic in terms of the northern and southern gyres that essentially shaped the routes of transatlantic sailing ships.[14] While the gyres were indeed the most fundamental environmental factor, a close study of ship types, trading practices, shipboard rebellions, and voyage durations points to the emergence of a Portuguese system of acquiring and moving labor across the Atlantic that no other Europeans were ever able to emulate. The unusual investment structure supporting this system is explored in Chapter 2, but the Portuguese advantage extended beyond financing and into superior methods of shipping their human commodities.[15] Their system dominated the Atlantic world after 1807, partly because Portuguese nationals retained a critical organizing role beyond the point at which their main market in the Americas – Brazil – was closed to the transatlantic business. Clearly, the gyres determined the maritime routes, but there were more important political and cultural factors that ensured Portuguese dominance in Atlantic slaving in the more than four centuries after 1450 – a dominance that remained unchallenged except for the British interlude in the six or seven decades prior to abolition.[16]

These same factors also ensured that African slaves and African slave traders experienced the slave trade very differently from their counterparts who engaged with and helped sustain the northwest European system of slave trading. As we have seen the French, British, Dutch, and Danes are best viewed not only as latecomers to the slave trade, but intruders, condemned to fall back on second-best options in the business. The fact that they were rarely able to adopt the preferred system of the

---

[14] Domingues da Silva, "The Atlantic Slave Trade to Maranhão."
[15] Hicks, *Captive Cosmopolitans*, chapter 3. Hicks spells out the unique features of Brazilian slave trading but without making the broader argument that these features enabled the Portuguese to maintain their dominance in the traffic.
[16] Data-driven work on the Portuguese slave trade dates from Herbert S. Klein, "The Portuguese Slave Trade from Angola in the Eighteenth Century," *Journal of Economic History*, 32 (1972): 894–918.

Portuguese ensured that they faced inefficiencies and higher costs in accessing slaves, costs that were absorbed ultimately by their planters and consumers. The traditional view of how the slave trade of the Atlantic world evolved needs revision.

At the very outset of their slave-trading activities the Iberian slave traders (mainly Portuguese) traded from their ship, but soon established permanent factories, some like those at Mina and Axim dealing in gold. The early slave trade to Europe came to rely heavily on what Curtin called "bulking centers," or assembly points for captives.[17] As the early direct trade in slaves from Africa to the Americas developed, the Spanish and Portuguese used several such stations. All were on islands under the full control of Iberians. Tenerife in the Canaries and Santiago in the Cape Verde islands were added to Arguim, with the first two being the most important down to the end of the sixteenth century. Thus, Tenerife and Santiago pulled in Africans from regions ranging from the Senegal River to what became Sierra Leone, and when the southern rivers emerged as the most important source in the region some transatlantic vessels collected their complement of slaves directly from Cacheu rather than Santiago. Luanda, founded in 1575 and later to become the single largest embarkation point for overseas markets in the whole of Africa, was also first settled on an island, initially supplying slaves to São Tomé.

Until 1720, Benguela dispatched all its slaves destined for the Americas to the "bulking center" of Luanda, before the volume of this traffic warranted Benguela's direct trade connections with Brazilian ports.[18] Later in the century, as the St. Domingue rebellion and the ensuing international conflict erupted, French withdrawal from the Indian Ocean allowed Mozambique island to assume its major role in the transatlantic business. The three southern bases of Luanda, Benguela, and Mozambique became well-fortified Portuguese enclaves that together accounted for three-quarters of all captives carried off from Africa south of the Congo River. At each location, when enough captives were acquired, the Portuguese would embark the full complement of enslaved persons in a single embarkation. A Capuchin friar in Luanda, Laurent de Lucques, described the scene in 1708 as he boarded a slave vessel to Bahia:

---

[17] Philip D. Curtin, *Economic Change in PreColonial Africa: Senegambia in the Era of the Slave Trade* (Madison, WI, 1975), p. 335.
[18] Roquinaldo Amaral Ferreira, "Slavery and Resistance to Slaving in West Central Africa," in Eltis and Engerman (eds.), *CWHS*, vol. 3: 116; Ferreira, "Transforming Atlantic Slaving: Trade, Warfare and Territorial Control in Angola, 1650–1800," *África*, 24–26 (2009): 85.

There was assembled there not only a large number of whites, but also a multitude of blacks who were to be embarked for America. On this island, all these blacks were reviewed, and a census of them was taken by the superintendent and ministers of the royal revenues. On my return the boarding began of these blacks, whose numbers amounted to 742.[19]

Slave-ship captains could thereby receive all their captives much more quickly than in, say, the Bights of Benin and Biafra. The exceptionally large barracoons (or *quintais*) in Luanda and Benguela were noted by several observers.[20] For Bissau and Cacheu, Antônio Carreira makes no reference to shipboard revolts, or measures taken to suppress them, but does reproduce a document cataloguing 100 deaths and escapes per year "*antes do embarque*" in the factories over the period 1768 to 1777, many of them the result of "uprisings."[21] Hans Christian Monrad, a Danish pastor, who, like Laurent de Lucques, had also travelled on a Brazilian slave vessel during a four-year stay on the Gold Coast, 1804–1809, wrote that he knew "not a single example of the Portuguese ships being, as they say, overrun (the crew attacked and killed by the slaves.)"[22]

Portuguese ship trade, or the gradual accumulation of slaves on board the vessel over several weeks, became largely confined to the smaller coastal craft that connected the bases with the adjacent African mainland. In Angola, the bulking centers drew on land-based networks, rather than coastal seaborne and river traffic. Through warfare and treaties, the Portuguese were able to extend a degree of sovereignty, or at least influence, inland, and maintain a handful of forts and factories strategically located on trade routes. In all other parts of sub-Saharan Africa, European

---

[19] "13th Relation," *Relations sur le Pére Laurent de Lucques (1700–1718)* (Brussels, 1953), edited by Jean Cuvelier. The vessel ID is 40839. For further examples of this embarkation procedure from the sixteenth through eighteenth centuries, see the 1667 voyage on the same route described in Michael Angelo of Gattina and Denis Carli of Piacenza, in Awnsham Churchill and John Churchill, *Collection of Voyages and Travels: Some Now First Printed from Original*, 4 vols (London, 1704), I: 637 where six hundred slaves were loaded when the ship was ready to sail; also Miller, *Way of Death*, pp. 405–406; the *Senhora do Cabo*, ID 40839, in Newson and Minchin, *From Capture to Sale*, pp. 72–100; Francesco Carletti, *My Voyage around the World*, trans by Herbert Weinstock (London, 1965), p. 15, writes of a similar process in Santiago, Cape Verde Islands, in 1594.

[20] Miller, *Way of Death*, pp. 389–91.

[21] Antônio Carreira, *A Companhia Geral do Grão-Pará e Maranhão*, 2 vols (Sao Paulo, 1988), vol. 1, p. 77; vol. 2 *Documentos*, pp. 133–34.

[22] For this and other aspects of the Portuguese system, see Hans Christian Monrad, *Two Views from Christiansborg Castle*, 2 vols, trans. by Selena Axelrod Winsnes (Legon, Accra, 2009), vol. 1: 223.

authority extended only as far as a cannon shot, and on most of the West African coast the cannon was located on a vessel. Even the famous Gold Coast forts amounted to no more than a large, anchored ship with a well-armed crew; there were few Mulattoes, and few European factories in their hinterlands. By contrast, Luanda had a population of 5,000 at the end of the eighteenth century, one-quarter of whom were Whites and Mulattoes. Though Benguela and Mozambique were half the size of Luanda, compared to the Gold Coast forts both comprised major communities under European jurisdiction that anchored trading routes extending into the interior.[23]

Moreover, as Mary Hicks has argued, there is a case to be made for the differences in Portuguese/African relations in the acquisition of slaves spilling over into captor-captive interactions on the voyage itself. As noted in Chapter 2, many members of the crew on Brazilian slave vessels were freedmen or former slaves, some of whom had a financial interest in the venture. Indeed, some crew were themselves enslaved.[24] They frequently spoke the language of the enslaved, in sharp contrast to crews on northern European slavers. Notwithstanding the harsh conditions in the Goias and Minas Gerais gold regions – which he admitted – Monrad wrote that the enslaved:

> show little fear of their fate of being sold ... They see that their comrades frequently come back to the coast as sailors and conclude that the condition of all of them is equally fortunate ... Never did I see anyone actually flog the slaves ... Rather I often saw the sailors make as much of the small Negro children as if they had been their own ... On the whole, a freedom and equality holds sway on Portuguese ships which I have met nowhere else among the other nations.[25]

He went on to contrast these conditions with those on Dutch, US, and British slave ships. There were no French vessels on the coast when he made his comments, but a few years earlier, the Le Havre vessel, *Bosquet*

---

[23] José C. Curto, and Raymond R. Gervais, "The Population History of Luanda during the Late Atlantic Slave Trade, 1781–1844," *African Economic History*, 29 (2001): 57; Mariana P. Candido, *An African Slaving Port and the Atlantic World: Benguela and Its Hinterland* (Cambridge, 2013), p. 6.

[24] Hicks, *Captive Cosmopolitans*, chapter 3; Mariana P. Candido, "Different Slave Journeys: Enslaved African Seamen on Board of Portuguese Ships, c. 1760–1820s," *Slavery and Abolition*, 31 (2010): 395–409; Herbert S. Klein, *The Middle Passage: Comparative Studies of the Atlantic Slave Trade* (Princeton, NJ, 1978), p. 86. There were a few examples of enslaved crew on British slavers, see Richardson, *Principles and Agents*, pp. 97–98.

[25] Monrad, *A Description of the Guinea Coast*, vol. 1: 223–25.

d'Or (ID 32803) sailed from Isles de Los to St. Marc, St. Domingue. On board was American Nathaniel Cutting, who observed in his journal:

> If every vessel bound to the Coast of Africa to Trade for Slaves Should have on board one or two Slaves, that had been already convey'd to, & had resided sometime in the West Indies, it might be of great service by encouraging the New Slaves that one takes on Board; preventing their apprehensions of being sacrificed etc... They cannot converse with their purchasers; and if they could it would be difficult to convince... that no harm was intended him by keeping him in Irons under constant guard of arm'd men...[26]

Monrad's encomium to Portuguese slave traders may be over-egged, but the interactions between crew and enslaved are consistent with what we know of the strong ties between Bahia and the Mina Coast and Rio de Janeiro and Luanda. The high proportion of slaves and former slaves among the crew of Brazilian slave ships, some of whom held a small equity interest in the voyage and others who could speak to captives in their own language must have reduced the terrors of the unknown. Divisions between Portuguese captors and their captives were likely never as sharp as Cutting and many others observed on board the slavers of other nations, but differences in interactions between crew and enslaved, certainly existed.[27]

In any event the skewed distribution of African resistance across national flags is startling. TSTD contains 572 incidents of violent resistance (including ninety-seven cases of attacks by Africans on shore). Only eleven out of the 572 involved vessels flying the Portuguese or Brazilian flag compared to 488 British, French, Dutch, and Danish slave ships.[28] Many of the reports of violence are retrieved from newspaper reports and until late in the period Portugal and Brazil did not possess vibrant press cultures. Moreover, both British and Dutch slave traders were well aware of the need for interpreters so that Africans would have some awareness of the fact that, as a minimum, they were not to be cannibalized.[29] Yet communication between crew and the enslaved on Portuguese slave

---

[26] Massachusetts Historical Society, "Nathaniel Cutting Journal and Letterbooks," *Journal*, December 10, 1789.

[27] For the extensive use of slaves as crew on Portuguese slavers see Hicks, *Captive Cosmopolitans*, chapter 3; Candido, "Different Slave Journeys" 395–409.

[28] https://slavevoyages.org/voyages/rOW3NIFt.

[29] See the discussion of languages on British slave ships in Jane Webster, *Materializing the Middle Passage: A Historical Archaeology of British Slave Shipping, 1680–1807* (Oxford, 2023), pp. 328–38. For the Dutch case, Pieter Emmer, personal communication, May 19, 2022.

voyages must have been greater than in any other branch of the slave trade, and it is plausible that a discrepancy such as this indicates that violent resistance on slave ships was much less common in the Luso-Atlantic.

There is no need here to reenter the old debates over attitudes toward race in the different European and African Atlantic worlds, but differences there were and still are.[30] The Portuguese freed all slaves living in their own country over a decade before the well-known English Somerset case.[31] As important, the British, French, Dutch, and Danes had fewer equivalents to the *lançados*. The British came closest in Upper Guinea on the coast ranging from Rio Pongo to Galinhas in the later eighteenth century where families emerged bearing the names of minor Liverpool slave traders. Such families – the Ormonds, the Holmans, and the Frasers – might have owned plantations on both sides of the Atlantic, but they were intermediaries, not traders who brought captives from the interior. Can one imagine the English or Dutch presiding over the mixed society that quickly emerged in the Cape Verde Islands?[32] Moreover, this region was not a major source of slaves compared to the Bight of Biafra and Angola.[33] Such descent groups could be quite large, but the extensive documentation of slave purchases by the northern Europeans on the West African coast points to the sellers of slaves being African, with fewer equivalents of *lançados*.[34] Except for parts of the Gambia and Senegal

---

[30] The old adage, "[i]f you are not quite White in the US, then you are Black; in Brazil, if you are not quite Black, then you are White" has been disrupted in recent years. In 2012 Brazil's federal and state universities began to reserve a tranche of admissions for Black and mixed-race students; and since 2014 the federal public service also has affirmative-action requirements.

[31] See the discussion in Chapter 6 below.

[32] Toby Green, "The Emergence of a Mixed Society in Cape Verde in the Seventeenth Century," in Green and Nafafé (eds.), *Brokers of Change*, pp. 217–36.

[33] Bruce Mouser writes the "priests and teachers associated with the mission of the Spiritan (Holy Ghost) Fathers (Archives Générales du Congrégation du Saint-Esprit) in the 1930s and 1940s kept records that contain elaborate genealogies of more than twenty influential families in the Pongo, nine of which were founded by slave traders who had arrived on the coast by the beginning of the nineteenth century," in "Towards a Definition of Transnational as a Family Construct: A Historical and Micro Perspective," in Jacqueline Knörr and Christoph Kohl (eds.), *The Upper Guinea Coast in Global Perspective* (New York, 2016), pp. 21–39, quote is pp. 29–30.

[34] Ibid; For other Africans with some European descent in Upper Guinea, see Brooks, *Eurafricans in Western Africa*, pp. 68–101. There were sometimes European factors on the coast with whom captains dealt (like Richard Miles), but for the most part especially in the Bight of Biafra and the major embarkation points north of the Congo River, captains traded directly with Africans. See Radburn, *Traders in Men*, pp. 59–90; Anne Ruderman,

Rivers, there were no European-controlled factories or trade routes in the African interior. It is extraordinary that the British and French not only carried off over 3 million captives from what is today Ghana, Benin, and Nigeria, but followed this with the imposition of a century of colonial rule. Yet they have left little genetic trace in the modern populations of these countries. Nor have the northwestern Europeans left anything comparable to the Afro-Brazilian presence in, say, Porto Novo – where commercial contact with Bahia began only in 1760.[35] We would not expect to find many English, French, and Dutch names among families today in Bonny, Old Calabar, Cabinda, and Loango from which the French, Dutch, and English carried off millions of African captives. And to refer briefly to the larger canvas, why, after three centuries of colonial occupation, there are no Dutch speakers in modern Indonesia?

The Portuguese had perhaps the most completely exploitative colonial system in world history in place by the early seventeenth century. They had a wider range of interactions with Africans than any of the other European slave-trading powers. While "interaction" here could mean unsuccessful wars, with African polities it more often meant an uneasy trading relationship with Africans in the often-distant hinterlands of the major slave trading ports of Angola and Upper Guinea that the French, Dutch, and English could not match. The *lançados* were vital to the system. They were largely independent of the Portuguese state, and, for the most part, purchased captives rather than enslaved them. They helped ensure that from the late sixteenth century, the Portuguese method of converting African labor in the interior of the continent into sugar, coffee, and tobacco consumed in the Old World gave them an advantage that their competitors were not able to match. Their dominance of sugar before 1650 and coffee in the first half of the nineteenth century was equivalent to French domination of world sugar output before 1792 and the subsequent British predominance, thereafter.[36] Between 1650 and 1800, the Portuguese system may have intermittently lost its preeminence

---

"Supplying the Slave Trade: How Europeans Met African Demand for European Manufactured Products, Commodities and Re-exports, 1670–1790," unpublished PhD thesis, Yale University (2016), chapter 3; and the numerous examples in Stephen D. Behrendt, A. J. H. Latham, and David Northrup, *The Diary of Antera Duke, an Eighteenth-Century African Slave Trader* (New York, 2012), passim.

[35] Visitors to the colonial section of modern Porto Novo might easily imagine that they were in colonial northeastern Brazil.

[36] Note that Cuban sugar production did not exceed that of the British until the 1833 abolition of slavery in the British Empire denied British unrestricted access to slave labor.

in plantation produce, but the literature on this topic in the Atlantic world invariably ignores the role of gold and silver production. As argued in Chapter 2, Brazil from the late 1690s to 1760, and of course the Spanish down to 1800, had colonial bullion production that vastly exceeded that of the northwestern European possessions in the Americas.

Three distinct phases of the slave trade emerged. If the pre-1560 era of mixing the traffic in commodities and enslaved people slave trading constituted the first, and a second comprised the Portuguese-controlled links just described, then a third and quite different method emerged as other European nations entered the business from 1640. The English and Dutch had initially built (or in the Dutch case, taken control of) forts on the Gold Coast to facilitate trade in African produce rather than slaves, though gold exports never matched those of Brazil beginning in the late 1690s. Together with the French they gradually wrested some of the smaller Caribbean islands and South American mainland from Spanish control to establish their own plantation systems and slave trades. The African forts did eventually become assembly points for slaves, but the major source of slaves lay east and south of the Gold Coast extending to the mouth of the Congo. Except possibly for eighteenth-century Anomabu, Gold Coast forts were never able to play the role of Tenerife, Santiago, Luanda, Benguela, and, later, Mozambique. Apart from Ouidah (and even there, the kings of first, Ardra, and then, Dahomey, were always very much in control) no European power was able to establish a permanent foothold beyond coastal lodges. The Dutch attack on Luanda, temporarily successful in the 1640s, was a recognition of the advantages of system two over system three. If Dutch *lançados* (something of an oxymoron) had existed, the occupation might have endured. But as Phyllis Martin noted, "[t]he Dutch probably never realized the intricacies of the trade network which the Portuguese had established over 150 years until they had to operate it themselves."[37] With the Brazilian reconquest of Luanda, the massive British, Dutch, and French slave trades between Cape Palmas and the Congo River that developed after 1640 were, of necessity, based on ships, not islands, much less, small segments of mainland Africa.

Over a wide range of the coast the slave ship – which had hitherto been a means of transportation – was, with arrival of the northern Europeans, now adapted to additional roles. The ship ferried merchandise in one

---

[37] Phyllis Martin, *The External Trade of the Loango Coast 1576–1870: The effects of Changing Commercial Relations on the Vili Kingdom of Loango* (Oxford, 1972), p. 63.

direction and slaves in another, but it also became a trading platform where wares could be displayed and clients entertained, as well, most importantly, as a floating stockade or barracoon. A vessel might now expect to spend many months accumulating slaves, often at more than one location. In Curtin's phraseology, bulking costs were now transferred from the coastal hub to the vessel itself. The implications of this for the design and construction of slave vessels, for slave resistance, for the African experience of transportation to the Americas, and more broadly yet, for imperial rivalries and economic development in the Atlantic world were significant.

For several thousand cases in TSTD it is now possible to calculate the duration of different phases of a slave voyage. As we might expect, round-trip voyages from Brazil during the eighteenth century (when data first become available) were 21 percent shorter than those setting out from Europe and ultimately the Caribbean (n = 5,707). It is also clear that voyage length declined in the nineteenth century as part of the general pattern of transoceanic sailing times.[38] But the key question in terms of shipping cost is how long the slaves were on board. The passage from Africa to the Americas accounts for much of the difference in round-trip times. Voyages from both the Bight of Benin and west central Africa to the Caribbean were 50 percent longer than those sailing to Brazil (n = 2,378). Nevertheless, the major factor in separating the Portuguese from the northern Europeans was what happened before the transoceanic passage began. In West African ports between 1640 and 1807, Dutch, French, and English vessels received their first captive eighty days after leaving home port on average. Accumulating a full complement of captives via trading from the ship took a further 140 days. Typically, therefore, the very first captive purchased would be on board the vessel for seven months, and severe crowding below decks usually began a month or so before departure when the captain began to pay higher prices for slaves to get off the coast as quickly as possible.[39] There are many voyages in TSTD where captives spent a year aboard the slave vessel between first boarding and disembarkation.

---

[38] Morgan Kelly and Cormac Ó Gráda. "Speed Under Sail during the Early Industrial Revolution (c. 1750–1830)," *Economic History Review*, 72 (2019): 459–80. Slave ships powered by steam were of course faster again. In 1863 the *Cicerón* (Figure 3.1) sailed from Godomey, near Whydah in the Bight of Benin, to Cuba with 1,600 slaves in just 24 days when the average time in the eighteenth century between Whydah and Jamaica was 67 days (n = 588, sd = 26,6).

[39] For this process see Radburn, *Traders in Men*, pp. 78–87.

By contrast, most vessels bound for Brazil had slaves on board for just a few days more than the duration of the crossing – less than two months overall. Despite this, Portuguese and northern European ships spent similar amounts of time on the African coast; but the Portuguese vessels were frequently empty during this time or had very few slaves on board. The competition between captains in places such as Luanda was over the order of embarkation, not about who should claim the last few captives that would make up a full complement. It might seem that for the captive there was little to choose between a stockade and the confined hold of a sailing vessel. Both were unhealthy environments that made extensive use of shackles and offered few opportunities for escape. Given that the slave-ship captain had the power to refuse captives who were not in prime condition, it could be argued that shore-based imprisonment was more lethal. Yet, as discussed below, a slave deck was without parallel in the annals of inhumanity; a tightly restricted space with some gratings for light, occupied for months by hundreds of people so that no part of the deck was visible. As the Antigua agent wrote to Bristol owner James Rogers, "[e]very commendation is due to Cpt. Rogers [no relation] for his assiduity and cleverness in bringing off so many people, in so small a vessel." The cutter sloop *Fly* (ID 17969) was just 27 tons and had disembarked fifty-three people.[40] Can any environment created by humans in global history have offered harmful pathogens a better opportunity to multiply and kill than this one? As noted below such conditions were never replicated in any other transoceanic movements of people whether convicts, troops, indentured servants, Asian contract workers, or modern illegal migrants. In the northern European based-trade the closest land-based parallel to the Portuguese system was the holding cell of a Gold Coast fort, which relatively few of those entering the transatlantic slave trade experienced, though we do have instances of the Danes, for example, boarding a complete complement of enslaved people from a fort just prior to departure.[41]

The differences between the Portuguese and the rest had major implications for costs. A ship that was expected to imprison captives for months instead of weeks required additional fortifications, crew, and armament. We have surprisingly little information on the design of slave vessels before 1670, but for the long eighteenth century the sources

---

[40] BNA, Jarvis to James Rogers, April 2, 1787, C107/1.
[41] See Lief Svalesen, *The Slave Ship Fredensborg*, trans. by Pat Shaw and Selena Winsnes (Bloomington. IN, 2000), 99–100 (ID 35181).

provide relatively abundant data and several pictorial illustrations. For vessels trading in West Africa in the second half of the eighteenth century when the transatlantic traffic reached its apogee, the slave deck contained two key features designed to control resistance. First, the spiked barricado, a huge timber barrier straddling midships, dominated the slave ship sailing from northern Europe. If it was not already in place from a previous voyage, then the ship's carpenter would build it on the way to Africa. Typically, it was topped with swivel guns and pierced with peashot-loaded cannon, all pointing directly at the men as their space in front of the barrier filled up during loading.[42] The barricado's chief purpose, as surgeon Alexander Falconbridge and Captain John Newton pointed out, was to stymie revolts, but it also served to separate the men from the women and child captives.[43] A second security feature comprised two chains running fore and aft along the main deck to which the men were always shackled in fair-weather daytime hours. At night, captives would be forced below – the men unshackled, but only two at one time allowed through the hatchway, whereupon they would be immediately reshackled. By far the best and most measured descriptions of the life of the enslaved at sea can be found in the recent books by Nicholas Radburn and Jane Webster.[44] Here, we are essentially adding some additional reflections on how experiences on Portuguese slave vessels differed from what these scholars describe. Fear of revolts was such that when sailors succumbed to disease, their bodies were committed to the deep at night when the men slaves were below deck and would not realize the diminishing numbers of their jailers.[45]

---

[42] For the aftermath of a rebellion quelled with peashot see the surgeon of the *Saint Michael* (ID 76203): "One boy gott some hundreds of peas lodged in him, Most of which I took out Immediately after, & yt very soon cured, but those yt were left in were more troublesome to cure." Hispanic Society of America, New York, mss. "Journal and Logbook of an Anonymous Scotch Sailor held on his voyage from London to Jamaica, and From London to Madagascar," entry for January 5, 1727.

[43] Alexander Falconbridge, *An Account of the Slave Trade on the Coast of Africa* (London, 1788), p. 6; John Newton, *Journal of a Slave Trader (John Newton), 1750–1754: with Newton's Thoughts upon the African Slave Trade*, edited by Bernard Martin and Mark Spurrell (London, 1962), p. 22. For the barricado in combat see Paul Erdmann Isert, *Letters on West Africa and the Slave Trade. Paul Erdmann Isert's Journey to Guinea and the Caribbean Islands in Columbia (1788)*, trans and edited by Selina Axelrod Winsnes (Legon, Ghana, 2007), pp. 234–38.

[44] Webster, *Materializing the Middle Passage*. For the evolution of the barricado, see Radburn, *Traders in Men*, pp. 99–103.

[45] "We concealed the death of the sailours from ye Negroes by throwing them overboard in ye night, lest it might give them a temptation to rise upon us so much weakened by ye death

The Portuguese System 171

Women and children by contrast, were held on the quarterdeck during daylight hours, and below deck at night, but in both cases once at sea, normally without restraint of any kind, but always divided from the men by the barricado. Women did take advantage of their relative freedom. Slave vessels that left open waters and ventured up rivers, accounting for perhaps 14 percent of the total traffic, faced particular problems heading downstream, a process that could take days. Slaves were normally held below deck at this stage, but small groups were brought up for feeding, The *Gezegend Suikerriet* was one of the few Dutch voyages to sail up the Gambia. It also had a captain on his first command. On its return downstream in late 1746 enslaved women brought up at feeding time attacked the sailors with billets of firewood and attempted to jump overboard,[46] which explains why vessels leaving riverine embarkation points would normally put women in chains. A similar incident on a 1714 voyage where two-thirds of the captives were female in the Cross River near what is today the Nigerian-Cameroon border, elicited the following poignant entry in the journal of an anonymous crew member:

All the men had shackles on their legs to prevent them from swimming ashore as we went down the river which were taken off when ... [at] sea. Not suspecting ye women we left them at their liberty, but before we got out of the river, 3 or 4 of them shew'd us how well they could swim to give us the slip tho we took one of them again that could not shift so well as the rest being big with child[47]

When below deck, women were adjacent to the officer's quarters and cook's workspace. Thus, firewood was not the only weaponry available. The arms' chest was normally in the captain's cabin and there are instances of women gaining access when the armorer forgot to lock the chest. There are records of three rebellions occurring when the women successfully passed along guns, swords, kitchen knives and an axe to the men's deck. Henry Schroeder, himself a boy on the *Hudibras* (ID 81890)

---

of eight and most of ye rest sick but myself, we being but twelve in all that were left," Anon, "Account of the voyage of Captain Samuel Pain, *Florida*," ID 75489, BrL, Add. Mss, 39946, pp. 12–13. See also Marcus Rediker's *The Slave Ship*, pp. 291–301, for a description of resistance and the precautions against revolts.

[46] ID 10605, GAA, NA, 5075, v. inv. nr. 11697, deed 126, 21 April 1746.

[47] "Account of the voyage of Captain Samuel Pain" (Payne), BrL, Add.mss, 39946 (ID 75489); William Butterworth (aka Henry Schroeder), *Three Years Adventures of a Minor* (Leeds, 1822), pp. 123, 124, wrote that on the *Hudibras* (ID 81890) in 1787 females would "seize upon the cook's knives, forks, axe, and other implements used in cooking, capable of being converted into ... weapons." See also Webster, *Materializing the Middle Passage*, pp. 342–44.

on his first voyage in 1787, found Africans of his own age able to pass weapons through the barricado to the men.[48]

Women spent more time above deck than did men. The famous Akan drum from Virginia in the British Museum that formed one of the items featured in the BBC Radio 4/British Museum series "A History of the World in 100 Objects" is often cited as a device used by slave traders to "dance the slaves" (in other words force captives to exercise).[49] This may have been the prime purpose of the drum, but for women on the quarterdeck there was a voluntary function associated with the instrument. An entry in the diary of Captain Ferentz of the *Fredensborg* (ID 35181) five days after departure states "female slaves entertain themselves by dancing their 'negro dances' on the quarterdeck."[50] This would have been quite unimaginable in the men's areas beyond the barricado both above and below deck where shackling was the norm. Confinement to a slave vessel did not mean complete disruption of the roles of African women. Food preparation, food consumption in groups of five to ten, and birthing (parturition) also occurred. On the *Eliza*, described below with 168 captives, three women gave birth but only one child survived.

Not depicted is the sexual molestation to which the crew subjected the enslaved. In 1840 the *Jesus Maria* (ID 2071) was adjudicated at the Havana Court of Mixed Commission. Only five of the 246 on board were adults. Court officials recorded the graphic testimony of eight girls aged 11 to 15 whom the crew had raped and beaten. The captain had distinguished himself by covering the nose and mouth of a 13-year-old Sherbro girl named "Mania" "to keep her from screaming."[51] On this ship like many others of the period, there were children everywhere above and below the quarterdeck throughout the voyage, though in only a few

---

[48] For the *Thomas*, 1797 (ID 83761), see Richard Brooke, *Liverpool as it was During the Last Quarter of the Eighteenth Century, 1775 to 1800* (Liverpool, 1853), pp. 236–7. For the *Convert*, 1680 (ID 9910), see BNA, Stede and Gascoigne to the Royal African Company, July 28, 1680, T70/15, f. 41. Boys caused the fire that destroyed the Luxemburg in 1726 (ID 78858), on its return journey, but while they were black it is not clear they were enslaved [Nigel Tattersfield, The Forgotten Trade (London, 1991), pp. 209–11]. Note that on the *Hudibras* the boys' room was built adjacent to the men's room.

[49] www.bbc.co.uk/ahistoryoftheworld/. For the drum, see www.bbc.co.uk/programmes/bo ov1mvt#:~:text=This%20drum%2C%20the%20earliest%20African,Britain%20by%2 oa%20slave%20owner.

[50] Svalesen, *The Slave Ship*, p. 109.

[51] The case of the *Jesus Maria* in BNA, FO 313/49 (ID 2071). I thank Marial Iglesias Utset for drawing my attention to this source. See Sowande' M. Mustakeem, *Slavery at Sea: Terror, Sex and Sickness in the Middle Passage* (Urbana, IL, 2016), pp. 85–90 for a review of sexual abuse in the women's quarters.

cases can we link mother and child. The most detailed and dependable guide to the child component of the Africans carried off to the Americas are the registers of British Vice Admiralty and Mixed Commission Courts in the four decades after 1807 (see Chapter 7 for details) that spell out ages and, very occasionally, relationships. The newly born would not normally survive on a slave vessel, nor would they be counted. Data taken from the registers of Liberated Africans show that only 115 of those listed were infants – aged 1 or below – but no less than 27 percent of captives were classed as children. As discussed below, this ratio was higher than recorded in previous centuries.

In some respects, the space on and below the quarterdeck was more restricted than on the men's side of the barricado.[52] Crew and children slept here and, especially upon leaving Africa, space was severely confined. The *Eliza* (ID 81194) left Galinhas in southern Sierra Leone in 1805 with nearly five tons of rice, beans, and palm oil in addition to 823 billets of firewood (each billet approximately 3 foot 4 inches long and 7.5 inches round), all stored below the quarterdeck. Unusually, the *Eliza's* captain kept a record of daily consumption of provisions during the sixty-three-day voyage, as well as slave mortality. His data allows an assessment of the rate of consumption and an estimate of daily nutritional intake. After allowing for deaths at sea, the barque had on board an average of 168 captives over the course of the voyage, of whom 157 reached Demerara. Africans consumed just over 3 tons of rice and 1.25 tons of beans plus 100 gallons of palm oil. Assuming that the rice was dehulled but not otherwise refined – ergo brown rice – and that cooking doubled its volume, then we have a per capita consumption figure of 0.64 pounds of rice and .026 pounds of beans per day. Even allowing for occasional shark flesh and traces of palm oil, this two-meal-a-day diet would not have provided much beyond 1,100 calories every 24 hours. People around the Atlantic world were of shorter stature two centuries ago than they are today. The average height of men leaving the Sierra Leone region, 1808–1848, was 64.5 inches and of women, 60.4 inches.[53] Moreover, one-quarter of those on board were children with somewhat lower nutritional requirements, and despite dancing, compulsory or not, the adults could hardly be described as anything other than sedentary. But even after considering such factors, the provisions on the *Eliza* appear carefully calibrated to

---

[52] See Radburn, *Traders of Men*, pp. 106–19.
[53] Calculated from 11,121 records of those carried off from Sierra Leone prior to recapture at www.slavevoyages.org/resources/names-database.

keep people alive at minimum expense.⁵⁴ Modern nutritionists claim that an adult can survive on a daily intake of 1,500 calories. We need more than one case, but the frequently observed skeletal figures that emerged from the holds of slave vessels in the Americas were more likely succumbing to amoebic and bacillary dysentery-induced dehydration rather than starvation.

One major difference in the voyage experience of men as opposed to women and children emerges sharply from the 230 French, British, and Dutch voyages in TSTD, where the data is sufficient to compare voyage mortality across the age–sex groupings. Men were almost three times more likely to die than women during the voyage, and 60 percent more likely than children. Such differences are more suggestive of the losing side of a savage war than of a mode of transportation. With 36.3 percent of men dying during a crossing and a mean duration of just two months, the men's deck of a slave ship was a virtual charnel house, especially as this data takes no account of deaths in the immediate aftermath of disembarkation. Given that shipboard mortality was the single most important factor determining the profitability of a slave-trading venture, it is extraordinary that over 350 years northwestern European enslavers could not find another solution to the problem of retaining control of a transatlantic voyage.⁵⁵ Mortality on transoceanic voyages generally declined over these centuries across the world as ship design and navigational aids improved. Convict voyages to Australia beginning in 1787 saw deaths on board fall dramatically after rates of 10 percent or more recorded in the first decade of transportation. At the height of the Irish famine, average annual rates on voyages to Quebec rarely exceeded 5 percent. In the slave trade, however, the 6,430 voyages for which mortality data has survived indicate that, after some improvement in the seventeenth century, onboard slave deaths as a proportion of those embarked remained the same between 1700 and 1864 – the years in which 80 percent of the slave trade occurred. This, despite a significant reduction in voyage duration after 1800, discussed more fully below, and the higher value of men compared to women and children.

---

⁵⁴ BNA, T70/1220/1, "Eliza. Ship's log and journal of the barque Eliza under Robert Hall ..." Vessels leaving from other regions would have loaded millet, yams, or cassava. For the agricultural activity that supported the provisions trade see the literature cited in David Eltis, "The Slave Trade and Commercial Agriculture in an African Context," in Robin Law, Suzanne Schwarz, and Silke Strickrodt (eds.), *Commercial Agriculture, the Slave Trade and Slavery in Africa* (Cambridge, 2013), pp. 28–53.

TABLE 4.1 *Mortality rates by age/sex groupings. Data from TSTD.*

	t-score	Degrees of freedom	Significance. (2-tailed)	Mean mortality
Boys	6.575	115	0	0.21296
Girls	6.146	78	0	0.22935
Men	3.194	229	0.002	0.36305
Women	8.058	223	0	0.13181

Notes: For comparative transoceanic mortality rates see Herbert S. Klein, Stanley L. Engerman, Robin Haines, and Ralph Shlomowitz, "Transoceanic Mortality: The Slave Trade in Comparative Perspective," *The William and Mary Quarterly*, 58 (2001): 93–118.

In the broader Atlantic picture, resistance was crucial in ending the slave trade, but the resistance came from several sources. The first was from those imprisoned on the vessel. The measures taken on board to control enslaved people raised the costs of transportation – and therefore the price of an enslaved person in the Americas. Because transportation formed a wedge between slave prices on either side of the Atlantic, measures to control captives on slave ships also lowered slave prices on the African coast, and this in turn reduced the number of Africans pulled into the transatlantic slave trade.[56] It is safe to assume that other things being equal the supply of slaves varied directly with price. Because of its influence on costs and therefore prices, shipboard resistance has been estimated to have prevented the departure of 1 million Africans to the Americas.[57] A second factor was the St. Domingue Revolution and subsequent rebellions of captives in the Americas explored more fully in Chapter 6. These, too, raised the costs of producing plantation products, reduced the amount consumed, and ultimately reduced the numbers of people pulled into the traffic. But resistance also came from other sources. Third, was the massive half-century-long naval campaign to suppress the slave trade that destroyed 1,600 slaving vessels and "liberated" (however qualified the resulting "freedom") more than 200,000 Africans found on

---

[55] David Eltis, Frank Lewis, and Kimberley McIntyre. "Accounting for the Traffic in Africans: Transport Costs on Slaving Voyages," *Journal of Economic History*, 70 (2010): 940–63.

[56] For a full exposition of this argument see David Richardson, "Shipboard Revolts, African Authority, and the Atlantic Slave Trade," *William & Mary Quarterly*, 58 (2001), 69–92; Steven D. Behrendt, David Eltis, and David Richardson, "The Costs of Coercion: African Agency in the Pre-modern Atlantic World," *Economic History Review*, 54 (2001): 454–76.

[57] Behrendt et al., "Costs of Coercion," 473–75.

board. This, too, increased the costs of carrying slaves across the Atlantic.[58] The total cost to the British of this naval campaign plus subsidies and bribes to foreign slave powers to ban the traffic was £12.4 million pounds between 1816 and 1865 (in constant pounds 1821=100) – somewhat less than the £20 million that they paid out in compensation to slave owners when slavery was abolished.[59] Finally, behind the naval campaign was an abolitionist movement that spread around the Atlantic world during the nineteenth century and helped eliminate the demand for slave labor. The interaction of these factors and their relative importance is discussed in Chapter 6. The underlying point in this discussion – ignored by almost all historians – is that resistance did not have to destroy the slave ship or overthrow the slave system to be effective. Higher costs anywhere in the pipeline that converted labor in Africa to the contents of the sugar bowls of Europe always meant fewer Africans carried off from Africa – in the above examples, millions fewer.

One of the widely cited findings to emerge from the first appearance of the TSTD on a 1999 CD-ROM, was that African resistance to the slave trade as expressed through onboard slave revolts displayed a strong regional bias. Rebellions, in short, were much more likely to occur on vessels leaving from Upper Guinea – the coast ranging from modern Senegal to the western limits of Côte d'Ivoire – than from the more southerly regions of sub-Saharan Africa. Moreover, compared to these other regions, Upper Guinea was not a major source of captives, supplying fewer than 12 percent of total embarkations over a period of 350 years.[60] The twenty-five years of research since 1999 that have both lengthened and thickened the TSTD have simply reinforced this finding. While Upper Guinea may have supplied only 12 percent of all captives carried off, more than 40 percent of the vessels experiencing revolts came from that same area. In addition, we now know that uprisings on Hispaniola in the 1530s involved Muslim Wolof slaves, all embarked in Upper Guinea, whom

---

[58] Richard Huzzey, "The Politics of Slave-Trade Suppression," in Richard Huzzey and Robert Burroughs (eds.), *The Suppression of the Atlantic Slave Trade: British Policies, Practices and Representations of Naval Coercion* (Manchester, UK, 2015), pp. 18–51.

[59] Eltis, *Economic Growth*, pp. 91–94. A different calculation would take the share of naval ships committed to the suppression of the slave trade and apply that share to the total naval budget. Such a procedure would generate a figure in excess of £20 million. For further discussion of these figures and their significance see the discussion in chapter 7 below.

[60] Behrendt et al., "Costs of Coercion," 454–76; Richardson, "Shipboard Revolts, African Authority," pp. 69–92.

slave traders were for a time banned from introducing into Spanish America.[61]

Were Europeans avoiding what to them were troublesome sources of slaves and thus tolerating longer and more costly voyages to the south and east to reduce the incidence of rebellion? Were enslaved Africans therefore helping to shape the distribution of the transatlantic slave trade? There can be no doubt that Africans influenced the size and direction of the traffic. But the association between revolts on the one hand and the coastal origins (or religions) of slaves on the other, probably has a more mundane explanation.

As Marcus Rediker has noted, "the greater the number of people in the plot, the greater the chance of success, but at the same time, the greater the chance that someone would snitch." In short, there was a collective action problem, where, because of the high risk and the horrendous consequences of failure, individual captives had an incentive not to participate in a revolt. It turns out that insurrection was more likely on vessels containing smaller numbers of slaves, spending more time on the coast, and carrying a higher ratio of males. These were all characteristic of slaving ventures to Upper Guinea markets, which lacked the supply networks that allowed relatively quick turnaround times in places further south.[62] Particularly striking is the relative absence of rebellions in that portion of the slave trade that operated between Bissau and Cacheu to Amazonia after 1750 – a branch of the trade conducted entirely under the Portuguese flag. Though both locations were in Upper Guinea, the Portuguese had a significant land-based presence there. As we have seen there is evidence of runaways and rebellion in the barracoons of both places, but not a single voyage leaving this port is recorded as experiencing a revolt. Rebellions were never successful, if by success we mean that those imprisoned escaped back to Africa or at least to freedom.[63] For successful in this sense we must turn to the intra-American traffic. Rebels in three cases – the *San Juan Nepomuceno* in 1800–1801, the *Amistad* in 1839, and

---

[61] Eagle, "Early Slave Trade to Spanish America," pp. 144–45.

[62] For the collective action problem, see Rediker, *Slave Ship*, pp. 292–93. For a formal analysis see Peter T. Leeson, "Rational Choice, Round Robin, and Rebellion: An Institutional Solution to the Problems of Revolution," *Journal of Economic Behavior & Organization*, 73 (2010): 297–307. For Leeson's hypotheses applied to the slave ship rebellions, see Andrew Marcum and David B Skarbek, "The Collective Action Problem of Onboard Slave Revolt," *Rationality and Society*, 26 (2014): 236–62.

[63] A possible exception – depending how one defines the slave trade – is the successful escape of 391 *engagés* from the French ship *Regina Coeli*, discussed in chapters 1 and 5. See Renault, *Liberation d'esclaves*, pp. 66–67.

the *Creole* in 1841 – really did escape.⁶⁴ Ships in this traffic lacked barricados, had smaller crews, slave numbers that averaged fewer than 40, and typically carried a larger proportion of males than vessels in the transatlantic traffic.⁶⁵ In other words they shared a lot of the characteristics of transatlantic vessels off the Upper Guinea coast. Shipboard resistance may have had a major influence on the transatlantic slave trade, but the determinants of rebellions had little to do with social structures, religion, or values of the societies from which captives were drawn. The desire to escape captivity was a constant and we need only look for the circumstances that created opportunities.

Resistance of enslaved people on Portuguese and Brazilian slave ships was expressed differently. As already noted, it was more likely to be manifested in the holding centers on the African coast than on the slave ship itself because that is where the enslaved spent most of the time between capture in Africa and sale in Brazil. On South Atlantic routes to Brazil a barrier such as the barricado is never mentioned in the sources. We have three images of a Portuguese slave ship between 1743 and 1830 when the Portuguese traffic was still legal. Two paintings hung in Brazilian churches because the owner of the vessel believed a miracle had ensured the success of his venture are of the *Nossa Senhora de Nazaré e S Antônio* (ID 8148), and

---

⁶⁴ The *San Juan Nepomuceno* left Montevideo for Lima in late 1800. As the vessel approached Cape Horn, the slaves rose up, killed five officers, transferred a section of the crew to a passing coastal vessel, and ordered the remainder to take the *San Juan* to Senegal, the home region of several of the rebels. Five months later, in April 1801, this improbable voyage ended at the island of Saint-Louis just weeks after a pro-abolitionist revolutionary governor had taken over the administration of this French colony. About forty surviving captives were freed and disappear from the record (Greg Grandin, *The Empire of Necessity: Slavery, Freedom and Deception in the New World* [New York, 2014], pp. 182–85). The second was the famous *Amistad*, sailing with fifty-three newly arrived Africans from Havana to Puerto Principe (now Camagüey) in Cuba. The rebellion, on July 2, 1839, three days after leaving Havana, gave Africans control of the schooner, which was eventually detained by a US naval vessel off Long Island, New York. Three subsequent court cases, the last one heard before the Supreme Court, resulted in the freeing of the captives, and thirty-five survivors returned to Sierra Leone (Howard Jones, *Mutiny on the Amistad: The Saga of a Slave Revolt and Its Impact on American Abolition* [New York, 1987], but for a more African perspective see Arthur Abraham at www.sierra-leone.org/Books/Amistad.pdf). Also well-known was the *Creole*, en route from Virginia to New Orleans in 1841: After taking possession of the vessel, the former captives brought it into Nassau, knowing that the British had recently abolished slavery and had freed slaves on other US ships in British waters (George Hendrick and Willene Hendrick, *The Creole Mutiny: A Tale of Revolt Aboard a Slave Ship* [Chicago, IL, 2003]). The three cases are viewable at www.slavevoyages.org/voyages/qlxJpPeR.

⁶⁵ The overall male ratio in the I-Am traffic was 75 percent; in TSTD it is 64.5 percent. See https://slavevoyages.org/voyage/database#statistics; and https://slavevoyages.org/american/database#statistics.

the *Nossa Senhora do Rozario do Castello* (not yet identified). Both had a full complement of slaves on board yet show no sign of this large defensive work, although it must certainly have existed below decks to separate men from women.[66] Robert Walsh's drawing of the Bahian slaver, *Veloz* (ID 1126), made just prior to the 1830 ending of the legal trade to Brazil, also shows no barricado, but it does have a cannon, presumably loaded with peashot, pointing at the slave deck. The shorter voyages around the South Atlantic gyre, together with the practice of embarking captives just prior to departure, made it unnecessary.[67]

As already discussed, there was one area where the Portuguese slave trade overlapped with that of the French, British, and Dutch – and that was the Bight of Benin. During the whole period of the slave trade, the Portuguese obtained more than 1 million slaves there, about 18 percent of all the Africans they carried off to the Americas. Here, the Portuguese came closest to the ship-based slave trade of their northern competitors and, not surprisingly, they began to face the same problems. According to TSTD, before 1760 this Portuguese Mina trade was confined to just three locations – the Dutch castle of Elmina, Epe, and Ouidah – locations with rapid turnaround times, especially for Brazilian vessels offering preferred trade goods in the form of gold and tobacco rolls.[68] In addition, in the early decades of the eighteenth century Portuguese slave ships carrying gold to the Mina Coast would often buy the complete slave cargo of English ships, thus compensating for their relative lack of factories in the region and reducing the time that slaves spent on board.[69] Nevertheless, immediately before Brazilian gold

---

[66] *Para Nuncer Esquecer: Negras Memórias, Memórias de Negros* (Rio de Janeiro, 2001), frontispiece; Portugal. Comissão Nacional para as Comemorações dos Descobrimentos Portugueses, *Estórias de dor esperança e festa: O Brasil em ex-votos portugueses (séculos XVII–XIX)* (Lisbon, 1998), "Milagre de Nossa Senhora do Rosário do Castelo a Francisco de Sousa Pereira."

[67] Robert Walsh, *Notices of Brazil in 1828 and 1829*, 2 vols (London, 1830), vol. 2: facing title page, and pp. 260–67. Walsh was on board the slaver (ID 895) for only a few hours, long enough to take measurements and make a sketch, but not to make a scale diagram.

[68] http://slavevoyages.org/voyages/EqJ9oqon; vessels from Bahia typically called at Dutch Elmina to pay a levy amounting to 10 percent of their outbound cargo. According to TSTD, between 1720 and 1740 such vessels also took on board an average of 95 slaves at Elmina (n=42), before proceeding to Epe or Ouidah in the Bight of Benin to purchase a further two or three hundred captives. For more information, see Verger, *Flux et reflux*, chapter 1; Stuart B. Schwartz and Johannes Postma, "The Dutch Republic and Brazil as Commercial Partners on the West African Coast during the Eighteenth Century," in Postma and Enthoven (eds.), *Riches from Atlantic Commerce*, pp. 171–99.

[69] Mitchell, *Prince of Slavers*, Appendix; voyage IDs 76418, 76954, 76433 are examples of this practice.

began to arrive on the coast, say between 1670, when Bahian slave vessels first begin to show up in West Africa, and 1700, the Portuguese – like their northwestern European competitors – were without significant coastal bases in the region and were forced to trade from the ship in the same way as their competitors. Interestingly, they lost four ships to slave rebellions in four years in the Ouidah road, presumably while they were assembling their full complement of captives.[70] The first permanent Portuguese fort at Whydah dates from 1721. Moreover, this is the one branch of the traffic where an illustration of a Portuguese slave ship complete with a northwestern European style barricado has survived.[71] Thus, for these few years a fragment, at least, of Portuguese slave trading was ship-based.[72]

As well as a regional bias in resistance, a second major finding to emerge from the CD-ROM version of TSTD was the strong temporal pattern in shipboard rebellions and attacks from the African shore. More than one-quarter of the total number of people carried off from Africa embarked after British and US abolition of the slave trade in 1807. Yet fewer than 5 percent of the 565 resistance incidents recorded in the current TSTD occurred in this same period.[73] Part of the explanation for this extraordinary decline is simply the southward shift in the center of gravity of the nineteenth-century traffic.[74] Upper Guinea outlets to the Atlantic, along with those on the Gold Coast, were among the first to withdraw from the business – either because of British naval pressure, or, according to some scholars, an independent Islamic and African-based abolitionist impulse.[75] By 1830, almost the whole transatlantic slave trade drew on the

---

[70] Willem Bosman, *New and Accurate Description of the Coast of Guinea, Divided into the Gold, the Slave, and the Ivory Coasts* (London, 1705), p. 366. Bosman was highly disparaging of Portuguese slave traders before the Minas Gerais gold began to reach Africa (see p. 334).

[71] *Transport des Nègres dans les Colonies.* Color-tinted lithograph by Pretextat Oursel, second quarter of the 19th century, now in the Musée d'Histoire de la Ville et du Pays Malouin, Saint Malo. Jane Webster in *Materializing the Middle Passage*, pp. 344–45 has identified the vessel in Oursel's lithograph as Portuguese; Robin Law, Adam Jones, Paul E. Hair (eds.), *Jean Barbot on Guinea: The Writings of Jean Barbot on West Africa, 1678–1712*, 2 vols (Farnham, UK, 2010), vol. 2: 655. www.culture.gouv.fr/public/mistral/joconde_fr?ACTION=CHERCHER&FIELD_98=AUTR&VALUE_98=PRETEXTAT%20Oursel%20&DOM=All&REL_SPECIFIC=1.

[72] It is likely that the Bahia-Bight of Benin branch of the slave trade had many other slave ship rebellions. We do not have information on these partly because of the absence of a Brazilian newspaper culture prior to 1808.

[73] https://slavevoyages.org/voyages/rOW3NIFt.

[74] Eltis and Richardson, *Atlas*, p. 92.

[75] For Islam as a source of nineteenth-century abolitionism see Rudolph T. Ware, *The Walking Qur'an* (Chapel Hill, NC, 2014), pp. 110–62; Jennifer Lofkrantz and Paul

African coast stretching from Dahomey east and south through to the Makonde region of what is now northern Mozambique. But by this stage over this vast region the community of slave traders had embraced the Portuguese system.

The nineteenth century brought major changes to the way slaves were carried off from Africa. The French transatlantic slave trade closed with the outbreak of war with England in 1793 and Dutch involvement, already in decline since the 1770s, followed suit with the French invasion of 1795. The Danes, British, and US had made participation of their own citizens illegal by 1807, and the legislative measures of all three countries did have a major impact. While the French rejoined the trade in 1813 for a further eighteen years, harassment from first the British and then the French authorities meant that the northern European practice of trading from the ship gradually disappeared. In the era of illegal slave trading the presence of slaves on board a vessel was usually incriminating. Slaves were therefore increasingly held on shore until the vessel was ready to depart – the system described above that the Portuguese had established in the sixteenth century. Thus, in the final half-century of the traffic, slaves were spending much less time on the vessel.

Table 4.2 compares the average number of captives found on board slave ships captured off Africa with the average carried off by vessels that escaped capture. In the early phase of suppression, the detained slave ships contained relatively few captives. At this point captains in West Africa were still trading in the northwestern European style by putting people in the slave hold as they purchased them. At the point of detention, many vessels were only partly loaded. Over the next few decades, the number on board captured vessels rose steadily as traders held their captives in shore-based establishments until all were ready to board. In other words, an increasing share of the vessels that the British captured contained a full complement of slaves on board because of the widespread adoption of the Portuguese system. The fact that column 1 never quite matched column 3 on Table 4.2 is explained by several detentions taking place just as the slaves were in the process of embarking. In the resulting confusion traders were able to abort embarkation or land some of the captives prior to capture.

E. Lovejoy, "Maintaining Network Boundaries: Islamic Law and Commerce from Sahara to Guinea Shores," *Slavery & Abolition*, 36 (2015): 211–32. But see Bernard K. Freamon, *Possessed by the Right Hand: The Problem of Slavery in Islamic Law and Muslim Cultures* (Leiden, 2019), for a different view.

TABLE 4.2 *Impact of naval suppression on average number of slaves captured per vessel, 1808–1850, compared to mean number of captives on vessels not captured*

	Mean no. of slaves found on board captured vessels	No. of captured vessels	Mean no. of slaves leaving Africa on board vessels not captured	No. of vessels not captured
1801–1810	88.8	19	328.9	8
1811–1820	138.8	106	312.6	99
1821–1830	234.4	137	322.2	30
1831–1840	309.6	132	398.7	13
1841–1850	373.8	113	457.5	12

Source: Calculated from TSTD

But the major explanation for the apparent decline in resistance lies with an unrecognized and unexpected impact of British naval tactics. The first anti-slave trade patrol began in 1808 but comprised just two warships that cruised only as far south as the southern limit of what is today Sierra Leone. From 1810, however, the Admiralty increased the size of the squadron and extended the patrol range to north of the equator, partly in response to their misinterpretation of a clause in the 1810 Anglo-Portuguese Treaty.[76] Where the British detained just five slave vessels north of the line in 1809, they took twenty-nine in 1810 and over the next quarter-century averaged eighteen detentions per year, despite the fact that for most of this period, only Spanish, Portuguese, and Dutch vessels with slaves on board were liable to capture.[77] These initiatives could not prevent the volume of the transatlantic traffic reaching its highest annual level ever in 1829, but it did induce slave traders to spend less time on the West African coast. Compared to the long eighteenth century (1701–1809), the number of days spent on the coast in the following quarter-century (1810–1834) declined by one-quarter. In effect, African sellers of slaves or land-based European slave traders were holding enslaved people in barracoons onshore for longer periods of time and were thereby absorbing the risks of rebellion (and escape) that had previously been borne by the owners, captains, and crew of the slave ship.

Given that vessels would land an agent, unload merchandise, and then put out to sea again before returning to collect enslaved persons, a good

[76] Eltis, *Economic Growth*, pp. 106–107.
[77] http://slavevoyages.org/voyages/pDYbgGUY.

part of time on the coast was now spent not at anchor, but in cruising without slaves (and sometimes without slave-trading equipment) while the vessel's intended "payload" was assembled onshore. The opportunities to stage a shipboard rebellion were now restricted to just the length of the middle passage. But this, too, was sharply cut from sixty-eight days between 1701 and 1809 to just forty between 1835 and 1866, as copper sheathing on the hull, improved design, iron fittings replacing wood, and even steam propulsion all came into use. As we might expect, advances in maritime technology applied to legal and illegal activity alike.[78] If slave ships in the nineteenth century spent far less time sitting on the coast accumulating a full complement of captives than their eighteenth-century predecessors, then the collective action problem identified by Rediker and other scholars moved from the slave deck to the stockade. In effect, the British navy helped reduce the incidence of shipboard rebellions by limiting the opportunities for them to occur. West African slave traders had adopted the Portuguese system in response to British naval pressure after 1809.

The trend in sex and age ratios also contributed to a decline in the incidence of revolts. TSTD contains 4,273 voyages with some information on the proportion of men and children carried during the last two centuries of transatlantic slave trading. Prior to serious attempts to suppress the traffic, men had typically comprised half of those on board. After 1809, this ratio declined to 42 percent by mid-century. More important was the sharp increase in the share of children, from 16 percent before abolition to 32.5 percent from 1810 to the Anglo-Spanish Treaty of 1835, and then a further jump to 42.2 percent in the last three decades of the business. Several voyages carried only children in this era.[79] The only eighteenth-century parallel to such a pattern was the small and specialized traffic in children to serve as house slaves, that operated down to mid-century from the Gambia and the southern rivers of Senegambia to Lisbon. The causes of the nineteenth-century decline in average age remain unclear. Perhaps slave traders were attempting to make their ventures more secure, or possibly, as

---

[78] We lack systematic data on escapes and rebellions in barracoons, though slave protests against human sacrifice did emerge in Calabar in 1850. See Augustine S.O. Okwu, *Igbo Culture and the Christian Missions, 1857–1957: Conversion in Theory and Practice* (Lanham, MD, 2010), pp. 47–49. On voyage times it should be noted that while the Mozambique to Brazil voyage was longer at sixty-six days (n = 284), it was still an average of ten days shorter than its West African-Caribbean counterpart of the previous century.

[79] Three-quarters of the nineteen voyages in TSTD recorded as having at least four out of five captives classed as children sailed after 1814, see (https://slavevoyages.org/voyages/QdRzqbfd). See the *Minerva* in 1842 (ID 3175), which had no slave deck.

with non-human commodities, more efficient transoceanic transportation allowed the movement of lower-cost items – in this case, from a slave merchant's perspective – children. Either way, opportunities for revolt were far fewer after 1809 than before.

The word "barracoons" (shore-based stockades) appears infrequently in the English and French records before 1810; just as the word "barricado" disappears after 1809. Paintings and sketches of captured slave ships constituted a sub-genre of maritime art in the aftermath of abolition. Not one of these illustrations – usually executed by a naval officer present at the time of detention – show a barricado. The 1835 Anglo-Spanish Convention was the single most important slave trade treaty of the post-abolition era in terms of interfering with the traffic as opposed to making it formally illegal. It allowed for the detention of vessels on the grounds of equipment rather than slaves on board. Article X specified that the presence of any one of nine items was sufficient grounds for condemnation. These included shackles, open gratings, an excess of water barrels, bulkheads, or spare planks, but the purpose of the "spare planks" was described as "for[the] laying down of ... a slave deck," not a barricado.[80] All nine items specified would have been familiar to crews and captives from the very beginning of the traffic, but nowhere in this period is there reference to what had been the main defensive work of West African slave vessels prior to abolition. Adult males of course remained in chains, within the field of fire of armament when above deck. William Doherty, a liberated Yoruba taken from a Portuguese slave ship in the mid 1840s recalled "[e]ach morning they were called up & fed on dry gari & salt beef, with one measure of water, five men fed at once one bucket of gari. After they had eaten, they were allowed to stay up & catch the breeze for one or two hours ... then they were put down in the hold which was so full they had to fit in close together."[81] But as the time spent bringing captives on board and crossing the Atlantic fell, along with the average age of captives, West African slave traders dispensed with the barricado. Paradoxically, in contrast to the pattern in the plantation Americas, abolitionist pressures were apparently associated with a decline in African resistance, on ships at least, rather than an increase.[82]

---

[80] Great Britain, PP, 1850, vol. L: 507–508.
[81] Richard P. Anderson, "Slavery, Emancipation, and the Mission: Narratives from Nineteenth-Century Africa," unpublished manuscript supplied by the author, p. 112.
[82] Rebellions, however, did not disappear. An unnamed vessel (ID 4162) lost 200 captives to a series of revolts in early 1853 en route from Mozambique to Cuba. BNA, Consul Crawford to Lord John Russell, March 3, 1853, FO84/905.

Shorter voyages and fewer slave rebellions gave the Portuguese an advantage over their northern competitors, not least because they resulted in lower shipboard mortality, with implications for profits. In addition, Portuguese slave ships were much less susceptible to capture. The eighteenth-century wars that severely disrupted the slave trade of the northern powers at regular intervals were rarely fought in the South Atlantic – where the Portuguese predominated. Between 1660 and 1807, TSTD contains records of 5,535 Portuguese slaving ventures. Only forty-seven of these terminated in capture by a pirate, or by another European power – usually the Dutch – yielding an extraordinarily low capture ratio of less than 1 percent. By contrast, further north frequent wars ensured that the French and English lost 7 percent of their ventures to enemy capture over the same period.[83]

As one might expect from these findings, the crews of Portuguese slavers were smaller than average, and, as Table 4.3 shows, they carried more slaves per crew member than did their French, English, and Dutch counterparts between 1750 and 1810 (the only years for which comparative crew data are available). Nothing approaching the rich accounting data available for the Dutch Middelburg Company, the London-based Royal African Company, and some Liverpool and Bristol slave traders, has survived for Portuguese and Brazilian slavers. We cannot therefore make direct cost comparisons across national flags, much less create a comparative price series for slaves, but all the physical (as opposed to

TABLE 4.3 *Slaves embarked per crew member on board when vessel left home port, by national flag, 1751–1810*

Country in which ship registered	Mean	Number of vessels	Std. deviation
Portugal/Brazil	12.2	76	9.5
Great Britain	9.8	828	3.1
Netherlands	7.2	65	1.7
France	9.1	713	2.7
Total	9.5	1,682	3.6

Source: Calculated from TSTD

[83] For the Portuguese, see http://slavevoyages.org/voyages/yYCDfaMO; for the British, https://slavevoyages.org/voyages/MAbW94N5; for the French, https://slavevoyages.org/voyages/NNitkFLW.

financial) productivity data – voyage length, shipboard rebellions, capture ratios, and crew sizes – suggests that the many private slave-trading merchants in Brazilian ports (and at least one of the several Portuguese monopoly trading companies) were able to deliver captives to planters in Brazil at a lower cost than could northwestern Europeans to their own Caribbean colonies.[84]

The British and Dutch were the most successful of the northern nations, with the former as we have seen taking over from the Portuguese intermittently as the leading transatlantic slave-trading nation for much of the eighteenth century. But the British never succeeded in displacing the Portuguese in Upper Guinea, the Bight of Benin, and Angola. The secret to the partial British and Dutch success was strong economic growth in Europe, their growing maritime power, and their associated ability to make the metals and some of the textiles that Africans wanted. The northwestern Europeans were able to tap into Brazilian exports of tobacco rolls and gold by trading with Portuguese ships on the West African coast to create the right assorted cargo. There may have been few traders of English-, Dutch- and French-African descent within Africa, but these northwestern European nations tended to develop close friendships and business relationship with key Africans living on the African littoral. In the seventeenth and eighteenth centuries the British and Dutch used their naval and economic powers to attempt to break into Iberian domination of the Americas and of the slave trade. In the end, they had to make do with the temperate Americas (plus Jamaica and some of the lesser Antilles) for their markets. Their trafficking on the African coast always remained based on ships rather than bulking centers.

By the nineteenth century, the British at last achieved the power to seriously penetrate the Portuguese slave-trading system, but apparently no longer had the will to do so. Indeed, they spent most of that century trying to suppress the traffic. In a counterfactual world, one can easily imagine a pro-slave trade Anglo-Portuguese Treaty as the British fleet carried off

---

[84] Some of the costs of the shore-based barracoons and the networks that fed them were absorbed by the Portuguese government. Just as the north European nations paid for the naval forces that protected their Caribbean possessions and were the ultimate defense against plantation slave revolts, so the Portuguese government put resources into warfare in Angola and defense of their Portuguese African outposts. Export duties on slaves covered part of this expense and therefore would have been reflected in slave prices paid by the Brazilian planters. It should also be stressed that shorter voyages had few positive implications for the health of the enslaved. Mortality rates remained high, the best description of which by firsthand observers of Portuguese slavers disembarking in Sierra Leone after capture is in Anderson, *Abolition in Sierra Leone*, pp. 82–88.

the Bragança royal family from Lisbon in November 1807. Such a treaty would not only have allowed British goods into Brazil but would likely have seen English investors based in Liverpool and London become the dominant slave traders supplying nineteenth-century Bahia and Rio de Janeiro with captives – perhaps moving part of their operations to Brazil. After all, French and London-based English slave traders had been trying to ship slaves to both ports in the previous century.[85] If, as Manolo Florentino and João Fragoso have argued, Brazilian slave owners and slave traders squandered their gains pursuing the "aristocratic idea," an influx of British investors and capital just as the slave-enabled coffee revolution was gathering speed would surely have set Brazil on to a radically different path of development as well as improving the fortunes of the British.[86]

But this was an economic opportunity lost, given that 1807 was also the year that the transatlantic slave trade became illegal for British subjects. The actual Anglo-Portuguese Treaty (in 1810) that followed on from the flight of the royal family to Rio de Janeiro contained an *anti*-slave trade clause. The relationship between capitalism and slavery once more appears complicated. The northern Europeans were latecomers to Atlantic slavery; it was their manufacturing capabilities, financial intermediaries and state support that allowed them to take a few islands from the Spanish, break into the Atlantic slave trade, and develop a West African alternative, albeit temporary, to the Portuguese enslaved procurement system.[87] But it did not have to be temporary. Access to Brazilian ports in the nineteenth century could have provided a bonanza for British slave traders.

Did the differences between the Portuguese and the rest matter? They should matter for historians interested in the African experience. More than 7 million Africans embarked on slave ships between 1701 and 1809, and almost half as many again from 1810 through to the end of the trade. A large literature exists on crowding, mortality, and the horrors of the

---

[85] See Ernst Pijning, "Regulating Illegal Trade: Foreign Vessels in Brazilian Harbors," *Portuguese Studies Review*, 15 (2007): 321–66. For cases not mentioned by Pijning see BNA, William Hickes, to RAC, Dec. 12, 1709, T70/5, ff. 65–6; James Blaney to RAC, Nov. 14, 1706, ibid, 25; Joseph Blaney to RAC, Jan. 12, 1714, T70/3, p. 10.

[86] João Luís Ribeiro Fragoso and Manolo Florentino, *O arcaísmo como projeto: mercado atlântico, sociedade agrária e elite mercantil no Rio de Janeiro, c. 1790–c1840*, 4th ed. (Rio de Janeiro, 2001), p. 21 – I thank Leo Marques for drawing my attention to this reference.

[87] For fuller discussions of the connection between economic growth and both slavery and its abolition, see Chapter 5 below.

middle passage, most of it derived from first, the extensive investigations of a committee of the British Privy Council in the late 1780s, second, the narratives of the crews of anti-slave trade cruisers, and third, the massive seven volumes of evidence collected by the British Parliamentary Select Committees on the trade, between 1847 and 1850.[88] This literature presents a single middle passage experience comprising physical violence, shortage of water and food, pestilential disease, periodic cataclysmic revolts, wastage of lives of all on board, and circulating sharks awaiting the next corpse to be dropped overboard. Above all, the image of the *Brooks* slave ship is still viewed as a reflection of reality rather than, as a comparison of Figure 4.1 and Figure 4.2 shows, an exaggerated, highly schematic, yet very successful attempt to attract public attention. Scholars and public alike have failed to recognize how captive experiences varied markedly over time and space. In short, despite the extensive (and mainly abolitionist) sources, many aspects of the typical lived experience of a slave transported to the Americas are not yet represented in the now extensive scholarship.

The slave experience on Portuguese vessels was not only different, but in the nineteenth century, very different yet again. Alonso de Sandoval collected information from hundreds of Africans in early seventeenth-century Cartagena and wrote what is probably the best ethnological treatise on early modern Africa. Scholars have taken his work to mean that adult males were held below deck throughout the voyage, which an abundance of later evidence makes extremely unlikely.[89] We have argued here that a key feature on all slave ships and probably the shore-based holding areas were long chains running across the space of imprisonment to which captives were shackled. Obviously, Africans spent a significantly shorter period of shipboard time in such conditions in the Portuguese trade, but no Portuguese slave ship has ever attracted the attention generated by their British and French counterparts.

For the abolitionist era historians have more images of Portuguese slavers on which to draw. But this was the period when, as our opening paragraphs suggests, the range of types of ships used in the traffic was at is

---

[88] Rediker, *Slave Ship*, and Daniel Mannix and Malcolm Cowley, *Black Cargoes: A History of the Atlantic Slave Trade, 1518–1865* (London, 1962) are probably the two most widely read books on the transatlantic slave trade in the last sixty years to which this comment applies.

[89] Alonso de Sandoval (ed. and translated by Nicole von Germeten), *Treatise on Slavery: Selections from De instauranda aethiopum salute* (Indianapolis, 2008), pp. 56–57. Such an interpretation is not supported by the original text,

greatest. The best-known image in Brazil is a lithograph of the hold of a slave ship created by Johan Moritz Rugendas in the early 1820s.[90] Unfortunately, there is no firm evidence that the engraver had ever set foot on a slave ship and his work could not have been executed from life. Numerous paintings hanging in maritime museums, often show a slaver accompanied by its naval captor, but at least we know the artists were present when the events they depicted occurred.

Three such illustrations allow us a closer examination of changes in slave accommodation during the nineteenth century. They are Figure 4.4, *Isla de Cuba* (1859, ID 4961), Figure 4.5, the *Albanez* (1845, ID 3483) and Figure 4.6, the *Diligente* (1838, ID 2588).

While it would be impossible to visually capture this variety in shipping practices, analyzing three images does give some sense of differences to the conditions shown in the *Brooks* and *Marie-Séraphique* images.[91] Slave vessels had never been large by transoceanic sailing ship standards. But in the quarter-century after 1820 the average standardized tonnage of a slave ship declined by 23 percent. Slave traders not only abandoned the barricado, some even abandoned slave decks after treaties allowing detentions based on the presence of slave trading equipment such as planks and extra water casks came into effect.

Figure 4.4 shows a plan of the hold of the *Isla de Cuba* (ID 4961) of 1859, which displays the barrels of water and provisions that occupied most of the space in a slave ship. Here the slave deck is in the form of planks stacked either side of the hold lying ready to be laid.[92] Attempting to escape a conviction for slave trading, the captain argued in a US court that the planks were intended for sale on the African coast rather than for

---

[90] "Négres a fond de calle," plate 1, 4e Div, in *Malerische Reise in Brasilien* (Paris, 1835). See the discussion in Jaime Rodrigues, *De Costa a Costa: Escravos, Marinheiros e Intermediários do Tráfico negreiro de Angola ao Rio de Janeiro (1780–1860)* (São Paulo, 2005), pp. 131–33.

[91] Not included here is the well-known image of the *Vigilante* from 1822. The unknown draftsman populated the vessel with images of Africans copied directly from the famous Brooks' poster except that their distribution is limited to midship. As a guide to how Africans traveled on a slave vessel, the published image was thus just as misleading as that of the Brooks. Nevertheless, the *Vigilante*'s sketch became accepted as authentic. As late as 1848, *The Illustrated London News* republished the drawing, without attribution, as representative of the conditions then existing in the slave trade (vol. 13, April 26, 1848, p. 123). Thus, the Brooks' diagram continued to dominate public perceptions of the slave trade in the last years of the traffic just as it does today, despite its obvious distortion of reality.

[92] "Return of Slavers Cruizing on the West Coast of Africa waiting for an opportunity to ship; vessels supposed to have shipped, and Slavers whose arrival is daily expected," February to July, 1859, FO84/1100, ff. 93, 242–44.

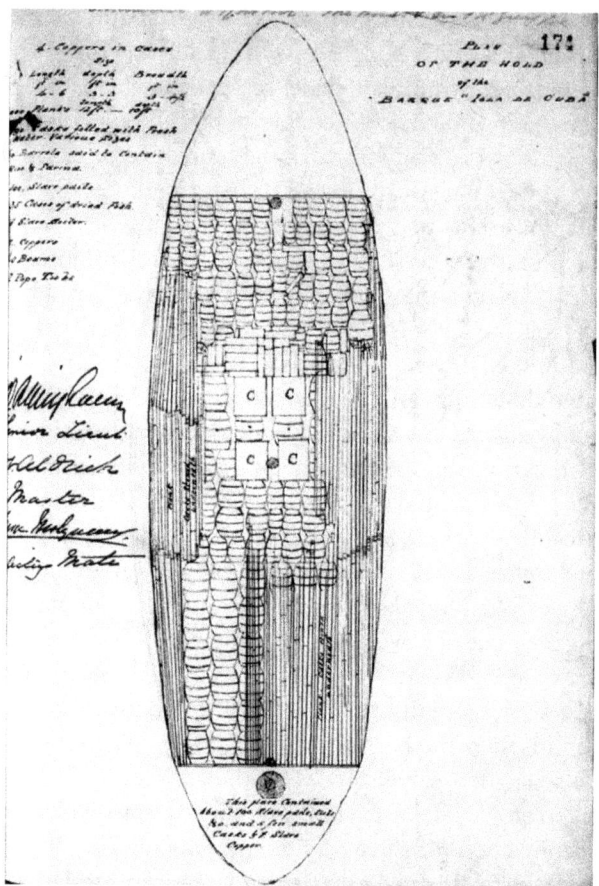

FIGURE 4.4 Contemporary image of the *Isla de Cuba* (ID 4961) showing planks stacked either side of the hold ready to be used for a slave deck. Reproduced with permission of the British National Archives, Kew.

use as a slave deck, and that the barrels of water were for ballast only.[93] A similarly sketched plan of the hold of the ironically named *Legítimo Africano* (ID 3049), detained in 1835 – not shown here – shows a 50-ton vessel without a slave deck (or the planks to make one) and built for speed. Yet it carried 190 people in an area of 400 square feet and with a deck height of just 1 foot 8 inches. How was this possible? Instead of a deck, the captain had formed a makeshift platform by filling the spaces between the

---

[93] Harris, *Last Slave Ships*, p. 104.

The Portuguese System

FIGURE 4.5 *Albanez* (ID 3483). Detained in 1845 with 600 captives, fewer than half of whom are shown in the image. Reproduced with permission of the National Maritime Museum, Greenwich, London.

FIGURE 4.6 Image of the *Diligente* (ID 2588), showing approximately half the number of captives on board at the time of detention. The other half are below deck and can be glimpsed through the open hatches. Reproduced with permission of the National Museum of African American History and Culture.

casks with bags of provisions. The key element that made this possible was that all but one of the 190 people on board were children. Such a pattern meant a dramatic reduction in security costs.[94] The British found an identical below-deck environment on the 45-ton *Jesus Maria* (ID 2071) with 246 Africans on board, of whom only five were adults – all, unsurprisingly, women.[95] Naval officers reported at least a dozen such cases after 1835 describing sand ballast or firewood filling the spaces between casks, or sometimes simply "hides laid on the tops of leaguers."[96] Scholars have addressed the issue of children in the slave trade by focusing on shifting cultural patterns within Africa, especially the large regional and ethnic variations in child ratios within Africa. However, the jump in the proportion of children carried from all regions in the nineteenth century was most likely a slave-trader response to naval activity.[97]

The painting of the slave hold of the *Albanez* (ID 3483) in Figure 4.5 shortly after its detention in the Congo River in 1845 captures how Africans may have been transported in vessels lacking a fixed slave deck. The painter, Francis Meynell, is probably sitting on the forward stairs looking aft and Africans can be seen on the casks. Frequently reproduced, the image is certainly authentic, and, in this respect, it matches the drawing of the *Marie-Séraphique*. The painting is not intended as a depiction of conditions in the middle passage because the apprehending cruiser, HMS *Albatross*, had taken on board many of the captives prior to the long voyage to adjudication in Freetown. Thus, the viewer sees the real belowdecks of a slaver, but only some of the captives. Even so, the image evocatively captures the chaos of a dimly lit slave deck. Africans are spread uncomfortably across the tops of barrels, some on mats, some on the bare wooden hoops; one captive sits on a latrine in the foreground, wrapping himself with his arms,

---

[94] Papers of Sir Thomas Fowell Buxton, BL, vol. 27, loose sheet; anon., "Report of the Case of the Portuguese schooner 'Legitimo Africano,'" BNA, FO84/169, ff. 67–75.

[95] Admiralty to Palmerston, March 31, 1840 (enc.), BNA, FO84/383; BNA, J. Kennedy and C.J. Dalrymple to Lord Palmerston, Jan. 20, 1841, FO313/18.

[96] For details, see the sources for the following voyageids in www.slavevoyages.org: 2097, 3466, 3458, 3483, 3484, 3629, 3689, 4057, 4072, 4073, 4082, 4940. The quote is from Charlotte Pilkington, Rio de Janeiro, September 23, 1840, in "Papers of the Anti-Slavery Society, 1757–1982," BL, MSS. Brit. Emp. S. 22, G79, "Leaguer" was a nautical term for a large water cask.

[97] David Eltis, "Fluctuations in the Age and Sex Ratios of Slaves in the Nineteenth-Century Transatlantic Slave Traffic," *Slavery and Abolition*, 7 (1986): 257–72; Eltis and Engerman, "Fluctuations in Sex and Age Ratios"; Paul E. Lovejoy, "The Children of Slavery – the Transatlantic Phase," *Slavery and Abolition*, 7 (2006): 197–217.

perhaps a dysentery victim. Above the barrels, slaves perch and lie on wooden beams, some with their legs dangling over the ledge. Many more captives are crammed together on platforms running along the vessel's side, one of the only commonalities with the *Marie-Seraphique*. Light pours in from the ceiling but only illuminates the captives in the center of the image. The fact that it is daylight gives some sense of how the Africans would have experienced the middle passage: packed below deck in whatever space they could find.[98]

While the *Albanez* and *Isla de Cuba* give some sense of the holds of illegal slavers, the recently unearthed painting of the *Diligente* (Figure 4.6) reveals the sheer mass of humanity that slave traders crammed onto their vessels. The *Diligente* (ID 2588) was a 174-ton brig depicted leaning in slightly toward the painter. It carried 475 Africans – survivors of 520 embarked at Lagos. Detained on its way to Cuba in 1838, the *Diligente* provides, at first glance, the most accurate depiction of the fair-weather daytime experience of captives for any period; not even the image of the *Marie-Seraphique* (Figure 4.3) provides such a view. But things are not quite what they seem. The deck shows fewer than half the number of captives that we can document as disembarking a few days after the detention. Furthermore, the seven blue-jacketed figures can only be the prize crew from HMS *Pearl*, not the original slave-ship crew. Thus, the artist's viewpoint is probably on the quarterdeck of HMS *Pearl* as the naval vessel conducts its prize to Nassau in the Bahamas – the capture having taken place in the Caribbean, not off the African coast. The missing two hundred or so Africans are probably below deck; some of them can be seen in the open hatch beside the mainmast. But here, as with all the other Portuguese vessels mentioned in this section, there is no sign of a barricado. There is no illustration of, nor indeed any documentary reference to, such a structure in the illegal era, something that makes sense given the need to conceal the vessel's intentions from the British navy. Crewmen likely enforced the separation of male and female slaves through restraints and violence or, alternatively, kept captives below deck for the voyage. To derive a perspective of crowding on the *Diligente* we need to imagine double the number of figures depicted in the painting, crammed below deck. As already noted, the belowdeck numbers can actually be glimpsed through two open hatches fore and aft of the mainmast that the painter has depicted.

---

[98] Francis Meynell, 1845, "Rescued Africans on deck of HM Sloop 'Albatross'," National Maritime Museum, Greenwich, UK, D9316.

Three illustrations cannot encapsulate the experience of captives in the nineteenth-century slave trade, but they can indicate change in that experience over time. The illegal phase of the trade as represented in the voluminous reports of British naval officers communicates a sense of the Wild West when, especially after the 1835 equipment clause, almost anything was possible. Apart from the open launches discussed earlier, slave traders used other strategies to economize on small spaces that fundamentally altered the African experience of the middle passage. In 1842, a 29-ton vessel bound from Ambriz to Brazil took off 127 captives – more than half of them children. The height between water casks and the underside of the main deck was just 1 foot 2 inches, and "one half of the slaves were obliged always to be on deck where they were so confined that every foot of the deck was occupied, while the reminder below were squeezed to excess."[99] Such variation in shipping practices does not permit easy distillation of the average experience, but scholars and the general public alike need to look beyond the *Brooks*.

In summary, European and Africa interaction on the coast generated three broad categories of slave experiences over 370 years. The first typically involved vessels carrying fewer than 100 captives and shipping, in addition, considerable produce to Europe from Upper Guinea, or, if going to the Americas, European merchandise and migrants. Confined mainly to the first half of the sixteenth century, the transatlantic voyages might have obtained their captives from the Iberian peninsula, or they might set out from Iberian ports and collect captives from the Canaries or Cape Verde Islands en route. In such cases the slave experience would have included an additional voyage of several hundred miles from the mainland to these offshore islands – as well as detention in barracoons. The vessels involved were caravels or galleons little different from their counterparts that plied the Atlantic and Pacific without slaves on board. The second category evolved from the first. The main difference being that as demand for slaves increased, the vessel became a recognizable slave ship, complete with dedicated slave deck, and often permanent shackles for the men. This system continued throughout the slave trade era, though it became increasingly a defining characteristic of the South Atlantic slave trade. In the nineteenth century, the slave deck might be abandoned. The third category, associated with the northwestern European incursion into the business, comprised the same dense crowding, but a more heavily fortified vessel, larger numbers of crew, long periods spent on the ship

---

[99] BNA, Admiralty to Lord Aberdeen, Sept. 15, 1842 (enc.), FO84/441.

both before and after leaving Africa, and greatly increased risk of slave revolts. We cannot be sure of the start date, but it was probably in effect for just 160 years, and it is likely that fewer than half the 12.5 million captives carried off from Africa experienced it.

This third category is certainly the best known of these experiences – partly because of the images of the *Brooks* and now the *Marie-Séraphique*. but in the end perhaps even accurate contemporary depictions must give way to 3D visualizations. The surviving plans of *L'Aurore*, published in 1984 by Jean Boudriot and the contemporary illustrations of the *Marie-Séraphique* are both incorporated into videos available on the home page of www.slavevoyages.org that begin to show what is possible in recreating the shipboard experience of the enslaved.[100]

---

[100] See www.slavevoyages.org/voyage/ship#3dmodel/o/en/. The emphasis on the Portuguese in this chapter is consistent with Michael Zeuske's recently published Afrika-Atlantik-Amerika: Slaverei und Sklavenhandel in Afrika, auf dem Atlantik und in den Amerikas Sowie in Europa (Berlin, 2022).

5

Africa, Africans, and the Slave Trade

AFRICAN CONCEPTIONS OF ENSLAVEMENT

African involvement in the transoceanic slave trades is today a particular sensitive topic, given the huge scale of the human traffic and the equally huge discrepancies in modern income levels between sub-Saharan Africa on the one hand and on the other the Old-World nations that organized the maritime segment of those trades. John Thornton has grappled with this dilemma in an essay that lays out what might be taken as a major subtheme of the present work as identified in Chapter 1.

> African rulers controlled states typical of their era throughout the world. Such states were often based on assumptions of power and authority that are no longer fashionable ... the right of governments to tax and take tribute without necessarily delivering any services, judicial systems that unashamedly protected the interests of the rich and powerful ... holding people as slaves ... and selling these rights. Today ... these ideas are repugnant, but rulers nevertheless ... had their principles and ethics, even if these were not the same as today.[1]

African states had very clear ideas about who could be enslaved and who among those enslaved could be forced into the hold of transoceanic slaving vessel.

For millennia before the onset of Atlantic slave trading, states with very different cultures across the Eurasian landmass had participated in slave markets with buyers and sellers each having different conceptions of what slavery meant. Such variations in comprehension at the time of the transaction have often meant that modern scholars are unable to agree on how

---

[1] John Thornton, "African Political Ethics and the Slave Trade," in Derek R. Peterson (ed.), *Abolitionism and Imperialism in Britain, Africa, and the Atlantic* (Athens, OH, 2010), p. 53.

to define slavery. In a sense the Venetian notary in the Sea of Azov's port of Tana in 1360 who recorded the sale of a Chinese girl – no doubt a "base" person in her country of origin – was no different from the Portuguese buying an African at Arguim a century later. In both instances the enslaved person was moving from one type of enslavement to a very different kind. What made such transactions possible was that the person traded was for both parties an outsider and accordingly eligible for slave status. As discussed in Chapter 1, Africans did not have a sub-continent-wide sense of identity or a shared affiliation with a world religion that prevented them from enslaving and selling other people living in Africa. In contrast, for sixteenth-century Europeans enslaving other Europeans was no longer possible, but for them any African was a potential slave. Yet on the African coast as the Portuguese quickly discovered Europeans could buy only those Africans that the sellers also considered to be outsiders.[2]

In the following centuries European newcomers to the business following in the Portuguese wake typically learned what might be called the eligibility rules for enslavement the hard way. In the absence of a land-based imperial presence in Africa the Hawkins slaving raids in Sierra Leone in the 1560s could not sustain a transatlantic slave trade. Likewise, a century and a half later as the English Royal African Company's monopoly crumbled, a host of London newcomers, called "ten-percenters" arrived on the coast without fully comprehending the rules. They did not raid African communities, but neither did they fully appreciate the often-narrow African eligibility requirements. Several of them panyarred (captured) free Africans, then sold them in Barbados, thereby temporarily wrecking the trading relationship for all English on the coast.[3] The RAC ordered its agents on the island to retrieve these individuals and then notified its Cape Coast Castle factors:

the *Guinea Hen* carries back (from Barbados) Seven free tradeing Negroes Panyared by Capt Jackman wch our factors have wth great difficulty Recovered them & sent home. Pray send us some affidavits of Capt. Jackman and other

---

[2] For the Chinese girl, see Hannah Barker, "The Trade in Slaves in the Black Sea, Russia and Eastern Europe," in *CWHS* 2: 112. For a fuller discussion of the general issue of African freedom with particular focus on the now well-known case of the enslavement of several Efik traders at Old Calabar in 1767, as well as the role of pawning slaves as a source of loss of freedom see Paul E. Lovejoy and David Richardson, "Anglo-Efik Relations and Protection against Illegal Enslavement at Old Calabar, 1740–1807," in Sylviane Diouf (ed.), *Fighting the Slave Trade: West African Strategies* (Woodbridge, UK, 2004), pp. 101–18.

[3] For the chaos at Old Calabar in 1701–1703 see Radburn, *Traders in Men*, pp. 59–60.

10 percent Men's miscarriages upon ye Coast in this or like manner wch may be of use to us.⁴

A similar situation occurred in the aftermath of South Carolina's reopening of the African slave trade between 1804 and the end of 1807 when several hundred inexperienced US and Cuban merchants arrived on the African coast to take advantage of this temporary window. What many of them did not know was that Vili societies on the Loango coast, a major source of slaves for transatlantic markets north of the Congo, had a law prohibiting "the sale of anyone born in Loango" other than criminals.⁵ Among the newcomers was a Captain Churchill who had previously "taken off some of the free natives of the Kingdom of Leango [Loango, north of the Congo]." Churchill had the temerity to return to the same port where the Vili Mafouks conspired in retaliation to put on board individuals who would start a rebellion while the vessel was still loading. The rebellion was unfortunately too successful – in the resulting melee the powder on board exploded killing all 240 captives. Churchill escaped but his supercargo later wrote "[t]he people are, in Congo, much exasperated against Captain Churchill, and if they can get possession of him, I have no doubt would murder him."⁶ Other documented cases of slave-ship captains ignoring African norms of eligibility involved equally inexperienced slave-ship's officers. Boston captains James Smith and Thomas Silk, on their only trips to Africa in 1645 and 1736 respectively, enslaved African or, more precisely, *lançado* slave traders with similarly violent outcomes.⁷

But perhaps the clearest and most poignant indicator of African ideas of freedom appears in the record just five years later – when Churchill was still fighting in court in his ultimately futile attempts to claim insurance on the destruction of his human cargo. In 1812 six "natives of Africa" placed on board the condemned slaver *S Miguel Triunfante* at Ouidah vigorously

---

⁴ Royal African Company to John Browne, Joseph Major, and Richard Willis, July 29, 1703, BNA, T70/51, p. 187. For another case see "Accounts of Squirrel" (ID 76191 then at Kingston, Jamaica), July 17, 1723, T70/958, f. 50, where "Cudjo a free Negro [is] sent home in [this] ship" He had been originally embarked on a slave ship at Ouidah and was probably Akan. For the request of a Cabinda mafouk to have his son returned to Africa on an RAC ship after attending school in London in the mid-1680s, see Donnan, *Documents*, vol. 1: 360.
⁵ Martin, *External Trade of the Loango Coast*, pp. 167–68.
⁶ Helen Tunnicliff Catterall, *Judicial Cases Concerning American Slavery and the Negro*, 4 vols (Washington, DC, 1926–1937), vol. 2: 300. This tactic was commonly used by the Chinese against Spanish traders embarking contract laborers from Chinese ports in the mid nineteenth century – see Arnold J. Meagher, *The Coolie Trade: The Traffic in Chinese Laborers to Latin America* (Philadelphia, 2008), chapter 5.
⁷ Kelley, *American Slavers*, pp. 30–31, 91. IDs are 25148 (Smith) and 28409 (Silk).

petitioned against being entered in the Liberated African register. How could they be "liberated," they argued when they had been wrongfully enslaved in the first instance? They "declared themselves freemen and never that they were slaves." The court agreed and indeed they do not appear in any of the court's registers and were not assigned apprenticeship duties. As discussed in Chapter 7, this was indeed a rare instance where rescue from a slave ship really did mean untrammeled freedom.[8]

Yet African conceptions of who was eligible for sale to offshore slave traders could also be porous. The Vai people of the Windward Coast dominated the traffic from Galinhas in the nineteenth century, and occupied territory extending 35 miles inland and comprising 3,300 square miles.[9] Thanks to the African-Origins database we know the ethnolinguistic associations of 2,756 people who left Galinhas in the hold of a slave ship in this era. Only forty of this sample were Vai – most presumably convicted of offenses within the Vai community. No clearer indication of the dominant Vai role as slave traders exists. British slave-trade suppression policies took effect here earlier than at most points further south. After 1850, only two slaving ventures left from the region – the last one in 1856.[10] Two years later, by which time slave supply lines to the coast would likely have atrophied, a French ship, the *Regina Coeli*, showed up off Cape Mount seeking *engagés* – or captives who would be bought from slave traders to serve ten years of indentured servitude on French Caribbean sugar plantations. In the absence of robust captive supply lines, the Vai elite responded by selling many of their own domestic slaves to the French. Disastrous consequences followed. While held on board off Monrovia the former domestic slaves staged a rebellion fueled, as they later claimed, by resentment at the violation of their status, which they understood to have constituted protection against alienation by sale, certainly into the Atlantic slave trade. Clearly, the Vai did not see themselves as fodder for plantations in the Americas. The captives killed all the crew and escaped, mostly into the Monrovia region.[11]

---

[8] BNA, HCA32/1836, part 2, the São Miguel Triunfante case (ID 7627).
[9] Jorge Felipe Gonzalez, "The Transatlantic Slave Trade and the Foundation of the Kingdom of Galinhas in Southern Sierra Leone, 1790–1850," *Journal of African History*, 62 (2021): 1–23. Svend E. Holsoe. "The Cassava-Leaf People: An Ethnohistorical Study of the Vai people with a particular Emphasis on the Tewo People," unpublished PhD thesis, Boston University (1967), pp. 5–9.
[10] https://slavevoyages.org/voyages/W2kAeNM7.
[11] Renault, *Liberation d'esclaves*, pp. 66–67; Philip Misevich and Konrad Tuscherer are writing a book-length analysis of the case. The complicated tensions around the rebellion are reported in BNA, Commodore Wise to the Adm, enc. Commander James Hunt to

As the above suggests, the African-Origins database can be used to identify not only protected groups, but also to provide a novel way to identify African slave traders and enslavers, at least for the nineteenth century. Susu peoples had a strong presence in the hinterlands of the Rio Pongos and Rio Nunez. Language identifications exist for 2,959 individuals embarking at these trading nodes.[12] Yet only thirteen of this group were Susu, thus providing numerical backing for Jorge Felipe's identification of several major Susu slave traders at both locations.[13] The same database provides language identifications of 3,645 people embarking at Malembo, Cabinda, and Loango, Atlantic outlets for the three separate states of Loango, Kakongo, and Ngoyo, and where Vili slave traders were dominant. Only one Vili is identified, suggesting that even Vili lawbreakers were not eligible for dispatch overseas. Likewise, among the 2,861 Africans on ships captured leaving Jakin and Whydah after 1807 whose language we can identify, only fifty Fon names appear. Further south, the distinction between slaves that could be alienated for sale overseas and those that could not was already well established in the major polities of Kongo and Ndongo in mid seventeenth-century West Central Africa. A partial ecclesiastical census in 1704 revealed many slaves in Angola who did not expect to be sold away from their families. And at the very end of the traffic Kosoko, king of Lagos, discovered that one of his palace officials had been enslaved and sent to Bahia. As with most attempts at recovery. his efforts to retrieve this formerly free man failed.[14]

The space for cultural misconceptions and malfeasance that might result in the free becoming unfree was undoubtedly greater on the African coast than in most slave markets in Eurasia discussed in Chapter 1. Children of African slave traders regularly accompanied their European counterparts to a vessel's home port for language and literacy training that could last several years before they returned home. Typically, they lodged in the homes of well-known slave traders in both French and

---

Commodore Wise, Nov. 6, 1858, in FO84/1070, f. 75, especially ff. 77–82. I thank Philip Misevich for this reference.

[12] www.slavevoyages.org/enslaved/ef2yls9D.
[13] Felipe Gonzalez, "The Transatlantic Slave Trade," 336.
[14] Linda M. Heywood and John K. Thornton, *Central Africans, Atlantic Creoles, and the Foundation of the Americas, 1585–1660* (Cambridge, 2007), pp. 78–79; Thornton, *History of West Central Africa*, pp. 252–53, 255; Olatunji Ojo, "Document 2: Letters Found in the House of Kosoko, King of Lagos (1851)," *African Economic History*, 40 (2012): 44. In contrast, nearly 10 percent of the captives leaving the Efik region of Old Calabar had Efik sounding names. Linguistic identifications may be inspected at www.slavevoyages.org/past/database.

British ports. But the Atlantic was a violent and unpredictable ocean, especially in wartime. Captain Cusack of the *Henry* (ID 81804), charged with carrying two 12-year-old sons of "kings" of Gabon to Liverpool "to be there educated," was captured by a Spanish schooner in 1798 and taken into Havana, where the two free African boys were sold along with the other 134 Africans on board, "in spite of all his (Cusack's) remonstrance." They probably ended their lives on a sugar plantation.[15] This and other incidents mentioned here speak to the tacit agreement between buyer and seller that must exist for market transactions to occur and be sustained over time. But they also underscore that the items being traded – human commodities – were not without influence on the transaction's outcome. Breakdowns in the agreement might result in violence, but the capacity for retaliation on both sides ensured that neither buyer nor seller held the upper hand for long.[16] Outside Angola White power on the oceans was matched by Black power on land.

The absence of permanent power imbalances between Europeans and Africans at the transaction point on the coast is consistent with the absence of hard evidence of either side imposing unequal trading terms on the other. Descriptions of the exchange of people for merchandise on the African coast have not survived for the first century and a half of transatlantic slave trading. Detailed accounts of the negotiations between African sellers and European buyers begin to show up only in the later seventeenth century. We have seen that in the first two decades after the British joined the slave trade in 1640 almost 70 percent of the Africans they carried off came from New Calabar, Old Calabar, and a few from Bonny, all in the Bight of Biafra.[17] The earliest accounts of this trade emerge only toward the end of the century, with the logbook of the *Vine* (1682), accounts from the journal of the *Fly* (1697), and the much fuller record of the *Albion* (1699).[18] We know from the names of the African traders listed in these documents that they were middlemen of mainly Qua and Efik origin, and that the people being traded were almost certainly largely Igbo and Ibibio. How did the Efik and English view each other? These documents clearly communicate a sense of equality between buyer

---

[15] Williams, *History of the Liverpool Privateers*, pp. 373–74.
[16] King Agaja of Whydah imprisoned Bulfinch Lambe for failure to repay a debt and he was not released for four years (Marion Johnson, "Bulfinch Lambe and the Emperor of Pawpaw: A Footnote to Agaja and the Slave Trade," *History in Africa* 5 (1978): 345–50. https://doi.org/10.2307/3171496).
[17] Chapter 3 above. See https://slavevoyages.org/voyages/KUL9Irpp.
[18] IDs 9894, 21416, and 20173, respectively.

and seller in the transaction. When conflicts developed between African families or houses of traders, Europeans certainly sought to aid one side or the other in their own self-interest.[19] But whatever the impact on societies from which slaves were drawn, at the point of sale and embarkation Europeans dealt with African traders as one merchant to another. Most compelling are the warm and familiar letters, written from 1760 to 1789, by Bristol and Liverpool merchants on the one hand and important African traders in Old Calabar on the other.[20] Bargaining over price and commodities, human and material, might include disputes and detention, with even violent deaths always possible, but the risk from such events was there for both, and resolution of disputes was never in the long run one-sided.

For the distinguished editors of the definitive edition of Jean Barbot's writings on Guinea, the journal of the *Albion* (ID 21073) "was probably the most detailed account of a slave-ship, in any century of the Atlantic trade, arriving at an African port, dealing with African traders, and embarking slaves." Of Old Calabar, Barbot wrote:

It is well furnish'd with villages and hamlets all about, where Europeans drive their trade with the Blacks, who are good civiliz'd people, and where we get, in their proper seasons, as at New Calabar, all sorts of eatables, yams, bananas, corn, and other provisions for the slaves, which we barter there, as well as elephants teeth.

The very detailed reports about Efik traders in the eighteenth century available in the correspondence of Liverpool traders and in the *Diary of Antera Duke: An Eighteenth-Century African Slave Trader* demonstrate that this assessment of the slave traffic as a trade between equals in the seventeenth century also holds good for the later period.[21] In August 1771

---

[19] For the clearest example of such behavior, see Randy Sparks, *The Two Princes of Calabar: An Eighteenth-Century Atlantic Odyssey* (Cambridge, MA, 2004). But the best discussion of negotiations between African sellers and European buyers is in Radburn, *Traders in Men*, pp. 59–90.

[20] Paul E. Lovejoy and David Richardson, "Letters of the Old Calabar Slave Trade 1760–1789," in Vincent Carretta and Philip Gould (eds.), *Genius in Bondage: Literature of the Early Black Atlantic* (Lexington, KY, 2001), pp. 89–115.

[21] Two scholarly tours de force, published since 2010, now dominate the contemporary writings of slave traders in West Africa in the late seventeenth and late eighteenth centuries. They are Hair et al., *Jean Barbot on Guinea* and Behrendt et al., *Antera Duke*. A third for the nineteenth century is currently under preparation: Marial Iglesias Utset, Philip Misevich, and Konrad T. Tuchscherer, *Diary of Theophilus Conneau*. These books do not get the attention they deserve. Scholars of the slave trade prefer instead to draw on the vast and essentially abolitionist narratives published in the House of Commons Sessional Papers in the late eighteenth century. Quotes are from *Barbot on Guinea*, pp. 677 and 712. For the sometimes turbulent, but usually harmonious, relations between Europeans

the London slave ship *Elizabeth* (ID 78857) ran aground at the entrance of the Bonny River. As was typically the case for ships in distress in coastal waters anywhere in the world, the local population attempted to exercise salvage rights and threatened to plunder the vessel. Captain Welch sought help from King Varrée of Bonny who immediately came in person with his retainers "*s'opposer à ce désordre.*" However, fighting broke out and the powder magazine exploded, killing all on board including King Varrée and the captain.[22] A few decades later, overtly racist effusions in the London press notwithstanding, the shift from the traffic in people to an even higher value traffic in palm oil after 1807 took place without disturbing that balance and indeed the respect of European buyers and African sellers for each other.[23]

Contrast these narratives of African-European interaction with the extreme power imbalance, accompanied of course by arrogance, that emerges from the account of the arrival of another British ship in the region. The flagship of Commodore Wilmot, Commanding Officer of the British anti-slave trade squadron dropped anchor in the Bonny River in 1865 – just a few years after the occupation of Lagos had established the first British land-based presence in what was to become Nigeria. Wilmot wrote a private letter to the head of the Slave Trade Department of the British Foreign Office describing his visit. He began "Bonny is settled satisfactorily" – by which he meant that the transatlantic slave trade had ended. He went on:

> I was there the other day and remained in the River 3 days. [King] Pepple was too ill to attend, but his son and principal chiefs attended. The first day they did not come to time, so I fined the King 20 puncheons, [of palm oil] and went out, returning again in 48 hours, when I found half the fine paid, and the other half forthcoming if I desired it. A most humble letter of apology was also sent promising good behavior for the future. I assembled all the traders, chiefs, etc., gave the latter a most severe lecture, which astonished their weak minds, after which I let them off the remainder of the fine ...[24]

If there was ever a single document that punctuated the shift from a trading relationship of equals to the master and subaltern connections

---

and Africans at Old Calabar in the eighteenth century, see Behrendt et al., *Antera Duke*, pp. 13–119.

[22] *Gazette de France*, November 17, 1771, https://digipress.digitale-sammlungen.de/view/b sb10485560_00383_u001/3?cq=nègre.

[23] Martin Lynn, *Commerce and Economic Change in West Africa: The Palm Oil Trade in the Nineteenth Century* (Cambridge, 1997), pp. 1–81.

[24] Wilmot, Fernando Po, to Wylde, May 14, 1865, Wylde Family Papers, University of Durham Library, WYL/28/22–24.

of imperialism, this is it. This private correspondence between the two most important permanent British officials charged with suppressing the slave trade, suggests that 1865 rather than 1851 – when the British took over Lagos in a close-fought assault – was the year that the British completed their transition from suppressor of the slave trade to the major imperialist power of sub-Saharan Africa.

In the slave trade era, any inequality, at least in terms of both market and military power, was typically experienced by Europeans, not Africans. At Ouidah, Bonny, and the embarkation points north of the Congo River, buyers negotiated a price with the political authority prior to the onset of trade. The Vili Mafouks (officials of the king of Loango) were frequently able to operate as an effective monopolist. For the earliest era of the traffic Ivana Elbl has noted "[t]he iron-handed control that the Oba of Benin exercised over slave supply to the Portuguese."[25] When the slave trade was its peak, the king of Dahomey and the king of Bonny played this role. Given the presence of other slave ships off the coast, almost all owned by different buyers of captives, there were frequently several prospective buyers, but only one African authority who could authorize trade. Only on the Upper Guinea coast was there a more openly competitive market structure. It is indeed, possible that the lack of significantly large state structures on the Upper Guinea littoral helps explain why this large and populous region contributed fewer than 12 percent of the nearly 13 million total that left the sub-continent. But even here there is nothing to indicate unequal trade. If on the coast of Western Africa, the advantage could lie with the seller rather than the buyer, in the Americas, European slave traders could sometimes find themselves temporarily as the only seller.[26]

Commodore Wilmot's report signified that several centuries of mutual respect between European and African on the sub-Saharan littoral had come to an end. Toby Green's argument that Europeans were the dominant partners in trade from the early eighteenth century is not supported by the thousands of individual transactions discussed below and now available online.[27] But just who were the African slave traders that participated in

---

[25] Elbl, "The Portuguese Trade with West Africa," p. 74.
[26] For a survey of market power see Robin Law, "'Here Is No Resisting the Country': The Realities of Power in Afro-European Relations on the West African 'Slave Coast,'" *Itinerario: European Journal of Overseas History*, 18 (1994): 50–64; Stacey J. M. Sommerdyk, "Trade and the Merchant Community of the Loango Coast in the Eighteenth Century," unpublished PhD thesis, University of Hull (2012), pp. 130–32.
[27] Green, *A Fistful of Shells*, pp. 234–39; www.slavevoyages.org/past/enslavers lists several thousand enslavers, both African and of European origin. The strongest sense of the equal

these transactions? Like merchants everywhere, slave traders had minimum requirements without which sustained trading activity was impossible. The first was ample supplies of the commodity to be traded, in this case a human commodity. The second was trust between both parties in a transaction that the terms of any agreement would be carried out. This was where the African political authority became centrally important. The crucial role of the African state in the external slave trade lay not with supplying enslaved people, but in underpinning and sustaining mercantile activity. African rulers certainly acquired and supplied captives to Europeans, especially after winning armed conflicts. both civil and interstate. King Agaja of Dahomey did establish a crown monopoly on slave sales in Ouidah that lasted for two decades, but it resulted in declining numbers of enslaved people leaving the port and could not endure. The main income of rulers derived from the fees and taxes levied on transactions in which they were not direct participants.[28] These prerequisites could be provided by very small polities such as those in Rio Pongo, Galinhas, and Casa Mansa in Upper Guinea, as well as Bonny and Old Calabar in the Bight of Biafra, all located in stateless regions.[29] But obviously larger states such as the Fante on the Gold Coast, Dahomey, and at different times, the kingdoms of Kongo and of Loango could also provide such an environment. Such polities of course could also refuse to participate in the slave trade as did the Kingdom of Benin in the early years of the transatlantic traffic.[30]

A third prerequisite that receives almost no attention from scholars is the larger population's acceptance of slavery and the slave trade. Though

---

status in coastal transactions emerges from Nick Radburn's *Traders in Men*, pp. 59–90; Robin Law, "Slaves, Trade and Taxes: The Material Basis of Political Power in Precolonial West Africa," *Research in Economic Anthropology*, 1 (1978): 37–52; Law, "The Origins and Evolution of the Merchant Community in Ouidah," in Robin Law and Silke Strickrodt (eds.), *Ports of the Slave Trade, Bights of Benin and Biafra* (Stirling, 1999), pp. 55–70.

[28] Paul E. Lovejoy and David Richardson, "African Agency and the Liverpool Slave Trade," in Richardson et al., *Liverpool and Transatlantic Slavery*, pp. 43–65. Lovejoy and Richardson, "'This Horrid Hole': Royal Authority, Commerce and Credit at Bonny, 1690–1840," *Journal of African History*, 45 (2004): 363–92; Lovejoy and Richardson, "Trust, Pawnship, and Atlantic History: The Institutional Foundations of the Old Calabar Slave Trade," *American Historical Review*, 104 (1999): 333–55.

[29] See Walter Hawthorne's description of the Casa Mansa in *Planting Rice and Harvesting Slaves: Transformations Along the Guinea-Bissau Coast, 1400–1900* (Portsmouth, NH, 2003), pp. 93–95. He cites André Donelha's 1625 comment about the king of Cassanga who "was so much a friend of the whites that they went around freely" in *Descrição da Serra Leoa e dos rios de Guiné do Cabo Verde* (Lisboa, 1977), p. 167.

[30] Nathaniel Uring, *A History of the Voyages and Travels of Captain Nathaniel Uring* (London, 1726), pp. 29–72 for the early history of trading at Loango. For Benin, see most recently Green, *A Fistful of Shells*, 168–69.

plantation slavery existed only in São Tomé and later in the Mascarene Islands, early modern Africa was no different from the rest of the world in its acceptance of the complete subordination of one human being to another that constituted slavery. Slavery itself is a matter primarily for the enslaved, the slave owner, and the community or state authority that sanctions it. The slave trade, however, involved a large segment of the African community. Manufacturing and assembling trade goods – or alternatively an army – feeding and transporting captives and manning barracoons until those captives embarked or were sold, demanded many more human resources than maintaining plantations where slaves sustained themselves. While the scholarly focus is very much on the organizational activities of slave-trading elites, many thousands of workers in Europe, the Americas, and Africa had no qualms in consuming slave-grown produce and finding employment in the sector that supplied enslaved labor to American plantations.

While we cannot enumerate such active participants in the business with precision, we can plausibly estimate nearly a million crew and owners of those slave ships leaving ninety-five different European ports over the slave trade era, with at least as many again involved in preparing these vessels for slaving ventures. Iron bars in Sweden, beads in Italy, linens in Silesia and the varied patterns of cotton and woolen textiles manufactured in all European countries created specifically for African markets over a 360-year period employed many times more than those preparing and working on slave ships. A similar exercise for the Americas produces even larger numbers. As argued in Chapter 2, the American population not only dispatched slave ships to Africa but also ensured the reception and distribution of their unwilling occupants at disembarkation. For every captive carried across the Atlantic there could easily have been months of employment for a worker in Europe and the Americas. As the petitions from textile workers in support of the early eighteenth-century slave trade discussed in Chapter 3 indicate, one can see only enthusiasm for the business, accompanied by a desire to avoid enslavement of oneself.

AFRICAN SLAVE TRADERS

The share of economic resources in Africa dedicated to obtaining and delivering captives was at least as great as those in Europe and the Americas. In the last decade researchers have uncovered trade books of sixty-four French, English, and Dutch slaving ventures buying captives at major embarkation outlets ranging from Galinhas on the Sierra Leone–Liberia border to Cabinda in an Angolan enclave north of the

Congo River. The trade books record a total of 5,500 transactions, in which 13,900 enslaved people changed hands. For this topic, their importance lies in that each transaction specifies the name of the African seller of the captive. Stacey Sommerdyck has undertaken the laborious task of converting thirty-two Middelburgse Commercie Compangie trade books into a usable database, and this is now augmented by similar records from an equal number of English, Portuguese, and French voyages.[31]

The African sellers of slaves fronted a large labor force ensuring the delivery of captives and supplying provisions. Table 5.1 shows that during the eighteenth century, slave vessels spent on average nearly five months on the African coast seeking to complete their complement of captives. Trading times did drop dramatically after 1810 partly in response to attempts to suppress the traffic but typically the African embarkation phase of the voyage was always of much greater duration than the disembarkation phase in the Americas. Captains hired a range of African help: pilots in riverine environments, canoes and the men to operate them where the surf was severe, and in the era of suppression, guards and canoes to shift embarkation points in response to naval cruiser activity. Kru men, living along what is now the Liberian coast, were essential for navigation

TABLE 5.1 *Time spent in days by vessels trading for slaves on African coast*

Years	Number of days on African coast	Number of voyages	
	Mean	N	Std. deviation
1661–1700	93.7	98	64.6
1701–1809	141.4	3,550	93.1
1810–1834	99.8	143	61.4
1835–1866	31.6	37	73.0
Total	137.5	3,728	92.4

Source: Calculated from www.slavevoyages.org.

[31] Sommerdyck, "Trade and the Merchant Community," pp. 139–46. For additional data see www.slavevoyages.org/past/database. African families that sold slaves have descendants embedded in the power structures of several modern African states. See Phyllis M. Martin, "Family Strategies in Nineteenth-Century Cabinda," *Journal of African History*, 28 (1987): 65–86; Adam Jones and Peter Sebald (eds.), *An African Family Archive: The Lawsons of Little Popo/Aneho (Togo), 1841–1938* (Oxford, 2005); Mouser, "Towards a Definition."

off the greater part of West Africa. Where Europeans had a land-based presence at locations ranging from Senegambia to the Bight of Benin, most of the personnel were African, usually Gromettoes and Guardians – to control the enslaved. Guardians usually originated in regions remote from the location of the fort or trading post itself to discourage fraternization with local populations. Some of these were enslaved, but most were not. All European establishments were heavily dependent on local labor for construction and maintenance of physical infrastructure, as well as provisions for both the European residents and most of the vast quantities of provisions that the 12.75 million crammed occupants of more than 40,000 slave ships needed to reach the Americas.[32]

African sellers of slaves were even more dependent on African labor. The trade books show hundreds of Africans receiving payments for small groups of captives, often just one or two per transaction as the above summary suggests. Indeed, the principals in the slave trade – buyers and sellers of people – were perhaps just as numerous in Africa as their counterparts were in the Americas and Europe. As Obikili has pointed out, "the opportunities and profits from the slave trade were open to everybody."[33] The older idea, shared by historians across the ideological spectrum, that mostly elite Africans sold slaves needs to accommodate this new evidence.[34] The system that held in Portuguese West Central Africa and the southern

---

[32] Stephanie E. Smallwood, "African Guardians, European Slave Ships, and the Changing Dynamics of Power in the Early Modern Atlantic," *William and Mary Quarterly*, 64 (2007): 679–716; Robin Law, "William's Fort: The English Fort at Whydah, 1690s to 1960," in John Kwadwo Osei-Tutu (ed.), *Forts, Castles and Society in West Africa: Gold Coast and Dahomey, 1450–1960* (Leiden, 2019), p. 141, but all the essays in this volume indicate a strong African presence within the forts. For provisions see Eltis, "The Slave Trade and Commercial Agriculture in African Context." The much smaller Dutch traffic was unusual in that it sourced most of their provisions in Europe, see Angus Dalrymple-Smith and Ewout Frankema, "Slave Ship Provisioning in the Long 18th Century: A Boost to West African Commercial Agriculture?" *European Review of Economic History*, 21 (2017): 185–235.

[33] Nonso Obikili, "The Trans-Atlantic Slave Trade and Local Political Fragmentation in Africa," *Economic History Review*, 69 (2016): 1159.

[34] The older view was established by Walter Rodney, "African Slavery and other Forms of Social Oppression on the Upper Guinea Coast in the Context of the Atlantic Slave Trade," *Journal of African History*, 7: 431–43 and *A History of the Upper Guinea Coast 1545–1800* (Oxford, 1970), but endorsed by Hopkins, *Economic History*, pp. 125–26; Martin, *External Trade of the Loango Coast*, pp. 33–72, and Martin, "The Trade of Loango in the Seventeenth and Eighteenth Centuries," in Richard Gray and David Birmingham (eds.), *Pre-Colonial Trade: Essays on Trade in Central and Eastern Africa before 1900* (Oxford, 1970), pp. 139–61. For the Dutch trade books, see MCC, NL-MdbZA_20_216_0004 to NL-MdbZA_20_938_0055, MCC Archief, first analyzed in Sommerdyk in "Trade and the Merchant Community," pp. 139–46.

rivers of Upper Guinea described in Chapter 2, which saw human cargoes assembled on land prior to embarkation may have conformed to this pattern, but we need to know more about how captives entered the Portuguese holding pens. Outside the Portuguese-dominated embarkation sites, the trade books show hundreds of sellers supplying captives to slave vessels, albeit often at a price previously established by negotiations between ship captain or supercargo on the one hand and the African ruler or his representatives on the other.

Many of these sellers were representatives of the head of state or members of the local nobility and appear in ten or more transactions per voyage often spread over two or three months. But a long tail of sellers always shows up in these documents, with the seller's name appearing just once or twice per vessel. Sixty-one percent of the transactions involved individuals who sold no more than five captives, usually to more than one ship. Indeed, 300 sellers sold just a single enslaved person. Some may have been employees, given that Stacey Sommerdyk has raised the possibility that the many Africans involved in guarding and delivering the enslaved to the coast were, like the Portuguese sailors on slave ships discussed in the previous chapter, paid in slaves.[35] But a more likely explanation for this exceptionally long tail is the involvement of numerous small merchants. Such a pattern appears nowhere in the existing literature, which tends to focus on the necessarily larger "warrior-merchants" found especially in the hinterland of the Bight of Benin–Dahomey, and the various factions in the wars following the collapse of Oyo. Perhaps the pattern that Tony Hopkins observed in the post abolition era – the "crisis of adaptation" that African warrior-merchants faced following the decline of the Atlantic slave trade and the shift to "legitimate commerce" was restricted to such hinterlands. Perhaps the small-scale "producer" was always a major component in the market for both enslaved people and African produce on the African coast, both before and after abolition.[36] Stacey Sommerdyk comments, "a large number of smaller traders also engaged in the trade ... there is an underlying story of minor merchants yet to be uncovered in Western African history," to which Mariana Candido adds in a study of Benguela, "there were also many smaller merchants who handled only a few slaves at a time."[37]

---

[35] Sommerdyk, "Trade and the Merchant Community."
[36] Hopkins, *Economic History*, pp. 124–38 and Robin Law, "The 'Crisis of Adaptation' Revisited: the Yoruba War, 1877–1893," in Toyin Falola and Emily Brownell (eds.), *Africa, Empire and Globalization: Essays in Honor of A. G. Hopkins* (Durham NC, 2011), pp. 125–43.
[37] Candido, *African Slaving Port*, pp. 165–66.

The largest number of enslaved were sold by Prins Tom in Malembo, north of the Congo River, who between 1749 and 1765 put 467 enslaved individuals on to seven different Dutch slave ships. Only ten African traders managed to sell more than one hundred individuals. But the exceptional size of these sales is highlighted by the overall average per trader, which was just eleven individuals per transaction. No less than eighteen cases involved fractions of an enslaved person. The major sellers established their status via multiple transactions of relatively small numbers of captives spread over the several weeks or months of a vessel's stay on the coast. But the African ruling authority was not always among this group. The king of Dahomey only appears eight times in our sample for a total of fifteen enslaved, but we know from Robin Law's work that he was often not a major supplier of captives to vessels trading at Ouidah. King Kosoko (Cocioko), the last independent ruler of Lagos, from which port far more enslaved people entered the transatlantic trade after 1800 than from Dahomey's outlet of Ouidah, presided over the departure of 32,000 captives during his reign of 1847–1851. Thanks to captured correspondence we know that the king himself sold only 212 of these. Of course, as with the king of Dahomey, direct sales never formed Kosoko's only income from the slave trade, though it is noticeable that he was never able to pay for his own slaving vessel, which he had ordered through merchants at Bahia.[38]

The new data do show a larger number of individual sellers on the Loango coast than appear further north. Nine hundred Africans sold slaves in the former region, but only 200 are identified in Bonny and Calabar, albeit with a smaller number of voyages. Nevertheless, for Igboland Northrup has argued that "the profits of the slave trade were distributed more widely ... than in parts of Africa where force and central control were more important."[39] Large caravans of captives did arrive at, say, Galinhas from the Fulani state of Fouta Djallon, and at Bonny as fleets of Ibani canoes arrived from interior markets. Lagos, too, saw caravans arriving, formed from the surges of people displaced by armed conflict as the final collapse of the Oyo Empire got underway in 1817.[40] Such sudden influxes of large numbers of captives into the coastal outlets represented in

---

[38] Robin Law, "Royal Monopoly and Private Enterprise in the Atlantic Slave Trade; The Case of Dahomey," *Journal of African History*, 18 (1977): 555–77; Ojo, "Letters Found in the House of Kosoko."

[39] David Northrup, *Trade Without Rulers: Pre-colonial Economic Development in Southeastern Nigeria* (Oxford, 1978), p. 175.

[40] Marial Iglesias Utset et al., *Conneau*, forthcoming; Lovejoy and Richardson, "This Horrid Hole," 380–81; Henry B. Lovejoy, "Mapping Uncertainty: The Collapse of

our sample must have occurred at times, but they were not the norm. And in centers stretching from the Gambia River to Benguela it seems that there was not just room for the smaller trader, but indeed the smaller trader provided most of the captives.

As in the numerous regions that sent ships to buy slaves in Africa, the principals involved such as ship owners, ship builders and captains, and, in Africa, sellers of slaves – all depended on hosts of support workers. To the smaller African traders must be added the armies of retainers that enabled the handing over of the captives to Europeans. Holding people in subjection and moving them is highly labor-intensive.

Figure 5.1 is a unique contemporary image of the trading post at Loango Bay, through which passed 435 individuals in our transactions dataset. This was painted by an officer of the *Marie-Séraphique* (ID 30941) in 1771. There are three sections to the painting. The top third comprises the merchandise unloaded from the vessel that prospective sellers are inspecting. The middle shows the trading activity, and the lower portion of the image shows chained captives leaving the compound, presumably on their way to the slave vessel. At the bottom right a tall man captive, and a woman slave, the former more heavily chained than the latter, are being led into the compound. Seventy-seven individuals are depicted, only nine of whom are captives traded, or to be traded. Three figures are European buyers, and a dozen appear to be African sellers

FIGURE 5.1 Slave-trading compound at Loango, north of the Congo estuary, 1771. Reproduced with the permission of the Musée d'histoire de Nantes. The image is part of a video accessible on the home page of www.slavevoyages.org.

Oyo and the Trans-Atlantic Slave Trade, 1816–1836," *Journal of Global Slavery*, 4 (2019): 127–61.

inspecting merchandise. Most of the figure are guards, attendants to sellers, or menials helping to display the merchandise.

As this suggests, delivering the captives to this point of sale must have been far more labor-intensive than bringing nonhuman commodities of equivalent value to the coast. The focus of historians on elite slave traders as the drivers of the traffic has resulted in the broad-based labor force, without whom the business could not have existed, not receiving the scholarly attention it deserves. As elsewhere in the Atlantic world, down to the late eighteenth century, no one in Africa wanted to be a slave, but acceptance of the enslavement and trafficking of others must have extended well beyond the elite and continued to do so in most of Africa at least until the traffic ended.[41] Here, too, we find that until late in the slave trade era a full acceptance of the slave trade in moral terms that was shared across, say, European textile workers and gunsmiths and African canoe men. And as discussed in Chapter 3 personal experience of enslavement made no difference to the attitudes of formerly enslaved Europeans and Africans.

Enslaved Africans of the slave trade era were no different to the European norm on this issue, as noted in Chapter 3. Recent scholarship on freed Africans originally embarked at Lagos and Ouidah and then returning to their homeland from Bahia and Sierra Leone has laid bare the movement of slave traders, many of them formerly enslaved persons. Kristin Mann has identified thirty freedmen in Lagos in the 1840s, most of whom were involved in the slave trade to Bahia.[42] Joaquim d'Almeida, a Mahi slave freed in Brazil and an associate of major slave trader Domingos José Martins, was key to redirecting the movement of captives through Agoué, thirty miles westward, when British pressure threatened Ouidah's role as a principal embarkation point.[43] Mann identifies several other smaller shippers. The typical pattern was displayed in the manifest of the *Santana* (ID 3850) where two or three owners accounted for more than half of the 311 enslaved persons on board and most of the remaining entries were for owners of just one or two captives. The major dealers were often of mixed Euro-African heritage, but few of these were former slaves. Most shippers are best described by Luis Nicolau Pares as "the

---

[41] Most of the fourteen essays in Sylviane Diouf's book *Fighting the Slave Trade* are about community strategies to hold the slave trade at bay – in other words effectively ensuring that other people/communities would be enslaved and sent overseas – rather than eliminating the slave trade altogether.

[42] Mann, *Transatlantic Lives* (forthcoming).

[43] BNA, Commodore Fanshawe to Admiralty, May 6, 1850, enc. Lt. Forbes, April 6, 1850, BNA, Adm 1/5605.

better off ... among the elite of Africans who managed to prosper ... a minority within what was already the minority of freedmen." Lisa Castillo has identified several freedmen employed on slave ships who bought a captive or two in Africa for resale in Brazil.[44] In Luanda, Dona Ana Joaquina Santos did not allow her former experience as a slave to prevent her from becoming one of the major slave traders in Luanda, or in attempting to redeploy her human property to a sugar-mill outside the city as the city's role in slave trade declined in the late 1840s.[45]

The phenomenon of freed persons resorting to trafficking in slaves was not restricted to Afro-Brazilians. Several thousand Africans "liberated" by the Freetown courts returned to their homes in Lagos and Abeokuta after 1840. In May 1857, during judicial proceedings against the recently captured *Abbot Devereux* (ID 4247) bound from Ouidah to Cuba, many Africans on board stated that they had been captured and sold by members of these relocated Yoruba communities.[46] Reports of such activity increased from 1855 to 1861 as the slave trade from the Bight of Benin reached its final crescendo, thus providing further evidence of the "precariousness of freedom" in the nineteenth-century Atlantic world, in Sidney Chalhoub's words.[47] As argued in Chapter 7, British policy toward former slaves, flawed as it was, aimed at turning Liberated Africans into quiescent workers responding to free market forces. British officials, of course, criticized the Africans they had freed from slave ships for working at slaving establishments from Rio Pongos to the Congo River, but the accused might have responded reasonably enough that following market signals and participating in a market economy was exactly what they were doing.

The largest African slave traders were likely in Angola. Linda Heywood and John Thornton have argued that Queen Njinga of Ndongo, a coastal

---

[44] Castillo, "Mapping the Nineteenth-Century Brazilian," 25–52, especially p. 32; Luis Nicolau Parés, "Entre Bahia e a Costa da Mina, libertos africanos no tráfico illegal," in Giuseppina Raggi, João Figueirôa-Rego, Roberta Stumpf (eds.), *Salvador da Bahia: Interações entre América e África (séculos XVI–XIX)* (Salvador, 2017), pp. 13–50. Quote is from p. 15.
[45] BNA, George Jackson and Edmund Gabriel to Palmerston, Feb. 18, 1847, BNA, FO84/671, ff. 109r–110.
[46] BNA, Stephen J. Hill to Clarendon, Sept 2, 1857, FO84/1011. For cases of Liberated Africans working in slaving establishments, see BNA, Admiralty to Lord John Russell, June 17, 1861, enc. Commodore Edmonstone to the Admiralty, May 7, 1861, FO84/1149 commenting on Mrs Lightbourne's establishment in the Rio Pongos.
[47] BNA, Benjamin Campbell, Lagos to Clarendon, Feb. 18, 1856, FO84/1002; H.G. Foote to Lord John Russell, Feb. 4, 1861, BNA, FO84/1141; Sidney Chalhoub, "The Precariousness of Freedom in a Slave Society (Brazil in the Nineteenth Century)," *International Review of Social History*, 56 (2011): 405–39.

state in northern Angola south of the Congo River, was associated with the embarkation of 190,000 captives between 1624 and 1663.[48] Such an exodus constitutes nearly half of those estimated to have left West Central Africa in these years and about one quarter of the population of Ndongo in 1623.[49] We have no record of Njinga interacting with ship captains, however, and many of the enslaved could have come from Njinga's periodically losing side in the civil wars of the period. But if only half that number comprised Njinga's share, her long life probably ensured that she was the African ruler who sold the largest number of people into the transatlantic slave trade.

Finally, scholars need to recognize that even beyond the limits of the Portuguese Atlantic, slave traders of African descent had a significant presence outside Africa. As already noted, major dealers often dispatched their offspring overseas for training in languages and the ways of foreign traders with whom they dealt. Some African slave traders extended their activities to the Americas. John Ormond was the son of a Susu woman and a man from Liverpool, England, who had sailed from Liverpool to West Africa as a cabin boy, but had remained first in Rio Nuñez and later the Rio Pongo, where he prospered from buying and selling slaves. After an education in England, John Ormond, Jr.,[50] returned to the Pongo from London in 1805 to run his father's slave-trading business.[51] His own son, John Ormond III, by another Susu woman, traveled to Havana and Matanzas frequently to further his business. John Ormond II was recognized as a plaintiff in a Cuban court and made an out-of-court settlement with a white Cuban. In 1764, Fenda Lawrence, a female slave trader in the Gambia, negotiated a passage to Charleston together with a letter from the captain affirming her free status. She received a confirmation of that status in a second letter from the acting governor of South Carolina.[52] The role of people of African descent in the slave trade outside the sub-continent has received scant

---

[48] Heywood and Thornton, pp. 123–68.

[49] www.slavevoyages.org/estimates/zTqfXo4r; John K. Thornton, "Revising the Population History of the Kingdom of Kongo," *Journal of African History*, 62 (2021): 201–12 doi:10.1017/S0021853721000451. The Njinga total is from a private communication to the author, January 11, 2023.

[50] Captain Theophilus Conneau, *A Slaver's Log Book or 20 Years' Residence in Africa* (Englewood Cliffs, NJ, 1976), pp. 76–77. For the Ormonds, see Jorge Felipe, "The Transatlantic Slave Trade and the Foundation of the Kingdom of Galinhas in Southern Sierra Leone, 1790–1820," *Journal of African History*, 61 (2021): 1–23.

[51] Bruce Mouser, "Trade and Politics in the Nunez and Pongo Rivers, 1790–1865," unpublished PhD thesis University of Indiana (1971), 25.

[52] Lilian Ashcraft-Eason, "She Voluntarily Hath Come: A Gambian Woman Trader in Colonial Georgia in the Eighteenth Century," in Paul E. Lovejoy (ed.), *Identity in the Shadow of Slavery* (London: 2000), pp. 202–21.

scholarly attention and is largely confined to exploring the roles of Black sailors on slave ships.[53] The "Black Atlantic" comprised more than enslaved people and Black crew. It is highly probable that north of Angola at least, there were always more Africans involved in the slave trade in non-African Atlantic ports than there were non-Africans located in African slave-trading centers.

QUESTIONING SOME BIG-PICTURE INTERPRETATIONS

So far in this chapter we have used data from www.slavevoyages.org to argue that neither side in the negotiations that put millions of Africans into the hold of a slave ship held a permanent advantage over the other. The concept of unequal trade is, however, only one of the strongly held but questionable beliefs about this horrific business that have become "established" in recent research. The balance of this chapter will examine some of the most prominent of these against the backdrop of new data that has become available in the last two decades. First, the conviction that African depopulation, either overall or regional, was offset by the introduction of New World crops, particularly maize and manioc. Second, that while slavery in Africa predated the Atlantic slave trade, exposure to the external demand for both people and commodities fundamentally altered the nature of Indigenous slavery. Third, that African economies were gutted by an influx of cheap European goods. Fourth, that the slave trade destroyed interpersonal trust to the point at which economic growth lagged the non-African world. Fifth, that as the slave trade expanded, slave routes penetrated ever further into the interior. Sixth and last, that as the slave trade came to a gradual close during the nineteenth century this non-Indigenous form of slavery in Africa expanded dramatically. According to this viewpoint, the abolition of the slave trade substantially increased the number of slaves within Africa, and those slaves worked in conditions closer to Americas-style plantation slavery. No single scholar espouses all these views together and it is certainly not possible to mention all those who embrace at least one of them. It is nevertheless worth querying the extent to which these six propositions hold in the face of new evidence embodied in databases on population trends, the size and

---

[53] Apart from the Candido essay, "Different Slave Journeys," the literature on Black crew members focuses on the English-speaking world, thus largely ignoring the more important and very different Portuguese traffic where Black crew, including the formerly and currently enslaved, were much more common.

direction of the slave trade and the ethnolinguistic identities of those who were enslaved in Africa prior to their forced exodus across the Atlantic.

Most Africanist scholars have only partially absorbed the implications of the mass of this new data. In my 1987 book, I pointed to the disconnect between what we knew then about the quantitative patterns of the slave trade on the one hand, and on the other, the positions assumed by most major scholars in the field as they developed their master narratives on why the slave trade happened, and, more particularly, the economic, political, and social impact of the traffic on African societies. In the thirty-seven years since that book appeared, the disconnect between new data and interpretations of relations between Africa and the Atlantic world has made that gap even wider. The more recent data in effect poses a numeracy test that is seldom applied to the work of Africanists. Africanists do draw on the voyage details available at www.slavevoyages.org, as well as the estimates of the volume and direction of the slave trade that the site provides, but they tend not to use this information to address the larger questions about the impact of the slave trade on Africa.

Population Decline?

Did the African population decline because of the slave trade? The discussion of global demographic patterns in Chapter 1, concluded that the overall African population was unlikely to have declined in response to the exodus of people via the Atlantic, the Indian Ocean, and the Sahara Desert, although these slave trades probably prevented the population growth that the rest of the globe experienced between 1500 and 1900. A fresh approach to these demographic issues is possible by distributing the numbers of captives carried off from Africa across modern countries and then computing the ratio of total departures to the population of each country in 1850 (as estimated by Frankema and Jerven).

Table 5.2 shows the results. Three obvious caveats are in order. Boundaries are a later and largely colonial addition, but it is easy to group the geocodes of embarkation points within them for the benefit of the general reader. Nation-states have the obvious advantage of familiarity and there is no intention here of projecting modern consequences of historical events. A second potential problem is that the ratios of people to population do not reflect the full demographic impact of the trade on African populations, given the deaths associated with warfare and kidnapping. We do not know how many casualties slave traders left in their wake. Age/sex data culled from slave ships suggest the very young and the old must often have been killed or

TABLE 5.2 *Transatlantic movement of people across the Atlantic from regions that became Western African nation-states, and from Portugal and Britain, 1519–1850*

Source country (modern)	Population in 1850	Cumulative number of people embarked	Column 2/ column 1
Mauritania	288,461	653	0.00
Senegal	931,646	202,966	0.22
Gambia	112,067	236,971	2.11
Guinea-Bissau	210,508	277,433	1.32
Guinea	1,028,675	132,406	0.13
Sierra Leone	778,717	329,117	0.42
Liberia	330,073	159,946	0.48
Ivory Coast	1,033,829	62,734	0.06
Ghana	1,981,047	1,551,034	0.78
Togo	506,578	68,262	0.13
Benin	791,150	1,308,401	1.65
Nigeria	13,539,371	1,837,883	0.14
Cameroon	2,767,547	91,853	0.03
Equatorial Guinea	108,342	2,907	0.03
Gabon	297,400	98,919	0.33
Congo-Brazzaville	507,653	226,454	0.45
Congo-Kinshasa	8,222,558	262,107	0.03
Angola	2,428,947	4,660,574	1.92
Total	35,864,569	11,510,620	0.24
Portugal	3,450,000	1,600,000	0.46
England	21,121,967	2,000,000	0.07

Sources: Calculated from https://slavevoyages.org/assessment/estimates; Census of Great Britain in 1851 at www.jstor.org/stable/2338356; Stanley L. Engerman and João César, "The Bricks of Empire, 1415–1999: 585 Years of Portuguese Emigration," *Journal of European Economic History*, 26 (1997): 471–508: Eltis (ed.), "Free and Coerced Migration from the Old World to the New," in Eltis (ed.), *Coerced and Free Migration*, pp. 60–74.

left to die, with prime-age males comprising battlefield deaths. The abolitionist Thomas Fowell Buxton suggested that such casualties amounted to one-half of those captured, so 25.5 million, of whom only 12.75 million survived to embarkation, but we will never know.[54] Final caveats are that the

---

[54] Thomas Fowell Buxton, *The African Slave Trade and Its Remedy* (London 1840), p. 169. Buxton's papers, now held in the Bodleian Library, University of Oxford, reveal no hard

table does not include the trans-Saharan and Indian Ocean traffic; Southeast African states are excluded from the table. In addition, the impact of the trans-Saharan trade on Upper Guinea is not assessed. The two leading slave-trading nations, Britain and Portugal, also happened to be the nations in Europe whose cumulative total of transatlantic emigrants leaving their own shores comprised the largest share of their respective 1850 populations. These two European countries are included in Table 5.2 for comparative purposes, but it should be noted that the large British population of 1851 was of very recent origin. Between 1500 and 1800, it was in the 5–8 million range and the ratio of migrants to populations was accordingly greater.

Even after allowing for the caveats, column 3 of Table 5.2 suggests that the overall demographic impact of the slave trade varied greatly by region. The greatest effects appear to have been on three areas occupied by the modern countries of the Gambia, Benin, and Angola. As column 3 shows, the area occupied by these modern nations lost more people to the slave trade over 350 years than lived there in 1850. The results are somewhat misleading, however. For Angola, combined populations, and population densities in the neighboring countries of Congo Kinshasa and Congo Brazzaville, were much greater than in Angola itself. Half the captives leaving the two Congo countries boarded ship in Cabinda and Malembo, both of which are now located in the Angolan enclave north of the Congo River.[55] It makes sense, therefore, to combine the data for Congo Kinshasa, Congo Brazzaville, and Angola. Doing so brings the ratio of total departures to the 1850 populations in this vast West Central African region to 0.46, or about the same as that imposed on Portugal by its migrants over the same period. A similar situation exists for Benin, many of whose captive deportees originated in its heavily populated neighboring region, now Nigeria. Applying a similar adjustment to captives and populations of these two countries shows that 350 years of cumulative departures amounted to approximately one-quarter of the combined 1850 population. This falls between the emigrants/population ratio of Portugal (0.46) and of Britain (0.07). Likewise, the Gambia, whose river was navigable for up to

---

data to support this estimate which has nevertheless become widely cited. John Thornton, "The Demographic Effect of the Slave Trade on Western Africa," *African Historical Demography, Volume II*: Proceedings of a Seminar Held in the Centre of African Studies, University of Edinburgh, April 24–25, 1981, p. 709 estimates 15 percent losses.

[55] Here, I follow John Thornton, who defines "West Central Africa largely by the watershed of the Congo River." *History of West Central Africa*, p. 1. Four of the largest six embarkation points for transoceanic captives leaving sub-Saharan Africa were in what is now Angola: Luanda, Benguela, Cabinda, and Malembo.

200 miles for oceangoing vessels, channeled many captives from what are today neighbors, especially Senegal. After these adjustments, Table 5.2 shows the region occupied by Ghana to have been most severely affected by the slave trade, with a departures-to-population ratio of 0.78, far greater than that of any country in Europe in the same period.

The slave trade from what is now Ghana spanned a shorter range of years than held in every other major coastal region in Africa. It began very gradually at just a few hundred people a year in the mid seventeenth century, intensifying only after 1700 before ending abruptly in 1808 in the aftermath of British and Danish abolition of the slave trade. Annual departures over 120 years averaged 13,000. West Central Africa and Benin/Nigeria saw larger numbers leaving annually, but their populations were several times the size of the Ghana region. Even in Ghana, however, the demographic impact of the traffic in those 120 years cannot have been great. Accepting the scholarly consensus that the sub-Saharan African population remained constant between 1650 and 1850, departures of 13,000 a year meant that natural population growth (i.e. births over deaths) was unlikely to have wholly offset transoceanic departures from eighteenth-century Ghana.[56] But the difference between departures and recovery rates was small. In all other regions affected by the transatlantic slave trade shown in Table 5.2, including Nigeria/Benin and the grouping of three West Central African nations, the average annual departure rate fell well below the Malthusian natural population growth recovery rate. This assessment does not reckon with the high male ratios in the traffic. Only one in three hauled off from Africa were female, a ratio that could only have enhanced recovery rates in the source population. The slave trade could therefore not have eroded populations in the region, unless the act of creating a captive resulted in extremely high death rates. For most of Africa, as with Europe, departures across the Atlantic did not mean population decline. The findings here offer new confirmation of a long-held scholarly consensus.

Comparisons between sub-Saharan Africa and Western Europe might not seem appropriate at first sight given the devastating impact of wars and slave raids on the former. But while the Atlantic slave trade carried off only Africans, violence and social disruption were not confined to Africa.

---

[56] If we assume that sub-Saharan Africa populations, as in most preindustrial societies, followed the Malthusian cycle of decline and recovery, demographers posit a maximum intrinsic population growth in the recovery phase of the cycle of 0.5 percent a year. The annual departure rate for Ghana implied by this discussion was close to two-thirds of 1 percent during the long eighteenth century.

Transatlantic migrants from Europe were not enslaved, and before 1820 were far fewer in number than slaves carried off from Africa, but within Europe widespread warfare, dispossession, and violent persecution, usually associated with religion, caused disruption, and triggered migration. Peoples of European descent not only organized a slave trade in Africans but between 1500 and 1850 were at war with each other almost continuously. Such wars killed 13 million combatants within Europe (or 7 million in Western Europe alone), and many more millions of civilians. The Thirty Years' War, part of which was fought in West Central Africa was particularly brutal. African casualties, in all conflicts, including noncombatants, were likely lower than in then contemporary Europe.[57] But Europe's population did grow between 1650 and 1850, as indeed did that of Asia. The overseas slave trades may have contributed to Africa's inability to share fully in the global increase in population of these two centuries, though disease factors within Africa would also have played a role.[58]

Impact of the Slave Trade on African Slavery

A second potential impact of the slave trade is that while slavery in Africa predated the Atlantic slave trade, exposure to the external demand for both people and commodities fundamentally altered the nature of Indigenous slavery. The core idea here can be found in Walter Rodney's influential work.[59] For him, slavery scarcely existed in Africa before European slave ships arrived. Paul Lovejoy, on the other hand, accepts its prior existence but the transformation he has in mind mirrors Rodney's argument on the slave trade's effect on African social structures, including slavery. The third edition of Lovejoy's *Transformations in Slavery* published in 2012, fully embraces the data in www.slavevoyages.org first made available at the end of 2008, the appearance of which may indeed have been one reason for this new edition. But nowhere does the author

---

[57] Quincy Wright, *A Study of War*, 2 vols, 2nd edition (Chicago, IL, 1965), vol. 1: 655, 665. The Wikipedia compilation offers higher figures, see https://en.wikipedia.org/wiki/List_of_wars_by_death_toll. Robert Jean Knecht, *The French Wars of Religion, 1559–1598*, 2nd ed. (London, 1996), and Nico Voigtländer and Hans-Joachim Voth, "Gifts of Mars: Warfare and Europe's Early Rise to Riches," *Journal of Economic Perspectives*, 27 (2013): 165–86.

[58] I am indebted to Ewout Frankema (personal communication) for his insights on African historical demography.

[59] Rodney's major contribution to scholarship was his 1966 essay "African Slavery and other Forms of Social Oppression," and *A History of the Upper Guinea Coast 1545–1800* (Oxford, 1970). His more polemical and best-known book is *How Europe Underdeveloped Africa* (London, 1972).

recognize that the now widely accepted profile of the slave trade projected by this new data undermines his core argument. The transformation that Lovejoy sees happening in Africa was one in which various forms of Indigenous slavery turned into a "slave mode of production," a phrase without a precise meaning, but which here is taken to refer to slaves employed in the production of commodities for a market.

We now know that West Central Africa had the longest association of any African region with an external slave trade – almost three centuries – and was the source of 45.7 percent of all captives dispatched to Atlantic destinations. The sheer volume of captives carried away from this one region over so long a period suggests that any change in African slavery should have happened first and be most apparent here. Yet this area that supplied by far the most enslaved people shows the least evidence of changes in the nature of slavery established in the sub-continent. The Congo Basin and Angola provide little evidence of captives employed in commodity production either before or after the external slave trade in the region came to an end. Coffee production in Angola expanded very slowly, and in the words of one recent reassessment based on Angolan slave census data "the widely accepted theory that the size and composition of slave populations in Western Africa changed under the influence of the maritime slave trade" is questionable.[60] To this we could add that except for limited parts of West Africa, the introduction of the "slave mode of production" was unlikely to have been an inevitable or generalized effect of transatlantic slave trading. Lovejoy's latest work tracks the connections between jihad in Africa and the Atlantic World, but overall, Paul Lovejoy might be seen as the least African-centered of the major Africanists in his ideas, with John Thornton perhaps occupying the opposite pole.[61]

Were Africans Subjected to Unequal Trade?

Were African economies gutted by an influx of cheap European goods, a third potential impact of the slave trade? Just as the scholarship on the impact of slavery and the slave trade on Western societies has come to

---

[60] Lovejoy, *Transformations*, pp. 271–73, argues that this process was complete only in West Africa and that for West Central Africa the change to a slave mode of production occurred in Brazil and in São Tomé, a strange concession in a book about slavery in the African sub-continent. For coffee, see Jelmer Vos and Paulo Teodora de Matos, "The Demography of Slavery in the Coffee Districts of Angola, c. 1800–1870," *Journal of African History*, 62 (2021): 213–34. Quote is from p. 230. Their data is from "Counting Colonial Populations: Demography and the Use of Statistics in the Portuguese Empire, 1776–1890" (http://colonialpopulations.iscte-iul.pt/).

[61] Paul E. Lovejoy, *Jihād in West Africa During the Age of Revolutions* (Athens, OH, 2016).

foreground the ideas of Eric Williams and his now eighty-year-old book, *Capitalism and Slavery*, so assessments of the impact of the external slave trade and slavery on Africa are underpinned by the only slightly more recent works of Rodney. His second book focused on the slave trade's destruction of African social structures and economies. Some of the most prolific and influential scholars on precolonial Africa's relations with the rest of the world since Rodney's early death continue to show more than just traces of his core ideas. And outside the scholarly community Rodney's influence had an immediate impact. Leaders of the Suriname maroon communities on a trip to Ghana in 1971 asked Akan leaders why their forefathers had been sold into slavery across the ocean – indeed "they felt some retribution was owed them."[62] Within the scholarly community we consider the work of Paul Lovejoy, Toby Green, Joseph C. Miller, and John Thornton in the light of the expanded version of slavevoyages.org.[63] Most Africanists see these consequences as strongly deleterious, socially as well as economically. If, as argued above, Africans and Europeans traded for the most part as equals, it is not likely that the merchandise exchanged for captives was inferior. Walter Rodney's account of the exchange now looks unsophisticated, especially its view of African traders implicit in his description of the merchandise they accepted as "cheap gin, cheap gunpowder, pots and kettles full of holes and assorted rubbish."[64] A half-century later, this now appears both inaccurate and patronizing to African traders and consumers. Like buyers and sellers in most locations, Africans were careful in their evaluation of quality and precise in defining their needs.[65] Yet Toby Green has recently reworked Rodney's position. Europeans, he argues got more from transactions on the African coast than did Africans. They dumped their goods in Africa ("the words dump, "dumping," and "dumped" appear frequently in his text) and were able to extract "capital and surplus value through circuits of long-distance trade

---

[62] Silvia W. de Groot, "The Bush Negro Chiefs Visit Africa: Diary of an Historic Trip," in Richard Price (ed.), *Maroon Societies: Rebel Slave Communities in the Americas* (Baltimore, 1973), pp. 389–98.

[63] Their most well received works are Thornton, *History of West Central Africa*; Miller, *Way of Death*; Lovejoy, *Transformations in Slavery*, 3rd edition, and Green, *A Fistful of Shells*. Discussion here is not restricted to these well-known works, however.

[64] Rodney, *How Europe Underdeveloped Africa*, p. 102.

[65] David Richardson, "West African Consumption Patterns and their Influence on the Eighteenth-Century British Slave Trade," in Gemery and Hogendorn, *Uncommon Market*, pp. 303–30; Domingues da Silva, *Atlantic Slave Trade*, pp. 122–41; Nick Radburn, *Traders in Men*, pp. 59–90.

[that] came to hold greater value than these material objects themselves."[66]

This statement is not supported with documentary evidence even though it is amenable to testing. Apart from the abundant papers of merchants, there is an extensive secondary literature on what trade goods cost, first at source, and second on the African coast as well as what captives cost on both sides of the Atlantic along with the prices of plantation produce in both the Americas and in Europe.[67] Without defining "dump," "surplus value," and "capital," much less providing even an approximate idea of their size and source, Green repeatedly restates the broader thrust of Rodney's argument: trading on the coast devastated African societies and in so doing generated Western economic growth. But given all the abundant documentation on transactions on the African coast now available, the reader is entitled to know how much "surplus value" was extracted and from where.

Green argues that vast quantities of capital were accumulated by Europeans in their trading activities with Africans. We could assume that the author is looking at differences in the price of slaves, gold, and African produce between their purchase in Africa and their sale in the Americas and Europe. But the literature makes clear that such differences are accounted for by transportation costs, not "surplus value," capital accumulation, or profits.[68] We should ask exactly what the sources were of "growing imbalances in capital accumulation." Green disparages "formalist economic rationality," but what he offers in its place to explain what was, for all participants, a transatlantic market for slaves is unclear. Most surprisingly, Green makes little use of Curtin's extensive work on Senegambia, which shows the terms of trade[69] turning strongly in Africa's

---

[66] Green, *A Fistful of Shells*, p. 469.
[67] Eltis et al., "Accounting for the Traffic in Africans," 940–63; Cheryl S. McWatters and Yannick Lemarchand, " Accounting Representation and the Slave Trade: The Guide Du Commerce of Gaignat de L'Aulnais," *The Accounting Historians Journal*, 33 (2006): 1–37, especially pp. 22–30.
[68] Joseph Kennedy, the British Commissary Judge in Havana, writing in 1850, at a time when the difference between slave prices in Cuba were many times greater than their cost in Africa, stated, "It is a great error to suppose that if a cargo of slaves may be purchased on the [African] coast for say $25, and sold again for $400 per head, that the intermediate sum is the real profit." He went on to itemize the additional costs, a major part of which were bribes (Joseph Kennedy to Palmerston, January 1, 1850, FO84/789).
[69] The commodity terms of trade are the relation between import and export prices. For the trend in Atlantic Africa from 1808 see Ewout Frankema, Pieter Woltier, Angus Dalrymple Smith and Leandre Bulambo, "An Introduction to the African Commodity Trade Database, 1730–2010," *Research Data Journal for the Humanities and Social Sciences*,

favor as the Industrial Revolution drove down the prices of all manufactured goods between the 1780s and 1850. It now seems that this pattern holds for the whole of West Africa and for the whole of the eighteenth century – the very period when Europeans were supposedly extracting most from Africa.[70]

The counterarguments to this position are straightforward. First, Green ties "dumping" by which he seems to mean selling cheaply, together with widespread depreciation of African commodity currencies such as the shells in the book's title.

Repeatedly throughout the book Green sees cheap goods flooding the African domestic markets but points out that they were in fact used as currencies in many African states – cowries, and pieces of cloth as well as gold, iron bars and copper. At the same time, Green argues these large quantities of commodity currencies stimulated rampant inflation far beyond that experienced in sixteenth and seventeenth century Europe as American silver and gold arrived. The economic tension in linking these two arguments is striking – to the point of impossibility. If currencies are depreciating because of inflation, then foreign-sourced goods cannot possibly be cheap for the domestic consumer. One argument makes sense by itself and so does the other, but not both at the same time. The reader is never told of the relative strength of each effect. If Africans found themselves spending more domestic currency to buy a given foreign good (depreciation) and at the same time the foreign seller was lowering prices (dumping), then the transaction price to the consumer might well have remained constant.[71] In addition, Green goes to great lengths to establish the economic, political, military, and cultural equivalence of sub-Saharan Africa and Europe at the outset of Atlantic contact between the two in the fifteenth and sixteenth centuries. This is plausible, but the amount of bullion flowing into Europe from the Americas between 1520 and 1800 was vastly greater than the total value of merchandise imported to Africa

---

3 (2018): 3. For the growth of commodity exports from Africa after 1750, see Angus E. Dalrymple-Smith, *Commercial Transitions and Abolition in West Africa 1630–1860* (Leiden, 2020), pp. 113–38.

[70] Curtin, *Economic Change in Precolonial Africa*, pp. 334–42. For Curtin's argument holding for all West Africa after 1700, see David Eltis and Lawrence C. Jennings, "Trade Between Western Africa and the Atlantic World in the Pre-Colonial Era," *American Historical Review*, 93 (1988): 939–44.

[71] For a different, but equally valid dismissal of the unequal trade argument, see John Thornton's assessment of European-African trade relations and the relative economic strength of Africans [*A Cultural History of the Atlantic World* (Cambridge, 2012), pp. 67–71, 78].

in the same period. Even if all African imports comprised shells, textiles, and gold (in other words currencies in Green's sense) how is it that devaluation on the scale posited by Green for Africa did not occur in Europe where on a per capita basis the boost to the money supply from American gold and silver was an order of magnitude greater?[72]

A second argument against Green's extraction of surplus position is that the slave trade does not appear any more profitable than other branches of long-distance trade. Averaging out wealthy merchants and planters in the Caribbean with bankruptcies in their respective businesses, investments in the slave trade and the plantation colonies were no more profitable than other sectors of comparable risk in Europe's complex economies.[73] Africa accounted for 3.6 percent of British exports in 1784–1786 and less than 1 percent in 1824–1826. Adding these African figures to exports to the West Indies to measure the impact of whole slave sector increases the share to 14 percent and 11 percent respectively.[74] Trade statistics for other European nations show much smaller shares of their exports going into the Atlantic slave systems. As shown in Chapter 3, some, like Germany and Italy, had shares close to zero; others, such as Spain and Portugal, had been drawing on the Atlantic slave system far longer than Britain without exhibiting any trace of a step change in economic development. And the surge in productivity in the domestic French economy occurred well after significant plantation activity had collapsed in the wake of the Haitian Revolution.[75] The question

---

[72] See Chapter 2 for estimates of the bullion inflows into Europe, especially TePaske and Brown, *New World of Gold and Silver*; John F. Richards "Introduction," in Richards (ed.), *Precious Metals in the Later Medieval and Early Modern Worlds* (Durham, NC, 1983), notes that only about one-fifth of American silver was re-exported to Asia (pp. 3–26). For Africa, see Philip D. Curtin, "Africa and the Wider Monetary World,1250–1850," in *Precious Metals*, pp. 231–68; Robin Law, *The Slave Coast of West Africa, 1550–1750* (Oxford, 1991), pp. 123, 134–6; Law, "The Gold Trade of Whydah in the Seventeenth and Eighteenth Centuries," in D. Henige and T. C. McCaskie (eds.), *West African Economic and Social History* (Madison, WI, 1990), pp. 110–11; Green, *A Fistful of Shells*, passim, but especially pp. 227–31.

[73] J. R. Ward, "The Profitability of Sugar Planting in the British West Indies, 1650–1834," *Economic History Review*, 31 (1978): 207–209; Richardson, *Principles and Agents*, pp. 43–44, 289–91; Radburn, *Traders in Men*, pp. 28–9, 206–13.

[74] Davis, *The Industrial Revolution*, p. 89. Davis converted official value to real values for three mid-decadal years in every decade from the 1780s to the 1850s. To avoid the distorting effects on transoceanic trade of the Revolutionary and Napoleonic Wars I have selected only the 1780s and 1820s. See also Chapter 3 above and Eltis, "Trade Between Western Africa," pp. 209–13.

[75] Réka Juhász, Mara P. Squicciarini, and Nico Voigtländer, "Technology Adoption and Productivity Growth: Evidence from Industrialization in France," NBER Working Paper (2020), 27503.

posed in Chapter 3 is again relevant here. Is it possible that Western Europe's economic development might have occurred without an Atlantic slave system, drawing on sub-Saharan Africa? Whether we take Africa alone or the whole Atlantic trading system, the answer must remain very likely yes.[76]

Did the Slave Trade Destroy Trust between Africans?

A fourth and quite different malevolent impact of the slave trade on the African economy focuses on loss of trust in commercial transactions. In two papers, the second coauthored with Leonard Wantchekon, Nathan Nunn has argued that countries that supplied the most captives during the slave trade era are also the most underdeveloped today. The second paper provided a possible explanation: Slave trading undermined interpersonal trust and thereby inhibited economic development so that "Africans whose ancestors were heavily raided during the slave trade era are less trusting today."[77] But raiding was not the major source of captives. Thornton's survey of the evidence on enslavement indicates that slightly more than one-third were prisoners of wars between African states or civil wars, and a further one-fifth entered the traffic via debt or judicial procedures. Extensive conflicts in Europe, already discussed, as well as in the Mediterranean and the Americas (within both Indigenous and settler societies) do not appear to have generated a similar lack of trust among modern descent groups. In Thornton's survey kidnapped individuals and those sold by relatives together – activities more likely to undermine trust – accounted for less than half of those dispatched. Also, scholars have yet to entertain the possibility that some unknown fraction of the exodus were already enslaved, although as above, we do have cases where African-owned "domestic" slaves in Liberia became outraged at their sale to overseas buyers.

---

[76] This constitutes a reprise of the argument in Chapter 3. Peter Coclanis has commented "Some exceedingly important (if rather more prosaic) European trades – the Baltic grain trade and the barge trade on the Rhine, most notably – have at a minimum suffered from relative neglect as a result of scholars' haste to focus on splashier developments in the Atlantic" in "The Disposal of Atlantic History," *New West Indian Guide/Nieuwe West-Indische Gids*, 88 (2014): 295. See also Deirdre McCloskey, *Bourgeois Dignity: Why Economics Can't Explain the Modern World* (Chicago, IL, 2010) pp. 179–238 for the relative unimportance of overseas markets in the development of Europe.

[77] Nathan Nunn, "The Long-Term Effects of Africa's Slave Trades," *Quarterly Journal of Economics*, 123 (2008): 139–76 and the second co-authored with Leonard Wantchekon, "The Slave Trade and the Origins of Mistrust in Africa," *American Economic Review*, 101 (2011): 3221–52.

A second problem with the Nunn/Wantchekon position is that it ignores the critical role of trust in both Indigenous African trade networks and in the organization of the slave trade itself both during and after the slave trade era. Curtin, Lovejoy, Richardson, and others have established the centrality of trust in the business of slave trading. In many parts of sub-Saharan Africa human pawns secured goods advanced on credit. European and African slave traders "appropriated and adapted" what was a local practice for the slave trade. A chain of credit could extend far into the interior and was based on the expectation that a debtor would pay off a creditor within an allotted time. Human pawns or not, this continent-wide system could not have worked without trust. This was one of the reasons that the shift from the slave trade to what quickly became a much more valuable trade in commodities, especially palm oil and groundnuts, occurred so seamlessly in the aftermath of the demise of slave trading. The trading networks, including the practice of human pawnship, were already in place.[78] Seymour Drescher states that Africanists have shown that "there were no more complex chains of trust, interlocking trade diasporas, long-term lines of credit ... and other recipes for economic transactions, than in the world of the slave trade," but this assessment also applies to the wide range of African products that gradually took the place of the trade in people after 1807.[79]

A third and more fundamental problem with the diminution of trust issue has to do with the econometrics that the two scholars employ in reaching this conclusion. In the last two decades the most prestigious journals in economics have published a range of studies covering a wide range of topics in world history all sharing the common theme of comparing an often-distant past with the same area in the present day. This research is now grouped under the label "persistence studies," all of which tend to come to the same conclusion: specifically, modern outcomes strongly reflect characteristics of the same places in the distant past. Morgan Kelly has subjected twenty such papers from the most prestigious journals, including Nunn and Wantchekon's work, to robustness checks.[80] He finds that in

---

[78] Thornton, *Cultural History*, pp. 71–74 drawing on the de Sandoval, Oldendorp and Sigismund Koëlle samples of interviews with captives. Curtin, *Economic Change in Precolonial Africa*, pp. 302–308; Lovejoy and Richardson, "Trust, Pawnship," 332–55; Randy J. Sparks, "Gold Coast Merchant Families, Pawning, and the Eighteenth-Century British Slave Trade," *William and Mary Quarterly* 70 (2013): 317–40; Radburn, *Traders in Men*, pp. 59–90.

[79] Seymour Drescher, *Capitalism and Anti-Slavery: British Mobilization in Comparative Perspective* (Oxford, 1987), p. 21.

[80] Morgan Kelly, "Persistence, Randomization and Spatial Noise" (2021). Available at www.researchgate.net/publication/355905391. As Kelly explains, persistence regressions are

more than half the studies, including the two Nunn papers, the high scores on significance tests are likely the outcome of underestimating standard errors or of fitting spatial trends. Kelly is at pains to distance himself from any intention to "disprove" the results of the twenty-five studies, but his corrective procedures do mean that the t-statistics in both slave trade papers are no longer significant. Indeed, Kelly's standard error adjustments and robustness checks generate results for the two slave trade papers that are among the most dramatic corrections in the twenty studies he examines. Finally, in this quantitative critique it is worth pointing to the miniscule ratio of the value of external trade per person in the Western African sub-continent shown in Table 5.3. Is it credible that the nature of a trade, even the slave trade, could have had such a profound long-range impact on attitudes to risk a century and a half after the cessation of that trade, especially given the very modest per capita values of the traffic compared to the rest of the Atlantic world?[81]

TABLE 5.3 *Value of imports per person in select regions in the Atlantic world c. 1800 in pounds sterling*

	The Netherlands*	France	United Kingdom	United States	Western sub-Saharan Africa
Imports (millions £)	11.4	20.6	56.0	20.6	25.2
Population (millions)	2.1	27.5	10.5	5.46	35.9
Imports per Person	5.4	0.75	5.3	3.77	0.08

Sources: Jan De Vries and Ad van der Woude, *The First Modern Economy: Success, Failure, and Perseverance of the Dutch Economy, 1500–1815* (Cambridge, 1997), pp. 51, 499.
Brian R. Mitchell, *European Historical Statistics, 1750–1970* (New York, 1975), pp. 4, 8.
Davis, *The Industrial*, p. 93.
Richardson, "Prices of Slaves," p. 55.
Frankema, and Jerven, "Writing History Backwards," 907–31. www.historicalstatistics.org/Currencyconverter.html

[effectively] spatial regressions and "spatial data ... tend to be strongly autocorrelated (p. 2). Further, while the correlations of Nunn and Wantchekon with GDP per capita in 2000 are significant, they are not so when run against 1960 or 2018 data. See Ewout Frankema, "Why Africa Is not *that* Poor," in Alberto Bisin and Giovanni Federico (eds.), *The Handbook of Historical Economics* (Amsterdam, 2021): 557–84, especially, p. 568.

[81] Frankema, "Why Africa," Figure 8, p. 24.

Was There a Slaving Frontier that Moved Inland over Time?

As the slave trade expanded, did slave routes penetrate ever further into the African interior? This constitutes the fifth questionable view of the slave trade's impact on the sub-continent. Joseph Miller made the strongest case for this pattern in Angola, though other historians had established this as a central theme of their work previously. Among the older generation of Africanists, only Patrick Manning questioned the emergence of more remote provenances of captives over time.[82] New data generated by Philip Misevich and Daniel Domingues da Silva provides a basis for revisiting Manning's position.[83] Further evidence of the proposed pattern is presented below in Chapter 7's maps. Generally, historians have taken insufficient notice of the time profile of regional departures of enslaved people. West Central Africa not only saw far more captives leave its shores than any other of the eight regions depicted on slavevoyages.org, but the volume of its departures built up steadily over time. From 150,000 in the half-century 1551 to 1600, the region reached its all-time peak of nearly 2 million between 1801 and 1850.[84] Just as with the transformation thesis, the impact of the slave trade on the slaving frontier and slave supply systems generally surely would have been at its most severe in West Central Africa during the first half of the nineteenth century. Miller tracks the slaving frontier as moving intermittently eastwards between 1730 and 1830.[85] Given the nearly 2 million captives carried off from the region in 1801–1850, his argument might lead us to expect that the frontier would have been at its furthest point from the "floating tombs" on the coast in say the second quarter of the nineteenth century. He also links this movement with state formation and disintegration. But, as with the transformation thesis, the historical evidence of this in West Central Africa is questionable.

---

[82] Patrick Manning, *Slavery and African Life: Occidental, Oriental and African Slave Trades* (Cambridge, 1990), pp. 63–72. Manning estimates an average distance from the coast of sixty miles for most of West Africa with captives marched 185–370 miles for West Central Africa.

[83] Miller, *Way of Death*, pp. 141–53, 234–41; Domingues da Silva, *Atlantic Slave Trade from West Central Africa*, pp. 73–99; Philip Misevich, *Abolition and the Transformation of Atlantic Commerce in Southern Sierra Leone, 1790s to 1860s* (Trenton, NJ, 2019), pp. 73–98; Misevich, "The Mende and Sherbro Diaspora in Nineteenth-century Southern Sierra Leone," in Philip Misevich and Kristin Mann (eds.), *The Rise and Demise of Slavery and the Slave Trade in the Atlantic World* (Rochester, NY, 2016), pp. 247–65.

[84] http://slavevoyages.org/estimates/KiaKJnQC.

[85] Miller mentions the term "slaving frontier" ninety-five times in his text (*Way of Death*, passim).

Since 2010 when www.african,origins.org went live,[86] students of the slave trade have had new material at their disposal to evaluate and refine interpretations of where people were enslaved. As noted in Chapter 1 and analyzed more fully in Chapter 7, one of the by-products of the British, then international, campaign against the slave trade after 1807 was the creation of registers of Africans released from detained slave vessels or held in coastal barracoons. Details of 95,000 individuals with 65,000 unique names are now available for analysis, plus 11,264 included in the Portuguese slave census counts of the mid 1850s, most of whom were originally intended for the Atlantic slave trade. For 35,300 individuals in this combined group, it is possible to link the African name with a language grouping. Such links throw new light on the sources of captives in three broad regions of the sub-continent for the period, 1808 to 1856: Sierra Leone and the Windward Coast (now Liberia) treated as a single region, and the hinterlands of the Bight of Benin and Biafra, including in the latter case, the Cameroon Highlands.[87] With the help of the www.ethnologue.com database of languages, we can locate the major groups in relation to their ports of embarkation.

For Sierra Leone and the Windward Coast Philip Misevich has drawn on this material for the period 1808–1844. The time profile of departures from these areas was quite different from that of the overall traffic. Although closer to both Europe and the Caribbean than most of sub-Saharan Africa, for two centuries they supplied relatively few transatlantic captives, but as the overall traffic peaked after 1750 slave traders moved into these regions to the extent of dispatching 422,000 people into New World slavery in the second half of the eighteenth century. After 1800, the volume of the traffic fell by 50 percent, with the creek systems of Rio Pongo and Galinhas replacing the offshore islands, Cape Mount, and the Sierra Leone, all of which were now more vulnerable to British attacks. Nevertheless, the half-century total was still the second highest of the slave-trading era. In this region at least, the Miller model appears to explain shifts in origins. Drawing on Barry Higman's analysis of the

---

[86] *African-Origins* is now folded into the Enslaved user interface of www.slavevoyages.org.
[87] For discussion of the construction of the Enslaved database and the methodology employed in linking names to language and ethnicity, see Richard Anderson, Alex Borucki, David Eltis, Daniel Domingues da Silva, Paul Lachance, Philip Misevich, Olatunji Ojo, "Using African Names to Identify the Origins of Captives in the Transatlantic Slave Trade: Crowd-Sourcing and the Registers of Liberated Africans, 1808-1862," *History in Africa*, 40 (2013): 165–91; Misevich, *Abolition and the Transformation*, pp. 245–48; and Domingues da Silva, *Atlantic Slave Trade*, pp. 172–75.

British Caribbean's slave registration data, plus a range of more conventional contemporary observations, Misevich finds a much wider range of origins before 1800 than after. He also notes much higher prices for captives in the earlier period. After 1800, lower prices and lower volumes meant that the local Mende/Sherbro language speakers predominated, with two-thirds of all captives embarked linked by language to locations within 100 miles of the coast. More recently, Jorge Felipe Gonzalez has tightly tied the rise and fall of the Kingdom of Galinhas under King Siaka to embarkations of captives in southern Sierra Leone.[88] Galinhas was thus one of the clearer, if smaller scale, examples of the transoceanic slave trade driving state formation. This pattern of proximity to the coast also emerges for a different segment of Upper Guinea which is now Guinea-Bissau and Guinea for the sixteenth and early seventeenth centuries.[89]

The slave-trading profile of the Cameroons shared some of the characteristics of Upper Guinea. Although some of its captive people had always left via Old Calabar, direct departures from the "Cameroons Estuary" or "Cameroon River" jumped after William Davenport, one of the largest Liverpool traders, moved a significant part of his business there in the late 1760s.[90] Identification of the ethnolinguistic links of 929 captives embarked between 1822 and 1837 indicate a more scattered range of linguistic origins but with four groups, Tikari, Douala-Bimbia (admittedly a coastal location rather than a language), Banyangi and Bakossi together, accounting for 60 percent of the total. But only one-third of the total likely traveled more than 125 miles. The coastal regions and grasslands of the northwest highlands supplied most captives, with much of the Cameroons, particularly what is now the French-speaking segment, not represented at all in this sample. As in the Igbo and Ibibio-speaking areas to the west, before, during and after the slave trade, political structures here were "stateless," and warfare was not a major source of slaves.[91]

The evidence for West Central Africa is much less clear-cut. As we have seen, this was by far the largest sub-Saharan African region that felt the impact of the transatlantic slave trade. Domingues da Silva has identified

---

[88] Misevich, *Abolition and the Transformation*, pp. 73–97; Felipe Gonzalez, "The Transatlantic Slave Trade."
[89] Wheat, Atlantic Africa and the Spanish Caribbean, pp. 20–67.
[90] Radburn, *Traders in Men*, pp. 36–38.
[91] G. Ugo Nwokeji and David Eltis, "Characteristics of Captives Leaving the Cameroons for the Americas, 1822–1837," *Journal of African History*, 43 (2002): 191–210; G. Ugo Nwokeji, *The Slave Trade and Culture in the Bight of Biafra: An African Society in the Atlantic World* (Cambridge, 2010), pp. 132–43.

the languages of 7,612 individuals who were enslaved here in the nineteenth century.⁹² He has been able to group his sample into twenty-one languages and 116 ethnicities distributed across the region's interior. His sample is small, but drawing mainly on vessels captured at sea, probably random. However, some of his identifications are questionable. The largest group in his sample, comprising one-sixth overall, is Ndongo. They are labelled as Kimbundu speakers, but a careful survey of eighteenth- and nineteenth-century contemporary sources by François Bontinck has them located in the vicinity of Lake Mai-Ndombe – far away from Kimbundu speakers. This region is 500 miles from the sea, rather than the 250 or less assumed as the center of linguistic gravity for Kimbundu speakers. We do not have the numbers to correct the distribution, but it does seem likely that the pattern established for West Africa of shorter distances from enslavement to the sea was, as a minimum, less pronounced in Angola.⁹³

For the Bights of Benin and Biafra west of the Cameroons after 1807 we now know that Yoruba names comprised 88 percent of those leaving from points lying between Keta in the west and the Kingdom of Benin in the east. Igbo names were not quite so dominant among those departing from ports located from the Niger Delta to Old Calabar coastline, but still comprised 69 percent of the total embarking. The maps in Chapter 7 use the www.ethnologue.com database to locate the geographic central point of these two languages and thus gives us a crude proxy for distance traveled on average by the typical Yoruba or Igbo captive. For the Yoruba this turns out to be a point northeast of Ibadan. No less than 87 percent of those forced to board a slave ship in the Bight of Benin passed through Lagos, Ouidah, and Grand Popo.⁹⁴ For the Igbo the modern central language point is 100 miles due north of Bonny – the major embarkation point in the Bight of Biafra. Of course, we cannot be sure that these modern language coordinates hold for the first half of the nineteenth century, but the major population shifts in the last two hundred years have been towards cities, not toward the coast. Lagos is already a mega-city, but cities in the interior of Nigeria have also grown rapidly. A striking feature of the identifications is how few could have come from north of the Yoruba–Igbo belt. Islamic, Hausa, Fulani, and

---

⁹² Domingues da Silva, *Atlantic Slave Trade*, pp. 172–75.
⁹³ "Les Mondongues," STVDIA, Lisboa, 53 (1994): 59–79. I thank John Thornton for drawing my attention to this source.
⁹⁴ Henry B. Lovejoy confirms that most captives taken in the wars associated with the collapse of the Oyo Empire originated close to the coast [Prieto: *Yorùbá Kingship in Colonial Cuba during the Age of Revolutions* (Chapel Hill, NC, 2018), pp. 20–24].

Nupe names comprise less than 9 percent of the Bight of Benin embarkations and just 2 percent of the Biafran group. Non-Yoruba and non-Igbo were mostly people from either east of Yorubaland, such as Akan, Ewe, Fon, or Gbe – or west of Igboland, the Efik, Ibibio, and some from the Upper Cross River. The Ethnologue central coordinates for all these languages lying to the east and west of the Igbo and Yoruba are much closer to the coast than are the equivalent Igbo and Yoruba geocodes.

But while the thrust of the new evidence is that most captives came from regions relatively close to the coast, there is at least one possible exception. After 1740 as we have seen in Chapter 3, Liverpool and Bonny, an island in the Niger Delta, developed close-knit trading ties that catapulted both to an extraordinary sixty-year dominance in the West African segment of the Atlantic slave trade. Liverpool dispatched more slaving voyages than any other port in the Atlantic world, while Bonny dispatched the second largest number of captives of any African port after Luanda.[95] Three-quarters of Bonny's captives left Africa on Liverpool ships between 1761 and 1807. The port's access to the interior via the Imo and Niger rivers was unparalleled, giving it effectively the largest slaving hinterland in sub-Saharan West Africa. But even here most of the Niger flowed through lightly populated regions and Igbo peoples from the forest zones further south and east always dominated Bonny's deportees. The Congo River was potentially of similar importance, but there was no port on its estuary that played a role like Bonny's. Instead, captives left Africa from several embarkation points north and south of the Congo.[96]

Did the End of the Slave Trade Drive up the Number of Enslaved Africans within Africa?

The final ingredient of this overview of the slave trade's impact on Africa is that the suppression of the slave trade increased the number of slaves held within Africa. The value of sub-Saharan African produce exports certainly came to exceed the value of captive embarkations in the immediate aftermath of slave trade suppression.[97] The shift to a produce trade

---

[95] Richardson, *Principles and Agents*, pp. 49–93.
[96] The Gambia and Senegal Rivers might be considered additional candidates (Kelley, *American Slavers*, pp. 139–41; Thornton, *Cultural History*, 61–2) but compared to the Niger and the Congo, and after allowing for the multiple oceanic outlets for captives pulled into the Niger and Congo systems, the two northern rivers together comprised a minor supply route.
[97] Eltis, *Economic Growth*, pp. 225–32.

happened first in the Bight of Biafra and last in the West Central Africa region. But the African labor that made this possible worked under a variety of labor regimes ranging from small farmers to slave owners. Perhaps slavery within Africa expanded temporarily as the shock of the 1826 Anglo-Brazilian Treaty took effect in 1830 and again as Brazil imposed serious measures to end the traffic twenty years later. Yet there is no evidence that the supply lines of the hinterlands that sent approximately 800,000 captives from Africa to Brazil during the two last crescendos of the Brazilian traffic – 1826–1830, and 1846–1850 respectively – suddenly found alternative markets in Angola and Benin in the succeeding quinquennia of 1831–1835 and 1851–1855.

We do not have sufficient census and other data to conclusively evaluate the impact of slave-trade suppression on slaveholdings within Africa, but we do have some evidence of movements of the enslaved from one part of Africa to another. We know that groundnuts, palm oil, and palm kernels comprised the major Western African commodity exports in middle decades of the nineteenth century.[98] Minor crops such as coconuts, wax, coffee, cloves, and an assortment of dyes and timber were much less important than these three. Moreover, slavery was only one form of labor used to produce these crops. Some slave labor was employed in the southern part of the Upper Guinea's groundnut region but was much less prevalent in the palm oil belt in the hinterlands of the Bights of Benin and Biafra.[99] Enslaved people could also be found cultivating cloves in Zanzibar, coffee in São Tomé, and sugar in the Mascarene Islands.[100] And in regions producing for domestic markets, the Sokoto Caliphate used slave labor to produce cotton, indigo, kola and shea nuts, grain, rice, and tobacco. An intra-African traffic in people did develop to the groundnut regions, and to São Tomé, as the transoceanic slave trade came under attack, and this, too, was susceptible to British disruption. Between 1820 and 1844, the British detained eighty-two small shipments of enslaved people destined for the groundnut areas of Upper Guinea, many in flotillas of canoes, carrying a total of 965 enslaved people, and a further sixteen voyages sailing for São Tomé with 697 on board. In the transatlantic trade

---

[98] This paragraph is based on Eltis, *Economic Growth*.
[99] Misevich, *Abolition and the Transformation*, pp. 160–79 for details of the spread of groundnut cultivation and the extent of slave use as well as further information on the slave traffic it generated.
[100] São Tomé's coffee output was so small that it merits scarcely a mention in William G. Clarence-Smith (ed.), *The Global Coffee Economy in Africa, Asia and Latin America, 1500–1989* (Cambridge, 2003).

the loss ratio due to captures was 20 percent.[101] If we assume that loss ratios were the same in these branches of the intra-African traffic, then we can estimate that Upper Guinea's groundnut region was the intended destination of 4,825 departures, and 3,485 left West Central Africa for São Tomé in these years.[102]

Such figures are, however, almost trivial when compared to the adjustment to suppression of the slave trade on the western side of the Atlantic. When plantation owners in the US and in Brazil had difficulty obtaining enough forced labor from Africa, after 1790 in one case and 1850 in the other, they quickly resorted to the intra-American traffic to supply their needs. Planters in Brazil's expanding coffee sector immediately turned to domestic sources of enslaved people via an intra-American traffic. They purchased 200,000 captives from the rest of the country in the three decades down to 1881. More than triple this number were moved from the Upper to the Lower Southern States of the US in the seventy years after 1790.[103] And within the British Caribbean, a further 25,000 were moved from long-established islands such as Jamaica to Trinidad, Grenada, and British Guiana between 1807 and 1833.[104] Mid nineteenth-century sub-Saharan Africa could well have contained at least as many bond-persons as Brazil and the United States put together, but the only substantial movement of slaves had been to the offshore islands such as the Mascarenes and São Tomé, where plantation complexes were established, and to the Cape of Good Hope.[105]

Table 5.3 displays the available data on populations and movement of people. Even if we include the enslaved labor introduced to grow cotton, indigo, kola and shea nuts, grain, rice, tobacco, and onion in the Sokoto Caliphate, the trade in enslaved persons within Africa could not have

---

[101] Eltis, *Economic Growth*, p. 101.
[102] Because 80 percent of British captures occurred off the African coast. Intra-African voyages were just as liable to capture as transatlantic ventures.
[103] Slenes, "Demography and Economics," pp. 145–58. As discussed in Chapter 2, the I-Am traffic had always been more active than its Intra-African counterpart. In addition to the Slenes data for post-suppression Brazil and the US we know that slave traders in British Caribbean islands sold 634,000 Africans into the intra-American slave trade between 1640 and 1807 (see row 8 of Table 2.4 above); O'Malley's estimates for the traffic to the North American mainland are in "Beyond the Middle Passage," pp. 125–72.
[104] Eltis, "Traffic in Slaves," 55–65; Higman, *Slave Populations*, pp. 80–81.
[105] Richard B. Allen, *European Slave Trading in the Indian Ocean, 1500–1859* (Athens, OH, 2015), table 1; Michael Charles Reidy, "VOC Slave Trading Strategies on the Madagascar to Cape Slave Route, 1676–1781," *HumaNetten*, 47 (2021), Special issue, "Enslavement in the Indian Ocean World," pp. 14–55. See especially the Appendix on "Africans in the Old World Slave Trade."

come close to the 850,000 enslaved people forced to move within the Americas over the same period. Nor could it have matched the size of the earlier traffic to Réunion and Mauritius, or the now expanded deportation of people across the Indian Ocean and the Sahara Desert that lasted until the early twentieth century. There is no evidence of an extensive intra-African traffic in people – either maritime or land based – during the nineteenth century to match these numbers either before or after European colonial powers carved up the continent. We can conclude that no surge in slave-produced African commodity exports in these years from any of these African regions was comparable to what happened in the Americas in the sugar, cotton, and coffee sectors in response to the transatlantic slave trade closing. This comparison suggests it is highly unlikely that the ending of the Atlantic slave trade triggered a massive increase in African slaveholdings.

Nevertheless, a substantial shift within Africa *was* triggered by suppression of the transatlantic slave trade, but it was not toward regions producing commercial produce for Europe, as happened in the Americas. Rather it was directed to locations that the British intended as sites safe from slavery – just how safe is taken up in Chapter 7. As part of the efforts to suppress the slave trade after the passage of the 1807 abolition acts of Britain and the US, 96,000 Africans were disembarked in Sierra Leone, 24,100 in St. Helena, 6,700 in Cape of Good Hope 5,100 in Liberia, and 2,200 in Luanda. While, as we shall see, many did not remain in these locations, this was not an economically rational deployment of labor by the standards of any of the imperial powers on the global stage referenced in Chapter 1, or indeed by the standards of early modern Europeans. On the contrary, did the labor power of 134,000 Africans diverted from the plantation Americas by the British navy constitute yet another significant foregone opportunity for British plantation owners? Perhaps not. Later in the century when Europeans divided up the continent, shedding most of their humanitarian sensibilities in the process, the position of African commodity exports relative to the rest of the world (and certainly the Americas) did not improve. From a long-run perspective, the outcome of the colonial partition of Africa was no different from the attempts of Europeans to bring sugar-growing technology to the African mainland in that compared to the Americas at least neither brought substantial gains to the imperialists.[106]

---

[106] Eltis, *Rise of African Slavery*, 139–40.

Suppression of the Atlantic slave trade might have had some small effect on slaveholdings south of the Sahara. Of course, overseas exports increased but not because more slave labor had become available. And major slave societies did appear in the form of the Sokoto Caliphate and in parts of French West Africa, but from an international perspective these made only modest contributions to African overseas exports. If slavery within Africa increased as the slave trade ended, that, too, must have been of modest proportions if it happened at all.

In summary, this rather lengthy review of how the positions of some leading Africanist scholars are at odds with recent scholarship on the slave trade points to a depressing conclusion. Major Africanists have exaggerated the impact of the Atlantic world on sub-Saharan Africa. They see cheap European goods devastating African economies, fundamental social practices such as slavery irrevocably altered, trust between strangers permanently undermined, states rising and falling in response to the slave trade, with the impact of all steadily increasing over time. What all this means is that the effect of much of the post-Rodney historiography as represented by Miller, Lovejoy, and Green is to severely reduce the agency of Africans in shaping their own history. In a sense, it suggests that for those not dispatched to the Americas, the impact of the Atlantic world was different from, but nevertheless comparably malevolent, for those that were forced to leave. In this sample of the post-Rodney literature Africans remain predominantly victims. Certainly, the argument that "a western 'capitalist mode of production' was fed by the African 'slave mode of production' over the course of the nineteenth century," becomes possible only by ignoring seventy years of painstaking data collection on the eighteenth- and nineteenth-century movement of commodities and people around the Atlantic world.[107]

Of the four influential scholars who have contributed most to current views of the effect of the slave trade on Africa, John Thornton is the one who has offered arguments most consistent with the wealth of new evidence that has recently become available.[108] He has long decentered the external slave trade in his interpretation of African history. In the

---

[107] Catherine Coquery-Vidrovitch, "African Slavery in the Nineteenth Century: Inseparable Partner of the Atlantic Slave Trade," in Dale Tomich and Paul E. Lovejoy (eds.), *The Atlantic and Africa: The Second Slavery and Beyond* (Stoneybrook, NY, 2021), p. 7.

[108] Readers may note that the recently published Howard French, *Born in Blackness: Africa, Africans, and the Making of the Modern World, 1471 to the Second World War* (New York, 2021) is not included in the following analysis. This book has received hugely favorable reviews in the leading English language press but has yet to be noticed in

words of David Gordon, Thornton sees "conquest and expansion from the sixteenth to the nineteenth centuries ... driven by efforts to control textile, copper, and salt production" within Africa rather than the external slave trade.[109] His long list of publications on specialist topics such as religion, warfare, and the transatlantic influence of the African diaspora, interspersed by his two major works of synthesis, have often been at odds with other major Africanists discussed here.[110] His most recent book generally avoids the big questions discussed in this chapter. Instead, it comprises a meticulous piecing together from primary sources of the political and military histories of the states of West Central Africa from Loango in the north to Banda and Ambuela in the south and stretching to Lake Tanganyika in the east.[111] Nevertheless, without drawing much on www.slavevoyages.org and related research it is more consistent with recent findings than are the works of other major figures in the field.

For Thornton, sub-Saharan Africa was abundant in land and wealth was expressed in ownership of people. Africans by and large took care of themselves before and during the Atlantic slave trade era without developing any dependency on overseas commerce whether in merchandise or people. As early as 1600 he can identify "some 200 known independent states along the African coast or in the inland areas where people who came into the slave trade lived." The involvement of these political entities in trafficking people was a choice, sometimes only occasionally exercised, as with the Kingdom of Benin. And as Thornton points out "most systems of African law that we have knowledge of today supported slavery and the sale of people into slavery ... [which] ... was both widespread and legally accepted, albeit with important reservations and safeguards."[112] Thornton makes frequent reference to transoceanic trade and politics as well as to population loss, but except for Portuguese diplomatic, military, and religious interventions, the

---

the scholarly community. Its arguments are not supported by references and thus cannot be evaluated.

[109] David M. Gordon, "States, Archives, and the Vivid Past – A History of West Central Africa to 1850," *Journal of African History*, 62 (2021): 285.

[110] John Thornton, *Africa and Africans in the Making of the Atlantic World* (Cambridge, 1998), and *A Cultural History*, pp. 60–99.

[111] Thornton, *History of West Central Africa* is an impressive work of archival scholarship, but it is pre-eminently about elite men and women, and their battles and treaties as they struggled for power. It is oddly old-fashioned in its approach. If it had been about Europe, the book would not have been out of place in the canon of the pre-social history historiography of the 1940s and 1950s!

[112] John Thornton, *A Cultural History of the Atlantic World, 1250–1820* (Cambridge, 2012), pp. 78, 81.

outside world is rarely the driver of, or even a participant in, African economic, social, and cultural change. In addition, Thornton is a strong proponent of the economic and demographic equivalence of Africans and Europeans at the onset of Atlantic slave trading, by which he means the economic well-being, life expectancy and military conflicts experienced by ordinary people in their respective sub-continents.[113]

John Thornton is not an economic historian and, except in his discussion of demographic trends, largely eschews numbers, but there is substantial support for his Africa-centered view of sub-Saharan history in the newly available quantitative evidence. Table 5.3 compares Western African imports with that of most of its main transoceanic trading partners – only the Brazilian data is missing. Just prior to British and US abolition of the slave trade the quantities of both slaves and African produce – mainly palm oil and ivory – as well as the prices of both commodities were close to their all-time peaks. African access to offshore merchandise was thus also at its peak and especially so given that, as already noted, the terms of trade were also swinging in Africa's favor. Yet on a per capita basis and, in comparison to other large regions bordering the Atlantic, the imports that these exports enabled were trivial even at their peak. African ratios fell well below those of their chief overseas trading partners and amounted to just over one-tenth of those of the West European nations that were least dependent on international trade, namely the French. In terms of per-capita income, Gemery and Hogendorn have calculated subsistence costs of £1 a year for eighteenth-century West Africa, so perhaps £1.20 after allowing for a margin beyond subsistence.[114] Thus, a little over 6 percent of average income was spent on ocean-borne merchandise and for most of the slave trade era before and after this peak late eighteenth-century period, import ratios would have been much smaller than this. As Thornton points out, Africans could feed, clothe, and house themselves, as well as sustain the savings and investment necessary to support these activities to a greater extent than European nations and their offshoots.

[113] *Africa and Africans* (2nd ed, Cambridge, 1998), pp. xii–xiv, xviii–xxxvii. For quotes, see *Cultural History*, pp. 78–9, 80–81. For the debates on the equivalency issue see his "Precolonial African Industry and the Atlantic Trade," *African Economic History*, 19 (1990): 1–19 and the responses in this issue from Ralph A. Austen, Patrick Manning, Jan Hogendorn, Henry A. Gemery, and E. Ann McDougall. Strangely, despite the fundamental differences between Miller, Lovejoy, and Green on the one hand and Thornton on the other, none of them have, to my knowledge, ever addressed these in print.

[114] Henry A. Gemery and Jan S. Hogendorn, "The Economic Costs of West African Participation in the Atlantic Slave Trade," in idem (eds.), *The Uncommon Market: Essays in the Economic History of the Atlantic Slave Trade* (New York, 1979), p. 153.

Of course, large quantities of foreign textiles, metals, alcohol, guns, and decorative goods did enter Africa in the slave-trade era. Their distribution across African regions was clearly skewed toward regions where the slave trade was most active, and Dahomey, accounting for one-fifth of the captives leaving the Bight of Benin in the mid eighteenth century, probably had a ratio of imports to total product as high as 15 percent. Yet Manning's careful assessment of the Dahomean economy concludes that while "the export of slaves [cannot] be dismissed as lacking real impact [neither] can it be taken as Dahomey's primary economic activity."[115] But such a skewed distribution also implies that most ordinary Africans living away from the major coastal trading sites would have had little experience of overseas merchandise.

Thornton addresses the question of why so many African states voluntarily participated in the overseas slave trade when that traffic had a clearly deleterious impact on their populations and general security. His answer lies in the political fragmentation of the sub-continent in coastal regions south of the Senegal and Niger valleys. Hundreds of mini-states or sometimes ethnolinguistic groups that could coalesce temporarily into larger polities or federations were more nearly the norm than were major state formations thriving on slave trading.[116] The lack of enduring overarching state structures meant that the potential pool of captives was probably greater in sub-Saharan Africa than at any point in the Old World since the Mongol expansions in Central Asia. In early nineteenth-century Upper Guinea a missionary observed that "[E]ach town has its own independent chief, who in time of war sometimes unite for the sake of mutual assistance and defence."[117] But to return to the demographic issue, might not an additional response to Thornton's question be the very fact that while local impacts of the slave trade could be and were devasting, the demographic consequences of the business on larger regions and in the longer term were less so? There is no clear evidence of a language group disappearing from West Africa during the slave trade era.[118]

---

[115] Patrick Manning, *Slavery, Colonialism and Economic Growth in Dahomey, 1640–1960* (Cambridge, 1982), pp. 44–45.
[116] Thornton, *Cultural History*, pp. 74–82.
[117] Reverend Leopold Butscher, *Account of the Mandingoes, Susoos, & Other Nations, about 1815* ed. Bruce L. Mouser (Leipzig, 2000), p. 15.
[118] Paul E. H. Hair, "Ethnolinguistic Continuity on the Guinea Coast," *Journal of African History*, 8 (1967): 247–68; Hair, "An Ethnolinguistic Inventory of the Lower Guinea Coast before 1700," *African Language Review*, 7 (1968): 47–73.

The northern interior of sub-Saharan Africa did contain larger states centered on the Niger, Gambia, and Senegal rivers. Thousands of non-Muslims were enslaved by the Islamic states Kaabu, Ségou, and eventually Futa Jallon, among others. Yet we know that after 1807 16 percent of those leaving Upper Guinea had Islamic or Arabic names, a ratio that shrinks to 5 or 6 percent if we broaden our base to West Africa. A simple backward projection into say, the sixteenth and seventeenth centuries, when very few Muslims could have entered the transoceanic trade, would suggest that probably fewer than two in every hundred of those boarding a slave vessel over the whole period could have been Islamic. Moreover, closer inspection of the nineteenth-century sample reveals a significantly higher ratio of men compared to the Yoruba, Igbo, and Mende diasporas. The jihads raging across central and western Sudan in the first half on the nineteenth century would certainly have raised the count of prisoners of war among those leaving Upper Guinea and Bight of Benin ports. In addition to the small numbers of Muslims, we can assume that the high ratio of men among them worked further to reduce the possibility of community-building and reproduction in those regions of the Americas receiving the Muslim influx. These sex ratios also comprise strong evidence of internecine Islamic conflict, some certainly jihadic in nature.[119] Such patterns were not the West African norm. Fewer than 9 percent of total transatlantic departures from Africa left from Senegambia and Sierra Leone together, and the majority of these came from coastal societies, not the interior.

Considerable scholarly effort has been put into tracking the African origins of captives brought to or intended for the Americas and how those captives came to be enslaved in the first instance. Thornton fully exploits the works of contemporary observers such as Christian Georg Andreas Oldendorp, Alonso de Sandoval, and Sigismund Köelle, as well as the many Portuguese officials in their ventures inland from Luanda. Frederick Bowser's book on early colonial Peru is also foundational.[120] But the range of "nations" that they found is such that perhaps the real challenge is to identify African ethnolinguistic groups that were *not* well represented

---

[119] Male ratios were .804 for Islamic names compared to .686 for Yoruba, Igbo, and Mende combined. Calculated from PAST data; for further discussion of the Islamic component of the transatlantic traffic see Daniel Domingues da Silva, David Eltis, Nafees Khan, Philip Misevich and Olantunji Ojo, "The Transatlantic Muslim Diaspora to Latin America in the Nineteenth Century," *Colonial Latin American Historical Review*, 26 (2017): 528–45.

[120] Bowser, *African Slave*.

in the Americas, other than known enslavers like the Vai, Fon, and Vili. If war and banditry were prime sources of captives, then as Thornton concludes, African states were "selling their opponents' subjects, and whatever damage [was] done [was] not done in their own country."[121] It is not surprising that, as in Europe and the Americas, a wide range of places on the sub-Saharan African coast were involved in putting captives on board a slave ship. The transatlantic slave trade database allows us to identify no fewer than 254 different sites on the sub-continent where vessels embarked captives.[122] In addition, while the sub-Saharan African population, comprised about 3 percent of the global total in 1850, it was home to at least one-quarter of the world's languages – and language is surely a key proxy for cultural diversity. No other region in the world of comparable size could come close to the degree of human diversity and political fragmentation that existed in Western Africa; sadly, these characteristics correlate well with potential for enslavement. The central point is that, in effect, everyone living in the sub-continent was an "outsider" and thus eligible for enslavement by one or more African polities or ethnolinguistic groups that were different from their own.[123]

The latest evidence for West Central Africa suggests that war was not the primary source of captives, at least after 1780. Domingues da Silva finds that minor conflicts, abduction, and judicial proceedings together accounted for most enslavements.[124] In other words Africans were at risk in their own communities, eligibility rules notwithstanding. These two views of the enslavement process – wars between states and slaves generated within the state – are not necessarily inconsistent with each other in the West Central African case. A large share of the conflicts that Thornton describes in his 2020 book were succession disputes, or civil wars after which many of the losing side found themselves in the hold of a slave ship.[125]

---

[121] Thornton, *Cultural History*, p. 83.

[122] I draw here on the CSV or SPSS versions of the TSTD (available from the download page of www.slavevoyages.org) as opposed to the online version, the maps for which identify only points that saw five or more voyages depart.

[123] For populations in 1850 I refer to Frankema and Jervens' research. Language counts are from contemporary Ethnologue.com estimates, which – given the severe erosion of language diversity around the globe in the last 150 years – means that 25 percent is likely an undercount. For a fuller discussion of the nineteenth-century Liberated African data, see Chapter 7 below.

[124] Domingues da Silva, *Atlantic Slave Trade*, pp. 142–66. Also, Badi Bukas-Yakabuul and Daniel B. Domingues da Silva, "From Beyond the Kwango: Tracing the Linguistic Origins of Slaves Leaving Angola, 1811–1848," *Almanack*, 12 (2016): 34–43.

[125] Thornton is not always consistent on this issue. In 2012, he wrote "for much of its history, the slave trade drew most heavily on populations within about 200 kilometers of

The recent data throw up three important specific questions for Thornton. First, his estimate that 7 million people were carried off from West Central Africa to the Americas is certainly too high. The figure that Paul Lachance and I generated is 5.7 million and we provided an essay, a separate spreadsheet and a database all downloadable from www.slavevoyages.org to explain its derivation. Thornton does not engage with this research. He relies instead on a "belief that the absence of crucial records makes the period before 1700 subject to serious undercounting which has not been fully considered in the database." In fact, the 5.7 million figure *does* attempt to take account of "serious undercounting" in the original sources.[126] The second issue is Thornton's assessment of the main demographic impact of the slave trade on West Central Africa, which for him was on the age and sex structure of its population rather than its size. He concludes "the slave trade had only a limited effect on the number of people living in the area."[127] While this is consistent with the current research, he nevertheless reports major imbalances in the sex ratio and a skewed age distribution in the remaining West Central African populations because of the removal of a preponderance of people of working age.[128]

But the numerical basis of this position is questionable. The estimated population of West Central Africa in Table 5.2 is 11.2 million (the sum of rows 16–18), and annual departures between 1776 and 1850, when these peaked, averaged 36,560 people. The overall region thus lost just under one-third of 1 percent of its population annually to the Atlantic slave trade (36,560/11.2 million) and most of these were males. Natural population

---

the coast" (*Cultural History*, 65), but his account of the rise and fall of the Lunda empire in *History of West Central Africa*, the origin of which was located 1,000 kilometers (620 miles) from the Atlantic coast (p. 85), leaves little doubt that between 1750 and 1850 the slave trade in his view was drawing heavily on regions east of the Kwanza River.

[126] Thornton, *History of West Central Africa*, p. 5. For the Eltis and Lachance materials, see https://slavevoyages.org/voyage/downloads#estimates-spreadsheet/2/en/.

[127] Thornton, "The Demographic Effect of the Slave Trade," pp. 693–721.

[128] Thornton, "An Eighteenth Century Baptismal Register and the Demographic History of Manguenzo," in African Historical Demography: Proceedings of a Seminar Held in the Centre of African Studies, University of Edinburgh, April 29–30, 1977, pp. 405–15; Thornton, "Demography and History in the Kingdom of Kongo, 1550–1750," *Journal of African History*, 18 (1977): 507–30; idem, "The Slave Trade in Eighteenth Century Angola: Effects on Demographic Structures," *Canadian Journal of African Studies / Revue Canadienne Des Études Africaines*, 14 (1980): 417–27; quote is from p. 418. In his recent revision of his earlier work, Thornton nevertheless retains his argument that the slave trade inflicted major imbalances of sex and age ratios on provenance zones. See his "Revising the Population," 201–12. In *History of West Central Africa*, p. 294, he suggests that this pattern held for the larger region.

growth must have at least replaced this loss because historians (including Thornton) see the African populations holding steady during the slave-trade era. On this Thornton is in line with the current consensus in arguing that slave trading did not reduce the total population. But it follows that births over deaths must have at least matched slave-trade losses and those births must necessarily have had an approximately equal sex ratio, thus offsetting the skewness of the group forced to leave.[129] It is possible to have a skewed sex and age ratio as a result of the slave trade as well as a constant population, but it would take a very peculiar population pyramid for this to happen. Under these circumstances, the ratio of seventy-one males per hundred females that Thornton calculates for the Portuguese Angolan slave population in 1777/1778 is not likely to have held for West Central Africa as a whole. Finally, new evidence from census data for 1797–1870 (with gaps) for Ambaca, São José de Encoge, Golungo, and Cazengo located in the coffee-growing belt shows no consistent indication that the slave populations left behind were predominantly female. In Encoge, the sex ratio was in most years somewhat biased to women, but in the other districts female captives were not predominant.[130] Either the assumptions underlying Thornton's demographic estimates are problematic or the communities for which he has found data are not representative of the wider region.

The latest version of slavevoyages.org includes databases that go beyond recording voyages and the people on board them. This new information permits an emphasis on African agency in the slave-trading business both in terms of participation in, and defense against, the ravages of the slave trade. Several Africanists have written interpretations consistent with the voyages data even before the full database became available online. In the stateless or politically "decentralized" areas of Upper Guinea as well as the hinterland of the Bight of Biafra, Walter Hawthorne, David Northrup, and Ugo Nwokeji give a strong sense of equality of status between African and European slave traders that is consistent with the new data.[131] Hawthorne finds that not only were

---

[129] In addition, Thornton's demographic profile of departures is not consistent with the sample of 7,045 Liberated Africans leaving West Central Africa and disembarking in either Havana, Sierra Leone, and St. Helena between 1811 and 1862. This sample shows a much younger demographic with many more children at risk. No less than 47.5 percent were below the age of 15, with 98 percent below the age of 31.

[130] Vos and de Matos, "Demography of Slavery."

[131] Hawthorne, *Planting Rice and Harvesting Slaves*; Northrup, *Trade Without Rulers*, pp. 65–84.

there many sellers of slaves, but that the Balanta people developed strategies to protect their communities against the impact of the Atlantic traffic. In a similar vein, at the end of his study of the Aro network in the Bight of Biafra hinterland, Nwokeji stresses "Africa's role in shaping the Atlantic slave trade."[132] For the areas dominated by what are often called "predatory states" we must dip into the older literature to find discussions that recognize the autonomy of African polities and the decision-making of their slave traders. Though written in the 1970s, the work of Boubacar Barry and Pat Manning recognizes the agency of the states of Kaabu and Dahomey respectively. While Barry writes within a Walter Rodney-type framework, both studies are broadly consistent with the data generated over the years by www.slavevoyages.org.[133]

As must now be obvious, the intent of this chapter is not to provide an alternative to the grand interpretations of Africa's involvement in the transoceanic slave trades that have dominated the historiography in recent years, but rather to ask more scholars to take on board new information, some of which contains a quantitative element. As Thornton has repeatedly pointed out, Africa had more in common with the Americas and Europe than it had differences during most of the slave-trade era. If this had not been the case, then the slave trade would not have happened. A widespread acceptance of slavery and the slave trade with, for most of the period, no evidence of a desire to abolish either, meant that hundreds of ports and millions of people on all continents bordering the Atlantic were available to organize and sustain the business. Further, each continent or sub-continent could generate the food, clothing, and shelter it needed to sustain its respective populations without reliance on long-distance trade, and for most of the period and with the dramatic exception of the Indigenous populations of the Americas and the 12.75 million people carried off from Africa, life expectancy and vital rates were not much affected by the transoceanic movements of people, except, obviously, those and their families caught up in the traffic. When a divergence in vital rates and income began to emerge between continents in the early nineteenth century, this, too, cannot easily be attributed to slavery and the transatlantic slave trade or, indeed, their abolition.

---

[132] *The Slave Trade and Culture in the Bight of Biafra: An African Society in the Atlantic World* (Cambridge, 2010), p. 207. Nwokeji, defines the Aro as a trade diaspora comprising a "nation of socially interdependent, but spatially dispersed, communities" (p. 17).

[133] Boubacar Barry, *Senegambia and the Atlantic Slave Trade*, trans. Ayi Kwei Armah (Cambridge, 1998), pp. 36–131; Manning, *Slavery, Colonialism, and Economic Growth*, pp. 1–12, 27–50.

The major figures in the historiography of course do not ignore the numbers, but the balance of the evidence they employ favors the opinions of contemporary observers – usually visitors to the sub-continent – and, to a lesser extent, African oral traditions. A consequence of relying on such evidence is that books for the general reader, blogs, and press reviews can promote the view that European exploitation of Africa was central to Western economic development. A proper response to the large questions raised in this chapter requires a synthesis that integrates these different methodologies or rather that recognizes that quantitative and qualitative approaches cannot be separated. My assessment of the current historiography is that we are still a long way short of attaining such a synthesis.

6

Abolition: A Leninist Interpretation

These are strange times for scholars of the struggle to end slavery and the slave trade in the Atlantic world. On the one hand, chattel slavery and its abolition have captured the interest of increasing numbers of historians – since 2006 new works from Christopher Brown, John Oldfield, David Ryden, Claudius Fergus, Robin Blackburn, Padraic X. Scanlan, David Richardson, and two each from David Brion Davis and Seymour Drescher have appeared, together with a much greater number of essays.[1] On the other hand governments, nongovernmental organizations, international organizations, and social commentators are raising the profile of modern trafficking and modern slavery. Most countries in recent

---

[1] Christopher Brown, *Moral Capital: Foundations of British Abolitionism* (Chapel Hill, NC, 2006); Drescher, *Abolition*; David Brion Davis, *Inhuman Bondage: The Rise and Fall of Slavery in the New World* (Oxford, 2006) and *The Problem of Slavery in the Age of Emancipation* (New York, 2014). Robin Blackburn's *The American Crucible: Slavery, Emancipation and Human Rights* (London, 2011) and "Debates on Slavery, Capitalism and Race, New and Old," in Banu Bargu, and Chiara Bottici (eds.), *Feminism, Capitalism, and Critique: Essays in Honor of Nancy Fraser* (London, 2017), pp. 43–65, update his earlier treatment of slave-trade abolition as a function of revolution in the Americas in *Overthrow of Colonial Slavery*; David Ryden, *West Indian Slavery and British Abolition, 1783–1807* (Cambridge, 2009); Padraic X. Scanlan, "Emancipation and Captivity in the British Empire," *History and Anthropology*, 30 (2019): 503–508; Scanlan, *Slave Empire: How Slavery Built Modern Britain* (London, 2020); John R. Oldfield, *The Ties that Bind Transatlantic Abolition in the Age of Reform* (Liverpool, 2020); Richardson, *Principles and Agents*. For a selection of the most important essays, see Marcel van der Linden, "Unanticipated Consequences of 'Humanitarian Intervention': The British Campaign to Abolish the Slave Trade, 1807–1900," *Theory and Society*, 39 (2010): 281–98; Tâmis Paron, "The British Empire and the Suppression of the Slave Trade to Brazil: A Global History Analysis," *Journal of World History*," 29 (2018): 1–36. Marcus Rediker's *The Slave Ship* is not about abolition, but it might be included here given its heavy use of evidence generated during the abolitionist era, and thus tells us as much about abolitionist attitudes as about the slave trade.

years have signed up to the United Nations Trafficking Protocol. The Walk-Free Foundation (an anti-slavery charity) has calculated that 28.9 million slaves live around the globe. The International Labor Organization, cited on anti-slavery.org (website of the British successor to two early nineteenth-century anti-slavery societies), estimates a lower number of 20.9 million. Kevin Bales, easily the most cited writer on this subject, now argues for 38.7 million, at least two-thirds of whom live in the Indian sub-continent or Southeast Asia in debt-bondage. He posits that more slaves live in today's world than at any point in global history, though passes over the point that the population today is eight times what it was in 1800.[2] In the century between the St. Domingue Rebellion of 1791 and Brazilian abolition in 1888 some 8 million people gained their freedom in the Americas, and many millions more followed suit thereafter as every nation made slavery illegal. How do we reconcile these two trends? How is it possible that so many people remain enslaved in the modern world?

At one level Orlando Patterson resolves the contradiction.[3] What most people today consider to be slave trading and slavery is not the same as the institutions that were suppressed in the Atlantic world after 1791. Patterson recognizes that "forms of forced labour and servitude in the world today may share some slave-like properties and are no doubt as pernicious in their victimization and exploitation," but, he argues, "they are not slavery." Patterson does see many forms of modern prostitution resulting in the "social death" of an individual (normally an ethnically distinct female), but most types of "human domination and forced labour" – as described by Bales – do not. The crucial underlying point in this exchange is that what was defined as slavery before, say, the mid twentieth century is not the same as what is defined as slavery today. And, as Patterson emphasizes, if it were the same, then the history of the world would also be the history of slavery.[4] Such a position is consistent with

---

[2] Kevin Bales, *Disposable People: New Slavery in the Global* Economy, 3rd edition (Berkeley, CA, 2017, first published in 1999), pp. 8–9; www.walkfree.org; see also Siddharth Kara, *Modern Slavery: A Global Perspective* (New York, 2017); www.antislavery.org/slavery-today/modern-slavery.

[3] Orlando Patterson, "Trafficking, Gender and Slavery: Past and Present," Kevin Bales, "Professor Bales' Response to Professor Orlando Patterson," and Patterson, "Rejoinder: Professor Patterson's Response to Professor Kevin Bales," in Jean Allain (ed.), *The Legal Understanding of Slavery: From the Historical to the Contemporary* (Oxford, 2012), pp. 322–74.

[4] "If we accept the fact that all forms of forced labour today amount to slavery, then we are compelled to view the entire history of the world, and especially of all the advanced

what observers from Jean Bodin through to Adam Smith and Arthur Young believed – that only 5 percent of the world's population was at that time free, mostly living in Western Europe.[5] Peasants owing obligations to landlords, state servitude – often in the form of mita labor – dependents of gerontocratic kin-groups, and indentured servitude were only some of the forms of unfreedom under which the great mass of people around the globe labored. But these forms of exploitation did not comprise slavery. Though neither author refers to it, the exchange between Patterson and Bales is a reprise of the tensions in the 1840s and 1850s between Black abolitionists on the one side and White labor reformers and women's rights activists on the other. Frederick Douglass took strong exception to the attempts of the latter to use the word "slavery" to describe workers in factories, and women in marriage. On the former, Douglass and William Wells Brown frequently invited White workers to apply for the job vacancy created by their own respective escapes from the slave South.[6]

Stretching definitions of slavery to include other forms of labor exploitation is not the only approach that effectively downgrades the significance of nineteenth-century abolition. For post-colonial and subaltern studies scholars, the nature of oppression – whether slavery, indentured servitude, or racism – is of less interest than is its continuity and the responses it evokes. A post-colonial study of abolition is indeed almost a contradiction in terms. One recent book on Trinidad in the first decade after British occupation in 1797 has close discussions of imperial mayhem, racism, and the competing visions for the development of the newly conquered island, including the viewpoint of then contemporary political radicals. Yet the question of why Trinidad was not immediately opened to the slave trade like the fifteen other Caribbean Island that the British acquired after 1650 is not even broached.[7] For many historians, abolition is unimportant because the slave trade was quickly replaced by an equally obnoxious

---

societies from Near Eastern antiquity up to the rise of modern industrial capitalism in the nineteenth century, as the history of slavery. Sauce for the goose of the present is sauce for the gander of the past." (Patterson in Allain [ed.], *Legal Understanding*, p. 334.) The previous quotes are from Patterson in Allain (ed.), *Legal Understanding* p. 359.

[5] Seymour Drescher, *Capitalism and Antislavery: British Mobilization in Comparative Perspective* (London, 1986), pp. 16–17.

[6] David Roediger, "Race, Labor, and Gender in the Languages of Antebellum Social Protests," in Stanley L. Engerman (ed.), *Terms of Labor: Slavery, Serfdom, and Free Labor* (Stanford, 1999), pp. 170–85.

[7] James Epstein, *Scandal of Colonial Rule: Power and Subversion in the British Atlantic during the Age of Revolution* (Cambridge, 2012).

transoceanic traffic in contract laborers that brought 2 million Asians to the plantation colonies of the Indian, Atlantic, and Pacific oceans. This was one of "many middle passages" that formed the modern world. As for abolition of slavery itself, Padraic Scanlan ignores the more than 50 percent drop in sugar production in Jamaica (from 1824–1833 to 1839–1846), and the withdrawal of women and children from plantation labor forces over the same period, to argue that captivity – albeit a "new kind" – simply continued unabated in the British Caribbean.[8] He has also pointed to the payments that abolitionists such as Zachary Macaulay and colonial officials in Sierra Leone received as part of the attempts to suppress the slave trade to suggest that the whole abolitionist enterprise was just another case of economic self-interest, surely not the most insightful way to deal with complex historical realities.[9]

A further oddity of the slavery and abolition field is that there has not been much movement in the major interpretations of abolition in recent decades. Most of the books cited at the beginning of this chapter provide abundant new detail and documentation but not much in the way of original overarching frameworks, even though most of the chief protagonists have modified their positions over the years. What has changed is the tone of the debate. Scholars now tend to cite others only when they agree with them. Publications aimed at demolishing the positions of those holding differing viewpoints have disappeared. Nothing published in the last decade or so has the cut and thrust of Eric Williams' *British Historians and the West Indies* (London, 1957), Paul David et al.'s, *Reckoning with Slavery: A Critical Study in the Quantitative History of American Negro Slavery* (New York, 1976) or Seymour Drescher's *Econocide: British Slavery in the Era of Abolition* (Pittsburgh, PA, 1977).

Interpretations of abolition usually hinge on the writer's view of slavery. Thus, Bales' conception of slavery, along with older categorizations of "wage slavery," has the effect of downgrading the importance of abolition. Eric Williams saw the West Indian slave system as in decline by 1800 and famously argued in his 1944 book *Capitalism and Slavery* that while the profits of that system had first made industrialization possible, by the early nineteenth century the British economy had outgrown its need for

---

[8] Christopher et al. (eds.), *Many Middle Passages* pp. 1–19; Scanlan, Emancipation and Captivity.
[9] Patrick X. Scanlan, "The Rewards of Their Exertions: Prize Money and British Abolitionism in Sierra Leone, 1808–1823," *Past & Present*, 225 (2014): 113–42; and Scanlan, *Slave Empire*.

a slave empire and the protective tariffs that supported it. Williams saw abolition as part of the British drive for free trade, wider markets, and more attractive investment options.[10] David Ryden rejects the decline thesis but nevertheless offers an economic explanation for abolition of the slave trade. He centers his work on what he sees as the overproduction of sugar in the few years before 1807, and attributes abolition of the slave trade to a "changing economic context that allowed abolition to be construed as having a positive effect on the colonial interest," by which he means mostly Jamaica. His study provides new information on the power of the Jamaican planter lobby and the war-induced disruption of trade patterns that made the Jamaican slave interest more amenable to abolition. But while Jamaica was easily Britain's most important slave colony, it was not the frontier or the future of British slavery by the time that Trinidad, Demerara, and Berbice came under British control in the 1790s.[11] To generalize about the relationship between British slavery and abolition on the basis of the Jamaican experience is rather like examining the prospects for slavery in the US in the 1790s by close inspection of Virginia and the Carolinas, or those in Brazil by looking only at Pernambuco and Bahia in the 1810s. The British invaded St. Domingue in the 1790s not to free slaves but to protect their own slave colonies. They had no doubt about the sustainability of New World slave systems.[12]

These new British possessions present a strong argument against seeing abolition as a response to either the overproduction of sugar or the economic decline of the British sugar complex. Together, they contained approximately the same amount of land suitable for sugar cultivation as did Cuba, though as late as 1750 none of them exported much sugar (again, like Cuba). Between 1745 and 1806 the three received 106,112 African captives direct from Africa. In the same period Cuba imported a comparable

---

[10] For other renditions of the decline argument see Selwyn H. H. Carrington's work, especially, "'Econocide' – Myth or Reality: the Question of West Indian Decline, 1783–1806" and "Post-Postscriptum," *Boletin de estudios latinoamericanos y del Caribe*, 36 (1984): 13–38, 66–67.

[11] Ryden argues that sugar production in Demerara was trivial compared to Jamaica prior to 1807 but ignores its role as a source of raw cotton. Between 1796 and 1805 it supplied 16.5 percent of British imports compared to 34.6 percent coming from North America [Seymour Drescher, *Econocide: British Slavery in the Era of Abolition*, 2nd. ed. (Chapel Hill, NC, 2010), pp. 84–85]. He also ignores its huge potential as a plantation economy. On the overproduction argument, see Richardson's critique in *Principles and Agents*, p. 247.

[12] Ryden, *West Indian Slavery*, 254; David Geggus, "Slavery in the French Caribbean," *CWHS*, vol. 4: pp. 321–43.

108,647 slaves.[13] After 1806, by contrast, only 8,600 Africans arrived in the British areas – almost all of them in 1807 and 1808, while Cuba brought in an estimated 660,000. Once British Guiana (the name given to the combined territories of Berbice, Essequibo and Demerara in 1833) and Trinidad gained access to labor in the form of Asian indentured workers from 1838, their sugar output expanded rapidly once more to reach 40 percent of Cuban output by mid-century. This was at a time when Cuba was accounting for almost half of global production. Obviously, abolition of the slave trade, together with a ban on the movement of slaves between British slave colonies, had a major impact on the ability of the British planters to compete with their Spanish counterparts.

Most modern British abolition clearly stimulated Cuban growth. holars (as well as then contemporary slave owners) have accepted the continued viability of slave labor as abolition approached. Robin Blackburn recognizes slavery's long presence in human history and its future potential in, say, 1790, but he also sees the institution reaching a climax in the New World, where it displayed major differences even from its Roman and Greek predecessors, not least because the trade and profits that it generated enabled industrialization. Where Ryden gives a modern (and more thoroughly evidence-based) depiction of the second part of the *Capitalism and Slavery* thesis, Blackburn rejects any direct economic impulse toward abolition, but fully embraces *Capitalism and Slavery*'s first hypothesis – that without the slave Americas there could have been no British industrialization. On abolition, he sees "popular" expressions of anti-slavery occurring well before 1780 though Blackburn is not much interested in why abolition emerged. His chief focus is on the circumstances that allowed it to become such a major force for change. The implication of his work is that the abolitionist impulse was always there, but needed the specific circumstances of the 1780s and 1790s to become a mass movement. For him, chief among these fortuitous and contingent events were the French Revolution and the St. Domingue Rebellion, even though four decades later the enslaved population of the Americas had more than doubled and the slave trade had just reached its all-time peak. Apart from these awkward facts, identifying contingencies does seem to be the easy part of the analysis. The much more interesting and difficult question is why, after three millennia, a universally accepted

---

[13] Cuba: http://www.slavevoyages.org/estimates/wxoi8PFT and http://www.slavevoyages.org/estimates/3b3PAtLZ. British areas: http://www.slavevoyages.org/estimates/RaP6YcSV and http://www.slavevoyages.org/estimates/phTD15fg.

human practice should suddenly be called into question. Moreover, the inception of British slavery in the mid seventeenth-century Caribbean occasioned no public discourse whatsoever, even among political radicals.[14] Whereas the destruction of the system less than two centuries later occurred in the context of massive public agitation for abolition.

In contrast to Blackburn, Davis and Drescher stress the continuities of slavery over the very long haul without perceiving a climax or crisis: Drescher's first chapter is entitled "A Perennial Institution." Both accept Orlando Patterson's perspective, according to which the devastating impact of slavery on personhood and perception of self are apparent in most historic societies. Their view of abolition does not require that slavery in the Americas was intensifying and expanding in the second half of the eighteenth century (even though it clearly was). Together with Christopher Brown, who eschews the very long-run perspective on slavery's growth, they largely avoid the class dialectic as incorporated into Marxist interpretations. They still center abolition as an epoch-making event.[15]

Blackburn's interpretation raises three questions about evidence. First, his section on "Popular Anti-Slavery and the Birth of Abolitionism" does not penetrate very far down the social scale. He very quickly gets into a discussion of middle-class attitudes to cruelty and the reading of novels, plays, and poetry. Neither he nor Brown have systematically used the online British Newspaper Archive's rich collection of early English newspapers that report on crowd activity and slavery.[16] Second, the term, "Slavery's New World Climax" is never precisely explained.[17] At no point between 1492 and 1888 did anything like the majority of the Earth's slaves live in the Americas, and between 1750 and 1830, a period straddling the American, French, Haitian, and Industrial revolutions, the number of *New World* slaves alone almost tripled in size. Moreover, in 1829 the transatlantic slave trade reached its highest annual total ever (310 slave vessels carrying off 118,000 captives). The Haitian Revolution may have struck fear in the hearts of slaveholders, but it had

---

[14] The radicals of the 1640s, including Levelers, had scant regard for human rights. They argued that anyone who did not contribute to the common welfare should be enslaved. See Eltis, *Rise of African Slavery*, pp. 15–16.

[15] In the British case the oft-quoted line from "Rule Britannia" (1740) – "Britons never shall be slaves" – was very much about eligibility for slave status, not whether slave status itself should exist.

[16] www.britishnewspaperarchive.co.uk.

[17] Blackburn, *American Crucible*, pp. 16, 150–59.

no apparent impact on their willingness to buy more enslaved people. Prices of slaves in the Atlantic slave trade surged to all-time highs in the fifteen years after August 22, 1791, when the rebellion began.[18] We can see slavery's foes massing in this era, but to portray any of the above upheavals as "a challenge it [the system of New World slavery] could not suppress" is a much bigger challenge.[19] Third, the largest export economy in the Americas by value remained Spanish, not British, through to the early nineteenth century. As well as the most valuable exports, the Spanish colonial Americas had larger cities, a much bigger population and labor force, and a much larger consumer market than did their British counterpart, both before and after 1776.[20]

Where Blackburn's view of abolition has changed little over the last four decades, other major contributors have shifted positions. Two works by David Brion Davis, *The Problem of Slavery in Western Culture* (1966) and *The Problem of Slavery in the Age of Emancipation* (2014), mostly bookend the historiography of the last half-century. They are part of a trilogy, the pages of which sparkle with paradoxes and insights and give more sheer pleasure than any other publication in the field. The first volume barely broached the era of politically active anti-slavery, but, reflecting the dominant views of mid 1960s, it did suggest that slave systems "helped prevent the growth of a balanced and healthy economy" and were in decline, at least in the British Caribbean, after 1750. This contributed to a broader and long-run shift in Western thinking (to which the book was devoted) that "undermined traditional religious and philosophical justifications of slavery."[21] Later, however, when Davis investigated the abolitionist era more closely, he came to recognize that the institution of slavery was economically efficient and durable. To resolve the paradox of an economically powerful country suppressing a legal and profitable activity he explored possible links between abolitionism and industrialization. Davis acknowledged the mass support for ending the slave trade in the late 1780s and against slavery itself after 1823. But he was especially interested in the fact that the country's elite abolished the

---

[18] Select www.slavevoyages.org/voyages/2yvutlMg and on the timeline tab select "Sterling cash price in Jamaica."
[19] Blackburn, *American Crucible*, 26. The author here is referring only to the St. Domingue revolt beginning in 1791. For slave trade data see the timeline tab on https://slavevoyages.org/assessment/estimates.
[20] See Chapter 2 above.
[21] David Brion Davis, *The Problem of Slavery in Western Culture* (Cornell, 1966), pp. 174–86. The quotes are from pp. 178 and 480.

slave trade, imposed a slave registration system on the colonies, and instituted measures to ameliorate slavery in the 1820s without much popular pressure. He argues that these were the *only* major social reforms implemented in a period when domestic exploitation of labor in factory environments was intensifying and class tensions were high. For Davis, "the colonial plantation system served as a projective screen or experimental theater for testing ideas of liberation, paternalism and controlled social change." Abolition was a cause that all classes could support and one that would have a minimal impact on British society. It also allowed elites to "demonstrate their commitment to decency and justice."[22]

In his final work, industrialization – indeed economic factors in general – are no longer central. Davis sees economic growth expanding demand for slave-supplied commodities and encouraging the glorification of free labor, but its restructuring effect on class relations as a major element in the ending of slavery is scarcely mentioned. Davis now defines his trilogy's thesis as a shift in moral perceptions triggered by the tension between Aristotle's ideal of a slave as a tool – a physical extension of their owners – and Hegel's observation that the master had a psychological need for the slave to recognize the master's status.[23] Davis noted "the truth of the master's independent consciousness lies in the dependent and supposedly unessential consciousness of the slave … the obsequious servant might also be a domestic enemy." This master–slave tension that Davis first brought to center stage in 1966 was to underpin Genovese's *Roll Jordan Roll: The World the Slaves Made* and indeed the two generations of scholarship on slave cultures thereafter.[24] In Davis' third volume industrialization and abolition are linked only in that both celebrated free labor, a system unique to Western Europe and its offshoots at the time. Davis' last words on abolition focused on racism as much as slavery and the damaging psychological effects of both on African Americans. Haiti, Liberia, and Black abolitionists are discussed extensively in terms of their value in counteracting this malignancy. The message of the Haitian Revolution "was as

---

[22] David Brion Davis, "Reflections on Abolitionism and Ideological Hegemony," *American Historical Review*, 92 (1987): 804–805. Davis' 2006 book added a further link between industrialization and abolition. The latter, he argued, allowed "British and later American culture … to dignify and honor [free] labor … a process that can cynically be seen as a way of disguising exploitation or … a way of genuinely recognizing elements of equality in people of subordinate status." (Davis, *Inhuman Bondage*, p. 248.)
[23] Davis, *The Problem of Slavery in the Age of Emancipation*, pp. 333–34.
[24] Eugene Genovese, *Roll Jordan Roll: The World the Slaves Made* (New York), 1974.

important for self-doubting blacks as for arrogant and self-deluding whites." Except on Haiti the Black elite's responses were hardly united, but Blacks were key members of a particularly fissiparous abolitionist movement in the US, ensuring the acceptance of immediatism and, ultimately, a critical erosion of support for the American Colonization Society. *The Problem of Slavery in the Age of Emancipation* is not the first to recount Black resistance to attempts of US Whites to animalize Blacks and remove them to Africa, but it is the first to argue that without such resistance Blacks would not have become full citizens of the US, briefly between 1865 and 1877, and permanently much later. Yet the book avoids central counterfactual questions: Would abolition have occurred when it did without Black abolitionists? Did Blacks become abolitionists before Whites, or were both affected at the same time?

Drescher's position on slavery has not shifted since he entered the field with a game-changing and dramatically entitled book, *Econocide* – arguing for the continuing vitality of slavery through to the forced ending of the institution.[25] His interpretation of abolition is, however, less settled. Whereas Blackburn and volume 2 of the Davis trilogy see industrialization as a key component in the ending of slavery, Drescher distances himself from revolutions of any kind.[26] In the 1980s Drescher attributed the sudden shift to activism in the late 1780s to the political mobilization of the new class of industrial artisans in the northern factory towns. Abolition was thus in one sense a cross-class alliance with the abolitionist sympathies of skilled workers in the north of England shaped by their exposure to exploitation in the early industrial factory,[27] but in his 2009 volume this explanation disappears.[28] "Manchester's workers" receive a single mention in its 462 pages. The narrative of abolition is laid out elegantly and insights abound, but counterpunching predominates. Factory workers as a source of the

---

[25] Seymour Drescher, *Econocide: British Slavery in the Age of Abolition* (Pittsburgh, 1977).
[26] Drescher, *Abolition*, p. 272.
[27] "[A] dramatic extension of public power to individuals whose opinion on slavery had never before been counted" was one of two "decisive changes (that) had to occur before British society turned against the slave trade" ("Capitalism and Abolition," p. 181), but the argument is developed more fully in Drescher, *Abolition* and Drescher, "Cart Whip and Billy Roller: Antislavery and Reform Symbolism in Industrializing Britain, *Journal of Social History*, 15 (1981): 3–24. See also his "Eric Williams: British Capitalism and British Slavery," *History and Theory*, 26 (1987): 195.
[28] Unless one accepts that the elite created a false consciousness among the non-elite – a now outdated idea – there is at least an irony in severely exploited peoples agitating first for improved conditions for others rather than themselves.

abolitionist impulse reappear in Drescher's latest work but are no longer the mainsprings and the reader who wonders why abolition happened when it did will continue to wonder.

For Christopher Brown the critical event is a different revolution. British failure to suppress the American Revolution meant that Britons attempted to reburnish their tarnished claim as the home and beacon of liberty. "Moral capital," the title of the book, was real enough and the British drew on it fully in their nineteenth-century imperial policies.[29] Eric Williams famously wrote, "British historians wrote almost as if Britain had introduced slavery solely for the satisfaction of abolishing it."[30] For Brown, the British appear to have invented abolition solely to gain the moral high ground and restore national esteem. Despite the superb research and the counterfactual exercises in the epilogue there remains a certain lack of clarity about the core argument. Was the American Revolution sufficient by itself to induce the onset of abolition or was it merely one of several prerequisites? Brown hunts down early anti-slavery attitudes in Britain more thoroughly than any other scholar but argues that turning scattered expressions into political action would not have been possible without the national trauma of the loss of the thirteen colonies.

The central problem here, as Seymour Drescher has argued, is lack of hard evidence of this trauma in the aftermath of defeat. For Drescher, electronic searching of thousands of 1780s British newspapers reveals only growing prosperity and a national self-esteem that required no bolstering.[31] Establishing motives for behavior – in this case abolition – is of course impossible, but given the thrust of his argument, Brown's discussion of post-war US independence Britain is surprisingly limited. His focus is very much on small numbers of abolitionists (Evangelicals and Quakers) and free Blacks who came within British purview during and after the conflict. And he makes no mention of the preceding decades-long commitment of Quakers to slavery, nor to the many thousands of free Blacks who, especially in the Portuguese Atlantic world, helped finance

---

[29] As Richard Huzzey, *Freedom Burning: Anti-Slavery and Empire in Victorian Britain* (Ithaca, NY, 2012), pp. 132–76, 206–13 has argued.
[30] *British Historians and the West Indies* (Port-of-Spain, Trinidad, 1964), p. 182.
[31] Brown, *Moral Capital*, pp. 451–62; Seymour Drescher, "The Shocking Birth of British Abolitionism," *Slavery & Abolition*, 33 (2012): 571–93. Drescher uses the digitized edition of the Burney collection of Early English Newspapers, a resource that became available only after the publication of *Moral Capital*.

hundreds of slave voyages to Brazil.[32] None of these scholars move out of the English-speaking world for very long.

A separate and increasing number of historians maintain that slaves freed themselves, as indeed Thomas Jefferson had predicted was inevitable. Violent slave resistance is certainly difficult to discount. C.L.R. James' book on St. Domingue first gave it prominence and Richard Hart's study of slave revolts in Jamaica extended its geographic range (though stripped of any discussion of James' ideology). In the US case, Herbert Aptheker simply stated that "the social system itself" caused rebellion. Steve Hahn has revived a different aspect of this argument in the context of the US Civil War, though in his case the violence that enabled slaves to escape was between largely White armies rather than between Black slaves and White authorities.[33] For the recent historiography, captives' resistance to enslavement sprang from one of the most basic of human instincts and was a constant. Yet one must ask how chattel slavery could have endured for millennia without a credible threat from the enslaved before succumbing rather suddenly in the Atlantic world of the nineteenth century. Slave resistance by itself and as conventionally interpreted was certainly a necessary prerequisite to such an event, but it cannot have been sufficient to explain a renouncement of slave labor beginning in 1777, the year Vermont's new constitution made slavery illegal.[34] Why did "the only successful slave revolt in history," in C.L.R. James' words, begin in 1791 and not centuries earlier?[35] James answered the question by drawing on a Marxist framework that cast St. Domingue slaves as hyper-exploited workers. More recently, Claudius Fergus and

---

[32] For the financial interest of both free and enslaved Blacks in the slave trade, see Chapter 4. Joseph Harbin's life (1667–1719) shows the limits of Quaker abolitionism. He was a Barbadian Quaker who was principal owner of five transatlantic slave voyages that carried off 1,076 Africans in the early eighteenth century. He owned twenty-one slaves at his death and while his Quaker beliefs meant that he would neither support nor serve in the colonial militia, he was apparently happy to be one of the island's major slave traders. (See www.slavevoyages.org/enslaver/PMcMHOby) and Joseph Besse, *Sufferings of the Early Quakers: America, West Indies, Bermuda* (York, UK, 2001), pp. 330 (2), 335, 336, 337 (2), 339 (2) 342 (2). I thank Patricia Stafford for this reference.

[33] Richard Hart, *Slaves Who Abolished Slavery: Blacks in Rebellion* (Kingston, Jamaica, 1980); Steven Hahn, *Political Worlds of Slavery and Freedom* (Cambridge, MA, 2009), pp. 55–114; Herbert Aptheker, *American Negro Slavery Revolts* (New York, 1943), p. 139.

[34] Stanley L. Engerman, *Slavery, Emancipation and Freedom: Comparative Perspectives* (Baton Rouge, LA, 2007), p. 5. This measure freed an estimated nineteen slaves.

[35] C. L. R. James, *Black Jacobins: Toussaint L'Ouverture and the San Domingo Revolution* (London, 1938), p. ix.

Simon Newman have made resistance central to their own interpretations of abolition in the British Caribbean.[36] But hyper-exploitation was not new in the late eighteenth century. Indeed, some scholars have argued that Enlightenment views had begun to ameliorate slave owners' treatment of captives in the late eighteenth-century British Caribbean.[37] Slave resistance may have been a vital element in the process of abolition as argued below, but it could not have been sufficient by itself to trigger an abolition movement.

Between 1787 and 1792, 1.7 million Britons signed petitions in favor of abolition of the traffic.[38] Suddenly, the attitudes of the British public toward the slave trade, as opposed to those of Europe's intellectuals become plain to see. The striking feature of this development is that it constituted a rather stunning reversal. The active support for and participation in the slave trade is described in Chapter 3. The Liverpool riots in favor of the slave trade as late as 1775, caused Gomer Williams, the late nineteenth century historian of the Liverpool slave trade, to comment "[w]ith the exception of the [1745 Jacobite] rebellion and the Gordon Riots, the annals of the eighteenth century cannot mention a more extraordinary and formidable popular outbreak in England than these riots."[39] Ringleaders were transported to the Americas in the aftermath of these disturbances. Most of them had no doubt crewed slave ships. Now shackled in the hold of a transatlantic voyage, they, too, were able to experience some of the horrors of the Africans they had formerly controlled. It is not likely that many of the rioters were among the 1.7 million signatories that flooded the House of Commons at the end of the following decade.

It is therefore surely undeniable that a dramatic change in British popular perceptions of the slave trade had occurred over the course of the eighteenth century, and more particularly in the last quarter of the

---

[36] Simon Newman, *A New World of Labor: The Development of Plantation Slavery in the British Atlantic* (Philadelphia, PA, 2013) and Claudius Fergus, *Revolutionary Emancipation: Slavery and Abolitionism in the British West Indies* (Baton Rouge, LA, 2013).

[37] Justin Roberts, *Slavery and the Enlightenment in the British Atlantic: 1750–1807* (Cambridge, 2013), pp. 49–52; Nicholas Radburn and Justin Roberts, "Gold Versus Life: Jobbing Gangs and British Caribbean Slavery," *William and Mary Quarterly*, 76 (2019): 223–56.

[38] John Oldfield, *Popular Politics and British Anti-Slavery: The Mobilization of Public Opinion against the Slave Trade, 1787–1807* (Manchester, UK, 1995), pp. 96–123; Huzzey, "Microhistory of British Antislavery," 599–623

[39] Williams, *History of Liverpool Privateers*, p. 555.

century. Moreover, if this relatively sudden emergence of hostility to the traffic had anything to do with the rebellious activities of slaves, such resistance was more likely to have taken place on board slave ships than in the slave colonies. Tacky's Rebellion in Jamaica in 1760, the center of Fergus' analysis, was certainly reported, but no newspaper linked the event to abolition. Until St. Domingue erupted, English newspapers focused on African shipboard resistance to the slave trade rather than the natural desire of the enslaved to overthrow the slavocracy. The abolition movement was well established before the St. Domingue conflagration.

It follows that to understand abolition we must account for the relatively sudden value shift in the second half of eighteenth-century Britain. With the advent of the British Newspaper Archive this is now easier to do. Richardson's contribution identifies the growing uneasiness with slavery among intellectuals and tracks a growing concern with personal rights in the literary world as represented in novels, poetry, and the theatre.[40] But it is the incorporation of newspaper content that distinguishes his contribution and is carried further below. Richardson's book is very much in the David Brion Davis tradition, but is able to get closer to accounting for the dramatic U-turn in British popular opinion.[41] Indeed, the British content in what follows below is essentially a supplement to Richardson's analysis.

All recent major contributors to the debate agree that after 1780 popular anti-slavery sentiments quickly crossed class lines (including the formerly enslaved and eventually all enslaved persons). There was no shortage of social issues that demanded attention during the Industrial Revolution, all of them closer to hand than the international slave trade. Just two years into the campaign a piece of doggerel verse in one of the larger circulation London newspapers asked why abolition of the slave trade had become so popular rather than some abuse closer to home?

> "Now freedom's grown to such a rage
> That thousands in its cause engage
> Altho' in every other matter
> They just agree like fire and water!"

The author went on to invoke the wage slavery hypothesis and to make a plea for ending exploitation at home *before* attacking African slavery:

---

[40] Richardson, *Principles and Agents*, pp. 118–64.
[41] Richardson, *Principles and Agents*, pp. 165–214.

> "They act as if no slaves there are,
> But what skin deep their sables wear;
> Or we two thousand leagues must roam
> In search of what abounds at home!
> Thus e'en at Birmingham, the great
> Seem zealous for poor Afric's fate!"
> Good tender souls! 'twould not enrage us
> If first at home you'd mend some wages,
> Among Christian Slaves, who, gainst their will
> Labour like horses in a mill . . . ."[42]

The striking feature of the verse is how little response it evoked. Other newspapers of the time ignored it, and while radical leaders prosecuted by the British government in the 1790s tried to propagate this line of reasoning there is little evidence of working-class support. It was perhaps thirty years ahead of its time but even when Robert Wedderburn and later, William Cobbett and the Chartist leaders began to make similar arguments after 1820, these radical luminaries had little effect initially in diverting working-class support from abolition to social issues closer to home. But by the mid nineteenth century this had changed.[43] The emergence of first an awareness and second an abhorrence of slavery across the eighteenth-century social spectrum is indeed remarkable.

The shift in moral perspectives tracked by Davis and Richardson is undoubtedly accurate and is in a sense shared by all scholars who have written on abolition, except that they differ on what is responsible. Davis begins with a fundamental tension in Western thought and describes how Blacks were eventually able to take advantage of this, first violently in what became Haiti, and then within the US abolitionist movement. For others, class struggle and violent resistance by themselves give birth to a new value system. It is as though the non-elite, especially the enslaved, had always been abolitionist (as opposed to wanting to be personally free) – abundant evidence to the contrary notwithstanding, especially in the Portuguese case. From this perspective the St. Domingue Revolution

---

[42] The author was William Hamilton Reid, a minor poet and controversialist. The poem appeared in the September 24, 1790, issue of the *Public Advertiser*, one of the larger circulation London newspapers. It was entitled "Lines on Domestic Slavery, occasioned by the late Attempts to emancipate (sic) the African Negroes." The poem is not included in any of the anthologies of anti-slavery literature that have appeared in recent years.

[43] Betty Fladeland, "'Our Cause Being One and the Same': Abolitionists and Chartism," in James Walvin (ed.), *Slavery in British Society, 1776–1846* (Baton Rouge, LA, 1982), pp. 69–99,

was necessary to make these values dominant or at least force the ruling class to accept them.

Violence would certainly appear to have a role in the disappearance of New World slavery. The two bloodiest conflicts ever fought in the Americas – one at the beginning of the abolition process in what became Haiti and the second in the US toward the end – were about slavery. But from a global perspective and given the widespread distribution of slavery over time and space, this does not seem adequate. Why would the abolitionist impulse emerge only in the Atlantic world? The conflict between the slave as an extension of the master and the master's need for recognition of his own status on the part of the slave (the Hegelian paradox) could not have been confined to the West. Written sources for Judaic, Islamic, early Christian, and several oriental cultures touched on in Chapter 1 indicate the ancient origins of slavery and the problems it generated.[44] It cannot have been only slaveholders in the Americas that crumbled in the face of the Hegelian paradox.

Some of the most recent contributions treat both Britain's creation of a slave empire and then later its abolition of the slave trade and slavery as one seamless method of extracting wealth from overseas possessions. They therefore constitute a return to Eric Williams' simple materialist approach. The slave systems (more precisely in Williams' case, the slave trade) powered the first Industrial Revolution, while abolition of slavery along with destruction of a protected market for British sugar accelerated the growth of a free-trade world in which British industry could thrive. For Padraic Scanlan and Bronwen Everill, an economy built on slavery became, in the nineteenth century, an empire enabled, sustained, and expanded by anti-slavery, especially in Africa.[45] As noted in Chapter 3, eighty years after the publication of *Capitalism and Slavery*, it seems most historians, as well as a large segment of social media and news outlets, accept that economic self-interest explain all.

The evidence against this position presented above is compelling yet largely ignored. First, as noted earlier, the preeminence of the value of the Iberian slavery and the slave trade throughout the colonial period is clear enough. Bahia and Rio de Janeiro both dispatched more slave vessels to Africa than Liverpool. Both ports had vast plantation or mining

---

[44] Most recently, see the forty-three essays in *CWHS*, vols 1 and 2.
[45] Scanlan, *Slave Empire*; Bronwen Everill, *Not Made by Slaves: Ethical Capitalism in the Age of Abolition* (London, 2020); Fara Dabhoiwala, "Speech and Slavery in the West Indies," *New York Review of Books*, 67 (August 20, 2020).

hinterlands surpassing those of the British Americas. Major slave systems long predated contact with the Americas; how is it possible that much larger slave systems than the British failed to trigger "prosperity and rise to global power" in the Iberian Atlantic? Moreover, but for abolition Britain could have continued to embrace the slave trade as well as moving to free trade, without ruining its own slave colonies. Second, it is now widely accepted that slavery and the slave trade remained highly profitable throughout the abolitionist era. Third, continuing British involvement in the traffic after 1807 would have seen the country quickly replacing Portugal as the premier slave-trading nation of the world, and if British Guiana and Trinidad had remained open to the transatlantic traffic, the British Empire would have remained the world's leading producer of tropical produce, except for cotton. Moreover, continuing support of slavery would have allowed the British to avoid the large direct costs of abolition: compensating slave owners for the loss of their human property in 1833 (£20 million), as well as an expensive and largely futile attempt to suppress the slave trade between 1808 and 1867 (£12.4 million).[46] The materialistic explanation for both a foreign trade-driven industrialization and an economically motivated abolition is unsustainable in the face of such arguments.

It is much easier to define and track the conundrum of the British switch from an unthinking but enthusiastic endorsement of the slave trade to equally enthusiastic abhorrence over the course of a few decades than to explain it. We need to recognize that even though the emergence of hostility to slavery is among the more startling and well-documented case studies, convincing explanations of shifts in widely held norms of morality will likely always lie beyond reach of historians. At the very least, such explanations will be easier to criticize than defend. In the Atlantic world, during the era 1787–1862, a period of seventy-five years, the slave trade passed from an activity no different from any other kind of business in the public mind to something beyond the pale. For modern parallels in the shift of public attitudes, think of how views of slavery and colonialism espoused by Caribbean and African American intellectuals like George Padmore and W. E. B. Du Bois in the 1940s have today become mainstream over a similar period. On June 6, 2013, the British government

---

[46] See Eltis, *Economic Growth*, pp. 3–16 for a counterfactual evaluation of this argument., and pp. 92–93 for the cost of attempts to suppress the slave trade. See also Frédérique Beauvois, trans by Andrene Everson, *Between Blood and Gold: The Debates over Compensation for Slavery in the Americas* (New York, 2017), pp. 202–204.

announced an historic settlement when they offered "sincere regret" for crimes perpetrated against Mau Mau detainees in the 1950s, including hundreds of executions. They paid nearly £20 million in reparations. In different arenas the change in sexual mores, normative family structures, and children's rights over the same period is even more astonishing. Alan Turing, the computer scientist, was posthumously pardoned in 2013 for his 1952 conviction for homosexuality. Seventy years after the publication of the photo of the US sailor kissing a nurse on VJ day in Times Square, *Time* magazine commented "many people view the photo as little more than the documentation of a very public sexual assault, and not something to be celebrated."[47] As discussed further in Chapter 7, Britain has also apologized for dispatching thousands of child migrants overseas without the consent of the child or the parent, a practice that continued into the 1970s.[48]

In all these cases, as with abolitionists in the mid nineteenth century, the public, as well as many scholars, see the changes as "right" and assume, too, that the new standards are immutable and should be used to judge past behavior.[49] Since the mid twentieth century a wide range of past evils has become the subject of apologies by the perpetrators (or their descendants), and in some cases the latter have paid reparations.[50] Today, a shift in values may be so rapid that certain long-lived individuals find themselves held to account in old age for offenses committed decades previously when their actions, while harmful to others, did not result in legal proceedings.[51]

Changes in moral values are no easier to explain than changes in taste. Consider the much simpler case of the clothes we wear or the way we cut our hair. One might think oneself totally indifferent to fashion, but a photograph of ourselves with others from thirty years ago would reveal immediately how we conformed to fashion then, and how much we have changed since. We would be utterly incapable of explaining why we dress or wear our hair differently today. Less trivially, but also a half century

---

[47] http://time.com/3517476/v-j-day-1945-a-nation-lets-loose/.
[48] www.barnardos.org.uk/who-we-are/our-history.
[49] Though the term "human rights" is very much of the twentieth century.
[50] Stanley L. Engerman, "Apologies, Regrets and Reparations," *European Review*, 17 (2009): 693–610.
[51] The German decision to prosecute aged Nazi war criminals in the twenty-first century is one example. At a different level of evil is the case of a Member of the Scottish Parliament, Bill Walker, whose twenty-three offenses against women straddling the years 1967 to 1995 were not brought to court until 2013. The travails of old pedophile priests need no documentation, and neither do the cases of Harvey Weinstein and Jeffrey Epstein.

ago, no one in the West could envisage same-sex marriage, much less that the US constitution could be invoked to support the institution, and that it would be accepted by an overwhelming majority of the electorate. How much more difficult it is to account for the profound shift in attitudes toward violence, or child abuse, or maltreatment of animals, or – between 1780 and 1807 – the slave trade. To presume to explain such changes whether via revolution (Brown, Blackburn), religion (Anstey), tectonic shifts in the economy (Williams, 1944; Eltis, 1987; Davis, 1975, 2006), or overproduction of sugar (Carrington, 2002; Ryden, 2009) is to trivialize the profound and poorly understood process of how and why shifts in social psychology and moral values occur over time.[52] We will likely never be able to do more than to group abolition with these other social issues and eschew simplistic explanations such as profit maximization. Nevertheless, here I suggest some potentially helpful parallels, and ultimately an alternative hypothesis, which will no doubt prove as ephemeral as all the others discussed here.

As the rash of state apologies on a wide range of topics over the opening decades of the twenty-first century suggests, any broad-based shift in norms of morality is going to manifest itself in more than one public issue. The focus of scholars on abolition of the slave trade is understandable in the light of the mass activism it elicited. But that focus also reduces context and emphasizes discontinuity. David Brion Davis has described abolition of the slave trade and then of slavery itself as reforms that "taught many Englishmen to recognize forms of systematic oppression ... closer to home." Yet significant social reforms occurred both before and during attempts to end the slave trade. Europeans had long linked slaves with three other subordinated categories – serfs, children, and domesticated animals.[53] Protection of animals first emerged only in the nineteenth century, but rights for the enserfed and protection of children were live issues well before the late eighteenth century. Here, too, however, long before 1800 serfs in mainland Europe were

---

[52] Blackburn, *American Crucible*; Roger Anstey, *The Atlantic Slave Trade and British Abolition* (London, 1975); Eltis, *Economic Growth*; Davis, *Inhuman Bondage*, pp. 245–49; Williams, *Capitalism and Slavery*: Selwyn H. H. Carrington, *The Sugar Industry and the Abolition of the Slave Trade, 1775–1810* (Gainesville, FL, 2002).

[53] Davis, *Problem of Slavery in the Age of Emancipation*, pp. 5–35. For the conceptualization of slaves as children or pupils see Ulrich Bonnell Phillips, *American Negro Slavery: A Survey of the Supply, Employment and Control of Negro Labor as Determined by the Plantation Regime* (New York, 1918), p. 342; Genovese, *Roll, Jordan, Roll*. For the animalization of slaves, see Davis, *Inhuman Bondage*, pp. 52–53, 62.

increasingly able to make decisions about the land on which they worked as well as their labor, with remuneration in cash gradually replacing seignorial obligations.[54] They were also, of course, far more numerous than the enslaved population of the Americas. In the British case, the so-called "second serfdom" that saw thousands of Scottish colliers bound to and sold along with their place of work was formally ended in 1775 by parliamentary legislation, an initiative that has received a tiny fraction of the scholarly attention paid to abolition of the slave trade.[55]

For children, particularly girls, the key decision was perhaps the ending of the global practice of exposing newborns for which parents could not or would not take responsibility. The Christian and Islamic establishments were officially opposed, but the practice of exposure remained widespread and, under the term "oblation," formed one recruitment stream for monasteries in medieval and early modern Europe. Exposure could result in death or a life of exploitation. Secular charitable child-care institutions were slow to appear in the aftermath of the dissolution of the monasteries in newly Protestant countries.[56] Online sources such as the Old Bailey records and the early English newspapers report a steady stream of executions of young women for infanticide (comprising 25 percent of all capital offences, according to one estimate), but very few references to foundlings and the institutions that dealt with them.[57] In England, orphaned and destitute children became the responsibility of the parish authorities, and farming out child indigents to local families (until age 21 for males and 25 for females) one of the major tasks of

---

[54] Edgar Melton, "Rural Subjection in East Central Europe ca. 1500–1800," in *CWHS*, vol. 3: 296–322.

[55] Paul E. H. Hair, "Slavery and Liberty: The Case of the Scottish Colliers," *Slavery & Abolition*, 21 (2000): 136–51; and Hair, "The Binding of the Pitmen of the North East, 1800–1809," *Durham University Journal*, 58 (1965): 1–13.

[56] John Eastburn Boswell, "Exposition and Oblation: The Abandonment of Children and the Ancient and Medieval Family," *American Historical Review*, 89 (1984): 10–33; Laila Williamson, "Infanticide: An Anthropological Analysis," in Marvin Kohl (ed.), *Infanticide and the Value of Life* (Buffalo, NY, 1978), pp. 61–75; Stephen Wilson, "Infanticide, Child Abandonment and Female Honour in Nineteenth Century Corsica," *Comparative Studies in Society and History*, 30 (1988): 762–83; Peter C. Hoffer and Natalie E. H. Hull, *Murdering Mothers: Infanticide in England and New England* (New York, 1981), p. 25 and chapter 3; Olwen H. Hufton, *The Poor of Eighteenth Century France* (Oxford, 1974), pp. 123, 206, 326–7.

[57] The *British Journal* (London), December 29, 1722, complained of women killing their newborns in London and contrasted this with the efforts of African slave mothers to protect their infants on board slave ships.

eighteenth-century local government.⁵⁸ The incidence of charity schools and hospitals increased in the mid eighteenth century, and the period also saw both state and voluntary associations begin to define as well as protect childhood. A letter in the London *Public Advertiser* on child chimney sweeps in 1760 saw Jonas Hanway, the founder of the Marine Society for boys, trigger a long campaign to abolish the practice. After an outbreak of fever in a textile factory in 1784, Manchester magistrates resolved not to apprentice out parish children to cotton mills that required night labor or more than ten hours work per day. Such initiatives would have been inconceivable a century earlier.⁵⁹

Protection of children and the weakening of feudal ties emerged at roughly the same time as questioning slavery. Spanish and later other Europeans' exclusions of Native Americans from the pool of people considered eligible for heritable chattel status began in the early sixteenth century, but this had nothing to do with abolition. Narrowing the eligibility pool meant that even more sub-Saharan Africans were pulled into the slave traffic to replace the now off-limits Indigenous people. In the English case historians have located anti-slavery voices and even abolitionist campaign tactics in the two centuries before the slave trade reached its peak. But they appear significant only from a much later perspective. The very earliest expression of doubts about slavery were strongly linked to the Black Legend of Spain generated by the English and Dutch as they both fought the most powerful nation in the Atlantic world. Post-1660 critiques of slave owners from a Christian perspective were usually associated with a concern for the souls of the enslaved or with how slaves were acquired, rather than attacking slavery. Scattered individual voices questioning slavery can be heard even as slavery became institutionalized in the Americas, but these do not constitute a discourse.⁶⁰ While the first

---

⁵⁸ Dorothy George's classic account, *London Life in the Eighteenth Century* (London, 1925) is still the best overview of this topic. For a survey of the Poor Law, see Paul Slack, *The English Poor Law, 1531–1782* (Houndsmill, UK, 1990).

⁵⁹ B. Leigh Hutchins and Amy Harrison, *A History of Factory Legislation* (London, 1903), pp. 7–9; Frederic Keeling, *Child Labour in the United Kingdom: A Study of the Development and Administration of the Law Relating the Employment of Children* (London, 1914), pp. 3–7; Stanley L. Engerman, "The History and Political Economy of International Labor Standards," in Kaushik Basu, Henrik Horn, Lisa Román, and Judith Shapiro (eds.), *International Labor Standards: History, Theory, And Policy Options* (Malden, MA, 2008), pp. 8–83.

⁶⁰ Philippe Rosenberg, "Thomas Tryon and the Seventeenth-Century Dimensions of Antislavery," *William and Mary Quarterly*, 61 (2004): 609–42; Davis, Problem of Slavery in Western Culture, pp. 228–30, 368–71, 402–405; Pettigrew, Freedom's Debt,

attempts to suppress the slave trade emerge in Massachusetts in the mid 1760s, the first tangible move on the British side occurred with the British East India Company's regulation against the traffic in the East in 1774, before either the American Revolution or any parliamentary initiative.[61]

But to put this in context, 1774 was also the year when a complete set of accounts for a small Bristol slave ship have survived. They identify the outset costs of the venture as well the names of the eight owners, the thirty-one crew, the thirty-seven skilled workers that prepared the vessel for sea and the thirty-one merchants and manufacturers that supplied the merchandise to be exchanged for captives, each of the latter group providing employment for numerous others at sites inland. Across British ports in that year at least 182 other slave vessels set out for Africa. Outset costs amounted to well over £1 million and the livelihoods of at least å35,000 people were at stake. In addition, the British navy had no problem with at least nine of its warships carrying slaves from Africa to the British Caribbean on behalf of British slave merchants between 1738 and 1763. Any serious questioning of the business was a remote prospect.[62] Attitudes to slavery and other social issues discussed here span many decades and range over a wide spectrum of human behavior. But most are manifestations of a gradual dissociation of physical compulsion from the terms of labor and a steady decrease in socially acceptable levels of violence over several decades.

We may not agree with Steve Pinker that "[t]he decline of violence may be the most significant and least appreciated development in the history of our species" or with his two-chapter explanation of changes in the brain as to why it happened, but we cannot dismiss the pattern he describes. The devastation of two world wars and the killing grounds of central Europe notwithstanding, the twentieth century witnessed a continuation in the very long-run fall in the incidence of violence perpetrated by states and

---

pp. 207–208 argues that by the 1730s the Royal African Company was able to "nurture antislavery sentiments."

[61] Richard B. Allen, "Suppressing a Nefarious Traffic: Britain and the Abolition of Slave Trading in India and the Western Indian Ocean, 1770–1830," *William and Mary Quarterly*, 66 (2009): 873–94. For the earliest New England moves against the slave trade, see Sean Wilentz, "The Revolution Within the American Revolution," *New York Review of Books*, October 23, 2023.

[62] Walter E. Minchinton, "The Voyage of the Snow 'Africa'," *The Mariner's Mirror*, 37 (1951): 187–96 and the sources cited in David Richardson, *The Bristol, Africa and the Eighteenth-Century Slave Trade to America*, 4 vols (Bristol, 1996), vol. 4: 50. For all British slave vessels in 1774, see https://slavevoyages.org/voyages/e4XmtoJw. For the Royal Navy slave ships, see https://slavevoyages.org/voyages/E1411h3J,

individuals alike. More important, the "moral commonplaces of our age, such as that slavery, war, and torture are wrong, would have been seen as saccharine sentimentality" in earlier centuries.[63] Historians have yet to link this profound change in human behavior with the rise and fall of the transatlantic slave system even though extreme violence permeated both the institution itself and the efforts of captives themselves to break free of it. European expansion into the Atlantic from the Iberian conquests to the establishment of Western Europeans in the major Antilles coincided with the expulsion of Islam from the peninsula and two centuries of bloody conflict between Catholics and Protestants. The bullion and produce from the Atlantic islands and the Americas that began to flow into Europe always came from labor that was violently coerced, if not formally enslaved.

When the European slave colonies in the Americas were created no one in metropolitan society questioned the brutality necessary to maintain the colonial system. State-inflicted violence on slaves seemed unremarkable. But by 1800 this was no longer the case. Writing at the end of both the Thirty Years' War and the English Civil War, and just prior to Cromwell's horrific engagement with the Irish, Thomas Hobbes thought he had witnessed a reversion to the state of savage nature that only the submission of the individual to the state could temper. As Orlando Patterson has pointed out, the true Hobbesian state of nature is to be found in eighteenth-century Jamaica.[64] As discussed more fully below, late eighteenth-century Britain no longer treated their convicts the way masters treated their slaves. Physical chastisement of servants by masters remained on the statute books but was no longer practiced, serfdom in Scottish coalmines was abolished, women were no longer burnt at the stake for killing their husbands or practicing witchcraft. We can plot this change by a systematic examination of newspapers.

Between 1650 and 1800, English awareness of the transoceanic world as reflected in references in newspapers increased to a far greater extent than did the value of long-distance trade. The information revolution, still largely undocumented, outran the well-recorded contemporaneous expansion in global flows of merchandise.[65] The Burney Collection of

---

[63] Steven Pinker, *Better Angels of Our Nature: Why Violence has Declined* (New York, 2011), chapter 10.
[64] Orlando Patterson, *The Sociology of Slavery: Black Society in Jamaica, 1655–1838*, 2nd edition (Cambridge, 2022), pp. xxxix–xli.
[65] Ian K. Steele, *The English Atlantic, 1675–1740: An Exploration of Communication and Community* (Oxford, 1986), pp. 273–78.

Early English Newspapers enables a preliminary gauge of the concerns and public interests of literate English people (largely Londoners) over 150 years. For the years 1637–1786, when England built up its first slave-based overseas empire, it is possible to track the use of certain key terms in this source across six quarter-century periods. The approach is crude but reveals three unexpected patterns that together give us a fresh perspective on slavery and the beginning of attempts to get rid of the institution in the Americas. First, the London public was not much engaged with the establishment of British slave colonies until well into the eighteenth century, despite the anchoring role of the city in the establishment of the English slave Atlantic. Second, even though violent street crime remained endemic in the eighteenth century, the English gradually came to perceive extreme violence as something that happened overseas. There is also evidence that London itself became less violent over this period. Third, violence in the slave colonies and on slave ships, on the part of both slaves and those charged with controlling them, continued unabated and was increasingly likely to be reported as the century wore on.

On the first of these patterns, a search of the Burney collection between 1637 and 1661 (a total of forty-seven titles) turned up just fifteen references to "Africa" (or sub-Saharan Africa – North Africa usually being described as "Barbary," "Algiers," or "Tripoli" which received sixty references), and eight to "negroes." This unawareness of matters overseas was not confined to Africa and Africans. "China" yielded just twelve hits and a valuable and understudied long-distance commodity, "whales," received just six mentions before 1662.[66] Prior to 1680 much of the Burney collection comprises broadsides and pamphlets. Religion in the form of sectarian disputes predominates, along with associated conflicts within England and between England and the Celtic fringe. Perhaps the most salient English overseas initiative in the mid seventeenth century was Barbados. Beginning as a producer of low-grade tobacco using European indentured servants, the island was transformed from the early 1640s into the most successful sugar-producing colony that the world had ever seen.[67] In the fifteen years or so down to 1661, as England emerged from a civil conflict fought over the nature of state authority, the relationship of the individual to the state, and religious freedom, the labor force of this colony came to be made up almost entirely of chattel slaves. More peculiarly still from the perspective of the long history of slavery, almost

---

[66] BrL, 17th–18th-century Burney Collection of newspapers.
[67] Eltis, *Rise of African Slavery*, pp. 193–223.

all captives were of African descent, and originated in a continent whose Mediterranean fringe, to the outrage of most European observers, contained at least 35,000 white slaves in the mid seventeenth century.[68]

Before 1700, then, the London reading public was no more aware of the slave trade than it was of the whaling business. The use of enslaved Africans had occasioned no discussion – if not an "unthinking decision," certainly one made without public debate. And such blindness would certainly make the violence that underpinned and sustained slavery pass unnoticed. Not only had slavery under English jurisdiction revived without public discussion but as shown below, for eighty years thereafter English newspapers scarcely mentioned Black slaves. This was the case even though there must have been around 200,000 African captives under British jurisdiction by 1720 compared to no more than a few thousand English captives in North Africa. The same point emerges startlingly with two reports a few days apart in the same newspaper as described in Chapter 3 when a slave ship in the sheltered anchorage of the Downs, was moored beside one carrying redeemed Britons from North Africa. The irony passed unnoticed, or at least without recorded comment. The "unthinking decision" to use Black slaves continued not to be thought about as late as the 1720s.

We can also measure the dramatic change in awareness of the overseas world 150 years later by comparing references in the first quarter-century of this period (1637–1661) to those in the last of six quarter-centuries (1762–1786). In this last quarter century Africa gets 18,299 references as opposed to just fifteen prior to 1662; references to "negro" jump from eight to 8,957 over the same period, China from twelve to 45,515; "whales" from six to 8,631. Comparing the decades 1651–1660 and 1791–1800, eleven references to "America" grew to 31,242 between 1791 and 1800, while mentions of "India" went from seventy-one to 85,341 over the same period. The growth curves are similar for all these terms – as with many others with overseas geographic and cultural connotations. Of course, there were hundreds of overseas projects sponsored by many thousands of London-based investors before 1637 – most of them failures – but few involved Black slaves or Africa. Such projects did not bring either topic into the foreground of English consciousness. What happened between 1637 and 1786 (more than a century and a half after Columbian contact) thus amounts to a revolution of perceptions of an

---

[68] Robert C. Davis, "Counting European Slaves on the Barbary Coast," *Past & Present*, 172 (2001): 87–124.

overseas world, and more especially the role of coerced labor in that world.

A second pattern to emerge from the Burney collection was the growth in English perceptions of violence as being an overseas phenomenon. Following the path of Phillipe Rosenberg's study of violence in seventeenth-century England it is possible to chart the use of three adjectives, "bloody," "cruel," and "inhumane" for the same years, 1637–1786, except when the English were engaged in international conflict (including 1776–1777). Such words were reserved for incidents seen as out of step with or beyond the norms of acceptable violence. They were not used to describe violence that had the support of the community. Rosenberg has found that such terms were used most frequently in relation to three topics in the pamphlet literature between 1640 and 1700 (he did not use the Burney collection). These three were the Civil War, rebellion in Ireland, and sectarian conflict between Protestants and Catholics.[69] The incidents to which they were applied occurred mostly within the British Islands, with Europe and the Islamic world accounting for almost all the rest. The Burney collection confirms this. Indeed, on the evidence of pamphlets, broadsides, and newspapers, "beyond the line" meant not so much an area to which a different code of conflict applied, but rather an area to be ignored except perhaps for Spanish atrocities in the Americas.

By the early eighteenth century sectarian religious disputes and, of course, civil conflict (except for Jacobean rebellions), are associated with these three terms much less frequently. Generally, reports of wars, particularly ones in which Britain was involved, see a marked rise in their employment. We can control for this, as already noted, by omitting years when the British state was formally at war. The pattern that emerges after the 1720s, quite different from the previous century, usually locates unacceptable levels of violence overseas. Whereas only one-quarter of the usages of "bloody," "cruel" and "inhumane" were applied to events outside the British Isles in the 1720s, by the period 1784–1790 that ratio had risen to 61 percent. The slave colony/slave ship share of all these foreign or overseas incidents was not large – just 15 percent in the 1780s. Most of the reported incidents outside Britain came from Europe and the Ottoman Empire. But the more fundamental point is that despite the enormous prevalence of street crime, home invasions, child molestation,

[69] Phillipe Rosenberg, "The Moral Order of Violence: The Meaning of Cruelty in Early Modern England, 1645–85," unpublished PhD thesis, Department of History, Duke University (1999), pp. 437–51.

and a violent judicial structure (all within Britain) the outcomes of which crowded the pages of a burgeoning press, extreme violence was increasingly associated with events that did not happen within England.

While community notions of acceptable violence shifted, so also did the reality of violence.[70] Whipping in the armed forces of Britain and the US continued until the mid nineteenth century (and birching in the Isle of Man prison until the 1970s). Nevertheless, despite the large number of offenses subject to capital punishment, Britain, like most European countries, was a less violent country in 1790 than it had been when the first English plantation owners established themselves in the Caribbean. Rules of war had evolved within Europe to the point where prisoners of war were released without ransom after the treaty of Westphalia, and dedicated prisoner-of-war camps were established during the Napoleonic Wars. The practice of the well-to-do visiting asylums for entertainment died out well before the relatively humane Hanwell institution opened in 1831.

Physical chastisement as a penalty for criminal offenses declined during the eighteenth century. The last recorded burning of a woman for murdering her husband (carried out in the London street opposite the house where the murder occurred) was in 1737; the last witch was similarly dispatched in Scotland a decade earlier. Mutilations of offenders became post-execution rituals and were then abandoned. Hanging, drawing, and quartering of servants for murdering their masters remained part of the criminal code until the mid eighteenth century, but do not appear to have been carried out after the seventeenth century. In fact, the broad pattern of change seems to have been one in which public attitudes to judicial violence moderated first, in response to which courts were less likely to apply such sentences, while formal abolition of the penalties occurred several decades later. The Master-Servant Act providing for whipping of recalcitrant servants was not repealed until 1875, but imprisonment had replaced whipping in the eighteenth century. Civil conflicts became less frequent and when they occurred, they were less bloody. While no one has made the comparison, the depredations of the Duke of Cumberland in the Scottish Highlands in 1746, much less the violence associated with the American Revolution, both pale in comparison to what Cromwell sanctioned in Ireland in the mid seventeenth century. The 1600s was England's

---

[70] For more detailed references, see David Eltis, "Abolition and Identity in the Very Long Run," in Willem Klooster (ed.), *Migration, Trade and Slavery in an Expanding World: Essays in Honour of Pieter Emmer* (Leiden, 2009), pp. 227–56.

century of bloodshed and revolution, patterns that fitted well with events in a continental Europe embroiled in the Thirty Years' War. Hardly surprising then that the establishment of the slave colonies thousands of miles away occurred without debate or indeed any serious attention in the nascent press.

By contrast, notions of acceptable violence had changed much more slowly in the Caribbean by the end of the eighteenth century. Thomas Thistlewood's diary shows that in the third quarter of the century enslaved people continued to be physically chastised, raped, and mutilated, and rebel leaders were routinely tortured to death in ways that were consistent with an earlier era in Europe.[71] However, even before the abolitionist critique of slavery began, Justin Roberts argues, planters in both the Caribbean and the slave South were trying to embrace ameliorative treatment of slaves as a way of preserving their increasingly valuable property and fostering agricultural improvement and profits. Included in this strategy was a diminished emphasis on corporal punishment amounting to "alternative visions of modernity" in which "slavery and enlightened civilization" were compatible.[72] Eventually, a planter and member of HM Council of Tortola, Arthur William Hodge, was hanged behind the island's jail in 1811 for the particularly revolting murder of a slave on the basis of evidence provided by a free colored.[73] Widely reported in Britain, it is difficult to imagine the trial and execution of a planter for such an offense in any earlier era of Caribbean history.

But there is no sign that efforts at "amelioration" in the slave Americas made any impression on the London newspapers. On the contrary, reports of revolts and reprisals from the Caribbean increased in the 1780s, and were particularly prominent in 1786, just prior to the political phase of abolition.[74] The press took the later Hodge case as a sign of the depravity

---

[71] Burnard, *Mastery, Tyranny & Desire*. See pp. 103–106 for a comparison of trends in and patterns of violence in England and Jamaica during Thistlewood's residence in the island (1750 to 1786) that differs from my assessment, at least with respect to England.
[72] Roberts, *Slavery and the Enlightenment*, pp. 44–56.
[73] *Aberdeen Journal*, July 17, 1811; *Morning Chronicle*, July 8, 1811.
[74] Reports of attacks by gangs of enslaved runaways in Jamaica and Dominica (*St. James's Chronicle or the British Evening Post*, January 28, 1786; January 31, 1786) were followed by the usually grizzly details of suppression a few weeks later (*General Evening Post*, April 1, 1786). The *St. James's Chronicle or the British Evening Post*, February 21, 1786, reported "The Insurrection of the Negroes in the West Indies is not confined to the British Settlement of Dominica. A very alarming Insurrection has also taken place in the French Settlement of Cape Francais, 12,000 Negroes having taken up arms, who are secretly supplied with Arms, Ammunition, etc. by the Spaniards. The French have sent [to] Martinico for a Supply of troops which went to their Assistance the end of December."

of the system, not that slaves were getting increased protection. The cataclysmic events in St. Domingue, beginning in 1791 and culminating in massacres preceding Haitian independence in 1804, would have made much less of an impression in say a seventeenth-century Europe emerging from the Thirty Years' War.[75]

The third pattern relevant to a new perspective on abolition apparent in the early English press was the coverage of violence between the enslaved and their controllers. Revolts in Danish St. John, in Berbice, in Surinam, in Jamaica, and on board thousands of slave vessels (and the brutality that followed on from these events) forced the issue before the domestic populace. At the outset of the eighteenth century, shipboard rebellions warranted only single-phrase reports in the shipping lists ("slaves rose," or "cut-off by slaves"). These were obviously intended as information for the merchants who had unluckily invested in the voyage. But by mid-century such cryptic references had developed into full-paragraph reports in the main news section of the newspaper. The incidence of slave revolts had not changed from the previous century, but the topic had found an audience beyond that of the business community. It is difficult to overestimate the long-term significance of this. Slavery and the slave trade necessary to sustain it could not exist without government sanction and the military power to enforce it. Abolitionist activism aimed first against the slave trade and eventually at slavery itself introduced the possibility of the erosion of that sanction – a circumstance that raised the prospect for the first time in the history of slave resistance of undermining the whole system.

The entry of slave revolts into the public record can be shown with some precision. In the sixteenth and seventeenth centuries, violent incidents on slave vessels – whether within the crew, among slaves, or between crew and slaves – appear in private correspondence, logbooks, and

---

Two years later the *Times* reprinted runaway advertisements from West Indian newspapers that used scars and deformities from punishments to identify the enslaved. This, the paper argued, was evidence of the "usage received by Negroes in captivity" (April 2, 1788).

[75] Publicly sanctioned burning and torturing of course continued beyond abolition in former slave societies, as in the case of the more than two thousand lynchings carried out in the US South in the late nineteenth and early twentieth centuries (with the incidence declining dramatically prior to the effective enforcement of legal sanctions against the practice). Capital punishment continued in several British Caribbean colonies after it was abolished in Britain. It is still part of the legal code of Barbados and Jamaica and is still practiced today in the Southern US states (thanks to Robert Goddard for pointing this out). Perhaps a split between metropolitan and enslaved (or formerly enslaved) societies in attitudes to violence is still to be observed.

occasionally in court records, but not generally in the nascent newspapers of the period. A slave rebellion was a misfortune of business, but not a matter of public interest. In fact, newspapers did not exist in Brazil (where most slaves arrived) until the nineteenth century, or in most ports around the Atlantic from which vessels cleared for slaving expeditions. A complete run of the *Lloyd's List* shipping newspaper exists for 1702–1704, a period for which other sources tell us that five instances of slave revolts on English vessels occurred. Not one of these was reported in *Lloyd's List*. By 1742, when continuous runs of the publication once more become available, such reports are frequent. In other newspapers the first references to violent resistance by slaves is in 1726 and are extremely cryptic – phrases such as "cut-off" or "slaves rose," and little else.[76] In the first quarter of the eighteenth century there was far more interest in the attacks of Barbary corsairs, the resulting enslavement of English sailors, and, of course at this time, violence involving pirates – including that against the enslaved.[77] Sources other than the newspapers make it clear that the resistance of captives was taking its toll of slaving ventures in these years, yet the incidents are not seen as worthy of publication.

Beginning in the late 1720s, public interest apparently increased, and more detail is provided on the incidents themselves. A typical report reads:

The Hester and Jane, Captain Bond from London, having taken on a considerable number of Slaves on the Coast of Africa, for the Leeward Islands, the Negroes rose and murdered all her crew, Except the Master and 4 Men, who by good Fortune made their Escape, and got on Shore in their Boat, leaving the Ship in the Possession of the Negroes.[78]

In 1731, the dramatic story of the Rhode Island sloop, the *Little George*, attracted wide attention on both sides of the Atlantic and has frequently been reported by several historians from different sources. The ninety-six captives gained control of the small vessel six days after leaving the Banana Islands south of Sierra Leone. The captain, three crew, and

---

[76] *Lloyd's List*, no. 167, 1703. There may well be earlier references, but until the extensive newspaper holdings of the Bodleian are digitized, it is beyond the means of any individual scholar to extract everything this material has to offer.

[77] See for example, *News Letter*, January 21, 1716; *The Weekly Journal or Saturday's Post*, March 15, 1718. *The Weekly Journal* of October 10, 1719, reported that off Whydah "the Pirates commit un-heard of Cruelties; they have hang'd Capt. Abraham Plumb of the Prince's Galley; and just as if they set themselves apart to study Cruelty, have hang'd several of the Negroes by the Legs, and afterwards shot 'em."

[78] *Daily Journal*, May 26, 1727, London.

a boy were trapped in the cabin under the quarterdeck in a stand-off while the captives managed to sail the sloop back to the coast, run the vessel ashore, and make their escape. The account was dramatic, filled with incident and, as with many of these early reports, written by a survivor. The *Daily Post Boy* devoted more than a column of its four pages to the story. The depth of coverage here and in other newspapers constitutes a watershed.[79] For land-based incidents the rebellion on St. John in the Danish West Indies in 1733, when slaves took control of the whole island, was given similar coverage in the London press. Thereafter, slave revolts, but particularly those on slave ships, are reported systematically in the English-language press on both sides of the Atlantic. The vessels concerned were mainly English, but what we know of rebellions on French, Dutch, and Danish vessels is also often carried by such newspapers.[80]

The tone of such reports was matter of fact, though the rebels were occasionally termed "barbarous." The content recalls notices of public executions or disasters or street crimes. There is a strong sense of placing the reader at the scene and being involved in the horrors of the events. A sense of sharing is the same as making the reader feel what those present must have felt, and while the captives are sometimes cast as the villains, this is not always the case. Later in the eighteenth century newspapers reported these events in more detail. There were no parallels in the non-human commodity trade of the Atlantic by this time – natural disasters and war apart.[81] In 1749, the *Scipio* suffered a similar fate to the *New Britannia* described in Chapter 3, but had no survivors.[82] Slave vessels found floating in the Atlantic with only a few captives on board and no crew fascinated the reading public. In one instance the facts became known because one of the crew had survived long enough to maintain a logbook during and after the slave uprising, but when the vessel was recaptured all the crew were dead. The fifty-four recaptured slaves were taken into Charleston to be sold.[83]

---

[79] *Daily Post Boy*, June 25, 1731. See inter alia Kenneth Scott, "George Scott, Slave Trader of Newport," *American Neptune*, 12 (1952): 222–28.

[80] Specific references may be found at https://slavevoyages.org/voyages/MPWyzSxb after configuring the columns to display the "Sources" variable. *Le Courrier*, the Paris newspaper, is also a good source for shipping news. See DIGIPRESS Bayerische Staatsbibliothek (https://digipress.digitale-sammlungen.de/view/bsb10502406_00099_u001/2?cq=nègre)

[81] *Gentleman's Magazine*, October 1773, p. 523; *Lloyd's List*, June 18, 1773; *South Carolina Gazette*, May 31, 1773.

[82] *Lloyd's List*, January 5, 1750.

[83] For these three cases see IDs 25486 in 1808, 25045 in 1785, and probably 32981 in 1770, in www.slavevoyages.org. Eric R. Taylor, *If We Must Die: Shipboard Insurrections in the Era of the Atlantic Slave Trade* (Baton Rouge, LA, 2006), p.128, mentions these cases.

For decades there is no hint of anti-slave trade sentiment, or links to issues of rights. Eric Slauter has tracked mentions of "natural rights," "rights of man," "human rights," and the "slave trade" in three major electronic collections of eighteenth-century publications – the Goldsmith-Kress Library of Economic Literature (for 1750–1849), Eighteenth Century Collections Online, and American Imprints, 1700–1819. "Human rights" comes into use slowly only in the nineteenth century, and prior to the late 1780s, as we might expect, usage of "rights of man" is rare.[84] An upward trend in mentions of "natural rights," however, is apparent from the 1720s, well before a modest increase in the trend line for mentions of the slave trade begins in the 1760s. Unfortunately, the collections Slauter consulted did not include any newspapers. While newspapers never link the topics of natural rights and the slave trade before the second half of the eighteenth century, it is suggestive that awareness of both topics apparently increases at about the same time.[85] By the 1760s and 1770s, when reports of slave revolts in newspapers are at their most frequent (and the incidence of revolts in the slave colonies is relatively low), references to "natural rights" are already at half or more of the level of usage attained between 1780 and 1808.

Equally important in separating Europe from the slave Americas was the emergence, in England at least, of checks on the abuse of power by people in authority. Legal historians have made little of this, probably because it required no new legislation, but rather changes in the application of existing laws. Ships' captains were increasingly brought to account for violence against their crew.[86] One poem that has appeared in anthologies of anti-slavery poetry turns out to have been written against the captain's abuse of his crew, not his slaves.[87] It was composed at a time

---

[84] Though notably, in 1776 David Ramsey proposed an easily defeated resolution in the House of Commons that the slave trade was "against the Laws of God and the Rights of man" (Richardson, *Principles and Agents*, p. 100).

[85] Eric Slauter, commentary, presented to the "The Bloody Writing is forever Torn," a Conference on the Abolition of the Slave Trade, held at Elmina, Ghana, August 2007). For the obliviousness of the English toward Black slavery during most of the eighteenth century see Richardson, *Principles and Agents*, p. 98.

[86] Eltis, "Abolition and Identity in the Very Long Run," p. 250.

[87] Parts of the poem "Essay on Humanity," 1735 reads:
> "You *Bristol Captains*, who no Mercy shew,
> Do you do what you wou'd have done to you?"

It includes the line "You feed your Cruelty with Christian Gore:"
Moira Ferguson, *Subject to Others: British Women Writers and Colonial Slavery, 1670–1834* (Abingdon, UK, 1992), p. 16, and James Basker, *Amazing Grace* (New

when several high-profile cases had ended in the conviction of captains for killing crewmen at sea. It is unlikely that such abuses were occurring for the first time in the 1720s, but the Burney collection provides no earlier cases that resulted in conviction.[88] In the same decade sheriff's officers were convicted of using excessive force while making an arrest, again a new phenomenon in the early newspaper reports.[89] Eventually cruelty to the shipboard enslaved made it to the courts. Prosecutions of captains for abuse of slaves do not appear until 1764, when John Burton of Bristol was charged with the murder of two "Negroes, on the High Seas, on board the *Royal Charlotte*, wherof he was master."[90] He was not convicted, and neither were those in three similar subsequent cases for which records have survived, but as the judge in the last of these in 1802 – also involving the murder of two slaves – commented, despite the acquittal "it was necessary that the affair should have been sifted to the bottom. When the Admiralty heard a charge made ... they were bound to institute an enquiry."[91] The appearance of slaves as murder victims in British courts may be seen as reflecting new community values, and could be grouped with the Somerset decision of 1772, the case of the slave ship *Zong*, involving the murder of 130 Africans, and the series of acts at the end of the eighteenth century regulating the slave trade (beginning in 1788).[92]

Haven, CT, 2002) have mistakenly interpreted this poem as an early example of anti-slavery poetry, but the "Christian gore" establishes the target as the tyrannical power of captains over the crew.

[88] In addition to the cases mentioned in Eltis, "Abolition and Identity in the Very Long Run," see the report of the trial of Captain Robert Elston for the murder of Joseph West and John Atkinson in Guinea in the *British Journal (1722)*, June 19, 1725. See also *The Proceedings of the Old Bailey, 1674–1913* at www.oldbaileyonline.org/search/keyword?text=Elston#results. Such cases support the argument that there was some equivalence in the violence meted out to crew and the enslaved. (Christopher, *Slave Ship Sailors*, pp. 96–102.)

[89] *London Daily Post and General Advertiser*, July 7, 1736: "On Thursday last was tried before Lord Hardwicke in the Court of King's Bench at Westminster, a Cause on an indictment against an Officer to the Sheriff of the County of Middlesex and his Follower, for assaulting a Person whom they had arrested, in a very cruel and barbarous manner, and after a long trial the Jury found them both guilty; and tis said they'll receive Judgment this term."

[90] *Public Advertiser*, June 5, June 7, and June 24, 1764. For the voyage see https://www.slavevoyages.org/voyages/BRi2B7jo.

[91] The *Times*, November 12, 1802. For a fuller report of the case see BNA, HCA, 1/61, ff. 348–57; see also HCA 1/24, ff 57–59; Christopher et al. (eds.), *Many Middle Passages*, p. 111, for Captain Thomas King killing a sailor on board the *Surry*.

[92] For the *Zong* case, see James Walvin, *The Zong: A Massacre, the Law and the End of Slavery* (New Haven, CT, 2011).

They represent the beginning of recognition, in England at least, that the enslaved could be *protected* by law as well as punished.

But if colonial and domestic norms of acceptable violence diverged in the eighteenth century, British awareness, recognition of, and engagement with Africans and their descendants followed quite a different path. The most compelling way of tracking this awareness is again via the press. The number of references to the word "slaves" in the Burney collection rises from forty-four in the decade 1641–1650 to 2,382 in the decade 1781 to 1790. This is as one would expect in the press of the capital of a country that in 1640 had no slave colonies and by 1790 controlled both the second largest enslaved population in the Caribbean, as well as the largest fleet of ships that supplied slaves to the New World. The unexpected point is demonstrated in Figure 6.1 which is based on the question to what kind of the enslaved do these many thousands of references refer. Many are to "slaves" in the figurative sense as in slaves to vice, or slaves to Rome, or slaves to the tyrannical powers of a political party that the author found not to his taste. Other references are to ancient slavery. When we limit the search to actual instances of slavery in existence at the time of writing, we find that from 1641 to 1700 – the period when the British rose to

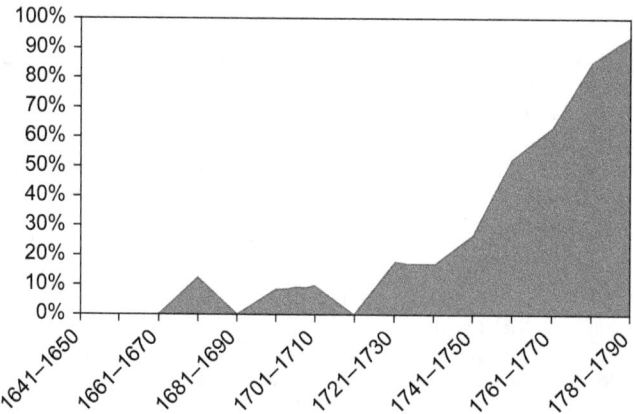

FIGURE 6.1 References to "slaves" in seventeenth- and eighteenth-century newspapers by decade distributed according to whether the slaves were European ("White") or African ("Black")
Legend: Unshaded area = share of references to White slaves
Shaded area = share of references to Black slaves Source: British Library, Seventeenth- and Eighteenth-Century Burney Collection of Newspapers

plantation preeminence in the New World, the Black enslaved are hardly ever mentioned.

So who were the enslaved preoccupying the early English press? Surprisingly, the answer is the mainly White galley slaves held in the Mediterranean by various Islamic polities. A simple chart illustrates the dramatic shift in awareness of Black slavery. Figure 6.1 plots the ratio of references to the enslaved who were White against the enslaved who were Black. Not only was the quite sudden revival of full chattel slavery under English jurisdiction in the mid seventeenth-century Caribbean carried out without public discussion, but as already noted, for eighty years thereafter English newspapers scarcely made any reference to enslaved Blacks.[93] The 1720s and 1730s thus saw newspapers begin to report violent incidents on slave vessels and on plantations more fully but these decades are also the period when the term "slaves" begins to mean people of African descent. However, not until mid-century did most references to "slaves" mean Black people in the Atlantic world. Even in the 1740s, when the British controlled the largest and most productive slave empire in the world, and when in the course of the previous century they had carried well over a million enslaved people across the Atlantic, the word "slaves" was used more often in relation to White captives than to Black, despite the fact that the latter had made possible the rapidly expanding British Empire in the New World. And as late as the 1770s and 1780s, as the prerequisites of the activist phase of abolition of the African slave trade emerged, references to White slaves in North Africa could easily be found in London newspapers. Indeed, one of the key prerequisites of an abolition movement was precisely that sufficient people *did* begin to be aware of Black slaves as well as white.

A trade in human beings can take place only if buyers and sellers can agree on a set of criteria that separate out those eligible for enslavement from those who are not. Apart from certain age, gender, and health requirements the basic criteria for European slave traders on what was called the Guinea Coast was that the person be African or of African descent and be offered for sale. References to and discussion of Black

---

[93] In addition to the Burney collection in the British Library, see the *Goldsmith-Kress Library of Economic Literature: A Consolidated Guide*, 4 vols (Woodbridge, CT, 1976–77). A search for the words "slave" or "slavery" in the titles in these sources for the years 1600 to 1710 generated 173 hits, but almost all use these terms either in a metaphorical sense, or refer to White slavery in North Africa, or to slavery in some part of the world other than the slave colonies. When the Caribbean is mentioned in connection to slavery the reference is usually to White servants being treated as slaves.

slaves in English newspapers to the point where these first appear beside and then begin to outnumber equivalent references to White slaves in the Mediterranean is the beginning of the erosion of Black skin as a key eligibility criterion.

A quite different reflection of the same phenomenon may be discerned rather paradoxically from the naming patterns of the vessels sent to Africa to obtain slaves.[94] Two developments are noteworthy. In the earlier period many of the names underscore the obliviousness of slave-ship owners to the existence of Africans as sensate beings – to put it differently, they show the status of Africans in European eyes as outsiders. Owners gave the names of favorite family members to their slave vessels, or for three centuries in the Portuguese case, the names of the holy family or saints – an attempt to invoke divine intervention to secure the success of the voyage. As noted earlier, one of the first New England slave ships, sent out from Boston in 1650 about the time that the colonial government was closest to being a theocracy was the *Gift of God*. There is no clearer demonstration of the accepted nature of the slave trade and the cultural remoteness of Africans to Europeans. In the early eighteenth century the *Negroes Nest* made several voyages from London and a few years later vessels named the *Black Joke* made several voyages from Liverpool and London. In the 1760s and 1770s *Liberty* was popular, followed by, in the Revolutionary era, French slavers (and two English slavers as well) named *Citoyen*, *Fraternité*, *Egalité*, or *Liberté* without hints of either irony or any appreciation of incongruity. After US independence, the *Fourth of July* made a pair of voyages. To the modern observer, the contrast between the abstract principles embodied in the name of the ship and the condition of its human cargo is astonishing, but the more important point is the obliviousness to which such names point. Less than a century later, however, in the last years of the slave trade (1850–1867), names that appear incongruous to the modern observer had disappeared completely. By then a consciousness of Africans as human beings meant that such names could only have been used ironically.

A second development in ships' naming patterns is the appearance of individual African names in the European record. For three centuries after ocean-born contact with sub-Saharan Africa, Africans in the European Atlantic world, whether enslaved or free, were either anonymous or

---

[94] This paragraph based on Eltis, "Abolition and Identity in the Very Long Run." All ships' names discussed here may be found in www.slavevoyages.org.

known by Europeanized names.[95] In the English slave Americas African names survived, albeit often in Europeanized form, to a much greater degree than has been appreciated.[96] Nevertheless, renaming, or in the Iberian worlds, formal christening was certainly the norm. Africans who received recognition or acceptance in European society did so under European names. African names emerge only in the 1780s when Ottobah Cugoano (baptized John Steuart in 1772) and Olaudah Equiano (Gustavus Vasa) reverted to their former (or what they claimed were former) names.[97] And in the next chapter we take up the post-1807 recording of African names of those found on board captured slave vessels. Outside the slave Americas, at least, this is indicative of a cultural recognition that would not have been possible a century earlier. Slave-ship names incorporating African references show a clear progression over two centuries from the general to the particular. Ships called the *Negro* or *Negro Merchant* or *Black Boy*, *Blackamoor* etc. in the seventeenth century are replaced in the following century with vessels named after particular peoples ("Fanteen" or Fanti), and after 1720, individual Africans. The *King Amboe*, was named after an eighty-year old Obong or "mayor" of Old Calabar and head of the most powerful ward in the community prior to the evolution of the Ekpe society. The *Roi Guinguin* assumed the title of the king of Badagry (1764–1766). The name of the *King Pepple* (ten voyages, 1786–1799) deriving from the head of the Anna Pepple house in Bonny are just three of many eighteenth-century examples. Clearly a small but growing number of Africans had come to hold a different status for Europeans. Overall, these naming patterns indicate some slight erosion of epidermal racism as the central separator of insider from outsider.[98]

More conventional indications of erosion of cultural separation between colonies and metropolis come from sermons, reports from the slave colonies, and anecdotes invoking the golden rule. As Michael

---

[95] For the African presence and status in fifteenth- and sixteenth-century England relative to southern Europe, see Gustav Ungerer, "Recovering a Black African's Voice in an English Lawsuit: Jacques Francis and the Salvage Operations of the *Mary Rose* and the *Sancta Maria* and *Sanctus Edwardus*, 1545–ca 1550," *Medieval and Renaissance Drama in England*, 17 (2005): 255–71.

[96] Kwesi L. DeGraft-Hanson, "Commemorating Hidden Landscapes of Slavery linked by Enslaved Africans and their American Descendants from the Butler Plantations in Georgia," unpublished PhD thesis, Emory University (2013), pp. 213–62.

[97] Even Ayuba Suleiman Diallo was known as Job Ben Solomon during his sojourn in England in 1733–1734.

[98] See Eltis, "Abolition and Identity in the Very Long Run," and p. 3 above.

Greenberg pointed out, the annual sermons preached before the Society for the Propagation of Christian Knowledge over the course of the eighteenth century provides a fascinating way of tracking what might be called a shift in the equivalency or the golden rule index in mid-century.[99] Governor Dunsmore's offer of freedom to Virginian slaves who escaped from their rebellious masters received favorable attention in the London press and triggered a series of anti-slavery articles.[100] At the end of the 1770s Jonas Hanway wrote to the *Public Advertiser*, perhaps a little prematurely, that he knew many "eminent" merchants "whose Minds revolt against the slave trade; and indeed the wonder is that the love of gain should ever have so prevailed in the Hearts of Men in the most civilized parts of Europe, that the same principle which they condemn in others, whom they call barbarous, should be adopted by them."[101] And in the 1780s newspapers began printing more overtly abolitionist material, well before the public and parliamentary campaigns began.[102] The absence of aggressive support for the trade after the widely cited mid-century statements of Malachy Postlethwaite are also striking. And Postlethwaite himself came to change his position on the traffic. Any defenses of the slave traffic were usually directly sponsored by the West India interest.[103]

Nevertheless, abolitionism was not a campaign for a multiracial society. Attitudes to Blacks normally associated with the West India interest are easily identified in the broader English society. Granville Sharp's

---

[99] Michael Greenberg, "Slavery and the Protestant Ethic," *Louisiana Studies*, 51 (1976): 209–39.

[100] *Morning Chronicle and London Advertiser*, February 28, 1776; See the series of "Letters" on the "Slavery of the Negroes" in *Lloyd's Evening Post*, especially March 11, 1776 by "An Enemy of Slavery," and "Letter V" in the May 1, 1776 issue.

[101] April 4, 1779.

[102] The *London Courant and Westminster Chronicle* April 20, 1780, reported a public debate in the Westminster Forum on the motion "Are there sufficient reasons to justify Englishmen continuing the Slave Trade?" The *Public Advertiser* became an outlet for anti-slavery sentiments.

[103] There was no equivalent to the eighteenth-century London press in other European cities and parallel analyses of public opinion are not possible for other major slave-trading countries. In Lisbon, however, the Marquis of Pombal decreed in 1761 that baptized Black slaves (thus, almost all slaves) landing in Portugal would henceforth be freed-persons and a further decree twelve years later emancipated all slaves living in the country. Black slavery in Brazil was ignored, but the enslavement of Indigenous people in the Empire had already been outlawed in 1755 and 1758. These measures were both less ambiguous than and predated the famous Somerset case in England. See A. J. R. Russell-Woods, "Iberian Expansion and the Issue of Black Slavery: Changing Portuguese Attitudes, 1440–1770," *American Historical Review*, 83 (1978): 40–41.

activities, according to the *St James Chronicle* were visiting "grievous injury ... upon this nation, by making it universally known that England is an asylum for those of the darker Colour to enjoy Liberty and Idleness," and that given that one in twenty in London were Black, "within a century there would be black judges, peers and peeresses, and members of parliament" (it actually took two centuries).[104] One of the two transports that brought free Blacks to Sierra Leone, in 1787 – to establish a "Province of Freedom" – purchased slaves on the African coast after disembarking its surviving emigrants, and subsequently sold them on the Musquito shore in Honduras – a voyage that appears nowhere in the extensive literature on the founding of Freetown.[105] Though the outcome of the voyage was reported in the newspapers, no one picked up the irony.

As developed further in the next chapter, elite leaders of the campaign to abolish the slave trade such as William Wilberforce and Zachary Macaulay believed that Africans were uncivilized and not ready for a free labor market.[106] Abolitionist and future Lord Chancellor Henry Brougham's commentary on the work habits of Africans in both Africa and the Americas, written in 1802, is indistinguishable in tone from Thomas Carlyle's anti-Black tirades in the late 1840s.[107] As the campaign to abolish slavery itself gathered strength in 1826, a London impresario staged the first known production of Othello with a distinguished African American, Ira Aldridge, in the title role. It closed within days, with the *Times* reporting "owing to the shape of his lips it is utterly impossible for him to pronounce English," and another newspaper describing Aldridge as "an unseemly nigger." As the abolition campaign reached its successful peak in 1833, with record numbers of petitions pouring into Parliament, a further production at the Covent Garden Theatre, also starring Aldridge, closed after just two performances, with the *Atheneum* objecting to "Desdemona [actress Ellen Tree] being pawed about the stage by a black man."[108] No

---

[104] *St. James's Chronicle or the British Evening Post*, December 21, 1784.
[105] *World and Fashionable Advertiser*, September 22, 1787. It was the *Belisarius* (ID 26327) It experienced a crew mutiny off Jamaica (a rare occurrence when slaves were on board) and was destroyed in a hurricane after selling its slaves (*General Evening Post*, January 8, 1788). The most comprehensive book on the subject is Alexander Byrd, *Captives and Voyagers: Black Migrants Across the Eighteenth Century, British Atlantic World* (Baton Rouge, LA, 2009).
[106] Ryan, Humanitarian Governance, pp. 15–17.
[107] Brougham, *Inquiry into the Colonial Policy*, vol. 2: 411–20.
[108] Yet Aldridge did play Macbeth and Richard III in white make-up and a wig without this abuse. For more on Aldridge, see Bernth Lindfors, *Ira Aldridge: The Early Years, 1807–1833* (Rochester, NY, 2011).

one should doubt that an underlying sense of racial distance was present in British society throughout the push for abolition of the slave trade and slavery from 1780 the mid nineteenth century.[109]

As this chapter stresses, abolition of the slave trade was one of many legislative changes that affected violent behavior and practices. Perhaps the traditional thinking of historians about the activist phase of abolition may owe something to one of the tyrannies of the French Revolution that Edmund Burke failed to anticipate, that of its impact on the historiography of the Atlantic world. One of the lingering central tenets in the field of coerced labor, from C.L.R. James to Laurent Dubois, is that significant reform was not possible until the ancien régime was destroyed, and when reform did occur, it was, of course, because of the Revolution. For French slave societies, this is undoubtedly the case, but even then, the position can be defended only by ignoring the transatlantic differentials in attitudes toward labor and violence that had developed during the eighteenth century. The shift in humanitarian sensibility – whether presented in terms of a growing awareness of others (Hunt, Richardson), or changing identities (as argued here) – was well underway by 1775.[110] A greater sensitization toward violence is apparent among eighteenth-century Europeans despite (or perhaps because of) the fact that Europe was one of the most violent regions in the world.[111] And to carry the argument forward and into the post-emancipation Caribbean, when ex-slaves left the sugar plantations, planters resorted to indirect means (taxation and Asian contract labor) rather than violence to secure a labor supply (the violent suppression of Black dissent at Morant Bay, Jamaica, in 1865 notwithstanding), a strategy much more in tune with the twenty-first century than the seventeenth. Rather than interpreting condemnation of the slave trade as a side effect of the American, French, Latin American, and Saint Domingue revolutions, we should see these as related phenomena, stemming from the same deep shift in values that began in the seventeenth century, at least as far as religious violence was concerned. The same phenomenon started to affect perceptions of slavery in England

---

[109] George Boulukos, "The Horror of Hybridity, "Enlightenment, Anti-Slavery and Racial Disgust in Charlotte Smith's 'Henrietta,'" in Bryccham Carey and Peter J. Kitson (eds.), *Slavery and the Cultures of Abolition: Essays Marking the Bicentennial of the British Abolition Act of 1807* (Chippenham, Wiltshire, UK, 2007), pp. 87–109.

[110] Lynn Hunt, *Inventing Human Rights: A History* (New York, 2007); Richardson, *Principles and Agents*.

[111] Stanley L. Engerman, "War, Colonization and Migration over Five Centuries," in Klooster (ed.), *Migration, Trade, and Slavery*, pp. 16–18.

in the 1720s and 1730s. The central point is that these shifts did not occur or were much less apparent in the slave colonies.

The divergence in norms of violence between the slave colonies and domestic metropolitan centers, and the increasing ability of some Europeans to think of extending the golden rule to West Africa and the plantation Americas, points most obviously to the fact that slave owners no longer had the unthinking support of the societies and power centers from which, in the English case, their ancestors had launched their slave initiatives. It was a support, moreover, upon which the slave system ultimately depended, as the revolts in both St. John and St. Domingue demonstrated. Small numbers of Whites could not prevail over large numbers of Blacks without at least the threat of outside imperial military intervention, and it was European navies that ultimately held the slaves in place. Clearly, doubts about the legitimacy of first the slave trade and then slavery itself did not mean the sudden withdrawal of the underpinning of imperial force on which the slave system depended. But it did provide opportunities for resistance from the enslaved, either in terms of violence or running away, to be more effective.

Abolitionist sympathies therefore constituted a split in the power structure that held slaves in subjection. Perhaps calling on his younger days when he and Eugene Genovese worked as communist organizers in New York City, Robert Fogel pointed out in relation to the US Civil War, "a revolution cannot be made at will. It requires a crisis within the ruling class."[112] For slaveholders around the Atlantic world, abolition was such a crisis. Violence and escape could be and were brutally repressed (except, ultimately for Haiti), but the repression inevitably had the effect of further widening the split in the imperial power structure. It did so by underlining the differing community norms of violence that had emerged in the eighteenth century between slaveholding and non-freeholding societies, continued racism in the latter notwithstanding. But if both resistance of slaves and ruling-class splits were necessary, perhaps neither by itself was sufficient to end slavery and the slave trade. And we should also note that the process played out rather differently in Africa than it did in the Americas. Rather than abolition eroding the

---

[112] Robert W. Fogel, *Without Consent or Contract: The Rise and Fall of American Slavery* (New York, 1989), p. 198. Robin Blackburn ("Debates on Slavery") agrees with this position, though he does not cite Fogel. The best account of the interdependence of the actions of slaves and abolitionists in the English case is Gelien Matthews, *Caribbean Slave Revolts and the British Abolitionist Movement* (Baton Rouge, LA, 2006).

underpinnings of the slave system, as happened in the Americas, in Africa it was a case of imperial governments eventually intervening in a system of slavery that never depended on them for its enforcement in the first place.

None of this means that abolition of the slave trade should be seen as a humanitarian initiative on the part of the British government. The success of the abolitionists – James Stephen, Henry Brougham, William Wilberforce, and others – hinged on their ability to persuade majorities in both Houses of Parliament that abolition was in the best economic and strategic interests of Britain, especially British slave owners in the Americas. Abolition was implemented in stages between 1805 and 1807 with an Order in Council and three laws.[113] These progressively limited the traffic first to the newly occupied foreign colonies like Guiana and Trinidad that in 1806 might still be returned to their original Dutch and Spanish owners in a subsequent peace treaty. A second measure restricted the traffic to ships that were already engaged in the business, while the third applied an outright ban on the business with almost immediate effect. And here, the declaration of Haitian independence on January 1, 1804, played an important role. The major impulse behind these measures was the need to address the demographic imbalance between Blacks and Whites in the Caribbean that was seen as the root cause of the St. Domingue Rebellion. As noted below, events in St. Domingue horrified Brougham in particular. Thus, as Richardson points out and as the debates clearly show, the package of legislation that ended the British slave trade was aimed primarily at the long-run preservation of the Caribbean colonies, a matter of state policy rather than a reflection of humanitarian sensibilities.[114] Despite the massive popular support for the measure, the British Parliament passed abolition primarily for reasons of state, and only secondarily alleviate the suffering of the enslaved.

The US did not have the same Black–White population imbalance as the British Caribbean colonies. In addition, anti-slavery societies in the northern colonies of North America predated those in Britain. Indeed, in 1776 they were likely world leaders in the anti-slavery movement, given

---

[113] 46 Geo III c.52; 46 Geo III c.119; 46 Geo III Sess. 2 c.44. c.52.

[114] Richardson, *Principles and Agents*, pp. 246–49; John R. Oldfield, *Transatlantic Abolitionism in the Age of Revolution: An International History of Anti-Savery c. 1787–1820* (Cambridge, 2013), pp. 180–88; Roger Anstey described the abolitionists' strategy as a device designed to secure a parliamentary majority ["A Re-Interpretation of the Abolition of the British Slave Trade, 1806–1807," *English Historical Review*, 87 (1972): 304–32], but this underplays the impact of Haitian independence on British security fears for its Caribbean possessions.

that Vermont freed its slaves in 1777, albeit with a twelve-year "apprenticeship" of unpaid labor to their former masters. Faced with Southern resistance, there was more room for the humanitarian impulse in the various US legislative initiatives on the slave trade beginning in 1794.[115] Nevertheless, secessionism in the US, ending with a particularly bloody and costly war, does in a sense confirm the importance of the "reasons of state" that underpinned the British government's decision to proceed with abolition. In the aftermath of the US conflict and the vast costs of that conflict, the British solution of compensating the slave owners for emancipating their human property looks distinctly preferable.[116] Dismantling slavery in the rest of the Atlantic world followed the British rather than the US model. Compensation to slave owners was the norm and, worse, that compensation was paid for in part by the enslaved themselves in the form of free womb laws and working without compensation for their former owners.[117]

Finally, given our inability to explain why these major value shifts occur, let us consider a broader implication. It might be argued that the single great issue for the English in the late eighteenth century and, for the Western Hemisphere, in the nineteenth, was the abolition of the slave trade and slavery; that in the twentieth, the great question was totalitarianism; and that in the twenty-first it may well be the treatment of women given that, except for sub-Saharan Africa, Japan, the state of Kerala in India and the Western world, census data suggest – in Amartya Sen's memorable title – "More Than 100 Million Women Are Missing."[118] Societies that distribute their resources so that a female ratio of 105 to 100 at birth becomes 80 or less to 100 in adulthood have long flourished – no doubt since the Neolithic revolution. The number of premature female deaths must always have greatly exceeded the number of enslaved people at any point in history. What form will the demands for reform take? Will the statues of politicians who opposed women's suffrage be demolished? Or perhaps animal rights will take center stage and the meat-eaters of today will assume the same status as the slave-owners of yesterday. If this

---

[115] See Paul Finkelman, "Regulating the African Slave Trade," *Civil War History*, 54 (2008): 379–405, for an overview of American anti-slave trade legislation.
[116] See Chapter 7 for a fuller discussion and Peter Coclanis, "The Civil War and its Aftermath," *CWHS*, vol. 4: 520–22.
[117] Rebecca J. Scott, *Slave Emancipation in Cuba: the Transition to Free Labor, 1860–1899* (Pittsburgh, 2000); Beauvois, *Between Blood and Gold*, pp. 247–53; Celso Thomas Castilho, "Abolition and its Aftermath in Brazil," *CWHS*, vol. 4: 488–503.
[118] *New York Review of Books*, December 20, 1990.

happens our current society can expect to be written about as disparagingly as the slave Americas are today. What on earth were those people thinking?

More fundamentally, what is it that makes one or another of such issues dominate the "public sphere"? Why does one issue take precedence? On this neither historians nor sociologists have begun to scratch the surface. The literature on shifts in moral attitudes is so thin, that it makes no sense to single out, say, the abolition of slavery and then look for economic, national, imperial, or class interests to explain all. Attempts to account for our history and deal with its consequences must surely be more complex than that.

CONCLUSION

The discussion here attempts to explain why one form of cruelty – the slave trade – received public attention and not another.[119] We can at least say that the emergence of abolition as a public issue cannot be understood by itself. It must be seen as part of the broad-based decline in violence that is easy to track across the Atlantic world from the fifteenth century to the present, the horrors of the twentieth century notwithstanding. Penal punishments, treatment of prisoners of war, care of abandoned children both before and after their employment, blood sports, and serfdom are just some of the issues that emerged at about the same time as an awareness of Black enslavement in the colonies. But increasing concern with cruelty was unevenly distributed geographically in that it occurred at a glacial pace in the slave- and serf-holding regions compared to the slave- and serf-free areas. Values that were shared by metropolitan centers and colonies on the issue of slavery that were apparent in 1700 were no longer shared by 1800. But why would reform of slavery seem to require the most urgent attention and why in England and the northern US and not in some other Atlantic country?

It is surely relevant that in the eighteenth century the English-speaking world developed the most vibrant newspaper and periodical culture on the planet and one with the fewest censorship restrictions. Literacy rates were

---

[119] Influential sociological texts such as Norbet Elias, *The Civilizing Process*, 2 vols, vol. 2 *State Formation and Civilization* (Oxford, 1982) and Jürgen Habermas (1962, trans. 1989) *The Structural Transformation of the Public Sphere: An Inquiry into a Category of Bourgeois Society* (Cambridge, MA, 1991) do not take up this issue and are therefore not included this discussion.

also among the highest in the world. But the key explanatory factor was the steady stream of reports of violence on slave-trading vessels and slave colonies described above. None of the other cruelties inflicted on children, women, prisoners, convicts, and animals received anything like the same attention, perhaps because these victim groups could not organize and violently resist. The French and St. Domingue revolutions may have split the metropolitan and colonial ruling class on the issue of slavery, as Fogel argued, and thus put an end to it in the Americas. But the more important and less dramatic cause of that split lies in the constant press reports of African resistance on slave ships and plantations, in 1720–1830, at a time when Britain itself had left behind the violent norms of the seventeenth century.[120] Despite the role of Haiti in the British decision to abolish the traffic in 1804–1807, those who wish to argue that slaves freed themselves should study these earlier decades, rather than focusing exclusively on events in St. Domingue after August 1791. They also need to account for the huge increase in slaveholdings across the Americas *after* the St. Domingue and French revolutions. Value shifts in Britain and the northern US are an essential part of the explanation.

---

[120] Thomas Haskell has argued that increasing market activity made the ultimate buyer of a product, for example sugar in Britain, more aware of how that product was produced. But the rest of Western Europe was in the same position as Britain on this issue and did not develop popular anti-slavery movements. Thomas L. Haskell, "Capitalism and the Origins of the Humanitarian Sensibility, Part 1," *American Historical Review*, 90 (1985): 339–61; Thomas Bender, *The Antislavery Debate,* Capitalism and Abolitionism as a Problem in Historical Interpretation (Berkeley, CA, 1992), pp. 111–12, 137–43.

7

Freedom?

For historians of the Black Atlantic in the last half century, accurately representing the humanity and resourcefulness of the millions of people pulled into the maelstrom of New World slavery might be described as the Holy Grail.[1] Photographic evidence has formed a small part of this quest. For the last years of the slave trade when slave ships carrying thousands of captives were detained, photography provides unexpected insights for the many thousands of Liberated Africans, as the re-captives on board came to be known. This large group of people experienced a slow transition from the slave deck to a severely circumscribed form of freedom on land. Photographs from the period give us a view, however limited, into their experience.

Dispatches from naval officers to the Admiralty describing slave-trading activities in the Indian Ocean continued after the transatlantic traffic closed in 1867. The occasional report included photographs. For the Africans involved, conditions in the two oceans were almost identical. Figures 7.1 through 7.3 show enslaved people disembarked in 1868 (7.1 and 7.2) and 1883 (7.3). The standard slaver off East Africa both for coastal and transoceanic voyages was a dhow typically smaller than a transatlantic carrier. Naval commanders often transferred the enslaved to their own vessel, as happened with the HMS *Daphne* shown in Figure 7.1. This could make crowding just as severe as on the slave ship.[2] Figure 7.2, also taken on HMS

---

[1] Parts of this chapter draw on Daniel Domingues da Silva, David Eltis, Philip Misevich, and Olatunji Ojo, "The Diaspora of Africans Liberated from Slave Ships in the Nineteenth Century," *Journal of African History*, 55 (2014): 347–69, and Philip Misevich, David Eltis, G. Ugo Nwokeji, and Adenike Ogunkoya, "The Origins and Destinations of Captives from the Bight of Biafra, 1807–1843," *Slavery & Abolition*, (May 2024), 1–28, https://doi.org/10.1080/0144039X.2024.2335144.

[2] BNA, Admiralty to Earl of Granville, Feb. 10, 1869, enc. Sir Leopold Heath, Jan. 16, 1869, FO84/1310, ff. 72–73. The photographs are detached at ff. 192 through 194 of the volume.

Freedom?

FIGURE 7.1 Liberated Africans on board HMS *Daphne*, 1868. Source: BNA, FO84/1310, f. 192. Reproduced with permission of the British National Archives, Kew.

Daphne, shows the appalling physical condition of the Africans. The distended stomachs of the malnourished and dehydration-induced emaciation of dysentery are plain to see. We know that the captured dhow had been at sea for only three days when detained. Nevertheless, the image surely reflects the typical condition of those disembarking from the 40,000 or so transatlantic voyages in the preceding three-and-one-half-centuries.

The *Daphne* subsequently sailed to the Seychelles, where it left a further 409 Oromo people of Ethiopia, speaking a Cushitic language, many of whom were also photographed (see Julien Durup, "The Diaspora of 'Liberated African Slaves'! In South Africa, Aden, India, East Africa, Mauritius, and the Seychelles," pp. 13–14, unpublished, nd, but available at https://www.blacfoundation.org/pdf/Libafrican.pdf.

294 Atlantic Cataclysm

FIGURE 7.2 Liberated African children on board HMS *Daphne*, 1868. Source: BNA, FO84/1310, f. 194. Reproduced with the permission of the British National Archives, Kew.

FIGURE 7.3 Liberated Africans on board HMS *Undine*, 1883. Source: Photo Lot 97 DOE: Africa: General: Unid: Artwork National Anthropological Archives, Smithsonian Institution.

Figure 7.3 shows 100 individuals removed from a second dhow fifteen years later, off Ndzwani (then called Johanna), one of the Comoros Islands. They had embarked 200 miles to the south, in what is now Mozambique. The prize officer's report identifies them as Makua people, speakers of Emakhuwa. This is not represented in the African-Origins database, but is the dominant language of modern Mozambique.[3] There, too, are the distended stomachs and emaciation on display in the front row, but the overall physical condition of the group seems better than its 1868 predecessor, possibly due to the artistic license of the engraver.[4] It should be noted that the naval report tells us that 20 percent of this group had already died in the interval between detention and the time of the photograph, probably a few short weeks later in Zanzibar. We know, too, that all but twenty of the Makua had been too ill to disembark unaided. A man and woman, likely parents, rest their arms on a child. The back row shows two crewmen, one of whom carries an African infant, possibly an orphan. This gives a human touch to the interaction of sailors and Africans, to be considered alongside evidence below of the occasional Liberated African rebellion against the prize crew as they sailed to the nearest court location. The high ratio of children and women, 77 percent in this instance, also obvious in these images, no doubt inhibited violent resistance.

These images are likely the closest we will get to representing the nearly 3 million African captives that were forced to leave Africa for the Americas in the sixty years after 1807. By that time Denmark, the United States, and Britain, in that order, had prohibited their citizens from engaging in the transatlantic slave trade. Three million is a surprisingly large number given that these same nations had withdrawn from the trade after financing almost two-thirds of total departures in the few years before 1807. It points to the inability of international law at the time to accommodate relatively sudden shifts in values, especially those relating to human rights, that enabled formal abolition of the traffic.[5] Though the British had been the leading transatlantic slave-trading nation at the end of the eighteenth century, they now led a campaign to capture hundreds of slave ships containing thousands of captives. Here we will

---

[3] Captured on May 5, 1883. See BNA, Admiralty to Earl of Granville, Oct. 9, 1883, enc. Lt. Cutfield, July 23, 1883, FO84/1648, ff. 107–10.
[4] The original photograph does not appear to have survived.
[5] See https://slavevoyages.org/voyages/xzEoQX3Y for 1804 to 1807, and https://slavevoyages.org/voyages/GdS4KvDx for 1808 to 1866.

first examine the structure of the post-1807 slave trade from West Africa with an emphasis on re-captives, in other words, those Africans for whom such naval intervention meant they never reached the slave markets of the Americas. We track the reactions, fate, and composition of the more than 200,000 Liberated Africans that the new British policy created, most of them released from slave vessels or rescued from coastal barracoons. We also draw comparisons with ex-slaves freed in parts of the British Empire by the 1833 abolition act, by the US Civil War, and to a lesser extent, *libertos* in the non-British Atlantic.[6] The main thrust of the chapter is evaluating how the Liberated Africans fared against the background of the broader struggles that were taking place over freedom in the nineteenth-century Atlantic world.

But first we need to track the geography of this huge diaspora, or rather, these diasporas. In almost every instance, captives liberated from slave vessels passed through a legal process that formally proclaimed their new status. The best known such process was adjudication in the so-called Courts of Mixed Commission – international courts established by treaties between the British and, eventually, twenty other nations; the term "mixed" deriving from the involvement of more than one nation. Mixed Commissions operated at different times in Sierra Leone, Luanda, Cape Town, Rio de Janeiro, and Havana to adjudicate vessels suspected of slave trading. Together they declared 90,988 Africans as "Liberated."[7] Additional courts existed in Paramaribo (Surinam), Kingston (Jamaica), and New York but none of these freed any slaves.

---

[6] Not taken up here are the naval campaigns, for which see most recently Anthony Sullivan, *Britain's War Against the Slave Trade: The Operations of the Royal Navy's West Africa Squadron, 1807–1867* (Barnsley, UK, 2020); Peter Grindal, *Opposing the Slavers: the Royal Navy's Campaign Against the Atlantic Slave Trade* (New York, 2016), and for the US campaign, Donald L. Canney, *The Africa Squadron: the U.S. Navy and the Slave Trade, 1842–1861* (Washington, DC, 2006). For the French see Paul Michael Kielstra, *The Politics of Slave Trade Suppression in Britain and France, 1814–48* (London, 2000), pp. 56–58, 79–80, 130–33. For the costs and ultimate ineffectiveness of these naval and diplomatic efforts see Eltis, *Economic Growth*, pp. 92–93.

[7] See www.slavevoyages.org/voyages/EEsRIeUb for vessels and their captives condemned by the Mixed Commission Courts. Historians still see the Courts of Mixed Commission as the major judicial weapon in the fight against the slave trade, but they accounted for fewer than half of all vessels condemned (though more than half of the Liberated Africans on those vessels). Note that for Sierra Leone and Havana the figures for re-captive Africans provided here are often greater than those generated by a count of Africans listed in the court registers. This is explained first, by deaths immediately after disembarkation and second, by the fact that several thousand captives whom the courts declared free, disembarked from the slave ship before the vessel was conducted to Sierra Leone or Havana.

A second large group assumed Liberated African status via domestic proceedings, the most important of which were British Admiralty Courts – domestic tribunals that had jurisdiction over maritime matters. At least one of these existed in every British possession with a coastline. In the colonies, they were called Vice-Admiralty Courts with those in Freetown and St. Helena dominating this group. All told, they determined the fate of a further 80,024 Africans.[8] Domestic courts and administrative decisions of other nations created Liberated status for 27,000 Africans, though this figure is an approximation, given that research on this topic in some of these countries is still incomplete. Brazil and the United States formed the core of this group, but Portuguese courts in Africa and French courts on both sides of the Atlantic also contributed. The Haitian navy captured four slave vessels and Argentinian privateers another four in the 1825–1828 war with Brazil.[9] In addition, the British freed 2,300 other people without apparently going through any formal process, most of them having survived shipwreck on islands in the British Caribbean while bound for Cuba. In summary, approximately 216,000 enslaved people fell into the hands of various anti-slave trade forces operating in the Atlantic after 1807. As some 10 percent of these comprised the Brazilian and Cuban authorities, we should perhaps say "nominal" anti-slave trade forces.

A third group, called *engagés* (nominally contracted workers) receives less attention in what follows because those involved have received much less scholarly scrutiny. Between 1831 and 1870 the Dutch and French governments authorized the "recruitment" of Africans for in one case military service in Dutch Indonesia, and in the other labor service on the sugar plantations of French colonies in the Americas and the Indian Ocean. French and Dutch agents negotiated with slave merchants in various parts of East and West Africa for the purchase of enslaved people who were then declared nominally free prior to their forced embarkation on transoceanic voyages. Each *engagé* and prospective soldier was given a contract that specified a term of service: ten years for the 19,900 dispatched in this fashion to Martinique, Guadeloupe, Guyane plus 34,258 sent to Réunion. The Dutch exacted fourteen years' service from the 3,085 sent to the Dutch East Indies. Both nations added the promise of a return voyage to Africa at completion of service. The combined total of 57,243 people caught up in these French- and Dutch-forced migrations, made it easily the largest source of Liberated Africans in the nineteenth century after the Sierra Leone

[8] See www.slavevoyages.org/voyages/kp3AKdNx.
[9] See www.slavevoyages.org/voyages/uz1BNwJR.

courts.[10] A final and not yet systematically investigated group are the tens of thousands taken off Arab dhows in the Indian Ocean, a few of whom are represented in Figures 7.1 to 7.3. Mixed Commission and Vice-Admiralty Courts from Cape Town to Bombay, and many points in between, assigned Liberated African status to an unknown number of Africans. The African names in the court registers of Zanzibar, Mombasa, Aden, Seychelles, the Mascarene Islands, and several Indian locations have yet to be analyzed. These mainly Indian Ocean sources could easily add a further 30,000 to the PAST enslaved database.

Of the overall total of more than a quarter-million Africans displaced by Atlantic voyages, we have personal details of fewer than half – 95,183 – mostly landing in Freetown and Havana. The PAST enslaved database on slavevoyages.org (formerly african-origins.org), gives readers access to this personal information. Some were liberated by the US Civil War a year or two after their slave ship arrived illegally late in the ante-bellum era.[11] Overall we can trace 95,165 Africans after they left Africa. As with all the databases on slavevoyages, this number will continue to grow as new documentary evidence surfaces.[12] Column 3 of Table 7.1 provides an overview of the initial location of Liberated Africans after their recapture or in some instances, last known location. Column 4 shows the net impact of their subsequent movements as far as we can tell. The plus sign indicates additional arrivals. The minus sign shows subsequent departures, insofar as these can be determined.

As discussed in Chapter 5, for many listed in the registers, we can also say something about their linguistic identities, and thereby their African

---

[10] Larry W. Yarak, "New Sources for the Study of Akan Slavery and Slave Trade: Dutch Military Recruitment in Asante and the Gold Coast, 1831–72," in Robin Law (ed.), *Source Material for Studying the Slave Trade and the African Diaspora* (Stirling, UK, 1997), pp. 35–60; Gareth Austin, Joerg Baten, and Bas Van Leewen, "The Biological Standard of Living in Early Nineteenth-Century West Africa: New Anthropometric Evidence for Northern Ghana and Burkina Faso," *Economic History Review*, 65 (2012): 1280–1302; Renault, *Liberation d'esclaves*, pp. 34–92; David Northrup, "Freedom and Indentured Labor in the French Caribbean, 1848–1900," in David Eltis (ed.), *Coerced and Free Migrations: Global Perspectives* (Stanford, 2002), pp. 204–28.

[11] Readers will not find Equiano (aka Gustavus Vasa) among this group because while liberated, he does not appear to have been African, given the documents that show he was born in North America. See Vincent Carretta, *Equiano the African: Biography of a Self-Made Man* (Athens, GA, 2005). The most balanced discussion of this contentious issue is Alexander Byrd, "Eboe, Country, Nation and Gustavus Vassa's Interesting Narrative," *William and Mary Quarterly*, 63 (2006): 123–48. Carretta's research is persuasive, and readers should note that additional evidence on his American birthplace has appeared since this was written.

[12] The database is at www.slavevoyages.org/past/database. It accepts any record of an enslaved person that can be linked to one of the voyages shown on the site.

TABLE 7.1 *Regions of disembarkation of Liberated Africans: Initial place of arrival and subsequent movements, 1800–1867*

	Place of arrival	Arriving after recapture/ shipwreck	Subsequent movement (net)
The Americas			
British Caribbean	Tortola	2,122	−107
	Antigua	1,583	0
	Dominica	443	0
	Barbados	433	0
	St. Vincent	0	+1,036
	St. Lucia	0	+730
	St. Kitts/Nevis	0	+455
	Grenada	1,100	+1,609
	Trinidad	195	+8,961
	Jamaica	2,950	+8,437
	Bahamas	6,217	+900
	British Guiana	314	+13,746
	Honduras	677	+500
US	US	5,051	−1,737
Spanish America	Cuba	27,538	−3,685
	Puerto Rico	650	0
	Buenos Aires/ Patagonia	1,437	0
Haiti	Haiti	1,048	0
French America	Martinique	993	0
Brazil	Rio de Janeiro	9,246	−1,718
	Bahia	729	0
	Maranhão	265	0
	Pernambuco	136	0
	Alagoas	97	0
	Ceará	160	0
	Rio Grande do Norte	49	0
	Rio Grande do Sul	25	0
Africa and Asia			
	Senegambia	71	+3,478
	Sierra Leone[1]	99,752	−24,322
	Liberia	5,457	+1,737

(continued)

TABLE 7.1 (continued)

Place of arrival	Arriving after recapture/ shipwreck	Subsequent movement (net)
Cape Coast Castle	45	0
Fernando Po	1,258	Unknown
Luanda	1,655	0
St. Helena	25,233	−17,687
Cape Town	5,598	0
Durban	600	0
Mauritius	1,186	0
Aden	3,600	−64
Seychelles	2,600	
Zanzibar	1,600	
Mombasa	1,600	
Bombay	1,100	0
Bagamoyo	170	
Grand Total	214,983	

Notes:
[1] Arrivals in Sierra Leone are the number disembarked wherever possible. Such numbers were usually greater than those surviving long enough to be entered in the registers of the Mixed Commission Courts and the British Vice-Admiralty Courts. In the case of Havana, some condemned vessels had disembarked slaves prior to capture and therefore not all those on board became *emancipados*.

Sources: This table has appeared in several forms since first publication in 2014. This most recent version is largely taken from Richard Anderson, "Liberated Africans," *Oxford Research Encyclopedias, African History* (Oxford, 2021), Appendix 1, https://doi.org/10.1093/acrefore/9780190277734.013.741, for which see references to earlier versions. Five modifications of data that do not appear in Anderson's 2021 compilation are:
United States:
www.slavevoyages.org/voyages/D4efjb2y plus 306 on board the Putnam (a) *Echo* (ID 4284), which entered Charleston. Those on board were held in quarantine before dispatch to Liberia on a different vessel.
Liberia:
Initial disembarkations are from IDs 4653, 4654, 4655, 4656, 4911, 4925, 4955, 4764; Subsequent movements are from the arrivals of IDs 4284, 4362, 4363, and 4364.
Senegambia:
www.slavevoyages.org/voyages/aEbnkclJ
French Americas:
www.slavevoyages.org/voyages/QULDqrjE, and Willendorf, *Affranchissements en Guadeloupe*, chapter 4.
St. Helena:
Andrew Pearson kindly made available his own compilations of Africans landed at St. Helena – unpublished spreadsheet: "St_Helena_V_Ad_Court_2017#12#05.xlxs,"
A worksheet incorporating these modifications is available from the author. Note that Henry B. Lovejoy is at work on further modifications of this table.

homeland. Court proceedings typically involved government clerks helped by African interpreters, transcribing into large bound registers the names, age, height, and, for many, probable languages of each enslaved person on board the detained ship.[13] Unfortunately, in the Portuguese south Atlantic world clerks entered only the post-baptismal Christian names rather than the Indigenous African name. The labels and the bound registers were intended to provide protection against re-enslavement in an Atlantic world in which slave populations in several parts were still expanding, and where 7 million people of African descent remained enslaved as late as 1830. The registers, sometimes along with multiple copies, had an almost identical format.[14] In what was for most African languages a pre-orthographic era, the African names were taken down phonetically. Modern native speakers of English, Spanish, or French have recorded the names and users can listen to these recordings. Crowdsourcing enables the identification of their modern counterparts and thus the likely linguistic association of the name.[15] In addition to the registers, there are missionary commentaries and reports of occasional interventions by the British imperial government such as the "Commissioners of Inquiry into the State of Africans in the West Indies," who interviewed a selection of 886 Liberated Africans a decade or more after release from their slave ship.[16]

---

[13] For the years and places that the extant registers covered and a fuller discussion of what they offer, see, Anderson et al., "Using African Names," 165–91, but especially Figure 1. Note that the Liberated Africans analyzed here include only those caught up in the Atlantic slave trades.

[14] There is a fine parallel here with the millions of baptismal certificates used across the centuries in the Iberian Atlantic, also in a standardized format. These have been described and partially digitized by Jane Landers. See www.vanderbilt.edu/quantumpotential/ai-unearths-untold-stories/

[15] See the PAST interface on slavevoyages for these data. Additional registers were kept in Luanda and Rio de Janeiro. For the usefulness of these documents in tracking down the origins of re-captives, see Anderson et al., "Using African Names," pp. 165–91.

[16] Reports by Commissioners of Inquiry into State of Africans apprenticed in the West Indies, I, *Papers Relating to Captured Negroes*, PP, 1825 (114), XXV, 193, 68; and PP, *Papers Relating to Captured Negroes*, No. 115, XXV (1825). The original documents based on these interviews are in BNA, CO 318/82–83 and CO 318/85 to 93. See Anita Rupprecht, "'When He Gets Among his Countrymen, They Tell Him That He Is Free': Slave Trade Abolition, Indentured Africans and a Royal Commission," *Slavery & Abolition*, 33 (2012): 435–55; Sean Kelley, "Precedents: The 'Captured Negroes' of Tortola, 1807–22," in Richard Anderson and Henry B. Lovejoy (eds.), *Liberated Africans and the Abolition of the Slave Trade, 1807–1896* (Martlesham, UK), pp. 25–44; Suzanne Schwarz, "The Impact of Liberated African 'Disposal' Policies in Early Nineteenth-Century Sierra Leone," in Anderson and Lovejoy (eds.), *Liberated Africans*, pp. 47–48.

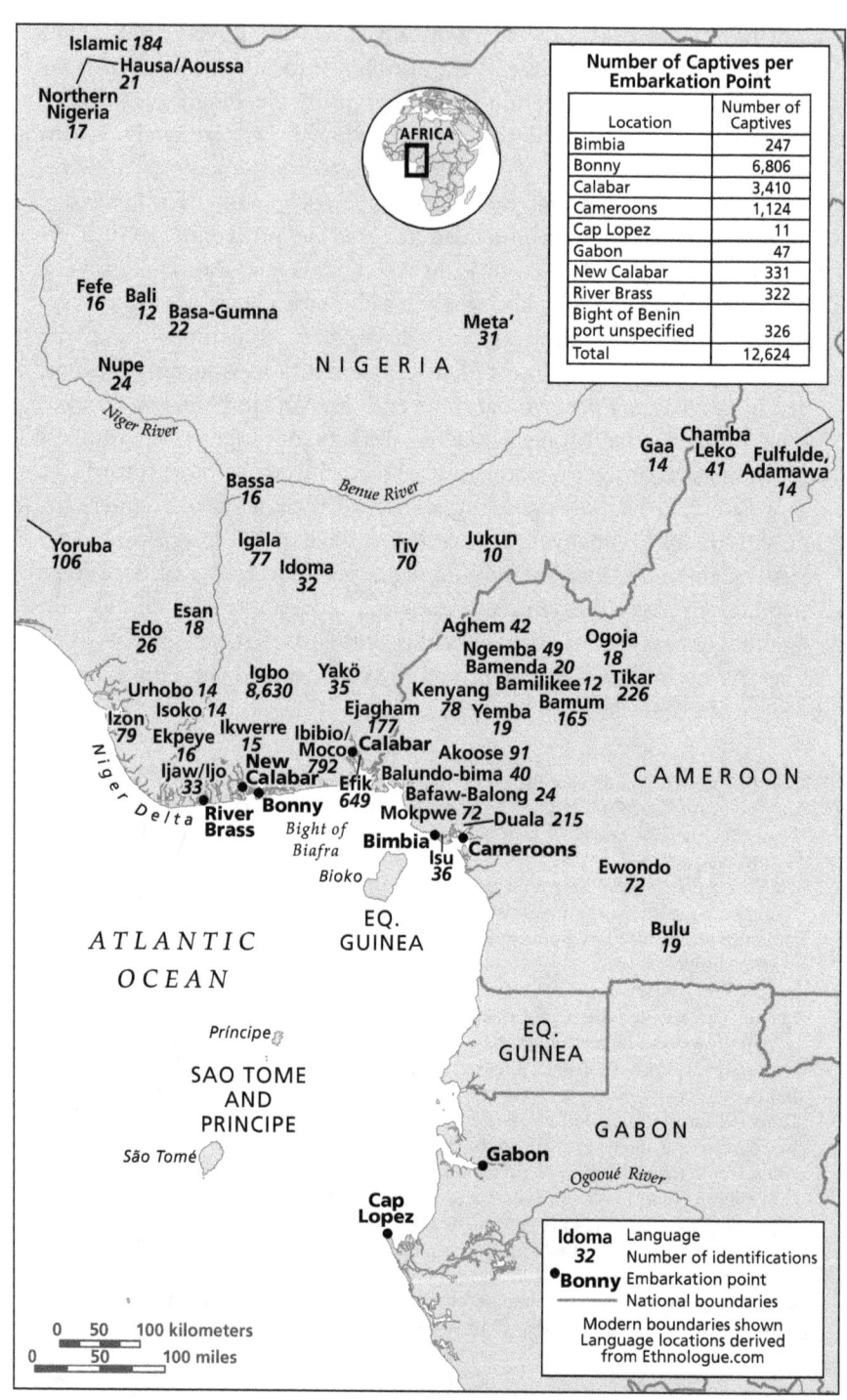

MAP 7.1 Locations of languages of Liberated Africans leaving northern Bight of Biafra ports, 1808–1847. Source: Data from the African-Origins database. For 1808 selection see www.slavevoyages.org/enslaved/yYcoFdQ6.

Twelve years of crowd-sourcing the African names in the registers, primarily through the former African-Origins site have allowed researchers to link 35,300 African names with a specific language, or in the case of Islam, a religion. The Ethnologue website (www.ethnologue.com) provides a modern-day coordinate for almost every one of the identified languages. Given the geographic continuity of coastal populations over centuries of slave trading and colonial rule, this in turn provides an approximate indication of the original geographic location of the Liberated African.[17] Up to this point, scholars have focused on the wide range of languages and cultures of Liberated Africans. Sigismund Koelle listed more than 200 languages and dialects in Sierra Leone as the influx of Liberated Africans to the colony approached its end in the mid-1850s. He and subsequent scholars have made such identifications, and the captive narratives that often went with them, the core of their work.[18] Misevich, Nwokeji, and I have taken the analysis a step further by using the surviving registers to estimate the size and relative importance of those language groups and to estimate their diasporas.[19]

Maps 7.1 to 7.3 distribute the identified languages across three major African regions caught up in the African slave trade after 1807. The italicized number beside the language label in the maps is the total of Liberated Africans associated with that language, as of 2023. The maps therefore draw directly on the names taken from the registers maintained by the Vice-Admiralty and Mixed Commission Courts and subsequently identified on the African-Origins site. These are now displayed in the PAST interface of slavevoyages.[20] For this large segment of West Africa, it is probable that the roughly 94,000 captives that naval forces detained

---

[17] For ethnolinguistic continuity over time, see Hair, "Ethnolinguistic Continuity." For a fuller discussion of the validity of this methodology, see Domingues da Silva et al., "Diaspora of Africans," Domingues da Silva et al., "Transatlantic Muslim Diaspora," pp. 530–31; and Anderson et al., "Using African Names."

[18] Koelle, *Polyglotta Africana* (Graz, Austria, 1963).

[19] Misevich, et al., "Origins and Destinations of Captives." The database of 35,300 used here is substantially smaller than the one assembled by Nathan Nunn in "Long-Term Effects of Africa's Slave Trades," which collates fifty-four different samples for a total of 80,656 captives over the whole slave trade era. Moreover, the African-Origins database covers only the nineteenth century. Nevertheless, our data is preferred here. Only seven of the Nunn samples are from Africa. In the turbulent field of African ethnography few Africanists accept at face value ethnolinguistic identifications made by observers in the Americas.

[20] Departures from West Central Africa, the major source of captives in the nineteenth century, cannot yet be mapped. For the languages and origins of Africans who embarked south of the equator after 1807 see Domingues da Silva, *Atlantic Slave Trade*, pp. 73–97

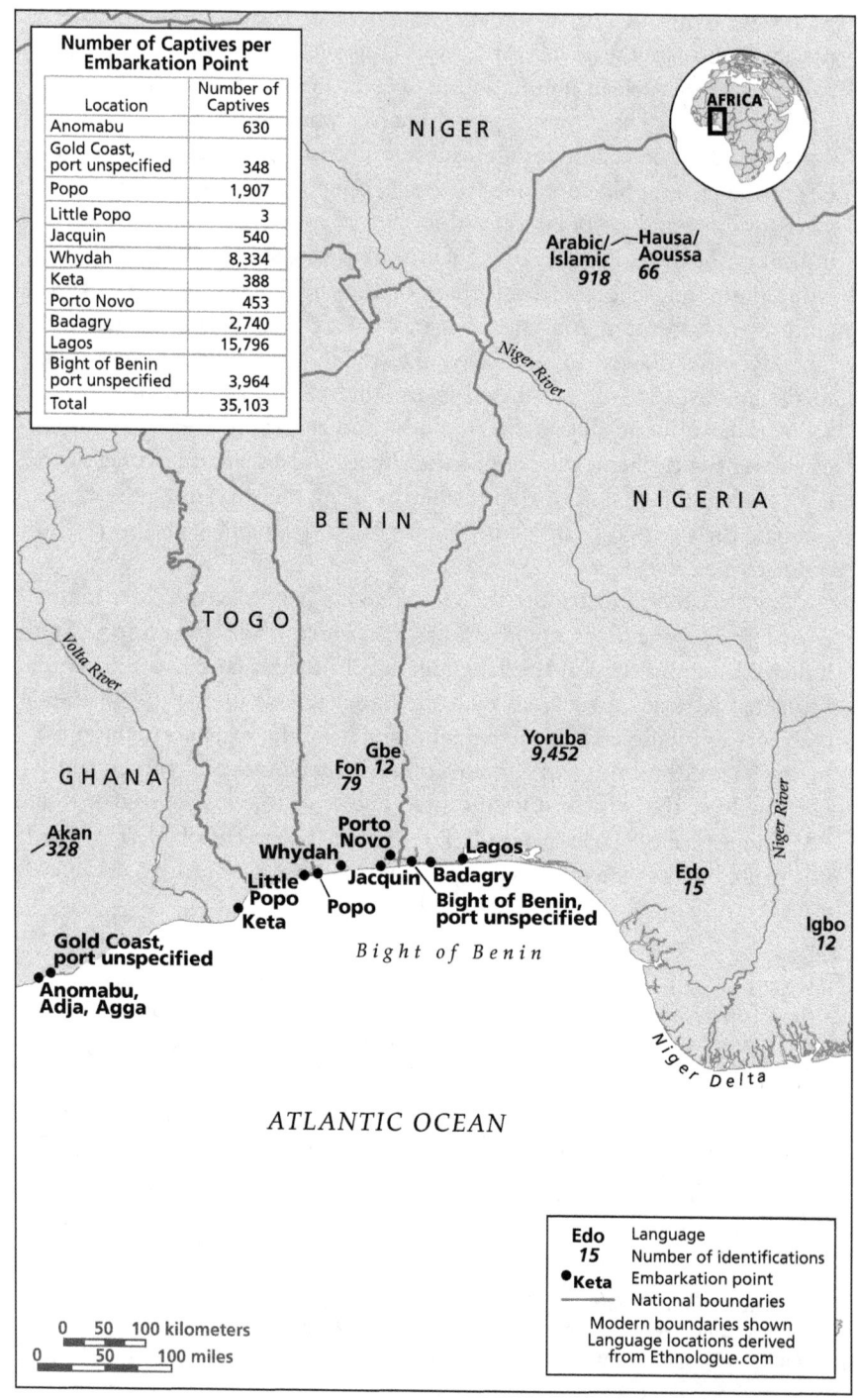

MAP 7.2 Locations of languages of Liberated Africans leaving the Bight of Benin and the Gold Coast, 1810–1848. Source: Data from the African-Origins database. For selection see www.slavevoyages.org/enslaved/IxIfqroC.

Freedom?

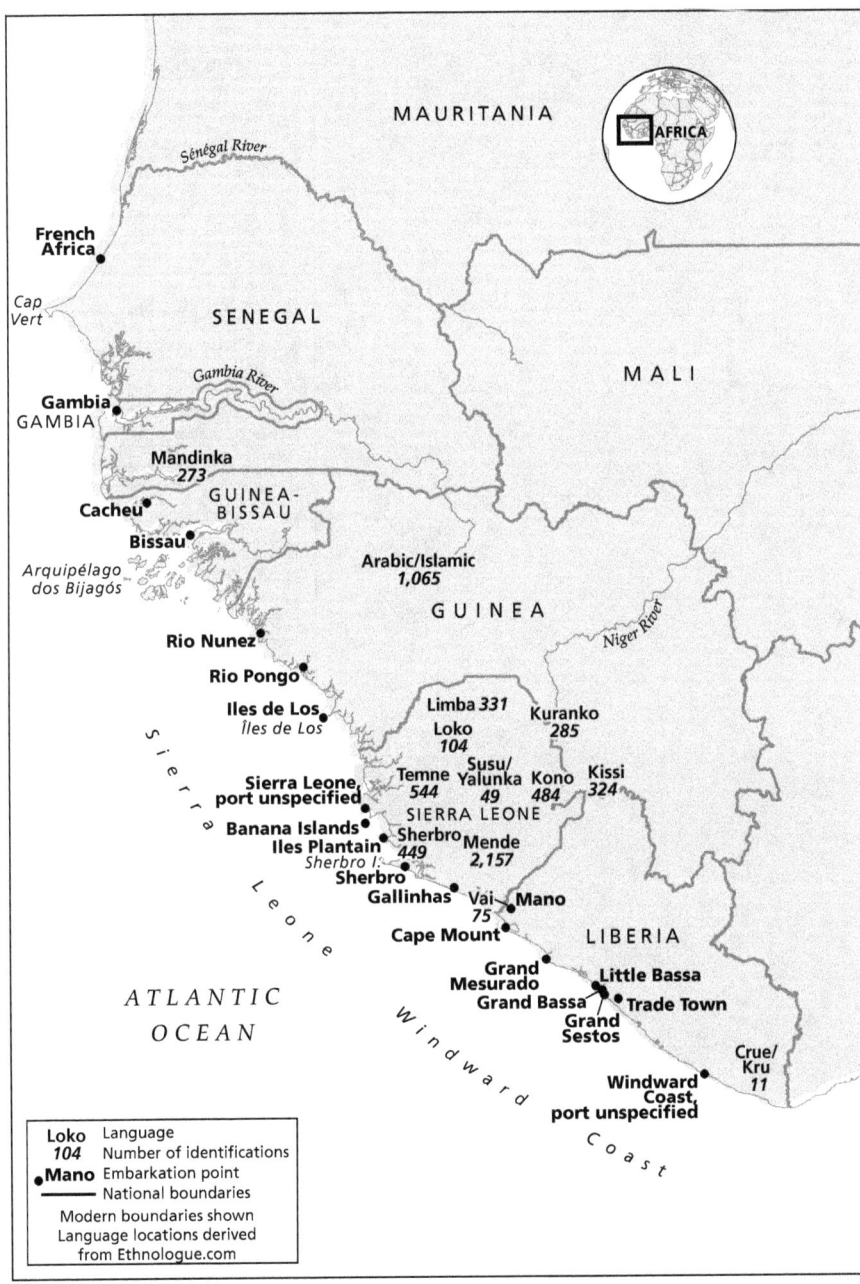

MAP 7.3 Locations of languages of Liberated Africans leaving Upper Guinea, 1808–1847. Source: Data from the African-Origins database. For selection see www.slavevoyages.org/enslaved/ybLOmhCN. https://www.slavevoyages.org/enslaved/69HG6ADC

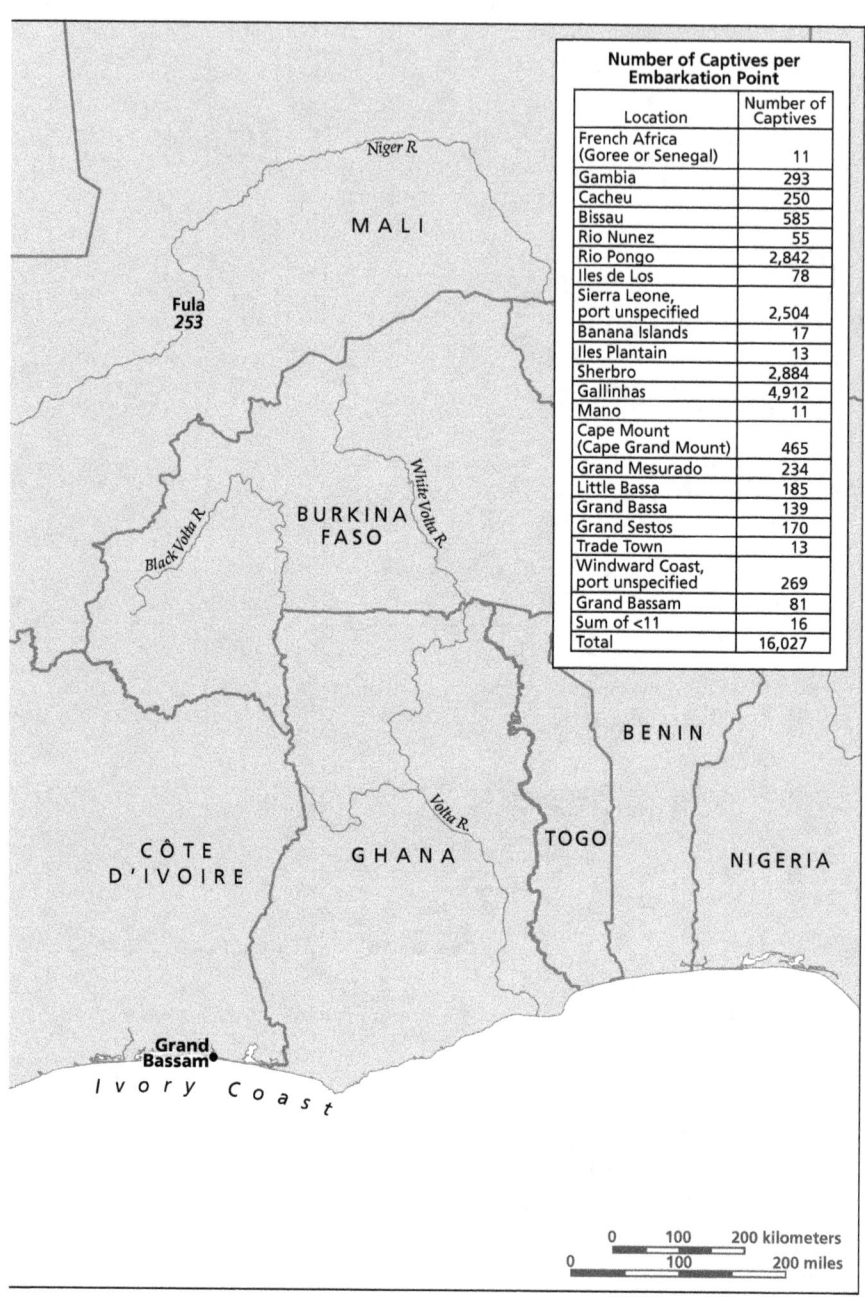

MAP 7.3 (cont.)

after 1807 comprised a representative sample of the total traffic from West Africa.[21] Further, the Bights of Benin and Biafra and most of Upper Guinea accounted for 95 percent of the West African Atlantic slave trade after 1807. By calculating a ratio for each language in the maps and applying this to the total number of people estimated to have embarked in each region in the given years from the slavevoyages.org estimates page we can derive numbers of departures for each language group. Thus, we can posit that 232,500 Igbo speakers left the northern Bight of Biafra (from the Rio Nun to the Cameroons), of whom 200,000 survived the voyage. We can also say something about where they went. In addition to 30,600 diverted to Freetown, the rest were scattered across the Americas with the largest number (69,600) disembarking in Cuba.[22] The Igbo language map shows that they accounted for about two-thirds of departures from the northern Bight of Biafra ports comprising Bimbia, Bonny, Calabar, New Calabar, the River Brass, and the Cameroons.[23] This is broadly consistent with data from 1821 to 1822 when the Sierra Leone Mixed Commission clerks briefly identified the "country of origin" of several hundred of the captives in the registers.[24]

The Efik, Ibibio, Moco, and other non-Igbo peoples leaving mainly from Calabar, and a second group leaving mainly from the Cameroons accounted collectively for a further 24 percent. Of course, the term "Igbo" covers a wide range of mutually intelligible dialects, but the relative linguistic homogeneity of the large exodus from western ports such as Bonny contrasts strongly with linguistic diversity of the regions to the east and to the west of Igboland. In the west multiple languages in the Niger Delta region today still makes the region something of a paradise for linguists. To the east diversity increases dramatically among those leaving from the Cross River and other points now in the Cameroun Republic. Captives arriving in Freetown from the northern Bight of Biafra had names that have been associated with no fewer than 107 unique languages. But seventy-seven of these were in the Cameroon Highlands and

---

and Andrew Pearson, *Distant Freedom: St. Helena and the Abolition of the Slave Trade, 1840–1872* (Liverpool, 2016), pp. 137–43.

[21] The 95,000 re-captives removed from slave vessels and barracoons made up 11.6 percent of all Africans that disembarked from slave vessels leaving West Africa between 1808 and 1848. See www.slavevoyages.org/past/database.

[22] Misevich et al., "Origins and Destinations of Captives."

[23] A total of 12,139 names of captives leaving these ports can so far be linked to a language, of which 8,294 are identified as Igbo.

[24] Northrup, *Trade without Rulers*, pp. 60–61; Anderson, *Abolition in Sierra Leone*, p. 48.

a further dozen among the just forty-four individuals that originated in the Niger Delta region.

The same procedure for the Gold Coast and Bight of Benin embarkation points reveals an even greater dominance of a single language group, this time for Yoruba speakers. The Gold Coast ports were largely closed in this period. Three-quarters of all captives left from just two ports in the Bight of Benin, Lagos, and Whydah. It appears that 261,500 enslaved Yoruba were carried off from the region, of whom 240,800 arrived, mostly in Brazil rather than Cuba. However, they formed the largest language group arriving at Freetown. It is not yet possible to break down the large Yoruba-speaking group into dialects. So far Yoruba-Ijebu were the most numerous, but sample sizes were too small to support generalization. This is particularly unfortunate because we know that unlike the Igbo, internecine warfare played a large role in the enslavement of the Yoruba. Thus, eighty-three of the 103 currently identified as Yoruba-Oyo left during the collapse of the Oyo empire between 1817 and 1835. Another sixty-three departed in the years 1832 to 1835 as the cataclysm of war faded with the abandonment of Old Oyo.[25]

Despite the Yoruba dominance, thirty-two other languages were spoken by enslaved people leaving the Bight of Benin. But the second largest group was not linguistic, but rather religious. Arabic and Islamic names are recorded in the registers for 8 percent of those embarking in the Bight of Benin. Of course, some with Islamic names were likely Yoruba as well as Islamic, suggesting that the Yoruba data may be upper bound and the Islamic ratio might be a lower-bound figure. Finally, as we might expect, the two most westerly embarkation sites, Keta and Little Popo, saw 328 Akan and a few Ewe embark, while in the east 137 Igbo and small numbers of Ijaw, Ijo, Urhobo and others from Delta region were carried away from the Rio Nun.

Map 7.3 presents the data on Upper Guinea, defined here as Senegambia, Sierra Leone, and the Windward Coast. It shows that almost four out of five of the region's captives passed through the Rio Pongo, Sherbro, and Galinhas, albeit places ranging over 300 miles of coastline. Nevertheless, captives also embarked from at least sixteen additional points along this stretch of coast, probably because mangrove swamps provided some cover from the attentions of naval vessels. The Mende

---

[25] See the literature reviewed in Anderson, *Abolition in Sierra Leone*, pp. 51–59; Misevich, *Abolition and the Transformation*, pp. 73–97; Misevich, "The Mende and Sherbro Diaspora," pp. 247–65.

language, famously spoken by the *Amistad* captives in their sojourn in the US in 1839–1841 was the most common of the twenty-four unique languages identified in the region. Mende accounted for one-third of the names with a unique linguistic link. This, too, is almost certainly a lower-bound estimate, given that Sherbro speakers share many names with their Mende neighbors. Grouping Mende and Sherbro together with Temne names, all from languages centered within 100 miles of the coast, accounts for half the sample of identified languages. The hundred or so names from outside the region, mainly Igbo, may point to individuals who fell into the hands of slave traders a second time after being resettled in one of the villages in the Freetown hinterland.[26] Like the Yoruba and Igbo, and indeed, those with Islamic names, more than half the Mende-speakers went to Cuba, which was easily the dominant destination for enslaved Africans in the nineteenth-century North Atlantic. The Mende diaspora was only one-third the size of its Yoruba and Igbo counterparts, but there must have been Mende-speaking groups on most Cuban plantations. Nevertheless, as Map 7.3 shows, after 1807 Upper Guinea comprised a smaller regional source of captives relative to the rest of West Africa. Probably 70,300 Mende left from twenty embarkation points. Some 62,500 surviving the voyage. Yet Mende-speakers made up only one-third of all Upper Guinea deportees. The impact of this group on nineteenth-century Sierra Leone was no doubt lessened by the many Liberated Africans who spoke local languages and absconded to their nearby homelands, among whom the Mende would have been well represented.[27]

The insets in each of three maps show the extraordinary dominance of just three African languages spoken by those pulled into the transoceanic traffic. Overall, 63 percent of all linguistically linked Liberated Africans spoke dialects of Igbo, Yoruba, or Mende. This proportion runs counter not only to the work of Koelle and others for the nineteenth century, but to the dominant narrative for the pre-1800 slave trade where historians have typically argued that captives of diverse backgrounds were bundled

---

[26] For examples of Liberated Africans that were re-enslaved, see Randy J. Sparks, *Africans in the Old South: Mapping Exceptional Lives Across the Atlantic World* (Cambridge, MA, 2016), pp. 134–56; Misevich, *Abolition and the Transformation*, pp. 86, 96, 153, 212–17, 253.

[27] The colonial authorities made intermittent attempts to track the fate of Liberated Africans, including those who absconded. For 209 of these runaways, a language identification is available. As we would expect, ninety-two or 44 percent spoke languages common to the areas within relatively easy reach of Freetown, even though only 20 percent of all identified Liberated Africans came from such areas (see slavevoyages.org).

together on slave decks without being able to speak to each other. Because the languages were so regionally specific, the great majority of vessels leaving from the Bights, especially, must have shared a language to the same extent as the Portuguese and Spanish crews that controlled the ship. Homogeneity in both language and culture among arrivals in the Americas was probably greater than at any other period of the slave trade except possibly for those expelled in the Kongo civil wars of the second half of the seventeenth century.[28]

There are some wider implications to be drawn from this pattern. Many scholars see the influence of the St. Domingue Rebellion and Haitian independence on the age of revolution in the Black Atlantic as seminal. Perhaps just as important to the struggle of Blacks for freedom was the appearance of this less dramatic pattern of a widespread shared cultural and linguistic background among the tens of thousands of new arrivals in Cuba and Bahia suggested by the maps above. As the Bahia uprising in 1835 demonstrated, resistance and revolution were always more likely in such an environment.[29] During the nineteenth century slave vessels leaving Africa contained people who shared a much greater cultural homogeneity than those in earlier centuries. Perhaps the armed resistance of people of African descent that characterized the nineteenth century was enabled and inspired not so much by Haiti as by a shared linguistic and cultural background among newly arriving Africans. One further broad point is that the analysis here would not be possible for free migrants travelling to the Americas in the first half of the nineteenth century. This is possibly the one area where the historical data is richer for Africans leaving the Old World than for Europeans.

For the Liberated African segments of these three diasporas (four if we were to include Islam) the quality of the subsequent lives depended heavily on where their slave vessel was first detained. As with modern commercial airliners, vessels were most at risk of calamity shortly after departure or shortly before arrival. Almost all captured slave vessels were intercepted near the beginning or the end of their voyage from Africa.

British detentions off Africa when the naval campaign was at its height in the late 1840s are shown in Map 186 of the Eltis-Richardson Atlas.[30]

---

[28] For the civil wars in seventeenth-century Angola, see John K. Thornton, *The Kingdom of Kongo: Civil War and Transition, 1641–1718* (Madison, WI, 1983), pp. 84–113.

[29] João José Reis, *Slave Rebellion in Brazil: The Muslim Uprising of 1835 in Bahia* (Baltimore, 1993), pp. 3–69.

[30] Eltis and Richardson, *Atlas*, pp. 284–85. Note that the British navy carried out just under 10 percent of its total captures in the two-year period 1847–1848, shown on the map.

On the western side of the ocean almost all detentions occurred in the Caribbean Sea or off major ports in South America. Capture locations are important because naval commanders would usually dispatch their prizes to the nearest "safe" port, one with a court that would condemn the vessel, to minimize loss of life and ensure Liberated African status.[31] They favored Sierra Leone or St. Helena in the east, and Havana, Rio de Janeiro, and the British Caribbean in the west. When the British began to detain slave vessels in 1808, slavery was present everywhere in the Americas south of the Mason-Dixon line. The single exception was Haiti. Abolitionist pressures, not least stemming from the success of the St. Domingue slave rebellion, meant that except possibly for Brazil, slaveholders would not easily accommodate the arrival of large numbers of free Blacks in their midst. There was no room in the hierarchy of most slave societies for such a group. From the Southern US states south to the Rio de la Plata, governments on the western Atlantic littoral, saw freed slaves as a threat. In the absence of court intervention, officials in Brazil, Cuba, and the Southern US imposed draconian "apprenticeship" terms on the newly arrived Africans that differed little from slavery. Governments also imposed apprenticeships on the eastern side of the Atlantic, especially where unoccupied land was available. But as in Sierra Leone, these were loosely administered societies, The restrictions were much less draconian and allowed for greater agency on the part of the re-captives.

In what follows we discuss the restrictions imposed on these Africans as they disembarked from their captured slave vessels. We try to locate such restraints on the nineteenth-century range of the terms of labor that linked full chattel slavery at one extreme with free labor at the other – what Clare Anderson has called a "continuum of labour exploitation."[32] But then what do we mean by "free labor"? The mid nineteenth-century North Atlantic provides an obvious model. Millions of free European migrants were beginning to flood across the North Atlantic just as the slave trade

---

[31] David Northrup has stressed the high mortality on board slave vessels after capture ("African Mortality in the Suppression of the Slave Trade: The Case of the Bight of Biafra," *Journal of Interdisciplinary History*, 9 (1978): 47–64). Updated estimates of shipboard mortality among the 136,866 Africans re-captives taken by the British to Freetown and St. Helena show 11.0 percent succumbed between capture and arrival. See https://www.slavevoyages.org/voyages/Ry9DMsoL.

[32] Clare Anderson, "After Emancipation: Empires and Imperial Formations," in Catherine Hall, Nick Draper, and Keith McClelland (eds.), *Emancipation and the Remaking of the British Imperial World* (Manchester, UK, 2014), pp. 113–27.

was approaching its zenith. Three million of them were Irish.[33] They, too, were crowded on to sailing ships, experienced shipboard mortality that reached a mean of 5 percent on vessels leaving Liverpool in the late 1840s, though averaged 1.0 to 1.5 percent on ships arriving in Quebec between 1833 and 1855.[34] Many of the survivors arrived in poor health, without contacts or immediate prospects. Their situation was unenviable. But even the destitute Irish landing in New York and Quebec City had rights, options, and most important, a level of volition, that were not available to Africans stepping off a captured slave ship. In stark contrast, very few of the 215,700 people in the African re-captive diaspora were allowed to leave their slave decks with futures free of encumbrances, especially "apprenticeships." And if they survived the apprenticeship obligations, most Liberated Africans chose to occupy smallholdings wherever land was available.

We begin our analysis of the African response to their new and imperially imposed status with a review of the reactions of re-captives to detention of their slave vessel. Africans on board could at least hope that detention of their vessel would improve their prospects compared to those whose voyage was not interrupted. Uprisings against the prize crew during the several weeks' journey to Freetown, St. Helena, or Simon's Bay were not unknown. On the *Ventura* (ID 4031), detained off Quicombo in Angola en route to Rio de Janeiro, the original Brazilian cook – who was very likely himself a recently freed person and who spoke the language of some of the captives – persuaded the shortly-to-be-liberated men to revolt. Five of the prize crew were wounded and five captives were killed. Their motive, according to the naval officer in charge, was "an ardent desire to return to their own country," a sentiment no doubt shared by almost all those found on detained vessels.[35]

Once before the court, however, captive people responded less predictably. The remarkable case of captives successfully questioning the court's jurisdiction is described in Chapter 5. But the most startling evidence derives from *L'Amélie* (ID 34281), a slave vessel captured in the

---

[33] Marjolein Hart, "Irish Return Migration in the Nineteenth Century," *Tijdschrift voor economisches en sociale geografrie*, 76 (1985): 223–31.
[34] Eltis, "Free and Coerced Transatlantic Migrations": 273.
[35] BNA, Commodore Fanshawe to the Admiralty, March 19, 1850, enc. Lt. H.B. Hodgkinson, Feb. 2, 1850, FO84/826. For the voyage to Sierra Leone after capture, including some firsthand accounts and a second revolt on the *Veloz* (ID 3068 – see www.slavevoyages.org/voyages/tvUt2hRg). Also, see Anderson, *Abolition in Sierra Leone*, pp. 66–95.

Freedom? 313

Caribbean and taken into Fort Royale, Martinique in 1822. The 214 survivors from Bonny were duly registered. Some of the disembarked refused or were too traumatized to speak at all, as was the case in all such tribunals.[36] The document nevertheless allows us to come as close as will ever be possible to hearing the voice of Africans almost immediately after leaving their slave ship.

An Igbo scholar working with a native French-speaker has listened to the pronunciation of their responses to the clerk's request for a name. He has found that some of the responses are not names at all, but rather segments of dialogue. These reflect the tensions between the colonial officials creating the record and the African subject, and perhaps more broadly in the Atlantic world context, between abolitionists and the people whose status the abolitionists were attempting to change. Thus, nearly 10 percent of the "names" taken down in Martinique in 1822 were not names but rather terms of anger, protest, and abuse. As translated by Chukwuma Azuonye, this segment of the mainly Igbo people on board responded with defiant challenges such as "whatever you write," "do not oppress me" and "leave my name alone." Then there were confrontational declarations like "abomination," or "what are you talking about." In Freetown, Africans sometimes responded with, "as you like" or the plea, "We beseech."[37] Another 300 refused to give any name at all. In the Martinique case there were common Igbo exclamatory metaphors of abuse such as "corpse" and "sheep," as well as one vow of self-consolation, "cry no more." Finally, in a startling two-century-old insight into the transatlantic slave system, which resonates today: one Igbo proclaimed, "undone by wealth."[38]

Tribunals adjudicating captured slave vessels almost never granted those on board full and immediate freedom as we understand it today – except of course to the crew who were never punished. There were always

---

[36] For the voyage, see https://slavevoyages.org/voyages/sws9W9vA. In the PAST database, see unique IDs 45326, 16192, 12258, 13881, 14937, 16192, 18066, 18774, 22264 for cases outside the French Atlantic where Africans are labelled as unable to speak, or "dumb."

[37] See www.slavevoyages.org/voyages/fPCgTh69.

[38] Chukwuma Azuonye, "Igbo Names in the Nominal Roll of *Amelié*, an Early 19th Century Slave Ship from Martinique: Reconstructions, Interpretations and Inferences," at https://scholarworks.umb.edu/cgi/viewcontent.cgi?article=1007&context=africana_faculty_pubs; for the voyage itself and the subsequent fate of this group, see Francoise Thésée, *Les Ibos de l'Amélie: Destinée d'une cargaison de traite clandestine à la Martinique, 1822–38* (Paris, 1986). Nevertheless, to complicate things further, in 1858 for some Africans already enslaved in their Vai homeland, the prospect of voluntarily moving to Martinique as an *engagé* for a ten-year term was an opportunity to escape a cruel African master. See Northrup, "Freedom and Indentured Labor," pp. 216–17.

compulsory terms of service attached to "Liberated African" status. These are discussed more fully below. Such "apprenticeships," as they were termed, provided further indications of the re-captives' relative agency. Initially, Liberated Africans were assigned to work or serve for a limited term or under a quasi-formal indenture. But most were eventually able to exercise some choice. Many exercised this choice before the expiry of the term. In Sierra Leone and Tortola, the colonial and imperial authorities initially attempted to keep track of apprentices. We know that many hundreds of re-captives absconded from their assigned masters.[39] As already suggested, most such runaways would have boarded their slave vessel in regions adjacent to Sierra Leone and were attempting to return home.

Runaways probably explain the absence of communities in the colony associated with local Susu and Temne peoples (although there was a Krutown) – unlike most villages that were majority Igbo and Yoruba. The remoteness of the latters' homelands helps to explain the dominance of the Yoruba and Igbo in Sierra Leone, especially the Yoruba. In addition, there is now a burgeoning field of study that explores the return of freed slaves to their point of origin, often after several decades. This literature focuses on the Iberian Americas, particularly Brazil and Cuba, but also on Sierra Leone where, by the 1830s, groups of Yoruba *were* able to contemplate returning to their homeland despite the risk of re-enslavement. Such individuals were clearly hoping to pick up the threads of their lives from which they had been summarily and violently torn. Yoruba people organized return ventures in both Brazil and Cuba, as well as Sierra Leone.[40] As late as 1904 Cilucängy (aka Ward Lee, African ID

---

[39] The registers do not systematically track the re-captives' activities after their assignment. Most of the later information comes from irregular colonial censuses and is incomplete. Some of this is available in PAST. For running away as a rejection of apprenticeship, see Michael J. Turner, "The Limits of Abolition: Government, Saints and the 'African Question', c. 1780–1820," *English Historical Review*, 112 (1997): 335–36, and for a closer and more recent analysis see Schwarz, "Impact of Liberated African 'Disposal'," in Anderson and Lovejoy (eds.), *Liberated Africans*, pp. 45–49.

[40] Olatunji Ojo, "Amazing Struggle: Dasalu, Global Yoruba Networks, and the Fight against Slavery, 1851–1856," *Atlantic Studies*, 12 (2015): 5–25; Mann, *Transatlantic Lives* (forthcoming); Kwesi Kwaa Prah, *Back to Africa: Afro-Brazilian Returnees and Their Communities* (Cape Town, 2009). They returned despite the dangers. In 1856, Consul Campbell reported the arrival at Whydah from Bahia of "40 self-emancipated Africans ... where they were first plundered of their property and on account their being Egbas, they were subsequently sent up to the King of Dahomey who put to death all the adults and retained the children as slaves." (BNA, Benjamin Campbell to the Earl of Clarendon, Jan. 21, 1856, FO84/1002.)

202544, Figure 7.10) then living in Trenton, South Carolina, and who had arrived on the *Wanderer* in 1858 (ID 4974) printed up and circulated a public appeal for funds that would enable his return to the Congo.[41]

The policy of suppressing the traffic was meant to create freedom from slavery. So it is appropriate to evaluate how close the different streams of Liberated Africans came to experiencing full control over their own lives. We should take Frederick Douglass' view of the effects of slavery as a starting point. After a rhetorically powerful indictment of the material impact of slave status on a man, Douglass zeroed in on the loss of freedom of action as by far the most important evil. Slavery, he argued, "leaves him to grope his way from time to eternity in the dark, under the arbitrary and despotic control of a frail, depraved and sinful fellow-man."[42] In its immediate effects therefore the Liberated African and apprenticeship statuses imposed on former slaves in so many jurisdictions as part of abolition appeared no different to slavery from Douglass' perspective. But there were nevertheless different levels of disabilities imposed. The discussion that follows here begins with the most restrictive outcomes, for example an enslaved person purchased by a Cuban sugar estate owner, through to the least restrictive: perhaps the options open to say a successful runaway.

As Table 7.1 shows, about one-third of the re-captive Africans were detained in coastal waters in the Americas, and most subsequently disembarked in the slave societies of the New World. Africans released from slave ships into Cuba and the early nineteenth-century US came closest to experiencing full chattel slavery. Their prospects were particularly bleak. Release from a slave ship meant little change in their circumstances.[43] Their subsequent lives were not much different from what they would have been if sold into the slave markets of the Americas. Indeed, many of the re-captive people in Cuba *were* auctioned off. Thus, several hundred slaves detained by the US coastguards off the Florida and Georgia coasts in the late 1810s quickly became part of the burgeoning US slave population. The single exception was the case of the *Phoebe* [ID 36992], detained

---

[41] It read in part "I beg every one who will please help me. I will be glad of whatever you will give me. I have been trying to make some arrangements to go ever since it was revealed to me to go. I am bound for my old home if God be with me" cited in Charles J. Montgomery, "Survivors from the Cargo of the Negro Slave Yacht *Wanderer*," *American Anthropologist*, 10 (1908): 621.
[42] Philip S. Foner and Yuval Taylor (eds.), *Frederick Douglass: Selected Speeches and Writings* (Chicago, IL, 1999), p. 166.
[43] Turnbull, *Cuba: Travels in the West*, pp. 161–65, 190.

in August 1800, shortly after the second US slave trade abolition act of that year, with 118 Africans on board.[44] The *Phoebe* was taken into Philadelphia by a naval officer, who happened to be an abolitionist. In accordance with the 1780 Pennsylvania Abolition of Slavery Act, all Africans on board would have been apprenticed to residents of the city. They were not re-enslaved, but the terms of their apprenticeship are unknown.[45]

The 27,538 re-captives landed in Cuba, after detention by either the British navy or the Cuban authorities, were assigned the promising title of *negros emancipados*. After British abolition of slavery took effect in 1834, 3,700 of them were dispatched from Cuba to British Caribbean colonies within months of disembarkation. There, they were subject to two- or three-year apprenticeships that, in accordance with the British Abolition of the Slave Trade Act, could not to be served on sugar estates. However, the unfortunate 24,000 who remained in Cuba found that their *emancipado* status was not only involuntary, but it was also subject to continuous renewal. Nor did it prevent the *emancipados* from being traded on the open market just like slaves. Thus, captives found on the first vessel brought before the Havana Court of Mixed Commission in 1824 were not freed in Douglass' sense until 1869. Until 1835 these *emancipados* were employed in the Havana region and worked largely as domestics. But after this date many were sold to sugar estates. The 1835 changes thus eliminated the last remaining practical difference between *emancipado* and slave status.[46]

---

[44] Paul Finkelman, "Regulating the African Slave Trade," *Civil War History*, 54 (2008): 398.

[45] See the cases of the *Tentativa*, *Politina*, and *Monserrate* in US, NARA, Southeast Region (Atlanta, GA): RG21, Box 23; and the General Ramirez, aka *Antelope*, in US, NARA, Southeast Region (Atlanta, GA): RG21, Box 28, "Mixed Cases, 1790–1860." Also US, NARA, US Southern District of Alabama, Mobile, Mixed Cases, 1820–1840, Box 10 for slaves imported from Cuba and West Florida in 1818. For the *Phoebe*, taken into Philadelphia, see www.slavevoyages.org/voyages/4GmhZBE6. See also John D. Fair, "Governor David B. Mitchell and the 'Black Birds' Slave Smuggling Scandal," *The Georgia Historical Quarterly*, 99 (2015): 253–89.

[46] Babatunde Sofela, *Emancipados: Slave Societies in Brazil and Cuba* (Trenton, NJ, 2011), pp. 199–259; Inés Roldán de Montaud, "En los borrosos confines de la libertad: el caso de los negros emancipados en Cuba, 1817–1870," *Revista de Indias*, 71 (2011): 159–92, which views *emancipados* as slaves; de Montaud, "The Misfortune of Liberated Africans in Colonial Cuba, 1824–76," in Anderson and Lovejoy (eds.), *Liberated Africans*, pp. 153–66; Anderson and Lovejoy, "Introduction," in *Liberated Africans*, pp. 9–10. The colonies were Trinidad (1,173), the Bahamas (1,098), British Honduras (484), Grenada (172), and Jamaica (146). In one respect *emancipados* who remained in Cuba as well as many in Brazil were worse off than slaves, given that they were not legally enslaved, and thus could not gain access to *coartacion* – the self-purchasing option

In Brazil, a similar scenario played out whereby fourteen-year apprenticeships that turned out to be renewable, eventually with no term limits whatsoever, despite Africans in this predicament frequently and unavailingly applying for "full freedom." Brazilian re-captives were typically sold to private individuals and public institutions in and around Rio de Janeiro. However, unlike in Cuba, very few worked in the main export sector – coffee in Brazil's case. They toiled, nonetheless, alongside enslaved people and their lives differed little from those of their workmates. Moreover, any children born to them had the same ambiguous status as their parents. In both Cuba and Brazil conditions for *emancipados* worsened over time. Cuban and Brazilian tribunals replaced the Mixed Commission Courts from the mid 1840s. Those adjudicated by the Mixed Commission Courts in the quarter-century after 1819 were more likely to be released from apprenticeship than anyone adjudicated later. The major difference between the Brazilian and Cuban administration of re-captives emerged in late 1853, when pressures from the British and the re-captives themselves resulted in a Brazilian decree allowing those who had served private hirers for fourteen years to petition for their "full freedom." But for the next ten years there were no guarantees of the success of such petitions. Not until 1864 did the Brazilian government grant unconditional emancipation to Liberated Africans.[47] Modest and hesitant as these measures were, it would be hard to imagine the Cuban slaveocracy instituting a similar policy. In summary, about 37,000 "Liberated" Africans (23,853 in Cuba, 10,833 in Brazil, and 2,500 in the US and Liberia), or about 15 percent of the overall total in Table 7.1, found that rescue from a slave ship gave them no more control over the balance of their lives than their compatriots had as enslaved people on plantations.

In addition to the US South, Cuba, and Brazil, a fourth region to receive re-captives who subsequently experienced severely encumbered terms of

---

available throughout the Iberian Americas. For Brazil, see Beatriz G Mamigonian, "Conflicts over the Meanings of Freedom: The 'Liberated Africans' Struggle for Emancipation in Brazil, 1840s–1860s," in Rosemary Brana-Shute and Randy J. Sparks (eds.), *Paths to Freedom: Manumission in the Atlantic World* (Columbia, SC, 2009), p. 238, and Castilho, "Abolition and its Aftermath in Brazil," *CWHS*, vol. 4: 486–509.

[47] Jennifer Nelson, "Apprentices of Freedom: Atlantic Histories of the *Africanos Livres* in Mid-Nineteenth Century Rio de Janeiro," *Itinerario*, 39 (2015): 349–69; Mamigonian, "Conflicts over the Meanings of Freedom," pp. 235–90; Mamigonian, *Africanos livres: A abolição do tráfico de escravos no Brasil* (São Paulo, 2017); Daryle Williams, *The Broken Paths of Freedom: A Spatial History of Free Africans in Nineteenth-Century Brazilian Slave Society* (forthcoming).

labor was South Africa's Cape Colony. A total of 5,598 Liberated Africans arrived there after 1807, 2,100 down to 1816 and the rest after 1838, with the second group including some transferred from St. Helena. On the Cape, we see the familiar pattern of renewable fourteen-year apprenticeships, sale on open markets, and work alongside the legally enslaved. This was the only Old-World site where a Cuban-style pattern emerged.[48]

Faring only slightly better than those falling under the authority of plantation regimes were the 1,437 re-captives removed from Brazilian slave vessels by Argentinian privateers during the Brazil–Argentine War, 1825–1828. Independence for the Rio de la Plata region had brought with it abolition of the slave trade and a free womb law of 1813, which freed newly born children, but also created a *liberto* status that ensured obligations to former masters that were not abolished until 1853. All this group disembarked at Carmen de Patagones, in the modern province of Buenos Aires at the northern edge of Patagonia. Some were conscripted into the army on the spot and remained in Patagonia, but most were transferred north to the city of Buenos Aires. All were required to serve as "apprentices" for ten years. Despite the slave trade having been abolished, the privateers were able to sell their prizes on an open market. Moreover, apprenticeship terms were extended in some cases to 1853. Survivors of this long-drawn-out process were eventually able to embrace a fuller version of freedom than was possible in, say, Cuba, very likely because neither sugar nor coffee did well in Argentina.[49]

Liberated Africans detained by the French navy between 1814 and the 1838, and US cruisers in the late 1850s were similarly discharged to plantations. They found themselves in the plantation colonies of French Guiana, Martinique, and Guadeloupe, some of them working on sugar estates – in Guadeloupe on the plantations Grand Marigot, Petit-Marigot, Basse-Terre, and Pointe-à-Pitre. When the Igbo on board the *L'Amelie* (ID 34281) arrived in Martinique in 1822, two abandoned sugar refineries, Rivière-Monsieur and Morne Vanier, came back into production.[50]

---

[48] Ryan, *Humanitarian Governance*, pp. 75–81; Christopher Saunders, "'Free Yet Slaves': Prize Negroes and the Cape Revisited," in Nigel Warden and Clifton Crais (eds.), *Breaking the Chains: Slavery and its Legacy in the 19th Century Cape Colony* (Johannesburg, 1994), pp. 99–115.

[49] Alex Borucki, *From Shipmates to Soldiers: Emerging Black Identities in the Rio de la Plata* (Albuquerque, NM, 2015), pp. 50, 136, 140 and personal communication from the author.

[50] Thésée, *Les Ibos de l'Amélie*, pp. 50–53.

A recent study tracks the fate of re-captives on two voyages taken into Guadeloupe in the mid 1820s showing the same pattern. The 207 on the *Jeune Adèle* (ID 2768) and another 100 on *L'Anémone* were first declared "released" before the decree was changed to require *un engagement de travail forcé* for seven years, which was then renewed upon expiry. Freedom for survivors was delayed until 1838. As the study's author succinctly states, "*ce group est dupé.*"[51]

The US began sustained efforts to capture slaving vessels later than other nations, but the outcome for Africans was no different. The detention of four large slave ships in the late 1850s, all bound for Cuba, resulted in the disembarkation of 1,541 re-captives in Florida's Key West. Within weeks and in accordance with the 1820 Slave Trade Piracy Act, the survivors were returned to Africa. For Americans, "Africa" meant Liberia, but here, too, after a second transatlantic passage with further mortality, many re-captives found themselves apprenticed for seven to fourteen years to Liberian settlers, most of whom were former US slaves. In Sharla Fett's words, "apprenticeships, agricultural and industrial labor, militia service, and Christian proselytization exposed re-captives to new forms of exploitation." In a great double irony, some of the "apprentices" were put to work on estates in the small Liberian sugar-growing sector, with formerly enslaved persons being among the probable owners.[52]

The next step down in the severity ranking of encumbrances that Liberated Africans faced is a group that scholars typically ignore in this context and are not to be found in Table 7.1. The Dutch recruits for the East Indies and the 65,000 *engagés* that the French sent to their tropical colonies endured years of hard labor after their supposed liberation as explained earlier. The parallels with slave trading are obvious, yet the eventual outcome for survivors was significantly less onerous than for those serving out time as *emancipados* in Cuba and Brazil. Perhaps because the Dutch and the French had become sensitive to international criticism that the *engagé* system sustained a slave trade within Africa, the

---

[51] Sandra Willendorf, *Affranchissements en Guadeloupe de 1826–1848: Le Rôle des Personnes Affranchies avant 1848 dans la société de la Guadeloupe* (Norderstedt, 2021), chapter 4.

[52] Karen Younger, "Liberia and the Last Slave Ships," *Civil War History*, 54 (2008): 424–42, especially p. 438; David Eltis "The U.S. Transatlantic Slave Trade, 1644–1867: An Assessment," *Civil War History*, 54 (2008): 347–78; Sharla M. Fett, *Recaptured Africans: Surviving Slave Ships, Detention, and Dislocation in the Final Years of the Slave Trade* (Chapel Hill, NC, 2017), pp. 156–85. Quote is p. 159. For references to work on sugar and coffee crops see, p. 171.

term limits of the service were respected in both jurisdictions. Significantly, 54 percent of Africans taken to Guadeloupe, Martinique, and Guyane elected to remain in their respective colonies at decision time, even though return voyages were available.[53] These additional degrees of freedom available to *engagés* clearly separated them off from their counterparts in Brazil and Cuba, and those arriving in Guadeloupe in the 1820s.

Liberated Africans arriving in the British Caribbean colonies might plausibly be assigned to the next category closer to freedom in our range of outcomes. Table 7.1 reveals that British possessions received more re-captives than any other jurisdiction in the Americas. But this is not surprising, since British sugar colonies experienced the greatest declines in output because of imperial antislavery policies. Liberated Africans arrived in three ways. Column 3 of the table shows a total of 23,700 disembarking because of shipwreck or capture and then adjudication in one of the islands' Vice-Admiralty Courts, mainly in the Bahamas, Jamaica, and Tortola.[54] To these should be added the secondary arrivals in column 4 who were sent to the British Caribbean after first disembarking in other jurisdictions. Finally, fifteen thousand came in from Sierra Leone and St. Helena, and a further influx of four thousand from Cuba and Brazil as those slave societies rid themselves of unwanted "free" Blacks after the Mixed Commission Courts there had assigned them Liberated African status. All told, 51,000 re-captives came into the British Americas from a wide variety of locations in the North and South Atlantic after 1807, when the slave trade with Africa was no longer an option. Most joined the labor forces of Trinidad, Grenada, British Guiana, and Jamaica after the original enslaved laborers had abandoned their sugar estates in the wake of British abolition of slavery.

Almost all the re-captives involved in these secondary movements from Sierra Leone, St. Helena, Brazil, and Cuba, shown in column 4 of Table 7.1 arrived after the premature termination of the apprenticeship

---

[53] Northrup, "Freedom and Indentured Labor," pp. 216–17.
[54] For details of the ninety-two voyages involved, see www.slavevoyages.org/voyages/7xC PZ3av. For the Liberated Africans involved, see Kelley, "Precedents" and Shantel George, "Diaspora Consciousness, Historical Memory, and Culture in Liberated African Villages in Grenada, 1850s–2014," in Anderson and Lovejoy (eds.), *Liberated Africans*, pp. 25–44, 384–408; for landings in Jamaica, BNA, CO137/188, ff. 352–57v, Earl of Mulgrave, April 30, 1833; in Grenada, BNA, CO101/81, ff. 213–30 and CO101/82, ff. 30–105; in the Bahamas and Trinidad, see Roseanne M. Adderley, *"New Negroes from Africa": Slave Trade Abolition and Free African Settlement in the Nineteenth-Century Caribbean* (Bloomington, IN, 2006), pp. 23–91.

phase of British abolition of slavery itself in 1838. The crucial question is what choice did they have in making this move? A definitive answer is not possible, but as with the choice of master in the assignment of apprenticeship, volition was no doubt a rarity.[55] Their situation was little different from the *engagés* that the French bought between 1853 and 1870, if not worse, given that no return passages were offered.[56] While they were sent to the British colonies experiencing the worst labor shortages, such as Guiana, Trinidad, Grenada, and Jamaica, their contracts were usually for one year, though sometimes up to three, much shorter than in the French and Dutch cases, although 5,475 were forcibly recruited into the British military for longer terms.[57] British policy toward the post-emancipation labor problems of its sugar colonies was usually aimed at increasing the colonial populations and thus putting downward pressure on wages, rather than overt coercion of individuals. On balance, those Liberated Africans sent to the British colonies were subjected to the second lightest post-emancipation set of labor encumbrances.

Was this apparently concerted movement of potential laborers to the British Caribbean an imperial government plot designed to offset the crippling effects of abolition of first the slave trade and then slavery in the British islands? To some extent, of course, it was. However, compared to the millions of enslaved people pouring into Brazil and Cuba, the Liberated African inflows into the British Caribbean after 1807 were numerically trivial and never came close to meeting the needs of British planters. The pre-1820 arrivals in Tortola and Trinidad did face fourteen-year apprenticeship terms and employers did attempt with limited success to renew these terms as expiry approached. But the stipulations in the 1807 abolition act and the March 1808 Order in Council that they should not work on sugar estates were largely respected. Most of the early arrivals began their new lives in colonies that lacked sugar plantations, such as Tortola and the Bahamas. They were able to form communities

---

[55] The best discussion of this is in Ryan, *Humanitarian Governance*, pp. 117–119.
[56] George, "Diaspora Consciousness," p. 386; Rosanne M. Adderley, "Interpreting Repatriation Projects among Free African Communities in the 19th-Century Caribbean," in Serge Mam Lam Fouck (ed.), *Regards sur l'histoire de la Caraibe, des Guyanes aux Grandes Antilles* (Guadeloupe. 2001), pp. 403–19; Ryan, *Humanitarian Governance*, pp. 92–99.
[57] Richard Anderson, "Diaspora of Sierra Leone's Liberated Africans, Enlistment, Forced Migration, and 'Liberation' at Freetown, 1808–1863," *African Economic History*, 41 (2013): 105; Kyle Prochnow, "Saving an Extraordinary Expense to the Nation": African Recruitment for the West India Regiments in the British Atlantic World," *Atlantic Studies*, 18 (2021): 149–71.

with obvious parallels to the villages in the Freetown hinterland. Given the severe labor shortages on the sugar estates, it is surprising not that so many Liberated Africans were dispatched across the Atlantic, but rather that the imperial government sent so few. In a counterfactual world, the British could have diverted all 125,000 Africans discharged from slave vessels at Sierra Leone and St. Helena to these colonies and subjected them to, say, a ten-year apprenticeship, thus emulating French policy toward *engagés*. Instead, they inaugurated what turned out to be a much larger and more expensive influx of more than a million indentured Asian laborers to Trinidad, Jamaica, Guiana, South Africa, and Mauritius that endured to 1918. Nevertheless, this inflow of indentured labor never allowed British planters to match the output of Cuban sugar plantations.[58]

Those emancipated in the Americas with the fewest restrictions were probably the more than 1,000 captives on four slave vessels disembarking in Haiti after shipwreck or capture by the Haitian navy between 1811 and 1820. But we cannot yet be certain given that we know nothing of their subsequent fates. It is entirely possible that they, too, found themselves apprenticed, but at least we can be reasonably certain that they would not have been employed on sugar estates as these had largely disappeared in the aftermath of independence in 1804.[59] Haiti apart, not only were the Liberated Africans who first disembarked in the Americas not immediately freed, but many thousands died before they were allowed to claim the "full freedom" that appears in so many of their petitions to the authorities, particularly in Brazil. "Full freedom" may have come most quickly in Haiti, or in the marginal British colonies that lacked a sugar sector, but the typical experience was a delay in reaching this status that was measured in decades rather than years.

In the Old World, for those who were not dispatched to another continent or to the Cape Colony, prospects were somewhat brighter. Table 7.1 shows that 60 percent of the Africans found on slave ships disembarked in just two centers, Sierra Leone, and St. Helena, with Freetown the main recipient. In Sierra Leone and St. Helena most of the Liberated Africans who were not summarily dispatched to the British sugar colonies settled in villages in the Freetown hinterland, and in

---

[58] Stanley L. Engerman, "Contract Labor, Sugar, and Technology in the Nineteenth Century," *Journal of Economic History*, 43 (1983): 635–59, especially 642–43; Lai, "Asian Contract and Free Migration," pp. 229–58.
[59] For voyage details, see www.slavevoyages.org/voyages/XQhNQ9GP.

a community that evolved in Rupert's Valley, St. Helena. The St. Helena government exacted *corvée* labor on the island for public works, comprising buildings and roads, or more accurately, trails. The British effectively evacuated most of the African occupants of this barren outpost between 1841 and 1867. Government-funded compulsory emigration to the British Caribbean and Cape Town occurred between 1841 and 1872, with terms limited to mostly one year and never more than three. The Rupert's Valley settlement survived this policy with 500 inhabitants in 1875, but they could not sustain a permanent community. As the island's economy declined, the re-captives voluntarily emigrated to Natal, the Cape, and Lagos. The side effect of these relocations was that no permanent Liberated African settlement took hold in St. Helena. The last surviving African re-captive died in 1929 and no African descent group exists today to take ownership of the recently excavated burial grounds.[60]

In the early days of African disembarkations in Sierra Leone the apprenticeships to which the colonial officials assigned the new arrivals reflected British expectations that they would learn skills that would prepare them for the labor market. The Freetown registers show that between 1808 and 1810, 519 mainly male Liberated Africans were assigned to masters with a wide range of occupations such as carpentry, fishing, masonry, and husbandry. But there were simply not enough skilled tradesmen in the small colonial economy to absorb the large number of arrivals. Within two years officials no longer even listed the occupation of the master. Children continued to be apprenticed or, in a rudimentary sense, educated, but for adults the "Disposal" column in the registers usually listed the armed forces or settlement in villages with the provision of rations for a limited term without specifying an occupation.[61] Peace in 1815 shut down army recruitment and left settlement in villages as the only long-run option. Similar patterns of village settlement occurred in the Bahamas with the encouragement of the colonial authorities at least after the early years. In Trinidad and Grenada, too,

---

[60] Pearson, *Distant Freedom*, pp. 201–90; Anderson, *Abolition in Sierra Leone*, pp. 96–126.
[61] Anderson, *Abolition in Sierra Leone*, pp. 101–105. For children, see Anderson, "Abolition's Adolescence: Apprenticeship as 'Liberation' in Sierra Leone, 1808–1848," *English Historical Review*, 137 (2022): 763–93. Christopher Fyfe has commented that "many apprenticed children in the colony remained drudges, virtually domestic slaves, to masters and mistresses who treated them harshly, even cruelly," in his *A History of Sierra Leone* (London, 1962), pp. 182–83; Maeve Ryan, "A Moral Millstone"?: British Humanitarian Governance and the Policy of Liberated African Apprenticeship, 1808–1848," *Slavery & Abolition*, 37 (2016): 399–422, DOI:10.1080/0144039X.2015.1130323.

villages rapidly emerged once the required one-to-three-year term of service was complete. The options for Liberated Africans in most British possessions were absconding, the choice of many in Sierra Leone, or self-sufficiency through smallholding and some casual labor.

A small minority who became merchants in Freetown or clerics in churches or missions prospered, though some might consider them to have been "Bridgeheads of Empire," a phrase John Darwin used to describe sub-imperial agents in the expansion of the British Empire.[62] Merchants buying and selling the trade goods auctioned off from captured slave ships were able to obtain property in Freetown. The 1853 assessment list of a new property tax reveals that well over half the wealthiest 194 owners were Liberated Africans.[63] Emmanuel Cline, a Hausa, and Igbo, James Godfrey Wilhelm, had the eighth and ninth largest assessments. James Will, with the Yoruba name Kealoo, was both a successful shopkeeper and a Wesleyan preacher who left behind his own memoir.[64] Examples of those who did very well are shown in Figure 7.4 and Figure 7.5, as well as the marble memorials in Freetown churches in Figure 7.6.[65] Missionaries were sent as far afield as the Cameroons with the most famous, Samuel Ajayi Crowther, shown in Figure 7.4, an 1874 photograph taken on one of his visits to London.[66] Equally well documented is Catherine Zimmerman Mulgrave, a Basel missionary, shown in Figure 7.5. Catherine was apprenticed out as a child to the Basel mission in Kingston after surviving a shipwreck and spent most of her adult life in Africa. The headstones, the expensively dressed principals, and the elegant furniture suggest a prosperity far beyond what their compatriots in the villages could have hoped for and, more important, has no parallel uncovered so far in the Liberated African communities that evolved in the Americas. This small group certainly came closest to meeting Douglass' idea of freedom.

No images of the Sierra Leone villages or of their inhabitants survive, but for St. Helena we have a photograph of five who arrived on the island

---

[62] Bronwen Everill, "Bridgeheads of Empire? Liberated African Missionaries in West Africa," *Journal of Imperial and Commonwealth History*, 40 (2012): 789–805; John Darwin, "Imperialism and the Victorians: The Dynamics of Territorial Expansion," *English Historical Review*, 112 (1997): 617.

[63] Christopher Fyfe, "Four Sierra Leone Recaptives," *Journal of African History*, 2 (1961): 81.

[64] Richard Anderson, "James Will, alias Kealoo: The Unpublished Narrative of a Liberated African Boy" in Stephen Rockel and Martin Klein (eds.), *The Life Histories of Enslaved Africans and Their Descendants in Africa* (Columbus, OH, 2025).

[65] For which, see Anderson, *Abolition in Sierra Leone*, pp. 274–75.

[66] David Killingray, "Beneath the Wilberforce Oak, 1873," *International Bulletin of Missionary Research*, 21 (1997): 111.

FIGURE 7.4 Catherine Zimmerman Mulgrave, seated third from the left. Photograph, 1873. Disembarked (shipwrecked) in 1833 from the *Heroina* (ID 41890) in Jamaica. Source: Reproduced with the permission of the Basel Mission Archives, QS-30.002.0237.02.

in 1850 on the *Aventureiro* (ID 4031) shown in Figure 7.7. They had embarked in Nova Redondo, a remote location lying between Luanda and Benguela. Traffickers tended to avoid what had been the major Portuguese slave-trading centers in the last years of the Brazilian slave trade.[67] These Africans remained on St. Helena after the forced relocation of their shipmates and were photographed fifty years later. In the absence of images of Sierra Leonian villagers, we might take the St. Helena residents as surrogates. To these we can add a range of photographs of survivors of the last two voyages to disembark slaves in the US, freed by Union forces in the Civil War. They disembarked from the *Wanderer* (ID 4974) in 1858 and the *Clotilda* (ID 36990) in 1860. While they did not have formal Liberated African status, they are included here because they faced the same challenges as other formerly enslaved Africans.[68]

---

[67] Roquinaldo Ferreira, "The Suppression of the Slave Trade and Slave Departures from Angola, 1830s–1860s." in Eltis and Richardson (eds.), *Extending the Frontiers*, pp. 321–25.

[68] The most comprehensive and accessible coverage of Africans on the *Clotilda* is Diouf, *Dreams of Africa*, but additional details can be found in Raquel Kennon, "In de Affica Soil": Slavery, Ethnography, and Recovery in Zora Neale Hurston's Barracoon: The Story

FIGURE 7.5 Samuel Ajayi Crowther (center) visiting the "Wilberforce Oak" (Keston, Kent) in 1873, along with leading members of the Church Missionary Society in Sierra Leone and Nigeria. Crowther probably disembarked at Freetown, Sierra Leone, from the *Esperanza Feliz* (ID 2919) in 1822. Unknown photographer, Wilberforce House, Hull City Museums and Art Galleries, UK/ © Wilberforce House Museum. Reproduced with permission of Bridgeman Images.

The gulf between Figure 7.4 through Figure 7.6 showing on the one hand, evidence of a bourgeois family and friends, and on the others, ranging from Figure 7.7 to Figure 7.13, needs no explication. It is what we would expect. More interesting are the differences between the former US slaves and the five in St. Helena. Several of the *Wanderer* survivors still lived on the South Carolina side of the Savannah River near Augusta,

---

of the "Last Black Cargo," *MELUS*, 46 (2021): 75–104; Hannah Durkin, "Zora Neale Hurston's visual and textual portrait of middle passage survivor Oluale Kossola/Cudjo Lewis," *Slavery & Abolition*, 38 (2017): 601–19, DOI: 10.1080/0144039X.2017.1279416; Durkin, "Uncovering the Hidden Lives of Last Clotilda Survivor Matilda McCrear and her Family," *Slavery & Abolition*, 41 (2020): 431–57, DOI: 10.1080/0144039X.2020.17418

33. Hannah Durkin claims the last surviving formerly enslaved African in the Americas died in 1940, but the Euro/US-centric focus of North American scholarship on slavery means that the many survivors of the Cuban slave trade who lived into the 1950s and beyond are ignored. See, for example, Esteban Montejo at https://g.co/kgs/JXhQBU.

Freedom? 327

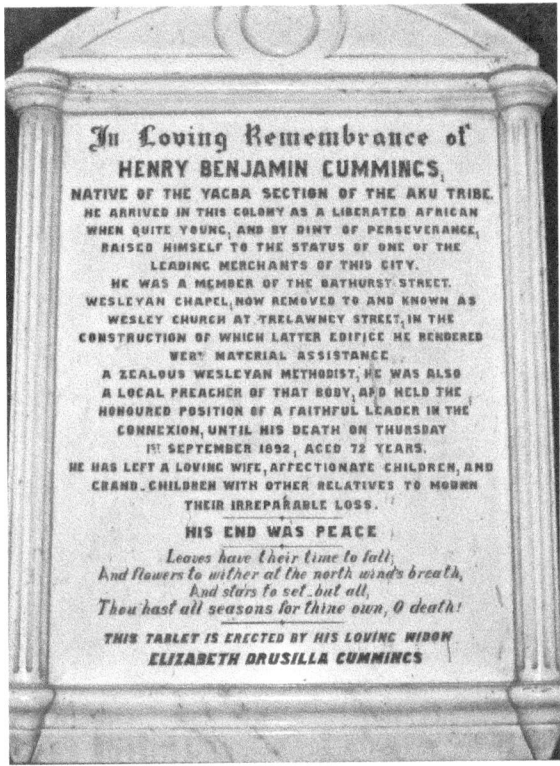

FIGURE 7.6 Headstones of a prominent Liberated African in Freetown, Sierra Leone. Reproduced with the permission of Richard Anderson.

Georgia, at the beginning of the twentieth century, where they had disembarked from the steamer that had transported them from the Atlantic coast in 1858. The Africans in the US wear Sunday-best suits and dresses, neckties, eyeglasses, a watch and chain, and furnishings in Kossola's (aka Cudjo) house that could not have been found in the average village hut and canvas-covered dwellings in Sierra Leone and St. Helena. Most freed in the US South were widely distributed, in the *Wanderer*'s case on plantations in Alabama, Florida, and Mississippi, and after the Civil War some still lived on the plantations of Senator Ben Tillman, one of the instigators of the new 1895 Alabama constitution that effectively disenfranchised Black voters. The fate of the *Clotilda* Africans is better known, thanks to Sylviane Diouf's careful work. Their purchase of land to build a house and grow produce followed on from their realization that returning to Africa was beyond their means. This group comprised not

SLAVERY.
(Africans still living on St. Helena who were captured by H.M. Cruisers and freed.)

FIGURE 7.7 Liberated Africans in St. Helena fifty years on from their arrival on the *Aventureiro* (ID 4031) in 1850: www.slavevoyages.org/voyages/LS5GY4QR. Image from Emma L. Jackson, *St. Helena: The Historic Island from Its Discovery to the Present Date* (New York, 1903), facing p. 264.

sharecroppers, but day workers at mills and shipyards in the Mobile area. The women sold produce grown on one- or two-acre lots.[69] Income from these activities was modest, but as the photographs suggest it would have

[69] Diouf, *Dreams of Africa*, pp. 126–81. The absence of shoes in some of the photos should not be taken as an indicator of poverty. On one occasion when Zora Neale Hurston asked if she could take his photograph, Kossalo (Cudjo Lewis) put on his best suit but

Freedom?

FIGURE 7.8 Survivors of the *Wanderer* (ID 4974) photographed in 1908: Kacāngy (Ward Lee), Pucka Geata (Tucker Henderson), and Tabro (Romeo). Arrived at Jekyll Island, Georgia, in 1858. Source: Charles J. Montgomery, "Survivors from the Cargo of the Negro Slave Yacht Wanderer," *American Anthropologist*, 10 (1908): 614.

FIGURE 7.9 A further survivor of the *Wanderer* (ID 4974) in 1908, disembarked at Jekyll Island, Georgia, in 1858: Manchuella (Katie Noble). Source: Charles J. Montgomery, "Survivors from the Cargo of the Negro Slave Yacht Wanderer," *American Anthropologist*, 10 (1908): 612, 614.

FIGURE 7.10 Survivor of the *Clotilde* (ID 36990): Oluale (Charlie Lewis) disembarked at Twelvemile Island, Alabama, in 1860; photographed in 1900. Source: The Erik Overbey Collection, University of South Alabama Archives, the Doy Leale McCall Rare Book and Manuscript Library. C-17165.

been greater than what was possible in either St. Helena or the infertile hinterland of Freetown.

Other evidence of the relative well-being of peoples in the Old and New Worlds supports this assessment. Anthropometric data on heights of recruits in the Revolutionary Wars have shown that those born in the Americas had a close to 2-inch advantage in terminal height over their European-born adversaries that can only be attributed to better nutrition. The recent upload of the Oceans of Kinfolk database drawing on the maritime shipment of enslaved people from the Old South to New Orleans in the nineteenth century, along with the expansion of the African-Origins database allows us to make similar comparisons of

removed his shoes because "I want to look lak I in Affica cause dat where I want to be" (Zora Neale Hurston, *Barracoon: The Story of the Last "Black Cargo"* [New York, 2018], p. 80).

Freedom? 331

FIGURE 7.11 Survivors of the *Clotilde* (ID 36990): Abache (Clara Turner) and Kossola (Cudjo Lewis) disembarked at Twelvemile Island, Alabama, in 1860; photographed in 1912. Source: Schomburg Center for Research in Black Culture, New York Public Library.

African American men with Old-World Africans. Selecting only those males aged 25–40 measured between 1838 and 1860 (to eliminate the African-born from the New World group) produces substantial samples of 4,906 Africans and 3,027 African Americans. African Americans turn out to have been 2.4 inches taller than their African counterparts.[70] Thus the Old-New World difference for Europeans observed as far back as the

---

[70] Africans = 64.96", sd = 3.04; African Americans = 67.33", sd = 2.97. Difference is significant at the .001 level; t-score = -33.996. For the anthropometric literature and findings consistent with the new data based on Africans in Trinidad, see Robert W. Fogel, Stanley L. Engerman, and James Trussell. "Exploring the Uses of Data on Height: The Analysis of Long-Term Trends in Nutrition, Labor Welfare, and Labor Productivity." *Social Science History* 6 (1982): 401–21,

Poleete.

FIGURE 7.12 Survivor of the *Clotilde* (ID 36990): Pollee Allen disembarked at Twelvemile Island, Alabama, in 1860; shown in c. 1912. Source: Emma Langdon Roche Historic Sketches of the South (New York, 1914) facing p. 72.

US Revolutionary War, also held for African-born and African-descent peoples separated by the Atlantic Ocean. Given the fact that both groups came from the same regions of Africa and that they shared the same gene pool, the difference is likely explained by a higher-protein diet and perhaps the pathogen-killing winter on the North American mainland. The ex-captives in Sierra Leone and St. Helena did not have to endure the horrifying violence of US slavery and the somewhat less systemic violence and disenfranchisements of the post-reconstruction era. But this cannot alter the fact that African Americans were more nutritionally secure and probably better off materially than their African counterparts.

especially 415–16. https://doi.org/10.2307/1170970; David Eltis, "Nutritional Trends in Africa and the Americas: Heights of Africans, 1819–1839," *Journal of Interdisciplinary History*, 12 (1982): 453–75; Eltis, "Welfare Trends Among the Yoruba at the Beginning of the Nineteenth Century: The Anthropometric Evidence," *Journal of Economic History*, 50 (1990): 521–40. For the importance of stature in human development, see most recently Manuel Llorca-Jaña, Damian Clarke, Roberto Araya-Valenzuela, Juan Navarrete-Montalvo, "Adult Female Height and the Gender Gap in Chile, 1860s–1990s," *Journal of Interdisciplinary History*, 53 (2022): 289–318. doi: https://doi.org/10.1162/jinh_a_01835.

FIGURE 7.13 Survivor of the *Clotilde* (ID 36990): Kossola (Cudjo Lewis) disembarked at Twelvemile Island, Alabama, in 1860; shown at home c. 1927. Source: Erik Overbey Collection, University of South Alabama Archives, the Doy Leale McCall Rare Book and Manuscript Library.

The striking, indeed, fascinating paradox to emerge from the foregoing is that the formerly enslaved facing the most long-run hardships in the form of systemic racism and denial of opportunities were those in the US South. Those with the fewest obstacles, given the disintegration of the apprenticeship system discussed below, were probably the inhabitants of the Sierra Leone villages. Yet materially, African Americans were clearly ahead.

Perhaps the more important point is that the anti-Black attitudes that enabled the onset of the transatlantic slave trade referred to in Chapter 1 and elaborated in my *Rise of African Slavery* book, continued into the nineteenth-century Atlantic and beyond. Emancipation did not change that. Even in the Caribbean, brown elites emerged over the largely Black non-elite. How, other than racism, can one explain that no ex-slave had the freedom of, say, the Irish immigrant fresh off the boat in New York or Quebec City, who were themselves hemmed in by the poverty common to immigrant communities?⁷¹ Though they became full citizens of the US, African Americans were denied the rights that could be routinely claimed by European immigrants. In Eric Foner's words, they had *Nothing but Freedom* and even that freedom was severely delayed.⁷² Racist officials and lack of capital prevented Black people taking significant advantage of the 1862 Homestead Act and its giveaway of 500 million acres of land between 1862 and 1904.⁷³ Nor could they move out of the South in significant numbers until the US land frontier had closed and European immigration was severely curtailed by World War I. Poor Whites in contrast could migrate to London, Quebec City, and New York, even in the teeth of anti-immigrant attitudes. Throughout the Americas, the huddled masses of Europeans were acceptable. The huddled masses of Africans shown in Figures 7.1 to 7.6 were certainly not. Migration to the more prosperous parts of the Atlantic world where slavery did not exist was an option for Irish and Jews, but not for Africans. Africans and African Americans were liable to expulsion from Brazil and massacre in Cuba, and in the US, subjected to systematic attempts to persuade them to move to Liberia. For this last group, the lack of equal opportunities could only have reinforced the desire of many to return to Africa.⁷⁴

Like their counterparts in the Americas, Liberated Africans in the Old World had to navigate a wide range of encumbering terms of labor before exercising the options of a fully free person. The stipulations of the 1807 Act and the accompanying Orders-in-Council may have in theory applied equally to British territories and vessels across the Atlantic world. Nevertheless, the average experience of a re-captive disembarking in the Old World was markedly closer to authentic liberation than the options open to their counterparts in the Americas. While the Civil War did bring full freedom briefly in the US, post Reconstruction, and the virulent racism thereafter largely demolished it. The four recently published foundational works on slavery and re-captives in Sierra Leone and St. Helena by Richard Anderson, Philip

---

[71] Tyler Anbinder, Cormac Ó Gráda, and Simone A. Wegge, "'The Best Country in the World': The Surprising Social Mobility of New York's Irish-Famine Immigrants." *Journal of Interdisciplinary History*, 53 (2022): 407–438. https://doi.org/10.1162/jinh_a_01869.

[72] Eric Foner, *Nothing but Freedom: Emancipation and its Legacy* (Baton Rouge, LA, 2007).

[73] Black ownership of land in the US has continued to decline in the last century, during which Black farmers have lost 14 million acres of agricultural land. See Eternal Polk's 2023 film *Gaining Ground: The Fight for Black Land*. (Director Eternal Polk, John Deere and Al Roker Entertainment (2023).

[74] African returnees from the Americas lived mostly in Latin America. Little data on this return movement exist. Emigration to Liberia from the US totaled c. 20,000, but much of this was subsidized, unlike the movement to other parts of Africa from Brazil and Cuba.

Misevich, Maeve Ryan, and Andrew Pearson contain extensive discussions on the volition of Liberated Africans and, though written quite independently they come to remarkably similar conclusions, with which this author is in broad agreement. The kind of volition enjoyed by the Irish immigrant, however constrained, scarcely existed for Black people.[75]

To the British naval officers who took possession of crowded slave ships, the people below deck were effectively like children – wards of the state, the capture of whom would nevertheless earn the crew a bounty. Indeed, to a greater extent than at any point in the slave trade the occupants of a transatlantic slave deck *were* children, given that after 1807 42 percent of re-captives *were* under the age of 17.[76] The analogy here is with the barges full of destitute and abandoned children that London Poor Law commissioners and magistrates dispatched to the Lancashire cotton mills in the late eighteenth century, or the Dr. Barnardo's children that as late as the 1970s were deported from Britain to Australia or Canada in numbers comparable to African re-captives, and with a similar absence of consultation.[77] We can assume that no representative of the British state asked any of these groups to which port, colony, or to which mill they would like to be sent, much less whether they wanted to be sent anywhere. Certainly, when African re-captives stepped off their vessel, none of them were consulted about what should happen next.[78] An estimated 25,000 of those passing through the Liberated African yard in Freetown were females over 14 years of age. Colonial officials resorted to arranged marriages to reduce expenses. For a fee Sierra Leonians could effectively buy a spouse.[79]

---

[75] Pearson, *Distant Freedom*, 201–11; Anderson, *Abolition in Sierra Leone*, pp. 96–105; Misevich, "'Freetown and 'freedom'? Colonialism and Slavery in Sierra Leone, 1790s to 1861," in Paul E. Lovejoy and Suzanne Schwarz (eds.), *Slavery, Abolition and the Transition to Colonialism in Sierra Leone* (Trenton, NJ, 2015), pp. 189–216.

[76] www.slavevoyages.org/enslaved/FpW2MOBs. For a discussion of Liberated African children, see Anderson, "Abolition's Adolescence."

[77] For a full assessment, see Ellen Boucher, *Empire's Children: Child Emigration, Welfare and the Decline of the British World, 1869–1967* (Cambridge, 2014).

[78] For the best discussions of volition in the context of the liberated African yards at Freetown and Lemon Valley, see Adderley, *New Negroes from Africa*, pp. 81–83, Anderson, *Abolition in Sierra Leone*, pp. 82–88; Pearson, *Distant Freedom*, pp. 224–30; and Maeve Ryan, "'It Was Necessary to Do Something with Those Women': Colonial Governance and the 'Disposal' of Women and Girls in Early Nineteenth-Century Sierra Leone," *Gender & History* (2021): 1–20.

[79] In a different contemporary context, but equally without volition there were the thousands of impoverished Italian boys purchased by the Vatican and other churches over the era of the slave trade and castrated for potential service as castrati in the choir of the Sistine Chapel. Many of the operations did not produce the required voice [Patrick Barbier, *The World of the Castrati: The History of an Extraordinary Operatic Phenomenon* (London, 1996)].

To fully understand the plight of Liberated Africans we need to reckon with what freedom meant in the early nineteenth-century Atlantic world and to consider the aspirations of both British officialdom and the Africans that fell at least temporarily within officialdom's remit. We also need to recognize the difference between decisions made in London and how local circumstances determined how those decisions were implemented. The vast resources that the British, especially, and eventually other nations committed to suppressing the slave trade were comparable to what the British spent to free the slaves in their large empire in 1833. As already noted, famously the British paid out £20 million to slaveholders as compensation for the loss of their human property. They paid nothing at all to the slaves themselves despite the labor that had been forcibly extracted from both them and their ancestors.[80]

Of the two British policies, compensating former owners to free slaves and "freeing" people from slave ships, there can be no doubt which was most successful, even though both were detestable from the standpoint of modern values. Abolition of slavery was much the easier policy to implement because it did not require any international agreements. But what most modern commentary on the subject ignores is that property rights were central to the British economy. Without legislation that respected property rights – in other words paying the slave owners – abolition could not have become law when it did.[81] In the US case slaves were freed after a war that cost an estimated $12.74 billion in 1860 dollars plus three-quarters of a million deaths.[82] If, instead of war, the US had fully compensated slave owners, costs would not have exceeded $4 billion in 1861, assuming 4 million slaves valued at $1,000 each. Thus, the costs of "buying" the freedom of nearly 4 million people in 1861 would have been far less than the costs of the Civil War to both sides. While there was no serious question of war between Caribbean slave owners and the British state in 1833, the British House of Lords would not have passed the abolition bill without compensating the slave owners and thus

---

[80] Stanley L. Engerman and Robert W. Fogel, "Philanthropy at Bargain Prices: Notes on the Economics of Gradual Emancipation," *Journal of Legal Studies*, 3 (1974): 377–401; Beauvois, *Between Blood and Gold*, pp. 158–253.

[81] Beauvois, *Between Blood and Gold*, pp. 20, 52–8.

[82] Claudia D. Goldin and Frank D. Lewis, "The Economic Cost of the American Civil War: Estimates and Implications," *Journal of Economic History*, 35 (1975): 299–326; Goldin and Lewis, "The Post-Bellum Recovery of the South and the Cost of the Civil War: Comment," *Journal of Economic History*, 38 (1978): 487–92; death toll is from J. David Hacker, "A Census-Based Count of Civil War Dead," *Civil War History*, 57 (2011): 307–48.

respecting the cornerstone of capitalism. British slaves were required to work for their former owners as unpaid "apprentices" for six years, thereby paying for part of their freedom via unremunerated labor. This term was later reduced to four, and 667,000 enslaved persons in the British Empire (excluding India) became free in 1838.[83]

The long campaign to suppress the slave trade by comparison must be judged a failure. The British navy captured nearly sixteen hundred slave ships and the warships of other countries another 100, but after more than a half-century of naval patrols and blockades, slave ships in the single year of 1859 were still able to carry off 36,000 people from Africa. Worse, many thousands more were forcibly removed to Indian Ocean destinations in the four decades after the transatlantic traffic ended in 1867. Moreover, while the costs of the anti-slave trade campaign were nominally somewhat lower than the £20 million compensation to former slave owners, they were comparable. As already noted in Chapter 4, direct costs for the African squadron and payments to other countries in return for their cooperation amounted to £12.4 million.

But this figure does not include the thousands of lives lost. Liberated Africans drafted into the navy were among those killed in attempts to detain slave ships. Slave ship crews frequently resisted capture and both African captives and naval personnel were also victims in the resulting conflicts. Even after detention several instances occurred of captive slaver crews re-taking possession of their vessel and murdering the prize crews on the voyage to Sierra Leone or St. Helena. But the greatest source of mortality for both Africans and Europeans was undoubtedly disease. At one point in the 1840s the African squadron absorbed 15 percent of the navy's ships and 10 percent of its personnel. Overall, about 50,000 seamen served off Africa in the nineteenth century, far more than if the only object had been to protect the small British commodity trade with the sub-continent. About 5 percent of them died each year, given that mortality was greater than on any other naval station. Enslaved people obviously suffered most, but among those opposed to the slave trade they were not alone.[84] Also excluded from this and most other cost assessments are the

---

[83] For India, see Indrani Chaterjee, "British Abolitionism from the Vantage of Pre-colonial South Asian," *CWHS*, vol. 4: 441–65.

[84] Ryan, *Humanitarian Governance*, p. 231, argues that the diplomatic costs of British anti-slavery costs were negligible, but this ignores the large subsidies paid to Spain and Portugal. For Portuguese and Spanish slave traders killing complete prize crews of captured slave ships as they were conducted to adjudication, see Eltis, *Economic Growth*, pp. 90–94, and Emily L. Jackson, *St. Helena: the Historic Island from Its Discovery to the*

heavy subsidies that the colony of Sierra Leone received from the British government, especially in the first two decades of its existence.[85] Overall, suppressing the slave trade may well have been as costly as compensating British slave owners in 1833.

As with slavery itself, the traffic ended only when citizens in the receiving countries of the Americas decided it should: Brazil in 1851, the US at the outset of the Civil War, and Cuba (or at least metropolitan Spain) in 1867.[86] Overall, the captured slaving vessels and raided barracoons contained an estimated 215,700 Africans, or approximately one in twelve of those embarked on the African coast for the Americas between 1809 and 1866.[87] Even if all 215,700 had achieved freeperson status, and as we have seen most did not, the British anti-slave trade initiatives did not constitute an efficient way of spreading freedom, however defined, around the Atlantic world. The British could not suppress the Atlantic slave trade and historians have never recognized the full costs of their attempt to do so. Perhaps compensating British slave owners cost more than the largely unsuccessful attack on the slave trade, but possibly not after full allowance of lives lost.[88]

British anti-slavery policies, naval suppression, and abolition of slavery, together nominally freed 667,000 people on land and 215,700 on board slave ships and in barracoons. Two competing visions of what the nearly 900,000 people of African descent freed by these two British policies should be doing with their new lives were at play in the first half of the nineteenth century. Both visions, as we shall see, appear fundamentally flawed to modern readers. Further, both were internally inconsistent. Neither British officialdom, nor for the most part the newly freed, got what they wanted. However, both sides might have agreed that what *was*

Present Date (New York, 1905), pp. 264–65. For mortality data on the West Coast of Africa only, see Christopher Lloyd, *The Navy and the Slave Trade: The Suppression of the African Slave Trade in the Nineteenth Century* (London, 1949), pp. 288–89.

[85] Padraic X. Scanlan, "The Colonial Rebirth of British Anti-Slavery: The Liberated African Villages of Sierra Leone, 1815–1824," *American Historical Review*, 121 (2016): 1097–1100, https://doi.org/10.1093/ahr/121.4.1085

[86] Eltis, *Economic Growth*, pp. 223–40. For the 1859 volume of the transatlantic trade, see www.slavevoyages.org/voyages/mSqhILCz.

[87] https://slavevoyages.org/voyages/164P6wzZ.

[88] Of course, like rebellions on slave ships, the chief impact of the navy must be measured in terms of the increasing costs imposed on slave traders. All such increases would push up slave prices and reduce the numbers of enslaved crossing the Atlantic (see the discussion in Chapter 4). For an estimate of this effect see Behrendt et al., "Costs of Coercion." Allowing for these additional numbers, however, does not shift the assessment in this paragraph significantly.

achieved was worth something given that 90 percent of those granted qualified liberation were able to avoid spending the balance of their lives working without pay and under duress on coffee or sugar plantations in the Americas. Such a fate would have been the inevitable consequence of a nineteenth-century world with no abolitionist intervention.

The official British position was broadly aligned with British public opinion, but was conceived by a few senior permanent officials in the Colonial Office and their abolitionist associates, albeit under pressure from the enslaved in the British Americas.[89] Key figures were James Stephen the elder, his son, also James Stephen, and the latter's associate, Henry Taylor. The first was a Member of Parliament, a lawyer, and widely believed to be the author of the Slave Trade Abolition Act, while the other two were permanent officials of the Colonial Office.[90] On the other side lay the hopes and expectations of the formerly enslaved people who were directly affected by these policies. For the most part, their aspirations were expressed not via position papers and publications, but rather via their reactions to colonial policies as we have seen already in those absconding from apprenticeship obligations. Abolitionists expected the suppression of the slave trade to lead to improved treatment of the enslaved – as owners could no longer access Africa for replacement labor – and their eventual peaceful transition to free laborer status. In one important sense the failure of the abolition of the slave trade to achieve these aims precipitated the abolition of slavery itself. The British, as with all colonial powers, wished to see their colonies prosper, which for them meant at least maintaining colonial exports after abolition, and for this a labor force was essential. Most abolitionists, along with Enlightenment luminaries such as Adam Smith, believed free labor to be more productive than slavery. The nearly 900,000 formerly enslaved people impacted by the British, on the other hand, generally wished to avoid plantation labor, whatever the terms of labor. The only element common to both visions was that slavery, and the slave trade should disappear.

---

[89] See Chapter 6 for the impact of slave rebellions on British policy.
[90] See CO318/117 for the various position papers that preceded the 1833 abolition act, especially those by Henry Taylor and James Stephen. Their authority was made clear when Colonial Secretary, Lord Stanley, later "commented that he was the first Secretary of State who had refused to transfer Stephen's reports on Colonial Acts into dispatches to the Governors." Cited in Green, *British Slave Emancipation*, pp. 124, 129, as well as William L. Burn, *Emancipation and Apprenticeship in the British West Indies* (London, 1937), pp. 110–11.

There can be no doubt that the authors of the 1807 Slave Trade Abolition Bill had no idea that, along with subsequent international treaties, abolition would bring more than 200,000 Africans into the British orbit, at least temporarily. Section VII of the British Slave Trade Abolition Act required that re-captives either enlist in the armed forces or be bound "whether of full Age or not, as Apprentices, for any Term not exceeding Fourteen Years." Further, this arrangement should have "the same Force and Effect as if the party thereby bound voluntarily so enlisted or entered [the apprenticeship]." As its author made clear, the clause was intended to protect Africans; it nevertheless empowered the Government to establish 'Regulations for the future Disposal and Support of such Negroes as shall have been bound Apprentices ... after the term of their Apprenticeship shall have expired ... as may prevent such Negroes from becoming at any Time chargeable' to the public purse."[91] An Order in Council issued in March 1808 laid out the guidelines. Masters and mistresses should be "prudent and humane" and should impart "trades, handicrafts or employment" that would enable the apprentices "to gain their livelihood ... when their apprenticeship should expire."[92] Military recruitment was to have priority, however, perhaps because the Act was passed in the middle of the Napoleonic Wars. Females could not be employed in plantation agriculture. Above all, re-captives should in "no case be liable to be sold, disposed of, treated or dealt with as Slaves."

At a deeper level the motives behind Section VII were the same as those behind first, the British poor law; second, the truncated apprenticeship scheme that followed slavery in British territories; and third, various devices such as head taxes and restrictions on land use that were to evolve in the non-settler parts of all European empires in the nineteenth and

---

[91] *Statutes at Large,* 47th George III, Session 1, cap. XXXV. The probable author of this clause, James Stephen the elder, explained its provenance with heavy condescension: "The reason for it was [that] ... Africans or new negroes as they are called, neither being intelligent enough to protect their own freedom, nor able immediately to work for their own subsistence (unless perhaps in such hard manual labour as they are wholly unused to in Africa and will not without compulsion submit to in the degree exacted from them in our colonies) it was necessary in respect of them to give for their own sakes, the power of enlisting or apprenticing." (BNA, Stephen to the CO, July 11, 1811, ff. 140–53, CO23/58). In Sierra Leone an 1808 colonial act declared that apprenticeship would be legal only if the names of both the apprentice and his or her employer be entered into a register kept by the Governor. Moreover, the Governor had to be notified in writing of any changes by either party within 24 hours. See BNA, CO 267/24, f. 30, Sierra Leone Gazette, 20 Aug. 1808.

[92] Robert R. Kuczynski, *Demographic Survey of the British Colonial Empire*, 3 vols (London, 1948), vol. 1: 113.

twentieth centuries. Section VII of the Act was both a harbinger of and a direct link between domestic and overseas policies toward labor. The intention in all cases was to extract more labor service from people than they would have been prepared to offer voluntarily.

To understand this point, a brief digression on the evolution of free labor in this period is necessary. Much of literature on Liberated Africans has focused, appropriately enough, on the denial of freedoms after disembarkation. The first part of this chapter has shown that there is an abundance of evidence to support this approach.[93] But there is a broader context, rarely considered, that provides some new insights. Between the seventeenth century and the early nineteenth centuries British elite attitudes to free labor had undergone a revolution that was fully reflected in the economic literature of the time. In the preindustrial era mercantilist intellectuals assumed that low wages were essential to the growth of exports, and that any increase in wages would reduce the supply of labor as workers found they were able to cover their basic needs with fewer hours of work. This phenomenon, termed "satisficing," was famously illustrated half a century ago in Marshall Sahlins' essay on the San people of the Kalahari entitled the "The Original Affluent Society."[94] The San, said Sahlins, were able to meet their basic needs in a few hours of work each day: their affluence was enjoyed via relaxation, not consumption. Accordingly, for the British elite, poor houses, vagrancy laws (including the whipping of vagrants), parish apprenticeships for children, and even slavery on occasion were deemed necessary to extract labor from the poorest segments of English society.

In the eighteenth century, elite attitudes began to shift toward approval of a high-wage economy as a culture emerged in which, as wages increased, consumers substituted merchandise, some of which was tropical produce, for leisure.[95] Higher wages now elicited more labor, not less.

---

[93] Turner, "Limits of Abolition"; Samuel Coghe, "The Problem of Freedom in a mid-Nineteenth Century Atlantic Slave Society," *Slavery and Abolition*, 33 (2012): 479–500; Rupprecht, "When He Gets Among His Countrymen"; Beatrice G. Mamigonian, "In the Name of Freedom: Slave Trade Abolition, the Law and the Brazilian Branch of the African Emigration Scheme (Brazil–British West Indies, 1830s–1850s)," *Slavery & Abolition*, 30 (2009): 41–66; Suzanne Schwarz, 'Reconstructing the Life Histories of Liberated Africans: Sierra Leone in the Early Nineteenth Century', *History in Africa*, 39 (2012): 194–200.

[94] Marshall Sahlins, *Stone Age Economics* (New York, 1974), pp. 1–37.

[95] Jan de Vries, "Between Purchasing Power and the World of Goods: Understanding the Household Economy in Early Modern Europe," in John Brewer and Roy Porter (eds.), *Consumption and the World of Goods* (London, 1993), pp. 85–132 for the short version

Scarcely surprising, then, that British elites became convinced of the superiority of free over slave labor and that this helped enable abolition. Instead of slave owners and slaves, they now wanted employers and a contented though subservient laboring population that would supply the labor that the new economy needed. Consumption of consumer goods instead of leisure on the part of workers now made higher wages tolerable for the elite.

The experiences of former slaves in the nineteenth century Atlantic world need to be placed in this broader spectrum of relations between capital and labor. We must first recognize that from a global history perspective the concept of free labor was of recent origin and in the sense that we understand the term today, it was largely confined to parts of Western Europe. Within Africa, in particular, kinship ties defined an individual in economic as well as social terms, and to be free of such ties meant marginal status and increased risk of enslavement.[96] Thus newly disembarked re-captives in Freetown quickly formed communities and kin groups that attempted to recreate such ties, though not always around their own ethnolinguistic groups. The possessive individualism, to use Macpherson's terminology, that had evolved in parts of Western Europe was not part of the experience of the rest of the world.[97] In Africa and elsewhere to be a full member of society meant having strong kinship and other communal ties, in other words to belong and to a degree be dependent on others. For British observers like Arthur Young, Patrick Colqhoun, and their contemporaries on the other hand, freedom meant the absence of such ties, leaving the individual free to enter European-style labor markets and respond to wage signals. This was why Young could claim that the 95 percent of the world's population outside Europe and North America was unfree though, as this discussion suggests, that does not mean that he saw them all as enslaved.

The British state's position was captured by mercantilist Sir James Steuart's aphorism in 1767 that to increase national product people

---

and de Vries, *The Industrious Revolution: Consumer Behavior and the Household Economy, 1650 to the Present* (Cambridge, 2008), for the full exposition of this shift as a factor in the onset of industrialization. See Eltis, *Rise of African Slavery*, pp. 258–80, for the implications of this shift for slavery in the Atlantic world.

[96] Igor Kopytoff and Suzanne Miers, "African Slavery as an Institution in Marginality," in Suzanne Miers and Igor Kopytoff (eds.), *Slavery in Africa: Historical and Anthropological Perspectives* (Madison, WI, 1977), pp. 3–81.

[97] Crawford B. Macpherson, *The Political Theory of Possessive Individualism: Hobbes to Locke* (Oxford, 1962).

should "be slaves to others or slaves to want" with, in the latter case, an increase in consumption leading to a greater work effort and more hours offered in the labor market.[98] By the early nineteenth century being "slaves to others" was becoming increasingly unacceptable, which meant that the state had to fall back on other measures to ensure adequate "voluntary" labor. These included attempting to limit access to land in those colonies that had an open land frontier, including several slave colonies in the Americas. In summary, for those at the low end of society, elites wanted an environment where, in another epigram – this one by an abolitionist – "fear of want had replaced dread of the lash."[99]

At root this view was internally inconsistent in that while it diverted people from slavery, the freedom it offered was predicated on freed people behaving in ways most of them had little interest in adopting. It allowed people to avoid plantation labor, but it also systematically attempted to restrict their freedom to choose alternatives. In fact, British anti-slave trade policy was shot through with contradictions. In addition to restricting the freedom of Liberated Africans, it was inconsistent with the emerging international law of the seas. The British detained and convicted many slave vessels in violation of that law given that the Palmerston and Aberdeen Acts of the 1840s allowed British warships to detain slave vessels belonging to Portugal and Brazil on the high seas. Such actions would have been *casus belli* if the detained ships had belonged to the US or the French.[100]

Before addressing the inconsistencies of the Liberated African standpoint, it is worth asking whether the "modernization" of the British labor force (substituting the purchase and consumption of goods for leisure) was as complete as Arthur Young believed. The largest early mass movement for domestic reform in Britain was Chartism, the goal of which was working-class suffrage. But Chartism also embraced a Land Cooperative scheme to settle workers on small plots of land and reduce their dependence on waged labor. In the US the land frontier remained open until the 1890s, but until the Homestead Act of 1862 the terms on which free land

---

[98] James Steuart, *An Inquiry into the Principles of Political Economy*, 2 vols (Chicago, IL, 1966), vol. 1: 52. For a fuller analysis of these positions, see Stanley L. Engerman, "Introduction," and David Eltis, "Slavery and Freedom in the Early Modern World," both in Engerman (ed.), *Terms of Labor*, pp. 1–23, 24–49.

[99] Brougham, *Inquiry into the Colonial Policy*, vol. 1: 507–18; David Eltis, "Abolitionist Perceptions of Society after Slavery," in James Walvin (ed.), *Slavery and British Society, 1795–1846* (London, 1982), pp. 195–213.

[100] Eltis, *Economic Growth*, pp. 113–14.

was made available were very restrictive. Nevertheless, Eric Foner has argued that working-class support of the Republican Party was based in part on the expectation that Republicans would reduce these restrictions and make land more accessible. In effect members of the working class saw their waged work in the eastern US as a stepping stone to accessing this "free" western land.[101] The Jeffersonian vision of a nation of small farmers also comes to mind.

There are obvious parallels here with aspirations of the formerly enslaved, though historians have failed to make them. The well-known – and never widely implemented – forty acres and a mule policy that emerged from a meeting in January 1865 between Black ministers and the Union leaders General William Tecumseh Sherman and Secretary of War Edwin Stanton certainly reflected like-minded aspirations.[102] Like many formerly enslaved people, the survivors of the *Clotilda,* the last slaving vessel to disembark captives from Africa in the US, sought to buy small landholdings in Mobile when they were freed in 1865 five years and six months after their arrival. Kossola (aka Cudjoe Lewis), interviewed between 1927 and 1931, explained how his community felt in 1865. "We ain in de Affica soil no mo' we ain' gottee no lan." Consequently, he continued, "We workee hard and save, and eat molasse and bread and buy de land from de Meaher (their former part-owner, Timothy Meaher). Kossola himself received 1.5 acres. Almost a century earlier, a captive called Broteer Furro, better known as Venture Smith, purchased his first 26-acre parcel of land in Connecticut and owned a hundred acres at his death in 1805. After buying his freedom he became one of the most successful Africans in the ante-bellum US but in no sense could he be considered wealthy.[103]

---

[101] In Canada, this frontier remains open in that the acquisition of land for agricultural purposes is still possible in the Yukon (see https://yukon.ca/en/apply-agriculture-land). One assumes that the length of the growing season has inhibited takers, but global warming will surely re-open this frontier. For working class support for Republicans, see Eric Foner, *Free Soil, Free Labor, Free Men: The Ideology of the Republican Party before the Civil War* (New York, 1996), pp. 21–39.

[102] Henry Louis Gates, Jr, "The Truth Behind '40 acres and a Mule,'" *The Root,* Jan. 7, 2013; Eric Foner, *Reconstruction: America's Unfinished Revolution, 1863–1877* (New York, 1988), pp. 70–71.

[103] See the chapter entitled "Freedom" in Zora Neale Hurston, *Barracoon: The Story of the Last 'Black Cargo* (New York, 2018). For personal details, see Chandler B. Saint, George A. Krimsky, and James O. Horton, *Making Freedom: The Extraordinary Life of Venture Smith* (Fishers, IN, 2009). Also see Diouf, *Dreams of Africa;* For two other survivors of the *Clotilde,* see Hannah Durkin, "Finding Last Middle Passage Survivor Sally 'Redoshi' Smith on the Page and Screen," *Slavery & Abolition,* 40 (2019): 631–58, and Durkin,

A further example of the desire for land by the newly liberated is labor's large-scale abandonment of plantations in the British Caribbean when the forced apprenticeship period ended prematurely in 1838. Wherever possible former slaves opted to set up smallholdings on unoccupied land rather than work for wages on sugar estates. In Sierra Leone the economic base of the numerous villages established by Liberated Africans was also smallholding, with any modest surplus being sold in Freetown or the export market that lay beyond.[104] A similar drive for land in Europe generated poverty in rural Ireland, and a peasant economy in rural France that inhibited industrialization until late in the nineteenth century. Across many cultures and societies in the wider Atlantic world, workers saw possession of smallholdings as a bulwark against waged labor and a guarantee of a measure of independence. But of course former slaves always had far fewer options than the rising number of free-labor factory workers in North America and Western Europe. Nevertheless, an examination of the goals of the two groups does reveal some unexpected similarities.

Haiti was a smaller version of Ireland in the Americas, though crucially without the migration option. Its 1805 constitution may have banned slavery and racial discrimination, but it unfortunately provides the best-known example of autarkic tendencies among those pushing back against the drive to create a "contented though subservient laboring population" in the era of abolition. The Haitian elite attempted to revive the plantation economy in the early years of independence. In the aftermath of the revolution, sugar output nevertheless almost disappeared, and production of coffee, indigo, and other tropical exports plummeted. The refusal of France to engage with the new state until its former colony paid out crushing reparations to former slave owners of course greatly exacerbated the situation. Yet the pattern was set before the reparation payments began in 1826. In the absence of a bigger land frontier, average plot sizes in Haiti rapidly diminished as the population grew, and by any measure of human welfare, living standards steadily declined.

Over the same period Sierra Leone also fared badly. Two thousand formerly enslaved migrants arrived in Sierra Leone from Britain, Jamaica,

---

"Uncovering the Hidden Lives of Last *Clotilda* Survivor Matilda McCrear and Her Family," *Slavery & Abolition*, 41 (2020): 431–57. For Broteer, see Chandler B. Saint and George A. Krimsky, *Making Freedom: The Extraordinary Life of Venture Smith* (Middletown, CT, 2009).

[104] Misevich, *Abolition and the Transformation*, pp. 115–30.

and Nova Scotia between 1787 and 1800, followed by nearly 100,000 from other parts of Africa after 1807. Nearly all who stayed pursued the smallholding option, though in contrast to Haiti this first British African colony, established in 1807, began with significant imperial subsidies, rather than crippling reparation claims imposed by their former exploiters. Also relevant here is that the West African settlement began life with a much weaker natural resource base than Haiti. Nevertheless, in Sierra Leone, as in Haiti, population grew more rapidly than output. These patterns probably have something to do with modern income levels. In 2020, GDP per capita in current prices was $509 in Sierra Leone, and $1,272 in Haiti.[105]

Consistent with the argument earlier in this chapter, jurisdictions where the smallholding option was difficult to establish have done better in generating welfare gains for their populations over the years. By 1807 Antigua, Barbuda, and Barbados had no unoccupied land available for former slaves. While we must be careful about any backward projection from contemporary data, it cannot be completely irrelevant that modern per capita GDP averages $14,500 in these islands. Jamaica was the major British Caribbean case that combined significant unoccupied land that would support a peasant economy with only minor inflows of Asian labor to former slave plantations. That island's modern per capita GDP of $4,665 is closer to Haiti/Sierra Leone levels than to those of Antigua/Barbuda and Barbados.[106] In short, smallholding has not provided a path to development anywhere in the world. If in the 1865 US South the policy of forty acres and a mule had been implemented, it may have done wonders for Black people in terms of social justice, political power, and, just maybe, the racist attitudes they faced during Reconstruction and beyond, but it would not likely have provided a route to higher incomes.[107] The Jeffersonian ideal of a nation of small independent landowners was always likely to be a developmental dead end.

Was there a homesteading option for the British and the eastern US working classes? For the former, Australia, Canada, and the American West certainly provided opportunities to abandon or curtail their engagement with the wage economy. The 1862 Homestead Act allowed for 160

---

[105] All data in current prices from the IMF, conveniently available from the Knoema site, https://knoema.com/pjeqzh/gdp-per-capita-by-country-forecast-from-imf-2020-2024.

[106] Jamaica's National Income in the century after 1831–1832 has been estimated via a series of benchmark years. GDP declined by about one-quarter in the aftermath of the abolition of slavery, while population growth accelerated. See Eisner, *Jamaica*, pp. 25, 43.

[107] https://projectreconstructionus.com/items/show/12.

acres per individual (Black or White) under strict provisions on occupancy and improvement. In the bigger picture, even a limited and distant homesteading option has typically acted as a safety valve en route to increasing incomes. For developed countries, including the UK, US, and in the EU, agriculture has experienced dramatic productivity gains, but these advances have occurred behind complex systems of protective subsidies, quotas, and tariffs that have inflated the size of their agricultural sectors and raised farm incomes at the expense of non-farmers. Such barriers should not prevent us from recognizing that a universal underlying feature of sustained long-run economic development has been the movement of labor *out of* the agricultural sector.[108]

Hence the central tension in the aspirations of Liberated Africans. The contradiction was as striking as for the English Chartists' land-bank lottery, and those Irish immigrants that returned to Ireland to buy a cow or a piece of land.[109] Except for the Mende, Susu, Temne, and other Upper Guinea peoples, returning home was not possible in West Africa, at least initially. Vibrant communities sprang up in the Freetown hinterland, as well as Grenada, Trinidad, and the Bahamas in the Americas. In each location, individuals forged new ethnolinguistic identities. Nevertheless, the aspirations of ex-slaves were as internally inconsistent as were the Liberated African policies of Western, and especially British, governments. As the winners of the Chartist land lottery and the returning Irish immigrants discovered, smallholding allowed them to avoid the labor market, but it was not the road to prosperity.

Faced with the prospect of large numbers of former slaves of African descent, the question for the British state, however misguided, was whether ex-slaves would behave like contemporary British workers, or even the poorest elements of preindustrial society. Maeve Ryan has pointed out that none of the Wilberforce generation of abolitionists – the Clapham Sect luminaries, together with Henry Brougham, Stephen Lushington, and the Quakers who initiated the 1783 Anti-Slavery Committee – believed that "uncivilized" Africans could not be given the same rights as, say, the European poor.[110] Nevertheless, the position papers in BNA CO318/117 referred to earlier are strikingly free of the

---

[108] One implication of this discussion is that if former slaves had had access to farmlands in the US West, Canada, and Australia on the same terms as European migrants as well as opportunities in urban areas, White/Black income differentials might have disappeared.
[109] Hart, "Irish Return Migration," 229–30.
[110] Ryan, *Humanitarian Governance*, p. 41.

overt racist attitudes that were shortly to re-emerge in the mid-century scientific racism literature, the best-known public face of which were the noxious writings of Thomas Carlyle.[111] But the specter of the backward-bending supply curve for labor certainly hovers over the discussions in the Colonial Office of 1832–1833 as the British prepared to abolish slavery. While astonishing to modern eyes in its naivete and injustice, the Colonial Office and the domestic and international courts saw apprenticeship primarily as a way of making the former slave pay for at least part of his or her own freedom. But it was also conceived as a way of repairing the perceived damage that slavery had inflicted on the individual's work ethic and thus it somehow prepared the apprentice for wage earning. Most slave owners, of course, were more likely to see apprenticeship as a way of prolonging, or even reinstituting slavery.[112]

British policy toward Liberated Africans and emancipated laborers was a success only in that it prevented tens of thousands of Africans from working on plantations in the Americas. Its broader aim of shaping a quiescent wage-seeking labor force was a failure. Padraic Scanlan describes the "liberal empire" that emerged from emancipation as "built on the same greed that made the slave empire" that had preceded it.[113] But if greed was so dominant, why did the British spend an unnecessary £32 million on destroying slavery and the slave trade? Why did the British destroy their own plantation colonies and those of other nations – instead of absorbing them into their own empire as they had done throughout the previous century and a half? And why did David Brion Davis spend a lifetime of brilliant scholarship wrestling with such issues? Does singling out profit maximization even get us out of the starting gate of historiographical explanations? "Greed" alone would have meant the continuing involvement of all Atlantic powers in slavery and the slave trade in the nineteenth century, a much simpler and less expensive British foreign policy, booming tropical colonies in the British Empire, and in the US, of course, no Civil War.

On the side of the exploited, Africans and people of African descent were the only group with ready access to the smallholding option, even

---

[111] The popular manifestation of this prevailing attitude was Thomas Carlyle's essay "Occasional Discourse on the Negro Question," *Fraser's Magazine for Town and Country of London* in December 1849.

[112] As the Governor of the Bahamas put it "a strict enforcement of the condition of the Indentures [apprenticeships]with frequent inquiries to ensure it would in all probability bring about the giving up of the most of them." BNA, Major General Lewis Grant to the Colonial Office, Nov. 11, 1823, CO23/80.

[113] Scanlan, *Slave Empire*, p. 322.

though as we have seen Europeans also had an interest in avoiding wage labor. Unfortunately, the lands available to former slaves, whether Liberated Africans or those freed in the Americas as slavery came to an end, were not available in large enough units, nor were they of the best quality. Within the British sphere, Jamaica, the Bahamas, Trinidad, and Guiana saw the best land remain in the hands of Whites and free Coloreds.[114] Sierra Leone simply had poor natural resources.

The failure of British policy did not stop officials blaming the newly liberated. A stipendiary magistrate sent out from Britain to oversee the apprenticeship system between 1834 and 1838 in Grenada summed up the British standpoint toward its mid-century tropical Atlantic possessions. Africans, he said, sought to avoid the "control of authority and to work at their own pleasure." A few years later, with scientific racism on the rise the lieutenant-governor of Grenada wrote:

there is so great a disposition among those people to separate themselves from the rest of the community and to settle down on small patches of land from which they derive their maintenance. The tendency of such a mode of life is undoubtedly to barbarize its followers; and least of all are the liberated Africans in a condition to fend off the miserable consequences of living in this, it may be independent, but savage state.[115]

Outside the British possessions, Haiti came to face the then contemporary Irish problem of the diminishing size of landholdings. The freed population of the US South were forced to deal with the end of reconstruction, though as already noted forty acres and a mule was not likely to have led to prosperity. European labor was tried in the tropical empire – Cornish miners were sent to the Gold Coast, workers from villages on the English estates of aristocratic planters were persuaded to labor in Jamaica in the 1840s, Canary Islanders were shipped to Cuba in the post-abolition years. But in the British sphere, at least, it was only indentured Asian labor that prevented the complete collapse of the plantation sector in the face of Cuban and Brazilian competition. In the early twentieth century, in another great irony, the poverty of autarky and the diminishing size of smallholdings drove Haitians to return to work on sugar, and eventually coffee plantations, a century after their

---

[114] For the Bahamas, see Adderley, *New Negroes from Africa*, especially the references to villages on p. 33; Isaac Dookhan, *A History of the British Virgin Islands, 1672 to 1970* (Epping, UK, 1975), pp. 97–119. Grenada quote is in George, "Diaspora Consciousness," p. 388.
[115] George, "Diaspora Consciousness," pp. 384–408, quote is on p. 390.

predecessors had liberated themselves from the hell of St. Domingue's cane fields. The workers were seasonal and this time the plantations were Cuban, not French.[116]

CONCLUSION

As the above quotes of officialdom indicate, identifying the differing and internally inconsistent worldviews of both the European state and the masses of Black, White, and Asian migrants on the move in the post-1800 world, will only get us so far in understanding the outcome of suppressing slave trading and slavery. The missing element is racism. To return to Figure 1.1, a sense of difference from others seems as innate to humanity as the need to reproduce and the pursuit of self-interest. The sense of difference from others shaped much of the premodern world discussed in the opening chapter of this book. Today, difference between insiders and outsiders in the form of bloodlines and religion are no longer the basis of citizenship in the developed world. Difference is no longer enshrined in laws and constitutions, except in the case of Israel, some Islamic states, and increasingly India. But in the nineteenth century constructions of racial difference and the discrimination based on these determined the fate of Liberated Africans and, for many, continue at the informal level to mold our social interactions in both developed and developing worlds.

No one got all they wanted from the freeing of enslaved people that perhaps constituted the major social revolution of the nineteenth century Atlantic world. Governments, plantocracies, and captains of industry faced wage rates higher than would have been the case if all potential workers had been able to move freely, without anti-Black prejudice. Cuba drew on slave labor until 1886, Brazil until 1888, and British plantation owners were unable to compete. The combined sugar output of Trinidad, and British Guiana, colonies now forced to draw on Asian contract workers, amounted to no more than 40 percent of Cuban output at mid-century. Jamaica's sugar exports did not recover to pre-abolition levels of output until the 1930s, and today buffeted by EU protective policy on sugar beets, it is once more in serious decline.

[116] See the cryptic comment in BNA, T70/7, f. 31v, a summary of letters from the Cape Coast Castle headquarters of the Royal African Company: "Advizes abt Miners who are almost all dead as well as the Pirates that were condemned to work in the Mines. Followed by "Success of the mines does not yet answer" (f.33); Matthew Casey, *Empire's Guestworkers: Haitian Migrants in Cuba during the Age of the US Occupation* (Cambridge, 2017), pp. 1–24.

In the US, the Immigration and Nationality Act of 1965 finally abolished most restrictions on the origins of immigrants. In the following half-century, the African-born component of the US population increased by 2.1 million, or five-times total arrivals in the 189-year-long era of the slave trade to the US. As already noted, the Irish and eventually poor Eastern European Jews were acceptable, but destitute Liberated Africans were not, and until 1920, nor were significant numbers of African Americans. The fifteen hundred occupants of the slave ships disembarked in Key West in 1860 were returned to Africa as quickly as possible. None of the other numerous and relatively prosperous countries offered to take in the people that the US rejected. On this score African immigrants were in the same situation as Haitians. Millions of Germans and Eastern Europe emigrants boarded ship in Bremen, headed for ports in the United States. Given that the distance from Sierra Leone to New York City was only slightly greater than from Bremen to New York, the influx of high-achieving African and Caribbean immigrants into the US that has occurred recently could have got underway long before 1965 if economics alone had been the only determinant of immigration policy. Euro-American conceptions of race that permitted this form of intensely discriminatory behavior toward migrants from Africa were present at the inception of Atlantic slavery. But four centuries later at a time when aliens arriving from a wide range of European countries were automatically and unthinkingly accorded free status, severe anti-Black attitudes clearly remained in place long after the abolition of slavery. Such attitudes reflect a near-universal pattern observed by Orlando Patterson when he pointed out that in very few slave societies in history has emancipation brought full freedom to the formerly enslaved people. In most instances, the former master continued to hold residual rights and the stigma of descent from slave status persisted for several generations. In this respect, societies in the Americas are no different to those in modern Africa.[117]

Opportunities open to black and white migrants after 1800 were not the same, and nor were those open to migrant Asian workers. Between the independence of Haiti in 1804 and the ending of slavery in Brazil in 1886 about 9 million people of African descent had to find some way of

---

[117] Patterson, Slavery and Social Death, pp. 240–61. Frederick Cooper, Thomas C. Holt, and Rebecca Scott, *Beyond Slavery: Explorations of Race, Labor, and Citizenship in Post-Emancipation Societies* (Cambridge, 2000) is the best survey of the disabilities experienced by the formerly enslaved in the Americas but makes no reference to Patterson's broader point about the ubiquity of residual rights of former owners and the stigma of descent.

supporting themselves independently of their former owners. Meanwhile, approximately 13 million Europeans and 0.5 million Asians arrived in the Americas after extensive transoceanic journeys. Labor markets in the Americas (plus some in African enclaves such as Sierra Leone and the Cape of Good Hope) could have been thereby inundated with millions of potential laborers at a time when most polities in the Atlantic world still had an open land frontier. Such a resource frontier offered the possibility of a landholding alternative to waged labor, but the reality was that the good land was open only to White people.

If land-labor ratios and transportation costs had constituted the only shaping influence over the decisions of these 22 million Black and White people on the move, then the Atlantic world would have looked very different in 1880 from the historical reality. A large segment of the 4 million freed slaves in the US would have taken advantage of the Homestead Act and moved west, instead of delaying their exodus from the South until World War I, by which time the land frontier in the US had been closed for two decades. Very few Liberated Africans would have chosen to relocate in the subtropical Americas, the Mascarene Islands, and Dutch Indonesia, much less Patagonia. The population of Sierra Leone would have been two or three times larger in 1880 if the 50,000 recaptives forced to leave for the Americas had remained in the colony and the disastrous satellite settlement in the Gambia, launched from Freetown, had never occurred.[118]

The reason these relatively benign patterns remained as mere counterfactuals leads us to the second shaping influence over the decisions of 9 million people of African descent: the failure of societies to accept Liberated Africans and other formerly enslaved as full citizens.[119] Initially for some it did seem that full freedom might happen. Reconstruction in the US moved former slaves closer to full membership of society than anywhere else in the Americas, but was soon superseded by the Jim Crow laws and two or three thousand lynchings, 95 percent of which killed Black people. In Cuba, likewise, the status of former slaves improved after abolition in 1886, and racial discrimination was barred in

---

[118] This estimate assumes that no forced military recruitment would have occurred, no forced movement from Sierra Leone to the sugar colonies and the Gambia, and that all those removed from St. Helena would have gone to Freetown instead of the Americas.

[119] Coghe, "Problem of Freedom," 492; Thomas C. Holt, *The Problem of Freedom: Race, Labor, and Politics in Jamaica and Britain, 1832–1938* (Baltimore, MD, 1992), pp. 56–57; Cooper et al, Beyond Slavery: Explorations of Race, pp. 21–22. Jeremy Ball, "Colonial Labor in Twentieth-Century Angola," *History Compass*, 3 (2005): 1–9.

the 1902 constitution, but several thousand Blacks were nevertheless massacred ten years later, an event that "damages forever the myth of Cuban racial equality."[120] The many thousands of *libertos* freed gradually in Portuguese Angola experienced first disenfranchisement and eventually the imposition of forced-labor systems later in the nineteenth century. Only Blacks in Brazil escaped direct violence. Such problematic transitioning from slavery to freedom was clearly not confined to the early nineteenth century.

The above discussion leaves us with a paradox. Full citizenship, at least in terms of voting rights and equal economic opportunity existed nowhere in the mid nineteenth-century Atlantic world. Nevertheless, the 13 million European emigrants enjoyed more legal protections and experienced far less overt discrimination than did the 9 million formerly enslaved people, or the 1 million or so Asian migrant workers. Not all the 24 million (13 million White migrants, 9 million former slaves, 2 million Asians) affected by uprooting or changes in status might have opted for forty acres and a mule if offered, but perhaps the majority had reservations about competing for wages in a labor market. The paradox is simply that, as the Irish and Haitian cases suggest, small landholdings or tenancies might have brought a measure of independence, but they could not bring enduring, much less increasing, prosperity. Imperial elites, for their part could not get the labor they needed without shutting down, or at least restricting access to alternatives to the free labor market – chief of which was land on which to settle.

Clearly, then, neither of the two visions of post-slavery society came to predominate. Exports in most of the sugar-producing colonies collapsed in the aftermath of abolition, and very few Africans released from slave ships or emancipated worked as contract laborers on sugar estates for more than three years. Most managed to avoid even that. It can be argued that the 900,000 people of African descent perhaps did more to shape the post-emancipation economic and social environment of the tropical colonies than did abolitionists and the British state. But freed people still faced considerable hardships and huge disruptions to their lives. They got little help from the colonial powers that had enforced their new status.

I have drawn here on Winthrop Jordan's idea of an "unthinking decision" on the part of the English to buy slaves in Africa and put them to

---

[120] Aline Helg, *Our Rightful Share: The Afro-Cuban Struggle for Equality, 1886–1912* (Chapel Hill, NC, 1995), pp. 193–226. Quote is on p. 226.

work in the Americas. If economics alone had shaped the search of European imperialists for labor at the outset of their respective conquests of the Americas, then the enslaved would have comprised European outcasts – condemned criminals, heretics, sexual deviants, and prisoners of civil and possibly international wars. The cost advantages of enslaving and dispatching this group over the expensive alternative of going to Africa are obvious. Instead, Europeans limited their coercion of other Europeans to indentured servitude. This, then, was far from a perfect labor market where wages reflected productivity and people responded to wage signals. Racism against those with Black skin informed the "unthinking decision" at the onset of transatlantic slavery. That same racism also shaped the policies of European imperialists and North American policymakers in the aftermath of the dismantling of Atlantic slavery nearly four centuries later. The erosion of such explicit discrimination gathered pace in the twentieth century. Since the 1965 Immigration and Nationality Act, the anti-Black manifestations that restricted opportunities for freedmen are no longer central to immigration policy. Voting rights appear to be surviving attempts to impose racially driven restrictions, and the minority component of the various societal elites is slowly growing. Nevertheless, racism is still manifest in the various indicators of well-being such as income, life-expectancy, prison populations, and educational opportunities. Major Black–White discrepancies in these vital social measurements live on and, given that we should all have access to the same opportunities share the genetic base of *Homo sapiens*, what other explanation can there be apart from racism?[121] Frederick Douglass' idea of freedom as expressed in 1845 implicitly assumed equality of opportunity. Even though, as argued in Chapter 1, we must all be descended from Black people, that has not yet happened.

---

[121] The position of Ta-Nehisi Coates, in *Between the World and Me* (New York, 2015).

Conclusion

The book is an attempt to rewrite Atlantic history by reassessing the story of the slave trade. As already noted, it is based on the digital humanities project www.slavevoyages.org, which at the time of writing is fourteen years old. If we include its CD-ROM predecessor published by Cambridge University Press in 1999, the data it provides have been in the public domain for a quarter-century. In that time many millions of visitors, whether scholars, students, the media, or interested members of the public have drawn on it in ways that its compilers and editors could never have imagined. Many more again have passed through exhibitions around the Atlantic world, including the permanent display of Washington, DC's National Museum of African American History and Culture, and the Nantes Memorial to the Abolition of Slavery that have incorporated its offerings. Few discussions of the slave trade fail to cite this resource. It is often described as a model of what the social sciences should be trying to achieve – presenting reliable, accessible, and renewable data to the interested public along with some basic interpretations. Consistent with this assessment, it has received financial support from a range of countries that almost matches the reach of the slave trade itself. In what many will see as appropriate, the only continent that has not contributed funding to its development is Africa. Public and private financial support over the years amounts to several million US dollars. Since 2018 the site has featured voyages that carried the enslaved from one part of the Americas to another. Perhaps most important, it has established separate databases on individuals who were on those voyages either as captives, or, who, like buyers and sellers of the enslaved, investors, and crew members, were responsible for the voyage itself. Moreover, it has now obtained funding to expand its coverage from destinations in the Americas to destinations in the Indian Ocean.

Yet as the preceding pages have shown, on so many major issues, general knowledge of the Atlantic slave trades is at odds with what the site's databases demonstrate. After a quarter-century of usage and as its core databases on voyages and the people involved in them continue to grow, there is not much sign of this situation changing. This book has highlighted tensions between what the data suggests, and what is received wisdom among scholars of Atlantic history. Perhaps the most striking is that the anti-quantitative turn in the study of Atlantic slavery noted in Chapter 1 has occurred even as users draw on the site in increasing numbers. Much of the site's traffic comes from users sampling the site to support their micro-historical studies or to note the scale of the slave trade in particular regions and time periods. While important, such usage often bypasses some major reinterpretations of the Atlantic slave trades that need to be explored.

Slavevoyages.org in fact, supports a radical revision of Atlantic history. In the current scholarship, the North Atlantic continues to appear as the center of both the transatlantic and intra-American slave trades. More precisely the North American and Northwest European role in the Black Atlantic gets by far the most scholarly attention. Yet perhaps the most important single new finding of slavevoyages is the central importance of the South Atlantic and that part of the North Atlantic trade that supplied the Spanish Americas. More transatlantic captives disembarked in South America than in the Caribbean. Within the Caribbean, Cuba, Puerto Rico, and the Spanish circum-Caribbean brought in more Africans than either Jamaica or St. Domingue. The availability since 2018 of the intra-American voyages database has further accentuated the Spanish, and beyond that, the Iberian role by providing evidence of the large flows of Africans from the British Americas to the Spanish Americas. This should surely undermine the long-held view that northwest Europeans, especially the British, were the most efficient practitioners and chief beneficiaries of Atlantic slavery. More fundamentally still, the new data displaces the old idea of the more capitalist-driven Northwest Europeans taking over a dominant role in the Atlantic from pre-capitalist Iberians at some point in the seventeenth century.

The slavevoyages data is also at odds with the current historiography in its foregrounding of the Americas rather than Europe as the organizational center of the traffic. The Americas were not only the source of a massive increase in demand for labor in the sixteenth-century Atlantic world, but the continent also had a major role in increasing supply. The reference here is not to the enslavement of Indigenous Americans – though that, too, occurred on a grand scale – but rather to the organization of transatlantic slave-trading voyages. The term "middle passage" to describe the slave trade no longer seems appropriate given that most voyages comprised just two legs, out and back, rather than three. And all this is without considering the central importance of the intra-American traffic in establishing where the displaced Africans were forced to spend the rest of their lives. Europe increasingly appears as an appendage to the system rather than its beating heart. Nevertheless, the idea that Europe was not the organizational center of the slave trade will likely be the last part of the traditional view of the slave trade to crumble in the face of slavevoyages' data.

The Portuguese were firstcomers in the Atlantic just as the Spanish were firstcomers in the Americas. They established connections with the regions of Africa that apparently could produce the most enslaved people (West Central Africa) and conceded little to the Northwest Europeans who joined the slave trade over a century later. British dominance in the slave trade was restricted to the period 1730–1800, and even then was intermittent and never pronounced – the Portuguese carrying off 1.49 million Africans as opposed to 1.73 million on British vessels. Apart from the brief Dutch incursions into Brazil and Angola, the Northwest Europeans did not displace the Portuguese system, but rather learned to live with it. The dominant Portuguese role emerged naturally from Portuguese preeminence in the late medieval and early modern Atlantic Ocean. They took sugar cultivation out of the Mediterranean world and into first, Madeira, the Canaries, São Tomé in the Gulf of Guinea, and then to Brazil. In each case they supplied enslaved African labor, as well as the technology to turn sugar cane into raw sugar. Their maritime expertise enabled them to become the major supplier of slave labor to Spanish America.

TSTD allows us to pinpoint some of the practices that permitted the Portuguese to maintain their dominant slave-trading position in the Atlantic world. First, as we have seen, Africans spent less time on board Portuguese slave ships than did captives on Northwest European vessels. Typically, Portuguese slavers leaving Guinea/Bissau, West Central Africa, and Mozambique filled their slave decks just prior to departure before sailing to ports in the Americas that were closest to Africa. Even in the highly competitive Bight of Benin environment, Portuguese vessels were often able to fill their slave decks quickly by exchanging Brazilian gold for complete shipments of people already on board British slave ships. In the major African supply centers of West Central and Southeast Africa, which together supplied half of all captives entering the Atlantic slave trade, the Portuguese had a land-based presence, albeit tenuous, and, except for regions north of the Congo, were able to exclude all European competitors.

Perhaps even more important, the core of the Portuguese slave supply system from the interior of Africa to the sugar plantations of Brazil and eventually gold from the far interior of Brazil hinged on a set of relations with Africans and Afro-Portuguese that none of their competitors could match. Luso slave traders did not have the financial intermediaries that underpinned the British and Dutch slave trades, and did not have partnerships that like the Gregson, Aspinall, and Boats families of Liverpool trans-shipped 50,000 Africans each to the Americas. But they did have large numbers of small investors, some of whom were crew members, including even enslaved crew members, and others who had formerly been enslaved. In other words, a crew member would be assigned a part-share in an enslaved individual instead of wages. Crew also frequently shared languages with captives. A shorter time spent on board and crew with a financial interest in the enslaved and/or able to converse with captives meant that violent resistance was much less common on Portuguese vessels than on the vessels of their competitors – this even though in the eighteenth century the number of captives per crew member was much greater on Portuguese than Dutch or French slavers. Not surprisingly, there is evidence of rebellion in the Portuguese onshore holding pens rather than on Portuguese ships. The key defensive work on a British, French, or Dutch slave ship was a barricado, a strong wooden barrier built amidships that sealed off enslaved men from the rest of the vessel. A documented example on a Portuguese vessel has yet to surface.

In the Americas, the Spanish position mirrored that of the Portuguese in Africa. Outside the North American mainland (and even there not until post-1800) the Spanish retained control of the richest parts of the Americas. The value of their commodity exports from the Americas, driven by silver mining but not bullion alone, exceeded that of all their European competitors combined until the late eighteenth century. Thereafter, Spanish America continually outproduced every other American empire down to 1800, and Cuban sugar supplied half the world market by the mid nineteenth century, surpassing in value even the output of the dominant Brazilian coffee sector. By this time, of course, cotton had permitted the US to assume the mantle of the leading plantation economy in the world. Captives entering the Spanish Americas with certain exceptions were not put to work in the silver mines, but the bullion produced by Indigenous labor did facilitate the purchase of enslaved Africans in a wide spectrum of occupations in lowland Spanish America, where the largest cities in the Americas were located. Moreover, when Spanish America was heavily dependent on the intra-American traffic to replenish its labor force, Spanish merchants had a major role in this traffic. And Spanish-flagged ships were far more prominent in this business than in the transatlantic trade. In sharp contrast to the transatlantic business, almost as many Africans arrived from other ports in the Americas under the Spanish flag as under the British.[1] It is unfortunate that the US, and the slave empires of the Northwestern Europeans still dominate the research into slavery and the slave trade in the Atlantic World.

All business activity depends on linking ultimate borrowers with ultimate lenders. The credit and insurance instruments that the Northwest Europeans developed across their respective economies, especially the British, eventually enabled them to compete with the Portuguese in long-distance trade without ever replacing them. The Portuguese had their own methods of financing and of manning slaving voyages. These methods survived the Northwestern intrusion. To put this point differently: It was economic growth that enabled British intervention in the Atlantic slave systems, rather than the slave systems that enabled British economic growth. The same was certainly true for the Dutch and the French, neither of whom showed any quickening of economic activity that can be linked to slavery and the slave trades in the Atlantic.

One of the most persistent myths in recent scholarship on the slave trade that can now be questioned is the belief in a clear causal link between slavery and the slave trade on the one hand and modern income disparities across the Atlantic world on the other. As Chapter 1 explains, slavery and slave trading were universal across the globe until very recently, at least in epochal terms.

In 1804, 45 million enslaved people lived on Earth, and all but a few million lived outside the Americas. Table C.1 shows that the African-descended share of the enslaved in the Americas comprised just 6.6 percent, or 3 million of the global total. The British held about 750,000 of these.[2] People holding slaves were far more numerous in the United States and

---

[1] See www.slavevoyages.org/voyages/IGBKuXkI. The evolution of the intra-American slave trade system to Spanish America is impressively described in García-Montón, *Genoese Entrepreneurship*. One of the few points that escapes the attention of the author is the large role of Spanish merchants in the business in contrast to the transatlantic slave trade.

[2] B. W. Higman, "Demographic Trends," in *CWHS* vol. 4: 23–4; Higman, *Slave Populations*, pp. 413–8.

TABLE C.1 *Enslaved populations of the African diaspora and Indian Ocean c. 1800*

	Year	Enslaved population
French		
St. Domingue	1793–1794	465,400
Guadeloupe	1790	90,139
Martinique	1789	81,130
French Guiana	1789	10,748
Bourbon/Ile de France	1788	55,154
Total		702,571
British		
Jamaica	1800	328,000
Other British Caribbean	1800	401,500
Total	1800	729,500
Brazil	1872	1,510,806
US	1800	1,002,000

Sources:
French: Christian Schnakenbourg, "Statistiques pour l'histoire de l'économie de plantation en Guadeloupe et Martinique (1635–1835)," *Bulletin de la Société d'Histoire de la Guadeloupe*, 31 (1977): 3–121. https://doi.org/10.7202/1044044ar; Alex Moreau de Jonnnes, *Recherches statistiques sur l'esclavage colonial et sur les moyens de le supprimer* (Paris, 1842), pp. 21, 27.
British: B. W. Higman, *Slave Population and Economy in Jamaica, 1807–1834* (Cambridge, 1976), p. 61; Higman, *Slave Population of the British Caribbean, 1807–1834* (Baltimore, 1984), p. 417, multiplied by 0.94 based on the difference between the Jamaican figures for 1800 and 1807.
Brazilian: Slenes, "Demography and Economics," p. 689. For the global population of slaves see B. W. Higman, "Demographic Trends," in *CWHS*, vol. 4: 23–24.

Brazil than in Britain, and absentee owners would have been as common in Portugal as in Britain. Until the St. Domingue Rebellion in 1791, in France, too, a similar pattern emerged. How very odd that such a small proportion of slaves and their owners that were British (1.7 percent of the enslaved global population, about the same proportion as the pre-1792 French, and somewhat lower than the US and Brazil ratios) should have triggered an Industrial Revolution. Why could not the larger proportions of global slaves that lived in Brazil or the Spanish Americas have triggered the first industrialization in Portugal and Spain, centuries earlier?

Adopting these larger perspectives makes it beyond credulity that slavery or the slave trade that supported it could have kick-started economic growth. It is far more likely that the key to such development lay in conditions within Britain, and eventually the Netherlands and the US, that enabled slaveholdings and other overseas activities to have had such an impact.[3] Enslaved people and their owners could not by themselves have been critically important to industrialization. As the experience of Germany, Italy, and other countries that industrialized without slavery, without Africa, and without the Americas, the evolution of the Dutch, British, and indeed all European economies could have been little different if slave colonies had never existed.

Studies of the role of the slave trade in Atlantic economic development must move beyond endless computations of how profits and trade goods in the slave trade, or any other business for that matter, enabled industrialization. Selecting any specific economic activity, for example whaling, the grain trade, the trade in hemp and iron bars from Russia, or almost any infrastructure project, including railroads – would similarly establish the indispensability of the activity to general economic growth – if subjected to an analysis that ignores the concept of value-added that is now so central to modern measurements of human welfare.[4]

In crude terms the sum of all the value added by all activity comprises the Gross Domestic Product. Unfortunately, the practical implications of this very simple concept are ignored by most historians and all journalists. Given the interests of most historians, this matters little. But for those writing about slavery, capitalism, and we could add, the slave trade, the consequences are frequently disastrous. One result is that the new historians of capitalism, the authors of the 1619 project, most scholars of the slave trade, and all the media, frequently distort the history of slavery by greatly exaggerating its economic importance.[5] At the very least, given the

---

[3] There are strong echoes here of the Maurice Dobbs–Paul Sweezy debates on industrialization beginning in the 1940s; for which, see Meenaxi Phukan, *Rise of The Modern West: Social and Economic History of Early Modern Europe* (New Delhi, 1998).

[4] For the view that the Russian trade enabled industrialization rather than the slave colonies or Africa, see Arcadius Kahan, "Eighteenth-Century Russian-British Trade: Russia's Contribution to the Industrial Revolution in Great Britain," in Anthony G. Cross (ed.), *Great Britain and Russia in the Eighteenth Century: Contacts and Comparisons* (Newtonville, MA, 1979), pp. 181–89. A view widely held in the Indian sub-continent is that it was the drain of riches from India that was the real trigger of English development.

[5] Peter A. Coclanis, "Capitalism, Slavery, and Matthew Desmond's Low-Road Contribution to the 1619 Project," *The Independent Review*, 26 (2022): 485–511. As noted in Chapter 3, all the essays in the special issue of *Slavery & Abolition* on this topic (vol. 42 [2021]: 1–178),

value of colonial exports from the Americas and the fact that most enslaved people ended their lives in the Iberian world, we would not have expected industrialization to have appeared first in Britain.

The implications of the slavevoyages set of estimates of the traffic have yet to be assessed for Africa, even though those estimates have been available since 2010. Plausible estimates of the sub-Saharan African population in 1850 became available in 2014. These constitute the result of several decades of research into precolonial African demography. A comparison of the 2014 findings with slavevoyages' estimates of those forcibly removed from the sub-continent raises questions about the size of the impact of the traffic on African populations. A review of some of the most widely read English-language Africanists indicates that some of their ideas are inconsistent with the data in TSTD. Because we have estimates of departures from Africa and data on the prices of captives on both sides of the Atlantic, we can say that the slave trade was not highly profitable compared to other long-distance trades and, moreover, accounted for a small part of the total product of all Euro-American slave-trading nations and, indeed, most African states that were involved in the business. TSTD's estimates of the volume of the slave trade also cast doubt on the argument that external pressures from the Atlantic world transformed the nature of slavery within Africa. We know that the largest number of captives left from West Central Africa, but there is little evidence that Indigenous slavery in its vast hinterland differed in the nineteenth century from earlier forms of enslavement.

Finally, some historians interpret abolition as a way for European states to have transitioned seamlessly into a new and equally exploitative form of imperialism, especially on the African continent.[6] Data from slavevoyages.org on the fate of Liberated Africans after 1807 used in Chapter 7 clearly establishes the profoundly anti-Black attitudes of all the former slave powers in the Atlantic world, including the British.

---

edited by Tamira Combrink and Matthias van Rossum ignore national accounting principles and thus hugely inflate the contribution of slavery and the slave trade to the Dutch economy. Imagine the impact of applying the same approach to any of the industries outside the slavery sector. Every single one of these others would be seen as the *sine qua non* of industrialization if subjected to the same analysis as has been applied to the slave trade.

[6] See Scanlan, *Slave Empire* and French, *Born in Blackness*. Also, Fara Dabhoiwala, "Slavery was Foundational to Britain's Prosperity and Rise to Global Power," *New York Review of Books*, August 20, 2020. Scanlan cites Seymour Drescher's, *Econocide*, a careful book-length destruction of Eric Williams' thesis of British slavery in decline as having "quibbled" with the famous author (p. 10), and apart from the Haitian Revolution largely ignores slavery in the non-British Atlantic, and indeed, the world.

Nevertheless, no one should be in any doubt that in strictly economic terms the ending of 350 years of the enslavement of a cumulative total of 12.75 million people constituted a significant break with the past. The data in www.slavevoyages.org showing 1,568 British captures of slave ships beginning in 1807 are consistent with the very high costs of trying to suppress slavery and the slave trade. Such an assessment is based not just on the costs of wars of liberation, on payments of compensation to slave owners, and on dispatching fleets to attempt suppression of the slave trade. The full costs must also include the higher prices for sugar, coffee, cotton, indigo, and other plantation produce that were the results of abolition. Consumers around the world would have continued to benefit if slavery itself had continued and the Liberated Africans had remained enslaved: Labor would have been less costly, plantation profits greater, plantation produce cheaper, and the Gross National Products of Western countries higher. The continuation of slavery in the nineteenth century would have accelerated, not hindered the industrialization of the North Atlantic world.[7] If abolition was not a sharp break with the past, then what is?

To return to the core theme of this book, anti-Black attitudes helped ensure that Europeans would not be among the captives carried across the Atlantic on the slave decks of ships. But as Chapter 7 shows, in the aftermath of abolition of both slavery and the slave trade, these same attitudes persisted and denied Blacks equality of opportunity. In yet another counterfactual, full equality post-abolition would surely have allowed the economy to draw on the full talents of Africans and African Americans, with all the resulting social and economic benefits. And the most important of these benefits would certainly have been stronger economic growth. In strictly economic terms, then, the path taken by formerly slave-holding nations after abolition was probably, in income terms, the worst of the three options open to them. What were these options? First, the historical reality described above; second, no abolition and thus continuation of slavery and slave trading; and third, full and equal rights for all after abolition, regardless of epidermal color. To return to Chapter 1, *Homo sapiens* migrated from Africa and populated the world. A century and a half since the ending of slavery in the Americas

---

[7] See David Brion Davis' exploration of the consequences of a British victory in the American Revolutionary War in "American Slavery and the America Revolution," in Ronald Hoffman and Ira Berlin (eds.), *Slavery and Freedom in the Age of the American Revolution* (Charlottesville, VA, 1983), pp. 262–80.

is surely long enough for us to realize that we are all descended from Black people and that we all carry genes of both slave owners and slaves. But apparently not. Racial discrimination persists.

Such speculations cannot be tested with the data in slavevoyages.org, but the project has at least brought us to the point of posing them, and it is appropriate to end with a plea for its more effective use. The project is very much a community resource in the hands of all scholars and interested contributors in the field. It is hosted by a single institution which, like the home of a learned journal, is subject to periodic change. However, it is controlled by a consortium of ten institutions comprising governments and museums as well as academic institutions. The site has no named authors or editors and has received thousands of contributions from users who are not all identified. New contributions of course require vetting and frequently editing. The editorial team at slavevoyages has dedicated many unpaid hours to this task as it seeks to expand and maintain the integrity of the core databases. In short, it is a resource both supported and drawn on by the scholarly community. The site's editors are experts in the field, but they, too, remain unnamed in citations to the data. Of course, every edit to its databases must have a verifiable source. But the broad acceptance of the project in the scholarly community suggests that the reliability of the site is widely recognized.

Apart from recognizing the horrors of the business, the team supports no single explanation or interpretation of the different Atlantic slave trades. The arguments made in the foregoing pages are my own, not the collective opinions of its professional and volunteer workers. But I am sure most would agree with me that if we ask anything of our users, it is that their own opinions about what happened be consistent with a greater share of slavevoyages' several million datapoints than has so far been the case. As outlined in the preceding pages, not only should the scholarly focus on this topic be switched from North to the South Atlantic, but, most important, if we are to get closer to delineating the African experience, we need to pay more attention to the people who survived the ordeal, as well as those who imprisoned them. Herein lies the site's huge potential for rewriting parts of Atlantic history.

Index

Entries in "*Italics*" refer to tables; entries in "**Bold**" refer to images/pictures.

Abbasid Caliphate, 24
Abbot Devereux (slave ship), 213
Abd al-Rahman, Mawlay, 138
Aberdeen Act, 343
abolition
   French, 126
   increase in intra-American slave trade and, 85
   of slavery, 33, 83, 151, 262, 336, 338
   of slavery and apprenticeships, 321
   of slavery and compensation payment, 140
   of slavery, British, 316
   of the slave trade, 262, 265–78, 285–90
   resistance to the slave trade and, 287
abolitionism, 140, 284
   and industrialization links, 254–56
abolitionist activism, 275
abolitionist dog, the, 125n52, 125
abolitionists, 85
   Black, 255, 256
   British, 91
Abrahamic religions, prejudice against Black people and, 25
absentee ownership, 94, 360
Accompong Town Maroons, Jamaica, request for compensation, 141
acquits de Guinée, 122
Admiralty Courts. *See also* Vice-Admiralty Courts
Admiralty Courts, British, 297

Africa
   agriculture in, 14
   annual population loss in, 14
   continental population of, 13
   cultural diversity and, 43
   impact of external slave trade and slavery on, 221–26
   impact of suppression of slave trade on, 233–36
   population decline and the slave trade, 216–20
   suppression of slave trade and increase in number of slaves, 233–36
African American men, comparison with Old World African men, 330–32
African Americans
   expulsion from Brazil, 334
   height of versus Africans, 331
   psychological effects of racism on, 255
   share of global population, 1800, 23
   viral infection rates among, 36
African depopulation, 215
African-descended people, in Islamic regions, 23
African diaspora and Indian Ocean, enslaved populations, *360*
African economies
   impact of European goods on, 221–26
   loss of trust in, 226–28
African enslavement, 29, 33, *See also* slavery
African immigrants, in the US, 351

African populations
  demographic impact of slave trade on, 216
  impact of slave trade on, 14, 216, 362
  natural population growth of, 244
  sub-Saharan, 219, 242, 362
African slave traders, 206–15
  experience of the slave trade, 160
African slavery, impact of slave trade on, 220–21
African slaves, 56
  arrival in St. Kitts, Martinique, and Guadeloupe, 120
  Brazilian gold production and, 88
  British slave traders and, 115
  direct arrival from Africa, 158
  early arrival in Brazil, 56
  experience of the slave trade, 160
  from Bahia (Salvador), 83
  in Bahia (Salvador), 81
  in Cuba, 69
  in Eastern Europe, 26
  in Spanish territories, 103
  sent to Brazil, 89
  silver mining in the Americas and, 48
African soldiers, early Islam and the use of, 24
African women
  disruption of role of, 172
  married to Portuguese men, 104
Africanist scholars, 216
  views on the impact of slavery on Africa, 237–46
African-Origins database/site, 200, 295, 303, 330
  ethnolinguistic associations and the, 199
Africans
  death at sea, 2
  disembarkment to safe sites, 236
  expulsion from Brazil, 334
  involvement in the transoceanic slave trades, 196–206
  not identifying as, 2
  resistance to the slave trade, xviii–xix, 3–4, 164–65, 176–81, 276, 287, 291
  risk of enslavement and eligibility rights, 242
age/sex data, 216, *See also* mortality rates
agricultural slavery, 22
agriculture
  African, 14
  Brazilian agricultural renaissance, 98
  in Bahia (Salvador), 69
Akan, 222
  Akan linguistic group, 233, 308
  drum, 172
Alabama constitution (1895), 327
Albanez (slave ship), 189, 193
  painting of, 192
Albion (slave ship), 201, 202
Aldridge, Ira, 285
American Colonization Society, 256
American Revolution, 268, 273
  abolition and, 257
  British failure in the, 257
Americas
  arrival of *Homo sapiens* in, 31
  demographic disasters on the, 20
  economic significance of slave trade to the, 94–100
  importance of in the slave trade, 50
  natural population growth in, 13
  repeopling of the, 5
Amistad (slave ship), 177
  captives and the Mende language, 309
Anderson, Clare, 311
Anderson, Richard, 334
Anglo-Brazilian Treaty (1826), 234
Anglo-French conflicts, 121
Anglo-Spanish Treaty (1835), 183
Angola, 58, 357
  coffee production, 221
  Dutch occupation of, 57
  European manufacturers and, 65
  forced labor systems, 353
  population densities of, 218
Anna (slave ship), 138
Anna Pepple house, 283
Anne (Queen), 140
Antera Duke, diary of, 202
anthropometric evidence, of Liberated Africans' welfare, 330
anti-Black attitudes, 285, 333, 351, 362, 363
Antigua, 50, 169, 346
  Blacks' natural population growth, 5
  slave ships dispatched from, 61
anti-slave trade campaign, 337
anti-slavery policies, British, 338
Antonil, André João, 81
apprenticeship system/apprenticeships, 289, 311, 316, 340–41, 349
  abolition of slavery and, 320
  absconding from, 339

Africans aboard the *Phoebe* and, 316
assignment of duties, 199
British abolition of slavery and, 321
British expectations of in Sierra Leone, 323
disintegration of the, 333
in Brazil, 317
in South Africa's Cape Colony, 318
in Tortola and Trinidad, 321
Liberated Africans and, 312, 314, 315
premature ending of, 340, 345
slave owners' views about, 348
terms of in Brazil, 318
Aptheker, Herbert, 258
Arab world, 8
African slaves in, 26
sugar cultivation in the, 28
Ardennes (slave ship), 3
Argentinian privateers, 297, 318
Arguim, 103, 106, 144, 158, 161, 197
Arte da Guerro do Mar (Oliveira), 125
Ashley, John, 79
Asia, status of enslaved peoples, 9
Asian contract labor. *See* Asian contract workers
Asian contract workers, 169, 286
colonies using, 350
indentured laborers, 252, 322, 349
asientistas, 115
Aspinall family (of Liverpool), 132, 358
Atheneum, 285
Atkins, John, 137
Atlantic and Indian oceans, 28
Atlantic gyres, 28, 122
Brazilian use of, 57
Atlantic islands, 6, 106, 269
Atlantic slave trade, 52, 356, *See also* slavery
Africa and Africans during the, 238
Africa's role in the, 245
British attempt at the suppression of the, 338
decline of the, 209
importation of Africans to the Americas, 86
incorrect information concerning the, 101–2
Portuguese and Spanish peoples and the, 92, 135
scale of, 5
slave ships used in, 153–57
slavery in Africa and the, 215

small investors in the North, 74
suppression of the, 237
survivors of the, 92
the Dutch and the, 58
the northern Europeans and the, 187
the Portuguese and the, 114, 358
Vais and the, 199
West Africa and the, 233
Atlantic Triangle, 106
Australia, 335
autarky, poverty of, 349
Aventureiro (slave ship), 324, **328**
Aztecs, 17
Azuonye, Chukwuma, 313

Bahia (Salvador), 55, 56, 58, 59, 71, 81, 85, 87, 116, 164, 166, 187, 212, 251, 262, 310
Bakossi (ethnolinguistic group), 231
Bales, Kevin, 248
concept of slavery, 250
Patterson and, 249
Bantu-speaking people, 23
Banyangi (ethnolinguistic group), 231
Barbados, 61, 79, 88, 113, 346
Blacks' natural population growth, 5
per capita production in, 95
slave arrivals to, 90
slave ships dispatched from, 61
Barbary corsairs/pirates, 137, 138, 139, 276
Barbot, Jean, 202
Barbuda, 346
Barry, Boubacar, 245
Begouën, Jacques-François, 132
Benguela, 58–59, 144, 167, 209, 211
Portuguese control of, 71
sending slaves to Luanda, 161–63
Berardi brothers, 127
Berbice, 83, 128, 251, 275
Asian indentured workers, 252
Berg, Maxine, *Capitalism and the Industrial Revolution*, 145
Bimbia, 307
birth/births
as a source of slaves, 17–19
female ratio at, 289
into servitude, 18
sex ratios in slave populations, 244
Bissau, 108, 111, 116, 135, 162, 177, 357
Black abolitionists, 249, 255, 256

Black Atlantic, 215, 292, 310
  northwest European role in the, 356
Black Boy (slave ship), 283
Black crew members, 215n53
  as investors, 73
  on slave ships, 73
Black Death, 12n25, 105
Black enslavement. *See also* slavery
Black enslavement, cruelty of, 290–91
Black farmers, 334n73
Black Joke (slave ship), 282
Black migration, 30
Black mortality, 5
Black people
  as citizens of the US, 256
  as non-Indigenous people, 33
  as surrogate settlers, 33
  black skin and enslavement, 25
  equality of opportunity, 354
  expulsion of by Britain, 31
  full citizenship and, 27
  Homestead Act (1862) and, 334
  in Lisbon, 125
  massacre of in Cuba, 353
  people descended from, 36
  prejudice against, 25
  reference to slaves, 281
Black Sea markets, Chinese captives in the, 11
black skin
  association with slavery, 26–27
  climatic factors and, 25
  eligibility criterion for enslavement, 282
  preoccupation over causes of, 30
  stigma of, 25
Black/white income differentials, 36
Black/white ratios, in prison, 36
Blackamoor (slave ship), 283
Blackburn, Robin, 247, 252–54, 256
  "Popular Anti-Slavery and the Birth of Abolitionism," 253
Blacks. *See* Black people
Blaney, James (RAC agent), 117
Boats family (of Liverpool), 358
Boats, William, 71, 132
Bodin, Jean, 137, 249
Bonny, 134, 166, 201, 204, 205, 210, 232, 307
  Anna Pepple house in, 283
  captives of, 233
  linguistic homogeneity and, 307
  survivors from, 313
Bonny River, 203
Bordeaux, 121, 130, 132, 134
  ratio of small investors in, 134
Bosquet d'Or (slave ship), 164
Boston, 47, 61, 62, 87, 282
Boudriot, Jean, 195
Bourbon reforms, 69
Bowsers, Frederick, 241
Brandenburg African Company, 128, 137
Brazil, 98, 168, 314
  abolition in, 248
  Africa-born slaves in, 18
  Africans and African Americans from, 334
  agricultural renaissance, 98
  apprenticeships in, 317
  Black people in, 353
  Brazilian slave trade, 19
  demographic structure in, 18n44
  fertility of the Brazilian slave population, 19
  free Black people before abolition, 94
  gold and silver production in, 167
  gold production, 88
  intra-America slave trade, 235
  invasion of, 101
  number of slaves sent to, 234
  plantation produce from, 149
  southern, 5
Brazil Frigate (slave ship), 73
Brazil–Argentine war, 318
Breda, Treaty of, 58
"bridgeheads of Empire," 324
Bridgetown, 50, 60, 89
  Royal African Company voyage from, 61
  slaves per annum arriving at, 79
Bristol (England), 4, 37–38, 49, 59, 118, 169, 185
  Black sailors in slave trade from, 74n76
  letters from, 202
  merchants from, 68
  sugar refinery in, 119
Bristol (Rhode Island), 47
Britain, slavery and perceptions of violence, 272–74
British abolition, 91
  Accompong Town Maroons and, 141
  and decision to abolish slavery, 291
  apprenticeship system and, 320
British Abolition of the Slave Trade Act, 316

British Admiralty, 297
British American shipbuilding sites, 68
British Americas, 115, 263, 339, 356
  re-captives in the, 320
British anti-slave trade policy, 343
British Caribbean, 49
  Africa-born slaves in, 18
  creditors and debtors in, 67
  economic impact of slavery on, 150
  intra-American traffic, 235
  slave markets, 68
  slave registration data, 231
British Columbia, mark of slavery in, 35
British East India Company, 268
British Evening Post, 274n74
British Guiana, 88, 96, 235, 252, 263, 350
British labor force, modernization of the, 343
British naval campaign, 175–76, 310
British Newspaper Archive, 253, 260
British plantation
  opportunities for owners of, 236
British plantation economies, 149
British plantations
  inability of owners to compete, 350
Bronze Age, the, 32
Brooks (slave ship), 76, 194
  images of, 195
  public perceptions of images of, 154, 188, 189
Broteer Furro (aka Venture Smith), 344
Brougham, Henry, 148, 285, 288, 347
  St. Domingue events and, 288
Brown, Christopher, 247, 253, 257
  Moral Capital, 257
Brown, Vincent, 44
Brown, William Wells, 249
Buddhist societies
  Buddhist monastic lineages, 10
  temple slavery in, 8
Buenos Aires/Montevideo axis, 85
bulking centers, 161, 186
  in Angola, 162
  of Luanda, 161
  off-shore, 158, 162
Burke, Edmund, 286
Burney Collection of Early English Newspapers, 270, 272, 279, 280
Burns, Robert, *Poems, Chiefly in the Scottish Dialect*, 140
Burton, John, 279

Bush, George Herbert Walker, 37
Bush, George W., 37
Buxton, Thomas Fowell, 217
Byzantine Empire, 15

Cacheu, 108, 111, 116, 135, 161, 162, 177
Calabar, 210, 307
Caldwell, John, 14
Callao (Peru), 47, 79
Cambini bank, 127
Cameroon Highlands, linguistic diversity in, 307
Cameroun Republic, 307
Canada, 157, 335
  French, 134
  land for agriculture, 344n101
Canaries, 7, 127, 161, 194, 357
  Indigenous people of, 106
Candido, Mariana, 92, 163n24, 164n27, 209, 215n53
Cape of Good Hope, the, 235, 236, 352
Cape Verde Islands, the, 54, 72, 103, 158, 161, 194
  mixed society in the, 165
Capitalism and Slavery (Williams), 222, 250, 262
captives carried from Africa, 49
Caribbean
  brown elites in, 333
  North Atlantic income gap between, 96
  notions of acceptable violence in, 274
  number of slaves sent to the, 89
Caribbean immigrants, into the US, 351
Caribbean-based ventures, illicit, 61
Carlyle, Thomas, 348
  anti-Black tirade of, 285
Carmen de Patagones, Argentina, 47, 318
Carreira, Antônio, 162
Cartagena, 80, 85, 188
Castilian code, Siete Partidas (1265), 32, 94
Castillo, Lisa, 59, 213
castrati singers, 335n79
catastrophic cruelties, 5
catchment zones, 13
Catholics, and conflict with Protestants, 269, 272
Central Asia, 11, 12, 15, 24
  Mongol expansions in, 240
Chalhoub, Sidney, 213
Chandos, Duke of, 76

Chartism, 343
  Chartist land lottery, 347
  Chartist leaders, 261
Chatham Islands, 40, 138
chattel bondage/slavery, 9, 105, 151, 247, 315
  in China, 13, 15
  linked to free labor, 311
  revival of in the seventeenth century, 281
  slave resistance to, 258
Chesapeake plantocracy, 76
child indigents, 266
child migrants, Britain and, 264
child ratios, 192
Child Slaves in Late Antiquity and the Middle Ages (Grubbs), 18n41
children
  abandoned, 17n40
  apprenticeships and, 323, 341
  as captives, 173
  child indigents, 266
  protection of, 267
China, 9, 11, 35
  chattel slavery in, 15
  Korean women as concubines, 34
  medieval population, 15
  source of enslaved peoples in mid-millennium, 11
  vs. United States and slavery, 12–14
Chinese captives, 11
Chinggis Khan, 12
Chinookan and Wakashan-speakers Indigenous societies, 36
Christendom, 25, 33, 106
  color symbolism and, 25
  no slaving zones in, 29
  perceptions of self within, 34
Christianity, 26, 262
Christians, held in slavery, 137
Churchill (captain), 198
Cicerón (slave ship), 168n38
Cilucängy (aka Ward Lee), 314
circum-Caribbean, 48
citizenship, 27, 353
Citóyen (slave ship), 282
Civil War, 287, 296, 298, 334
  cost of, 336
  in Ireland, 272
  US, 258
Clapham sect luminaries, 347
Clarkson, Thomas, 148

Cline, Emmanuel, 324
Clotilda (slave ship), 2, 325, 327, 344
coartación (self purchase), 33, 94, 316n46
Cobbett, William, 261
Cock, Francis, 116
Coclanis, Peter, 145
coerced labor, 7. *See also* forced labor
coffee production, 221
Côlonia do Sacramento, 80
colonial bullion production, 167
colonial income, 99n140
color symbolism, 25
Colqhoun, Patrick, 342
Columbus, 31, 52
"comfort women," Korean, 35
commodity exports, 236
commodity exports, Western African, 234
Compagnie de Guinée, 129
Compagnie de l'Asiente, 129
Compagnie des Îles d' Amérique, 89
Compagnie des Indes Occidentales, 129
Compagnie du Sénégal, 129
Companhia Geral de Pernambuco e Paraíba, 130
Companhia Geral do Grão Pará e Maranhão, 130, 135
Company of Royal Adventurers, 115, 130
compensation
  Accompong Town Maroons' request for, 141
  to former slave owners, 140, 176, 187, 289, 336–37, 345, 363
concubines, 34
Congo River, 233
consumer behavior, 141
consumer goods, 342
  demand for tropical, 141
convicts, 1, 51, 138, 169, 291
  change in treatment of, 269
  on plantations, 112
  source of, 9
Coopstad and Rochussen, 132
Coromandel Coast, 110
corsairs, Barbary, 137, 138, 139, 276
Costa, Roberto de, 117
Courland, Duchy of, 128
court slavery, 10
Courts of Mixed Commission, 296n7
Creole (slave ship), 178
creoles, 19

crew members
  Black, 215n53
  enslaved persons per, 67
  former, 153
  private investments and, 73
Cromwell, 269
  sanctioned violence in Ireland and, 273
Crowther, Samuel Ajayi, 324, 326
Cuba, 252, 307, 314
  African slaves into, 69
  Canary Islanders sent to, 349
  emancipado status of re-captives, 316
  expulsion of Africans and African Americans from, 334
  Mende-speakers and, 309
  myth of racial equality, 353
  rise and fall of the Cuban slave trade, 91
  sugar revolution in, 19n47
  use of slave labor, 350
Cugoano, Ottobah, 283
cultural diversity, 31
  Africa and, 43
Cumberland, Duke of, 273
Curse of Ham, 25
Curtin, Philip, xiii, 6, 161, 168, 223
Cush, Black descendants of, 25
Cutting, Nathaniel, 164

d'Almeida, Joaquim, 212
Dahomean economy, 240
Daily Post Boy, 277
Darwin, John, 324
Davenport, William, 132, 135, 231
  Davenport papers, 135
David, Paul, *Reckoning with Slavery*, 250
Davis, David Brion, 247, 253, 254–57, 260, 261, 265, 348
  The Problem of Slavery in the Age of Emancipation, 254, 256
  The Problem of Slavery in Western Culture, 254
Deane, Stephen (slave ship captain), 139
deaths
  cause of on slave ships, 2
  during slave traffic, 13
debt financing, 67
debt-bondage/debt slavery, 37n85, 248
degredados, 32, 113
Delhi Sultanate, 8, 24
Demerara, 83–84, 128, 173, 251
  Asian indentured workers in, 252

  impact of abolition on planters in, 91
demographic disasters, 20
  Spanish invasion and, 51
demographic material, shortage of, 15
demographic patterns/trends, of European colonies, 13, 239
Desire (slave ship), 62
destitute children, 266
developed country status, 150
digital humanities project, 355
Diligente (slave ship), 189, 193
  crowding on, 193
Diouf, Sylviane, 327
disabilities, of Liberated Africans, 351n117
discrimination, 354
disease environments, 5, 13
DNA analysis, 30
Doherty, William, 184
Domesday Book, 38
domestic labor, 8
Douglass, Frederick, 249, 315, 316, 354
  Liberated Africans and freedom, 324
Downing, George, 60
dracunculiasis (Guinea worm), 2
Drescher, Seymour, 227, 247, 253, 256–57
  Econocide, 250, 256
Du Bois, W. E. B., 263
Dubois, Laurent, 286
Duchy of Courland, 128
Duke of Cumberland, 273
Dutch
  Dutch Caribbean Islands, 116
  intra-American slave trade and, 78
  role in the slave trade, 101
Dutch East India Company, 135
Dutch Indonesia, 352
Dutch Middelburg Company, 185
Dutch migration, 112
Dutch Sephardic Jews, 120
Dutch slave ships, 89
Dutch West India Company, 3

Eagle, Marc, 107
Earl family, 132
Earl of Inchiquin, 138
East Indian
  textiles, 65, 143
  trade, 149
East Indies, 52
East–West trade, 12n25
Econocide (Drescher), 256

economic development
  Europe's, 225
  importance of slavery to Western, 145
  in the Atlantic world, 168
  movement of labor from agricultural sector and, 347
  role of the slave trade in the Atlantic world, 361–62
  slave trade impact on Africa's, 226
  Western, 246
economic expansion, slavery and, 8
Efik
  and English view of each other, 201
  linguistic group, 307
  traders, 197n2, 201, 202
Egypt, 34
Ehinger, Heinrich, 127
Eighteenth-Century Collections Online, and *American Imprints*, 278
Eisner, Gisela, 96
Eliza (slave ship), 172–74
Elizabeth (slave ship), 203
Elizabeth and Sarah (slave ship), 49
Ellen (slave ship), 139
Eltis-Richardson Atlas, 310
Emancipation, 18, 333
  Brazil granting unconditional, 317
  full freedom and, 351
  post-emancipation Caribbean, 286
embarkation points, 216
emigration
  compulsory, 323
  impact of on population, 14
  restricted, 115
  to Liberia, 334n74
engagés, 120, 199, 297
  freedoms available to, 320
  French, 89, 112, 319, 321
  French policy toward, 322
England, 105, 110, 138
  as a racial state, 32
  Bristol, 4, 37, 169
  Captain Deane return to, 139
  check on abuse of power in, 278
  Cuba's per capita income compared to, 96
  in the 1600s, 273
  letters from Bristol, 202
  Liverpool, 148
  Liverpool and Bristol, 185
  Liverpool, London, and Bristol, 49, 59
  London and Bristol, 68
  neutrality in war between the Netherlands and Portugal, 88
  orphaned and destitute children in, 266
  per capita production in, 95
  protection of the enslaved in, 280
  real wages in, 104
  reform of slavery in, 290
  riots in, 259, 270
  slave trade and, 125
  slave-based empire building of, 270
  study of violence in, 272
  transoceanic migration from, 115
  war with France, 181
  white servitude in, 112
English Caribbean, 55
  English indentured servants to the, 115
  European settlers in, 120
  sugar cultivation in, 120
English Chartists' land-bank lottery, 347, *See also* Chartism
English Civil War, 269
English Committee for Foreign Plantations, 96
Enlightenment, 259
enslaved Africans, 78, *See also* slaves
  Brazil and, 58–59, 84
  Cuba and, 69
  English public and, 271
  first recorded landing in the US, 46
  in Spanish Americas, 359
  markets for, 108
  number transported from the Gold Coast to Barbados, 126
  numbers of in Jamaica and St. Domingue, 90
  Portuguese and, 32
  production and, 87–88
  slave traders as former, 212
  Spanish Americas and, 92
  transported to Cuba, 309
  transported to Suriname, 132
  used of in gold mining, 98
enslaved people, 18, *See also* slaves
  Africa-born, 18
  as wages, 74
  collective ownership of, 10
  Cuban merchants and, 157n8
  disembarking from steam-powered ships, 70
  ratio of with African descent, 22
  vs. free people in the Americas, 12

enslaved persons. *See* enslaved people
enslaved population, of the Old World vs. the New World, 26
enslavement
　eligibility for, 32, 33, 41, 197, 242, 267, 282
　raids and conquest and, 17
enslavement mechanisms, 17
Epic of Gilgamesh, the, 7
epidemiological apocalypse, 51
epidermal racism, 25
　erosion of, 283
Equiano, Olaudah, 283
Espindola, Polo de, 127
Essequibo, 83, 128
　Asian indentured workers, 252
ethnolinguistic associations, 199
ethnolinguistic groups, 23, 240, 342
　African, 241
ethnolinguistic identities, 216, 347
ethnolinguistic links, 231
ethnologue.com database, 230, 232, 303
Eurasia
　medieval, 11, 12, 23
　movement of enslaved peoples within, 16
　slavery in the medieval millennium, 22
Euro-American
　conceptions of race, 351
　slave-trading nations of, 362
Europe
　economic significance of slave trade to, 94–100
　impact of slave trade on, 142–52
　Muslims held as slaves in, 137
European colonies, demographic patterns of, 13
European consumers. and the slave trade, 42
European emigrants, legal protections for, 353
European immigration, World War I and, 334
European incursions, 22, 103, 194
　resulting violence and, 12
European migrants, 311
European migrants, homesteading option for, 346
European overseas expansion, 8
European prejudice, 1–2
European Union protective policy, 350
European war, impact of on the Atlantic slave trades, 86

European welfare, slave trade contribution to, 142–52
Evangelicals, 257
Everill, Bronwen, 262
Ewe linguistic group, 308
exports
　African commodity, 236
　impact of abolition on, 353
　Western African commodity, 234

Felipe Gonzalez, Jorge, 231
female slaves. *See also* women slaves
　sexual exploitation of, 21
　value of, 20
　vs. male slaves, 20
females
　apprenticeship and, 340
　component of the forced migration, 14
　human trafficking and, 27
　Liberated Africans in Freetown, 335
Ferentz (captain), 172
Fergus, Claudius, 247, 258
Ferreira, Roquinaldo, 92
fertility rate, 19
Fett, Sharla, 319
flattened heads, 35–36
Florentino, Manolo, 187
Fly (cutter sloop), 169
Fogel, Robert W., 146, 287
Foner, Eric, 334, 344
food, non-Indigenous in sub-Saharan Africa, 14
foodstuffs, nutritional content of, 14
forced labor
　abandonment of, 12–14
　in Angola, 353
　medieval Eurasia and, 7
　Patterson's views on, 248
forced labor, 248n4
forced migration/migrations, 6, 16–17, 45, 52
　female component of, 14
　French and Dutch, 297
　of Africans to the Americas, 101
　to Liberia, 334
forty acres and a mule, 344
fossil jawbone, 30n75
Fourth of July (slave ship), 282
Fouta Djallon, 210
Fragoso, João, 187

France, 79, 99, 121, 141, 151, 360
  cessation of St. Dominigue to, 98
  economic impact of slavery on, 150–51
  hostilities with Spain, 86
  industrialization in, 151, 345
  investors in the slave trade from, 133
  per capita income of, 96
  reparations from Haiti, 345
  slave trade and, 125
  subsidization of slave trade of, 122
Franc-maçon (slave ship), 68
Frankema, Ewout, 13, 216
Fraternité (slave ship), 282
Fredensborg (slave ship), 172
free labor, 255, 289, 311, 341
  concept of, 342
  factory workers and, 345
  in silver mines, 123
  vs. slavery, 339
free migrants, 1
free womb laws, 289
freed persons, trafficking in slaves, 213
freedmen
  as crew on Brazil vessels, 163
  involved in slave trade, 212, 213
  restricted opportunities for, 354
Freemasons, 68
Freetown
  churches in, 324
  communities in, 347
  Liberated Africans in, 324
French Canada, 134
French economy, 150
French *engagés* (indentured servants), 89, 112
French navy, Liberated Africans and, 318
French Revolution, 252, 291
  tyrannies of the, 286
French slavers, 282, 358
  contribution to non-French territories, 121
French West Africa, slave societies in, 237
full freedom, 322, 351, 352
  in the US, 334
  petitioning for in Brazil, 317
Fynn-Paul, Jeffrey, 23, 29

Galinhas, 199, 206
galley slaves, 29, 32
General Ramirez (slave ship), 316n45
Geniza documents, 20, 21, 23
Genoa, 32, 78, 127

Gezegend Suikerriet (slave ship), 171
Ghaznavids, 11, 17
Gift of God (slave ship), 61, 282
Gini coefficient, 72
global plague, 8
global populations, reintegration of, 31
Goiás, 77
gold and silver, 88n112
  American, 225
  difficulties mining, 57
  export to southeast Asia, 87
  need for slave labor to get, 80
  production of, 167
  production of American, 54
gold, riverine, 77
gold-bearing regions, 77
golden rule, and European-African relations, 287
Goldsmith-Kress Library of Economic Literature, 278
Gordon, David, 238
Gottschall, Jonathan, 41
Goulart, Mauricio, 91
Gouvenot, Laurent de, 127
greed, discussions about, 348
Green, Toby, 44, 204, 222–25, 237
  views on benefits gained by Europeans in African transactions, 222–26
Greenberg, Michael, 284
Gregson family (of Liverpool), 132, 358
Grenada, 235, 349
Grillo, Domenico, 78, 115
Grootschaar, Pieter, 139
groundnut areas (Upper Guinea), slavery and the, 234
Grubbs, Judith Evans, 18n41
grumetes, 104
Guadeloupe, 61, 89, 120, 297
  Dutch Sephardic Jews in, 120
Guangzhou, China, Africans in, 11
Guinea worm (dracunculiasis), 2
Guinea-Bissau, 231
Gulf of Guinea islands, 104
gyres, 28, 53, 160
  Brazilian, 57
  North Atlantic, 108
  northern and southern, 160
  northern Atlantic, 135
  South Atlantic, 65, 122, 179

Hahn, Steve, 258

Haiti, 90, 287, 311, *See also* St. Domingue
　autarky, 349
　GDP per capita, 346
　Haitian elites and the plantation economy, 345
　Haitian independence declaration, 275, 288, 310
　independence of, 351
　landholdings in, 345
　payment of reparations to France, 345
　per capita product in, 96
　role in British abolition decision, 291
　size of landholdings in, 345, 349
Haitian navy, 297
Haitian Revolution, 91, 225, 253
　message of, 255
Hall, Robert, 174n54
Hanson Jones, Alice, 95
Hanway, Jonas, 267, 284
Harris, John, 70
Hart, Richard, 258
Hausa, 324
Hawaii, 30, 88
Hawthorne, Walter, 244
He, Zheng (Admiral), 11, 31
Hegelian paradox, 262
Heng, Geraldine, 32
Hermano & Cía firm (slave traders), 100
Heywood, Linda, 213
Hibbard, Robert, 76
Hicks, Mary, 72–74, 163
　book of, 74
　crew members as investors, 74
Highlands, the Spanish American, 54
Higman, Barry W., 16, 22, 230
Hilt, Eric, 151
Hindu monastic lineages, 10
Hispaniola, 85
History of the World in 100 Objects, A, 172
HMS *Albatross*, 192
HMS *Pearl*, 193
Hodge, Arthur William, 274
　Hodge case, 274
Hodgson, Thomas, 71
　Hodgson family, 132
Homestead Act (1862), 343, 346, 352
　Black people and the, 334
homesteading option, European migrants and, 346
Homo sapiens, 30, 40, 354
　arrival into the Americas, 31
　migration of, 363
homosexuality, 264
Hudson, Pat
　Slavery, Capitalism and the Industrial Revolution, 145
　slavevoyages and, 145
Huggins, Nathan, 1–2
human pawns/pawnship, 227
human trafficking, 27
　transatlantic slave trade as, 3
Hurston, Zora Neale, 328n69
Hutson, Alaine S., database of, 26n65

Iberian Americas, 53, 314
　dominance of, 74
　enslaved persons arriving in, 150
　financing and hiring strategies of traders of the, 74
　impact of *coartación* on, 94
　Jesuit slaveholdings in, 8
　survivors of Atlantic slave trade living in the, 92
Iberian nations, slave trade and the, 102
Ibibio, 201
　enslaved, 118
　ethnolinguistic group, 231, 233
　linguistic group, 307
Ibn Battuta, 16
Igbo, 201, 210, 241, 318, 324
　as a term, 2
　enslaved, 118
　ethnolinguistic group, 231–33, 307, 308–10, 313–14
　peoples, 307
Ijaw linguistic group, 308
Ijo linguistic group, 308
illegal migrants, 169
Immigration and Nationality Act (1965), 354
Imo River, 233
imports per person, value of, 228
Inchiquin, Earl of, 138
income levels
　discrepancies in modern, 196
　modern, 346
indentured servants, 1, 51, 118, 169, 199
　Asian contract laborers, 322
　Asian indentured workers, 252, 349
　English, 115
　European, 270
　French *engagés* as, 112
　French equivalent of, 89

indentured servants (cont.)
  slaveries and, 112
indentured servitude, 354, *See* indentured servants
India, 11, 350
  enslaved military units in, 25
Indian Ocean World (IOW) slave trades, 14
Indian sub-continent
  debt-bondage in, 248
  slavery in, 10
Indigenous African trade networks, trust and, 227
Indigenous American, 33
Indigenous peoples, 2, 92, 267
  great dying of, 19
  in Spanish Americas, 359
  of the Canaries, 106
  work in silver mines, 98
Indigenous populations
  decline of, 1
  enslavement of, 1
  epidemiological apocalypse and the, 51
  population growth, 20
  slavery of, 215, 220, 362
  slavery of in Africa, 221
Industrial Revolution, 145, 224, 260
  English, 148
  slavery and the first, 262
industrialization, 8, 60, 148, 360–62, 363
  and the end of slavery, 256
  British, 252
  deterrence to in France, 345
  European fabric during, 143
  foreign trade-driven, 263
  impact of slavery on, 147, 152, 250–51
  links between abolitionism and, 254–56
  Netherlands, 151
  of France, 151
  second slavery and, 44
infanticide, punishment for, 266
Inikori, Joseph, 112, 134n80
International Labor Organization, 248
intra-American slave trade, 115
  database, 46
  Portuguese merchants and, 80
intra-American traffic, 84
investment
  British direct investment in, 132
  Gini coefficient and research in slave trade, 72
  in Brazilian slave trade center, 72
  in the slave trade, 66–76, 119, 127–37, 225
  larger investors in the slave trade, 134
  Portuguese plantation, 100
  private, 73, 131
  small investor ratio, 134
  small investors in the slave trade, 133–34
  unusual investment patterns in the slave trade, 160
Ireland, 38, 115, 148, 345
  cause of poverty in, 345
  immigrants returning to, 347
  rebellion in, 272
Irish immigrants
  compared to Liberated Africans, 333, 335
  smallholdings of, 347
Irving, James (slave ship captain), 138
Isla de Cuba (slave ship), 189, 193
Islam, 26
  color symbolism and, 25
  Islamic conflict effect on sex ratios, 241
  Islamic influences on slavery, 10
  Islamic populations, 15
  Islamic powers and no slaving zones in, 29
  Islamic slaves, 24
  source of slaves in the medieval Islamic world, 25
Islamic regions
  people of African descent in, 23
  slave markets in, 23
Israel, 350
Italian boys, 335n79

Jacobs, Claas, 138
Jamaica, 235, 258
  Asian labor to, 346
  cession to England, 98
  English workers sent to, 349
  Maroon communities in, 141
  modern per capita GDP, 346
  per capita production in, 95
  slave arrivals in, 78–79
  slave entrepot, 79
  slave population of, 91
  Tacky's Rebellion, 260
  Thomas Thistlewood in, 22
James, C. L. R., 258, 286
Janissaries, 8
Jefferson, Thomas, 258
  Jefferson's Louisiana purchase, 82
Jerven, Morten, 13, 216

Jesus Maria (slave ship), 172, 192
Jeune Adèle (slave ship), 319
Jews
　Eastern European, 351
　expelled from Pernambuco, 89
　expulsion of, 31
　Jewish rituals of, 34
Jim Crow laws, 352
Jins, 15
Jones, Alice Hanson, 100n140
Jordan, Winthrop, 125, 353
Jurchens, 15

Kealoo, 324
Kelley, Sean, 63, 135
Kelly, Morgan, 227
Kennedy, Joseph, 223
Key West, 351
　disembarkation of re-captives in, 319
Khmer Empire, 9, 11
King Agaja of Dahomey, 205
King Amboe (slave ship), 283
King Kosoko (Cocioko), 210
King of Bonny, 204
King of Dahomey, 204
King Pepple, 283
King Varrée of Bonny, 203
kinship groups, 37, 342
　economic and social status, 342
Koelle, Sigismund W., 17, 241, 303, 309
　Polyglotta Africana, 2
Korea, 9, 26
　Korean "comfort women" (women as concubines), 34, 35
Kossola (Cudjoe Lewis), 327, 328n69, 331, 333, 344

L'Amélie (slave ship), 312, 318
L'Anémone (slave ship), 319
L'Aurore (slave ship), 195
La Escalera conspiracy, 33n81
La Rochelle, 121, 130
labor
　labor debts, 1
　labor exploitation, 249, 311
　labor markets, 342
　labor markets in the Americas, 352
　post-emancipation labor problems, 321
　servile, 15, 20
　shortages, 1, 105, 138, 321
　shortages on the sugar estates, 322

Laborde, Jean-Joseph de, 76
Lachance, Paul, xiii, 243
lançados, 104, 116, 165–67
　as traders, 71
　Dutch, 167
　equivalents of, 165
Lancashire, 148
Lancaster, 119
Land Cooperative scheme, 343
land ownership, by Blacks, 334n73
land-to-labor ratios, 19, 31, 51, 66, 104, 105, 352
Lane, Paul, 12
larger investors. *See* investment
Latin America, 123
　creditors and debtors in, 67
　mestizo in, 34
　revolutions in, 286
　slaves in, 19
Latin West
　African slaves in, 26
　diversity of enslaved people, 27
Law, Robin, 210
Lawrence, Fenda, 214
Lea (slave ship), 138
Leach, Edmund, 9
Lee, Ward. *See* Cilucängy (aka Ward Lee)
"Legacies of British Slave-Ownership," 124
"Legacies of the British Slave Trade: The Structure and Significance of British Slave Trade Investment, 1550–1807," 124
Legacy of British Slavery group, 36
Legítimo Africano (slave ship), 190
Lesser Antilles, 61, 120
lettres patentes, of the Crown, 130
Leusden (slave ship), slaves murdered on the, 3
Levelers, the, 105
Liberated Africans, 303, 320n54, 335
　acceptance of, 352
　apprenticeship status of, 315
　arriving in the British Caribbean, 320
　assignment of status, 298
　assignment of status by default, 325
　Brazilian government emancipation of, 317
　British policy toward, 348
　disabilities of, 351n117
　freedoms after disembarkation, 341
　French navy and, 318

Liberated Africans (cont.)
  going to Sierra Leone, 324
  in Freetown, 324
  in Sierra Leone, 2, 17
  in South Africa's Cape Colony, 318
  in the Old World, 334
  inflow into the British Caribbean, 321
  languages of, 309
  photographic evidence of, 292
  plight of, 336
  racism and violence after freedom, 352–53
  rebellion against the crew, 295
  regions of disembarkment, 299
  register of, 199
  smallholdings of, 312, 324, 345
  status of, 297, 311, 314, 320
Liberia, 236
  domestic slaves in, 226
  emigration to, 334n74
  forced migration to, 334
libertos, 353
Liberty (slave ship), 282
Lima, Jose de Cerqueira, 71
Lisbon, 55, 65
  Black population of, 125
  center of slave trade, 107
  embarkment ports of Luanda and Benguela, 58, 59
  population of, 32
  ships leaving from, 58
  transatlantic slave trade in, 47
Little George (slave ship), 276
Liverpool, 131, 144, 148, 185, 233
  Black sailors in slave trade from, 74n76
  ownership of voyages from, 147
  riot, 126
Lloyd's List shipping newspaper, 276
Lomellino, Ambrosio, 78, 115
loss ratio, due to captures, 235
Lovejoy, Paul, 222
  Transformations in Slavery, 220
Lower Columbia River, 36
Lowlands of Spanish America, the, 54
Luanda, 58, 73, 103, 161–63, 164, 167, 169, 233, 236, 241, 296
  Dutch loss of control over, 114
  Dutch occupation of, 116
  former slave as slave trader in, 213
  imports of, 65
  population of, 163
  Portuguese control of, 71
  Portuguese transshipment point at, 57
  trade of goods from, 143
Lucques, Laurent de, 161, 162
Lushington, Stephen, 347
lynchings, 352

Macaulay, Zachary, 250, 285
Madanela Cansyna (slave ship), 72, 136
Madeira, 7
Maillard, Thomas, 127
Mali, 23n58
Malthusian demographic patterns, 219
  cycle of decline and recovery, 219n56
Mamluk Egypt, 8, 20, 24
  elite, 25
Mann, Kristin, 59, 212
Manning, Patrick, 13, 229, 240, 245
manumission rates, 19
Maori, 40–41, 138
Maranhão, 130
Marchionni, Bartolomeo, 127
Marie-Séraphique (slave ship), 155, 189, 192, 193, 211
  images of, 193, 195
maritime bondage, expansion of, 12
maritime slave trade, 221
  Africa and, 125
  number of slaves during, 18
marketplace, for trading people, 10
Maroon communities
  in Jamaica, 141
  in Suriname, 141, 222
Marques, Leonardo, xiii, 70, 77n83, 77, 187n86
marriage, 9
Martin, Phyllis, 167
Martinez, Pedro, 100
Martinique, 61, 120, 297, 313
  Africans who stayed in, 320
  Dutch Jews in, 89, 120
  Igbo terms/names, 313
  Liberated Africans in, 318
  main destination for Africans, 121
  slave arrivals to, 90
Martins, Domingos José, 212
Mascarene Islands, 234
Mason-Dixon line, 311
Master-Servant Act, 273
Mato Grosso (of Brazil), 77
Mau Mau detainees, settlement to, 264

Mauro, Frederic, 91
McCormick, Michael, 23
Meaher, Timothy, 344
medieval millennium
  Eurasian slavery of the, 22
  movement of enslaved people during, 16
  plantation slavery in, 20
  slavery before and after the, 7
  trading of people during the, 10
Mediterranean and Black seas, 32
Mediterranean Atlantic, 106
Meillassoux, Claude, 16
Mellis, John Charles, 3
Mende, 241, 308–9
  diaspora, 309
  language, 309
  Mende traders, 143
  Sherbro language, 231
Menz, Max, 58
merchandise
  shipped to Africa, 142
  textile as, 143–45
Mesopotamia, 8
mestizaje, 34, 92
Methuen Treaty, 115
Middelburg, 126, 144
Middelburgse Commercie Compangie, 207
Middle Ages, 27
  no-slaving zones during, 29
  prejudice against Black people in the, 25
  terms for slave during, 24
migrant Asian workers, 351
migration
  as an option for Irish and Jews, 334
  from Europe to the tropical Americas, 115
military service
  recruitment of Africans for, 297
  use of slaves in, 8, 10
military slavery, 10
  in India, 25
Miller, Joseph C., 91, 222, 229, 230, 237
  specification of slavery and, 9
Mina Coast, 164
Minas Gerais, Brazil, 77, 80, 85, 163
  discovery of gold in, 81
"Miracle of San Marco, The" (painting), 26
miscegenation, 34
Misevich, Philip, 229, 230, 303, 335
missionaries, 324

Mixed Commission Courts, 153, 173, 296n7, 296, 298, 303, 320
  Cuban and Brazilian tribunals and, 317
  Havana, 172, 316
  Sierra Leone, 307
"mobby" (alcohol), 66
Mobile, 328, 344
Moco linguistic group, 307
modern income
  discrepancies in, 196
  disparities across the Atlantic world, 359
  levels of, 346
modern prostitution, 248
Mongol Empire/Mongols, 12–13, 15, 20, 23, 24, 34, 39
  enslaved Eurasian people and the, 12
  Europeans as, 41
  expansions in Central Asia, 240
  slave trade and the, 36
  victories of, 17
Monserrate (slave ship), 316n45
Montaudoin family, 132
Moral Capital (Brown), 257
moral perspectives, on slavery, 261–62
moral values, shifts in, 264–72
morality, 33
"More Than 100 Million Women Are Missing," (Sen), 289
More, Thomas, 105
Morgan, Jennifer, 45
Morice, Humphry, 66n53, 140
Moriori, 40
mortality rates, by age-sex groupings, 174, 175
mortality, slave, 173
Mozambique Island, 161
Mulgrave Zimmermann, Catherine, 325
Muslim Middle East, 15
Muslims, 106
  held as slaves in Europe, 137
  involvement in the slave trade, 241
  Wolof slaves, 176

Naïade (slave ship), 76
Nairac family, 132
Nantes (French port), 59, 62, 121, 130, 131, 132, 144
  families, 135
  small investors in, 134
Nantes Memorial to the Abolition of Slavery, 355

Napoleonic Wars, 83
National Museum of African American History and Culture, Washington, 355
Native Americans, 267
Native American labor, 53, 57
natural resources
  Americas, 53
  Sierra Leone, 349
  West African settlements and, 346
naval campaign
  against the slave trade, 175–76
  British detentions, 310
Negro Merchant (slave ship), 283
Negroes Nest (slave ship), 282
negros emancipados, 316
Netherlands, 58, 104, 107–8, 110, 122, 141, 361
  economic growth of, 111
  expulsion from Pernambuco, 120
  industrialization in the, 151
  investors in the slave trade from the, 133, 136
  slave trade and, 125
  small investors in the slave trade from the, 133–34
  transatlantic war with Portugal, 88
Neves, José Paes Falcão das, 78
New Calabar, 118, 201, 307
New England rum ships, 50
New England slave traders, 55
New World
  enslaved population of the, 26
  slavery, 230, 254, 262, 292
New Zealand, 30, 40
Newman, Simon, 259
Newport, 63
newspapers, 278
  African shipboard resistance reports in, 260
  English awareness of the transoceanic world through, 269–72
  mention of Blacks in English, 271
  reports incidence of slave revolts in, 275
  reports on the depravity of slavery, 274
Newton, John (slave ship captain), 139, 170
Niger River, 233
Njinga of Ndongo (Queen), 213
Nombre de Dios, 85
non-Indigenous foodstuff, 14
non-Indigenous population, 33

Norman conquest, 32
North Africa, 11, 87, 103, 139
  Christians as slaves in, 137
  English captives in, 271
  European captives in, 105
  Europeans liable to enslavement in, 106
  no-slaving zones in, 29
  white slaves in, 281
North Atlantic gyre, 108, 135
North Atlantic slave trades, small investors in, 74
northern Europe
  female slaves in, 21
  slavery in, 7
northern India, 15
northern Iraq, 7
Northrup, David, 210, 244
no-slaving zones, 17, 29
Nossa Senhora de Nazaré e S Antônio (slave ship), 178
Nossa Senhora do Rozario do Castello (slave ship), 179
Nova Redondo, 325
NS da Penha de França (slave ship), 74
NS do Monserrat e Piedade (slave ship), 117
Nuestra Señhora de los Remedios (slave ship), 54
Nunn, Nathan, 226
Nunn/Wantchekon position, 227
Nwokeji, Ugo, 244, 303

O'Malley, Greg, 84
Oceans of Kinfolk database, 330
Old Calabar, 118, 166, 201, 202, 205, 231, 232, 283
  Efik traders at, 197n2
Old Testament, the, 34
Old World, the, 8
  diseases of, 5
  enslaved population of the, 26
  Liberated Africans in the, 334
Oldendorp, Christian Georg Andreas, 241
Oldfield, John, 247
Oliveira, Fernão, *Arte da Guerro do Mar*, 125
opportunities
  denial of, 333
  differences based on race, 351
  equality of, 354
Original Affluent Society, The (Sahlins), 341
Orion (slave ship), 153, 155

Ormond, John, 214
Ormond, John Jr., 214
Orr, Leslie, 20
Orthodox Christians, 106
outsiders
  Africans as, 197
  and insiders and citizenship, 350
  Europeans' view of Africans as, 282
  slavers as, 10
Oyo Empire, 210, 308

Padmore, George, 263
palenques, 141
Palmer, Colin, 92
Palmerston Act, 343
pan-African identity, 2
pan-American identity, 2
Para and Maranhäo company, 135
Parés, Luis Nicolau, 59
Parzival (von Eschenbach), 25
PAST database, 72, 131, 134, 298
  interface of slave voyages of, 303
  user interface of, 133
PAST enslaved database. *See* PAST database
Patagonia, 102, 318, 352
Patterson, Orlando, 15, 37, 248–49, 253, 269, 351
  Kevin Bales and, 249
Pax Mongolica, 12n25
Pearce, Adrian, 85
Pearson, Andrew, 335
Pennsylvania Abolition of Slavery Act (1780), 316
Pepple, Anna, 283
Pequot War, 62
per capita GDP averages, modern, 346
per capita income, Caribbean vs. in England, 95
Pernambuco (Recife), 55, 56, 58, 73, 130
  Dutch attack on, 57
  Dutch Jews expelled from, 89
  Dutch loss of control over, 114
  Dutch occupation of, 56, 57
  expulsion of the Netherlands from, 120
  Portuguese retaking of, 58
  tobacco, 142
Phillips, Ulrich Bonnell, 4, 41
Phoebe (slave ship), 315
photographic evidence, of Liberated Africans, 292
Pierre Soulé (slave ship), 62

Pinellis, of Genoa, 127
Pinker, Steve, 268
pirates, 276
  Barbary, 138, 139
plantation complex/complexes, 6–7, 33, 44, 55, 90, 98, 145, 235
  consumer choice and, 28
  Dutch and the, 58
  Europe as instigator of, 52
plantation economies, 19, 94
  based on tobacco and cotton, 60
plantation produce, 52, 363
  Brazil production of, 149
  consumer demand for, 141
  exported to Europe, 87
  Portuguese system and, 167
  prices of, 223
  St. Domingue output, 101
plantation slavery, 9
  in the medieval millennium, 20
Plymouth, 60, 119
Poems, Chiefly in the Scottish Dialect (Burns), 140
Poest, Andries van der, 134
police shootings, Black/White victims of, 36
polygamy, 9
Polyglotta Africana (Koelle), 2
Pombal, Marquis de, 117, 130, 284n103
pombeiros, 104
Pope Gregory I, 38
Popular Anti-Slavery and the Birth of Abolitionism (Blackburn), 253
population
  Brazilian slave in the, 19
  decline in Africa and the slave trade, 216–20
  discussions about during slavery era, 13–16
  medieval global, 15
population densities
  Angola, 218
  fall in, 19
  in the New World, 51
population growth
  African populations, 244
  in Africa, 14
  in the Americas, 13
  Indigenous populations, 20
  natural, 20, 91, 150, 219
  natural rate of growth in Antigua, 5
  of female slaves, 21

population growth (cont.)
   of the US Black population, 91
   of US slave population, 150
   recovery rate, 219
   slave trade prevention of, 216
population loss, due to slave trade in Africa, 14
portmanteau biota, 52
Portugal
   baptized Black slaves in, 284n103
   emigrants/population ratio of, 218
   transatlantic war with the Netherlands, 88
Portuguese Empire, 53
Portuguese merchants, intra-American slave trade, 80–81
Portuguese sea loans, 136
Portuguese slave vessels, 170
Portuguese South Atlantic, 70
possessive individualism, 342
post Reconstruction, 334
Postlethwaite, Malachy, 284
post-slavery society, 353
Price, Jacob, 66
prison populations, Black/white ratios in, 36
prisoners of wars, 17, 29, 226, 273
   treatment of, 290
   Upper Guinea and, 241
private investment, 131
privateers, 318
   Argentinian, 297, 318
   Dutch, 109
   North America-based, 73
Problem of Slavery in the Age of Emancipation, The (Davis), 254, 256
profit maximization, 2
profits, 112, 185, 223, 274
   from the slave trade, 62, 208, 210, 250, 252, 361
   plantation, 42, 363
property tax list (1853), 324
proselytization, religious, 41
prostitution, modern, 248
Protestants, and Catholic conflict, 269, 272
Public Advertiser, 267
Puerto Rico, 85, 90, 107
   captives in, 356
   first slave voyage and, 54
   number of captives arriving in, 158
   recorded landing of slaves in, 46

Qua middlemen, 201
Quakers, 257, 347
   abolitionism of, 258n32
quilombos, 140

Rabah, Bilal ibn, 25
race
   attitudes toward, of Iberian and other Europeans, 92
   racial inequalities, 36
racial discrimination. *See* racism
racism, 36, 249, 287, 333, 334, 350, 364
   against
      Black people, 354
   among abolitionists, 124
   and slavery decisions of Europeans, 354
   barring of in Cuba, 352
   epidermal, 25, 283
   psychological effects, 255
   scientific literature and, 348
Radburn, Nicholas, 170
raids, 11–12
Reconquista, in Iberia, 32
Reconstruction, 346, 349, 352
Reconstruction, post, 332, 334
Rediker, Marcus, 44, 177, 183
Regina Coeli (slave ship), 4, 199
Regulations for the future Disposal and Support of such Negroes, 340
reparations, 264, 345
Republican Party, working-class support of the, 344
Réunion, 236, 297
Revolutionary Wars, 121, 330
   US, 332
Rhode Island, 50
   Black sailors in slave trade from, 74n76
   slave ships from, 64
   slave traders from, 135
Richardson, David, 247
Rio de Janeiro, 59, 87, 164, 262
Rio de la Plata, 78
Río Platense merchants, 48
Riva, Juan Pérez de la, 95
riverine gold, 77
Roanoke Island, 102
Roberts, Justin, 274
Rodney, Walter, 220, 221–26, 245
   post-Rodney literature, 237
   Toby Green's views on position of, 222
Rogers, James, 169

Roi Guinguin, 283
Roll Jordan Roll (Genovese), 255
Rosenberg, Phillipe, 272
Royal African Company, 61, 68, 126, 130, 131, 134, 138, 143, 185, 197
  capture of rum ship by, 65
  English monopoly of slave trade and, 61
  slave voyages of, 140
Royal Charlotte (slave ship), 279
rum ship, 65
runaways, 140, 314–15
  in Jamaica and Dominica, 274n74
Rupert's Valley, St. Helena, 323
Rus, arrival of the, 21
Ryan, Maeve, 124n50, 335, 337n84, 347
Ryden, David, 247, 251

S Miguel Triunfante (slave ship), 198
Sahlins, Marshall, *The Original Affluent Society*, 341
Saint George (slave ship), 134
Salé (Morocco), 138
Salvador de Bahia, 59
Samanids, 11
San Fortunato el Nuevo (slave ship), 78
San Juan Nepomuceno (slave ship), 177, 178n64
San Miguel del Gualdape, 46
Sandoval, Alonso de, 188, 241
Santa Catalina (slave ship), 107
Santana (slave ship), 212
Santos, Dona Ana Joaquina, 213
São Tomé, 6, 55, 56, 103, 159, 234
  slave rebellion in, 56
  source of sugar from, 55n17
satisficing, definition of, 341
Sayler, Hieronymus, 127
Scanlan, Padraic, 247, 250, 262, 348
Scheidel, Walter, 6
Schindlmayr, Thomas, 14
scientific racism, 349
  literature, 348
SCIR. *See Slavery, Capitalism and the Industrial Revolution*
Scott, James C., 16
Scottish colliers, 266
sea loans, Portuguese, 136
seas, as slave routes, 11
self-enslavement, 17
self-purchase (coartación), 19, 33, 94
  institutionalized, 34

semi-precious beads and brass bracelets, 143
Sen, Amartya, "More Than 100 Million Women Are Missing," 289
Sephardic Jews, Dutch, 120
serfdom, 290
  abolishment in Scottish coalmines, 269
  decline of, 105
  early Eastern Europe, 105
  second, 266
servile labor. *See* servitude
servitude, 15, 20, 248
  born into, 18
  use of term, 112–13
settled society, enslaved people and, 8
Seville
  center of slave trade, 107
  transatlantic slave trade in, 47
sex and age ratios
  effect of on revolts, 183
  imbalances of, 243n128
sex ratios. *See also* mortality rates
  in slave populations, 244
  internecine Islamic conflict and, 241
  Portuguese Angolan slave population, 244
  West-Central African populations, 243–44
sexual assault
  and rape, 22
  public, 264
sexual exploitation, 10
  female slaves and, 21
sexual labor, 8
Shaddad, Antarah ibn, 25
Shammas, Carole, 141
Sharp, Granville, 284
Sherbro, 309
Sherman, William Tecumseh, 344
Siaka (King of Galinhas), 231
Sierra Leone, 161, 236, 314, 334, 346, 352
  ex-captives in, 332
  GDP per capita, 346
  languages and dialects in, 303
  Liberated Africans going to, 324
  population of, 352
Silk, Thomas, 198
Silva, Carlos da, 92
Silva, Daniel Domingues da, 229, 231, 242
Silva, Pablo Miguel Sierra, 92
silver export sector, 48

slave
  multiethnic conception of the eligibility of, 32
  other meanings of, 10
  terms for a, 24
slave decks, 310, 312, 363
  changes on, 189
  children on, 335
  Portuguese slavers and, 357
slave labor, 1
  creoles as, 19
  effect of sugar production on, 28
  market for, 77
  of the Caribbean sugar colonies, 18
  renewing slave status of, 75
  sources of, 17
  transition from white indentured to Black, 60
slave markets, 11–12, 38, 47, 82, 114, 296
  British Caribbean, 68
  Eurasia and, 196
  in Cairo, 23
  in Eastern Europe, 21
  in Eurasia, 200
  re-captives and, 315
  Scandinavian Dublin, 38
slave mortality, 173
slave owners
  compensation to, 289, 336–37, 363
  compensation to former, 36, 127n59, 187, 252, 267, 287, 337, 338, 342, 348
slave populations, 110, 244, 301
  Cuba, 94
  females in, 20
  global, 22
  Iberia's Black component of, 106
  in Western Africa, 221
  Jamaica's total, 91
  non-French territories, 121
  US, 91, 315
slave resistance/revolts, 3, 42, 139, 168, 258–59
  abolitionist activism and, 275
  regional bias and, 176
  reports of in English newspapers, 275–76
  risks of on slave ships, 195
  study of in Jamaica, 258
slave routes, 11, 38, 215
  in the African interior, 229–33

slave ship owners, 68, 126, 282
slave ship rebellion, 178n64
  on the *Regina Coeli*, 4
slave ships, 153–57
  Abbot Devereux, 213
  Albanez, 189, 192, 193
  Albion, 201, 202
  Amistad, 177
  Amistad captives and the Mende language, 309
  Anna, 138
  Ardennes, 3
  Aventureiro, 324
  Black Boy, 283
  Black Joke, 282
  Blackamoor, 283
  Brooks, 76, 154, 188, 189, 194, 195
  Clotilda, 325
  Creole, 178
  Desire, 62
  Diligente, 189, 193
  Eliza, 172–74
  Elizabeth, 203
  Elizabeth and Sarah, 49
  Ellen, 139
  Fourth of July, 282
  Fraternité, 282
  Fredensborg, 172
  General Ramirez, 316n45
  Gezegend Suikerriet, 171
  Gift of God, 61, 282
  Isla de Cuba, 189, 193
  Jesus Maria, 172, 192
  Jeune Adèle, 319
  King Amboe, 283
  L'Amélie, 312, 318
  L'Anémone, 319
  L'Aurore, 195
  Legítimo Africano, 190
  Leusden, 3
  Liberty, 282
  Little George, 276
  Madanela Cansyna, 136
  Marie-Séraphique, 155, 189, 192, 193, 195, 211
  Monserrate, 316n45
  Naïade, 76
  Negro Merchant, 283
  Negroes Nest, 282
  Nossa Senhora de Nazaré e S Antônio, 178

Nossa Senhora do Rozario do Castello, 179
NS da Penha de França, 74
NS do Monserrat e Piedade, 117
Nuestra Señhora de los Re, 54
Orion, 153, 155
Phoebe, 315
Regina Coeli, 4, 199
Royal Charlotte, 279
S. Miguel Triunfante, 198
Saint George, 134
San Fortunato el Nuevo, 78
San Juan Nepomuceno, 177, 178n64
Santa Catalina, 107
Santana, 212
Snow Tulip, 69
Veloz, 179
Ventura, 312
Vergulde Zon, 134
Wanderer, 325, 326
slave soldiers, 8
slave trade
  barriers to, 54–55
  Brazilian traffic, 234
  class-based/race-based interpretation of, 73
  cruelty of, 290–91
  direct British investment in, 132
  economic significance of, 94–100
  impact of African slavery on, 220–21
  impact of on African population, 216–20
  impact of suppression of the, 233–36
  investment in, 66–76, 119, 127–37, 148
  investment in Brazilian slave center, 72
  larger investors in the, 134
  morality of the, 33
  new data and questions about, 215–16
  petition in favor of the, 125
  phases of the, 167
  private investment in, 73
  profits from, 62, 208, 210, 250, 252, 361
  role of people of African descent and, 214
  small investments in the, 133–34
  statistics and, 1
  suppression of, 233
  unusual investment patterns in, 160
Slave Trade Abolition Act, 339, 340
Slave Trade Abolition Bill (1807), 340
Slave Trade Department of the British Foreign Office, 203
Slave Trade Piracy Act (1820), 319

slave traders
  African, 213
  female, 214
  New England, 55
slave vessels, 50, *See also* slave ships
  capture of, 297
  from West Indian ports, 50
  Portuguese, 170
  reports of violence on, 291
slave voyages, 47, 68, 107, 111, 129, 131, 157, 159
  Americas and, 52
  Black crew leaving Brazil, 74
  captained by John Newton, 139
  disembarking in Barbados, 61
  dispatching, 53–55
  English, 119
  European and American-based, 48
  European territories, 58
  financing, 75, 258
  French Americas, 120
  from French ports, 110
  from Kingston, Jamaica, 61
  investment, 133
  leaving Lisbon, 108
  PAST interface of, 303
  Portuguese, 165
slaver/slavers. *See* slave ships
slavery, 112, *See also* slaves
  abolition of, 33, 151, 262, 316, 320, 336, 338
  agricultural, 22
  court, 10
  debates over definition of, 10
  definition of, 9
  economic expansion and, 8
  French abolition of, 126
  geographic patterns in movement, 11
  history of, 7
  in global history, 9
  in temples, 15, 37
  Indigenous, 215
  industrialization and the ending of, 256
  Islamic influences and, 10
  Meillassoux's model of, 16
  military, 10
  moral perspectives on, 261–62
  New World, 230
  psychological effects of, 255
  study of slavery and the slave trades, 4
  temple, 8

Slavery and Abolition's annual bibliography, 7
Slavery, Capitalism and the Industrial Revolution (Berg & Hudson), 145
slaves
  African-born, 18
  demographic scenarios of African descent, 18–21
  effect of wars on, 17
  estimated arrival of in the Americas, 89
  freeing themselves, 258–59
  galley, 32
  major source of, 17–19
  price of, 223
  prices of in Atlantic slave trade, 254
  rights of some, 10
slaves per crew member/ratio, 68, 185
slavevoyages.org, 86, 102, 145, 195, 215, 216, 220, 229, 238, 355–64
  expanded version of, 222
  slave ship database of, 36
  slaving ventures records in, 71
  slaving ventures to Brazil in, 58
Slavic labor, 51
Slavic regions, Latin slave trading in, 35
Slenes, Robert W., 19, 82
small landholdings, 346, 348, 353
  former slaves and ownership of, 346
  Haitians and, 349
  in Mobile, 344
  Irish immigrants and, 347
  Liberated Africans and, 345
  preferred by Liberated Africans, 312, 324
smallholding. *See* small landholdings
Smallwood, Stephanie, 44
Smith, Adam, 249, 339
Smith, James, 198
Smith, Venture, 344
Smitt, Coenraad, 132
Smitt, Matthijs, 132
Snow Tulip (slave ship), 69
social death, 248
social dependency, 10
social leakage, 37
Society for the Propagation of Christian Knowledge, 284
Sokoto Caliphate, 43, 234, 235
  slave societies in, 237
Sommerdyk, Stacey, 207, 209
Song dynasty, 15
  Atlantic slave trade, 58

South Africa, Cape Colony, 318
South Asian labor, 51
South Atlantic gyre, 65, 179
South Atlantic slave trade, 194
South Carolina, 139
  Cilucängy (Ward Lee) living in, 315
  reopening its ports to the transatlantic traffic, 99
  reopening of slave trade, 198
  slave ships from, 54
  survivors of the *Wanderer* in, 326
South Sea Bubble, 131
South Sea Company, 130–31, 140
Southeast Asia, debt-bondage in, 248
southern Brazil, 5
Souza, João Ferreira, 71
Soyo army, 27
Spanish Americas, 87
  Africa's contribution to the population of, 92
  economies of, 54
  galley slaves in, 29
  importance of the South Atlantic to, 356
  Lowland, 359
  non-Indigenous population, 33
  palenques in, 141
Spanish Caribbean
  European slaves, 32
  pre-plantation, 32
Spanish Casa de la Contractión (House of Trade), 107
Spanish circum-Caribbean, 86, 87, 356
Spanish conquistadors, 53
Spanish Empire, 80, 98, 101, 122
  British supply of slaves to, 115
Spanish invasion
  demographic disaster and the, 51
  of the Americas, 107
St. James Chronicle, 285
St. Domingue
  invasion of by the English and the French, 150
  plantation produce from, 101
  slave economy of, 151
St. Domingue rebellion, 90, 126, 175, 248, 252, 288, 291, 310, 360
St. Domingue revolution. *See* St. Domingue rebellion
St. Eustatius, 79
St. Helena, 236, 334
  ex-captives in, 332

Index

St. James's Chronicle, The, 274n74
St. Kitts, 49, 60, 61, 120
St. Lawrence River, 102
St. Maurice, 25
Stanton, Edwin, 344
steam-powered ships, 70, 109, 168n38
steam-powered slave ships. See steam-powered ships
Stephen, James, 288
Stephen, James (the younger), 339, 340n91
Steuart, James, 342
Steuart, John, 283
Strangford Treaty, 115, 118
sub-Saharan Africa/Africans
  European prejudice and, 1–2
  first sale of as chattel, 26
  non-Indigenous foods in, 14
  population, 219
  population of, 242, 362
  produce exports value, 233
sugar
  boycotts of, 137
  slavery and, 5
sugar plantation complex, 28, 55
sugar plantations, 339
  Asian contract workers on, 286
  Cuban, 96, 322
  in Barbados, 68, 88
  in Brazil using slave labor, 108
  in the lowland Vera Cruz region, 80
  indentured laborers on French Caribbean, 199
  of French colonies, 297
  Portuguese slave supply system and, 358
  transatlantic slave trade and, 76
sugar production
  enforced labor and, 6
  in the Caribbean, 60
Suriname, 128
  Maroni River in, 3
  Maroon communities in, 141, 222
  slaves carried to, 132
surplus value, 222–23
surrogate settlers, 33
Sweden, 96, 105, 143, 206
systemic racism, in the US South, 333

Tacky's Rebellion, 260
Tamerlane, 12
tangomãos, 104
Tarleton family, 132
Taylor, Henry, 339
temples, slavery in, 8, 15, 37
Thirty Years' War, 220, 269, 274, 275
Thistlewood, Thomas, 140, 274
  accounts of sexual assault, 22
Thorne, Robert, 127
Thornton, John, 196, 213, 221, 222, 226, 237–40, 241–45
  estimate of slaves from West Central Africa, 243
  undermining of trust of Africans, 226
Thurloes, Thomas (RAC agent), 116
Tigris–Euphrates region, 11
Tikari (ethnolinguistic group), 231
Tillman, Ben, 327
Time magazine, 264
Times, the, 285
Tintoretto, 27n66
  "The Miracle of San Marco" (painting), 26
tobacco rolls, 117, 179
  Brazilian exports of, 186
Tom, Prins, 210
tons per crew ratios, 66, 67, 68
Tønsborg, 131
trading posts, 57
transatlantic migration, 112
  Europeans and, 1
transatlantic slave trade, 29, 58
  estimated size of, *108*
  impact of demand for plantation produce on, 34
  intra-American slave trade and, 76–85
transatlantic slave voyages, *129*
  atrocities of, 2–4
  receiving countries, 85–94
Transformations in Slavery (Lovejoy), 220
transoceanic migration, impact of, 31
transoceanic slave trades/voyages, 119, 157, 238
  Africans' involvement in, 196–206, 245
  dispatching, 53–55
  sea loans and, 136
transoceanic transportation, 28
transoceanic voyages, deaths on, 2
trans-Saharan and Indian Ocean, exodus of Africans via the, 23
trans-Saharan slave trade, 14
Treaty of Breda, 58
Treaty of Utrecht, 130
triangular trade, 46, 47, 59

Trinidad, 83, 235, 251, 263, 350
  Asian indentured workers in, 252
trust, 237
  interpersonal, 215, 226
  loss of, 226–28
Tryon, Thomas, 137
TSTD Enslavers database, 66, 71–73, 145, 157, 159–60, 168, 174, 176, 357
  British Caribbean ports information in the, 68
  CD-ROM version of, 180
  information on violence on slave vessels, 164
  Liverpool slave vessels information in the, 147
  records of Portuguese slaving ventures, 185
  records on Brazil, 56
  sex and age ratios information in the, 183
Turing, Alan, 264
twelve tribes of Israel, 34

Umayyad Caliphate, 17
United Mongol Empire, 24
United Nations Trafficking Protocol, 248
United States
  dependence on slave trade, 91
  expulsion of Africans and African Americans from, 334
  first slaves received, 46
  Germans and Eastern Europe emigrants to, 351
  intra-American traffic, 235
  shipping industry, growth of, 100n140
  systemic racism in the South, 333
  US Civil War, 258, 287, 296, 298
  US Immigration and Nationality Act (1965), 351
  US Revolutionary War, 332
  vs. China and slavery, 12–14
Upper Cross River, 233
urbanization, 8
Urhobo linguistic group, 308
US. *See* United States
Usselinx, Willem, 137
Utrecht, Treaty of, 130

Vai people, 199, 242
Vallodolid debates, 105
value of captives, 75
Vasa, Gustavus, 283

Veer, Albert van der, 134
Veloz (slave ship), 179
Venice, 11, 26, 32, 41
Ventura (slave ship), 312
Venture Smith, 344
Veracruz, 80
  disembarkation in, 85
Vergulde Zon (slave ship), 134
Vice-Admiralty Courts, 297, 303, 320
  Cape Cod, 298
Vieira, João, 73
Viking raiders/raids, 17
  victims of, 11
Vili Mafouks (Loango), 198, 204
violence
  Caribbean and notions of acceptable, 274
  effect on disappearance of New World slavery, 262
  notions of acceptable, 273
  publicly sanctioned, 275n75
violence of abstraction, 44
VJ Day kiss, in Times Square, 264
von Eschenbach, Wolfram, *Parzival*, 25
voting rights, 354
voyage mortality rates, by age–sex groupings, 174
Voyages database, 48
voyages, funding in the South Atlantic, 71
Vries, Jan de, 228

W. E. B. Du Bois Institute, 1
Wakashan and Chinookan-speakers Indigenous societies, 36
Walker, Thomas, 37
  ancestor of, 37n87
Walk-Free Foundation, 248
Wallerstein, Immanuel, 44
Walsh, Lorena S., 76
Walsh, Robert, 179
Walvin, James, 44
Wanderer (slave ship), 315, 325, 329
  survivors from the, 326
Wantchekon, Leonard, 226
Ward Lee. *See* Cilucängy (aka Ward Lee)
warrior-merchants, 209
Webster, Jane, 170
Wedderburn, Robert, 261
Welch (captain), 203
Welser family, 127
West African nation states, transatlantic movement from, 217

West African settlement, natural resources available to, 346
West Central Africa, 27, 142, 159, 168, 200, 214, 218, 219, 221, 231, 234, 243, 357
　Portuguese, 208
　sex ratios in, 243–44
　Thirty Years' War in, 220
Western economic growth, 223
Western Europe, 31, 141, 219, 255, 345
　economic development and slave trade, 226
　population of, 144, 249
　statistics on enslaved peoples, 15
West-Indische Compagnie, 128, 131, 139
Westphalia, Treaty of, 273
Wheat, David, 32, 107
white galley slaves. *See* white slaves
white servitude, in England, 112
white slaves, 271, 281
　in North Africa, 281
　in the Mediterranean, 282
Whitehaven, 119
Wickevoort, Pieter van, 134
Wilberforce, William, 285, 288
Wilhelm, James Godfrey, 324
Will, James, 324
Williams, Eric, 152n129, 257, 262
　British Historians and the West Indies, 250
　Capitalism and Slavery, 222, 250, 252, 262

Wilmot, Arthur Eardley (Commodore), 203, 204
women
　sale of, 20
　seizures of, 17
　treatment of, 289–90
women slaves
　in northern Europe, 21
working-class suffrage, 343
World Systems school, 8, 44
World War II, Korea
　Korean "comfort women" (women as concubines), 35
World War I, 334, 352
Woude, Ad van der, 228
Wyatt, David, 21

Yoruba, 241, 308
　relocated communities, 213
Yoruba-Oyo, 308
Young, Arthur, 249, 342, 343

Zacetecas, 80
Zangronis, Hermano (slave trader), 100
Zanj, 23
　Zanj people, 7
Zanzibar, 234
Zimmermann-Mulgrave, Catherine, 94, 324
Zuluetta, Julián (slave trader), 100

For EU product safety concerns, contact us at Calle de José Abascal, 56–1°,
28003 Madrid, Spain or eugpsr@cambridge.org.

www.ingramcontent.com/pod-product-compliance
Lightning Source LLC
LaVergne TN
LVHW011007250326
834688LV00004B/124